Principles of Management Version 2.0

By

Mason Carpenter, Talya Bauer, Berrin Erdogan and Jeremy Short

P-1227483-BW-1

Principles of Management Version 2.0

Mason Carpenter, Talya Bauer, Berrin Erdogan and Jeremy Short

Published by:

Flat World Knowledge, Inc.
1111 19th St NW, Suite 1180
Washington, DC 20036

Brief Contents

Exam 1 1-5 (P)

(O)

(L)

Inc: non-financial controls / balanced score card (C)

Contents

Dedications

About the Authors

MASON CARPENTER

April 13, 1961–September 22, 2011

Mason A. Carpenter (PhD, 1997, University of Texas at Austin) was the M. Keith Weikel Professor of Leadership in University of Wisconsin Madison's Wisconsin School of Business. He was responsible for the MBA and executive MBA courses in business, corporate, and global strategy, and the curriculum offered through Wisconsin's Strategic Leadership Institute. He was coauthor of the second edition of *Strategic Management: A Dynamic Perspective*, with Dr. Gerry Sanders and published by Prentice Hall. His research concerning corporate governance, top management teams, social networks, and the strategic management of global start-ups was published widely in top management and strategy journals. He was associate editor of the *Academy of Management Review*, the strategic management area editor for Business Expert Press, and served on a handful of editorial boards. His teaching accomplishments included MBA Professor of the Year, notoriety as one of the two most popular professors in several *Business Week* MBA program polls, the Larson Excellence in Teaching Award from the School of Business, and a Distinguished Teaching Award from the University of Wisconsin–Madison.

TALYA BAUER

Talya Bauer (PhD, 1994, Purdue University) is the Gerry and Marilyn Cameron Professor of Management at Portland State University. Dr. Bauer is an award-winning teacher who specializes in teaching organizational behavior, management, power and influence, and negotiations, as well as training and development at the graduate and undergraduate level. She conducts research about relationships at work. More specifically, she works in the areas of leadership, selection, and new employee onboarding, which have resulted in dozens of journal publications. She has acted as a consultant for a variety of government, *Fortune* 1000, and start-up organizations. She has served as a visiting professor in France, Spain, and at Google, Inc. Dr. Bauer is involved in professional organizations and conferences at the national level, such as serving on the Human Resource Management Executive Committee of the Academy of Management, SIOP Program Chair, and member-at-large for SIOP. She is the former editor of *Journal of Management* and is on the editorial boards for the *Journal of Applied Psychology*, *Journal of Management*, *Personnel Psychology*, and *Industrial and Organizational Psychology: Perspectives on Science and Practices*. Dr. Bauer was recognized as one of the most published authors of the 1990s, and is a Fellow of SIOP and APS.

BERRIN ERDOGAN

Berrin Erdogan (PhD, 2002, University of Illinois at Chicago) is the Express Employment Professionals Endowed Professor at Portland State University. Dr. Erdogan is an award-winning teacher of management, organizational behavior, and human resources management. Her research interests focus on individual attachment to organizations through fairness, leader-subordinate relations, contextual factors such as organizational culture, and person-organization fit. Her work has been published in journals such as *Academy of Management Journal*, *Journal of Applied Psychology*, and *Personnel Psychology*. She has conducted managerial seminars on the topics of motivation, organizational justice, performance appraisals, training and development, and has worked as a corporate trainer. She is a visiting professor at Koc University (Istanbul, Turkey) and regularly teaches courses at ALBA Graduate Business School at the American College of Greece. She is currently an associate editor of *European Journal of Work and Organizational Psychology* and serves on the editorial boards of *Journal of Applied Psychology*, *Journal of Management*, *Journal of Organizational Behavior*, and *Personnel Psychology*.

JEREMY SHORT

Jeremy Short (PhD, 2000, Louisiana State University) is the Rath Chair in Strategic Management at the University of Oklahoma. His award-winning teachings include classes on principles of management, strategic management, entrepreneurship, and management history. Dr. Short's research focuses on the determinants of firm and organizational performance. He has published more than fifty articles in journals such as *Strategic Management Journal*, *Organization Science*, *Personnel Psychology*, *Organizational Behavior and Human Decision Processes*, *Academy of Management Learning and Education*, and *Journal of Management Education*, among others. He is an associate editor for the *Journal of Management* and serves on the editorial board of *Organizational Research Methods*. He also coauthored the first Harvard Business School case in graphic novel format.

What's New

WHAT'S NEW FOR *PRINCIPLES OF MANAGEMENT*, 2ND EDITION?

In this edition, you'll find a new author, a new look and feel, new content, and new as well as updated end-of-chapter cases.

We are excited that Jeremy Short has joined the author team. Dr. Short has a wealth of experience with teaching and learning. He has authored several textbooks including *Mastering Strategic Management*, as well as two management graphic novels titled *Tales of Garcón: The Franchise Players* and *Atlas Black: The Complete Adventure*. He also cowrote the first Harvard Business Case in graphic novel format. You can view him giving a Ted-X talk on his work in the area of graphic novels at http://www.youtube.com/watch?v=U7yybHtbCb8. In addition, he has published research on a variety of management topics in top-tier outlets.

© Thinkstock

This edition of the book has a whole new look and feel. For example, the following changes have been made:

- Dozens of new concept pages have been added. These concept pages visually bring important management content to life by illustrating key points both in text and in vibrant images. Research shows that 65% of individuals are *visual learners*. These concept pages add another layer of learning prompts for those who learn best visually. Some research shows that the addition of visual aids can improve learning by up to 400%. One reviewer of our new edition said the following about the addition of these new pages: "I will tell you that the addition of pictures in this edition is brilliant! I compared this text to the previous one (page by page)…the pictures truly help bring the 'black and white' pages to life!"

- All end-of-chapter cases were either rewritten to include the latest content or newly written. New cases include Rovio, the company behind the wildly popular Angry Birds game, UK-based Pret a Manger sandwich shop, bestselling author and management consultant Guy Kawasaki, and investment firm TIAA CREF's CEO, Roger Ferguson.

- Those who loved the cases that were replaced need not fear. We have updated these cases as well and they can now be found within the all-new Instructor's Manual.

- This edition is streamlined to make key points more quickly and powerfully than ever before. Chapters have been updated to include the most relevant information while removing distractions.

- New video links have been added throughout the book.

- All facts and figures have been updated with the most current information.

- New businesses are featured throughout the book.

- New business examples are included throughout the book.

Strategic planning, usually in the form of a business plan, is a key aspect of creating a new venture. Many well-known firms, however, owe their success more to their ability to adapt than to their original plan. Most firms begin by pursuing their plans (also known as intended strategy), but unexpected opportunities that arise over time can lead firms in much different directions than could have ever been anticipated (emergent strategy). Ultimately, the intended and emergent strategies each contribute to a firm's realized strategy. In the cases below, the original intended strategy can barely be detected within today's strategy.

	Intended Strategy	Emergent Strategy	Realized Strategy
	David McConnell aspired to be a writer. When his books weren't selling he decided to give out perfume as a gimmick.	The perfumes McConnell gave out with his books were popular, inspiring the foundation of the California Perfume Company.	The company changed its name to Avon in 1939, and its direct marketing system remained popular for decades. Avon is now available online and in retail outlets worldwide.
	When father and son team Scott and Don Rasmussen were fired from the New England Whalers, they envisioned a cable television network that focused on sports events in the state of Connecticut.	As the network became successful, ESPN has branched out beyond the local softball games and demolition derbies that were first broadcasted.	ESPN is now billed as the worldwide leader in sports, owning several ESPN affiliates as well as production of ESPN magazine, ESPN radio, and broadcasting for ABC.
	In 1977, a cash-strapped advertiser gave a radio station managed by Lowell Paxson 112 electric can openers to pay off an overdue bill. The can openers were offered over the air for $9.95 and quickly sold out.	An idea emerged. Soon the radio station features a regular show called "Suncoast Bargaineers." In 1982, Paxson and a partner launched the Home Shopping Club on local cable television in Florida.	Today the Home Shopping Network has evolved into a retail powerhouse. The company sells tens of thousands of products on television channels in several countries and over the Internet.

Source: Image courtesy of Ketchen, D., & Short, J. (2011). Mastering strategic management. Irvington, NY: Flat World Knowledge.

Other content changes include the following:

- The social networks chapter is now included in the Instructor's Manual and not included in the book, so now there are 15 chapters.
- Chapter 2 and Chapter 3 have been reordered so that "History, Globalization, and Ethics" comes before "Personality, Attitudes and Work Behaviors."

What hasn't changed is our commitment to writing in a concise, accessible, and engaging manner to communicate the latest findings and best practices related to mastering the principles of management. We hope you and your students enjoy this edition as much as we enjoyed writing it!

—Talya Bauer, Berrin Erdogan, and Jeremy Short

Preface

Given that principles of management is likely to be one of the first management courses, if not one of the first business courses, that students take, our objective in developing this material was to provide students and instructors with a solid and comprehensive foundation on the fundamentals of management. Each of the 15 chapters is comprehensive, succinct, and action-oriented, but not busy (as in *busy work*). Moreover, the book and supplements have been written in a direct, active style that we hope students and instructors find both readily accessible and relevant.

So how are we delivering on these promises? Let's consider the top three ways cited by instructors and students.

First, this principles of management book is organized around the well-established **planning**, **organizing**, **leading**, and **controlling** framework (or, simply, P-O-L-C). The P-O-L-C structure provides a number of benefits. Each chapter opens with a brief discussion of how the chapter topic fits in P-O-L-C. For instructors, the use of P-O-L-C as an overarching framework helps with organizing class material, developing the class calendar, and making choices about adding or removing readings and real-life examples. It also provides them with an invaluable reference point at the beginning and conclusion of each class session to share with students "where we've been, and where we're going next." Pedagogically, this is a simple yet powerful tool to aid and promote student learning. For students, the P-O-L-C typology provides them with an enduring framework for processing and organizing just about everything they will learn and experience, during and beyond their classroom-based education, related to the management of organizations.

Second, there are **three underlying themes** carried through all the chapters. These themes are *strategic thinking*, *entrepreneurial thinking*, and *active management*. Strategy, for instance, is explicitly concerned with the determinants of high performance. Most importantly, you will find that we treat performance using the notion of the triple bottom line—the idea that economic performance allows individuals and organizations to perform positively in social and environmental ways as well. The triple bottom line is financial, social, and environmental performance. The entrepreneurial dimension reflects an underlying and growing trend showing that students and instructors see themselves as entrepreneurs and active change agents, not just as managers. By starting fresh with an entrepreneurial/change management orientation, we provide an exciting perspective on the principles of management. Starting with the opening chapter, we incorporate an active management perspective to show how leaders and leadership are essential to personal and organizational effectiveness and effective organizational change. Moreover, the concluding section of each chapter is focused on the assessment and development of particular management skills. Students and instructors are active as leaders at an increasingly early age and are sometimes painfully aware of the leadership failings they see in public and private organizations. It is the leader and leadership that bring principles of management together.

Third, your author team is bringing a truly **interdisciplinary perspective** to your principles of management course. The book that is the foundation for how you learn about, study, and teach the principles of management is titled *Principles of Management: A Behavioral Approach*. This book has very important implications for our emphasis on skills and decision making, coupled with the strategic, entrepreneurial, and leadership orientations. Your authors are award-winning teachers who harbor a deep knowledge and experience about the book's conceptual underpinnings with a sincere appreciation for experiential teaching approaches.

Only with Flat World Knowledge learning platforms do you have the power to choose what your principles of management book looks like, when and how you access material, what you use and don't use, when it will be changed, how much you pay for it, and what other study vehicles you leverage. These innovative study vehicles range from book podcasts and flash cards to peer discussion groups organized in social network formats. Nowhere else on the planet can this combination of user friendliness, user choice, and leading edge technologies be found for business education and learning. An extensive author-prepared instructors' manual and excellent set of PowerPoint slides provide teaching support for instructors. A test item file developed using state-of-the-art assessment techniques supports faculty in evaluating student performance.

Acknowledgments

VERSION 2.0

We would like to thank the following colleagues whose comprehensive feedback and suggestions for improving the material helped make the second edition of *Principles of Management* a better text:

- Lynn Addison, Brewton-Parker College
- Jay Azriel, York College of Pennsylvania
- Kevin Cavanagh, Bismarck State College
- Anjali Chaudhry, Saint Xavier University
- Linda Davenport, Klamath Community College
- John Girard, Minot State University
- Jeff Haynie, Nicholls State University
- Ghadir Ishqaidef, University of Wisconsin, Green Bay
- George Klemic, Lewis University
- Anita Leffel, University of Texas at San Antonio
- Gregory Luce, Bucks County Community College
- Bryan Jon Maciewski, Fond du Lac Tribal and Community College
- Arlene Nicholas, Salve Regina University
- Marvin (Tony) Parker, Fort Valley State University
- Anthony Racka, Oakland Community College
- Sherry Robinson, Penn State University, Hazleton
- Renee Rogers, Forsyth Technical Community College
- Kelly Sell, Bucks County Community College
- P. Gerard Shaw, Dean College
- Wayne Smith, California State University, Northridge
- Karel Sovak, University of Mary
- Atul Teckchandani, California State University, Fullerton
- Dennis Veit, University of Texas, Arlington

VERSION 1.0/1.1

While *Principles of Management* v. 2.0 has a new look and feel as well as a significant amount of new content, we would be remiss to not acknowledge the work of those who helped make v. 1.0 and 1.1 a huge success. We want to thank Margaret Lannamann for doing such a great job keeping all the balls in the air with the earlier version, and Jeff Shelstad and Eric Frank for having this book be among the first books Flat World Knowledge published. Many thanks, too, to the talented Andrea Meyer, who was an invaluable resource in providing background content for several of our chapters. We also thank Elsa Peterson for her tireless and amazing developmental editing; Brett Guidry for helping to keep everything on track; and Sharon Koch and Evelyn Forte for their expertise and contagiously positive perspectives. We further thank Dean Scott Dawson and Portland State University, as well as Michele Yoder and the University of Wisconsin–Madison for supporting our work.

We would also like to thank the following colleagues whose comprehensive feedback and suggestions for improving the material helped make the earlier versions of *Principles of Management* a better text:

- Erin Atchley, University of Tennessee at Knoxville
- Laura Bulas, Central Community College
- Val Calvert, San Antonio College
- Sylvia Charland, Fitchburg State College
- Dexter Davis, Niagara University
- Matt DeLuca, Baruch College

- Charles Englehardt, St. Leo University
- Jeff Fahrenwald, Rockford College
- Carolyn Fausnaugh, Florida Institute of Technology
- Don Furman, SUNY New Paltz/SUNY OCCC
- Shelly Gardner, Augustana College
- Bruce Gillies, California Lutheran University
- Hugh Graham, Loras College
- Susan Greer, Horry-Georgetown Technical College
- Dewey Hemphill, Crichton College
- Kirk Heriot, Columbus State University
- Betty Hoge, Bridgewater College
- Gerald Hollier, University of Texas at Brownsville
- Kathleen Jones, University of North Dakota
- Claire Kent, Mary Baldwin College
- Daniel Kent, Northern Kentucky University
- Anita Leffel, The University of Texas at San Antonio
- Damian Lonsdale, University of South Dakota
- Daniel Morrell, University of South Carolina
- Francine Newth, Providence College
- Roy Pipitone, Erie Community College
- Michael Provitera, Barry University
- Linda Sargent, University of Texas Pan American
- Mukesh Sud, Augustana College
- Nicholas Twigg, Coastal Carolina University
- Nkuma Uche, Central Community College
- Donna Waldron, Manchester Community College
- Carolyn Youssef, Bellevue University

The authors appreciate the efforts of those instructors who have contributed to the project with their work on supplementary materials. Anita Leffel from the University of Texas at San Antonio developed the Student Quizzes and the Test Item File.

In addition, two instructors assisted the development of this material by using it in their classrooms. Their input, along with their students' feedback, has provided us with valuable feedback and confirmation that the material is effective in the classroom:

- Dexter Davis, Niagara University
- P. Gerald Shaw, Dean College

The cadre of copyeditors, graphic designers, and technical designers involved in this first-of-its-kind global publishing project also garner our heartfelt thanks. Finally, this book would not have the incredible value and meaning it does without the support and interest of the faculty and students who have commented on early iterations and will serve to make this "their book" in the many years to come.

CHAPTER 1
Introduction to Principles of Management

FIGURE 1.1
The restaurant industry poses many challenges to the successful management of individuals and groups.

© Thinkstock

Thomas Edison once quipped, "There is a way to do it better—find it." This simple challenge is at the heart of the study and practice of management. Perhaps you've already considered ways to do things better in the organizations, teams, schools, clubs, or social groups in your life. Most of us have thought of better ways to manage others at work or perhaps at home. As you've visited or worked at restaurants, coffee shops, schools, or other organizations, it's likely you've encountered many instances where different interactions with individuals would have led to a better experience.

management

The art and science of accomplishing individual and organizational goals through the efforts of individuals and groups using planning, organizing, leading, and controlling.

principles of management

The concepts managers use in an effort to accomplish management goals.

Management is the art and science of managing others. Knowledge of management will help you identify and develop the skills to better manage your career, relationships, and the behavior of others in organizations. A manager's primary challenge is to solve problems creatively, and **management** often refers to "the art of getting things done through the efforts of other people."[1] The **principles of management**, then, are the means by which you actually manage, that is, get things done through others—individually, in groups, or in organizations. Formally defined, the principles of management are the activities that "plan, organize, and control the operations of the basic elements of [people], materials, machines, methods, money and markets, providing direction and coordination, and giving leadership to human efforts, so as to achieve the sought objectives of the enterprise."[2] For this reason, principles of management are often discussed and learned using a framework called P-O-L-C, which stands for planning, organizing, leading, and controlling. While managers do not necessarily spend all their time managing, the managerial function is required in all aspects of organizations. Everyone employed in an organization is affected by management principles, processes, policies, and practices as one is either a manager or a subordinate to a manager, and usually both. Consequently, finding a "way to do it better" is a challenge that helps all individuals to meet their personal and professional goals.

1. WHO ARE MANAGERS?

L E A R N I N G   O B J E C T I V E S

1. Know what is meant by the term "manager."
2. Be able to describe the types of managers.
3. Understand the nature of managerial work.

1.1 Types of Managers

empowerment

The process of enabling or authorizing an individual to think, behave, take action, and control work and decision making in autonomous ways.

We tend to think about managers based on their position in an organization. This tells us a bit about their role and the nature of their responsibilities. Figure 1.2 summarizes the historic and contemporary views of organizations with respect to managerial roles.[3] In contrast to the traditional view of management where the manager is seen as the "boss" who wields unquestioned power over employees, in the contemporary view, top managers support and serve other managers and employees through a process called empowerment, just as the organization ultimately exists to serve its customers and clients. **Empowerment** is the process of enabling or authorizing an individual to think, behave, take action, and control work and decision making in autonomous ways.

FIGURE 1.3 Types of Managers

We illustrate the different types of managers using examples drawn from fact and fiction below.

Top managers are responsible for developing the organization's strategy and acting as a steward for its vision and mission. Michael Dell showed this type of visionary leadership by founding Dell, Inc. after successfully selling computers out of his dorm room as a freshman student at the University of Texas.

Functional managers are responsible for the efficiency and effectiveness of a specific area such as accounting or marketing. Functional managers at marketing-intensive companies such as Kellogg's, General Mills, and Post must carefully manage many similar but competing brands. In fact, these individuals are typically called *brand managers*.

Supervisory managers, or *team managers*, are responsible for coordinating a subgroup with a particular function or a team composed of members from different parts of the organization. Hotel managers are responsible for all aspects of their hotel, from staffing and customer service to the flowers on display in the hotel lobby.

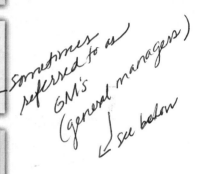

sometimes referred to as GM's (general managers) ↙ *see below*

Line managers, often referred to as product or service managers, lead a team that contributes directly to the products or services the organization creates. Line managers often serve critical roles in keeping assembly line manufacturing on track to meet the organization's production goals as in the auto industry.

A *staff manager* leads a group that creates indirect inputs. Staff managers usually provide an advisory role. The White House chief of staff (an office held by Jacob Lew among others during the Obama administration) provides a high profile example of this important managerial type.

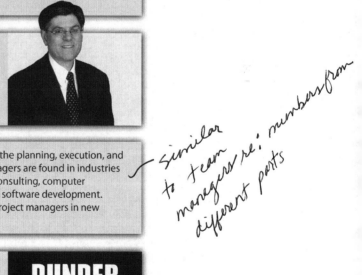

Project managers are responsible for the planning, execution, and completion of projects. Project managers are found in industries such as construction, architecture, consulting, computer networking, telecommunications, or software development. General contractors often serve as project managers in new housing construction.

similar to team managers re: members from different parts

General managers are responsible for managing a clearly identifiable, revenue-producing unit, such as a store, business unit, or product line. Michael Scott served as general manager of the Scranton branch of paper merchant Dunder-Mifflin in the first several seasons of the popular TV series *The Office*.

Source: http://en.wikipedia.org/wiki/File:Jacob_Lew.jpg (third from bottom); http://en.wikipedia.org/wiki/File:Dunder_Mifflin,_Inc.svg (bottom); all other images © Thinkstock.

FIGURE 1.2

Many restaurants empower employees to offer a free dessert to dissatisfied patrons in order to gain long-term customer allegiance.

© *Thinkstock*

A number of different types of managers can be found in organizations. *Top managers* are responsible for developing the organization's strategy and being a steward for its vision and mission. *Functional managers* are responsible for the efficiency and effectiveness of an area, such as accounting or marketing. *Supervisory managers*, or *team managers*, are responsible for coordinating a subgroup of a particular division or a team composed of members from different parts of the organization.

Line and staff managers serve two distinct functions. A *line manager*, often called a product or service manager, leads a team that contributes directly to the products or services the organization creates. For example, a line manager at Procter & Gamble (P&G) is responsible for the production, marketing, and profitability of the Tide detergent product line. In contrast, a *staff manager* leads a function that creates indirect inputs. For example, finance and accounting are critical organizational functions but do not typically provide a clear input into the final product or service a customer buys, such as a box of Tide detergent. Instead, they serve a supporting role. A *project manager* is responsible for the planning, execution, and closing of any project. Project managers are often found in construction, architecture, consulting, computer networking, telecommunications, and software development.

A *general manager* is responsible for managing a clearly identifiable revenue-producing unit, such as a store, business unit, or product line. Typically, general managers make decisions across various functions and have rewards tied to the performance of the entire unit. General managers take direction from their top executives and must first understand the executives' overall plan for the company. Then they set specific goals for their own departments to fit in with the plan. The general manager of production, for example, might have to increase certain product lines and phase out others. Moreover, general managers must describe their goals clearly to their support staff. Supervisory managers see that the goals are met.

FIGURE 1.4 The Changing Roles of Management and Managers

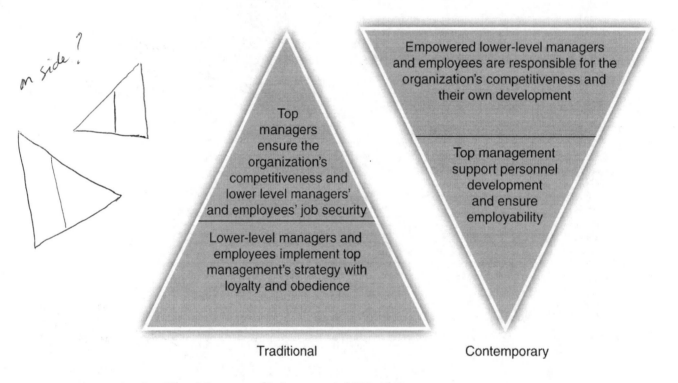

Traditional   Contemporary

1.2   The Nature of Managerial Work

Managers are responsible for the processes of getting activities completed effectively and efficiently with other people while setting and achieving the firm's goals through the execution of four basic management functions: planning, organizing, leading, and controlling. Both sets of processes utilize human, financial, and material resources.

Why are some managers more effective than others? There have been a number of studies on what managers actually do, with one of the most famous conducted by Professor Henry Mintzberg in the early 1970s.[4] After following managers around for several weeks, Mintzberg concluded that, to meet the many demands of performing their functions, managers assume multiple roles (a role is an organized set of behaviors). Mintzberg identified 10 roles common to the work of all managers. As summarized in Figure 1.5, the 10 roles are divided into three groups: interpersonal, informational, and decisional. The informational roles link all managerial work together, while the interpersonal roles ensure that information is provided. The decisional roles make significant use of the information. The performance of managerial roles and the requirements of these roles can be played at different times by the same manager and to different degrees, depending on the level and function of management. The 10 roles are described below.

The three interpersonal roles are primarily concerned with interpersonal relationships. In the figurehead role, the manager represents the organization in all matters of formality. The top-level manager represents the company legally and socially to those outside of the organization. The supervisor represents the work group to higher management and higher management to the work group. In the liaison role, the manager interacts with peers and people outside the organization. The top-level manager uses the liaison role to gain favors and information, while the supervisor uses it to maintain the routine flow of work. The leader role defines the relationships between the manager and employees.

FIGURE 1.5 Ten Managerial Roles

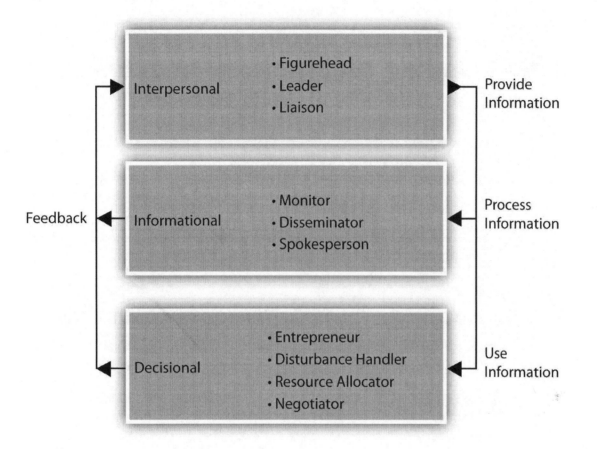

The direct relationships with people in the interpersonal roles place the manager in a unique position to get information. Thus, the three informational roles are primarily concerned with the information aspects of managerial work. In the monitor role, the manager receives and collects information. In the role of disseminator, the manager transmits special information into the organization. The top-level manager receives and transmits more information from people outside the organization than the supervisor. In the role of spokesperson, the manager disseminates the organization's information into its environment. Thus, the top-level manager is seen as an industry expert, while the supervisor is seen as a unit or departmental expert.

The unique access to information places the manager at the center of organizational decision making. There are four decisional roles managers play. In the entrepreneur role, the manager initiates change. In the disturbance handler role, the manager deals with threats to the organization. In the resource allocator role, the manager chooses where the organization will expend its efforts. In the negotiator role, the manager negotiates on behalf of the organization. The top-level manager makes the decisions about the organization as a whole, while the supervisor makes decisions about his or her particular work unit.

The supervisor performs these managerial roles but with different emphasis than higher managers. Supervisory management is more focused and short-term in outlook. Thus, the figurehead role becomes less significant and the disturbance handler and negotiator roles increase in importance for the supervisor. Since leadership permeates all activities, the leader role is among the most important of all roles at all levels of management.

FIGURE 1.6

A master of interpersonal roles, Herb Keller made the skies friendlier by knowing the names and faces of each of his employees when he was CEO of Southwest Airlines.

Source: http://www.flickr.com/ photos/jordanvuong/6858046853

KEY TAKEAWAY

Managers are responsible for getting work done through others by using the key managerial functions of planning, organizing, leading, and controlling. The nature of management has evolved from the traditional hierarchical relationship between managers and employees to a climate better characterized as an upside-down pyramid, where top executives support middle managers and middle managers, in turn, support the employees, who innovate and fulfill the needs of customers and clients. Through all four managerial functions, the work of managers ranges across 10 roles, from figurehead to negotiator. While actual managerial work can seem challenging, the skills you gain through principles of management—consisting of the functions of planning, organizing, leading, and controlling—will help you to meet these challenges.

EXERCISES

1. Alone or in a group, think about the following questions: Why do organizations need managers? Can you imagine an organization with no managers? Does this seem better or worse than what you see there now in terms of organizational performance? What are some different types of managers and how do they differ?

2. Alone or in a group, reflect on Mintzberg's 10 managerial roles. What are they? Which have you personally held? Which seem easier and which seem harder for individuals to do effectively?

3. Imagine you are designing a new restaurant or retail store. Now that you have the idea for your business in your mind, which managerial roles do you think you'll need? Who do you want to fill them? Are any of them unimportant, or are they all important at different times?

4. What four general managerial functions are included in the principles of management? Think of an effective organization you know about in some depth as either an employee or a customer. Now, do you think they do a good job in all four of these managerial functions? Why or why not?

---

2. LEADERSHIP, ENTREPRENEURSHIP, AND STRATEGY

LEARNING OBJECTIVES

1. **Know the roles and importance of leadership, entrepreneurship, and strategy in principles of management.**
2. **Understand how leadership, entrepreneurship, and strategy are interrelated.**

The principles of management are drawn from a number of academic fields, principally, the fields of leadership, entrepreneurship, and strategy.

2.1 Leadership

leadership

The act of influencing others toward a goal.

Leadership is defined as the social and informal sources of influence that you use to inspire action taken by others. Leadership involves actions taken to mobilize others to want to work toward a common goal. Leadership also includes an understanding of when, where, and how to use more formal sources of authority and power, such as position or ownership. Increasingly, we live in a world where good *management* requires good *leaders* and *leadership*. While these views about the importance of leadership are not new, competition among employers and countries for the best and brightest, increased labor mobility, and the nature of global competition puts pressure on firms to invest in present and future leadership capabilities.

General Electric exemplifies a corporation with an excellent reputation for developing leaders. In contrast to many companies, GE has always filled the CEO position with individuals who have been developed through their experience with the company. This practice of developing leaders from within dates back to the influence of their first CEO—Thomas Edison. Whereas GE has been around for more than 100 years, another winning firm in terms of leadership—Google—has only been around since 1998. Both firms emphasize leadership in terms of being exceptional at developing people. Google has topped *Fortune's* 100 Best Companies to Work For several times. Google's founders, Sergey Brin and Larry Page, built a company around the idea that work should be challenging and the challenge should be fun.[5] Google's culture is unique in corporate America, and Google espouses the practice of putting employees first when it comes to daily life in all its offices. There is an emphasis on team achievements and pride in individual accomplishments that contribute to the company's overall success. Ideas are traded, tested, and put into practice quickly. Observers and employees note that meetings that would take hours elsewhere are frequently little more than a conversation in line for lunch and few walls separate those who write the code from those who write the checks. This highly communicative environment fosters a productivity and camaraderie fueled by the realization that millions of people rely on Google results. Leadership at Google amounts to a deep belief that if you give the proper tools to a group of people who like to make a difference, they will.

Views on Managers versus Leaders

Source: http://en.wikipedia.org/wiki/File:Harry-truman.jpg.

My definition of a leader…is a man who can persuade people to do what they don't want to do, or do what they're too lazy to do, and like it.

- *Harry S. Truman (1884–1972), 33rd U.S. president*

Source: http://en.wikipedia.org/wiki/File:Booker_T_Washington_retouched_flattened-crop.jpg.

There are two ways of exerting one's strength; one is pushing down, the other is pulling up.

- *Booker T. Washington (1856–1915), educator, author, and African American civil rights leader*

The first job of a leader is to define a vision for the organization…Leadership is the capacity to translate vision into reality.

- *Warren Bennis (1925–), author and leadership scholar*

FIGURE 1.7

Hope Solo emerged as a leader of the U.S. women's soccer team, winning two gold medals despite her controversial leadership style.

Source: *Photo courtesy of Ampatent, http://en.wikipedia.org/wiki/File:Hope_Solo_USA_Training.jpg.*

Source: http://en.wikipedia.org/wiki/File:Rose_Carter,_official_color_photo,_1977.jpg.

A manager takes people where they want to go. A great leader takes people where they don't necessarily want to go but ought to.

- *Rosalynn Carter (1927–), First Lady of the United States, 1977–1981*

Managers have subordinates—leaders have followers.

- *Chester Bernard (1886–1961), former executive and author of Functions of the Executive*

 Great Quotes from Great Leaders

More quotes by famous leaders.

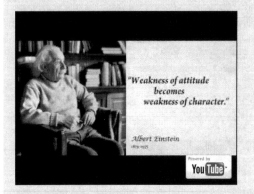

View the video online at: http://www.youtube.com/embed/ZCE_9hoRWlk

2.2 Entrepreneurship

entrepreneurship

The recognition of opportunities (needs, wants, problems, and challenges) and the use or creation of resources to implement innovative ideas for new, thoughtfully planned ventures.

entrepreneur

A person who engages in the process of entrepreneurship.

Entrepreneurship is defined as the recognition of opportunities (needs, wants, problems, and challenges) and the use or creation of resources to implement innovative ideas for new, thoughtfully planned ventures. An **entrepreneur** is a person who engages in the process of entrepreneurship. Entrepreneurship is best understood as a process because it often involves more than simply coming up with a good idea—someone also has to convert that idea into action. As an example of both, Google's leaders suggest that its point of distinction "is anticipating needs not yet articulated by our global audience, then meeting them with products and services that set new standards. This constant dissatisfaction with the way things are is ultimately the driving force behind the world's best search engine." [6]

Entrepreneurs and entrepreneurship are the catalysts for value creation. They identify and create new markets, as well as foster change in existing ones. However, such value creation first requires an opportunity. Indeed, the opportunity-driven nature of entrepreneurship is critical. Opportunities are typically characterized as problems in search of solutions, and the best opportunities are big problems in search of big solutions. "The greater the inconsistencies in existing service and quality, in lead times and in lag times, the greater the vacuums and gaps in information and knowledge, the greater the opportunities." [7] In other words, bigger problems will often mean there will be a bigger market for the product or service that the entrepreneur creates. The problem-solving, opportunity-seeking nature of entrepreneurship is a fundamental building block for effective principles of management.

2.3 Strategy

(handwritten note: Could be a problem people do not ever realize they have…)

Strategy refers to the creation of an organization's long-term purpose, articulated in clear goals and objectives that can be incorporated into a coherent plan of action. It has a *good* or even *great* strategy when this plan also takes advantage of unique resources and capabilities to exploit a big and growing external opportunity. **Strategy**, then, is the central, integrated, externally-oriented concept of how an organization will achieve its objectives.[8] **Strategic management** is the body of knowledge that answers questions about the development and implementation of good strategies.

Strategic management is important to all organizations because, when correctly formulated and communicated, strategy provides leaders and employees with a clear set of guidelines for their daily actions. This is why strategy is so critical to understanding the principles of management. Simply put, strategy is about making choices: What do I do today? What should my organization be doing? What should it stop doing?

2.4 Synchronizing Leadership, Entrepreneurship, and Strategy

Leadership, entrepreneurship, and strategy are the inspiration for important, valuable, and useful principles of management that relate to each other in meaningful ways. In terms of principles of management, you can think of leadership, entrepreneurship, and strategic management as answering questions about "who," "what," and "how." Leadership helps you understand who helps lead the organization forward using the critical characteristics of good leadership. Entrepreneurial firms and entrepreneurs in general are fanatical about identifying opportunities and solving problems—for any organization, entrepreneurship answers big questions about "what" an organization's purpose might be. Strategic management aims to make sure that the right choices are made—specifically, that a good strategy is in place—to exploit those big opportunities.

(handwritten note: how)

KEY TAKEAWAY

The principles of management are drawn from three specific areas—leadership, entrepreneurship, and strategic management. Leadership helps us understand who leads the organization forward and what the critical characteristics of good leadership might be. Entrepreneurs are fanatical about identifying opportunities and solving problems—for any organization, entrepreneurship answers big questions about "what" an organization's purpose might be. Strategic management aims to make sure that the right choices are made—specifically, that a good strategy is in place—to exploit those big opportunities.

EXERCISES

1. Alone or in a group, think about leadership beyond what you've read in this chapter. How do you define leadership, and who would you identify as a great leader? How much does your personal experience help shape your responses to this question?

2. Have you ever had an idea for a new product or service? If so, did you pursue it? Why or why not? Now that you've read this section, what is entrepreneurship and how is it similar to or different from the idea of it you held before this course?

3. Now that you've read this section, what is strategy and how is it similar to or different from the idea of it you held before this course?

4. Address the following alone or in a group. What roles do leadership, entrepreneurship, and strategy play in good principles of management? Can you be an effective organization by employing strong leadership, entrepreneurship, or strategy? Explain your answer.

3. PLANNING, ORGANIZING, LEADING, AND CONTROLLING

LEARNING OBJECTIVES

1. **Know the dimensions of the planning-organizing-leading-controlling (P-O-L-C) framework.**
2. **Know the general inputs into each P-O-L-C dimension.**

A manager's primary challenge is to solve problems. Four major functions at the heart of management are planning, organizing, leading, and controlling (the P-O-L-C framework). The four functions are highly integrated when carried out in the day-to-day realities of running an organization. Although these functions may not accurately depict the day-to-day actions of actual managers on any given day,[9] the P-O-L-C categorization of management functions continues to serve as an effective framework for classifying the activities managers engage in as they attempt to achieve organizational goals.[10]

FIGURE 1.9 The P-O-L-C Framework

Principles of Management at Work throughout History: Applying the P-O-L-C Framework to the Roman Empire

The P-O-L-C framework has been a popular structure since the first principles of management books were written less than a century ago. However, the four functions can be seen as critical management elements in antiquity. Here, we explain how elements of the P-O-L-C were utilized to manage the Roman Empire for nearly a thousand years.

Planning involves setting objectives and determining a course of action for achieving those objectives. Hallmarks of planning in the Roman empire include impressive architectural feats like bridges, roads, aqueducts, baths, and other structures that multitudes of people visit to this day. The city grid used in modern-day city planning was popularized in Roman colonies.

Organizing is the management function that involves developing an organizational structure and allocating human resources to ensure the completion of objectives, often through the design of individual jobs within the organization. Organization in the Roman Empire is best illustrated through their military. The Roman military was composed of legions of about five thousand soldiers; these were then organized into smaller units (e.g., cohorts of about six centuries or a hundred men).

Leading involves social and informal sources of influence used to inspire others to take action utilizing knowledge of personalities, values, attitudes, and emotions. Leadership in the Roman Republic was headed by two consuls elected annually and advised by a senate. This system of checks and balances is often emulated in both governments and corporations today.

Controlling involves ensuring that managerial actions do not deviate from standards by creating processes and procedures that ensure consistent behavior. The establishment of Roman Law allowed for the peaceful control of citizens, conquered lands, and property rights in a manner that kept peace more efficiently than previous global powers.

Source: http://en.wikipedia.org/wiki/File:Maccari-Cicero.jpg (Roman senate picture); all other images © Thinkstock.

3.1 Planning

Planning is the function of management that involves setting objectives and determining a course of action for achieving those objectives. Planning requires that managers be aware of environmental conditions facing their organization and forecast future conditions. It also requires that managers be good decision makers.

Planning is a process consisting of several steps. The process begins with environmental scanning, where planners must be aware of the critical contingencies and trends facing their organizations in terms of economic conditions, their competitors, and their customers. Planners must then attempt to forecast future conditions. These forecasts form the basis for planning.

Planners must establish objectives, which are statements of tangible actions that need to be achieved, and a timeline for their completion. Planners must then identify alternative courses of action for achieving objectives. After evaluating the various alternatives, planners must make decisions about the best courses of action for achieving objectives. They then formulate necessary steps and ensure effective implementation of plans. Finally, planners must constantly evaluate the success of their plans and take corrective action when necessary.

There are many different types of plans and planning.

Strategic planning involves analyzing competitive opportunities and threats, as well as the strengths and weaknesses of the organization, and then determining how to position the organization to compete effectively in their environment. Strategic planning has a long time frame, often three years or more. Strategic planning generally includes the entire organization and includes formulation of objectives. Strategic planning is often based on the organization's mission, which is its fundamental reason for existence. An organization's top management most often conducts strategic planning.

Tactical planning is intermediate-range (one to three years) planning that is designed to develop relatively concrete and specific means to implement the strategic plan. Middle-level managers often engage in tactical planning.

Operational planning generally assumes the existence of organization-wide or subunit goals and objectives and specifies ways to achieve them. Operational planning is short-range (less than a year) planning that is designed to develop specific action steps that support the strategic and tactical plans.

3.2   Organizing

Organizing is the function of management that involves developing an organizational structure and allocating human resources to ensure the accomplishment of objectives. The structure of the organization is the framework within which effort is coordinated. The structure is usually represented by an organization chart, which provides a graphic representation of the chain of command within an organization. Decisions made about the structure of an organization are generally referred to as organizational design decisions.

Organizing also involves the design of individual jobs within the organization. Decisions must be made about the duties and responsibilities of individual jobs, as well as the manner in which the duties should be carried out. Decisions made about the nature of jobs within the organization are generally called "job design" decisions.

Organizing at the level of the organization involves deciding how best to departmentalize, or cluster, jobs into departments to coordinate effort effectively. There are many different ways to departmentalize, including organizing by function, product, geography, or customer. Many larger organizations use multiple methods of departmentalization.

Organizing at the level of a particular job involves how best to design individual jobs to most effectively use human resources. Traditionally, **job design** was based on principles of division of labor and specialization, which assumed that the more narrow the job content, the more proficient the individual performing the job could become. However, experience has shown that it is possible for jobs to become too narrow and specialized. For example, consider how much you would like to screw lids on jars one day after another, as you might have done many decades ago if you worked in a company that made and sold jellies and jams. When job fatigue results from such processes, negative outcomes are often the result, including decreased job satisfaction and organizational commitment, increased absenteeism, turnover, and accidents.

---

environmental scanning

The act of analyzing the critical external contingencies facing an organization in terms of economic conditions, competitors, and customers.

strategic planning

The process of analyzing competitive opportunities and threats, as well as the strengths and weaknesses of the organization, and then determining how to position the organization to compete effectively in its environment.

tactical planning

Intermediate-range planning that is designed to develop relatively concrete and specific means to implement the strategic plan.

operational planning

Assumes the existence of goals and objectives and specifies ways to achieve them.

job design

The process of putting together various elements to form a job, bearing in mind organizational and individual worker requirements.

Recently, many organizations have attempted to strike a balance between the need for worker specialization and the need for workers to have jobs that entail variety and autonomy. Many jobs are now designed based on such principles as empowerment, **job enrichment** and **teamwork**. For example, HUI Manufacturing, a custom sheet metal fabricator, has done away with traditional "departments" to focus on listening and responding to customer needs. From company-wide meetings to team huddles, HUI employees know and understand their customers and how HUI might service them best.[11]

job enrichment

A job redesign technique that allows workers more control over how they perform their own tasks.

teamwork

Cooperative effort by the members of a group or team to achieve a common goal.

3.3 Leading

Leading involves the social and informal sources of influence that you use to inspire action taken by others. If managers are effective leaders, their subordinates will be enthusiastic about exerting effort to attain organizational objectives.

Behavioral sciences, such as psychology and sociology, have made many contributions to understanding this function of management. Personality research and studies of job attitudes provide important information as to how managers can most effectively lead subordinates. For example, this research tells us that to become effective at leading, managers must first understand their subordinates' personalities, values, attitudes, and emotions.

Studies of motivation and motivation theory provide important information about the ways in which workers can be energized to put forth productive effort. Studies of communication provide direction as to how managers can effectively and persuasively communicate. Studies of leadership and leadership style provide information regarding questions, such as, "What makes a manager a good leader?" and "In what situations are certain leadership styles most appropriate and effective?"

3.4 Controlling

Controlling involves ensuring that performance does not deviate from standards. Controlling consists of three steps, which include (1) establishing performance standards, (2) comparing actual performance against standards, and (3) taking corrective action when necessary. Performance standards are often stated in monetary terms such as revenue, costs, or profits but may also be stated in other terms, such as units produced, number of defective products, or levels of quality or customer service.

The measurement of performance can be achieved in several ways, depending on the performance standards, including financial statements, sales reports, production results, customer satisfaction, and formal performance appraisals. Managers at all levels engage in the managerial function of controlling to some degree.

The managerial function of controlling should not be confused with control in the behavioral or manipulative sense. This function does not imply that managers should attempt to control or to manipulate the personalities, values, attitudes, or emotions of their subordinates. Instead, this function of management concerns the manager's role in taking necessary actions to ensure that the work-related activities of subordinates are consistent with and contributing toward the accomplishment of organizational and departmental objectives.

Effective controlling requires the existence of plans, since planning provides the necessary performance standards or objectives. Controlling also requires a clear understanding of where responsibility for deviations from standards lies. Two traditional control techniques are budget and performance audits. An audit involves an examination and verification of records and supporting documents. A budget audit provides information about where the organization is with respect to what was planned or budgeted for, whereas a performance audit might try to determine whether the figures reported are a reflection of actual performance. Although controlling is often thought of in terms of financial criteria, managers must also control production and operations processes, procedures for delivery of services, compliance with company policies, and many other activities within the organization.

The management functions of planning, organizing, leading, and controlling are widely considered to be the best means of describing the manager's job, as well as the best way to classify accumulated knowledge about the study of management. Although there have been tremendous changes in the environment faced by managers and the tools used by managers to perform their roles, managers still perform these essential functions.

FIGURE 1.10

The old adage "measure twice and cut once" refers to the importance of quality control. Quality control ensures that the organization delivers on its promises.

© Thinkstock

KEY TAKEAWAY

The principles of management include four critical functions: planning, organizing, leading, and controlling. This P-O-L-C framework provides useful guidance for common managerial roles.

4. ECONOMIC, SOCIAL, AND ENVIRONMENTAL PERFORMANCE

LEARNING OBJECTIVES

1. Be able to define economic, social, and environmental performance.
2. Understand how economic performance is related to social and environmental performance.

stakeholders

Individuals and organizations who are actively involved in the organization or whose interests may be positively or negatively affected as a result of what the organization does.

A stakeholder approach to management focuses on the desire to satisfy multiple, often competing, constituents who have a claim on an organization's actions and outcomes. Economic performance is a very important outcome to a firm's **stakeholders**, such as investors or owners, because this performance eventually provides them with a return on their investment. Other stakeholders, like the firm's employees and society at large, are also deemed to benefit from such performance. Increasingly, noneconomic accomplishments, such as reducing waste and pollution, are also viewed as critical performance targets that managers must meet to satisfy stakeholders. The notion of the triple bottom line refers to the measurement of business performance along social, environmental, *and* economic dimensions. We discuss economic, social, and environmental performance in the following section and conclude it with a brief discussion of the interdependence of economic performance with other forms of performance.

FIGURE 1.11

The triple bottom line emphasizes the three Ps: people (social concerns), planet (environmental concerns), and profits (economic concerns).

Social   Environmental   Economic

Source: Reproduced with permission from Short, J., Bauer, T., Ketchen, D., & Simon, L. (2010). Atlas Black: Managing to succeed. Irvington, NY: Flat World Knowledge.

4.1 Economic Performance

Traditionally, economic performance of a firm is a function of its success in producing benefits for its owners in particular, accomplished through product innovation and the efficient use of resources to produce some form of profit. Simply put, an organization makes a profit when its revenues are more than its costs in a given period of time, such as three months, six months, or a year. It is important to note that *customers* play a big role in economic profits. Profits accrue to firms because customers are willing to pay a certain price for a product or service, as opposed to a competitor's product or service of a higher or lower price. If customers are only willing to make purchases based on price, then a firm, at least in the face of competition, will only be able to generate profit if it keeps its costs under control.

FIGURE 1.12 Examples of Leading Firms with Strong CSR Orientations[12],[13],[14]

"We've taken time each year since 1989 to compile this [Social Audit] report because we continue to believe that it keeps us in touch with our Company's stated Social Mission. By raising the profile of social and environmental matters inside the Company and recording the impact of our work on the community, this report aids us in our search for business decisions that support all three parts of our Company Mission Statement: Economic, Product, and Social. In addition, the report is an important source of information about the Company for students, journalists, prospective employees, and other interested observers. In this way, it helps us in our quest to keep our values, our actions, and public perceptions in alignment."

"It's nice to live next door to a family that cares about its neighbors, and at S. C. Johnson we are committed to being a good neighbor and contributing to the well-being of the countries and the communities where we conduct business. We have a wide variety of efforts to drive global development and growth that benefit the people around us and the planet we all share. From exceptional philanthropy and volunteerism to new business models that bring economic growth to the world's poorest communities, we're helping to create stronger communities for families around the globe."

"Community giving is and always has been a cornerstone of our company. Since 1946, Target has given 5 percent of our income—which today equals more than $3 million a week—to our communities. We also invest in the career development and well-being of our 355,000 team members worldwide, knowing that their diverse perspectives, talent, and commitment enhance our company and our communities. And we engage with a broad range of public and private partners to make our communities strong, healthy, and safe. Working side by side with those around us and sharing Target's expertise with local partners, we help drive results that benefit all."

Source: (From top to bottom) http://www.flickr.com/photos/nine17com/2586708755/in/photostream/; http://www.flickr.com/photos/chicagogeek/6712820771/; http://en.wikipedia.org/wiki/File:Target_in_Miami.jpg

4.2 Social and Environmental Performance

Corporate social responsibility (CSR) is a concept whereby organizations consider the interests of society by taking responsibility for the impact of their activities on customers, suppliers, employees, shareholders, communities, and the environment in all aspects of their operations. This obligation is seen to extend beyond the statutory obligation to comply with legislation and sees organizations voluntarily taking further steps to improve the quality of life for employees and their families, as well as for the local community and society at large. Such actions result in the corporate social performance of an organization.

Three notable companies in terms of CSR are Ben & Jerry's, S. C. Johnson, and Target Corporation. Their statements about why they do this, summarized in Figure 1.12, capture many of the facets just described.

4.3 Integrating Economic, Social, and Environmental Performance

FIGURE 1.13

The use of socially responsible practices has been a key to the success of The Body Shop.

Source: http://en.wikipedia.org/wiki/File:The_Body_Shop_in_the_Prudential_Center,_Boston_MA.jpg

FIGURE 1.14

TOMS shoes exemplifies a venture based on social goals by donating a pair of shoes to a child in need for every pair of shoes purchased.

Source: http://www.flickr.com/photos/ohnodoom/5202639102

Managing a firm's actions to achieve a triple bottom line in a way that actually builds up all three facets of performance—economic, social, and environmental—is challenging. Advocates of CSR argue that achieving success in each type of performance is possible, and consideration of all stakeholders should be the way all firms are evaluated. Increasingly, evidence is mounting that attention to a triple bottom line is more than being "responsible"; instead, it's just good business. Critics argue that CSR detracts from the fundamental economic role of businesses; still, others argue that it is an attempt to preempt the role of government as a watchdog over powerful multinational corporations.

A review of nearly 170 research studies on the relationship between CSR and firm performance reported that there appeared to be no negative shareholder effects of such practices. In fact, this report showed that there was a small positive relationship between CSR and shareholder returns.[15] Similarly, companies that pay good wages and offer good benefits to attract and retain high-caliber employees "are not just being socially responsible; they are merely practicing good management."[16]

The financial benefits of social or environmental CSR initiatives vary by context. For example, environment-friendly strategies are much more complicated in the consumer products and services market. For example, cosmetics retailer The Body Shop and StarKist Seafood Company, a strategic business unit of Heinz Food, both undertook environmental strategies but only the former succeeded. The Body Shop goes to great lengths to ensure that its business is ecologically sustainable.[17] It actively campaigns against human rights abuses and for animal and environmental protection and is one of the most respected firms in the world, despite its small size. Consumers pay premium prices for Body Shop products, ostensibly because they believe that it simply costs more to provide goods and services that are environmentally friendly. The Body Shop has been wildly successful.

StarKist, too, adopted a CSR approach when it decided to purchase and exclusively sell dolphin-safe tuna. At the time, biologists thought that the dolphin population decline was a result of the thousands killed in the course of tuna harvests. However, consumers were unwilling to pay higher prices for StarKist's environmental product attributes. Moreover, since tuna were bought from commercial fishermen, this particular practice afforded the firm no protection against imitation by competitors. Finally, in terms of credibility, the members of the tuna industry had launched numerous unsuccessful campaigns in the past touting their interest in the environment, particularly the world's oceans. Thus consumers did not perceive StarKist's efforts as sincerely "green."

KEY TAKEAWAY

Organizational performance can be viewed along three dimensions—financial, social, and environmental—collectively referred to as the triple bottom line, where the latter two dimensions are included in the definition of CSR. While there remains debate about whether organizations should consider environmental and social impacts when making business decisions, there is increasing pressure to include such CSR activities in what constitutes good principles of management. This pressure is based on arguments that range from CSR helps attract and retain the best and brightest employees, to showing that the firm is being responsive to market demands, to observations about how some environmental and social needs represent great entrepreneurial business opportunities in and of themselves.

EXERCISES

1. Why is financial performance important for organizations?
2. What are some examples of financial performance metrics?
3. What dimensions of performance beyond financial are included in the triple bottom line?
4. How does CSR relate to the triple bottom line?
5. Alone or in a group, answer whether or not you agree with the triple bottom line approach. Why or why not?

---

5. PERFORMANCE OF INDIVIDUALS AND GROUPS

LEARNING OBJECTIVES

1. Understand the key dimensions of individual-level performance.
2. Understand the key dimensions of group-level performance.
3. Know why individual- and group-level performance goals need to be compatible.

Principles of management are concerned with organization-level outcomes such as economic, social, or environmental performance, innovation, or ability to change and adapt. However, for something to happen at the level of an organization, something must typically also be happening within the organization at the individual or team level. If you are an entrepreneur and the only person employed by your company, the organization will accomplish what you do and reap the benefits of what you create. Normally, though, organizations have more than one person, and in such cases, understanding concepts of individual and group performance is key to effective management.

5.1 Individual-Level Performance

Individual-level performance draws upon those things you have to do in your job, or **in-role performance**, and those things that add value but are not part of a formal job description. These "extras" are called extra-role performance, or **organizational citizenship behaviors (OCBs)**. Generally, in-role performance relates to productivity and quality dimensions associated with certain standards that you must meet to do your job. In contrast, OCBs can be understood as individual behaviors that are beneficial to the organization and are discretionary, but not directly or explicitly recognized by the formal reward system.[18]

In comparison to in-role performance, what constitutes OCBs seems to be growing. In a recent review, for example, management researchers identified 30 potentially different forms of OCB, which they collapsed into seven common themes: (1) Helping Behavior, (2) Sportsmanship, (3) Organizational Loyalty, (4) Organizational Compliance, (5) Individual Initiative, (6) Civic Virtue, and (7) Self-Development.[19] Definitions and examples for these seven themes are summarized in Figure 1.15.[20]

in-role performance

The things that you have to do as part of your job and its job description.

organizational citizenship behaviors (OCBs)

Voluntary behaviors employees perform to help others and benefit the organization.

FIGURE 1.15 Organizational Citizenship Behaviors

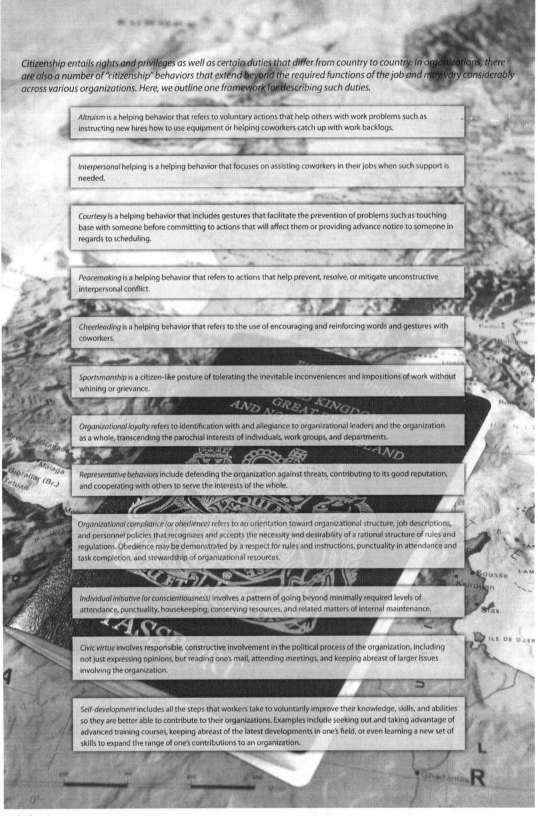

Citizenship entails rights and privileges as well as certain duties that differ from country to country. In organizations, there are also a number of "citizenship" behaviors that extend beyond the required functions of the job and may vary considerably across various organizations. Here, we outline one framework for describing such duties.

Altruism is a helping behavior that refers to voluntary actions that help others with work problems such as instructing new hires how to use equipment or helping coworkers catch up with work backlogs.

Interpersonal helping is a helping behavior that focuses on assisting coworkers in their jobs when such support is needed.

Courtesy is a helping behavior that includes gestures that facilitate the prevention of problems such as touching base with someone before committing to actions that will affect them or providing advance notice to someone in regards to scheduling.

Peacemaking is a helping behavior that refers to actions that help prevent, resolve, or mitigate unconstructive interpersonal conflict.

Cheerleading is a helping behavior that refers to the use of encouraging and reinforcing words and gestures with coworkers.

Sportsmanship is a citizen-like posture of tolerating the inevitable inconveniences and impositions of work without whining or grievance.

Organizational loyalty refers to identification with and allegiance to organizational leaders and the organization as a whole, transcending the parochial interests of individuals, work groups, and departments.

Representative behaviors include defending the organization against threats, contributing to its good reputation, and cooperating with others to serve the interests of the whole.

Organizational compliance (or obedience) refers to an orientation toward organizational structure, job descriptions, and personnel policies that recognizes and accepts the necessity and desirability of a rational structure of rules and regulations. Obedience may be demonstrated by a respect for rules and instructions, punctuality in attendance and task completion, and stewardship of organizational resources.

Individual initiative (or conscientiousness) involves a pattern of going beyond minimally required levels of attendance, punctuality, housekeeping, conserving resources, and related matters of internal maintenance.

Civic virtue involves responsible, constructive involvement in the political process of the organization, including not just expressing opinions, but reading one's mail, attending meetings, and keeping abreast of larger issues involving the organization.

Self-development includes all the steps that workers take to voluntarily improve their knowledge, skills, and abilities so they are better able to contribute to their organizations. Examples include seeking out and taking advantage of advanced training courses, keeping abreast of the latest developments in one's field, or even learning a new set of skills to expand the range of one's contributions to an organization.

© Thinkstock

Principles of management are primarily concerned with an individual's in-role performance, but those principles should help you better manage OCBs of employees as well.

5.2 Group-Level Performance

A **group** is a collection of individuals. Group-level performance focuses on both the outcomes and process of collections of individuals, or groups. In some cases, individuals might be expected to work on their own agendas in the context of a group. Groups might also consist of project-related groups, such as a product group or an entire store or branch of a company. The performance of a group consists of the inputs of the group minus any process loss that result in the final output, such as the quality of a product and the ramp-up time to production or the sales for a given month.

What is the difference between a *group* and a *team*? A collection of people is not a team, though they may learn to function in that way. A **team** is a cohesive coalition of people working together to achieve the team agenda (i.e., teamwork). Being on a team is not equal to total subordination of personal agendas, but it does require a commitment to the vision and involves each individual directly in accomplishing the team's objective. Teams differ from other types of groups in that members are focused on a joint goal or product, such as a presentation, completing in-class exercises, discussing a topic, writing a report, or creating a new design or prototype. Moreover, teams also tend to be defined by their relatively smaller size. For example, according to one definition, "A team is a *small* number of people with complementary skills who are committed to a common purpose, performance goals, and approach for which they are mutually accountable."[21]

The purpose of assembling a team is to accomplish bigger goals that would not be possible for the individual working alone or the simple sum of many individuals' independent work. Teamwork is also needed in cases where multiple skills are needed or where buy-in is required from certain key stakeholders. Teams can, but do not always, provide improved performance. Working together to further the team agenda seems to increase mutual cooperation between what are often competing factions. The aim and purpose of a team is to perform, to get results, and to achieve victory in the workplace and marketplace. The very best managers are those who can gather together a group of individuals and mold them into an effective team.

5.3 Compatibility of Individual and Group Performance

As a manager, you will need to understand the compatibility of individual and group performance, typically with respect to goals and incentives. What does this mean? Looking at goals first, there should be compatibility between individual and group goals. For example, do the individuals' goals contribute to the achievement of the group goal or are they contradictory? Incentives also need to be aligned between individuals and groups. A disconnect between these is most likely when individuals are too far insulated from the external environment or rewarded for action that is not consistent with the goal. For example, individuals may be seeking to perfect a certain technology and, in doing so, delay its release to customers, when customers would have been satisfied with the current solution and put a great priority on its timely delivery. Finally, firms need to be careful to match their goals with their reward structures. For example, if the organization's goal is to increase group performance but the firm's performance appraisal process rewards individual employee productivity, then the firm is unlikely to create a strong team culture.

group

A collection of individuals who interact with each other such that one person's actions have an impact on the other informal groups.

team

A cohesive coalition of people working together to achieve mutual goals.

FIGURE 1.16

The 1980 U.S. Olympic hockey team earned the gold medal and gained international fame after defeating the USSR in the game known as the "Miracle on Ice."

Source: http://en.wikipedia.org/wiki/ File:TeamUSA1980_stamp.png

KEY TAKEAWAY

Individual and group performance are important components of organizational performance. Principles of management incorporate two key facets of individual performance: in-role performance and OCB (or extra-role performance). Group performance is a function of how well individuals achieve a combination of individual and group goals. A team is a type of group that is relatively small with members who are willing and able to subordinate individual goals and objectives to those of the larger group.

1. What is in-role performance? In your opinion, what can managers do to increase in-role performance of employees?
2. If extra-role performance is not directly recognized by reward systems, what motivates employees to display these behaviors?
3. Can you think of any situations in which in-role and extra-role performance may not be beneficial for the work group or the organization? Provide examples.
4. What differentiates a team from a group? Is this distinction an important one?
5. Consider the definitions of different types of citizenship behaviors. Who are the targets or beneficiaries of these behaviors? Do you feel that behaviors with different beneficiaries may have different causes? Why or why not?

6. MANAGING LEARNING STYLES

L E A R N I N G   O B J E C T I V E S

1. **Know your learning style.**
2. **Know how to match your style to the circumstances.**
3. **Use the gauge-discover-reflect framework.**
4. **Learn about journaling as a tool.**

Principles of management courses typically combine knowledge about skills and the development and application of those skills. For these reasons, it is helpful to develop a strategy for learning about and developing management skills. The first part of this strategy should be based on your own disposition toward learning. The second part of this section will offer some specific frameworks and tools to help you be more effective.

6.1 Assess Your Learning Style

In order to maximize your learning in this course and in any learning situation, it is important to understand what type of learner you are. Some people learn better by seeing information. For example, if you notice that you retain more information by reading and seeing diagrams and flow charts, you may be a *visual learner*. If you primarily learn by listening to others, such as in lectures, conversations, and videos, you may be an *auditory learner*. Finally, if you have a preference for actually doing things and learning from trial and error, you may be a *kinesthetic learner*. If you are unaware of what your primary learning style is, take a moment to diagnose it at the following Web site.

What Is Your Learning Style?

Take the following online learning style quiz to find out what type of learner you are:

http://www.vark-learn.com/english/page.asp?p=questionnaire

VARK

FIGURE 1.17 Learning in Style

The learning style of individuals has numerous implications for how to best manage the learning experience. We provide some learning recommendations for each style below.

Effective techniques for *visual learners* (individuals who acquire knowledge through images, pictures, colors or other graphic presentations of material.)

Draw pictures and diagrams

Take careful notes during class

Summarize key points using charts

Effective techniques for *auditory learners* (individuals who acquire knowledge through listening.)

Join study groups so you can discuss your questions and ideas and hear responses

Write down any oral instructions right away

Consider taping lectures

Effective techniques for *kinesthetic learners* (individuals who acquire knowledge through application.)

Schedule your homework and study sessions so you can take breaks

Take good notes during class

Avoid scheduling long classes that require too much sitting and listening when possible to avoid boredom

For various reasons, using flash cards seems to help with all three learning styles. For example, for an auditory learner, saying the answers aloud when using flash cards helps to solidify concepts. For a visual learner, seeing the answers written down on the flash card can be helpful. And for the kinesthetic learner, the act of creating and organizing flash cards helps the concepts stick.

© Thinkstock

6.2 Gauge-Discover-Reflect

Individuals can maximize the value of learning about learning styles by embracing the gauge-discover-reflect process. You have already begun to apply the spirit of what we recommend in this part of the development of your principles of management survival kit, by gauging your learning style. The three essential components are (1) *gauge*—take stock of your knowledge and capabilities about a topic; (2) *discover*—learn enough about a topic so that you can set specific development goals that you can apply and practice, and later gauge again your progress toward your set goals; and (3) *reflect*—step back and look at the ways you have achieved your goals, take the opportunity to set new ones, and chronicle this experience and thought process in a daily journal.

Journaling

It has been established that a way to document your learning and achievement regarding your goals is to chronicle your progress in some form of a journal.[22] A journal may be a required component of a principles of management course, so there may be extrinsic as well as intrinsic motives for starting a journal.

FIGURE 1.18

Famous for their journaling efforts, Lewis and Clark chronicled their adventures on their groundbreaking transcontinental journey to the Pacific coast.

Source: http://en.wikipedia.org/wiki/ File:Lewis_and_Clark.jpg

There are also various exercises that you can partake in through your journaling. These allow you to challenge yourself and think more creatively and deeply. An effective journal entry should be written with clear images and feelings. You should aim to include your reactions along with the facts or events related to your developmental goals. The experience of certain experiments may not necessarily be what you thought it would be, and this is what is important to capture. You are bound to feel turmoil in various moments, and these feelings are excellent fodder for journaling. Journaling allows you to vent and understand emotions. These types of entries can be effective at giving yourself a more rounded perspective on past events.

In addition to the goals you are evaluating, there are numerous things to write about in a journal. You can reflect on the day, the week, or even the year. You can reflect on events that you have been a part of or people you have met. Look for conclusions that you may have made or any conflicts that you faced. Most important, write about how you felt. This will allow you to examine your own emotional responses. You may find that you need to make a personal action or response to those conflicts. The conclusions that you make from your journal entries are the ingredients to self-growth. Facing those conflicts may also change your life for the better, as you are able to grow as a person.

You should also always go back and review what you have written. Think about each journal entry you have made and what it means. This is the true aspect of self-growth through journaling. It is easy to recognize changes in yourself through your journaling. You may find that you had a disturbing idea one day, but the next your attitude was much better. You may also find that your attitude grows and improves day by day. This is what makes journaling a true self-growth tool.

Journaling may be inexpensive, but it does require time and commitment. The time factor itself can be small, only about 10 minutes a day or maybe 30 minutes a week, depending on how you would like to summarize your life. You do, however, have to be motivated to write on a regular basis. Even if you do not have a lot of time to write, you will still be able to enjoy the large amount of personal growth that is available through journaling. Perhaps this suggests that your first goal set relates to time set aside for journaling.

KEY TAKEAWAY

You have seen how different individuals approach the learning process and that an understanding of these differences can help you with your objectives related to principles of management. Beyond this general understanding of your own learning style, you also have an opportunity to put together your own survival kit for this course. Your kit will have answers and resources based on the gauge-discover-reflect framework.

EXERCISES

1. What is your learning style?
2. Were you surprised by your learning style?
3. What target learning issue could you use to experiment with the gauge-discover-reflect framework?

7.   CASE IN POINT: DOING GOOD AS A CORE BUSINESS STRATEGY

FIGURE 1.19

Source: http://en.wikipedia.org/wiki/File:Goodwill_Industries_thrift_shop_Canton_Michigan.JPG

The nonprofit organization Goodwill Industries International has been an advocate of diversity for more than 100 years. In 1902 in Boston, a young missionary set up a small operation enlisting struggling immigrants in his parish to clean and repair clothing and goods for resale. This provided workers with the opportunity for basic education and language training. His philosophy was to provide a "hand up," not a "hand out." Although today you can find retail stores in more than 2,600 locations worldwide, and in 2010, more than 74 million people in the United States and Canada donated to Goodwill, the organization has maintained its core mission to respect the dignity of individuals by eliminating barriers to opportunity through the power of work. Goodwill accomplishes this goal, in part, by putting 84% of its revenue back into programs to provide employment, which in 2010 amounted to $4 billion. As a result of these programs, every 42 seconds of every business day, someone gets a job and is one step closer to achieving economic stability.

Goodwill is a pioneer of social enterprise and has managed to build a culture of respect through its diversity programs. If you walk into a local Goodwill retail store, you will likely see employees from all walks of life and with different genders, races, physical abilities, sexual orientations, and ages. Goodwill provides employment opportunities for individuals with disabilities as well as those who lack education or job experience. The company has created programs for individuals with criminal backgrounds who might otherwise be unable to find employment, including basic work skill development, job placement assistance, and life skills. In 2010, more than 170,000 people obtained employment, earning $2.7 billion in wages and gaining tools to be productive members of their community. Goodwill has established diversity as an organizational norm, and as a result, employees are comfortable addressing issues of stereotyping and discrimination. In an organization of individuals with such wide-ranging backgrounds, it is not surprising that there are a wide range of values and beliefs.

Management and operations within the organization are spread out with 179 independent, community-based Goodwill stores. These regional businesses are autonomous, not-for-profit human services organizations. Despite its decentralization, the company has managed to maintain its core values. Seattle's Goodwill is focused on helping the city's large immigrant population and those without basic education and English language skills. Furthermore, at Goodwill Industries of Kentucky, the organization recently invested in custom software to balance daily sales at stores to streamline operations so managers can spend less time on paperwork and more time managing employees.

Part of Goodwill's success over the years can be attributed to its ability to innovate. As technology evolves and such skills become necessary for most jobs, Goodwill has developed training programs to ensure that individuals are fully equipped to be productive members of the workforce. In 2010, Goodwill was able to provide 2.4 million people with career services. As an organization, Goodwill has entered into the digital age. You can now find Goodwill on Facebook, Twitter, and YouTube. Goodwill's business practices encompass the triple bottom line values of people, planet, and profit. The organization is taking advantage of new green initiatives and pursuing opportunities for sustainability. For example, in 2010, Goodwill received a $7.3 million grant from the U.S. Department of Labor, which provided funds to prepare individuals to enter the rapidly growing green industry of their choice. Oregon's Goodwill Industries has partnered with the Oregon Department of Environmental Quality and its Oregon E-Cycles program to prevent the improper disposal of electronics. Goodwill discovered long ago that diversity is an advantage rather than a hindrance.

Case written by Carlene Reynolds, Talya Bauer, and Berrin Erdogan to accompany Carpenter, M., Bauer, T., Erdogan, B., & Short, J. (2013). Principles of management (2nd ed.). New York: Flat World Knowledge. Based on information from Goodwill Industries International, Inc. (2010). Goodwill Q & A. Retrieved August 28, 2012, from http://www.goodwill.org/wp-content/uploads/2011/01/QandA.pdf; Walker, R. (2008, November 2). Consumed: Goodwill hunting. New York Times Magazine, 18; Tabafunda, J. (2008, July 26). After 85 years, Seattle Goodwill continues to improve lives. Northwest Asian Weekly. Retrieved March 1, 2010, from http://www.nwasianweekly.com/old/2008270031/goodwill20082731.htm; Slack, E. (2009). Selling hope. Retail Merchandiser, 49(1), 89–91; Castillo, L. (2009, February 24). Goodwill Industries offers employment programs. Clovis News Journal. Retrieved April 22, 2010, from http://cnjonline.com/cms/news/story-536506.html; Oregon E-Cycles Web site. Retrieved April 22, 2010, from http://www.deq.state.or.us/lq/ecycle.

CASE DISCUSSION QUESTIONS

1. How might the implications of the P-O-L-C framework differ for an organization like Goodwill Industries versus a firm like Starbucks?

2. What are Goodwill's competitive advantages?

3. Goodwill has found success in the social services. What problems might result from hiring and training the diverse populations that Goodwill is involved with?

4. Have you ever experienced problems with discrimination in a work or school setting?

5. Why do you think Goodwill believes it necessary to continually innovate?

ENDNOTES

1. We draw this definition from a biography of Mary Parker Follett (1868–1933) written by Graham, P. (1995). *Mary Parker Follett: Prophet of Management*. Boston: Harvard Business School Press. Follett was an American social worker, consultant, and author of books on democracy, human relations, and management. She worked as a management and political theorist, introducing such phrases as "conflict resolution," "authority and power," and "the task of leadership."

2. The fundamental notion of principles of management was developed by French management theorist Henri Fayol (1841–1925). He is credited with the original planning-organizing-leading-controlling framework (P-O-L-C), which, while undergoing very important changes in content, remains the dominant management framework in the world. See Fayol, H. (1916). *General and Industrial Management*. Paris: Institute of Electrical and Electronics Engineering.

3. Ghoshal, S. & Bartlett, C. (1996). *The Individualized Corporation: A Fundamentally New Approach to Management*. New York: Collins Business.

4. Mintzberg, H. (1973). *The Nature of Managerial Work*. New York: Harper & Row.

5. Retrieved October 15, 2008, from http://www.google.com/intl/en/corporate/tenthings.html.

6. Retrieved August 28, 2012, from http://www.google.com/intl/en/corporate/tenthings.html.

7. Timmons, J. (1999). *The Entrepreneurial Process*. (p. 39) New York: McGraw-Hill.

8. Hambrick, D., & Fredrickson, J. (2001). Are you sure you have a strategy? *Academy of Management Executive, 15*(4), 2.

9. Mintzberg, H. (1973). *The Nature of Managerial Work*. New York: Harper & Row; Lamond, D. (2004). A matter of style: Reconciling Henri and Henry. *Management Decision, 42*(2), 330–356.

10. Lamond, D. (2004). A matter of style: Reconciling Henri and Henry. *Management Decision, 42*(2), 330–356.

11. Retrieved August 28, 2012, from http://www.huimfg.com/abouthui-yourteams.aspx.

12. Retrieved October 15, 2008, from http://www.benjerrys.com/our_company/about_us/social_mission/social_audits.

13. Retrieved October 15, 2008, from http://www.scjohnson.com/community.

14. Retrieved August 28, 2012, from http://sites.target.com/site/en/company/page.jsp?contentId=WCMP04-031084.

15. Margolis, J., & Elfenbein, H. H. (2008). Doing well by doing good? Don't count on it. *Harvard Business Review, 86*, 1–2.

16. Reich, R. (2007). *Supercapitalism: The transformation of business, democracy, and everyday life*. New York: Knopf.

17. Retrieved August 28, 2012, from http://www.bodyshop.com.

18. Organ, D. W. (1988). *Organizational citizenship behavior: The good soldier syndrome*. Lexington, MA: Lexington Books.

19. Podsakoff, P. M., MacKenzie, S. B., Paine, J. B., & Bachrach, D. G. (2000). Organizational citizenship behaviors: A critical review of the theoretical and empirical literature and suggestions for future research. *Journal of Management, 26*, 513–563.

20. These definitions and examples are adapted from Organ, D. W. (1990). The motivational basis of organizational citizenship behavior. *Research in Organizational Behavior, 12*, 43–72; Graham, J. (1991). An essay on organizational citizenship behavior. *Employee Responsibilities and Rights Journal, 4*, 225, 249–270; George, J. M., & Jones, G. R. (1997). Experiencing work: Values, attitudes, and moods. *Human Relations, 50*, 393–416; George, J. M., & Jones, G. R. (1997). Organizational spontaneity in context. *Human Performance, 10*, 153–170; Graham, J. W. (1991). An essay on organizational citizenship behavior. *Employee Responsibilities and Rights Journal, 4*, 249–270; Organ, D. W. (1994). Personality and organizational citizenship behavior. *Journal of Management, 20*, 465–478; Moorman, R. H., & Blakely, G. L. (1995). Individualism-collectivism as an individual difference predictor of organizational citizenship behavior. *Journal of Organizational Behavior, 16*, 127–142.

21. Katzenbach, J. R., & Smith, D. K. (1993). *The wisdom of teams: Creating the high-performance organization*. Boston: Harvard Business School Press.

22. Bromley, K. (1993). *Journaling: Engagements in reading, writing, and thinking*. New York: Scholastic.

CHAPTER 2
History, Globalization, and Ethics

FIGURE 2.1

For every English-speaking college graduate in the United States, there are approximately three English-speaking college graduates in India each year.

© Thinkstock

The planning-organizing-leading-controlling (P-O-L-C) framework is summarized in Figure 2.2. In this chapter, you'll learn that some principles of management are enduring, but you'll also see that managers need to be continually adapting to changing times. Each facet of the framework—from planning, to organizing, to leading, to controlling—has to be adapted to take advantage of, and to manage in, our changing world. Global trends affect both the style and the substance of management. As the world becomes more global, managers find themselves leading workforces that may be distributed across the country—and the world. Workers are more educated, but more is expected of them.

FIGURE 2.2 The P-O-L-C Framework

Planning	Organizing	Leading	Controlling
1. Vision & Mission 2. Strategizing 3. Goals & Objectives	1. Organization Design 2. Culture 3. Social Networks	1. Leadership 2. Decision Making 3. Communications 4. Groups/Teams 5. Motivation	1. Systems/Processes 2. Strategic Human Resources

The realm of managers is expanding. Wise leaders realize the critical task of acting as a leader, thus setting the tone not just for *what* gets done but for *how* it gets done. Increasingly, good business practice extends to stewardship, not just of the organization, but of the environment and community at large. Ethics and values-based leadership are vital to attracting talent and retaining loyal customers and business partners.

1.　ANCIENT HISTORY: MANAGEMENT THROUGH THE 1990S

LEARNING OBJECTIVES

1. Explain the early motivation for the development of principles.
2. Know what problems these principles solved.
3. Recognize the limitations of these early views.

1.1　Early Management Principles

Henri Fayol,

Fayol was one of the most influential contributors to modern concepts of management, having proposed that there are five primary functions of management: (1) planning, (2) organizing, (3) commanding, (4) coordinating, and (5) controlling.

Early management principles were born of necessity. The most influential of these early principles were set forth by **Henri Fayol**, a French mining engineer. In 1888, Fayol became director of a mining company. The company was in difficulty, but Fayol was able to turn it around and make the company profitable again. When he retired, Fayol wrote down what he had done to save the company. He helped develop an "administrative science" and developed principles that he thought all organizations should follow if they were to run properly.

FIGURE 2.3 Fayol's 14 Principles of (Restaurant) Management

French mining engineer Henri Fayol developed 14 key principles of management in the early 1900s that continue to influence management practices today. Here, we apply Fayol's principles to issues found in restaurant management.

1. *Specialization/division of labor.* By specializing in a limited set of activities, workers become more efficient and increase their output. Unless you are dining at the smallest of mom-and-pop restaurants, you will generally find the tasks of cooking food and waiting tables separated.

2. *Authority/responsibility.* Managers must have the authority to issue commands; however, with authority comes the responsibility to ensure that work gets done. Not surprisingly, many restaurant managers are less than forgiving when employees come in a few minutes late.

3. *Discipline.* Workers must obey orders if the business is to run smoothly. Good discipline is the result of effective leadership. Workers must understand the rules and management should use penalties judiciously if workers violate the rules. Employees who miss too many shifts or display other behaviors in conflict with company policy may find themselves looking for other job opportunities.

4. *Unity of command.* An employee should receive orders only from one boss to avoid conflicting instructions. This leads some restaurants to designate a single manager on duty, or shift manager, to make it clear who is in charge.

5. *Unity of direction.* Each unit or group has only one boss and follows one plan so that work is coordinated efficiently. This principle can be challenging in restaurants as different managers may emphasize different preferred workplace behaviors.

6. *Subordination of individual interest.* The interests of one person should never take precedence over what is best for the company as a whole. Although many employees may prefer to have weekends off, schedules are rotated to keep a full staff when restaurants are at their busiest.

7. *Remuneration.* Workers must be paid fairly for their services. While some claim the word "tips" is an acronym for "to insure proper service," this is unfortunately not related to the true origin of the word.

8. *Centralization*. Centralization refers to whether decisions are centralized—made by management—or decentralized—made by employees. Fayol believed that whether a company should centralize or decentralize its decision making depended on the company's situation and the quality of its workers. In most restaurants, decision making is fairly centralized, although some employees are empowered to offer a free meal to unsatisfied customers.

9. *Line of authority*. The line of authority moves from top management down to the lowest ranks. This hierarchy is necessary for unity of command, but communication can also occur laterally if the bosses are kept aware of it. The line should not be overextended or have too many levels. In restaurants, employees from busboy to cook to waiter can go directly to the manager on duty if workplace problems arise.

10. *Order*. Orderliness refers to the environment and materials as well as the policies and rules. People and materials should be in the right place at the right time.

11. *Equity*. Fairness, dignity, and respect should pervade the organization. Bosses must treat employees well, with a "combination of kindliness and justice." Treating employees with the same respect shown to customers is an important, although sometimes overlooked, policy that restaurant managers should embrace.

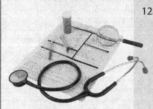

12. *Stability of tenure*. Organizations do best when tenure is high and turnover is low. People need time to learn their jobs and stability promotes loyalty. High employee turnover is inefficient. Rewarding excellent performance and engaging in fun events can help keep employees in the high-turnover restaurant industry. Offering employee benefits such as health insurance is one excellent way to keep employees in industries that face high turnover.

13. *Initiative*. Allowing everyone in the organization the right to create plans and carry them out will make employees more enthusiastic and will encourage them to work harder. Although restaurant employees, in general, have little discretion over daily operations, a suggestion box is always an positive symbol that an organization is open to new ideas.

14. *Esprit de corps*. Harmony and team spirit across the organization builds morale and unity. Look no further than the company softball team to see an example where workers could volunteer their free time based on the unity built at work.

Source: Fayol, H. (1914). Administration industrielle et generale.

Time and Motion

Frederick Winslow Taylor, a contemporary of Fayol's, formalized the principles of scientific management in his 1911 book, *The Principles of Scientific Management*. Taylor described how productivity could be greatly improved by applying scientific principles to management; for this reason, scientific management is sometimes referred to as Taylorism.

Taylor is most famous for his "time studies," in which he used a stopwatch to measure how long it took a worker to perform a task, such as shoveling coal or moving heavy loads. Then he experimented with different ways to do the tasks to save time. Sometimes the improvement came from better tools. For example, Taylor devised the "science of shoveling," in which he conducted time studies to determine how much weight a worker could lift with a shovel without tiring. He determined that 21 pounds was the optimal weight. But since the employer expected each worker to bring his own shovel, and there were different materials to be shoveled on the job, it was hard to ensure that 21-pound optimum. So, Taylor provided workers with the optimal shovel for each density of materials, like coal, dirt, snow, and so on. With these optimal shovels, workers became three or four times more productive, and they were rewarded with pay increases.

Husband-and-wife team **Frank Gilbreth and Lillian Moller Gilbreth** were associates of Taylor also interested in standardization of work to improve productivity.[1] They went one better on Taylor's time studies, devising "motion studies" by photographing the individual movements of each worker (they attached lights to workers' hands and photographed their motions at slow speeds). The Gilbreths then carefully analyzed the motions and removed unnecessary ones. These motion studies were preceded by timing each task, so the studies were called "time and motion studies."

Applying time and motion studies to bricklaying, for example, the Gilbreths devised a way for workers to lay bricks that eliminated wasted motion and raised their productivity from 1,000 bricks per day to 2,700 bricks per day. Frank Gilbreth applied the same technique to personal tasks, like coming up with "the best way to get dressed in the morning." He suggested the best way to button the waistcoat, for example, was from bottom up rather than top down. Why? Because then a man could straighten his tie in the same motion, rather than having to raise his hands back up from the bottom of the waistcoat.

Limitations of the Early Views

Fayol, Taylor, and the Gilbreths all addressed productivity improvement and how to run an organization smoothly. But those views presumed that managers were overseeing manual labor tasks. As work began to require less manual labor and more knowledge work, the principles they had developed became less effective. Worse, some argued that the principles of Taylorism tended to dehumanize workers. The writer Upton Sinclair, one of Taylor's vocal critics, raised awareness of deplorable working conditions in the meatpacking industry in his 1906 book *The Jungle*. Sinclair pointed out the relatively small increase in pay (61%) that workers received compared with their increased productivity (362%). Frederick Taylor answered Sinclair's criticism, saying that workers should not get the full benefit because it was management that devised and taught the workers to produce more. But Taylor's own words compare workers to beasts of burden: The worker is "not an extraordinary man difficult to find; he is merely a man more or less the type of an ox, heavy both mentally and physically."[2]

When work is primarily manual, there is considerable benefit to observing workers doing a task and to devise the most efficient motions and tools to do that task. As we moved from a manufacturing society to a service-based and knowledge-based one, that kind of analysis had less relevance. While researchers can examine companies such as McDonald's and Starbuck's to study ways their services can be delivered with greater speed and efficiency, managers cannot see inside the head of a software engineer to devise the fastest way to write code. Effective software programming depends on knowledge possessed by the engineer rather than simply typing speed.

Frederick Winslow Taylor

Developer of scientific management, which deals with the efficient organization of production in the context of a competitive enterprise that has to control its production costs.

Frank and Lillian Moller Gilbreth

Associates of Taylor also interested in standardization of work to improve productivity.

FIGURE 2.4

Lillian Gilbreth's work on the *Psychology of Management* led her to become one of the world's first management consultants. Lillian also invented the foot-pedal trashcan found in homes and dorms across the globe today.

Source: http://en.wikipedia.org/wiki/
File:Gilbreth_01.jpg

FIGURE 2.5

Frederick Taylor's work on scientific management in the early 1900s continues to influence management thought today. An example is his finding that the ideal shovel load was 21 pounds.

Source: http://en.wikipedia.org/wiki/ File:F._Taylor_1856-1915.jpg

FIGURE 2.6

Peter Drucker's writings and work with GE, Coca-Cola, IBM, and other corporations led him to become one of the leading management gurus in the last century.

Source: http://www.flickr.com/ photos/isaacmao/62322208

Peter Drucker

A prolific management guru and the first scholar to write about how to manage knowledge workers.

A services-based economy requires interactions between employees and customers. Employees have to be able to improvise, and they have to be motivated and happy if they are to serve the customer in a friendly way. Therefore, new management theories were developed to address the new world of management and overcome the shortcomings of the early views.

Early views of management were heavily oriented toward efficiency at the expense of attention to the manager-as-leader. That is, a manager basically acts as a foreman that directs resources to complete predetermined goals or projects. For example, a manager may engage in hiring, training, and scheduling employees to accomplish work in the most efficient and cost-effective manner possible. A manager is considered a failure if he or she is not able to complete the project or goals with efficiency or when the cost becomes too high. However, a leader within a company develops individuals to complete predetermined goals and projects. A leader develops relationships with his or her employees by building communication, by evoking images of success, and by eliciting loyalty. Thus, later views of management evoke notions of leaders and leadership in discussing the challenges and opportunities for modern managers.

1.2 Management Ideas of the 1990s

Peter Drucker was the first scholar to write about how to manage knowledge workers, with his earliest work appearing in 1969. Drucker addressed topics like management of professionals, the discipline of entrepreneurship and innovation, and how people make decisions. In 1982, Tom Peters and Robert Waterman wrote *In Search of Excellence*, which became an international best seller and ushered a business revolution by changing the way managers viewed their relationships with employees and customers. On the basis of the authors' research focusing on 43 of America's most successful companies in six major industries, the book introduced nine principles of management that are embodied in excellent organizations:[3]

1. Managing Ambiguity and Paradox

   The ability of managers to hold two opposing ideas in mind at the same time and still be able to function effectively.

2. A Bias for Action

   A culture of impatience with lethargy and inertia that otherwise leaves organizations unresponsive.

3. Close to the Customer

   Staying close to the customer to understand and anticipate customer needs and wants.

4. Autonomy and Entrepreneurship

   Actions that foster innovation and nurture customer and product champions.

5. Productivity through People

   Treating rank-and-file employees as a source of quality.

6. Hands-On, Value-Driven

   A management philosophy that guides everyday practice and shows management's commitment.

7. Stick to the Knitting

   Stay with what you do well and the businesses you know best.

8. Simple Form, Lean Staff

   The best companies have very minimal, lean headquarters staff.

9. Simultaneous Loose-Tight Properties

   Autonomy in shop-floor activities plus centralized values.

Following up, Peters wrote a *Passion for Excellence*, which placed further emphasis on leadership, innovation, and valuing people. His book *Thriving on Chaos*, published the day of the biggest stock market crash of the time ("Black Monday," October 19, 1987), addressed the uncertainty of the times; and *Liberation Management*, published in 1992, laid out 45 prescriptions for how to lead companies in a rapidly changing world. The book called for empowering people by involving everyone in decision making and eliminating bureaucratic rules and humiliating conditions. Peters urged organizational leaders (i.e., managers) to celebrate and recognize employees for their contributions. His advice to leaders was to "master paradox" (i.e., develop a level of comfort with complexity and ambiguity) and establish direction for the company by developing an inspiring vision and leading by example.

Beginning in the 1970s, **Warren Bennis** pioneered a new theory of leadership that addressed the need for leaders to have vision and to communicate that vision. More than just a manager, an effective leader was defined as someone with the ability to influence and motivate others not only to perform work tasks but also to support the organization's values and meet the organization's goals.

Warren Bennis
Pioneered a new theory of leadership that addressed the need for leaders to have vision and to communicate that vision.

FIGURE 2.7 Management History Timeline

The practice of management has existed throughout the ages. Here, we illustrate several key events in the timeline of management.

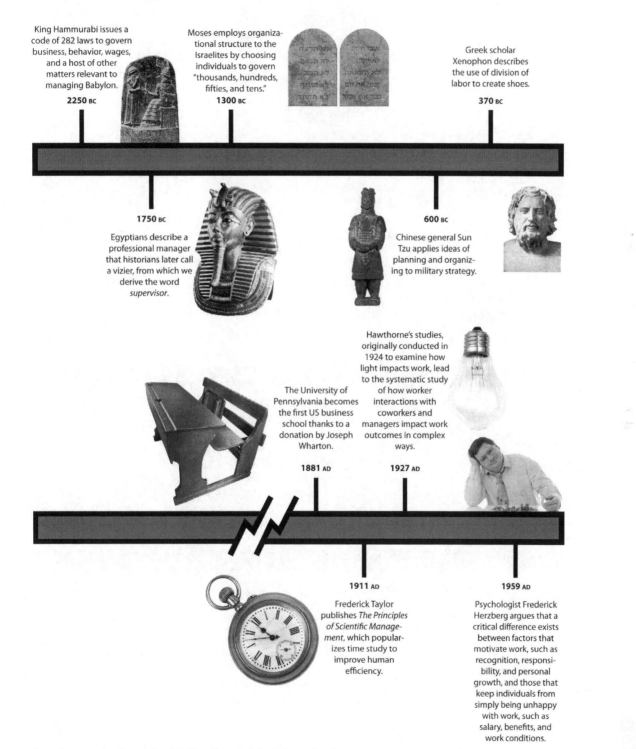

King Hammurabi issues a code of 282 laws to govern business, behavior, wages, and a host of other matters relevant to managing Babylon.
2250 BC

Moses employs organizational structure to the Israelites by choosing individuals to govern "thousands, hundreds, fifties, and tens."
1300 BC

Greek scholar Xenophon describes the use of division of labor to create shoes.
370 BC

1750 BC
Egyptians describe a professional manager that historians later call a vizier, from which we derive the word *supervisor*.

600 BC
Chinese general Sun Tzu applies ideas of planning and organizing to military strategy.

Hawthorne's studies, originally conducted in 1924 to examine how light impacts work, lead to the systematic study of how worker interactions with coworkers and managers impact work outcomes in complex ways.

The University of Pennsylvania becomes the first US business school thanks to a donation by Joseph Wharton.
1881 AD   **1927 AD**

1911 AD
Frederick Taylor publishes *The Principles of Scientific Management*, which popularizes time study to improve human efficiency.

1959 AD
Psychologist Frederick Herzberg argues that a critical difference exists between factors that motivate work, such as recognition, responsibility, and personal growth, and those that keep individuals from simply being unhappy with work, such as salary, benefits, and work conditions.

Source: http://en.wikipedia.org/wiki/File:Milkau_Oberer_Teil_der_Stele_mit_dem_Text_von_Hammurapis_Gesetzescode_369-2.png (top left); http://en.wikipedia.org/wiki/File:Xenophon.jpg (Xenophon bust); all other images © Thinkstock.

FIGURE 2.8

Harley-Davidson Motor Company embraces the concept of vision with their formal vision statement, which notes, "We fulfill dreams inspired by the many roads of the world by providing remarkable motorcycles and extraordinary customer service experiences."

Source: http://en.wikipedia.org/wiki/File:ZweiRadMuseumNSU_EasyRider.JPG; caption retrieved from http://www.harley-davidson.com/en_US/ Content/Pages/Company/company.html?locale=en_US&bmLocale=en_US

Views on Leadership through the Ages

A leader is a dealer in hope.
  - *Napoleon, leader of the French Empire in the early 19th century*

I suppose that leadership at one time meant muscle; but today it means getting along with people.
  - *Mahatma Gandhi, leader of the Indian Independence Movement*

What leaders really do: set direction, align people, and motivate people.[4]
  - *John Kotter, Harvard Business School professor and management consultant*

KEY TAKEAWAY

Early management theorists developed principles for managing organizations that suited the times. A century ago, few workers were highly educated; most work was manual, tasks were repetitive, and rates of change were slow. Hierarchy brought unity and control, and principles of management in which managers defined tasks and coordinated workers to move in a unified direction made sense. As the economy moved from manufacturing to services, the need for engaging workers' minds and hearts became more important. Drucker, Peters, and Waterman presented ideas on how managers could achieve excellence in a continually changing business environment, while Bennis encouraged managers to become inspiring leaders who empowered people.

EXERCISES

Alone or in a group, address the following questions:

1. What goals seem to dominate early management principles? Why do you think this is the case?
2. Do you see any commonalities between Fayol's principles of management from 1911 and those of Tom Peters in the 1990s? What do you think accounts for this?
3. Are there any jobs today for which time and motion studies would make sense to do? Would any other skills need to be taught as well?
4. How would you put some of the ideas of the 1990s into practice?
5. What aspects of P-O-L-C would be most likely to change based on what you have learned in this section?

2. CONTEMPORARY PRINCIPLES OF MANAGEMENT

LEARNING OBJECTIVES

1. Recognize organizations as social movements.
2. Understand the benefits of social networking.
3. Recognize learning organizations.
4. Understand virtual organizations.

2.1 Corporations as Social Movements

Traditionally, corporations have been conceptualized as organizations with clear boundaries, formal procedures, and well-defined authority structures. In contrast, social movements are seen as more spontaneous and fluid. The term social movement refers to a type of group action that is focused on specific political or social issues; examples include the civil rights movement, the feminist movement, and the Occupy Wall Street movement. Leaders of social movements depend on charisma rather than authority to motivate participants to action. Contemporary management theory, however, is showing that the lines between the two are blurring: corporations are becoming more like social movements, and social movements are taking on more permanence. Just as companies are outsourcing specific jobs, so social movements can contract out tasks like lobbying and fundraising.

Corporations can implement initiatives that mimic a social movement. Consider how the CEO of one bank described a program he introduced: "The hierarchical management structure will give way to some collective activities that will improve our effectiveness in the marketplace. Decisions won't flow from a management level to people on the line who are expected to implement those decisions....We're telling everyone, choose a process, figure out what and where the problems are, work together to come up with solutions, and then put your solutions to work."[5] Thus, more and more leading businesses are harnessing the mechanics of social movements to improve how they will manage their businesses in the future.

2.2 Social Networking

Social networking refers to systems that allow members of a specific site to learn about other members' skills, talents, knowledge, or preferences. Companies use these systems internally to help identify experts.

Social networks involve groups of individuals who share a common interest or passion. Poker players, dog lovers, and high school alumni are a few examples of social networks in action. In the corporate world, a social network is made up of individuals who share an employer and, potentially, other interests as well. In the pre-Internet age, managers lacked the tools to recognize or tap the business value of in-house social networks because social networks such as the company softball team had little to do with the organization's bottom line.

Today, social networks are starting points for corporate innovation: potentially limitless arrangements of individuals inspired by opportunities, affinities, or tasks. People feel better and work better when they belong to a group of people like themselves.[6] This new attitude toward social networks in the workplace has been fueled by the growth of social networking sites like Facebook.

Facebook was started by then-college student Mark Zuckerberg in 2004 as a way of connecting a social network—specifically, university students. Since then, Facebook has changed the way organizations connect as well. Some companies maintain a presence on Facebook that allows consumers to chime in about their passions (or lack of them) for corporate offerings, news, and products.

social movement

A type of group action that is focused on specific political or social issues.

FIGURE 2.9

The blurring between social movement and corporation is evidenced in the incorporation of Occupy Portland, an offshoot of the Occupy Wall Street movement in Portland, Oregon.

Source: http://en.wikipedia.org/wiki/ File:Occupy_Portland,_first_day.jpg

social networking

Systems that allow members of a specific site to learn about other members' skills, talents, knowledge, or preferences.

FIGURE 2.10

Launched in February 2004, Facebook boasted 900 million active users in May 2012, the month their initial public offering took place.

Source: http://en.wikipedia.org/wiki/ File:MarkZuckerberg.jpg

learning organization

An organization skilled at creating, acquiring, and transferring knowledge, and at modifying its behavior to reflect new knowledge and insights.

As Zuckerberg told the *Wall Street Journal*, "We just want to share information more efficiently."[7] And, in the information age, that's what social networks do best. Companies are applying the online social networking model of open and closed groups to their corporate intranets, creating secure sites for employees in different locations to collaborate on projects based on common interests, management directives, and incentives. For example, IBM's virtual world lets Big Blue employees use chat, instant messaging, and voice communication programs while also connecting to user-generated content in the public spaces of Second Life, another large social networking site. IBM also opened a virtual sales center in Second Life and, separately from the Second Life partnership, is building an internal virtual world where work groups can have meetings.

2.3 Learning Organizations

A **learning organization** is "an organization skilled at creating, acquiring, and transferring knowledge, and at modifying its behavior to reflect new knowledge and insights."[8] The following are the five building blocks of learning organizations:

1. *Systematic problem solving.* The company must have a consistent method for solving problems, using data and statistical tools rather than assumptions.

2. *Experimentation.* Experiments are a way to test ideas in small steps. Experiments let companies hunt for and test new knowledge, such as new ways of recycling waste or of structuring an incentive program.

3. *Learning from past experience.* It's essential for companies to review projects and products to learn what worked and what didn't. Boeing, for example, systematically gathered hundreds of "lessons learned" from previous airplane models, such as the 737 and 747, which it applied to the 757s and 767s, making those the most successful, error-free launches in Boeing's history.

4. *Learning from others.* Recognizing that good ideas come from anywhere, not just inside the company, learning organizations network with other companies in a continual search for good ideas to adapt and adopt.

5. *Transferring knowledge.* Sharing knowledge quickly throughout the organization is the way to make everyone a smart, contributing member.

2.4 Virtual Organizations

virtual organizations

Organizations with members who are geographically apart and who usually work by computer e-mail and groupware while appearing to others to be a single, unified organization with a real physical location.

A **virtual organization** is one in which employees work remotely—sometimes within the same city, but more often across a country and across national borders. The company relies on computer and telecommunications technologies instead of physical presence for communication between employees. E-mail, collaboration software, wikis, Web meetings (e.g., like Webex or GoToMeeting), phone, and instant messaging are used extensively to keep everyone in touch. Virtual companies present special leadership challenges because it's essential for leaders to keep people informed of what they are supposed to be doing and what other arms of the organization are doing. Communication in a commons area is preferable to one-on-one communication because it keeps everyone up to speed and promotes learning across the organization.

The Value of Wikis

Wikis provide companies with a number of benefits:[9]

- Wikis pool the talent of experts as well as everyone from across the company and beyond it—in all time zones and geographic locations.
- Input from unanticipated people brings fresh ideas and unexpected connections.
- Wikis let people contribute to a project any time, giving them flexibility in managing their time.
- It's easy to see the evolution of an idea, and new people can get up to speed quickly by seeing the history of the project.
- Co-creation of solutions eliminates the need to "sell" those solutions to get buy-in.
- Wikis cut the need for e-mail by 75% and the need for meetings by 50%.

With more and more companies outsourcing work to other countries, managers are turning to tools like wikis to structure project work globally. A wiki is a way for many people to collaborate and contribute to an online document or discussion (see "The Value of Wikis"). The document remains available for people to access anytime. The most famous example is Wikipedia. A "wikified" organization puts information into everyone's hands. Managers don't just talk about empowering workers—the access to information and communication empowers workers directly. Google is well known as a company that empowers employees to share information freely within the organization, but it also has strong deterrents, such as financial and legal consequences, to sharing information outside of the organization. People who are passionate about an idea can tap into the network to make the idea happen. Customers, too, can rally around an issue and contribute their opinions. Many companies that are not solely virtual use the principles of a virtual organization as a way to structure the work of globally distributed teams. VeriFone, one of the largest providers of electronic payment systems worldwide, has development teams working on software projects around the world. In what the company calls a "relay race," developers in Dallas working on a rush project send unfinished work at quitting time to another development center in Laupahoehoe, Hawaii. When the sun sets there, the project is handed off to programmers in Bangalore, India, for further work, and by morning, it's back in Dallas, 16 hours closer to completion. Similarly, midwestern Paper Converting Machine Co. (PCMC) outsourced some design work to Chennai, India. Having U.S. and Indian designers collaborate 24/7 has helped PCMC slash development costs and time, enabling the company to stay in business, according to CEO Robert Chapman. Chapman said, "We can compete and create great American jobs, but not without offshoring."[10] In fact, moving part of business operations to other locations because of lower costs, access to skilled labor, and growing markets is becoming more and more common. A 2011 study conducted by Deloitte showed that 83% of the research and development centers opened up by global multinationals between 2003 and 2007 were in India or China.[11]

Virtual organizations also pose management challenges. In practical terms, if everyone is empowered to be a decision maker but various people disagree, how can decisions be made? If all workers can work at the times they choose, how can management be sure that workers are doing their work—as opposed to reading Web sites for fun, shopping, or networking with friends—and that they are taking appropriate breaks from work to avoid burnout? There are also challenges related to the virtual environment's dependence on computers and Web security.

FIGURE 2.11

Wikis such as Wikipedia pool knowledge across numerous experts globally to collect and disseminate knowledge.

Source: *http://www.flickr.com/ photos/nojhan/3204073130*

wiki

An Internet-based method for many people to collaborate and contribute to a document or discussion.

KEY TAKEAWAY

In today's fast-changing world, organizations are becoming more like social movements, with more fluid boundaries and more participation in leadership across all levels. Social networks within corporations let employees find out about one another and access the people who have the skills, knowledge, or connections to get the job done. Continuous learning is important, not just for individuals but for organizations as a whole, to transfer knowledge and try out new ideas as the pace of change increases. Virtual organizations can speed up cycle time, but they pose new challenges for managers on how to manage remote workers. Communications technologies and the Web let employees work from anywhere—around the corner or around the world—and require special attention to managing communication.

EXERCISES

Alone or in a group, consider the following questions:

1. What commonalities do you see between organizations and social movements?
2. How could you use a social network to help with a specific task such as helping new employees to adjust to the organization?
3. Do intraorganizational social networks inspire employees or do they create more problems than they are worth? Please explain your position.
4. How can social networks help managers plan, organize, lead, and control?
5. What are the potential advantages and potential disadvantages of a virtual organization?
6. What aspects of P-O-L-C would be most likely to change based on what you have learned in this section?

3. GLOBAL TRENDS

LEARNING OBJECTIVES

1. Explain the top 10 ways the world is changing.
2. Describe the pace of these changes.

The world is changing in dramatic ways, and today's managers are in a good position to take advantage of these changes. Here we examine 10 major ways in which the world is changing.

Top Trends

Top 5 Challenge Trends

1. Increasing Concern for the Environment
2. Greater Personalization and Customization
3. Faster Pace of Innovation
4. Increasing Complexity
5. Increasing Competition for Talent

Top 5 Solution Trends

1. Becoming More Connected
2. Becoming More Global
3. Becoming More Mobile
4. Rise of the Creative Class
5. Increasing Collaboration

3.1 Top 5 Challenge Trends

Increasing Concern for the Environment

An analysis by the National Oceanic and Atmospheric Administration (NOAA) suggests that there have been more catastrophic weather events in recent years than 10–20 years ago.[12] People are debating the growing threat of global warming, with its potential to lead to failing crops, rising sea levels, shortages of drinking water, and increasing death tolls from disease outbreaks such as malaria and dengue fever. Currently, 191 nations have signed the Kyoto Protocol on climate change and pledged to begin the long process of reducing greenhouse gas emissions. According to McKinsey's Global Survey of Business Executives, executives across the world believe that business plays a wider role in society and has responsibility to address issues such as environmental concerns beyond just following the letter of the law to minimize pollution. Costa Rica has set a goal to become completely carbon neutral by 2021. Currently, 99% of their electrical energy comes from renewable sources. In addition to countries, more and more companies now watch the "triple bottom line"—the benchmark of how they benefit not just profits but also employees and the environment as a whole. Companies realize they have to take bold steps to minimize their carbon footprint, create environmentally friendly products, and manage the company for more than just the next quarter's profits. Companies are also realizing that they may increase their revenues and profitability by committing to environmental programs. For example, U.S.-based banana producer Chiquita forged a partnership with the Rainforest Alliance, and they worked together to find creative ways for satisfying both environmental and business needs, resulting in increased productivity and reduced costs.[13]

Greater Personalization and Customization

Consumers are demanding more say in products and services. One size no longer fits all, and that means tailoring products and services to meet specific customer preferences. And as companies sell their products globally, tailoring has to meet vastly different needs, cultural sensitivities, and income levels. Even something simple such as Tide laundry detergent can come in hundreds of potential variants in terms of formulations (powders, liquids, tablets), additives (whiteners, softeners, enzymes), fragrances (unscented, mountain fresh, floral), and package sizes (from single-load laundromat sizes to massive family/economy sizes). Customization and the growing numbers of products mean managing more services and more products. For example, for just $5.99 plus shipping, you can create your own personalized Kleenex tissue box![14]

Faster Pace of Innovation

We all want the next new thing, and we want it now. New models, new products, and new variations—companies are speeding new products to market in response to customer demands. The Finland-based mobile phone maker Nokia sells 150 different devices, of which 50–60 are newly introduced each year. The new variations are tailored to local languages, case colors, carriers, add-ons, and content. David Glazer, engineering director at Google, explained how his company adapts to this fast pace: "Google has a high tolerance for chaos and ambiguity. When we started OpenSocial [a universal platform for social-network applications], we didn't know what the outcome was going to be." So Google started running a bunch of experiments. "We set an operational tempo: when in doubt, do something," Glazer said, "If you have two paths and you're not sure which is right, take the fastest path."[15]

Increasing Complexity

Because we want more sustainability, more customization, and more innovation, companies face growing complexity. For example, Nokia's 50–60 new phone models a year all have 300–400 components, some of which contain millions or hundreds of millions of transistors. Those components have to arrive at the right manufacturing location (Nokia has 10 worldwide) from whichever country they originated and arrive just in time to be manufactured.

Increasing Competition for Talent

We need people who can solve all these tough problems, and that's a challenge all by itself. According to McKinsey's global survey of trends, business executives think that this trend, among all trends, will have the greatest effect on their companies in the next five years. Jobs are also getting more complex. Consider people who work in warehouses doing shipping and receiving. At Intel, these workers were jokingly called "knuckle-dragging box pushers" and known for using their brawn to move boxes. Now, the field of transportation and shipping has become known as "supply chain management" and employees need brains as well as brawn—they need to know science and advanced math. They're called on to do mathematical models of transportation networks to find the most efficient trucking routes (to minimize environmental impact) and to load the truck for balance (to minimize fuel use) and for speed of unloading at each destination. Intel now acknowledges the skills that supply chain people need. The company created a career ladder leading to "supply chain master" that recognizes employees for developing expertise in supply chain modeling, statistics, risk management, and transportation planning. Overall, demand will grow for new types of talent such as in the green energy industry. At the same time, companies face a shrinking supply of seasoned managers as baby boomers retire in droves. Companies will have to deal with shortages of specific skills.

3.2   Top 5 Solution Trends

Becoming More Connected

We can now use the Internet and World Wide Web to connect people with people as never before. By mid-2012, more than 2.3 billion people were online, and that number continues to increase each year as the developing world catches up with the developed world on Internet usage.[16] Through over 644 million Web sites, we can access information, words, sounds, pictures, and video with an ease previously unimaginable.

Becoming More Global

We can now tap into more global suppliers and global talent. Whatever problem a manager faces, someone in the world probably has the innovative products, the knowledge, or the talent to address the

FIGURE 2.12

The University of Oklahoma has committed to purchase 100% of its electricity from renewable sources such as wind farms beginning in 2013.

Source: http://en.wikipedia.org/wiki/ File:HolmbergHall2.jpg

problem. And the Internet gives managers the tools to help problems find solutions, customers find suppliers, and innovators find markets. The global problems we face will require people to work together to solve them. Ideas need to be shaped and implemented. Moving ideas around the world is a lot less costly and generates less greenhouse gases than moving people and products around the world. Organizations and social movements alike are using social networking to help people find others with the skills and talents to solve pressing problems.

Becoming More Mobile

We can now reach employees, suppliers, and customers wherever they are. By the end of 2011, 86.7% of the world's population—5.9 billion people—were using mobile phones.[17] And, like Internet use, mobile phone adoption continues to grow. The penetration of mobile phones is changing the way we do business because people are more connected and able to share more information. Two-way, real-time dialogue and collaboration are available to people anytime, anywhere. The low cost of phones compared with computers puts them in the hands of more people around the world, and the increasing sophistication of software and services for the phone expands its use in business settings. Phones are not just a voice communication device—they can send text as well as be a connective device to send data. The fastest mobile phone growth is in developing countries, bringing connectivity to the remotest regions. India has 929 million mobile users and is adding millions of new users every month. Fisherman off the coast of southern India can now call around to prospective buyers of their catch before they go ashore, which is increasing their profits by 8% while actually lowering the overall price consumers have to pay for fish by 4%.[18] In South Africa, 85% of small businesses rely solely on mobile phones. Nokia has 120,000 outlets selling phones in India, where half the population lives in rural areas, not cities.

Rise of the Creative Class

With blogs, Flickr, Instagram, Pinterest, and YouTube, anyone can post their creative efforts. And with open source and wikis, anyone can contribute ideas and insights. We have ubiquitous opportunities for creativity that are nurturing a new creative class. For example, *OhmyNews*, a popular newspaper, is written by 70,000 contributing "citizen reporters." It has become one of South Korea's most influential news sources, with more than 750,000 unique users a day.[19] The demand for workers and ability for workers to work from anywhere may lead to an "e-lance economy." Workers may become free agents, working temporarily on one project and then moving to another when that project is done. Mobile connectivity means these new workers can live anywhere in the world and can work from anywhere in their community. For you as a manager, this means managing workers who might be in a cubicle in Columbus, Ohio, an apartment in Amsterdam, or an Internet café in Bangalore.

Increasing Collaboration

These solution trends combine to foster a rise in collaboration across space and time. We can now bring more people together to solve more problems more quickly. To design new products quickly—and make sure they meet consumer needs—companies are now looking beyond their four walls for innovation. Google, for example, identifies itself as an organization that believes in open, decentralized innovation. "Google can't do everything. And we shouldn't," said Andy Rubin, senior director of Mobile Platforms. "That's why we formed the Open Handset Alliance with more than 34 partners."[20] While the handset alliance is about open cell phones (i.e., phones that aren't tied to any particular phone company and can be programmed by users just like Apple or Palm's "apps"), collaboration means much more than communications. People can collaborate, building coalitions, projects, and products.[21] Groups self-organize on the Web. For example, the MIT-based Vehicle Design Summit is virtual, so students from around the world can participate. The goal is to make a low-cost, 200-mpg four-seater for the Indian market; in 2008, about 200 students participated in this international open-source project.[22]

FIGURE 2.13 Trends in Higher Education

Trends capture general changes in various phenomena over time and help predict how companies and industries may need to adjust as the environment changes. Here we illustrate a number of trends in higher education from the last decade compiled by the College Board Advocacy & Policy Center.

Tuition is up. From 2001 to 2002 and from 2011 to 2012, published tuition and fees at private, nonprofit, four-year institutions rose at an average rate of 2.6 percent per year beyond inflation. The good news is that this is lower than the 4.8 percent per year in the 1980s and 3.1 percent per year in the 1990s.

Funding is down. Adjusting for inflation, state funding per full-time college student was 23 percent lower in 2010–11 than it had been in the previous decade.

Rent is up. Beyond increases in tuition and textbook costs, students can plan on forking over a little more overhead as room and board costs increased 2.9 percent per year.

For-profit organizations are on the rise. In 2008–9, 5 percent of the 1.6 million bachelor's degrees awarded were granted by for-profit institutes of higher education compared to just 1 percent of 1.2 million a decade earlier. Regarding associate degrees, the percentage increased from 11 percent to 18 percent over the same time period.

© *Thinkstock*

KEY TAKEAWAY

Today's world faces many challenges, from the need to protect the natural environment to the rapid pace of innovation and change. Technological connectivity is bringing the world closer together and enabling people to work from anywhere. Demand for talent and low-cost workers gives rise to outsourcing and employees working remotely, whether from home or from remote different countries. At the same time, information is now available to more and more people. This drives demand for personalization. It increases complexity but at the same time gives us the collaboration tools needed to solve tough problems.

EXERCISES

1. How do you manage innovation if ideas can come from anywhere, including people who aren't your direct employees—or aren't even part of the company?
2. If, according to some trends, you can work anytime and anywhere, how do you decide when to work? When do you stop working?
3. What advantages do you see from an increasingly global workforce?

4. GLOBALIZATION AND PRINCIPLES OF MANAGEMENT

4.1 Globalization and Cross-Cultural Lessons

Despite the growing importance of global business, there is a lack of managers with global leadership competencies. According to an American Management Association survey, only 38% of the nearly 1,000 companies surveyed had training programs in place to develop these competencies.[23] Some experts have argued that most U.S. companies are not positioned to implement global strategies due to a lack of global leadership capabilities.[24]

It's easy to understand the problem: communicating and working with people from different countries can be a challenge—not just because of language issues but also because of different cultural norms. For example, in the United States, we tend to be direct in our communication. If you ask a U.S. manager a question, you'll tend to get a direct answer. In other cultures, particularly in southern Europe and Japan, the answer to a question begins with background and context—not the bottom line—so that the listener will understand how the person arrived at the conclusion. Similarly, in some cultures, it is considered rude to deliver bad news or say "no" to a request—instead, the speaker would give a noncommittal answer like "we'll see" or "we'll try."

Country-by-country differences are so prevalent that a worldwide team of scholars proposed to create and validate a theory of the relationship between culture and societal, organizational, and leadership effectiveness. Called the GLOBE Project, it included 170 researchers working together for 10 years to collect and analyze data on cultural values and practices and leadership attributes from more than 17,000 managers in 62 societal cultures. In its 2006 report, GLOBE identified the following nine dimensions of culture.[25]

Performance Orientation

Should you reward people for performance improvement and excellence? In countries like the United States and Singapore, the answer is yes. Organizations in these countries use employee training and development to help people improve their skills and performance. In countries like Russia and Greece, however, family and background count for more than performance.

Uncertainty Avoidance

Life often brings unpredictable events, and with them anxiety. **Uncertainty avoidance** reflects the extent to which members of a society attempt to cope with anxiety by minimizing uncertainty. Should you establish rules, procedures, and social norms to help your employees deal with uncertainty? In countries where uncertainty avoidance is high, like Brazil and Switzerland, the answer is yes. People in such societies want strict rules, laws, and policies to eliminate or control the unexpected. Employees in these countries tend to seek order, consistency, and structure. Countries with low uncertainty avoidance, in contrast, are less rule-oriented. They tolerate a variety of opinions and are open to change and taking risks. Countries with low uncertainty avoidance include Hong Kong and Malaysia.

Assertiveness

How assertive, confrontational, or aggressive should you be in relationships with others? In highly assertive countries like the United States and Austria, competition between individuals and groups is encouraged. Managers may set up incentives that reward the best idea, even if it's contrary to established practices. People in less assertive countries, like Sweden and New Zealand, prefer harmony in relationships and emphasize loyalty and solidarity.

FIGURE 2.14

Our places of work are more diverse than ever before in terms of different ethnicities, gender mixes, backgrounds, cultures, and generations. This brings with it unique opportunities as well as management challenges.

© Thinkstock

uncertainty avoidance

The extent to which members of a society attempt to cope with anxiety by minimizing uncertainty.

Power Distance

Power distance reflects the extent to which the less powerful members of institutions and organizations expect and accept that power is distributed unequally. Should you distribute decision-making power equally among the group? In high-power-distance countries like Thailand, Brazil, and France, the answer is no. People in these societies expect unequal power distribution and greater stratification, whether that stratification is economic, social, or political. People in positions of authority in these countries expect (and receive) obedience. Decision making is hierarchical with limited participation and communication. Australia, in contrast, has a power distance rating that is much lower than the world average. The Australian view reinforces cooperative interaction across power levels and stresses equality and opportunity for everyone.

Gender Egalitarianism

Countries with low gender egalitarianism are male dominated. Men hold positions of power to a much greater extent in low-gender-egalitarianism countries like Egypt and South Korea. Companies operating in more gender-egalitarian countries such as the Nordic countries, Germany, and the Netherlands encourage tolerance for diversity of ideas and roles regardless of gender.

Institutional Collectivism

Institutional collectivism refers to the extent to which people act predominantly as a member of a lifelong group or organization. In countries with high institutional collectivism such as Sweden, a more effective motivational strategy is to reward groups rather than individuals. Countries with low institutional collectivism, such as in the United States, emphasize individual achievement and rewards.

Humane Orientation

Should you reward people for being fair, altruistic, generous, and kind to others? In countries such as Malaysia, this practice is more prevalent and encouraged than in low-humane-orientation countries such as Germany.

Future Orientation

Will your employees favor activities that involve planning and investing in the future for long-term payoff? Or do they want to see short-term results? **Future orientation** is defined as one's expectations and the degree to which one is thoughtful about the future. It is a multifaceted concept that includes planning, realism, and a sense of control. Companies in countries with high future orientation, such as China and Singapore, will have a longer-term planning horizon, and they will be more systematic about planning. Corporations in countries that are the least future-oriented, such as Argentina and Russia, will be more opportunistic and less systematic. At the same time, they'll be less risk averse.

Global Ventures Gone Awry

When Corning proposed a joint venture with a Mexican glass manufacturer, Vitro, the match seemed made in heaven. But just two years later, the venture was terminated. What happened? Cultural clashes eroded what could have been a lucrative partnership. To start, American managers were continually frustrated with what they perceived to be slow decision making by Mexican managers. Mexico ranks higher on the power distance dimension than the United States—company structures are hierarchical, and decisions are made only by top managers. Loyalty to these managers is a high priority in Mexico, and trying to work around them is a big taboo. Mexicans also have a less urgent approach to time. They see time as more abundant than their U.S. counterparts. As a result, Mexicans thought that Americans wanted to move too fast on decisions, and they perceived American directness in communication as aggressive.[26] Additional vignettes on managing across borders are shared next.

FIGURE 2.15

You are much more likely to hear "no problem" than "no" with Indian nationals who avoid delivering bad news.

© *Thinkstock*

power distance

The extent to which the less powerful members of institutions and organizations expect and accept that power is distributed unequally.

institutional collectivism

The extent to which people act predominantly as a member of a lifelong group or organization.

future orientation

One's expectations and the degree to which one is thoughtful about his or her future. It is a multidimensional concept that includes such dimensions as planning, realism, and control.

Managing across Borders

Lines on the Map Miss the Real Story

Diversity is deeper than variations between countries. Sometimes those differences appear in different regions of the same country. For example, some parts of Mexico don't use Spanish as the primary language. Walmart's Mexico's Juchitan store, therefore, conducts business in the local Zapotec tongue, encourages female employees to wear traditional Zapotec skirts, and does the morning company cheer in Zapotec.

Talent Abroad

With so much variation across countries, it's no surprise that countries vary in level of talent and the supply of managerial, skilled, and unskilled labor. Companies shouldn't assume that emerging market countries offer inferior labor pools. GM, for instance, found that 50% of its assembly-line workers in India have college degrees—a ratio much higher than in other countries.

Local Solutions by People Who Understand Local Needs

Nokia uses local designers to create country-specific handset models. The models designed in India for Indians are dust resistant and have a built-in flashlight. The models designed in China for the Chinese have a touch screen, stylus, and Chinese character recognition. Local designers are more likely to understand the needs of the local population than headquarters-located designers do.

Source: Strategies in emerging markets conference, held by the MIT Center for Transportation and Logistics (CTL) on March 7, 2007, Cambridge, MA.

KEY TAKEAWAY

Because the business environment increasingly depends on collaboration across regional and national borders, a successful global manager needs to be culturally sensitive and have an understanding for how business is done in different cultures. In some countries, loyalty to the group is key. Other countries celebrate mavericks and rule breakers if they can get things done. Knowing how best to communicate with your coworkers and employees—whether to be direct or indirect, whether to follow strict protocol or be more casual, whom to involve in decisions—are all important considerations.

EXERCISES

1. You've just been made a manager in Sweden, known for its institutional collectivism. What incentives and reward structures would you use to motivate your employees?
2. How might you prepare workers for an overseas assignment, helping them adjust to their new location and culture effectively?
3. Your company has 12 branches in the United States and will be opening its first branch in Brazil. Your company prides itself on its self-managed teams. Will you keep this policy in the new country? Why or why not?
4. You're a manager in Japan, and you've just discovered that a team leader under your supervision has made a mistake that will result in a quality problem. How will you handle this mistake?
5. You work in Hong Kong for a Swiss-owned firm. The Swiss are known for their high uncertainty avoidance. What differences might you expect to see from your Swiss bosses compared with your Hong Kong employees?
6. What aspects of P-O-L-C would be most likely to change based on what you have learned in this section?

5. DEVELOPING YOUR VALUES-BASED LEADERSHIP SKILLS

LEARNING OBJECTIVES

1. **Describe the ethical challenges managers are likely to face.**
2. **Understand why ethics are relevant to principles of management.**
3. **Discover what decision-making framework you can use to help integrate ethics into your own principles of management.**

5.1 Ethical Challenges Managers Face

It's late at night and the office is quiet—except that you've got a nagging voice in your head. Your product is already two weeks behind schedule. You've got to get it out this week or lose the deal. But you've discovered a problem. To correct the problem would mean another 3-week delay—and you know the client won't go for that. It's a small error—it'll probably never become an issue. What do you do?

Managers face these kinds of issues all the time. Ethical dilemmas can arise from a variety of areas, such as the following:

- Advertising (desire to present your product or service in the best light)
- Sourcing of raw materials (does the company buy from a supplier who may be underpaying their people or damaging the environment?)
- Privacy (should the company monitor private e-mails that employees write on company time? or the Web sites they visit during work hours?)
- Safety (employee and community)
- Pay scales (relation of the pay of top executives to the rest of the company)
- Product pricing policies (variable pricing, discounts)
- Communication (with stockholders, announcements of plant closings, etc.)

It's easy to think that people who behave unethically are simply bad apples or have a character flaw. But in fact, it's often the situation or circumstances that create the ethical pressures. A global study of business ethics, published by the American Management Association, found that the main reasons for a lapse of ethics are

1. pressure to meet unrealistic business objectives/deadlines,
2. a desire to further one's career,
3. a desire to protect one's livelihood.[27]

You may have developed your own personal code of ethics, but the social environment of the organization can be a barrier to fulfilling that code if management is behaving unethically. At Enron, vice president Sherron Watkins pointed out the accounting misdeeds, but she didn't take action beyond sending a memo to the company's chairman. Although she was hailed as a hero and whistleblower, she did not disclose the issue to the public. Similarly, auditors at Arthur Andersen saw the questionable practices that Enron was pursuing, but when the auditors reported these facts to management, Arthur Andersen's managers pointed to the $100 million of business they were getting from the Enron account. Those managers put profits ahead of ethics. In the end, both companies were ruined, not to mention the countless employees and shareholders left shattered and financially bankrupt.

Since 2002, when the **Sarbanes-Oxley Act** was passed, companies have been required to write a code of ethics. The act sought to reform corporate governance practices in large U.S. public companies. The purpose of the rules is to "define a code of ethics as a codification of standards that is reasonably necessary to deter wrongdoing and to promote honest and ethical conduct," including the ethical handling of actual or apparent conflicts of interest, compliance with laws, and accountability to adhere to the code.[28] The U.S. financial crisis of late 2008 pointed out that other areas, particularly in the financial services industry, needed stiffer regulations and regulatory scrutiny as well, and those moves began to take effect in early 2009. Some companies go a step further and articulate a set of values that drives their code of conduct, as "Procter & Gamble's Values and Code of Ethics" shows.

Sarbanes-Oxley Act

Government act that sought to reform corporate governance practices in large U.S. public companies.

FIGURE 2.16 Sarbanes Oxley Act of 2002 (SOX)

In the early 2000s, highly publicized fraud at Enron, WorldCom, Tyco, and other firms revealed significant issues including conflicts of interest by auditors and securities analysts, boardroom failures, and inadequate funding of the Securities and Exchange Commission. In response, Senator Paul Sarbanes and Representative Michael Oxley sponsored legislation that contained what former President George W. Bush called "the most far-reaching reforms of American business practices since the time of Franklin D. Roosevelt." We outline the eleven key aspects of the law below.

Source: Image courtesy of Ketchen, D., & Short, J. (2011). Mastering strategic management. Irvington, NY: Flat World Knowledge.

Procter & Gamble's Values and Code of Ethics

Procter & Gamble Company lives by a set of five values that drive its code of business conduct:

1. *Integrity*
   - We always try to do the right thing.
   - We are honest and straightforward with each other.
   - We operate within the letter and spirit of the law.
   - We uphold the values and principles of P&G in every action and decision.
   - We are data-based and intellectually honest in advocating proposals, including recognizing risks.
2. *Passion for Winning*
   - We are determined to be the best at doing what matters most.
   - We have a healthy dissatisfaction with the status quo.
   - We have a compelling desire to improve and to win in the marketplace.

3. *Leadership*

We are all leaders in our area of responsibility, with a deep commitment to delivering leadership results.

We have a clear vision of where we are going.

We focus our resources to achieve leadership objectives and strategies.

We develop the capability to deliver our strategies and eliminate organizational barriers.

4. *Trust*

We respect our P&G colleagues, customers and consumers, and treat them as we want to be treated.

We have confidence in each other's capabilities and intentions.

We believe that people work best when there is a foundation of trust.

5. *Ownership*

We accept personal accountability to meet our business needs, improve our systems, and help others improve their effectiveness.

We all act like owners, treating the Company's assets as our own and behaving with the Company's long-term success in mind.[29]

5.2 Importance of Ethics in Management

Ethical behavior among managers is even more important in organizations because leaders set the moral tone of the organization and serve as role models. Ethical leaders build trust in organizations. Thus it is no surprise that ethical leadership has been linked to employee motivation.[30] If employees see leaders behaving unethically, chances are the employees may be less inclined to behave ethically themselves. Companies may have printed codes of ethics, but the key standard is whether leaders uphold those values and standards. We tend to watch leaders for cues on appropriate actions and behavior that the company expects. Decisions that managers make are an indicator of their ethics. If the company says it cares about the safety of employees but then does not buy enough protective gear for them, it is not behaving in line with its code. Likewise, if managers exhibit unsafe behavior or look the other way when employees act unsafely, their behavior is not aligned with their stated code.

Without integrity, there can be no trust. Leadership is based on trust. Ethics drive effectiveness because employees know they can do the right thing decisively and with confidence. Ethical behavior earns the trust of customers and suppliers as well. It earns the public's good will. Ethical managers and ethical businesses tend to be more trusted and better treated. They suffer less resentment, inefficiency, litigation, and government interference. If top management cuts corners, however, or if they make shady decisions, then no matter how good the code of ethics sounds, people will emulate the questionable behavior, not the code.

As a manager, you can make it clear to employees that you expect them to conduct business in an ethical manner by offering seminars on ethics, having an ethics hotline via which employees can anonymously raise issues, and having an ombudsman office or ethics committee to investigate issues.

Integrating Ethics into Managerial Decision Making

Ethics implies making a choice between decision-making rules. For instance, when choosing between two suppliers, do you choose the cheapest (decision rule 1) or the highest quality (decision rule 2). Ethics also implies deciding on a course of action when no clear decision rule is available. Dilemmas occur when the choices are incompatible and when one course of action seems to better serve your self-interest but appears to violate a moral principle. One way to tackle ethical dilemmas is to follow an ethical decision-making process, like the one described below.

Steps in an Ethical Decision-Making Process

1. Assess the situation. What are you being asked to do? Is it illegal? Is it unethical? Who might be harmed?

2. Identify the stakeholders and consider the situation from their point of view. For example, consider the point of view of the company's employees, top management, stockholders, customers, suppliers, and community.

3. Consider the alternatives you have available to you and how they affect the stakeholders:

   - consequences

FIGURE 2.17

Supplemental insurance carrier Aflac has been listed as one of the world's most ethical companies by The Ethisphere Institute for five years in a row.

© *Thinkstock*

- duties, rights, and principles
- implications for personal integrity and character

4. How does the action make you feel about yourself? How would you feel if your actions were reported tomorrow in the *Wall Street Journal* (or your daily newspaper)? How would you explain your actions to your mother or to your 10-year-old child?

5. Make a decision. This might involve going to your boss or to a neutral third party (such as an ombudsman or ethics committee). Know your values and your limits. If the company does nothing to rectify the situation, do you want to continue working for the company?

6. Monitor outcomes. How did the decision work out? How did it turn out for all concerned? If you had it to do over again, what would you do differently?[31]

If you see unethical behavior in others, confronting it early is better. Early on, you have more of an opportunity to talk with the person in a fact-finding (rather than an accusatory) way. The discussion may nip the problem in the bud and prevent it from escalating. Keeping silent because you want to avoid offending the person may lead to much greater problems later on. As French playwright Jean-Baptiste Moliere wrote, "It's not only for what we do that we are held responsible, but for what we do not do."

KEY TAKEAWAY

Management involves decision making, and decisions often have an ethical component. Beyond personal ethics or a moral code, managers face making decisions that reflect the company as a whole, affecting its future success and vitality. Ethics doesn't just mean following the law but acting in accordance with basic values.

EXERCISES

1. What are the consequences of unethical behavior?
2. If you were writing a code of ethics for your company, what would you include?
3. In times of economic downturn, is ethical behavior a luxury or a mandate?
4. Imagine you just found out that one of your employees has lied on an expense report. He is a great employee and one of your best salespeople. How would you handle this ethical violation?
5. Nobel laureate economist Milton Friedman said that companies should focus on maximizing profits, not social responsibilities or purposes. Do you agree with this view? Why or why not?
6. What aspects of P-O-L-C would be most likely to change based on what you have learned in this section?

6.   CASE IN POINT: HANNA ANDERSSON CORPORATION CHANGES FOR GOOD

FIGURE 2.18

Source: Used by permission from Hanna Andersson Corporation.

Born from a desire to bring quality European-style children's clothing to the United States, Hanna Andersson Corporation has sold colorful clothing and accessories since 1983. Husband and wife cofounders, Tom and Gun (pronounced "g??n") Denhart, started the Portland, Oregon–based company by selling imported Swedish clothing from their home. Named for Gun's Swedish grandmother, the company now boasts over $100 million in annual sales and employs over 400 people. Growing from an exclusive mail-order catalog business in the early 1980s, today Hanna Andersson also distributes products online, in 37 retail stores nationwide, and through select specialty retailers.

Over the years, Hanna Andersson has shown that it deeply values its employees. The company provides supplemental child-care reimbursement to all employees—even part-time sales associates. Additional employee benefits include part-time and flexible work hours, considerable paid time off, and 8 hours per year of paid time for employees to volunteer in the community. More importantly, employees feel like they are part of the Hanna Andersson family. In fact, in the beginning, many of the employees were friends and family members of the Denharts.

It was important to the Denharts that they were involved in the decisions of the company and that those decisions took quality of life issues into account. Gun states, "If you can create balance among your work, your community, your family, and your friends, then you're going to be more satisfied." Examples of this philosophy infusing Hanna Andersson include the establishment of HannaDowns, a clothing recycling program where customers can return used clothing and receive a 20% off coupon for their next purchase. The charitable nature of Hanna Andersson has continued through to what is now the HannaHelps program. This program awards grants and donates products to schools and nonprofit groups, helping children in the community and around the world. In addition, under Gun's leadership, Hanna Andersson established ongoing donations, 5% of pretax profits, to charities that benefit women and children.

The considerable growth and development the business experienced did not come without its challenges and necessary organizational change. In the 1990s and early 2000s, increased competition from other retailers and the introduction of online commerce posed some challenges for Hanna Andersson. The Denharts found themselves without a solid growth plan for the future. They worried that they might have lost sight of market forces. Change was necessary if Hanna Andersson was to remain viable.

Realizing the need for help and direction, the Denharts promoted from within the company to help initiate change and strategic growth, and in 1995, Phil Iosca took the strategic lead as CEO. Hanna Andersson was then sold to a private equity firm in 2001 and has since changed ownership several times, leading to a new business direction for the company. After selling the business, Gun remained on the Hanna board of directors until 2007. She also served as chair of the Hanna Andersson Children's Foundation from 2001 to 2006. She still partners with the company from time to time on charitable events in the community.

Under Iosca's steady leadership, the company opened several retail stores throughout the country in 2002 and established online commerce. In 2009, Hanna Andersson began distributing merchandise wholesale through retail partners such as Nordstrom and Costco. The implementation of each of these new distribution avenues required a great deal of change within the company. HR Vice President Gretchen Peterson explains, "The growth of the retail business required the greatest shift in our internal processes from both technical systems, to inventory planning and buying to distribution processes to our organizational communication and HR processes (recruitment, compensation, etc.), as well as our marketing communication programs." Tenured employees throughout the company found themselves in unfamiliar territory, unsure of the company's future as the board and owners debated the risks and rewards of retail expansion. Fortunately, the changes were mostly offset by a consistent leadership team. Petersen, who has been with the company since 1994, explains, "From 1995 to 2010, we retained the same CEO (Iosca) and therefore, the face of the company and the management style did not fluctuate greatly."

When Iosca retired in early 2010, chief operating officer Adam Stone took over as CEO. He helped the company cope with yet another transition through a calm push for changes within the company. To understand different points of view at Hanna Andersson, Stone often sat in on inventory and operational planning meetings. Step by step, Stone was able to break down work initiatives so the continuing changes were not so overwhelming to the company and its valued employees. Over time, his and other company leaders' presence has helped employees make better, more strategic decisions. Rather than resisting change, they now feel heard and understood.

The decision to sell wholesale turned out to be a good one, as it has enabled the company to weather the recession's negative effect on retail and online purchases. Accounting for approximately 10% of total sales, the company's wholesale business is expected to boost yearly revenue by 5%. With more conscientious inventory purchases and strategic distribution initiatives, Hanna Andersson has realized a higher sales volume, lower inventory at year-end, and less liquidation. Through it all, company management has done an effective job at interpreting the desired growth goals of its owners while inspiring change within the company. With continued clear communication, direction, and willingness to try new techniques, Hanna Andersson is poised for growth and success in the future while not forgetting to take care of its employees.

Case written by Amy Wester, Talya Bauer, and Berrin Erdogan to accompany Carpenter, M., Bauer, T., Erdogan, B., & Short, J. (2013). Principles of management (2nd ed.). New York: Flat World Knowledge. Based on information from Bollier, D. (1996). Aiming higher: 25 stories of how companies prosper by combining sound management and social vision, 23–35; Boulé, M. (2009, July 16). Hanna Andersson employee can't say enough of a thank-you to co-workers who helped her through cancer. Oregonian. Retrieved March 4, 2010, from http://www.oregonlive.com/news/oregonian/margie_boule/index.ssf/2009/07/hanna_andersson_employee_cant.html; Hanna Andersson home page. Retrieved February 28, 2010, from http://www.hannaandersson.com; Muoio, A. (1998, November 30). Giving back. Fast Company. Retrieved March 1, 2010, from http://www.fastcompany.com/magazine/20/one.html?page=0%2C1; Goldfield, R. (2002, June 14). Hanna sees bricks-and-mortar future. Portland Business Journal; G. Peterson, personal communication April 5, 2010. Retrieved March 1, 2010, from http://www.answers.com/topic/hanna-andersson; Raphel, M., & Raphel, N. (1995). Up the loyalty ladder (pp. 83–90). New York: HarperCollins.

CASE DISCUSSION QUESTIONS

1. How has Hanna Andersson applied values-based leadership in terms of the company's choices related to P-O-L-C?

2. How did company leaders like Iosca, Petersen, and Stone help facilitate change within the company? Did they remain consistent with the values of the founders?

3. What were the reasons for organizational change within Hanna Andersson, both internally and externally?

4. What unique challenges do family-owned and -operated businesses face?

5. How did the mission of Hanna Andersson evolve over time?

ENDNOTES

1. Retrieved September 10, 2012, from http://en.wikipedia.org/wiki/ Cheaper_by_the_Dozen. *Cheaper by the Dozen* was made into a 1950 motion picture starring Clifton Webb and Myrna Loy as Frank and Lillian Gilbreth.

2. Sinclair, U. (1911, June). A criticism. *American Magazine*, 243–244; Taylor, F. W. (June 1911). An answer to the criticism. *American Magazine*, 243–244. Retrieved September 10, 2012, from http://stevens.cdmhost.com/cdm4/document.php?CISOROOT=/ p4100coll1&CISOPTR=244&REC=14&CISOSHOW=242.

3. Peters, T. J., & Waterman, R. H. (1982). *In Search of Excellence*. New York: Knopf.

4. Kotter, J. P. (1990, May–June). What leaders really do. *Harvard Business Review*, pp. 85–95.

5. Davis, G. F., McAdam, D., Scott, W. R., & Zald, M. N. (Eds.). (2005). *Social Movements and Organization Theory* (p. 283). Cambridge Studies in Contentious Politics. Cambridge, UK: Cambridge University Press.

6. Rummler, L. (2007, July). Corporate social networking updates definition of women's groups. Retrieved September 10, 2012, from http://www.talentmgt.com/ newsletters/recruitment_perspectives/2007/July/380/index.php.

7. Vara, V. (2007, May 21). Facebook opens its pages as a way to fuel growth. *Wall Street Journal*. Retrieved September 10, 2012, from http://online.wsj.com/public/article/ SB117971397890009177-wjdKPmjAqS_9ZZbwiRp_CoSqvwQ_20070620.html.

8. Garvin, D. (1993, July–August). Building a learning organization. *Harvard Business Review*, 78–91.

9. Tapscott, A., & A. D. Williams. (2006). *Wikinomics: How Mass Collaboration Changes Everything*. New York: Portfolio.

10. Engardio, P. (2006, January 30). The future of outsourcing. *BusinessWeek*.

11. Porter, M. E., & Rivkin, J. W. (2012, March, 2012). Choosing the United States. *Harvard Business Review, 90*(3).

12. Retrieved September 10, 2012, from http://www.ncdc.noaa.gov/oa/climate/ severeweather/extremes.html.

13. Unruh, G., & Ettenson, R. (2010, November). Winning in the green frenzy. *Harvard Business Review, 88*(11).

14. Retrieved September 10, 2012, from http://www.mykleenextissue.com/ ?WT.srch=1&WT.mc_id=5659768&iq_id=5659768.

15. Fast company. (2008, March). Retrieved September 10, 2012, from http://www.fastcompany.com/magazine/123/google.html.

16. Retrieved September 10, 2012, from http://www.internetworldstats.com/stats.htm.

17. Retrieved Septermber 10, 2012, from http://www.itu.int/ITU-D/ict/statistics/ at_glance/KeyTelecom.html.

18. Corbett, S. (2008, April 13). Can the cellphone help end global poverty? *New York Times*.

19. Hua, V. (2007, March 27). South Korea: Everyone's a Journalist. http://www.pbs.org/ frontlineworld/rough/2007/03/south_korea.html; Schonfeld, & Yi-Wyn Yen. It's a Web, Web, Web 2.0 world. *Business 2.0 Magazine*. http://money.cnn.com/galleries/ 2007/biz2/0707/gallery.web_world.biz2/14.html.

20. Fast company. (2008, March). Retrieved September 10, 2012, from http://www.fastcompany.com/magazine/123/google.html.

21. Friedman, T. (2005). *The World Is Flat: A Brief History of the Twenty-first Century* (p. 81). New York: Farrar, Straus & Giroux.

22. Retrieved September, 2012 from http://www.fastcompany.com/magazine/124/ the-amazing-race.html.

23. Edwards, S. (2011, February 24). Today's leaders should be global. *Chief Learning Officer*. Retrieved September 10, 2012, from http://clomedia.com/articles/view/4121.

24. Hollenbeck, G. P., & McCall, M. W. 2003. Competence, not competencies: Making global executive development work. In W. Mobley & P. Dorfman (Eds.), *Advances in Global Leadership* (Vol. 3; pp. 101–119). Oxford: JAI Press.

25. Javidan, M., Dorfman, P. W., de Luque, M. S., & House R. J. (2006, February). In the eye of the beholder: Cross cultural lessons in leadership from Project GLOBE. *Academy of Management Perspectives, 20*, 67–90.

26. Brake, T. (1996). *The Global Leader* (p. 203). New York: McGraw-Hill.

27. *The Ethical Enterprise: A Global Study of Business Ethics*. (2005). New York: American Management Association.

28. Retrieved September 10, 2012, from http://www.sec.gov/news/press/2002-150.htm.

29. Retrieved September 10, 2012, from http://www.pg.com/company/who_we_are/ ppv.jhtml;jsessionid=MCSCEC20KZGJTQFIASJXKZOAVACJG3MK.

30. Piccolo, R. F., Greenbaum, R., den Hartog, D. N., & Folger, R. (2010). The relationship between ethical leadership and core job characteristics. *Journal of Organizational Behavior, 31*, 259–278.

31. Hartman, L., and DesJardins, J. (2008). *Business Ethics: Decision-Making for Personal Integrity and Social Responsibility*. New York: McGraw-Hill.

CHAPTER 3
Personality, Attitudes, and Work Behaviors

FIGURE 3.1

Donald Trump's enigmatic personality has led him to extremes in terms of both personal and business successes and failures.

Source: http://en.wikipedia.org/wiki/File:Donald_Trump_by_Gage_Skidmore.jpg

CHAPTER LEARNING OBJECTIVES

Reading this chapter will help you do the following:

1. Understand the roles of personality and values in determining work behaviors.
2. Explain the process of perception and how it affects work behaviors.
3. Identify the major work attitudes that affect work behaviors.
4. Define the concept of person-organization fit and how it affects work behaviors.
5. List the key set of behaviors that matter for organizational performance.
6. Be able to develop your positive attitude skills.

FIGURE 3.2 The P-O-L-C Framework

Planning	Organizing	Leading	Controlling
1. Vision & Mission	1. Organization Design	1. Leadership	1. Systems/Processes
2. Strategizing	2. Culture	2. Decision Making	2. Strategic Human Resources
3. Goals & Objectives	3. Social Networks	3. Communications	
		4. Groups/Teams	
		5. Motivation	

Individuals are unique. Each person brings a number of different personality traits, values, and attitudes to the organizations in which he or she works. Stable as well as changing personality traits affect how individuals behave and perform. Moreover, companies hire people with the expectation that they have certain knowledge, skills, abilities, personalities, and values. Employees' personalities, attitudes, and work behaviors affect how managers approach each of the planning-organizing-leading-controlling (P-O-L-C) framework dimensions. Here are just a few examples:

- When scanning for important trends during the planning process, a manager's perceptions color the information that is absorbed and processed.

- Employee preferences for job design and enrichment (two aspects of organizing) may be a function of individuals' personalities and values.

- Leading effectively requires an understanding of employees' personalities, values, and attitudes.

- Absenteeism can challenge a manager's ability to control costs and performance (at the group and individual levels).

Therefore, it is important for managers to understand the individual characteristics that matter for employee and manager behaviors.

1. PERSONALITY AND VALUES

LEARNING OBJECTIVES

1. Identify the major personality traits that are relevant to organizational behavior.
2. Explain the potential pitfalls of personality testing.
3. Describe the relationship between personality and work behaviors.
4. Understand what values are.
5. Describe the link between values and work behaviors.

1.1 Personality

personality

The relatively stable feelings, thoughts, and behavioral patterns a person has.

Personality encompasses a person's relatively stable feelings, thoughts, and behavioral patterns. Each of us has a unique personality that differentiates us from other people, and understanding someone's personality gives us clues about how that person is likely to act and feel in a variety of situations. To manage effectively, it is helpful to understand the personalities of different employees. Having this knowledge is also useful for placing people into jobs and organizations.

When scholars discuss personality characteristics as being "stable," this does not mean that an individual's personality exhibits no degree of change. You probably remember how you have changed and evolved as a result of your own life experiences, attention you have received in early childhood, successes and failures you experienced over the course of your life, and other life events. In fact, personality does change over long periods of time. For example, we tend to become more socially dominant, more conscientious (organized and dependable), and more emotionally stable between the ages of 20 and 40, whereas openness to new experiences tends to decline as we age.[1] In other words, even though we treat personality as relatively stable over short periods of time, change occurs. Moreover, even in childhood, our personality matters, and it has lasting consequences for us. For example, studies show that part of our career success and job satisfaction later in life can be explained by our childhood personality.[2]

Is our behavior in organizations dependent on our personality? Yes and no. While we will discuss the effects of personality for employee behavior, you must remember that the relationships we describe are modest. For example, having a sociable and outgoing personality may encourage people to seek friends and prefer social situations. This does not mean that their personality will immediately affect their work behavior. At work, we have a job to do and a role to perform. Therefore, our behavior may be more strongly affected by what is expected of us, as opposed to how we want to behave. Especially in jobs that involve a lot of autonomy, or freedom, personality tends to exert a strong influence on work behavior.[3]

Big Five Personality Traits

How many personality traits exist? In the English language alone, more than 15,000 words describing personality have been identified. When researchers analyzed the traits describing personality characteristics, they realized that many different words might be used to describe a single dimension of personality. When these words were grouped, five dimensions emerged that explain much of the variation in our personalities.[4] These five are not necessarily the only traits that exist. Still, understanding them gives us a good start for describing personality.

FIGURE 3.3 The Big Five Personality Traits

Researchers have discovered that five key traits explain much of the variation in individual personalities. We outline each of these traits below.

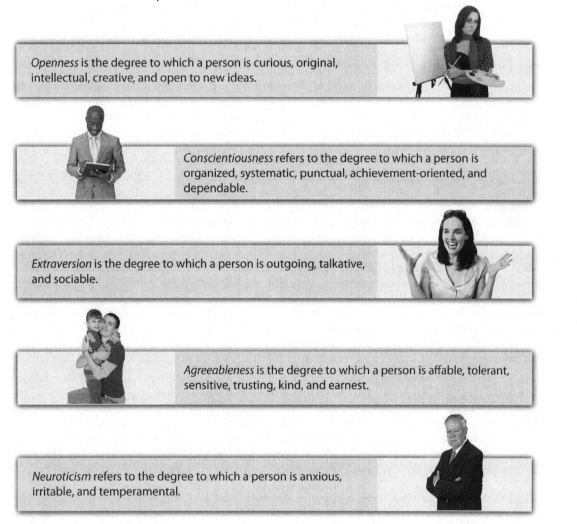

Openness is the degree to which a person is curious, original, intellectual, creative, and open to new ideas.

Conscientiousness refers to the degree to which a person is organized, systematic, punctual, achievement-oriented, and dependable.

Extraversion is the degree to which a person is outgoing, talkative, and sociable.

Agreeableness is the degree to which a person is affable, tolerant, sensitive, trusting, kind, and earnest.

Neuroticism refers to the degree to which a person is anxious, irritable, and temperamental.

© *Thinkstock*

The Big Five dimensions of Openness, Conscientiousness, Extraversion, Agreeableness, and Neuroticism can be remembered using the acronym OCEAN. Everyone has some degree of each of these traits; it is the unique configuration of how high a person rates on some traits and how low on others that produces the individual quality we call personality.

Openness is the degree to which a person is curious, original, intellectual, creative, and open to new ideas. People high in openness seem to thrive in situations that require flexibility and learning new things. In fact, individuals who have this trait are more likely to be drawn to jobs with a creative component. For example, students between the ages of 6 and 12 who were rated higher in openness by their teachers were likely to be working in artistic jobs when they grew up.[5] As employees, these individuals are highly motivated to learn new skills and do well in training.[6] They also have an advantage when they enter into a new organization. Their open-mindedness leads them to seek a lot of information and feedback about how they are doing and to build relationships, which leads to quicker adjustment to the new job.[7] They can utilize organizational resources and their own personal network to

openness

The degree to which a person is curious, original, intellectual, creative, and open to new ideas.

maximize creativity at work.[8] Compared with people low in openness, they are also more likely to start their own business.[9] The potential downside is that they may also be prone to becoming more easily bored or impatient with routine.

Conscientiousness refers to the degree to which a person is organized, systematic, punctual, achievement-oriented, and dependable. Conscientiousness is the one personality trait that uniformly predicts how high a person's performance will be across a variety of occupations and jobs. The ability of those high in conscientiousness to be reliable and rational decision makers has advantages on and off the job—for example, they tend to have higher credit scores compared to those low in conscientiousness.[10] Not surprisingly, conscientiousness is the trait most desired by recruiters, and highly conscientious applicants tend to succeed in interviews.[11] Once they are hired, conscientious employees not only tend to perform well, but they also have higher levels of motivation, lower levels of turnover, lower levels of absenteeism, and higher levels of safety performance at work.[12] In other words, conscientious employees are highly desirable to businesses. In return, companies tend to reward those who have this trait, which results in higher levels of career success and career satisfaction over time.[13] Finally, conscientiousness is a particularly valuable trait for entrepreneurs. Highly conscientious people are more likely to start their own business compared with those who are not, and their firms have longer survival rates and better performance.[14]

Extraversion is the degree to which a person is outgoing, talkative, sociable, and enjoys socializing. Interacting with others and being social energizes extraverts, whereas similar levels of stimulation and interactions may be viewed as draining to someone who is an introvert. One of the established findings is that extraverts tend to be effective in jobs involving sales. For example, when obligated to show "service with a smile," they are more effective and convincing, resulting in more tips from customers, whereas similar behaviors seem to backfire for introverts and result in less tips![15] Moreover, they tend to be effective as managers and they demonstrate inspirational leadership behaviors.[16] Extraverts do well in social situations, and, as a result, they tend to be effective in job interviews. Part of this success comes from preparation, as they are likely to reach out to their social network in order to prepare for the interview.[17] Extraverts have an easier time than introverts do when adjusting to a new job. Adjusting to a new job requires seeking out information and feedback early on, which extraverts are generally more comfortable with doing.[18] Interestingly, extraverts are also found to be happier at work, which may be because of the relationships they build with the people around them and their easier adjustment to a new job.[19] However, they do not necessarily perform well in all jobs; jobs depriving them of social interaction may be a poor fit. Moreover, they are not necessarily model employees. For example, they tend to have higher levels of absenteeism at work, potentially because they may miss work to hang out with or attend to the needs of their friends.[20]

Agreeableness is the degree to which a person is affable, tolerant, sensitive, trusting, kind, and warm. In other words, people who are high in agreeableness are likeable people and get along with others. Not surprisingly, agreeable people help others at work consistently; this helping behavior does not depend on their good mood.[21] They are also less likely to retaliate when other people treat them unfairly.[22] This may reflect their ability to show empathy and to give people the benefit of the doubt. Agreeable people may be a valuable addition to their teams and may be effective leaders because they create a positive environment when they are in leadership positions. In fact, they are regarded as highly ethical leaders by their subordinates.[23] At the other end of the spectrum, people low in agreeableness are less likely to show these positive behaviors. Moreover, people who are disagreeable are shown to quit their jobs unexpectedly, perhaps in response to a conflict with a boss or a peer.[24] If agreeable people are so nice, does this mean that we should only look for agreeable people when hiring? You might expect some jobs to require a low level of agreeableness. When hiring a lawyer, would you prefer a kind and gentle person or someone who can stand up to an opponent? People high in agreeableness may also be too trusting and submissive, sacrificing their own well-being for others. Research shows that agreeable individuals tend to have lower levels of financial credit ratings, which may be a result of making promises they are not able to keep or possibly cosigning loans for friends and family and then getting into financial trouble.[25] Because they avoid conflict, they may miss opportunities for initiating constructive change or get into difficulties while attempting to please others.

Neuroticism refers to the degree to which a person is anxious, irritable, temperamental, and moody. It is perhaps the only Big Five dimension where scoring high is undesirable. People high in neuroticism experience a number of problems at work, mostly because of their difficulties with handling stress. Neurotic people have a tendency to experience anger when confronted with the daily hassles of their work, including time pressure and red tape, and they respond to this daily stress by drinking after hours. Moreover, they have trouble forming and maintaining relationships and are less likely to be the ones that people go to for advice and friendship.[26] They tend to be habitually unhappy in their jobs and report high intentions to leave, but they do not necessarily actually leave their jobs.[27] Being high in neuroticism seems to be harmful to one's career, as these employees have lower levels of career

© *Thinkstock*

success (measured with income and occupational status achieved in one's career). Finally, if they achieve managerial jobs, they tend to create an unfair climate at work.[28]

Video Link

Evaluate Yourself on the Big Five Personality Factors

See how you score on these factors:

http://www.outofservice.com/bigfive

Other Personality Dimensions

In addition to the Big Five personality dimensions, researchers have proposed various other dimensions, or traits, relevant to understanding personality. These include self-monitoring, proactive personality, self-esteem, and self-efficacy.

Self-monitoring refers to the extent to which a person is capable of altering his or her actions and appearance in social situations. People who are self-monitors are social chameleons who understand what the situation demands and act accordingly, while low social monitors tend to act the way they feel. High self-monitors are sensitive to the types of behaviors the social environment expects from them. These individuals are rated as higher performers and emerge as leaders, and they tend to be very effective at networking—they constantly add new people to their social network and serve as social connectors between other people.[29] Self-monitors are effective in influencing other people and are able to get things done by managing their impressions. As managers, however, they tend to have lower accuracy in evaluating the performance of their employees. It seems that while trying to manage their impressions, they may avoid giving accurate feedback to their subordinates to avoid confrontations, which could hinder a manager's ability to carry out the controlling function.[30]

Proactive personality refers to a person's inclination to fix what is wrong, change things, and use initiative to solve problems. Instead of waiting to be told what to do, proactive people take action to initiate meaningful change and remove the obstacles they face along the way. Proactive employees also are more successful over the course of their careers because they use initiative and acquire greater understanding of how the politics within the company work.[31] Proactive people are valuable assets to their companies because they may have higher levels of performance.[32] They adjust to their new jobs quickly because they understand the political environment better, make friends more quickly, and are more responsive to feedback they receive.[33] For all their potential, under some circumstances a proactive personality may be a liability for a person or an organization. Proactive individuals, often perceived as too pushy, try to change things other people are not willing to let go of, use their initiative to make decisions that do not serve a company's best interests, or may have trouble in workplace situations. Research shows that a proactive person's success depends on his or her understanding of the company's core values, ability, and skills to perform the job and ability to assess situational demands correctly.[34]

Self-esteem is the degree to which a person has overall positive feelings about himself or herself. People with high self-esteem view themselves in a positive light, are confident, and respect themselves. In contrast, people with low self-esteem experience high levels of self-doubt and question their self-worth. High self-esteem is related to higher levels of satisfaction with one's job, higher levels of performance on the job, and higher levels of creativity at work.[35] People with low self-esteem are attracted to situations where they will be relatively invisible, such as large companies.[36] Managing employees with low self-esteem may be challenging at times because negative feedback given with the intention of improving performance may be viewed as a negative judgment on their worth as an employee. Therefore, effectively managing employees with relatively low self-esteem requires tact and providing lots of positive feedback when discussing performance incidents.

FIGURE 3.5

Rumored to have cut off his own ear, Vincent Van Gogh, one of the world's most famous—and most neurotic—artists, did not see success during his lifetime.

Source: http://en.wikipedia.org/wiki/ File:Vincent_Willem_van_Gogh_106.jpg

self-monitoring

The extent to which a person is capable of altering one's actions and appearance in social situations.

proactive personality

A person's inclination to fix what is wrong, change things, and use initiative to solve problems.

self-esteem

The degree to which a person has overall positive feelings about oneself.

FIGURE 3.6 Self-Esteem around the Globe

Self-Esteem Around the Globe

Which nations have the highest average self-esteem? Researchers asked this question by surveying almost 17,000 individuals across 53 nations, in 28 languages.

On the basis of this survey, these are the top 10 nations in terms of self-reported self-esteem:

1.	Serbia	6.	United States of America
2.	Chile	7.	Turkey
3.	Israel	8.	Mexico
4.	Peru	9.	Croatia
5.	Estonia	10.	Austria

The following are the 10 nations with the lowest self-reported self-esteem:

1.	South Korea	6.	Taiwan
2.	Switzerland	7.	Czech Republic
3.	Morocco	8.	Bangladesh
4.	Slovakia	9.	Hong Kong
5.	Fiji	10.	Japan

Source: Adapted from information in Denissen, J. J. A., Penke, L., & Schmitt, D. P. (2008, July). Self-esteem reactions to social interactions: Evidence for sociometer mechanisms across days, people, and nations. Journal of Personality & Social Psychology, 95, 181–196; Hitti, M. (2005). Who's No. 1 in self-esteem? Serbia is tops, Japan ranks lowest, U.S. is no. 6 in global survey. WebMD. Retrieved September 12, 2012, from http://www.webmd.com/ skin-beauty/news/20050927/whos-number-1-in-self-esteem; Schmitt, D. P., & Allik, J. (2005). The simultaneous administration of the Rosenberg self-esteem scale in 53 nationals: Culture-specific features of global self-esteem. Journal of Personality and Social Psychology, 89, 623–642.

FIGURE 3.7 The Pygmalion Effect, Self-Efficacy, and Seasickness

In Greek mythology, Pygmalion was a sculptor who created a statue of a woman so beautiful and realistic that he fell in love with it. Management scholars have applied the idea to a concept called the Pygmalion effect where individuals can shape a person's personality to expectations, much like Pygmalion shaped the statue to become his idea of a perfect woman.

Self-efficacy refers to an individual's belief in his or her own abilities. In one unique study, a researcher was trying to test the degree to which a self-efficacy could be changed in regard to a biological process. He tried to see if you could create seasickness self-efficacy where if you believed you wouldn't get seasick. Applying self-efficacy ideas to seasickness was unique because when the waters get really rough, everyone is subject to getting seasick eventually.

In the study, the researcher gave members of the navy a number of tests. Then, some soldiers were told they were less prone to seasickness based on their test results.

The other group was shown the standard military training videos that show soldiers puking once the waters started to get rough.

Key Takeaway: The Pygmalion effect (based on the expectations individuals place on others) has the ability to influence an individual's self-efficacy (the belief in one's own abilities.)

After they all went out to see for the first time, lo and behold, the group that was told they have a higher seasickness self-efficacy was less likely to lose their lunch.

Reprinted with permission from Short, J. C., Bauer, T., Ketchen, D. J., & Simon, L. (2011). Atlas Black: The complete adventure. Irvington, NY: Flat World Knowledge.

FIGURE 3.8

Organizations using personality tests should ensure that the questions they ask are not being used to discriminate based on sex, race, age, disability, or other legally protected characteristics.

© Thinkstock

FIGURE 3.9

The Wonderlic Cognitive Ability Test is used by the National Football League when evaluating the learning aptitude of new players entering the draft.

Source: http://en.wikipedia.org/wiki/
File:PNS_2707.jpg

Self-efficacy is a belief that one can perform a specific task successfully. Research shows that the belief that we can do something is a good predictor of whether we can actually do it. Self-efficacy is different from other personality traits in that it is job specific. You may have high self-efficacy in being successful academically, but low self-efficacy in relation to your ability to fix your car. At the same time, people have a certain level of generalized self-efficacy, and they have the belief that whatever task or hobby they tackle, they are likely to be successful in it.

Research shows that self-efficacy at work is related to job performance.[37] This is probably because people with high self-efficacy actually set higher goals for themselves and are more committed to their goals, whereas people with low self-efficacy tend to procrastinate.[38] Academic self-efficacy is a good predictor of your grade point average, as well as whether you persist in your studies or drop out of college.[39]

Is there a way of increasing employee's self-efficacy? In addition to hiring people who are capable of performing the required job tasks, training people to increase their self-efficacy may be effective. Some people may also respond well to verbal encouragement. By showing that you believe they can be successful and effectively playing the role of cheerleader, a manager may be able to increase self-efficacy beliefs. Empowering people—giving them opportunities to test their skills so that they can see what they are capable of—is also a good way of increasing self-efficacy.[40]

1.2   Personality Testing in Employee Selection

Personality is a potentially important predictor of work behavior. In job interviews, companies try to assess a candidate's personality and the potential for a good match, but interviews are only as good as the people conducting them. Unfortunately, research has shown that most interviewers are not particularly good at detecting the one trait that best predicts performance: conscientiousness.[41]

One method some companies use to detect the people who are potentially good job candidates is personality testing. Several companies conduct pre-employment personality tests. Companies using them believe that these tests improve the effectiveness of their selection and reduce turnover. For example, Overnight Transportation in Atlanta found that using such tests reduced their on-the-job delinquency by 50%–100%.[42]

Experts have not yet reached an agreement regarding the best way to select employees, and the topic is highly controversial. Some experts cite data indicating that personality tests predict performance, while others note important criteria such as job satisfaction. A key consideration in this debate is that how a personality test is used influences its validity. Imagine filling out a personality test in class. You will probably fill it out as honestly as you can. Then, if your instructor correlates your personality scores with your class performance, we could say that the correlation is meaningful. But now imagine that your instructor tells you, before giving you the test, that based on your test scores, you will secure a coveted student assistant position, which comes with a tuition waiver and a stipend. In that case, would you still fill out the test honestly or would you try to make your personality look as "good" as possible?

In employee selection, where the employees with the "best" personalities will be the ones receiving a job offer, a complicating factor is that people filling out the survey do not have a strong incentive to be honest. In fact, they have a greater incentive to guess what the job requires and answer the questions in a way they think the company is looking for. As a result, the rankings of the candidates who take the test may be affected by their ability to fake desired qualities. Some experts believe that this is a serious problem. In fact, it is estimated that 20%–50% of all job applicants give fake responses in personality tests.[43] Others point out that even with **faking** the tests remain valid because the scores are related to job performance.[44]

Scores on personality self-assessments are distorted for other reasons beyond the fact that some candidates can fake better than others. For example, using a survey assumes that individuals understand their own personalities, but this may not be the case. How supervisors, coworkers, and customers see our personality may matter more than how we see ourselves. Therefore, using self-report measures may not be the best way of measuring someone's personality, whereas asking our former colleagues or supervisors may reveal more accurate answers. In fact, observers are surprisingly accurate in assessing our personality. In one study, evaluators were able to accurately assess the personality of others simply by looking at and rating their Facebook pages.[45] In addition, individuals may be tempted to give aspirational answers to surveys. If you are asked whether you are honest, you may think, "Yes, I always have the intention to be honest." While this answer relates to how you value honesty, it may say nothing about your actual level of honesty in any given situation.

Another problem with personality tests is the uncertain relationship between performance and personality. Research has shown that personality is not a particularly strong indicator of how a person will perform at work. According to one estimate, personality only explains about 10%–15% of variation in job performance. Our performance at work depends on many factors, and personality does not seem to be the key factor for performance. In fact, cognitive ability (your overall mental intelligence) is a more powerful predictor of job performance. Instead of personality tests, cognitive ability tests may do a better job of predicting who will be good performers. Personality is a better predictor of job satisfaction and other attitudes, but screening people out on the assumption that they may be unhappy at work is a challenging argument to make in an employee selection context.

In any case, if an organization decides to use personality tests for selection, it is important to be aware of their limitations. If they are used together with other tests, such as tests of cognitive abilities, they may contribute to making better decisions. The company should ensure that the test fits the job and actually predicts performance. This is called validating the test. Before giving the test to applicants, the company could give it to existing employees to find out the traits that are most important for success in this particular company and job. Then, in the selection context, the company can pay particular attention to those traits.

Finally, the company also needs to make sure that the test does not discriminate against people on the basis of sex, race, age, disabilities, and other legally protected characteristics. Rent-a-Center experienced legal difficulties when the test they used was found to violate the Americans with Disabilities Act (ADA). The company used the Minnesota Multiphasic Personality Inventory for selection purposes, but this test was developed to diagnose severe mental illnesses; it included items such as "I see things or people around me others do not see." In effect, the test served the purpose of a clinical evaluation and was discriminating against people with mental illnesses, which is a protected category under ADA.[46]

1.3 Values

Values refer to people's stable life goals, reflecting what is most important to them. Values are established throughout one's life as a result of accumulating life experiences, and values tend to be relatively stable.[47] The values that are important to people tend to affect the types of decisions they make, how they perceive their environment, and their actual behaviors. Moreover, a person is more likely to accept a job offer when the company possesses the values he or she cares about.[48] Value attainment is one reason people stay in a company. When a job does not help them attain their values, they are likely to decide to leave if they are dissatisfied with the job.[49]

What are the values people care about? As with personality dimensions, researchers have developed several frameworks, or typologies, of values. One particularly useful framework includes 10 values outlined in Figure 3.10[50]

Values people hold will affect their employment. For example, someone who values stimulation highly may seek jobs that involve fast action and high risk, such as firefighter, police officer, or emergency medical technician positions. Someone who values achievement highly may be likely to become an entrepreneur. An individual who values benevolence and universalism may seek work in the nonprofit sector with a charitable organization or in a "helping profession," such as nursing or social work. Like personality, values have implications for Organizing activities, such as assigning duties to specific jobs or developing the chain of command; employee values are likely to affect how employees respond to changes in the characteristics of their jobs.

In terms of work behaviors, a person is more likely to accept a job offer when the company possesses the values he or she cares about. A firm's values are often described in the company's mission and vision statements, an element of the planning function. Value attainment is one reason people stay in a company. When a job does not help them attain their values, they are likely to decide to leave if they are also dissatisfied with the job.[51]

FIGURE 3.10 Valuing Your Career Choices

Values refer to the stable life goals held by individuals. The values individuals hold dear have implications for the types of industries and jobs individuals find interesting. Here, we pair values included in Schwartz's (1992) Value Inventory with examples of jobs that reflect those values.

Achievement—the desire for personal success. Careers in sales often focus on this value by offering commissions to align individuals with organizational outcomes.

Benevolence—the desire to protect the well-being of people who are close to the person. Allstate Insurance's pledge that "you're in good hands" demonstrates the role of benevolence common to many insurance agencies.

Conformity—being motivated through self-discipline and obedience to the will of others. Careers in the military might be a good fit for individuals who hold such values in high regard.

Hedonism—the desire for pleasure in life. The gaming industry has been referred to as a "sin" industry due to its ties with what many consider hedonistic activities. Such a perspective has been embraced by the Las Vegas Convention and Visitors Authority marketing slogan, "What happens in Vegas, stays in Vegas."

Power—the desire for control over others, attaining authority and prestige. The 2006 comedic drama *The Devil Wears Prada* illustrates the role of power within the fashion industry.

© *Thinkstock*

Security—valuing safety and stability. Firefighters and police officers undergo extensive training to help them achieve goals of protecting and serving others.

Self-direction—the desire to be free and independent. Many academics are drawn to a career in research because of the ability to independently pursue their intellectual curiosity on any number of topics with relatively little outside influence.

Stimulation—the desire for a stimulating and exciting life. Careers in big-game hunting, adventure travel, and deep-sea diving exemplify jobs that embrace the need for stimulation.

Tradition—acceptance of social customs and traditional ideas in society. Individuals valuing traditional ideas might enjoy working in event planning.

Universalism—the desire to protect the well-being of all people with a care for social justice. Groups that promote human rights, such as Amnesty International, demonstrate a potential career choice for individuals who value universalism.

KEY TAKEAWAY

Personality traits and values are two dimensions on which people differ. Personality is the unique, relatively stable pattern of feelings, thoughts, and behavior that each individual displays. Big Five personality dimensions (Openness, Conscientiousness, Extraversion, Agreeableness, and Neuroticism) are important traits; others that are particularly relevant for work behavior include self-efficacy, self-esteem, social monitoring, and proactive personality. While personality is a stronger influence over job attitudes, its relation to job performance is weaker. Some companies use personality testing to screen out candidates. Companies using personality tests are advised to validate their tests and use them to supplement other techniques with greater validity, such as tests of cognitive ability. Companies must also ensure that a test does not discriminate against any protected group. Values express a person's life goals; they are similar to personality traits in that they are relatively stable over time. In the workplace, a person is more likely to accept a job that provides opportunities for value attainment. People are also more likely to remain in a job or career that satisfies their values.

E X E R C I S E S

1. Think about the personality traits covered in this section. Can you think of jobs or occupations that seem particularly suited to each trait? Which traits would be universally desirable across all jobs?

2. What are the unique challenges of managing employees who have low self-efficacy and self-esteem? How would you deal with this situation?

3. What are some methods that companies can use to assess employee personality?

4. Have you ever held a job where your personality did not match the demands of the job? How did you react to this situation? How were your attitudes and behaviors affected?

5. Identify ways in which the Big Five (of the manager and/or the employees) may affect how you as a manager would carry out the Leadership function.

2. PERCEPTION

L E A R N I N G   O B J E C T I V E S

1. **Understand the influence of biases in the process of perception.**
2. **Describe how we perceive visual objects and how these tendencies may affect our behavior.**
3. **Describe the biases of self-perception.**
4. **Describe the biases inherent in our perceptions of other people.**

perception

The process by which individuals detect and interpret environmental stimuli.

Our behavior is a function not only of our personality and values but also of the situation. We interpret our environment, formulate responses, and act accordingly. **Perception** may be defined as the process by which individuals detect and interpret environmental stimuli. What makes human perception so interesting is that we do not solely respond to the stimuli in our environment. We go beyond the information that is present in our environment, pay selective attention to some aspects of the environment, and ignore other elements that may be immediately apparent to other people.

Our perception of the environment is not entirely rational. For example, have you ever noticed that while glancing at a newspaper or a news Web site, information that is especially interesting or important to you seems to jump out of the page and catch your eye? If you are a sports fan, while scrolling down the pages, you may immediately see a news item describing the latest success of your team. If you were recently turned down for a loan, an item of financial news may jump out at you. Therefore, what we see in the environment is a function of what we value, our needs, our fears, and our emotions. In fact, what we see in the environment may be objectively flat out wrong because of such mental tendencies. For example, one experiment showed that when people who were afraid of spiders were shown spiders, they inaccurately thought that the spider was moving toward them.[52] In this section, we will describe some common perceptual tendencies we engage in when perceiving objects or other people and the consequences of such perceptions.

2.1 Visual Perception

Our visual perception definitely goes beyond the physical information available to us; this phenomenon is commonly referred to as "optical illusions." Artists and designers of everything from apparel to cars to home interiors make use of optical illusions to enhance the look of the product. Managers rely on their visual perception to form their opinions about people and objects around them and to make sense of data presented in graphical form. Therefore, understanding how our visual perception may be biased is important.

For example, we extrapolate from the information available to us and may see things that are not actually there. Similarly, when we look at objects that are partially blocked, we see the whole.[53]

FIGURE 3.11

Danish psychologist Edgar Rubin created this famous image, which can be perceived as a vase form or two faces.

© *Thinkstock*

Look at Figure 3.11. What do you see? Most people look at this figure and see two faces *or* a goblet, depending on which color they focus upon. Our visual perception is often biased because we do not perceive objects in isolation. The contrast between our focus of attention and the remainder of the environment may make an object appear bigger or smaller.

This principle is shown here in Figure 3.12. At first glance, the circle on the left may appear bigger, but they are the same size. This is due to the visual comparison of the middle circle on the left with its surrounding circles, whereas the middle circle on the right is compared with the bigger circles surrounding it.

How do these tendencies influence behavior in organizations? The fact that our visual perception is faulty means that managers should not always take what they see at face value. Let's say that you dislike one of your peers and you think that you saw this person surfing the Web during work hours. Are you absolutely sure, or are you simply filling the gaps? Have you really seen this person surf unrelated Web sites, or is it possible that the person was searching for work-related purposes? The tendency to fill in the gaps also causes our memory to be faulty. Imagine that you have been at a meeting where several people made comments that you did not agree with. After the meeting, you may attribute most of these comments to people you did not like. In other words, you may twist the reality to make your memories more consistent with your opinions of people.

Video Link

View More Illusions Here:

http://www.squidoo.com/artistic-illusions

The tendency to compare and contrast objects and people to each other also causes problems. For example, if you are a manager who has been given an office much smaller than the other offices on the floor, you may feel that your workspace is crowded and uncomfortable. If the same office is surrounded by smaller offices, you may actually feel that your office is comfortable and roomy. In short, our biased visual perception may lead to inaccurate inferences about the people and objects around us.

FIGURE 3.12

Although our perceptions may suggest otherwise, the two circles in the middle of the six outer circles are the same size.

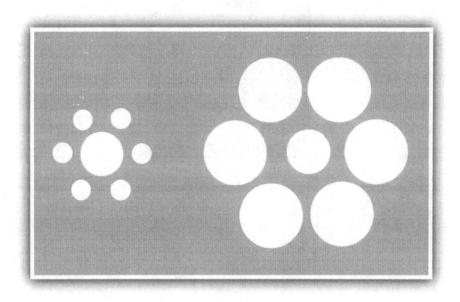

2.2   Self-Perception

Human beings are prone to errors and biases when perceiving themselves. The types of bias people have depend on their personality. Many people suffer from **self-enhancement bias**, in which individuals tend to overestimate performance and capabilities and see themselves in a more positive light than do others. People who have a narcissistic personality are particularly subject to this bias, but many others also have this bias to varying degrees.[54] At the same time, other people have the opposing extreme, which may be labeled as **self-effacement bias**, or modesty bias. This is the tendency to underestimate performance and capabilities and see events in a way that portrays them in a more negative light. Individuals with low self-esteem are more prone to making this error. These tendencies have real consequences for behavior in organizations. For example, people who suffer from extreme levels of self-enhancement tendencies may not understand why they are not getting promoted or rewarded, while those who have a tendency to self-efface may project low confidence and take more blame for their failures than necessary.

When human beings perceive themselves, they are also subject to the **false consensus error**. Simply put, such individuals overestimate how similar they are to other people.[55] An example of this error is when individuals assume that whatever quirks they have are shared by a larger number of people than in reality. People who take office supplies home, tell white lies to their boss or colleagues, or take credit for other people's work to get ahead may genuinely feel that these behaviors are more common than they are in reality. The problem for behavior in organizations is that, when people believe that a behavior is common and normal, they may repeat the behavior more freely. Under some circumstances, this may lead to a high level of unethical or even illegal behaviors.

2.3   Social Perception

How we perceive other people in our environment is also shaped by our biases. Moreover, how we perceive others will shape our behavior, which in turn will shape the behavior of the person we are interacting with.

One of the factors biasing our perception is **stereotypes**. Stereotypes are generalizations based on a group characteristic. For example, believing that women are more cooperative than men or that men are more assertive than women are stereotypes. Stereotypes may be positive, negative, or neutral. In the abstract, stereotyping is an adaptive function—we have a natural tendency to categorize the information around us to make sense of our environment. Just imagine how complicated life would be if we continually had to start from scratch to understand each new situation and each new person we encountered. What makes stereotypes potentially discriminatory and a perceptual bias is the tendency to generalize from a group to a particular individual. If the belief that men are more assertive than women leads to choosing a man over an equally qualified female candidate for a position, the decision will be biased, unfair, and potentially illegal.

Stereotypes often create a situation called **self-fulfilling prophecy**. This happens when an established stereotype causes one to behave in a certain way, which leads the other party to behave in a way that confirms the stereotype.[56] If you have a stereotype such as "Asians are friendly," you are more likely to be friendly toward an Asian person. Because you are treating the other person more nicely, the response you get may also be nicer, which confirms your original belief that Asians are friendly. Of course, just the opposite is also true. Suppose you believe that "young employees are slackers." You are less likely to give a young employee high levels of responsibility or interesting and challenging assignments. The result may be that the young employee reporting to you may become increasingly bored at work and start goofing off, confirming your suspicions that young people are slackers.

Stereotypes persist because of a process called selective perception. **Selective perception** simply means that we pay selective attention to parts of the environment while ignoring other parts, which is particularly important during the planning process. Our background, expectations, and beliefs will shape which events we notice and which events we ignore. For example, an executive's functional background will affect the changes he or she perceives in the environment.[57] Executives with a background in sales and marketing see the changes in the demand for their product, while executives with a background in information technology may more readily perceive the changes in the technology the company is using. Selective perception may also perpetuate stereotypes because we are less likely to notice events that go against our beliefs. A person who believes that men drive better than women may be more likely to notice women driving poorly than men driving poorly. As a result, a stereotype is maintained because information to the contrary may not even reach our brain.

Let's say we noticed information that goes against our beliefs. What then? Unfortunately, this is no guarantee that we will modify our beliefs and prejudices. First, when we see examples that go against our stereotypes, we tend to come up with subcategories. For example, people who believe that women are more cooperative may classify an assertive female as a "career woman." Therefore, the example to the contrary does not violate the stereotype and is explained as an exception to the rule.[58] Or, we may simply discount the information. In one study, people in favor of and against the death penalty were shown two studies, one showing benefits for the death penalty while the other disconfirming any benefits. People rejected the study that went against their belief as methodologically inferior and ended up believing in their original position even more![59] In other words, using data to debunk people's beliefs or previously established opinions may not necessarily work, a tendency to guard against when conducting planning and controlling activities.

One other perceptual tendency that may affect work behavior is **first impressions**. The first impressions we form about people tend to have a lasting effect. In fact, first impressions, once formed, are surprisingly resilient to contrary information. Even if people are told that the first impressions were caused by inaccurate information, people hold on to them to a certain degree because once we form first impressions, they become independent of the evidence that created them.[60] Therefore, any information we receive to the contrary does not serve the purpose of altering them. Imagine the first day that you met your colleague Anne. She treated you in a rude manner, and when you asked for her help, she brushed you off. You may form the belief that Anne is a rude and unhelpful person. Later on, you may hear that Anne's mother is seriously ill, making Anne very stressed. In reality, she may have been unusually stressed on the day you first met her. If you had met her at a time when her stress level was lower, you could have thought that she is a really nice person. But chances are, your impression that she is rude and unhelpful will not change even when you hear about her mother. Instead, this new piece of information will be added to the first one: She is rude, unhelpful, and her mother is sick.

As a manager, you can protect yourself against this tendency by being aware of it and making a conscious effort to open your mind to new information. It would also be to your advantage to pay careful attention to the first impressions you create, particularly during job interviews.

self-fulfilling prophecy

When an established stereotype causes one to behave in a certain way, which leads the other party to behave in a way that makes the stereotype come true.

selective perception

When we pay selective attention to parts of the environment while ignoring other parts.

FIGURE 3.13

A job interview is one situation where impressions formed during the first few minutes may have lasting consequences for your relationship with future colleagues. Research has shown that a firm handshake with three or four up-and-down pumps is key to making a positive impression.

© *Thinkstock*

first impressions

Initial thoughts and perceptions we form about people that tend to be stable and resilient to contrary information.

KEY TAKEAWAY

Perception is how we make sense of our environment in response to environmental stimuli. While perceiving our surroundings, we go beyond the objective information available to us and our perception is affected by our values, needs, and emotions. There are many biases that affect human perception of objects, self, and others. When perceiving the physical environment, we fill in the gaps and extrapolate from the available information. When perceiving others, stereotypes influence our behavior. Stereotypes may lead to self-fulfilling prophecies. Stereotypes are perpetuated because of our tendency to pay selective attention to aspects of the environment and ignore information inconsistent with our beliefs. Understanding the perception process gives us clues to understanding human behavior.

EXERCISES

1. What are some of the typical errors, or optical illusions, that we experience when we observe physical objects?
2. What are the problems of false consensus error? How can managers deal with this tendency?
3. Describe a situation where perception biases have or could affect any of the P-O-L-C facets. Use an example you have experienced or observed, or, if you do not have such an example, create a hypothetical situation. How do we manage the fact that human beings develop stereotypes? Is there such as thing as a good stereotype? How would you prevent stereotypes from creating unfairness in management decisions?
4. Describe a self-fulfilling prophecy you have experienced or observed in action. Was the prophecy favorable or unfavorable? If unfavorable, how could the parties have chosen different behaviors to produce a more positive outcome?

3. WORK ATTITUDES

LEARNING OBJECTIVES

1. **Define what work attitudes are.**
2. **Define and differentiate between job satisfaction and organizational commitment.**
3. **List several important factors influencing job satisfaction and organizational commitment.**
4. **Identify two ways companies can track attitudes in the workplace.**

attitude

Our opinions, beliefs, and feelings about aspects of our environment.

job satisfaction

The feelings people have toward their job.

organizational commitment

The emotional attachment people have toward the company they work for.

How we behave at work often depends on how we feel about being there. Therefore, making sense of how people behave depends on understanding their work attitudes. An **attitude** refers to our opinions, beliefs, and feelings about aspects of our environment. We have attitudes toward the food we eat, people we meet, courses we take, and things we do. At work, two job attitudes have the greatest potential to influence how we behave. These are job satisfaction and organizational commitment.

Job satisfaction refers to the feelings people have toward their job. If the number of studies conducted on job satisfaction is an indicator, job satisfaction is probably the most important job attitude. Institutions such as Gallup or the Society for Human Resource Management (SHRM) periodically conduct studies of job satisfaction to track how satisfied employees are at work. According to a recent SHRM study, 83% of respondents were at least somewhat satisfied with their jobs.[61]

Organizational commitment is the emotional attachment people have toward the company they work for. A highly committed employee is one who accepts and believes in the company's values, is willing to put out effort to meet the company's goals, and has a strong desire to remain with the company. People who are committed to their company often refer to their company as "we" as opposed to "they" as in "in this company, we have great benefits." The way we refer to the company indicates the type of attachment and identification we have with the company.

There is a high degree of overlap between job satisfaction and organizational commitment because things that make us happy with our job often make us more committed to the company as well. Companies believe that these attitudes are worth tracking because they often are associated with outcomes that are important to the Controlling role, such as performance, helping others, absenteeism, and turnover.

3.1   What Causes Positive Work Attitudes?

What makes you satisfied with your job and develop commitment to your company? Research shows that people pay attention to several factors of their work environment, including characteristics of the job (a function of Organizing activities), how they are treated (related to Leadership actions), the relationships they form with colleagues and managers (also Leadership related), and the level of stress the job entails. In addition, what people value at any given time may be a function of the economic circumstances and the job market. For example, a Global Workforce Study conducted during the late 2000s recession shows that 86% of workers felt a secure or stable position was most important to their happiness at work, surpassing factors that are more important in more prosperous times, such as growth opportunities.[62]

As we have seen earlier in this chapter, personality and values play important roles in how employees feel about their jobs.

FIGURE 3.14 Factors Contributing to Job Satisfaction and Organizational Commitment

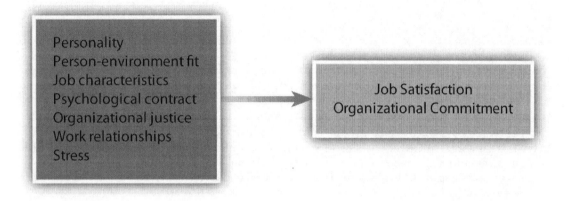

Person-Environment Fit

The fit between what we bring to our work environment and environmental demands influences both our behavior and our work attitudes. Therefore, person-job fit and person-organization fit are positively related to job satisfaction and commitment. When the abilities of individuals match those of the job's demands and the company's values, individuals tend to be more satisfied with the job and more committed to the company.[63]

When companies hire employees, they are interested in assessing at least two types of fit. **Person-organization fit** refers to the degree to which a person's personality, values, goals, and other characteristics match those of the organization. **Person-job fit** is the degree to which a person's knowledge, skills, abilities, and other characteristics match the job's demands. (Human resources professionals often use the abbreviation KSAO to refer to these four categories of attributes.) Thus someone who is proactive and creative may be a great fit for a company in the high-tech sector, which would benefit from risk-taking individuals, but may be a poor fit for a company that puts a high priority on routine and predictable behavior, such as a nuclear power plant. Similarly, a proactive and creative person may be a great fit for a field-based occupation, such as marketing manager, but a poor fit for an office job highly dependent on rules, such as accountant.

person-organization fit

The degree to which a person's values, personality, goals, and other characteristics match those of the organization.

person-job fit

The degree to which a person's skill, knowledge, abilities, and other characteristics match the job's demands.

psychological contract

The unspoken, informal understanding that an employee will contribute certain things to the organization and will receive certain things in return.

Some companies are in a great position to attract people who fit. For example, lifestyle retailers such as Patagonia, Columbia Sportswear, and Nike draw people who are attracted to the active, outdoorsy lifestyle these companies focus on. The core values of these businesses, such as preserving the environment, appeal to job candidates who enjoy spending much of their time in nature. To someone who enjoys surfing, being a product tester for surfing gear may be highly appealing. Thus it is no surprise that when people fit into their organization, they tend to be more satisfied with their jobs, more committed to their companies, and more influential, and they remain longer in their companies.[64]

Job Characteristics

Employees tend to be more satisfied and committed in jobs that involve certain characteristics. The ability to use a variety of skills, feeling empowered at work, receiving feedback on the job, and performing a significant task are some job characteristics related to satisfaction and commitment. However, the presence of these factors is not important for everyone. Some people have a high need for growth; these employees tend to be more satisfied when their jobs help them build new skills and improve.[65]

Organizational Justice and the Psychological Contract

A strong influence over our satisfaction level is how fairly we are treated. People pay attention to the fairness of company policies and procedures, fair and kind treatment from supervisors, and fairness of their pay and other rewards they receive from the company.[66] Organizational justice can be classified into three categories: (1) procedural (fairness in the way policies and processes are carried out), (2) distributive (the allocation of resources or compensation and benefits), and (3) interactional (the degree to which people are treated with dignity and respect). At the root of organizational justice is trust, something that is easier to break than to repair if broken.

The **psychological contract** is the unspoken, informal understanding that an employee will contribute certain things to the organization (e.g., work ability and a willing attitude) and will receive certain things in return (e.g., reasonable pay and benefits). Under the psychological contract, an employee may believe that if he or she works hard and receives favorable performance evaluations, he or she will receive an annual bonus, periodic raises and promotions, and will not be laid off. Since the "downsizing" trend of the past 20 years, many commentators have declared that the psychological contract is violated more often than not.

Relationships at Work

Two strong predictors of our happiness at work and commitment to the company are our relationships with coworkers and managers. The people we interact with, how friendly they are, whether we are socially accepted in our work group, and whether we are treated with respect by them are important to our happiness at work. Research also shows that our relationship with our manager, how considerate the manager is, and whether we build a trust-based relationship with our manager are critically important to our job satisfaction and organizational commitment.[67] When our manager and overall management listen to us, care about us, and value our opinions, we tend to feel good at work. When establishing effective relations with employees, little signals that you care about your employees go a long way. For example, San Francisco's Hotel Carlton was taken over and renovated by a new management group, Joie de Vivre Hospitality. One of the small things the new management did that created dramatic results was that, in response to an employee attitude survey, they replaced the old vacuum cleaners housekeepers were using and started replacing them every year. It did not cost the company much to replace old machinery, but this simple act of listening to employee problems and taking action went a long way to make employees feel better.[68]

Stress

Not surprisingly, the amount of stress present in a job is related to employee satisfaction and commitment. Stressors range from environmental ones (noise, heat, inadequate ventilation) to interpersonal ones (organizational politics, conflicts with coworkers) to organizational ones (pressure to avoid making mistakes, worrying about the security of the job). Some jobs, such as intensive care unit nurse and military fighter pilot, are inherently very stressful.

Another source of stress has to do with the roles people are expected to fulfill on and off the job. Role ambiguity is uncertainty about what our responsibilities are in the job. Role conflict involves contradictory demands at work; it can also involve conflict between fulfilling one's role as an employee and other roles in life, such as the role of parent, friend, or community volunteer.

Generally speaking, the higher the stress level, the lower job satisfaction tends to be. But not all stress is bad, and some stressors actually make us happier. For example, working under time pressure and having a high degree of responsibility are stressful, but they are also perceived as challenges and tend to be related to high levels of satisfaction.[69]

3.2   Assessing Work Attitudes in the Workplace

Given that work attitudes provide valuable clues about who will leave or stay with an organization, why some individuals will perform better, and which employees will be more engaged, tracking satisfaction and commitment levels is a helpful step for companies. If there are company-wide issues that make employees unhappy and disengaged, these need to be resolved. There are at least two systematic ways in which companies can track work attitudes: through **attitude surveys** and exit interviews. Companies such as KFC restaurants, the SAS Institute, Google, and others give periodic attitude surveys, which are used to track employee work attitudes. Companies can get more out of these surveys if responses are held confidential. If employees become concerned that their individual responses will be shared with their immediate manager, they are less likely to respond honestly. Moreover, success of these surveys depends on the credibility of management in the eye of employees. If management periodically collects these surveys but no action comes out of them, employees may adopt a more cynical attitude and start ignoring these surveys, hampering the success of future efforts. **Exit interviews** involve a meeting with the departing employee. This meeting is often conducted by a member of the human resource management department. If conducted well, this meeting may reveal what makes employees dissatisfied at work and give management clues about areas for improvement.

The connection between work attitudes and behaviors depends on the attitude in question. Your attitudes toward your colleagues may influence whether you actually help them on a project, but they may not be a good predictor of whether you quit your job. Second, attitudes are more strongly related to intentions to behave in a certain way, rather than actual behaviors. When you are dissatisfied with your job, you may have the intention to leave. Whether you actually leave will be a different story. Your leaving will depend on many factors, such as availability of alternative jobs in the market, your employability in a different company, and sacrifices you have to make while changing jobs. Thus, while the attitudes assessed through employee satisfaction surveys and exit interviews can provide some basis for predicting how a person might behave in a job, it's important to note that behavior is also strongly influenced by situational constraints.

FIGURE 3.16
Blame It on the Bridezillas

Event coordinator was listed among the top 10 highest-stress jobs, along with police officer, firefighter, and enlisted soldier.

© Thinkstock; caption retrieved from http://www.careercast.com/jobs-rated/10-most-stressful-jobs-2012

attitude surveys

Surveys that are given to employees tracking their work attitudes.

exit interview

A meeting with the departing employee.

FIGURE 3.17

Companies such as KFC track employee attitudes to ensure they remain finger lickin' good in the workplace.

Source: http://www.flickr.com/photos/elizaio/5631748475

KEY TAKEAWAY

Work attitudes are the feelings we have toward different aspects of the work environment. Job satisfaction and organizational commitment are two key attitudes that are the most relevant to important outcomes. In addition to personality and fit with the organization, work attitudes are influenced by the characteristics of the job, perceptions of organizational justice and the psychological contract, relationships with coworkers and managers, and the stress levels experienced on the job. Many companies assess employee attitudes through surveys of worker satisfaction and through exit interviews. The usefulness of such information is limited, however, because attitudes create an intention to behave in a certain way, but they do not always predict actual behaviors.

EXERCISES

1. What is the difference between job satisfaction and organizational commitment? How do the two concepts relate to one another?

2. In your opinion, of the factors that influence work attitudes, which three are the most important in making people dissatisfied with their jobs? Which three are the most important relating to organizational commitment?

3. How can companies assess person-job fit before hiring employees? What methods do you think would be helpful? What can they do to increase person-job and person-organization fit after they hire employees?

4. Do you think making employees happier at work is a good way of motivating people? When would high satisfaction not be related to high performance?

5. How important is pay in making people attached to a company and making employees satisfied?

4. WORK BEHAVIORS

LEARNING OBJECTIVES

1. Define job performance, organizational citizenship, absenteeism, and turnover.
2. Explain factors associated with each type of work behavior.

One of the important objectives in the field of management is to understand why people behave the way they do. We focus on four key work behaviors: job performance, organizational citizenship behaviors, absenteeism, and turnover. The first two behaviors are desirable ones, whereas the other two are often regarded as undesirable. While these four are not the only organizational behaviors managers are concerned about, if you understand these behaviors and the major influences over each type of behavior, you will gain valuable knowledge surrounding these key behaviors in the workplace.

FIGURE 3.18   Factors That Have the Strongest Influence over Work Behaviors

Job Performance	Organizational Citizenship	Absenteeism	Turnover
General mental abilities	Organizational justice and interpersonal relations	Health problems	Having low performance
Organizational justice and interpersonal relations	Personality	Work/life balance issues	Negative work attitudes
Stress (−)	Positive work attitudes	Negative work attitudes	Stress
Positive work attitudes	Older employee	Younger employee	Personality
Personality			Younger employee & shorter tenure

4.1   Job Performance

Job performance refers to the degree to which an employee successfully fulfills the factors included in the job description. For each job, the content of job performance may differ. Measures of job performance include quality and quantity of work performed by the employee, the accuracy and speed with which the job is performed, and the overall effectiveness of the person on the job.

In many companies, job performance determines whether a person is promoted, rewarded with pay raises, given additional responsibilities, or fired from the job. Therefore, most employers observe and track job performance. This is accomplished by tracking data on topics such as the number of sales the employee closes, the number of clients the employee visits, the number of defects found in the employee's output, or the number of customer complaints or compliments received about the person's work. In some jobs, objective performance data may not be available, and instead supervisor, coworker, customer, and subordinate assessments of the quality and quantity of work performed by the person become the indicators of job performance. Job performance is one of the main outcomes studied in organizational behavior and is an important variable managers must assess when they are engaged in the controlling role.

job performance

The performance level on factors included in the job description.

What Are the Major Predictors of Job Performance?

general mental ability

Our reasoning abilities, verbal and numerical skills, analytical skills, or overall intelligence level.

Under which conditions do people perform well, and what are the characteristics of high performers? The most powerful influence over our job performance is our **general mental ability** also known as cognitive ability or intelligence, and often abbreviated as "g." General mental ability can be divided into several components—reasoning abilities, verbal and numerical skills, and analytical skills—and it seems to be important across different situations. It seems that "g" starts influencing us early in our school days because it is strongly correlated with measures of academic success even in childhood.[70] In adult life, "g" is also correlated with different measures of job performance.[71] It seems that the influence of "g" on performance is important across different settings, but there is also variation. In jobs with high complexity, it is much more critical to have high general mental abilities. Examples of such jobs are manager, sales representative, engineer, and professions such as law and medicine. In jobs such as police officer and clerical worker, the importance of "g" for high performance is still important but weaker.

Perceptions of organizational justice and interpersonal relationships are factors determining performance level. When employees feel they are being fairly treated by the company, when management is supportive and rewards high performance, and when individuals trust the people they work with, performance is better. The primary reason seems to be that when individuals believe they are treated well, they want to reciprocate. Therefore individuals treat the company well by performing their jobs more effectively.

The *stress* experienced on the job also determines performance level. When individuals are stressed, mental energies are drained. Instead of focusing on the task at hand, individuals start concentrating on the stressor. Because attention and energies are diverted to dealing with stress, performance suffers. Having role ambiguity and experiencing conflicting role demands are related to lower performance.[72] Stress that prevents individuals from doing their jobs does not have to be related to experiences at work. For example, according to a survey conducted by Workplace Options, 45% of the respondents said that financial stress affects work performance. When people are in debt, worrying about their mortgage payments or college payments of their kids, their performance will suffer.[73]

Work attitudes, particularly job satisfaction, are also correlates of job performance. Many studies have been devoted to understanding whether happy employees are more productive. Some studies show weak correlations between satisfaction and performance while others show higher correlations.[74] The correlation between commitment and performance tends to be even weaker.[75]

It seems that happy workers have an inclination to be more engaged at work. They may *want* to perform better. They may be more motivated. But there are also exceptions, because the desire to perform better does not mean that individuals will actually perform better. Rather, skill level in performing the job is a major factor in job performance. There are also some jobs where performance depends on factors beyond an employee's control, such as the pace of the machine where they are working. For this reason, in professional fields such as engineering and research, as opposed to manual jobs such as assembly-line work, there is a stronger link between work attitudes and performance.[76] Does disliking a job mean that individuals will reduce their performance? Maybe up to a certain point, but there will be factors that prevent individuals from reducing performance, such as the fear of getting fired, the desire to get a promotion in order to get out of a job that they dislike, or a professional work ethic. As another example, among nurses, there seems to be a weak correlation between satisfaction and performance. Even when they are unhappy, nurses put a lot of effort into their work because they feel a moral obligation to help their patients. As a result, we should not expect a one-on-one relationship between satisfaction and performance. Still, the observed correlation between work attitudes and performance is important and has practical value.

Finally, job performance has a modest relationship with *personality* traits, particularly conscientiousness. People who are organized, reliable, dependable, and achievement oriented seem to outperform others in various contexts.[77]

FIGURE 3.19

The fact that general mental ability influences job performance may come as no surprise to singer Shakira, whose 140 IQ puts her at the genius level. When not performing, she is a UNICEF Goodwill Ambassador.

Source: http://en.wikipedia.org/wiki/ File:Shakira_Rio_02.jpg

4.2 Organizational Citizenship Behaviors

While job performance refers to the performance of duties listed in one's job description, organizational citizenship behaviors involve performing behaviors that are more discretionary. Organizational citizenship behaviors (OCB) are voluntary behaviors employees perform to help others and benefit the organization. Helping a new coworker understand how things work in the company and volunteering to organize the company picnic are some examples of citizenship behaviors. These behaviors contribute to the smooth operation of business.

What are the major predictors of citizenship behaviors? Unlike job performance, citizenship behaviors do not depend on one's general mental abilities. Job performance, to a large extent, depends on general mental abilities. When you add the education, skills, knowledge, and abilities that are needed to perform well, the role of motivation on performance becomes more limited. As a result, just because someone is motivated will not mean that the person will perform well. For citizenship behaviors, in contrast, the motivation-behavior link is clearer. Individuals help others if they feel motivated to do so, and managers, in the Leadership role, are responsible for motivating employees.

Perhaps the most important factor explaining citizenship behaviors is *organizational justice* and *interpersonal relationships*. When individuals have a good relationship with their managers; are supported, treated fairly, and attached to peers; and trust the people at work, they are more likely to engage in citizenship behaviors. In a high-quality relationship, individuals feel the obligation to reciprocate and go the extra mile to help out coworkers.[78]

Personality is yet another explanation for why individuals perform citizenship behaviors. Personality is a modest predictor of actual job performance but a much better predictor of citizenship. People who are conscientious and agreeable tend to perform citizenship behaviors more often than others.[79]

Job attitudes are also moderately related to citizenship behaviors—more so than they are to job performance. People who are happier at work, those who are more committed to their companies, and those who have overall positive attitudes toward their work situation tend to perform citizenship behaviors more often than others. When people are unhappy, they tend to be disengaged from their jobs and rarely go beyond the minimum that is expected of them.[80]

Interestingly, age seems to be related to the frequency with which we demonstrate citizenship behaviors. People who are older are better citizens. It is possible that with age we gain more experiences to share. It becomes easier to help others because we have more accumulated company and life experiences to draw from.[81]

4.3   Absenteeism

Absenteeism refers to unscheduled absences from work. Such absences are costly to companies because of their unpredictable nature, affecting a manager's ability to Control the firm's or department's budget. When an employee has an unscheduled absence from work, companies struggle to find replacement workers at the last minute. This may involve hiring contingent workers, having other employees work overtime, or scrambling to cover for an absent coworker. The cost of **absenteeism** to organizations is estimated at $153 billion.[82]

absenteeism

Failure to appear at work.

What causes absenteeism? Some absenteeism is unavoidable and is related to *health reasons*. For example, reasons such as acute or serious illness, lower back pain, migraines, accidents one may have on or off the job, or acute stress are important reasons for absenteeism.[83] Health-related absenteeism is costly, but it would be unreasonable and unfair to institute organizational policies penalizing such absences. When an employee has a contagious illness, showing up at work will infect coworkers and will not be productive. Indeed, companies are finding that programs aimed at keeping workers healthy are effective in dealing with this type of absenteeism. Companies using wellness programs, educating employees about proper nutrition, helping them exercise, and rewarding them for healthy habits have reported reduced absenteeism. In fact, a transportation authority in Austin, Texas, notes that the return on investment of their wellness program focusing on weight loss and nutrition is $2.50 for every dollar spent.[84]

Work-life balance is another common reason for absences. Staying home to care for a sick family member, attending the wedding or funeral of a loved one, and skipping work to study for an exam are all common reasons for unscheduled absences. Companies may deal with these by giving employees more flexibility in work hours. If employees can manage their own time, they are less likely to be absent. Conversely, when a company has "sick leave" but no other leave for social and family obligations, they may fake being sick and use their "sick leave." One solution is to have a single paid time off policy that would allow workers to balance work and life and allow companies to avoid unscheduled absences. Organizations such as Lahey Clinic at Burlington, Massachusetts, have found this to be effective in dealing with unscheduled absences. Some companies such as IBM got rid of sick leave altogether and instead allow employees to take as much time off as they need, so long as the work gets done.[85]

FIGURE 3.20

Understanding the value of corporate wellness, The Bridges wellness program at Rancho Santa Fe Gold Community in Southern California includes Wii Tennis.

Sometimes, absenteeism is a form of work withdrawal and a step followed by turnover. In other words, *poor work attitudes* lead to absenteeism. When employees are dissatisfied with their work, have low organizational commitment, or perceive that they are treated unfairly, they are likely to be absent more often. In this case, management may deal with absenteeism by investigating the causes of dissatisfaction and dealing with them.

Research does not reveal a consistent link between personality and absenteeism, but there is one demographic criterion that predicts absenteeism: age. Interestingly, and against some stereotypes that increased age would bring more health problems, research shows that age is negatively related to both frequency and duration of absenteeism. That is, younger workers are the ones more likely to be absent. Because of reasons that include higher loyalty to their company and a stronger work ethic, older employees are less likely absent from work.[86]

Source: http://www.flickr.com/ photos/imuttoo/325076189

4.4 Turnover

FIGURE 3.21

Although many view shopping as a fun activity, this feeling does not translate to employees as jobs in retail are historically among the highest in turnover.

© *Thinkstock*

Turnover refers to an employee's leaving an organization. Employee **turnover** has potentially harmful consequences, such as poor customer service and poor company-wide performance. When employees leave, their jobs still need to be performed by someone, so companies spend time recruiting, hiring, and training new employees, all the while suffering from lower productivity. Yet not all turnover is bad. Turnover is particularly a problem when high-performing employees leave, while a poor performer's leaving may actually give the company a chance to improve productivity and morale.

Why do employees leave? An employee's *performance* level is an important reason. People who perform poorly are actually more likely to leave. These people may be fired, may be encouraged to quit, or may quit because of their fear of being fired. Particularly if a company has pay-for-performance systems, poor performers will find that they are not earning much due to their below-standard performance. This gives poor performers an extra incentive to leave. This does not mean that high performers will definitely stay with a company. High performers may find it easier to find alternative jobs, so when they are unhappy, they can leave more quickly.

Work attitudes are often the primary culprit in why people leave. When workers are unhappy at work, and when they do not feel committed to their companies, they are more likely to leave. Loving the things you do, being happy with the opportunities for advancement within the company, being happy about pay are all aspects of our work attitudes relating to turnover. The link between work attitudes and turnover is not direct. When employees are unhappy, they will have the intention to leave and may start looking for a job. But their ability to actually leave will depend on many factors, such as their employability and the condition of the job market. For this reason, when national and regional unemployment is high, many people who are unhappy will still continue to work for their current company. Understanding the connection between employee happiness and turnover, many companies make an effort to make employees happy. Turner Construction in Chicago was able to reduce its turnover rate from 21% to 3.8% by focusing on flexibility and employee happiness and executing policies such as allowing employees to take off after 2 p.m. every Friday in the summer and giving employees their birthdays off. The focus on worker well-being had support from the highest levels of the business.[87]

People are more likely to quit their jobs if they experience *stress* at work as well. Stressors such as role conflict and role ambiguity drain energy and motivate people to seek alternatives. For example, call center employees experience a great deal of stress because of poor treatment from customers, long work hours, and constant monitoring of their every action. Companies such as EchoStar realize that one method that is effective in retaining their best employees is to give them opportunities to move to higher-responsibility jobs elsewhere in the company. When a stressful job is a step toward a more desirable job, employees seem to stick around longer.[88]

There are also individual differences in the reasons people leave or stay with organizations. For example, *personality* is a factor in the decision to quit one's job. People who are conscientious, agreeable, and emotionally stable are less likely to quit their jobs. Many explanations are possible. People with these personality traits may perform better at work, which leads to lower turnover. Or they may have better relations with coworkers and managers, which is a factor in their retention. Whatever the reason, it seems that some people are likely to stay longer at any given job regardless of the circumstances.[89]

Whether individuals leave a job or stay also depends on *age* and *how long they have been at an organization*. It seems that younger employees are more likely to leave. This is not surprising because people who are younger often have fewer responsibilities such as supporting a household or having dependents. As a result, they can quit a job they dislike much more easily. They may also have higher expectations and thus be more easily disappointed when a job proves to be less rewarding than they had imagined. Similarly, people who have been with a company for a short period of time can quit more easily. For example, Sprint Nextel found that many of their new hires were likely to quit within 45 days of their hiring dates. When they investigated, they found that newly hired employees were experiencing a lot of stress from avoidable problems such as unclear job descriptions or problems with hooking up their computers. Sprint was able to solve the turnover problem by paying special attention to orienting new hires. New employees experience a lot of stress at work, and there is usually not much keeping them in the company such as established bonds to a manager or colleagues. New employees may even have ongoing job interviews with other companies when they start working. This, too, gives them the flexibility to leave more easily.

Employees demonstrate a wide variety of positive and negative behaviors at work. Among these, four are critically important and have been extensively studied in the management literature. Job performance is the degree of success with which one accomplishes the tasks listed in one's job description. A person's abilities, particularly general mental ability, are the main predictor of job performance in many occupations. How we are treated at work, the level of stress experienced at work, work attitudes, and, to a lesser extent, our personalities are also factors relating to one's job performance. Citizenship behaviors are tasks helpful to the organization that go above and beyond one's job description. Performance of citizenship behaviors are less a function of our abilities and more of motivation. How individuals are treated at work, personality, work attitudes, and age are the main predictors of citizenship. Among negative behaviors employees demonstrate, absenteeism and turnover are critically important. People who experience health problems and work-life balance issues are prone to more absenteeism. Poor work attitudes are also related to absenteeism, and younger employees are more likely to be absent from work, especially when dissatisfied. Turnover is higher among low performers, people who have negative work attitudes, and those who experience a great deal of stress. Personality and being younger are personal predictors of turnover.

EXERCISES

1. What is the difference between performance and organizational citizenship behaviors? As a manager, how would you improve someone's performance? How would you increase citizenship behaviors?

2. Are citizenship behaviors always beneficial to the company? Can you think of any citizenship behaviors employees may perform with the intention of helping a company but that may have negative consequences overall?

3. Given the factors correlated with job performance, which employee selection methods should be better at identifying future high performers?

4. What are the major causes of absenteeism at work? How can companies minimize the level of absenteeism that takes place?

5. In some companies, managers are rewarded for minimizing the turnover within their department or branch. A part of their bonus is directly tied to keeping the level of turnover below a minimum. What do you think about the potential effectiveness of these programs? Do you see any downsides to such programs?

5. DEVELOPING YOUR POSITIVE ATTITUDE SKILLS

LEARNING OBJECTIVES

1. **Learn to be happier at work.**
2. **Leverage your attitudes for optimum work performance.**

Have you ever wondered how you could be happier at work and how greater work satisfaction could improve your overall effectiveness? Here are some ideas that may help you achieve a great sense of peace for yourself as well as when you are working with a negative coworker.

- *Leverage your Big Five traits.* Your personality is a big part of your happiness. Which of the Big Five positive traits are you strongest on? Be aware of them and look for opportunities to express them at work. Are you high on Neuroticism? If so, work to overcome this challenge: If you choose to find the negative side of everything, you will.

- *Find a job and company that fit you well.* Good fit with the job and company are important to your happiness. This starts with knowing yourself, your chosen career, and the particular job in question: What do you want from the job? What do you enjoy doing?

- *Get accurate information about the job and the company.* Ask detailed questions about what life is like in this company. Do your research. Read about the company; use your social network to understand the company's culture.

- *Develop good relationships at work.* Make friends. Try to get a mentor if your company does not have a formal mentoring program. Approach a person you admire and attempt to build a relationship with this person. An experienced mentor can be a great help in navigating life at a

FIGURE 3.22

Research shows that acting positive at work can actually help you become happier over time as emotions can be influenced by actions.

© Thinkstock

company. Your social network can help you weather the bad days and provide you with emotional and instrumental support during your time at a company as well as afterward.

- Pay is important, but *job characteristics matter more to your job satisfaction*. So don't sacrifice the job itself for a bit more money. When choosing a job, look at the level of challenge and the potential of the job to make you feel engaged.

- *Be proactive in managing organizational life.* If the job is stressful, cope with it by effective time management and having a good social network, as well as being proactive in getting to the source of stress. If you don't have enough direction, ask for it!

- *Know when to leave.* If the job makes you unhappy over an extended period of time and there is little hope of solving the problems, it may be time to look elsewhere.

KEY TAKEAWAY

Promoting a positive work attitude will increase your overall effectiveness as a manager. You can increase your own happiness at work by knowing yourself as a person, by ensuring that you work at a job and company where you fit in, and by building effective work relationships with your manager, coworkers, and subordinates. Concentrating on the motivating potential of the job when choosing a job and solving the problems you encounter in a proactive manner may be helpful as well.

EXERCISES

1. Do you believe that your own happiness at work is in your hands? What have you done in the past to increase your own satisfaction with work?

2. Consider the most negative person you work or interact with. Why do you think they focus more on the negative side of life?

3. On the basis of what you have read in this chapter, can you think of ways in which you can improve your effectiveness in dealing with negative coworkers?

6. CASE IN POINT: ADVICE FOR HIRING SUCCESSFUL EMPLOYEES FROM GUY KAWASAKI

FIGURE 3.23

Source: http://commons.wikimedia.org/wiki/File:Guy_Kawasaki,_2006.jpg.

When people think about entrepreneurship, they often think of Guy Kawasaki (http://www.guykawasaki.com), who is a Silicon Valley venture capitalist and the author of nine books as of 2010, including *The Art of the Start* and *The Macintosh Way*. Beyond being a best-selling author, he has been successful in a variety of areas, including earning degrees from Stanford University and UCLA; being an integral part of the creation of Apple's first computer; writing columns for *Forbes* and *Entrepreneur Magazine*; taking on entrepreneurial ventures, such as cofounding Alltop, an aggregate news site; and becoming managing director of Garage Technology Ventures. Kawasaki is a believer in the power of individual differences. He believes that successful companies include people from many walks of life, with different backgrounds and with different strengths and different weaknesses. Establishing an effective team requires a certain amount of self-monitoring on the part of the manager. Kawasaki maintains that most individuals have personalities that can easily get in the way of this objective. He explains, "The most important thing is to hire people who complement you and are better than you in specific areas. Good people hire people that are better than themselves." He also believes that mediocre employees hire less-talented employees in order to feel better about themselves. Finally, he believes that the role of a leader is to produce more leaders, not to produce followers, and to be able to achieve this a leader should compensate for their weaknesses by hiring individuals who compensate for their shortcomings.

In today's competitive business environment, individuals want to think of themselves as indispensable to the success of an organization. Because an individual's perception that he or she is the most important person on a team can get in the way, Kawasaki maintains that many people would rather see a company fail than thrive without them. He advises that we must begin to move past this and to see the value that different perceptions and values can bring to a company, and the goal of any individual should be to make the organization that one works for stronger and more dynamic. Under this type of thinking, leaving a company in better shape than one found it would become a source of pride. Kawasaki has had many different roles in his professional career and as a result realized that while different perceptions and attitudes might make the implementation of new protocol difficult, this same diversity is what makes an organization more valuable. Some managers fear diversity and the possible complexities that it brings, and they make the mistake of hiring similar individuals without any sort of differences. When it comes to hiring, Kawasaki believes that the initial round of interviews for new hires should be held over the phone. Because first impressions are so important, this ensures that external influences, negative or positive, are not part of the decision-making process.

Many people come out of business school believing that if they have a solid financial understanding, then they will be successful and appropriate leaders and managers. Kawasaki has learned that mathematics and finance are the "easy" part of any job. He observes that the true challenge comes in trying to effectively manage people. With the benefit of hindsight, Kawasaki regrets the choices he made in college, saying, "I should have taken organizational behavior and social psychology" to be better prepared for the individual nuances of people. He also believes that working hard is a key to success and that individuals who learn how to learn are the most effective over time.

If nothing else, Guy Kawasaki provides simple words of wisdom to remember when starting off on a new career path: don't become blindsided by your mistakes, but rather take them as a lesson of what not to do. And most important, pursue joy and challenge your own personal assumptions.

Case written by Carlene Reynolds, Talya Bauer, & Berrin Erdogan to accompany Carpenter, M., Bauer, T., Erdogan, B., & Short, J. (2013). Principles of management (2nd ed.). New York: Flat World Knowledge. Sources: Bryant, A. (2010, March 19). Just give him 5 sentences, not "War and Peace." New York Times. Retrieved September 12, 2012, from http://www.nytimes.com/2010/03/21/business/21corner.html?emc=eta1; Kawasaki, G. (2004). The art of the start: The time-tested, battle-hardened guide for anyone starting anything. New York: Penguin Group; Iwata, E. (2008, November 10). Kawasaki doesn't accept failure; promotes learning through mistakes. Retrieved September 12, 2012, from LexisNexis Academic database.

CASE DISCUSSION QUESTIONS

1. Describe how self-perception can positively or negatively affect a work environment.
2. What advice would you give a recent college graduate after reading Guy Kawasaki's advice?
3. What do you think about Kawasaki's hiring strategy?
4. How would you describe a "perfect" boss?
5. How would Kawasaki describe a "perfect" boss?

ES

W., Walton, K. E., & Viechtbauer, W. (2006). Patterns of mean-level change nality traits across the life course: A meta-analysis of longitudinal studies. *Psy- gical Bulletin, 132*, 1–25.

dge, T. A., & Higgins, C. A. (1999). The big five personality traits, general mental abil- ity, and career success across the life span. *Personnel Psychology, 52*, 621–652.

3. Barrick, M. R., & Mount, M. K. (1993). Autonomy as a moderator of the relationships between the big five personality dimensions and job performance. *Journal of Applied Psychology, 78*, 111–118.
4. Goldberg, L. R. (1990). An alternative "description of personality": The big-five factor structure. *Journal of Personality & Social Psychology, 59*, 1216–1229.
5. Woods, S. A., & Hampson, S. E. (2010). Predicting adult occupational environments from gender and childhood personality traits. *Journal of Applied Psychology, 95*, 1045–1057.
6. Lievens, F., Harris, M. M., Van Keer, E., & Bisqueret, C. (2003). Predicting cross-cultural training performance: The validity of personality, cognitive ability, and dimensions measured by an assessment center and a behavior description interview. *Journal of Applied Psychology, 88*, 476–489.
7. Wanberg, C. R., & Kammeyer-Mueller, J. D. (2000). Predictors and outcomes of pro-activity in the socialization process. *Journal of Applied Psychology, 85*, 373–385.
8. Baer, M. (2010). The strength-of-weak-ties perspective on creativity: A comprehensive examination and extension. *Journal of Applied Psychology, 95*, 592–601.
9. Zhao, H., & Seibert, S. E. (2006). The big five personality dimensions and entrepreneurial status: A meta-analytic review. *Journal of Applied Psychology, 91*, 259–271.
10. Barrick, M. R., & Mount, M. K. (1991). The big five personality dimensions and job performance: A meta-analysis. *Personnel Psychology, 44*, 1–26; Bernerth, J. B., Taylor, S. G., Walker, H. J., & Whitman, D. S. (2012). An empirical investigation of dispositional antecedents and performance-related outcomes of credit scores. *Journal of Applied Psychology, 97*, 469–478.
11. Tay, C., Ang, S., & Van Dyne, L. (2006). Personality, biographical characteristics, and job interview success: A longitudinal study of the mediating effects of interviewing self-efficacy and the moderating effects of internal locus of control. *Journal of Applied Psychology, 91*, 446–454.
12. Judge, T. A., & Ilies, R. (2002). Relationship of personality to performance motivation: A meta-analytic review. *Journal of Applied Psychology, 87*, 797–807; Judge, T. A., Zimmerman, R. D. (2008). Understanding the impact of personality traits on individuals' turnover decisions: A meta-analytic path model. *Personnel Psychology, 61*, 309–348.
13. Judge, T. A., & Higgins, C. A. (1999). The big five personality traits, general mental ability, and career success across the life span. *Personnel Psychology, 52*, 621–652.
14. Zhao, H., & Seibert, S. E. (2006). The big five personality dimensions and entrepreneurial status: A meta-analytic review. *Journal of Applied Psychology, 91*, 259–271; Zhao, H., Seibert, S. E., Lumpkin, G. T. (2010). The relationship of personality to entrepreneurial intentions and performance: A meta-analytic review. *Journal of Management, 36*, 381–404.
15. Chi, N. W., Grandey, A. A., Diamond, J. A., & Krimmel, K. R. (2011). Want a tip? Service performance as a function of emotion regulation and extraversion. *Journal of Applied Psychology, 96*, 1337–1346; Vinchur, A. J., Schippmann, J. S., Switzer, F. S., & Roth, P. L. (1998). A meta-analytic review of predictors of job performance for salespeople. *Journal of Applied Psychology, 83*, 586–597.
16. Bauer, T. N., Erdogan, B., Liden, R. C., & Wayne, S. J. (2006). A longitudinal study of the moderating role of extraversion: Leader-member exchange, performance, and turnover during new executive development. *Journal of Applied Psychology, 91*, 298–310; Bono, J. E., & Judge, T. A. (2004). Personality and transformational and transactional leadership: A meta-analysis. *Journal of Applied Psychology, 89*, 901–910.
17. Tay, C., Ang, S., & Van Dyne, L. (2006). Personality, biographical characteristics, and job interview success: A longitudinal study of the mediating effects of interviewing self-efficacy and the moderating effects of internal locus of control. *Journal of Applied Psychology, 91*, 446–454.
18. Wanberg, C. R., & Kammeyer-Mueller, J. D. (2000). Predictors and outcomes of pro-activity in the socialization process. *Journal of Applied Psychology, 85*, 373–385.
19. Judge, T. A. Heller, D., & Mount, M. K. (2002). Five-factor model of personality and job satisfaction: A meta-analysis. *Journal of Applied Psychology, 87*, 530–541.
20. Judge, T. A., Martocchio, J. J., & Thoresen, C. J. (1997). Five-factor model of personality and employee absence. *Journal of Applied Psychology, 82*, 745–755.
21. Ilies, R., Scott, B. A., & Judge, T. A. (2006). The interactive effects of personal traits and experienced states on intraindividual patterns of citizenship behavior. *Academy of Management Journal, 49*, 561–575.
22. Skarlicki, D. P., Folger, R., & Tesluk, P. (1999). Personality as a moderator in the relationship between fairness and retaliation. *Academy of Management Journal, 42*, 100–108.
23. Walumbwa, F. O., & Schaubroeck, J. (2009). Leader personality traits and employee voice behavior: Mediating roles of ethical leadership and work group psychological safety. *Journal of Applied Psychology, 94*, 1275–1286.
24. Zimmerman, R. D. (2008). Understanding the impact of personality traits on individuals' turnover decisions: A meta-analytic path model. *Personnel Psychology, 61*, 309–348.
25. Bernerth, J. B., Taylor, S. G., Walker, H. J., & Whitman, D. S. (2012). An empirical investigation of dispositional antecedents and performance-related outcomes of credit scores. *Journal of Applied Psychology, 97*, 469–478.
26. Klein, K. J., Beng-Chong, L., Saltz, J. L., & Mayer, D. M. (2004). How do they get there? An examination of the antecedents of centrality in team networks. *Academy of Management Journal, 47*, 952–963; Liu, S., Wang, M., Zhan, Y., & Shi, J. (2009). Daily work stress and alcohol use: Testing the cross-level moderation effects of neuroticism and job involvement. *Personnel Psychology, 62*, 575–597; Rodell, J. B., & Judge, T. A. (2009). Can "good" stressors spark "bad" behaviors? The mediating role of emotions in links of challenge and hindrance stressors with citizenship and counterproductive behaviors. *Journal of Applied Psychology, 94*, 1438–1451.
27. Judge, T. A., Heller, D., & Mount, M. K. (2002). Five-factor model of personality and job satisfaction: A meta-analysis. *Journal of Applied Psychology, 87*, 530–541; Zimmerman, R. D. (2008). Understanding the impact of personality traits on individuals' turnover decisions: A meta-analytic path model. *Personnel Psychology, 61*, 309–348.
28. Mayer, D., Nishii, L., Schneider, B., & Goldstein, H. (2007). The precursors and products of justice climates: Group leader antecedents and employee attitudinal consequences. *Personnel Psychology, 60*, 929–963.
29. Day, D. V., Schleicher, D. J., Unckless, A. L., & Hiller, N. J. (2002). Self-monitoring personality at work: A meta-analytic investigation of construct validity. *Journal of Applied Psychology, 87*, 390–401; Sasovova, Z., Mehra, A., Borgatti, S. P., & Schippers, M. C. Network churn: The effects of self-monitoring personality on brokerage dynamics. *Administrative Science Quarterly, 55*, 639–670.
30. Jawahar, I. M. (2001). Attitudes, self-monitoring, and appraisal behaviors. *Journal of Applied Psychology, 86*, 875–883.
31. Seibert, S. E. (1999). Proactive personality and career success. *Journal of Applied Psychology, 84*, 416–427.
32. Crant, M. J. (1995). The proactive personality scale and objective job performance among real estate agents. *Journal of Applied Psychology, 80*, 532–537.
33. Kammeyer-Mueller, J. D., & Wanberg, C. R. (2003). Unwrapping the organizational entry process: Disentangling multiple antecedents and their pathways to adjustment. *Journal of Applied Psychology, 88*, 779–794; Li, N., Harris, B., Boswell, W. R., & Xie, Z. (2011). The role of organizational insiders' developmental feedback and proactive personality on newcomers' performance: An interactionist perspective. *Journal of Applied Psychology, 96*, 1317–1327.
34. Chan, D. (2006). Interactive effects of situational judgment effectiveness and proactive personality on work perceptions and work outcomes. *Journal of Applied Psychology, 91*, 475–481; Erdogan, B., & Bauer, T. N. (2005). Enhancing career benefits of employee proactive personality: The role of fit with jobs and organizations. *Personnel Psychology, 58*, 859–891.
35. Judge, T. A., & Bono, J. E. (2001). Relationship of core self-evaluations traits—self esteem, generalized self efficacy, locus of control, and emotional stability—with job satisfaction and job performance: A meta-analysis. *Journal of Applied Psychology, 86*, 80–92; Keller, R. T. (2012). Predicting the performance and innovativeness of scientists and engineers. *Journal of Applied Psychology, 97*, 225–233.
36. Turban, D. B., & Keon, T. L. (1993). Organizational attractiveness: An interactionist perspective. *Journal of Applied Psychology, 78*, 184–193.
37. Bauer, T. N., Bodner, T., Erdogan, B., Truxillo, D. M., & Tucker, J. S. (2007). Newcomer adjustment during organizational socialization: A meta-analytic review of antecedents, outcomes, and methods. *Journal of Applied Psychology, 92*, 707–721.
38. Phillips, J. M., & Gully, S. M. (1997). Role of goal orientation, ability, need for achievement, and locus of control in the self-efficacy and goal-setting process. *Journal of Applied Psychology, 82*, 792–802; Steel, P. (2007). The nature of procrastination: A meta-analytic and theoretical review of quintessential self-regulatory failure. *Psychological Bulletin, 133*, 65–94.
39. Robbins, S. B., Lauver, K., Le, H., Davis, D., Langley, R., & Carlstrom, A. (2004). Do psychosocial and study skill factors predict college outcomes? A meta-analysis. *Psychological Bulletin, 130*, 261–288.
40. Ahearne, M., Mathieu, J., & Rapp, A. (2005). To empower or not to empower your sales force? An empirical examination of the influence of leadership empowerment behavior on customer satisfaction and performance. *Journal of Applied Psychology, 90*, 945–955.
41. Barrick, M. R., Patton, G. K., & Haugland, S. N. (2000). Accuracy of interviewer judgments of job applicant personality traits. *Personnel Psychology, 53*, 925–951.
42. Gale, S. F. (2002, April). Three companies cut turnover with tests. *Workforce, 81*(4), 66–69.
43. Morgeson, F. P., Campion, M. A., Dipboye, R. L., Hollenbeck, J. R., Murphy, K., & Schmitt, N. (2007). Reconsidering the use of personality tests in personnel selection contexts. *Personnel Psychology, 60*, 683–729; van Hooft, E. A. J., & Born, M. P. (2012). Intentional response distortion on personality tests: Using eye-tracking to understand response processes when faking. *Journal of Applied Psychology, 97*, 301–316.
44. Ones, D. S., Dilchert, S., Viswesvaran, C., & Judge, T. A. (2007). In support of personality assessment in organizational settings. *Personnel Psychology, 60*, 995–1027; Tett, R. P., & Christiansen, N. D. (2007). Personality tests at the crossroads: A response to Morgeson, Campion, Dipboye, Hollenbeck, Murphy, and Schmitt (2007). *Personnel Psychology, 60*, 967–993.
45. Kluemper, D. H., & Rosen, P. A. (2009). Future employment selection methods: Evaluating social networking Web sites. *Journal of Managerial Psychology, 24*, 567–580; Mount, M. K., Barrick, M. R., & Strauss, J. P. (1994). Validity of observer ratings of the big five personality factors. *Journal of Applied Psychology, 79*, 272–280.
46. Heller, M. (2005, September). Court ruling that employer's integrity test violated ADA could open door to litigation. *Workforce Management, 84*(9), 74–77.
47. Lusk, E. J., & Oliver, B. L. (1974). Research notes. American manager's personal value systems-revisited. *Academy of Management Journal, 17*, 549–554; Rokeach, M. (1973). *The nature of human values*. New York: Free Press.
48. Judge, T. A., & Bretz, R. D. (1992). Effects of work values on job choice decisions. *Journal of Applied Psychology, 77*, 261–271; Ravlin, E. C., & Meglino, B. M. (1987). Effect

of values on perception and decision making: A study of alternative work values measures. *Journal of Applied Psychology, 72*, 666–673.

49. George, J. M., & Jones, G. R. (1996). The experience of work and turnover intentions: Interactive effects of value attainment, job satisfaction, and positive mood. *Journal of Applied Psychology, 81*, 318–325.

50. Schwartz, S. H. (1992). Universals in the content and structure of values: Theoretical advances and empirical tests in 20 countries. In M. Zanna (Ed.), *Advances in experimental social psychology* (pp. 1–65). San Diego, CA: Academic Press.

51. George, J. M., & Jones, G. R. (1996). The experience of work and turnover intentions: Interactive effects of value attainment, job satisfaction, and positive mood. *Journal of Applied Psychology, 81*, 318–325.

52. Higgins, E. T., & Bargh, J. A. (1987). Social cognition and social perception. *Annual Review of Psychology, 38*, 369–425; Keltner, D., Ellsworth, P. C., & Edwards, K. (1993). Beyond simple pessimism: Effects of sadness and anger on social perception. *Journal of Personality and Social Psychology, 64*, 740–752; Riskind, J. H., Moore, R., & Bowley, L. (1995). The looming of spiders: The fearful perceptual distortion of movement and menace. *Behaviour Research and Therapy, 33*, 171.

53. Kellman, P. J., & Shipley, T. F. (1991). A theory of visual interpolation in object perception. *Cognitive Psychology, 23*, 141–221.

54. John, O. P., & Robins, R. W. (1994). Accuracy and bias in self-perception: Individual differences in self-enhancement and the role of narcissism. *Journal of Personality and Social Psychology, 66*, 206–219.

55. Fields, J. M., & Schuman, H. (1976). Public beliefs about the beliefs of the public. *The Public Opinion Quarterly, 40*(4), 427–448; Ross, L., Greene, D., & House, P. (1977). The "false consensus effect": An egocentric bias in social perception and attribution processes. *Journal of Experimental Social Psychology, 13*, 279–301.

56. Snyder, M., Tanke, E. D., & Berscheid, E. (1977). Social perception and interpersonal behavior: On the self-fulfilling nature of social stereotypes. *Journal of Personality and Social Psychology, 35*, 656–666.

57. Waller, M. J., Huber, G. P., & Glick, W. H. (1995). Functional background as a determinant of executives' selective perception. *Academy of Management Journal, 38*, 943–974.

58. Higgins, E. T., & Bargh, J. A. (1987). Social cognition and social perception. *Annual Review of Psychology, 38*, 369–425.

59. Lord, C. G., Ross, L., & Lepper, M. R. (1979). Biased assimilation and attitude polarization: The effects of prior theories on subsequently considered evidence. *Journal of Personality and Social Psychology, 37*, 2098–2109.

60. Ross, L., Lepper, M. R., & Hubbard, M. (1975). Perseverance in self-perception and social perception: Biased attributional processes in the debriefing paradigm. *Journal of Personality and Social Psychology, 32*, 880–892.

61. Society for Human Resource Management (2011). Employee job satisfaction and engagement. Retrieved August 29, 2012, from http://www.shrm.org/research/surveyfindings/articles/documents/11-0618%20job_satisfaction_fnl.pdf

62. Hollon, J. (2010, April). Worker "deal" is off. *Workforce Management, 89*(4).

63. Kristof-Brown, A. L., Zimmerman, R. D., & Johnson, E. C. (2005). Consequences of individuals' fit at work: A meta-analysis of person-job, person-organization, person-group, and person-supervisor fit. *Personnel Psychology, 58*, 281–342; Verquer, M. L., Beehr, T. A., & Wagner, S. H. (2003). A meta-analysis of relations between person-organization fit and work attitudes. *Journal of Vocational Behavior, 63*, 473–489.

64. Anderson, C., Spataro, S. E., & Flynn, F. J. (2008). Personality and organizational culture as determinants of influence. *Journal of Applied Psychology, 93*, 702–710; Cable, D. M., & DeRue, D. S. (2002). The convergent and discriminant validity of subjective fit perceptions. *Journal of Applied Psychology, 87*, 875–884; Kristof-Brown, A. L., Zimmerman, R. D., & Johnson, E. C. (2005). Consequences of individuals' fit at work: A meta-analysis of person-job, person-organization, person-group, and person-supervisor fit. *Personnel Psychology, 58*, 281–342; O'Reilly, C. A., Chatman, J., & Caldwell, D. F. (1991). People and organizational culture: A profile comparison approach to assessing person-organization fit. *Academy of Management Journal, 34*, 487–516; Saks, A. M., & Ashforth, B. E. (2002). Is job search related to employment quality? It all depends on the fit. *Journal of Applied Psychology, 87*, 646–654.

65. Mathieu, J. E., & Zajac, D. M. (1990). A review and meta-analysis of the antecedents, correlates, and consequences of organizational commitment. *Psychological Bulletin, 108*, 171–194; Seibert, S. E., Wang, G., & Courtwright, S. H. (2011). Antecedents and consequences of psychological and team empowerment in organizations: A meta-analytic review. *Journal of Applied Psychology, 96*, 981–1003.

66. Cohen-Charash, Y., & Spector, P. E. (2001). The role of justice in organizations: A meta-analysis. *Organizational Behavior and Human Decision Processes, 86*, 278–321; Colquitt, J. A., Conlon, D. E., Wesson, M. J., Porter, C. O. L. H., & Ng, K. Y. (2001). Justice at the millennium: A meta-analytic review of 25 years of organizational justice research. *Journal of Applied Psychology, 86*, 425–445.

67. Bauer, T. N., Bodner, T., Erdogan, B., Truxillo, D. M., & Tucker, J. S. (2007). Newcomer adjustment during organizational socialization: A meta-analytic review of antecedents, outcomes, and methods. *Journal of Applied Psychology, 92*, 707–721; Gerstner, C. R., & Day, D. V. (1997). Meta-analytic review of leader-member exchange theory: Correlates and construct issues. *Journal of Applied Psychology, 82*, 827–844.

68. Dvorak, P. (2007, December 17). Theory and practice: Hotelier finds happiness keeps staff checked in: Focus on morale boosts Joie de Vivre's grades from workers, guests. *Wall Street Journal*, B3.

69. Kinicki, A. J., McKee-Ryan, F. M., Schriesheim, C. A., & Carson, K. P. (2002). Assessing the construct validity of the job descriptive index: A review and meta-analysis. *Journal of Applied Psychology, 87*, 14–32; Podsakoff, N. P., LePine, J. A., & LePine, M. A. (2007). Differential challenge stressor-hindrance stressor relationships with job attitudes, turnover intentions, turnover, and withdrawal behavior: A meta-analysis. *Journal of Applied Psychology, 92*, 438–454.

70. Kuncel, N. R., Hezlett, S. A., & Ones, D. S. (2004). Academic performance, career potential, creativity, and job performance: Can one construct predict them all? *Journal of Personality and Social Psychology, 86*, 148–161.

71. Kuncel, N. R., Hezlett, S. A., & Ones, D. S. (2004). Academic performance, career potential, creativity, and job performance: Can one construct predict them all? *Journal of Personality and Social Psychology, 86*, 148–161; Lang, J. W. B., Kersting, M., Hülsheger, U. R., & Lang, J. (2010). General mental ability, narrower cognitive abilities, and job performance: The perspective of the nested-factors model of cognitive abilities. *Personnel Psychology, 63*, 595–640.

72. Gilboa, S., Shirom, A., Fried, Y., & Cooper, C. (2008). A meta-analysis of work demand stressors and job performance: Examining main and moderating effects. *Personnel Psychology, 61*, 227–271.

73. Anonymous. (2008, June). Financial stress: The latest worker risk. *HR focus, 85*(6), 12.

74. Iaffaldano, M. T., & Muchinsky, P. M. (1985). Job satisfaction and job performance: A meta-analysis. *Psychological Bulletin, 97*, 251–273; Judge, T. A., Thoresen, C. J., Bono, J. E., & Patton, G. T. (2001). The job satisfaction–job performance relationship: A qualitative and quantitative review. *Journal of Applied Psychology, 127*, 376–407; Riketta, M. (2008). The causal relation between job attitudes and performance: A meta-analysis of panel studies. *Journal of Applied Psychology, 93*, 472–481.

75. Mathieu, J. E., & Zajac, D. M. (1990). A review and meta-analysis of the antecedents, correlates, and consequences of organizational commitment. *Psychological Bulletin, 108*, 171–194; Riketta, M. (2002). Attitudinal organizational commitment and job performance: A meta-analysis. *Journal of Organizational Behavior, 23*, 257–266; Wright, T. A., & Bonnett, D. G. (2002). The moderating effects of employee tenure on the relation between organizational commitment and job performance: A meta-analysis. *Journal of Applied Psychology, 87*, 1183–1190.

76. Riketta, M. (2002). Attitudinal organizational commitment and job performance: A meta-analysis. *Journal of Organizational Behavior, 23*, 257–266.

77. Barrick, M. R., & Mount, M. K. (1991). The big five personality dimensions and job performance: A meta-analysis. *Personnel Psychology, 44*, 1–26; Dudley, N. M., Orvis, K. A., Lebiecki, J. E., & Cortina, J. M. (2006). A meta-analytic investigation of conscientiousness in the prediction of job performance: Examining the intercorrelations and the incremental validity of narrow traits. *Journal of Applied Psychology, 91*, 40–57; Vinchur, A. J., Schippmann, J. S., Switzer, F. S., & Roth, P. L. (1998). A meta-analytic review of predictors of job performance for salespeople. *Journal of Applied Psychology, 83*, 586–597; Cohen-Charash, Y., & Spector, P. E. (2001). The role of justice in organizations: A meta-analysis. *Organizational Behavior and Human Decision Processes, 86*, 278–321; Colquitt, J. A., Conlon, D. E., Wesson, M. J., Porter, C. O. L. H., & Ng, K. Y. (2001). Justice at the millenium: A meta-analytic review of 25 years of organizational justice research. *Journal of Applied Psychology, 86*, 425–445; Colquitt, J. A., Scott, B. A., & LePine, J. A. (2007). Trust, trustworthiness, and trust propensity: A meta-analytic test of their unique relationships with risk taking and job performance. *Journal of Applied Psychology, 92*, 909–927; Fassina, N. E., Jones, D. A., & Uggerslev, K. L. (2008). Relationship clean-up time: Using meta-analysis and path analysis to clarify relationships among job satisfaction, perceived fairness, and citizenship behaviors. *Journal of Management, 34*, 161–188; Hoffman, B. J., Blair, C. A., Meriac, J. P., & Woehr, D. J. (2007). Expanding the criterion domain? A quantitative review of the OCB literature. *Journal of Applied Psychology, 92*, 555–566; Ilies, R., Nahrgang, J. D., & Morgeson, F. P. (2007). Leader-member exchange and citizenship behaviors: A meta-analysis. *Journal of Applied Psychology, 92*, 269–277; Lepine, J. A., Erez, A., & Johnson, D. E. (2002). The nature and dimensionality of organizational citizenship behavior: A critical review and meta-analysis. *Journal of Applied Psychology, 87*, 52–65; Organ, D. W., & Ryan, K. (1995). A meta-analytic review of attitudinal and dispositional predictors of organizational citizenship behavior. *Personnel Psychology, 48*, 775–802; Podsakoff, P. M., MacKenzie, S. B., & Bommer, W. H. (1996). Meta-analysis of the relationships between Kerr and Jermier's substitutes for leadership and employee job attitudes, role perceptions, and performance. *Journal of Applied Psychology, 81*, 380–399; Riketta, M., & Van Dick, R. (2005). Foci of attachment in organizations: A meta-analytic comparison of the strength and correlates of workgroup versus organizational identification and commitment. *Journal of Vocational Behavior, 67*, 490–510.

78. Cohen-Charash, Y., & Spector, P. E. (2001). The role of justice in organizations: A meta-analysis. *Organizational Behavior and Human Decision Processes, 86*, 278–321; Colquitt, J. A., Conlon, D. E., Wesson, M. J., Porter, C. O. L. H., & Ng, K. Y. (2001). Justice at the millenium: A meta-analytic review of 25 years of organizational justice research. *Journal of Applied Psychology, 86*, 425–445; Colquitt, J. A., Scott, B. A., & LePine, J. A. (2007). Trust, trustworthiness, and trust propensity: A meta-analytic test of their unique relationships with risk taking and job performance. *Journal of Applied Psychology, 92*, 909–927; Hoffman, B. J., Blair, C. A., Meriac, J. P., & Woehr, D. J. (2007). Expanding the criterion domain? A quantitative review of the OCB literature. *Journal of Applied Psychology, 92*, 555–566; Ilies, R., Nahrgang, J. D., & Morgeson, F. P. (2007). Leader-member exchange and citizenship behaviors: A meta-analysis. *Journal of Applied Psychology, 92*, 269–277; Lepine, J. A., Erez, A., & Johnson, D. E. (2002). The nature and dimensionality of organizational citizenship behavior: A critical review and meta-analysis. *Journal of Applied Psychology, 87*, 52–65.

79. Chiaburu, D. S., Oh, I.S., Berry, C. M., Li, N., & Gardner, R. G. (2011). The five-factor model of personality traits and organizational citizenship behaviors: A meta-analysis. *Journal of Applied Psychology, 96*, 1140–1166; Ilies, R., Fulmer, I. S., Spitzmuller, M., & Johnson, M. D. (2009). Personality and citizenship behavior: The mediating role of job satisfaction. *Journal of Applied Psychology, 94*, 945–959.

80. Dalal, R. S. (2005). A meta-analysis of the relationship between organizational citizenship behavior and counterproductive work behavior. *Journal of Applied Psychology, 90*, 1241–1255; Fassina, N. E., Jones, D. A., & Uggerslev, K. L. (2008). Relationship clean-up time: Using meta-analysis and path analysis to clarify relationships among job satisfaction, perceived fairness, and citizenship behaviors. *Journal of Management, 34*, 161–188; Hoffman, B. J., Blair, C. A., Meriac, J. P., & Woehr, D. J. (2007). Expanding the criterion domain? A quantitative review of the OCB literature. *Journal of Applied Psychology, 92*, 555–566; Lepine, J. A., Erez, A., & Johnson, D. E. (2002). The nature and dimensionality of organizational citizenship behavior: A critical review and meta-analysis. *Journal of Applied Psychology, 87*, 52–65.

81. Ng, T. W. H., & Feldman, D. C. (2008). The relationship of age to ten dimensions of job performance. *Journal of Applied Psychology, 93*, 392–423.

82. Witters, D., & Agrawal, S. (2011). Unhealthy workers' absenteeism costs $153 billion. Gallup Wellbeing. Retrieved on June 17, 2012, from http://www.gallup.com/poll/150026/unhealthy-workers-absenteeism-costs-153-billion.aspx.

83. Farrell, D., & Stamm, C. L. (1988). Meta-analysis of the correlates of employee absence. *Human Relations, 41*, 211–227; Martocchio, J. J., Harrison, D. A., & Berkson, H. (2000). Connections between lower back pain, interventions, and absence from work: A time-based meta-analysis. *Personnel Psychology, 53*, 595–624.

84. Blackburn, G. L. (2009, December). The ROI on weight loss at work. *Harvard Business Review*, p. 30; Parks, K. M., & Steelman, L. A. (2008). Organizational wellness programs: A meta-analysis. *Journal of Occupational and Organizational Psychology, 13*, 58–68.

85. Cole, C. L. (2002, September). Sick of absenteeism? Get rid of sick days. *Workforce, 81*(9), 56–61; Conlin, M. (2007, November 12). Shirking working: The war on hooky. *Business Week, 4058*, 72–75.

86. Martocchio, J. J. (1989). Age-related differences in employee absenteeism: A meta-analysis. *Psychology and Aging, 4*, 409–414; Ng, T. W. H., & Feldman, D. C. (2008). The relationship of age to ten dimensions of job performance. *Journal of Applied Psychology, 93*, 392–423.

87. Griffeth, R. W., Hom, P. W., & Gaertner, S. (2000). A meta-analysis of antecedents and correlates of employee turnover: Update, moderator tests, and research implications for the next millennium. *Journal of Management, 26*, 463–488; Society for Human Resource Management (2011, November). The gift of time. Retreived from http://www.shrm.org/Publications/hrmagazine/EditorialContent/2011/1111/Pages/1111meinert.aspx.

88. Badal, J. (2006, July 24). "Career path" programs help retain workers. *Wall Street Journal*, B1; Griffeth, R. W., Hom, P. W., & Gaertner, S. (2000). A meta-analysis of antecedents and correlates of employee turnover: Update, moderator tests, and research implications for the next millennium. *Journal of Management, 26*, 463–488; Podsakoff, N. P., LePine, J. A., & LePine, M. A. (2007). Differential challenge stressor-hindrance stressor relationships with job attitudes, turnover intentions, turnover, and withdrawal behavior: A meta-analysis. *Journal of Applied Psychology, 92*, 438–454.

89. Salgado, J. F. (2002). The big five personality dimensions and counterproductive behaviors. *International Journal of Selection and Assessment, 10*, 117–125; Zimmerman, R. D. (2008). Understanding the impact of personality traits on individuals' turnover decisions: A meta-analytic path model. *Personnel Psychology, 61*, 309–348.

CHAPTER 4
Developing Mission, Vision, and Values

DEVELOPING MISSION, VISION, AND VALUES

Mattel Inc.'s vision of "creating the future of play" is evidenced in the constantly evolving designs found in their popular Hot Wheels cars.

© Thinkstock

CHAPTER LEARNING OBJECTIVES

Reading this chapter will help you do the following:

1. **Understand the roles of mission, vision, and values in the planning process.**
2. **Understand how mission and vision fit into the planning-organizing-leading-controlling (P-O-L-C) framework.**
3. **See how creativity and passion are related to vision.**
4. **Incorporate stakeholder interests into mission and vision.**
5. **Develop statements that articulate organizational mission and vision.**
6. **Apply mission, vision, and values to your personal goals and professional career.**

At the organizational level, a key part of planning (the first element of the P-O-L-C framework) is captured in verbal and written statements of an organization's mission and vision. With a mission and vision, firms craft a strategy for achieving their general purpose and afterward establish benchmarks for judging progress and success through clear goals and objectives. Mission and vision communicate the organization's values and purpose, and the best mission and vision statements have an emotional component that serves to incite employees and delight customers.

Mission and Vision as P-O-L-C Components

Planning	Organizing	Leading	Controlling
1. Vision & Mission	1. Organization Design	1. Leadership	1. Systems/Processes
2. Strategizing	2. Culture	2. Decision Making	2. Strategic Human Resources
3. Goals & Objectives	3. Social Networks	3. Communications	
		4. Groups/Teams	
		5. Motivation	

Mission and Vision in the Planning Process

The strategy is how the firm aims
to realize its mission and vision

Mission
&
Vision

Strategy

Goals & Objectives

Goals and objectives are the indicators of how well the strategy is succeeding

1. THE ROLES OF MISSION, VISION, AND VALUES

LEARNING OBJECTIVES

1. Be able to define mission and vision.
2. See how values are important for mission and vision.
3. Understand the roles of vision, mission, and values in the P-O-L-C framework.

1.1   Mission, Vision, and Values

Mission and vision both relate to an organization's purpose and are typically communicated in some written form. Mission and vision are statements from the organization that answer questions about who they are, what they value, and where they're going. A 2011 study by the consulting firm Bain and Company reports that 63% of the more than 1,000 firms surveyed globally reported using mission and values statements as a management tool.[1] Moreover, firms with a clearly communicated, widely understood, and collectively shared mission and vision have been shown to perform better than those without them, with the caveat that they related to effectiveness only when strategy, goals, and objectives were aligned with vision and mission.[2]

A **mission statement** communicates the organization's reason for being, and how it aims to serve its key stakeholders. Customers, employees, and investors are the stakeholders most often emphasized, but other stakeholders like government or communities (i.e., in the form of social or environmental impact) can also be discussed. Mission statements sometimes include a summation of the firm's values. **Values** are the beliefs of an individual or group, and in this case the organization, in which they are emotionally invested.

A **vision statement**, in contrast, is a future-oriented declaration of the organization's purpose and aspirations. In many ways, you can say that the mission statement lays out the organization's "purpose for being," and the vision statement then says, "based on that purpose, this is what we want to become." The strategy should flow directly from the vision, since the strategy is intended to achieve the vision and thus satisfy the organization's mission. Typically, vision statements are relatively brief, as in the case of Starbuck's vision statement, which reads: "Establish Starbucks as the premier purveyor of the finest coffee in the world while maintaining our uncompromising principles as we grow."[3] Or advertising firm Ogilvy & Mather, which states their vision as "an agency defined by its devotion to brands."[4] Similarly, Walmart's tag-line version of its vision statement is "Save money. Live better."[5]

A casual tour of business or organization Web sites will expose you to the range of forms that mission and vision statements can take. Mission statements answer the questions of "Who are we?" and "What does our organization value?" Vision statements typically take the form of relatively brief, future-oriented statements—vision statements answer the question "Where is this organization going?" Increasingly, organizations also add a **values statement** that either reaffirms or states outright the organization's values that might not be evident in the mission or vision statements.

mission statement

A statement of purpose, describing who the company is and what it does.

values

Shared principles, standards, and goals.

vision statement

A future-oriented declaration of the organization's purpose and aspirations.

values statement

A written statement that reaffirms or states outright the organization's values that might not be evident in the mission or vision statements.

FIGURE 4.4

Starbucks describes six guiding principles in their full mission statement that also communicate the organization's values:

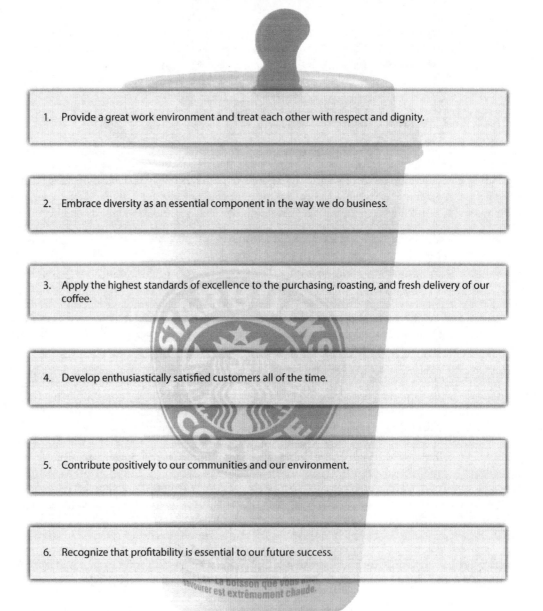

1. Provide a great work environment and treat each other with respect and dignity.

2. Embrace diversity as an essential component in the way we do business.

3. Apply the highest standards of excellence to the purchasing, roasting, and fresh delivery of our coffee.

4. Develop enthusiastically satisfied customers all of the time.

5. Contribute positively to our communities and our environment.

6. Recognize that profitability is essential to our future success.

FIGURE 4.5 Missions

While a vision describes what an organization desires to become in the future, an organization's mission is grounded in the past and present. A mission outlines the reasons for the organization's existence and explains what role it plays in society. A well-written mission statement captures the organization's identity and helps to answer the fundamental question of "Who are we?" As a practical matter, a mission statement explains to key stakeholders why they should support the organization. The following examples illustrate the connections between organizations and the needs of their key stakeholders.

Harley Davidson	We ride with our customers and apply this deep connection in every market we serve to create superior value for all of our stakeholders.	
Internal Revenue Service	Provide America's taxpayers top-quality service by helping them understand and meet their tax responsibilities and enforce the law with integrity and fairness to all.	
Starbucks	To inspire and nurture the human spirit – one person, one cup and one neighborhood at a time.	
The Estée Lauder Company	Bringing the best to everyone we touch and being the best in everything we do.	
Limited Brands	Limited Brands is committed to building a family of the world's best fashion brands offering captivating customer experiences that drive long-term loyalty and deliver sustained growth for our shareholders.	
Fender Musical Instruments	We will exceed the expectations of music enthusiasts worldwide and create a community for individual expression by focusing on our people, products, and business excellence.	

Source: Images courtesy of Ketchen, D., & Short, J. (2011). Mastering strategic management. Irvington, NY: Flat World Knowledge; Evb-wiki, http://en.wikipedia.org/wiki/File:Evb-my_hog.jpg (first); Internal Revenue Service, http://en.wikipedia.org/wiki/File:IRS.svg (second); Jeff Wilcox, http://www.flickr.com/photos/jeffwilcox/1882938710/ (third); Dwight Burdette, http://en.wikipedia.org/wiki/File:Victoria%27s_Secret_at_Briarwood_Mall.JPG (fifth); other images © Thinkstock.

FIGURE 4.6

An organization's vision describes what the organization hopes to become in the future. Visions highlight the values and aspirations that lay at the heart of the organization. Although vision statements have the potential to inspire employees, customers, and other stakeholders, vision statements are relatively rare and good visions are even rarer. Some of the visions being pursued by businesses today are offered below.

Alcoa – To be the best company in the world—in the eyes of our customers, shareholders, communities and people.

Avon – To be the company that best understands and satisfies the product, service and self-fulfillment needs of women—globally.

Chevron – To be the global energy company most admired for its people, partnership and performance.

Google – To develop a perfect search engine.

Kraft Foods – Helping people around the world eat and live better.

Proctor and Gamble – Be, and be recognized as, the best consumer products and services company in the world.

Source: Images courtesy of Ketchen, D., & Short, J. (2011). Mastering strategic management. Irvington, NY: Flat World Knowledge; David Herrera, http://www.flickr.com/photos/dph1110/2672793430/ (third from the top); bfishadow, http://www.flickr.com/photos/bfishadow/3458254707/ (fourth from the top); Thinkstock and Like_the_Grand_Canyon, http://www.flickr.com/photos/like_the_grand_canyon/2406679678/, http://www.flickr.com/photos/like_the_grand_canyon/4945749010/ (fifth from the top); Scott Ehardt, http://en.wikipedia.org/wiki/File:Crest_toothpaste.jpg (bottom); other images © Thinkstock.

1.2   Roles Played by Mission and Vision

Mission and vision statements play three critical roles: (1) communicate the purpose of the organization to stakeholders, (2) inform strategy development, and (3) develop the measurable goals and objectives by which to gauge the success of the organization's strategy.

First, mission and vision provide a vehicle for communicating an organization's purpose and values to all key stakeholders. Stakeholders are those key parties who have some influence over the organization or stake in its future. Some key stakeholders are employees, customers, investors, suppliers, and institutions such as governments. Typically, mission and vision statements would be widely circulated and discussed often so that their meaning is widely understood, shared, and internalized. The better employees understand an organization's purpose, through its mission and vision, the better able they will be to understand the strategy and its implementation.

Second, mission and vision create a target for strategy development. That is, one criterion of a good strategy is how well it helps the firm achieve its mission and vision. The best vision statements create a tension and restlessness with regard to the status quo—that is, they should foster a spirit of continuous innovation and improvement. London Business School professors Gary Hamel and C. K. Prahalad describe this tense relationship between vision and strategy as stretch and ambition. Indeed, in a study of such able competitors as CNN, British Airways, and Sony, they found that these firms displaced competitors with stronger reputations and deeper pockets through their ambition to stretch their organizations in more innovative ways.[6]

Third, mission and vision provide a high-level guide, and the strategy provides a specific guide, to the goals and objectives showing success or failure of the strategy and satisfaction of the larger set of objectives stated in the mission. Such objectives include profitability goals, metrics on customer and employee satisfaction, and social and environmental responsibility measures.

FIGURE 4.7

Founded by Anita Roddick, the mission of The Body Shop explicitly includes a broad understanding of stakeholders by providing a commitment "to the well-being of our fellow humans and the preservation of the planet."

Source: http://www.flickr.com/photos/homard/417370634/

FIGURE 4.8

Virgin Galactic provides an example of a company that embraces the ambitious vision of providing suborbital space flights to eager tourists.

Source: http://en.wikipedia.org/wiki/File:Spaceship_One_in_flight_1.jpg

KEY TAKEAWAY

Mission and vision both relate to an organization's purpose and aspirations, and are typically communicated in some form of brief written statements. A mission statement communicates the organization's reason for being and how it aspires to serve its key stakeholders. The vision statement is a narrower, future-oriented declaration of the organization's purpose and aspirations. Together, mission and vision guide strategy development, help communicate the organization's purpose to stakeholders, and inform the goals and objectives set to determine whether the strategy is on track.

1. Alone or in a group, think about the concept of a mission statement. Besides knowing what a mission statement is, do you feel it is important for organizations to have mission statements? Why or why not?
2. What about a vision statement? Is it as important as or less important than a mission statement?
3. How are values important to the content of mission and vision statements?
4. What happens if an organization's mission and vision statements don't seem sincere? How might this affect an organization?
5. How do mission and vision relate to a firm's strategy?
6. In what ways are mission and vision important for organizational goals and objectives?

2. MISSION AND VISION IN THE P-O-L-C FRAMEWORK

LEARNING OBJECTIVES

1. Understand the role of mission and vision in *organizing*.
2. Understand the role of mission and vision in *leading*.
3. Understand the role of mission and vision in *controlling*.

Mission and vision play a prominent role in the planning facet of the P-O-L-C framework. Beyond the relationship between mission and vision, strategy, and goals and objectives, mission and vision are also related to the organizing, leading, and controlling aspects as well. In this section, we describe each of these relationships.

2.1 Mission, Vision, and Organizing

organizing

The function of management that involves developing an organizational structure and allocating human resources to ensure the accomplishment of objectives.

organizational design

A formal, guided process for integrating the people, information, and technology of an organization.

Organizing is the function of management that involves developing an organizational structure and allocating human resources to ensure the accomplishment of objectives. The organizing facet of the P-O-L-C framework typically includes subjects such as organization design, staffing, and organizational culture. With regard to organizing, it is useful to think about alignment between the mission and vision and various organizing activities. For instance, **organizational design** is a formal, guided process for integrating the people, information, and technology of an organization. It is used to match the form of the organization as closely as possible to the purpose(s) the organization seeks to achieve. Through the design process, organizations act to improve the probability that the collective efforts of members will be successful.

Organization design should reflect and support the strategy—in that sense, organizational design is a set of decision guidelines by which members will choose appropriate actions, in terms of their support for the strategy. Strategy unifies the intent of the organization and focuses members toward actions designed to accomplish desired outcomes. The strategy encourages actions that support the purpose and discourages those that do not.

To organize, managers must connect people with each other as well as with information and technology in meaningful and purposeful ways to allow the success of such key human resources. Organization structure defines the formal relationships among people and specifies both their roles and their responsibilities. Administrative systems govern the organization through guidelines, procedures, and policies. Information and technology define the process(es) through which members achieve outcomes. Each element must support each of the others, and together they must support the organization's purpose, as reflected in its mission and vision.

For example, in 2006, Disney acquired Pixar, a firm renowned for its creative prowess in animated entertainment. Disney summarizes the Pixar strategy like this: "Pixar's [strategy] is to combine proprietary technology and world-class creative talent to develop computer-animated feature films with memorable characters and heart-warming stories that appeal to audiences of all ages."[7] Disney has helped Pixar achieve this strategy through an important combination of structural design choices. First, Pixar is an independent division of Disney and is empowered to make independent choices in all aspects of idea development. Second, Pixar gives its "creatives"—its artists, writers, and designers—great leeway over decision making. Third, Pixar protects its creatives' ability to share work in progress, up and down the hierarchy, with the aim of getting it even better. As a result, innovations gained through new projects can be shared with later projects, while at the same time sharing knowledge about potential pitfalls.[8]

Organizational culture is the workplace environment formulated from the interaction of the employees in the workplace. Organizational culture is defined by all the life experiences, strengths, weaknesses, education, upbringing, and other attributes of the employees. While executive leaders play a large role in defining organizational culture by their actions and leadership, all employees contribute to the organizational culture.

Achieving alignment between mission and vision and organizational culture can be very powerful, but culture is also difficult to change. This means that if you are seeking to change your vision or mission, your ability to change the organization's culture to support those new directions may be difficult, or, at least, slow to achieve.

For instance, in 2000, Procter & Gamble (P&G) sought to change a fundamental part of its vision in a way that asked the organization to source more of its innovations from external partners. Historically, P&G had invested heavily in research and development and internal sources of innovation—so much so that "not invented here" (known informally as NIH) was the dominant cultural mind-set.[9] NIH describes a culture that avoids using products, research, or know-how that originated anywhere other than inside the organization. It is normally used in a pejorative sense. As a sociological phenomenon, the "not invented here" syndrome is manifested as an unwillingness to adopt an idea or product because it originates from another culture. P&G has been able to combat this NIH bias by adopting a five-year stretch goal that at least 50% of their initiatives will include an external collaboration and moving to a hybrid research and development (R&D) structure that balances local focus and headquarter oversights.[10] P&G was gradually able to change its culture toward one that is more open to external contributions, and hence in much better alignment with its current mission and vision.

2.2 Mission, Vision, and Leading

Leading involves influencing others toward the attainment of organizational objectives. Leading and leadership are nearly synonymous with the notions of mission and vision. We might describe a very purposeful person as being "on a mission." As an example, Steve Demos had the personal mission of replacing cow's milk with soy milk in U.S. supermarkets, and this mission led to his vision for, and strategy behind, the firm White Wave and its Silk line of soy milk products.[11] Similarly, we typically think of some individuals as leaders because they are visionary. For instance, when Walt Disney suggested building a theme park in a Florida swamp back in the early 1960s, few other people in the world seemed to share his view.

FIGURE 4.9

Pixar's creative prowess is reinforced by Disney's organizational design choices leading to successful offerings, such as the Academy Award–winning film *Up*.

Source: http://en.wikipedia.org/wiki/File:John_Lasseter-Up-66th_Mostra.jpg

organizational culture

A system of shared assumptions, values, and beliefs showing people what is appropriate and inappropriate behavior.

leading

Involves influencing others toward the attainment of organizational objectives.

FIGURE 4.10
Got Silk?

Steve Demos has led the way in his mission to replace cow's milk with a soy alternative.

Source: http://www.flickr.com/photos/theimpulsivebuy/5262711697

controlling

Ensuring that performance does not deviate from standards. Controlling consists of three steps, which include (1) establishing performance standards, (2) comparing actual performance against standards, and (3) taking corrective action when necessary.

strategic human resources management (SHRM)

Management strategy that reflects the aim of tying the organization's human capital, its people, into the mission and vision.

Any task—whether launching Silk or building the Disney empire—is that much more difficult if attempted alone. Therefore, the more that a mission or vision challenges the status quo—and recognizing that good vision statements always need to create some dissonance with the status quo—the greater will be the organization's need of "change leaders"—people who will help diffuse the revolutionary philosophy even while the leader (i.e., the founder or CEO) is not present. Without real change leaders, a revolutionary vision would remain a mere idea of the visionary CEO—they are the ones who make the implementation of the transformation real.

In many cases, we can associate revolutionary companies with the organization's visionary leaders—for instance, Apple and Steve Jobs, Dell and Michael Dell, or Google and the team of Sergey Brin and Larry Page. In all three of these organizations, the leaders focused on creating an organization with a noble mission that enabled the employees and management team not only to achieve the strategic breakthrough but also to realize their personal dreams in the process.

Vision That Pervades the Organization

A broader definition of visionary leadership suggests that, if many or most of an organization's employees understand and identify with the mission and vision, efficiency will increase because the organization's members "on the front lines" will be making decisions fully aligned with the organization's goals. Efficiency is achieved with limited hands-on supervision because the mission and vision serve as a form of cruise control. To make frontline responsibility effective, leadership must learn to trust workers and give them sufficient opportunities to develop quality decision-making skills.

Mission and vision are also relevant to leadership well beyond the impact of one or several top executives. Even beyond existing employees, various stakeholders—customers, suppliers, prospective new employees—are visiting organizations' Web sites to read their mission and vision statements. In the process, they are trying to understand what kind of organization they are reading about and what the organization's values and ethics are. Ultimately, they are seeking to determine whether the organization and what it stands for are a good fit for them.

2.3 Mission, Vision, and Controlling

Controlling involves ensuring that performance does not deviate from standards. Controlling consists of three steps: (1) establishing performance standards, (2) comparing actual performance against standards, and (3) taking corrective action when necessary. Mission and vision are relevant to all three steps.

Actual versus Desired Performance

The goals and objectives that flow from an organization's mission and vision provide a basis for assessing actual versus desired performance. In many ways, such goals and objectives provide feedback that helps managers assess the degree to which the organization is succeeding and provide insights into areas where corrective action may be needed. This is one reason goals and objectives should ideally be specific and measurable.

Corrective Action

Finally, just as mission and vision should lead to specific and measurable goals and objectives and thus provide a basis for comparing actual and desired performance, corrective action should also be prompted in cases where performance falls short of performance objectives. While mission and vision may signal the need for corrective action, because they are rather general, high-level statements they rarely spell out what specific actions firms should take when performance is below expectations.

Strategic human resources management (SHRM) reflects the aim of integrating the organization's human capital—its people—into the mission and vision. Human resources management alignment means to integrate decisions about people with decisions about the results an organization is trying to obtain. Research indicates that organizations that successfully align human resources management with mission and vision accomplishment do so by integrating SHRM into the planning process, emphasizing human resources activities that support mission goals, and building strong human resources/management capabilities and relationships.[12]

KEY TAKEAWAY

In addition to being a key part of the planning process, mission and vision also play key roles in the organizing, leading, and controlling functions of management. While mission and vision start the planning function, they are best realized when accounted for across all four functions of management—P-O-L-C. In planning, mission and vision help to generate specific goals and objectives and to develop the strategy for achieving them. Mission and vision guide choices about organizing, too, from structure to organizational culture. The cultural dimension is one reason mission and vision are most effective when they pervade the leadership of the entire organization, rather than being just the focus of senior management. Finally, mission and vision are tied to the three key steps of controlling: (1) establishing performance standards, (2) comparing actual performance against standards, and (3) taking corrective action when necessary. Since people make the place, ultimately strategic human resources management must bring these pieces together.

EXERCISES

1. How might mission and vision influence organizational design?
2. How might mission and vision influence leadership practices?
3. Why might a specific replacement CEO candidate be a good or poor choice for a firm with an existing mission and vision?
4. Which aspects of controlling do mission and vision influence?
5. What performance standards might reinforce a firm's mission and vision?

3. CREATIVITY AND PASSION

LEARNING OBJECTIVES

1. Understand how creativity relates to vision.
2. Develop some creativity tools.
3. Understand how passion relates to vision.

FIGURE 4.11

The creative passion of James Dyson led him to develop the dual cyclone vacuum cleaner, which bears his name.

Source: http://en.wikipedia.org/wiki/File:James_Dyson.jpg

creativity

The generation of new ideas.

passion

An intense, driving, or overmastering feeling or conviction. Passion is also associated with intense emotion compelling action.

Creativity and passion are of particular relevance to mission and vision statements. A simple definition of **creativity** is the power or ability to invent. While creativity is often thought of as being largely an artistic attribute, creativity in business is critical to innovation and progress. **Passion** in business refers to an intense, driving, or overmastering feeling or conviction. Passion is also associated with intense emotion compelling action. We focus on the relationship between creativity, passion, and vision in this section because organizational visions are intended to create uneasiness with the status quo and help inform and motivate key stakeholders to move the organization forward. Consequently, a vision statement should reflect and communicate something that is relatively novel and unique, and such novelty and uniqueness are the products of creativity and passion.

FIGURE 4.12 Four Creativity Types

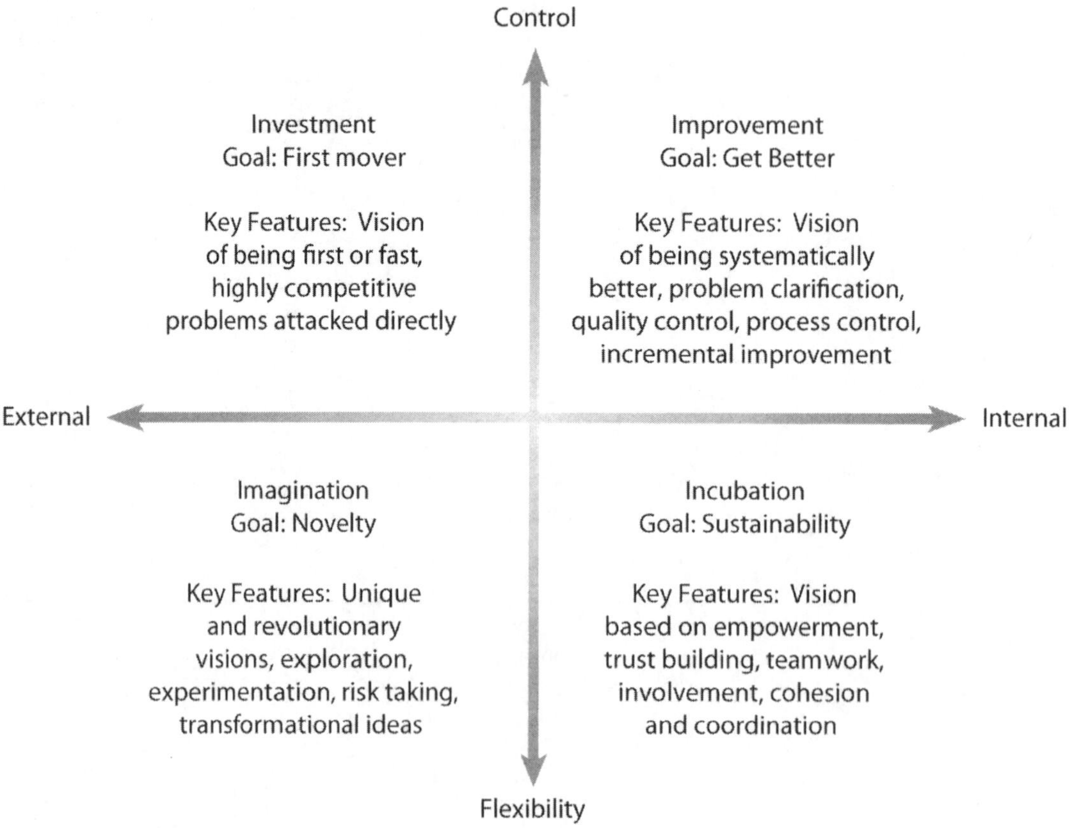

Control

Investment
Goal: First mover

Key Features: Vision of being first or fast, highly competitive problems attacked directly

Improvement
Goal: Get Better

Key Features: Vision of being systematically better, problem clarification, quality control, process control, incremental improvement

External ←——————————→ Internal

Imagination
Goal: Novelty

Key Features: Unique and revolutionary visions, exploration, experimentation, risk taking, transformational ideas

Incubation
Goal: Sustainability

Key Features: Vision based on empowerment, trust building, teamwork, involvement, cohesion and coordination

Flexibility

Adapted from DeGraf, J., & Lawrence, K. A. (2002). Creativity at Work: Developing the Right Practices to Make It Happen. San Francisco: Jossey-Bass.

3.1 Creativity and Vision

DeGraf and Lawrence present a framework consisting of four types of creativity.[13] They argued that creativity "types" could be clustered based on some combination of flexibility versus control and internal versus external orientation. For the manager, their typology is especially useful as it suggests ways to manage creativity, as in simply hiring creative individuals. As summarized in the figure, their research suggests that there are four types of creativity: (1) investment (external orientation with high control), (2) imagination (external orientation with flexibility emphasis), (3) improvement (internal orientation with high control), and (4) incubation (internal orientation with flexibility emphasis).

The first type of creativity, *investment*, is associated with speed—being first and being fast. It is also a form of creativity fostered from the desire to be highly competitive. Perhaps one of the most recent examples of this type of creativity crucible is the beer wars—the battle for U.S. market share between SABMiller and Anheuser Busch (AB; Budweiser). Miller was relentless in attacking the quality of AB's products through its advertisements, and at the same time launched a myriad number of new products to take business from AB's stronghold markets.[14]

The second type of creativity, *imagination*, is characterized by new ideas and breakthroughs: Apple's stylish design of Macintosh computers and then game-changing breakthroughs with its iPod and iPhone are examples of this type of creativity. Oftentimes, we can tie this type of creativity to the drive or genius of a single individual, such as Apple's Steve Jobs.

Where big ideas come from the imagination quadrant, *improvement* is a type of creativity that involves making an existing idea better. A great example of this is McDonald's Ray Kroc, who joined McDonald's as a franchise agent and then built it into the worldwide corporation it is today, utilizing the founding McDonald brothers' original idea of creating quality and cooking standards for preparing tasty burgers and fries. While there were many other burger restaurants around at the time (the 1950s), Kroc's unique process-oriented approach gave McDonald's a big advantage. The fourth type of creativity is referred to as *incubation*. Incubation is a very deliberate approach that concerns a vision of sustainability—that is, leaving a legacy. This type of creativity is more complex because it involves teamwork, empowerment, and collective action. In their chapter on problem solving, David Whetten and Kim Cameron provide Gandhi as an example of incubation creativity:

> *Mahatma Gandhi was probably the only person in modern history who has single-handedly stopped a war. Lone individuals have started wars, but Gandhi was creative enough to stop one. He did so by mobilizing networks of people to pursue a clear vision and set of values. Gandhi would probably have been completely noncreative and ineffective had he not been adept at capitalizing on incubation dynamics. By mobilizing people to march to the sea to make salt, or to burn passes that demarcated ethnic group status, Gandhi was able to engender creative outcomes that had not been considered possible. He was a master at incubation by connecting, involving, and coordinating people.[15]*

While no one of these four types of creativity is best, they have some contradictory or conflicting characteristics. For example, imagination and improvement emphasize different approaches to creativity. The size of the new idea, for instance, is typically much bigger with imagination (i.e., revolutionary solutions) than with improvement (i.e., incremental solutions). Investment and incubation also are very different—investment is relatively fast, and the other relatively slow (i.e., incubation emphasizes deliberation and development).

3.2 Creativity Tools

In this section, we introduce two creativity tools: SCAMPER and the Nominal Group Technique. This set of tools provides some good intuition and resources to develop new ideas—either to craft a vision for a new company or to revise an existing mission and vision. The first three tools can be used and applied individually or in groups; Nominal Group Technique is designed to bolster creativity in groups and can build on individual and group insights provided by the other tools.

FIGURE 4.13

Confederate Major General Nathan Bedford Forrest exemplified the investment type of creativity with his famous quote concerning military strategy: "I got there first with the most men."

Source: http://en.wikipedia.org/wiki/ File:NathanBedfordForrestportrait.jpg

programmed thinking

Thinking that relies on logical
or structured ways of creating
a new product or service
(often called left-brained
thinking).

lateral thinking

A thinking process that is
about changing patterns and
perceptions (often called
right-brained thinking).

SCAMPER

SCAMPER is a checklist tool
that helps you to think of
changes you can make to an
existing marketplace to
create a new one: a new
product, a new service, or
both.

All these tools help manage two divergent forms of thinking necessary for creativity—programmed thinking and lateral thinking. **Programmed thinking**, often called left-brained thinking, relies on logical or structured ways of creating a new product or service. In terms of mission and vision, this means a logical and deliberate process is used to develop the vision statement. **Lateral thinking** is a term coined by Edward DeBono in his book *The Use of Lateral Thinking* (1967), and it refers to changing patterns and perceptions; it is about ideas that may not be obtainable by using only traditional, step-by-step, programmed logic.[16] Lateral thinking draws on the right side of our brains.

Each type of approach—programmed versus lateral—has its strength. Logical and disciplined programmed thinking is enormously effective in making products and services better. It can, however, only go so far before all practical improvements have been carried out. Lateral thinking can generate completely new concepts and ideas and brilliant improvements to existing systems. In the wrong place, however, it can be impractical or unnecessarily disruptive.

SCAMPER

Developed by Bob Eberle, **SCAMPER** is a checklist tool that helps you to think of changes you can make to an existing marketplace to create a new one—a new product, a new service, or both.[17] You can use these changes either as direct suggestions or as starting points for lateral thinking. This, in turn, can inspire a new vision statement.

By taking a topic or problem and then applying SCAMPER, you can generate possible new products. It may be some combination of these SCAMPER changes that lead to highly innovative solutions. For instance, the entertainment company Cirque du Soleil has modeled its shows on the traditional circus. However, it has adapted aspects of theater and opera, eliminated animals, and reduced the number of rings from three to one. As a result, it offers a highly stylized (and much more expensive!) version of what, nostalgically, we call a circus today.

FIGURE 4.14

Was Cirque du Soleil created using the SCAMPER technique? The world may never know.

Source: http://www.flickr.com/photos/joaoa/3633786642

FIGURE 4.15 SCAMPER Your Way to Creativity

The following illustrates examples of how creativity can be fostered using the SCAMPER framework:

Definition	Example	
Substitute. What other ingredients, materials, times, or places can be used to create value?	Vegetarians can now enjoy soy versions of bacon cheese-burgers, once considered the sole domain of meat eaters, without any guilt. 	
Combine. How can products, services, or other elements be combined to create new arrangements?	Based on the two top interests of its founder, Sweets and Spurs is a boutique in Norman, Oklahoma, that caters to locals by selling cupcakes and cowboy boots. 	
Adapt. How can goods or services be altered to meet new needs?	E. L. James, best-selling British author of *Fifty Shades of Grey*, originally developed the book's ideas as online episodes of fan fiction based on the popular Twilight books and movies. James later removed the vampires and reworked and extended the plots of these episodes into a new trilogy—now the fastest-selling paperbacks of all time. 	
Modify. How can products be magnified, minimized, or otherwise given a different shape?	Perhaps even less likely to melt in your mouth than in your hands, M&Ms have found a new life through their miniature cousins. 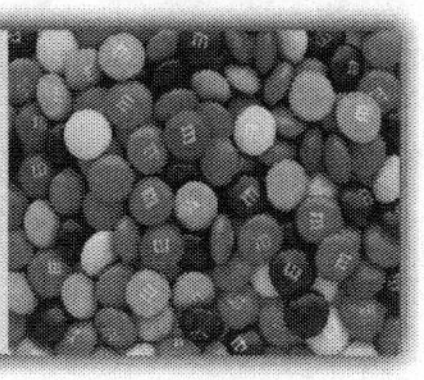	
Put to other uses. How can products created for one use be repurposed for another use?	Artists have recently found value in Lego blocks, originally developed for children, as a creative medium. 	
Eliminate. What can be omitted, deleted, or understated to add value?	Although it lacked apps, the ability to play music, and YouTube access, the cordless phone was an impressive innovation when it first hit the market in the 1980s. 	
Rearrange. Can other layouts, sequences, or patterns create value for organizations?	The idea of paying first and eating second was likely seen as ridiculous before McDonald's served billions in this manner. 	

Source: http://en.wikipedia.org/wiki/File:Plain-M%26Ms-Pile.jpg (fourth from the bottom); http://en.wikipedia.org/wiki/File:Harlem_Micky_Dz.jpg (bottom); all other images © Thinkstock.

Nominal Group Technique

The Nominal Group Technique (NGT) is a method of facilitating a group of people to produce a large number of ideas in a relatively short time.[18] In addition to using NGT to develop a mission and vision statement, it can be useful

- to generate numerous creative ideas,
- to ensure everyone is heard,
- when there is concern that some people may not be vocal,
- to build consensus,
- when there is controversy or conflict.

As shown in "NGT Preparation and Supplies," preparation and supplies are modest. The technique encourages contributions from everyone by allowing for equal participation among group members. A question is posed to the group. Individually and silently, each participant writes down his or her ideas. In round-robin fashion, each member supplies an idea until all ideas are shared. Generally, 6 to 10 people participate. "Nominal" means that the participants form a group in name only. For most of the session, they do not interact as they would in other group processes.

NGT Preparation and Supplies

Formulate your discussion question. Ensure that the wording prevents misunderstanding and is objective. Supplies needed include the following:

- Flip chart for each table
- Masking tape
- 3 × 5 cards for each participant
- Work tables
- Felt pens

The group is divided into small work groups, each with a leader. A flip chart and markers are needed at each table. Position the flip chart so that all can see the ideas. The remaining simple procedures are summarized in "NGT Procedure."

FIGURE 4.16 NGT Procedure

Here, we illustrate the steps of the nominal group procedure:

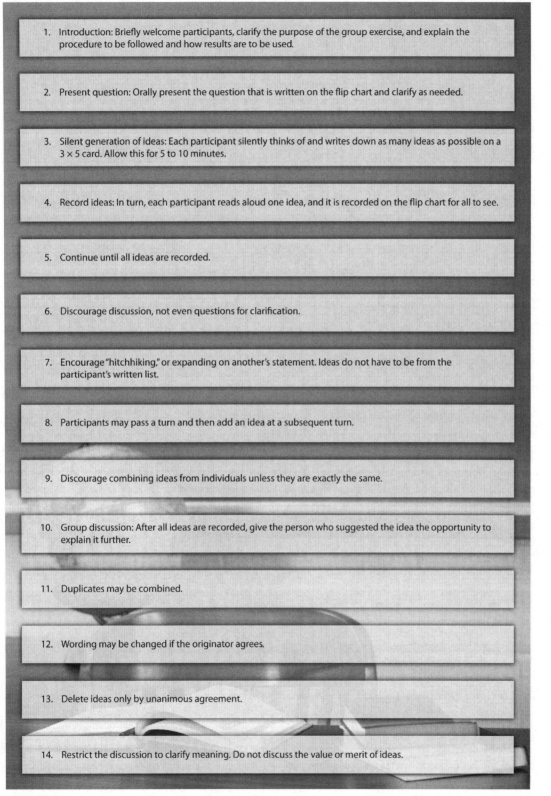

1. Introduction: Briefly welcome participants, clarify the purpose of the group exercise, and explain the procedure to be followed and how results are to be used.

2. Present question: Orally present the question that is written on the flip chart and clarify as needed.

3. Silent generation of ideas: Each participant silently thinks of and writes down as many ideas as possible on a 3 × 5 card. Allow this for 5 to 10 minutes.

4. Record ideas: In turn, each participant reads aloud one idea, and it is recorded on the flip chart for all to see.

5. Continue until all ideas are recorded.

6. Discourage discussion, not even questions for clarification.

7. Encourage "hitchhiking," or expanding on another's statement. Ideas do not have to be from the participant's written list.

8. Participants may pass a turn and then add an idea at a subsequent turn.

9. Discourage combining ideas from individuals unless they are exactly the same.

10. Group discussion: After all ideas are recorded, give the person who suggested the idea the opportunity to explain it further.

11. Duplicates may be combined.

12. Wording may be changed if the originator agrees.

13. Delete ideas only by unanimous agreement.

14. Restrict the discussion to clarify meaning. Do not discuss the value or merit of ideas.

© *Thinkstock*

Passion and Vision

Passion refers to intense, driving, or overmastering feeling or conviction. Passion is also associated with intense emotion compelling action. Passion is relevant to vision in at least two ways: (1) Passion about an idea as inspiration of the vision and vision statement and (2) shared passion among organizational members about the importance of the vision.

Passion about the Vision

Passion can help the entire business thrive. While there is little academic research on the relationship between passion and vision, studies suggest that fostering engagement, a concept related to passion, in employees has a significant effect on the corporate bottom line. Gallup, for instance, has been on the forefront of measuring the effect of what it calls employee engagement. **Employee engagement** is a concept that is generally viewed as managing discretionary effort; that is, when employees have choices, they will act in a way that furthers their organization's interests. Engaged employees are dedicated, passionate, and absorbed in their work.[19] The consulting firm BlessingWhite offers this description of engagement and its value (and clear relationship with passion): "Engaged employees are not just committed. They are not just passionate or proud. They have a line-of-sight on their own future and on the organization's mission and goals. They are 'enthused' and 'in gear' using their talents and discretionary effort to make a difference in their employer's quest for sustainable business success." (Employee Engagement Report 2008).[20]

Engaged employees are those who are performing at the top of their abilities and happy about it. According to statistics that Gallup has drawn from 300,000 companies in its database, 75%–80% of employees are either "disengaged" or "actively disengaged."[21] Disengagement from a strategic human resource perspective is an enormous waste of potential. Consider Gallup's estimation of the impact if 100% of an organization's employees were fully engaged:

- Customers would be 70% more loyal.
- Turnover would drop by 70%.
- Profits would jump by 40%.

Job satisfaction studies in the United States routinely show job satisfaction ratings of 50%–60%. But one recent study by Harris Interactive of nearly 8,000 American workers went a step further.[22] What did the researchers find?

- Only 20% feel very passionate about their jobs.
- Fewer than 15% agree that they feel strongly energized by their work.
- Only 31% (strongly or moderately) believe that their employer inspires the best in them.

Consciously creating an environment where passion is both encouraged and actively developed can yield an enormous competitive advantage. That environment starts at the top through the development and active communication of mission and vision.

KEY TAKEAWAY

Creativity relates to the power or ability to create, and passion is intense emotion compelling action. Creativity is important if the desired mission and vision are to be novel and entrepreneurial; passion is important both from the standpoint of adding energy to the mission and vision and to key stakeholders following the mission and vision.

EXERCISES

1. Think about a time when you have been especially creative. What factors do you think helped contribute to your creativity?
2. Why is creativity relevant to vision and vision statements?
3. What are some useful creativity tools?
4. What is passion, and how is passion relevant to vision and vision statements?
5. What is the relationship between passion and engagement?

4. STAKEHOLDERS

4.1 Stakeholders and Stakeholder Analysis

Stakeholders are individuals or groups who have an interest in an organization's ability to deliver intended results and maintain the viability of its products and services. A number of factors impact the degree to which various stakeholders may influence an organization. Influence reflects a stakeholder's relative power over and within an organization; importance indicates the degree to which the organization cannot be considered successful if a stakeholder's needs, expectations, and issues are not addressed.

One key stakeholder group comprises the CEO and the members of the top-management team. These are key managers, and they might be owners as well. This group is important for at least three reasons:

1. Top managers influence as either originator or steward of the organization's mission and vision.
2. Top managers are responsible for formulating a strategy that realizes the mission and vision.
3. Top managers play a key role in strategy implementation.

Typically, stakeholder evaluation of both quantitative and qualitative performance outcomes will determine whether management is effective. Quantitative outcomes include stock price, total sales, and net profits, while qualitative outcomes include customer service and employee satisfaction. As you can imagine, different stakeholders may place more emphasis on some outcomes than other stakeholders, who have other priorities.

4.2 Stakeholders, Mission, and Vision

Stakeholder analysis refers to the range of techniques or tools used to identify and understand the needs and expectations of major interests inside and outside the organization environment. Managers perform stakeholder analysis to gain a better understanding of the range and variety of groups and individuals who not only have a vested interest in the organization, and ultimately the formulation and implementation of a firm's strategy but also have some influence on firm performance. Managers thus develop mission and vision statements not only to clarify the organization's larger purpose but also to meet or exceed the needs of its key stakeholders.

Stakeholder analysis may also enable managers to identify other parties that might derail otherwise well-formulated strategies, such as local, state, national, or foreign governmental bodies. Finally, stakeholder analysis enables organizations to better formulate, implement, and monitor their strategies, and this is why stakeholder analysis is a critical factor in the ultimate implementation of a strategy.

Identifying Stakeholders

The first step in stakeholder analysis is identifying major stakeholder groups. As you can imagine, the groups of stakeholders who will, either directly or indirectly, be affected by or have an effect on a firm's strategy and its execution can run the gamut from employees, to customers, to competitors, to the government. Ultimately, we will want to take these stakeholders and plot them on a chart, similar to that shown in Figure 4.18.

FIGURE 4.17

The American Federation of Labor and Congress of Industrial Organizations (AFL–CIO) is a powerful stakeholder as a federation of unions that represented over 11 million workers in 2012.

Source: http://www.flickr.com/ photos/labor2008/3272687139

stakeholder analysis

The range of techniques or tools used to identify and to understand the needs and expectations of major interests inside and outside the organization environment.

FIGURE 4.18 Stakeholder Mapping

Influence of Stakeholder	Importance of Stakeholder			
	Unknown	Little/No Importance	Moderate Importance	Significant Importance
Unknown				
Little/No Influence				
Moderate Influence				
Significant Influence				

Source: Adapted from Freeman, R. E. (1984). Strategic management: A stakeholder approach. Boston: Pitman.

Stakeholders can be individuals or groups—communities, social or political organizations, and so forth. Groups can be broken down demographically, geographically, by level and branch of government, or according to other relevant criteria. A map of stakeholders will include such diverse groups as governmental bodies, community-based organizations, social and political action groups, trade unions and guilds, and even journalists. National and regional governments and international regulatory bodies will probably be key stakeholders for global firms or those whose strategy calls for greater international presence. Internally, key stakeholders include shareholders, business units, employees, and managers.

Steps in Identifying Stakeholders

Identifying all a firm's stakeholders can be a daunting task. A list of stakeholders that is too long actually may reduce the effectiveness of this important tool by overwhelming decision makers with too much information. Here, we illustrate three key steps in stakeholder analysis.

Step 1: Determining Influences on Mission, Vision, and Strategy Formulation. One way to analyze the importance and roles of the individuals who compose a stakeholder group is to identify the people and teams who should be consulted as strategy is developed or who will play some part in its eventual implementation. These are *organizational stakeholders*, and they include all types of employees ranging from high-level managers to frontline workers. *Capital-market stakeholders* are groups that affect the availability or cost of capital—sources of money to fund the firm—and they include shareholders, venture capitalists, banks, and other financial intermediaries. *Product-market stakeholders* include parties with whom the firm shares its industry, including suppliers and customers. Social stakeholders consist broadly of external groups and organizations that may be affected by or exercise influence over firm strategy and performance, such as unions, governments, and activist groups. The next two steps are to determine how various stakeholders are affected by the firm's strategic decisions and the degree of power that various stakeholders wield over the firm's ability to choose a course of action.

Step 2: Determining the Effects of Key Decisions on the Stakeholder. Step 2 in stakeholder analysis is to determine the nature of the effect of the firm's strategic decisions on the list of relevant stakeholders. Not all stakeholders are affected equally by strategic decisions. Some effects may be rather mild, and any positive or negative effects may be secondary and of minimal impact. At the other end of the spectrum, some stakeholders bear the brunt of firm decisions, good or bad.

In performing step 1, determine the stakeholders who are most important based on how the firm's strategy affects the stakeholders. You must determine which of the groups still on your list have direct or indirect material claims on firm performance or which are potentially adversely affected. For instance, it is easy to see how shareholders are affected by firm strategies—their wealth either increases or decreases in correspondence with the firm's actions. Other parties have economic interests in the firm as well, such as parties the firm interacts with in the marketplace, including suppliers and customers. The effects on other parties may be much more indirect. For instance, governments have an economic interest in firms doing well—they collect tax revenue from them. However, in cities that are well diversified with many employers, a single firm has minimal economic impact on what the government collects. Alternatively, in other areas, individual firms represent a significant contribution to local employment and tax revenue. In those situations, the effect of firm actions on the government would be much greater.

Step 3: Determining Stakeholders' Power and Influence over Decisions. The third step of a stakeholder analysis is to determine the degree to which a stakeholder group can exercise power and influence over the decisions the firm makes. Does the group have direct control over what is decided, veto power over decisions, nuisance influence, or no influence? Recognize that although the degree to which a stakeholder is affected by firm decisions (i.e., step 2) is sometimes highly correlated with their power and influence over the decision, this is often not the case. For instance, in some companies, frontline employees may be directly affected by firm decisions but have no say in what those decisions are. Power can take the form of formal voting power (boards of directors and owners), economic power (suppliers, financial institutions, and unions), or political power (dissident stockholders, political action groups, and governmental bodies). Sometimes the parties that exercise significant power over firm decisions don't register as having a significant stake in the firm (step 2). In recent years, for example, Walmart has encountered significant resistance in some communities by well-organized groups who oppose the entry of the megaretailer. Walmart executives now have to anticipate whether a vocal and politically powerful community group will oppose its new stores or aim to reduce their size, which decreases Walmart's per store profitability. Indeed, in many markets, such groups have been effective at blocking new stores, reducing their size, or changing building specifications.

Identifying stakeholder groups and differentiating them by how they are affected by firm decisions and the power they have to influence decisions may prompt some additional questions:

- Are there any vulnerable points in either the firm's strategy or its potential implementation based on the impact of overlooked stakeholders?
- Which groups are mobilized and active in promoting their interests?
- Which groups will benefit from successful execution of the firm's strategy and which may be adversely affected?
- Where are various groups located? Who belongs to them? Who represents them?

KEY TAKEAWAY

This section introduced stakeholders, their roles, and how to begin assessing their roles in the development of the organization's mission and vision. While any person or organization with a stake in your organization is a stakeholder, managers are most concerned with those stakeholders who have the most influence on, or will be most influenced by, the organization. On the basis of your assessment of stakeholders, you now can be proactive in involving them in the P-O-L-C stages.

EXERCISES

1. What are stakeholders, and why are they relevant to mission and vision?
2. Are stakeholders equally relevant to all parts of P-O-L-C, or only mission and vision?
3. What is stakeholder analysis? What are the three identification steps?
4. How does stakeholder analysis help you craft a mission and vision statement?
5. Which important stakeholders might you intentionally exclude from a mission or vision statement?
6. What are the risks of not conducting stakeholder analysis as an input to the formulation of your mission and vision?

5. DEVELOPING YOUR PERSONAL MISSION AND VISION

> ### LEARNING OBJECTIVES
>
> 1. Determine what mission and vision mean for you.
> 2. Develop some guidelines for developing your mission and vision.

Mission and vision are concepts that can be applied to you, personally, well beyond their broader relevance to the P-O-L-C framework. Personal mission and vision communicate the direction in which you are headed, as well as providing some explanation for why you are choosing one direction or set of objectives over others. Thinking about and writing down mission and vision statements for your life can help provide you with a compass as you work toward your own goals and objectives.

5.1 Your Mission and Vision

Note that the development of a personal mission and vision, and then a strategy for achieving them, are exactly the opposite of what most people follow. Most people do not plan further ahead than their next job or activity (if they plan their career at all). They take a job because it looks attractive, and then they see what they can do with it. We advocate looking as far into the future as you can and deciding where you want to end up and what steps will lead you there. In that way, your life and your career fit into some intelligent plan, and you are in control of your own life.

Guidelines

The first step in planning a career is obviously a long-term goal. Where do you want to end up, ultimately? Do you really want to be a CEO or president of the United States, now that you know what it costs to be either one? There are a couple basic parts to this process.

BHAG

First, set out a bold vision.

> Jim Collins, author of *Good to Great*, describes this as a **BHAG**: a big, hairy, audacious goal. Five guiding criteria for good BHAGs is that they

1. Are set with understanding, not bravado.
2. Fit squarely in the three circles of (a) what you are deeply passionate about (including your core values and purpose), (b) what drives your economic logic, and (c) what differentiates you (what you can be the best in the world at).
3. Have a long time frame—10 to 30 years.
4. Are clear, compelling, and easy to grasp.
5. Directly reflect your core values and core purpose.

Values

Second, sketch out your personal values, or "Guiding Philosophy"—a set of core values and principles like your own Declaration of Independence.

Schedule

Once the vision is set, you have to develop some long-term goal (or goals), then intermediate-term goals, and so on. If you want to be President, what jobs will you have to take first to get there and when do you have to get these jobs? Where should you live? What training do you need? What political connections do you need? Then you have to set up an orderly plan for obtaining the connections and training that you need and getting into these steppingstone jobs.

Finally, you need to establish short-term goals to fit clearly into a coherent plan for your entire career. Your next job (if you are now a fairly young person) should be picked not only for its salary or for its opportunities for advancement but for its chances to provide you with the training and connections you need to reach your long-term goals. The job that is superficially attractive to you because it has a high salary, offers the opportunity for immediate advancement, or is located in a desirable place may be

BHAG

A big, hairy, audacious goal.

FIGURE 4.19

Ford Motor Company's goals of democratizing the automobile is a commonly cited example of a BHAG.

© Thinkstock

a mistake from the standpoint of your long-term career. Following these steps can help you identify your core mission statement and values.

Step 1: Identify Past Successes. Spend some time identifying four or five examples where you have had personal success in recent years. These successes could be at work, in your community, or at home. Write them down. Try to identify whether there is a common theme—or themes—to these examples. Write them down.

Step 2: Identify Core Values. Develop a list of attributes that you believe identify who you are and what your priorities are. The list can be as long as you need. Once your list is complete, see whether you can narrow your values to five or six most important values. Finally, see whether you can choose the one value that is most important to you. We've added "Generating Ideas for Your Mission and Vision" to help jog your memory and brainstorm about what you do well and really like to do.

Step 3: Make a list of the ways you could make a difference. In an ideal situation, think about how could you contribute best to the following:

- The world in general
- Your family
- Your employer or future employers
- Your friends
- Your community

Generating Ideas for Your Mission and Vision

A useful mission and vision statement should include two pieces: what you wish to accomplish and contribute and who you want to be, the character strengths and qualities you wish to develop. While this sounds simple, those pieces of information are not always obvious. Try these tools for generating valuable information about yourself.

Part 1

1. Describe your ideal day. This is not about being practical. It is designed to include as many sides of you and your enthusiasms as possible: creative, competent, artistic, introverted, extraverted, athletic, playful, nurturing, contemplative, and so on.

2. Imagine yourself 132 years old and surrounded by your descendants or those descendants of your friends. You are in a warm and relaxed atmosphere (such as around a fireplace). What would you say to them about what is important in life? This exercise is designed to access the values and principles that guide your life.

3. Imagine that it is your 70th birthday (or another milestone in your life). You have been asked by national print media to write a press release about your achievements. Consider what you would want your family, friends, coworkers in your profession and in your community to say about you. What difference would you like to have made in their lives? How do you want to be remembered? This is designed to inventory your actions and accomplishments in all areas of your life.

Part 2

Review your notes for these three exercises. With those responses in mind, reflect on questions 1, 2, and 3 above. Then write a rough draft (a page of any length) of your mission statement. Remember that it should describe what you want to do and who you want to be. This is not a job description. Carry it with you, post copies in visible places at home and work, and revise and evaluate. Be patient with yourself. The process is as important as the outcome. After a few weeks, write another draft. Ask yourself whether your statement was based on proven principles that you believe in, if you feel direction, motivation, and inspiration when you read it. Over time, reviewing and evaluating will keep you abreast of your own development.

Step 4: Identify Goals. Spend some time thinking about your priorities in life and the goals you have for yourself. Make a list of your personal goals, perhaps in the short term (up to three years) and the long term (beyond three years).

Step 5: Write Mission and Vision Statements. On the basis of the first four steps and a better understanding of yourself, begin writing your personal mission and vision statements.

Here are some final thoughts: A personal mission and vision statement is, of course, personal. But if you want to see whether you have been honest in developing your personal mission and vision statement, we suggest sharing the results of this process with one or more people who are close to you. Ask for their feedback. Finally, remember that mission and vision statements are not meant to be written once and blasted into stone. You should set aside some time annually to review your career, job, goals, and mission and vision statements—and make adjustments as necessary.

EXERCISES

1. How does a personal mission and vision statement differ from one created for an organization?
2. What time period should a personal mission and vision statement cover?
3. What type of goals should you start thinking about in creating a personal mission and vision?
4. How are your strengths and weaknesses relevant to mission and vision?
5. What stakeholders seem relevant to your personal mission and vision?

6. CASE IN POINT: XEROX MOTIVATES EMPLOYEES FOR SUCCESS

FIGURE 4.20

Anne Mulcahy (left), former Xerox chairman of the board, and Ursula Burns (right), Xerox CEO.

Source: Photo courtesy of Xerox Corporation.

As of 2012, Xerox Corporation (NYSE: XRX) is a $23 billion, multinational company that owns more than 10,700 patents and operates in 160 countries. Xerox is headquartered in Norwalk, Connecticut, and employs 140,000 people. How does a company of such size and magnitude effectively manage and motivate employees from diverse backgrounds and experiences? Such companies depend on the productivity and performance of their employees. The journey over the last 100 years has withstood many successes and failures. In 2000, Xerox was facing bankruptcy after years of mismanagement, piles of debt, and mounting questions about its accounting practices.

Anne Mulcahy turned Xerox around. Mulcahy joined Xerox as an employee in 1976 and moved up the corporate ladder, holding several management positions until she became CEO in 2001. In 2005, Mulcahy was named by *Fortune* magazine as the second most powerful woman in business. Based on a lifetime of experience with Xerox, she knew that the company had powerful employees who were not motivated when she took over. Mulcahy believed that, among other key business changes, motivating employees at Xerox was a key way to pull the company back from the brink of failure. One of her guiding principles was the belief that in order to achieve customer satisfaction, employees must be treated as key stakeholders and become interested and motivated in their work. Mulcahy not only successfully saw the company through this difficult time but also was able to create a stronger, more focused company.

In 2009, Mulcahy became the chairman of Xerox's board of directors (until 2010, when she retired from her position) and passed the torch to Ursula Burns, who became the new CEO of Xerox. Burns became not only the first African American woman CEO to head a Standard & Poor's (S&P) company but also the first woman to succeed another woman as the head of an S&P 100 company. Moreover, Burns is a lifetime Xerox employee who has been with the company for more than 30 years. She began as a graduate intern and was hired full time after graduation. Because of her tenure with Xerox, she has close relationships with many of the employees, which provides a level of comfort and teamwork. She describes Xerox as a nice family. She maintains that Mulcahy created a strong and successful business yet encouraged individuals to speak their mind, to not worry about hurting one another's feelings, and to be more critical.

Burns explains that she learned early on in her career, from her mentors at Xerox, the importance of managing individuals in different ways and not intentionally intimidating people but rather relating to them and their individual perspectives. As CEO and chairman of the board, she wants to encourage people to get things done, take risks, and not be afraid of those risks. She motivates her teams by letting them know her intentions and priorities. The correlation between a manager's leadership style and the productivity and motivation of employees is apparent at Xerox, where employees feel a sense of importance and a part of the process necessary to maintain a successful and profitable business.

Case written by Carlene Reynolds, Talya Bauer, and Berrin Erdogan to accompany Carpenter, M., Bauer, T., Erdogan, B., & Short, J. (2013). Principles of management (2nd ed.). New York: Flat World Knowledge. Based on information from Tompkins, N. C. (1992, November 1). Employee satisfaction leads to customer service. AllBusiness. Retrieved September 12, 2012, from http://www.allbusiness.com/marketing/market-research/341288-1.html; Anonymous (2006). 50 most powerful women. Fortune. Retrieved September 12, 2012, from http://money.cnn.com/popups/2006/fortune/mostpowerfulwomen/2.html; Anonymous (2010). Profile: Anne M. Mulcahy. Forbes. Retrieved September 12, 2012, from http://people.forbes.com/profile/anne-m-mulcahy/19732; Whitney, L. (2010, March 30). Anne Mulcahy to retire as Xerox chairman. CNET News. Retrieved September 12, 2012, from http://news.cnet.com/8301-1001_3-20001412-92.html; Bryant, A. (2010, February 20). Xerox's new chief tries to redefine its culture. New York Times; Xerox at a glance. Retrieved September 12, 2012, from http://www.xerox.com/about-xerox/company-facts/enus.html; Retrieved September 12, 2012, from http://www.nytimes.com/2010/02/21/business/21xerox.html?pagewanted=18dpc.

CASE DISCUSSION QUESTIONS

1. In terms of the P-O-L-C framework, what values do the promotion and retention of Mulcahy and Burns suggest are important at Xerox? How might these values be reflected in its vision and mission statements?

2. How do you think Xerox was able to motivate its employees through the crisis it faced in 2000?

3. How do CEOs with large numbers of employees communicate priorities to a worldwide workforce?

4. How might Ursula Burns motivate employees to take calculated risks?

5. Both Anne Mulcahy and Ursula Burns were longtime employees of Xerox when they became CEO. How does an organization attract and keep individuals for such a long period of time?

ENDNOTES

1. Rigby, D., & Bilodeau, B. (2011). Management tools & trends 2011. Retrieved September 12, 2012, from http://www.bain.com/Images/BAIN_BRIEF_Management_Tools.pdf.

2. Bart, C. K., Bontis, N., & Taggar, S. (2001). A model of the impact of mission statements on firm performance. *Management Decision, 39*(1), 19–35.

3. Retrieved October 27, 2008, from http://www.starbucks.com/aboutus.

4. Retrieved October 27, 2008, from http://www.ogilvy.com/o_mather.

5. Retrieved October 27, 2008, from http://www.walmart.com.

6. Hamel, G., & Prahalad, C. K. (1993, March–April). Strategy as stretch and leverage. *Harvard Business Review*, 75–84.

7. Retrieved September 12, 2012, from http://www.pixar.com/companyinfo/about_us/overview.htm.

8. Catmull, E. (2008, September). How Pixar fosters collective creativity. *Harvard Business Review*, 1–11.

9. Lafley, A. G., & Charan, R. (2008). *The game changer*. Upper Saddle River, NJ: Crown Books.

10. Brown, B. (2010, November/December). Why innovation matters. *Research Technology Management, 53*, 18–23.

11. Carpenter, M. A., & Sanders, W. G. (2006). *Strategic management: A dynamic perspective*. (1st ed.). Upper Saddle River, NJ: Pearson/Prentice-Hall.

12. Gerhart, B. A., & Rynes, S. L. (2003). *Compensation:Compensation: Theory, evidence, and strategic implications*. Thousand Oaks, CA: Sage.

13. DeGraf, J., & Lawrence, K. A. (2002). *Creativity at Work: Developing the Right Practices to Make It Happen*. San Francisco: Jossey-Bass.

14. Retrieved October 27, 2008, from http://www.bizjournals.com/milwaukee/stories/2004/05/31/story7.html.

15. Whetten, D., & Camerson, K. (2007). *Developing management skills* (7th ed.). Upper Saddle River, NJ: Pearson/Prentice-Hall.

16. De Bono, E. (1992). *Serious creativity*. New York: Harper Business; Osborn, A. (1953). *Applied imagination*. New York: Scribner's.

17. Eberle, R. (1997). *Scamper: Creative games and activities for imagination development*. New York: Prufrock Press.

18. This section is reproduced with permission of the University of Wisconsin Extension Program. A circulation version can be found at http://www.uwex.edu/ces/pdande/resources/pdf/Tipsheet3.pdf (retrieved September 12, 2012). Additional information on NGT can be gained by reading the following: Delbecq, A., Van de Ven, A., & Gustafson, D. (1975). *Group techniques for program planning: A guide to nominal group and Delphi processes*. Glenview, IL: Scott, Foresman; Tague, N. (1995). *The quality toolbox*. Milwaukee, WI: ASQC Quality Press; Witkin, B., & Altschuld, J. (1995). *Planning and conducting needs assessment: A practical guide*. Thousand Oaks, CA: Sage.

19. Crawford, E. R., LePine, J. A., & Rich, B. L. (2010). Linking job demands and resources to employee engagement and burnout: A theoretical extension and meta-analytic test. *Journal of Applied Psychology, 95*, 834–848.

20. BlessingWhite. (2008, April). 2008 employee engagement report. Retreived from http://www.blessingwhite.com/eee___report.asp.

21. Retrieved October 28, 2008, from http://gmj.gallup.com/content/24880/Gallup-Study-Engaged-Employees-Inspire-Company.aspx.

22. Retrieved September 12, 2012, from http://www.agewave.com/media_files/rough.html.

CHAPTER 5
Strategic Management

FIGURE 5.1

Apple's unique strategy has enabled the company to capture the hearts and minds of music lovers worldwide.

© Thinkstock

CHAPTER LEARNING OBJECTIVES

Reading this chapter will help you do the following:

1. See how strategy fits in the planning-organizing-leading-controlling (P-O-L-C) framework.
2. Better understand how strategies emerge.
3. Understand strategy as trade-offs, discipline, and focus.
4. Conduct internal analysis to develop strategy.
5. Conduct external analysis to develop strategy.
6. Formulate organizational and personal strategy with the strategy diamond.

Strategic management is about understanding choices organizations make to achieve specific goals and objectives that fulfill a firm's mission and vision. Strategy is a central part of the planning function in P-O-L-C. Strategy is also about making choices that provide organizations with some measure of uniqueness that allows them to outperform competitors. This chapter primarily emphasizes strategy formulation (answers to the "What should be our strategy?" question) as opposed to strategy implementation (answers to questions about "How do we execute a chosen strategy?"). The central position of strategy is summarized in Figure 5.2. In this chapter, you will learn about strategic management and how it fits in the P-O-L-C framework. You will also learn some of the key internal and external analyses that support the development of good strategies. Finally, you will see how the concept of strategy can be applied to you personally and professionally.

FIGURE 5.2 The P-O-L-C Framework

Planning	Organizing	Leading	Controlling
1. Vision & Mission	1. Organization Design	1. Leadership	1. Systems/Processes
2. Strategizing	2. Culture	2. Decision Making	2. Strategic Human Resources
3. Goals & Objectives	3. Social Networks	3. Communications	
		4. Groups/Teams	
		5. Motivation	

1. STRATEGIC MANAGEMENT IN THE P-O-L-C FRAMEWORK

LEARNING OBJECTIVES

1. Be able to define strategic management.
2. Understand how strategic management fits in the P-O-L-C framework.
3. Broadly identify the inputs for strategy formulation.

1.1 What Is Strategic Management?

Strategic management reflects what a firm is doing to achieve its mission and vision as seen by its achievement of specific goals and objectives. The **strategic management process** "is the process by which a firm manages the formulation and implementation of its strategy."[1] The strategic management process is "the coordinated means by which an organization achieves its goals and objectives."[2] Others have described strategy as the pattern of resource allocation choices and organizational arrangements that result from managerial decision making.[3] Planning and **strategy formulation**, sometimes called *business planning* or *strategic planning*, have much in common, since formulation helps determine what the firm should do. **Strategy implementation** tells managers how they should go about putting the desired strategy into action. The concept of strategy is relevant to all types of organizations, from large, public companies like GE, to not-for-profit organizations, to religious organizations, to political parties.

1.2 Strategic Management in the P-O-L-C Framework

If vision and mission are the heart and soul of planning (in the P-O-L-C framework), then strategy, particularly strategy formulation, would be the brain. Figure 5.3 summarizes where strategy formulation (*strategizing*) and implementation fit in the planning and other components of P-O-L-C. We will focus primarily on the strategy formulation aspects of strategic management because implementation is essentially organizing, leading, and controlling P-O-L-C components.

---

strategic management process

A comprehensive and ongoing management process aimed at formulating and implementing effective strategies; it is a way of approaching business opportunities and challenges such that the firm achieves its vision and mission.

strategy formulation

Synonymous with business planning and strategic planning. The set of processes involved in creating or determining the strategies of the organization; it focuses on the content of strategies.

strategy implementation

The methods by which strategies are operationalized or executed within the organization; it focuses on the processes through which strategies are achieved.

FIGURE 5.3 Strategizing in P-O-L-C

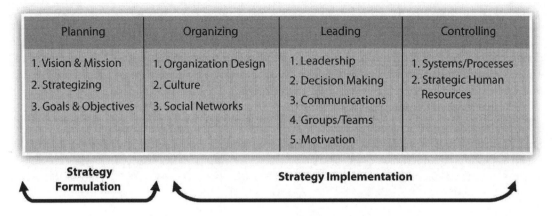

Planning	Organizing	Leading	Controlling
1. Vision & Mission	1. Organization Design	1. Leadership	1. Systems/Processes
2. Strategizing	2. Culture	2. Decision Making	2. Strategic Human Resources
3. Goals & Objectives	3. Social Networks	3. Communications	
		4. Groups/Teams	
		5. Motivation	

Strategy Formulation   **Strategy Implementation**

Planning starts with vision and mission and concludes with setting goals and objectives. In-between is the critical role played by strategy. Specifically, a strategy captures and communicates how vision and mission will be achieved and which goals and objectives show that the organization is on the right path to achieving them.

There are two aspects of strategizing for most organizations. The first, **corporate strategy**, answers strategy questions related to "What business or businesses should we be in?" and "How does our business X help us compete in business Y, and vice versa?" Corporate strategy considers an organization to be a portfolio of businesses, resources, capabilities, or activities. For example, McDonald's is well known for their golden arches, associated exclusively with their restaurants worldwide. McDonald's also had a majority stake in Mexican food favorite Chipotle for several years as well.[4] The McDonald's corporate strategy helped its managers evaluate and answer questions about whether it made sense for McDonald's set of businesses to include different restaurants such as McDonald's and Chipotle. While other food-service companies have multiple outlets—YUM! Brands, for example, owns Taco Bell, Pizza Hut, and KFC—McDonald's determined that one brand (McDonald's) was a better strategy for it in the future and sold Chipotle in 2006. Figure 5.5 provides a graphic guide to this kind of planning.

The logic behind corporate strategy involves the concepts of synergy and diversification. **Synergy** exists when the interaction of two or more activities, such as those in a business, create a combined effect greater than the sum of their individual effects. For example, synergy arises when each of the YUM! Brands' food outlets performs better because they have common ownership and can share valuable inputs into their businesses. The idea is that the combination of certain businesses is stronger than they would be individually because they either do things more cheaply or of higher quality as a result of their coordination under a common owner.

corporate strategy

The set of strategic alternatives that an organization chooses from as it manages its operations simultaneously across several industries and several markets.

synergy

The interaction of two or more activities, creating a combined effect greater than the sum of their individual efforts.

FIGURE 5.4

Synergy is evident in YUM! Brands' practice of sharing a physical location between two of their restaurant concepts.

Source: http://www.flickr.com/photos/dno1967b/6360169037.

Diversification exists when an organization participates in multiple businesses that are in some way distinct from each other, as Taco Bell is from Pizza Hut, for instance. Just as with a portfolio of stock, the purpose of diversification is to spread out risk and opportunities over a larger set of businesses. Some may be high growth, some slow growth or declining; some may perform worse during recessions, while others perform better. Sometimes the businesses can be very different, such as when fashion sunglass maker Maui Jim diversified into property and casualty insurance through its merger with RLI Corporation.[5] Perhaps more than a coincidence, RLI was founded some 60 years earlier as Replacement Lens International (later changed to its abbreviation, RLI, in line with its broader insurance products offerings), with the primary business of providing insurance for replacement contact lenses. There are two major diversification types. **Related diversification** occurs when a firm operates multiple businesses within the same industry. For example, Estée Lauder engages in multiple cosmetics-related businesses. In contrast, **unrelated diversification** occurs when a firm engages in businesses in different industries that lack similarities between each other. Warren Buffett's company, Berkshire Hathaway, engages in various businesses with little similarities to each other, such as GEICO, Fruit of the Loom, Justin Brands, Burlington Northern, and See's Candies.

FIGURE 5.5 Corporate and Business Strategy

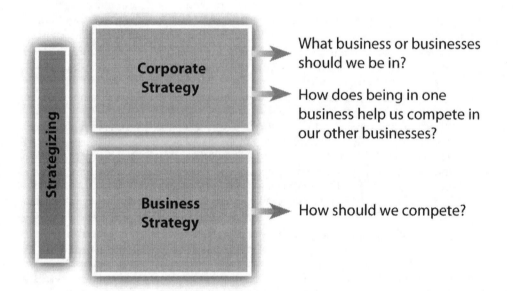

Whereas corporate strategy looks at an organization as a portfolio, **business strategy** focuses on how a given business needs to compete to be effective. All organizations need strategies to survive and thrive. A neighborhood church, for instance, may want to serve existing members, build new membership, and, at the same time, raise surplus monies to help with outreach activities that fulfill their mission. Its strategy would answer questions surrounding the accomplishment of these key objectives. In a for-profit company such as McDonald's, business strategy would help keep existing customers, grow its business by moving into new markets and taking customers from competitors like Taco Bell and Burger King, and do all this at a profit level demanded by the stock market.

FIGURE 5.6 The Sweet Fragrance of Success: The Brands That "Make Up" the Lauder Empire

Estée Lauder was a pioneer in the cosmetics industry. Estée Lauder summarized her zest for business by noting, "I have never worked a day in my life without selling. If I believe in something, I sell it, and I sell it hard." The company that bears her name has used related diversification and other growth strategies to create over two dozen brands of cosmetics, perfume, skin care, and hair care products. Below we illustrate some of the products that make up the Lauder empire.

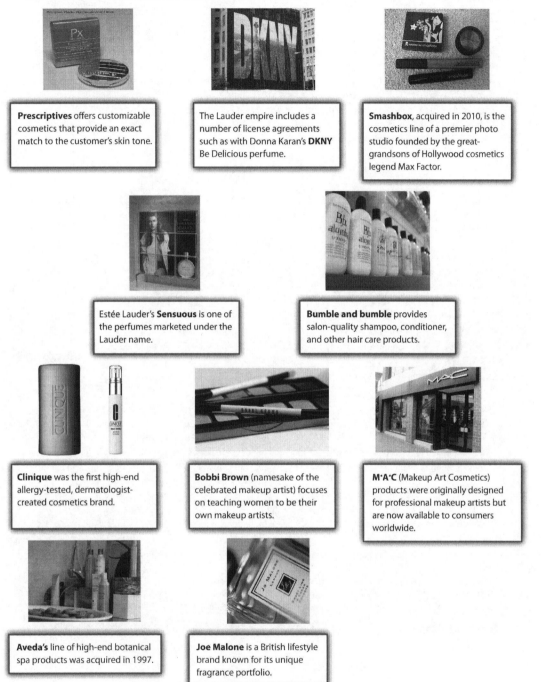

Prescriptives offers customizable cosmetics that provide an exact match to the customer's skin tone.

The Lauder empire includes a number of license agreements such as with Donna Karan's **DKNY** Be Delicious perfume.

Smashbox, acquired in 2010, is the cosmetics line of a premier photo studio founded by the great-grandsons of Hollywood cosmetics legend Max Factor.

Estée Lauder's **Sensuous** is one of the perfumes marketed under the Lauder name.

Bumble and bumble provides salon-quality shampoo, conditioner, and other hair care products.

Clinique was the first high-end allergy-tested, dermatologist-created cosmetics brand.

Bobbi Brown (namesake of the celebrated makeup artist) focuses on teaching women to be their own makeup artists.

M·A·C (Makeup Art Cosmetics) products were originally designed for professional makeup artists but are now available to consumers worldwide.

Aveda's line of high-end botanical spa products was acquired in 1997.

Joe Malone is a British lifestyle brand known for its unique fragrance portfolio.

Source: Image courtesy of Ketchen, D., & Short, J. (2011). Mastering strategic management. Irvington, NY: Flat World Knowledge.

1.3 SWOT Analysis

SWOT analysis, which stands for strengths, weaknesses, opportunities, and threats, is a tool to help organizations understand internal strengths and weaknesses and external opportunities of the environment. SWOT was developed by Ken Andrews of Harvard Business School in the early 1970s.[6] An assessment of strengths and weaknesses occurs as a part of organizational analysis; that is, it is an audit of the company's internal workings, which are relatively easier to control than outside factors. Examining opportunities and threats is a part of environmental analysis—the company must look outside of the organization to assess opportunities and threats over which it has lesser control.

SWOT analysis

An assessment of strengths, weaknesses, opportunities, and threats.

Andrews's original conception of the strategy model that preceded the SWOT asked four basic questions about a company and its environment: (1) What can we do? (2) What do we want to do? (3) What might we do? and (4) What do others expect us to do?

FIGURE 5.7 SWOT

Chess master Bruce Pandolfini has noted the similarities between business and chess. In both arenas, you must understand your own abilities as well as your flaws. You must also know your opponents, try to anticipate their moves, and deal with considerable uncertainty. A very popular management tool that incorporates the idea of understanding the elements internal and external to the firm is SWOT (strengths, weaknesses, opportunities, and threats) analysis. Strengths and weaknesses are assessed by examining the firm, while opportunities and threats refer to external events and trends. These ideas can be applied to individuals too. Below we offer examples of each element of SWOT analysis for organizations and for individuals who are seeking employment.

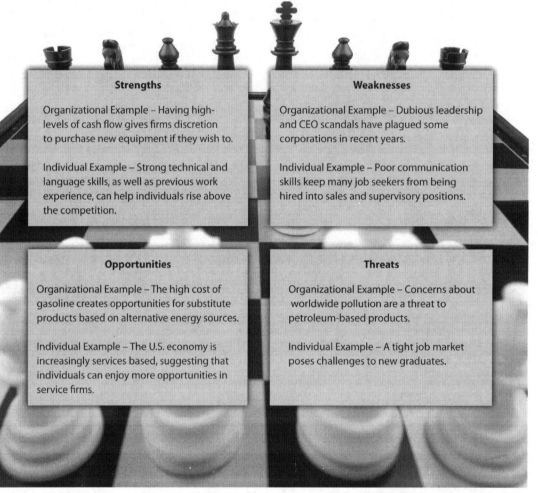

Source: *Image courtesy of Ketchen, D., & Short, J. (2011). Mastering strategic management. Irvington, NY: Flat World Knowledge.*

Strengths and Weaknesses

sustainable competitive advantage

A competitive advantage that will exist after all attempts at strategic imitation have ceased.

A good starting point for strategizing is an assessment of what an organization does well and what it does less well. In general, good strategies take advantage of *strengths* and minimize the disadvantages posed by any *weaknesses*. TOMS Shoes, for example, is known for its trendy footwear that helps others by donating a pair of shoes to a person in need for every pair of shoes sold. A weakness of TOMS Shoes is that its strategy can be easily duplicated. For example, Sketchers has launched BOBS Shoes with a similar style and mission to that of TOMS. As is evidenced by the competitive dynamics of these two shoemakers, the hardest thing for an organization to do is to develop its competitive advantage into a **sustainable competitive advantage** where the organization's strengths cannot be easily duplicated or imitated by other firms, nor made redundant or less valuable by changes in the external environment.

Opportunities and Threats

Understanding of the external environment is also critical to understanding strategic management. *Opportunities* assess factors external to the business that could enable a business to exist and/or prosper. For example, an aging population could lead to opportunities in numerous industries that cater to that demographic. *Threats* include factors beyond the firm's control that could place the strategy, or the business, at risk. Like opportunities, these are considered external because managers typically have no control over them, but may benefit from having plans to respond to these opportunities or threats. For example, the struggling world economy has posed challenges for countless firms within multiple industries.

Internal Analysis Tools

Internal analysis tools help identify an organization's strengths and weaknesses. Two tools for internal analysis are the *value chain* and *VRIO* tools. The value chain dissects the organization and then identifies areas of unique strength or weakness. Sometimes these parts take the form of functions, like marketing or manufacturing. For instance, Disney excels at developing and profiting from its branded products, such as *Cinderella* or *Pirates of the Caribbean*. This is a marketing function, as well as a design function, another Disney strength.

Value chain functions are also called *capabilities*. VRIO—which stands for Value, Rarity, Imitability, and Organization—is a framework that suggests that a capability, or a *resource*, such as a patent or a desirable location, is likely to yield a competitive advantage to an organization when it can be shown that it is valuable, rare, difficult to imitate, and supported by the organization. Where the value chain might suggest internal areas of strength, VRIO helps predict whether those strengths will give it a competitive advantage. For example, while other movie studios can copy Disney's strategy by marketing their films, they are unlikely to successfully imitate the iconic status Disney has developed over years of marketing commitment and through association with their well-known theme parks.

External Analysis Tools

Two primary tools to examine the external environment are *PESTEL* and *industry analysis*. PESTEL is an acronym that stands for Political, Economic, Sociocultural, Technological, Environmental, and Legal environments. The PESTEL framework directs managers to collect information about, and analyze, each environmental dimension to identify the broad range of threats and opportunities facing the organization. Industry analysis, in contrast, maps out the different relationships that the organization might have with suppliers, customers, and competitors. Whereas PESTEL provides you with a good sense of the broader macro-environment, industry analysis informs you about the organization's competitive environment and the key industry-level factors that seem to influence performance.

FIGURE 5.8

Disney's marketing excellence has spread the tales of Captain Jack Sparrow across the globe.

Source: http://www.flickr.com/ photos/sandrascherer/6921198621/

PESTEL

Stands for the political, economic, social, technological, environmental, and legal dimensions of an organization's external environment.

FIGURE 5.9 PESTEL

Examining the general environment involves gaining an understanding of key factors and trends in broader society. PESTEL analysis is a popular framework for organizing these factors and trends and isolating how they influence industries and the firms within them. Below we describe each of the six dimensions associated with PESTEL analysis: political, economic, social, technological, environmental, and legal.

Political factors include elements such as tax policies, changes in trade restrictions and tariffs, and the stability of governments.

Economic factors include elements such as interest rates, inflation rates, gross domestic product, unemployment rates, levels of disposable income, and the general growth or decline of the economy.

Social factors include trends in demographics such as population size, age, and ethnic mix, as well as cultural trends such as attitudes toward obesity and consumer activism.

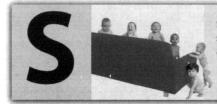

Technological factors include, for example, changes in the rate of new product development, increases in automation, and advancements in service industry delivery.

Environmental factors include, for example, natural disasters and weather patterns.

Legal factors include laws involving issues such as employment, health and safety, discrimination, and antitrust.

Source: Image courtesy of Ketchen, D., & Short, J. (2011). Mastering strategic management. Irvington, NY: Flat World Knowledge.

EXERCISES

1. What is the difference between strategy formulation and strategy implementation?
2. What is the difference between business strategy and corporate strategy?
3. What are some of the forms of diversification, and what do they mean?
4. What do you learn from a SWOT analysis?
5. In SWOT analysis, what are some of the tools you might use to understand the internal environment (identify strengths and weaknesses)?
6. In SWOT analysis, what are some of the tools you might use to understand the external environment (identify opportunities and threats)?

2. HOW DO STRATEGIES EMERGE?

LEARNING OBJECTIVES

1. Understand the difference between intended and realized strategy.
2. Understand how strategy is formulated.
3. Understand the need for a balance between strategic design and emergence.

How do business strategies come into being? In this section, you will learn about *intended* and *realized* strategies. The section concludes with discussion of how strategies are made.

FIGURE 5.10 Strategic Planning and Learning: Intended, Emergent, and Realized Strategies

Strategic planning, usually in the form of a business plan, is a key aspect of creating a new venture. Many well-known firms, however, owe their success more to their ability to adapt than to their original plan. Most firms begin by pursuing their plans (also known as intended strategy), but unexpected opportunities that arise over time can lead firms in much different directions than could have ever been anticipated (emergent strategy). Ultimately, the intended and emergent strategies each contribute to a firm's realized strategy. In the cases below, the original intended strategy can barely be detected within today's strategy.

	Intended Strategy	Emergent Strategy	Realized Strategy
	David McConnell aspired to be a writer. When his books weren't selling he decided to give out perfume as a gimmick.	The perfumes McConnell gave out with his books were popular, inspiring the foundation of the California Perfume Company.	The company changed its name to Avon in 1939, and its direct marketing system remained popular for decades. Avon is now available online and in retail outlets worldwide.
	When father and son team Scott and Don Rasmussen were fired from the New England Whalers, they envisioned a cable television network that focused on sports events in the state of Connecticut.	As the network became successful, ESPN has branched out beyond the local softball games and demolition derbies that were first broadcasted.	ESPN is now billed as the worldwide leader in sports, owning several ESPN affiliates as well as production of ESPN magazine, ESPN radio, and broadcasting for ABC.
	In 1977, a cash-strapped advertiser gave a radio station managed by Lowell Paxson 112 electric can openers to pay off an overdue bill. The can openers were offered over the air for $9.95 and quickly sold out.	An idea emerged. Soon the radio station features a regular show called "Suncoast Bargaineers." In 1982, Paxson and a partner launched the Home Shopping Club on local cable television in Florida.	Today the Home Shopping Network has evolved into a retail powerhouse. The company sells tens of thousands of products on television channels in several countries and over the Internet.

Source: Image courtesy of Ketchen, D., & Short, J. (2011). Mastering strategic management. Irvington, NY: Flat World Knowledge.

2.1 Intended and Realized Strategies

The best-laid plans of mice and men often go awry.
  - *Robert Burns, "To a Mouse," 1785*

This quote from Scottish poet Robert Burns is applicable to how strategies are often developed. While some strategies are the outcome of a rational, predictable, analytical process, a fine plan does not guarantee a successful outcome. Many things can happen between the development of the plan and its realization, including (but not limited to) (1) the plan is poorly constructed, (2) competitors undermine the advantages envisioned by the plan, or (3) the plan was good but poorly executed. You can probably imagine a number of other factors that might undermine a strategic plan and the results that follow.

How organizations create strategies has emerged as an area of intense debate within the field of strategic management. Henry Mintzberg and his colleagues at McGill University distinguish intended, deliberate, realized, and emergent strategies.[7] **Intended strategy** is strategy as conceived by the top management team. Even here, rationality is limited and the intended strategy is the result of a process of negotiation, bargaining, and compromise, involving many individuals and groups within the organization. However, **realized strategy**—the actual strategy that is implemented—is only partly related to that which was intended (Mintzberg suggests only 10%–30% of intended strategies actually become a reality).

The primary determinant of realized strategy is what Mintzberg terms **emergent strategy**—the decisions that emerge from the complex processes in which individual managers interpret the intended strategy and adapt to changing external circumstances.[8] Thus the realized strategy is a consequence of **deliberate** and emerging factors. Analysis of Honda's successful entry into the U.S. motorcycle market has provided a battleground for the debate between those who view strategy making as primarily a rational, analytical process of deliberate planning and those that envisage strategy as emerging from a complex process of organizational decision making.[9]

FIGURE 5.11 Intended, Deliberate, Realized, and Emergent Strategies

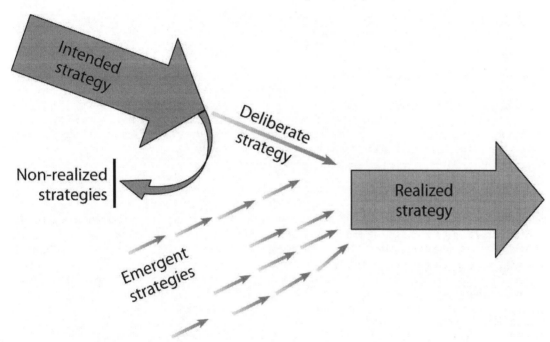

What's the Best Way to Develop a Strategy?

Mintzberg's advocacy of strategy making as an iterative process involving experimentation and feedback is not necessarily an argument against the rational, systematic design of strategy. The critical issues are, first, determining the balance of design and emergence and, second, how to guide the process of emergence. The strategic planning systems of most companies involve a combination of design and emergence. Thus headquarters sets guidelines in the form of vision and mission statements, business principles, performance targets, and capital expenditure budgets. However, within the strategic plans that are decided, divisional and business unit managers have considerable freedom to adjust, adapt, and experiment.

KEY TAKEAWAY

Strategy development is a process. Most organizations use planning to create intended strategies that they hope to follow. Managers must exercise flexibility in their strategies, as changes in an organization's situation may give rise to new opportunities and challenges. Organizations often respond by using emergent strategies. The realized strategies ultimately embraced by organizations are a product of both intended and realized strategies.

intended strategy
The strategy conceived of by managers and the impetus for initial attempts at strategy implementation.

realized strategy
The actual strategy that is implemented and comes to fruition as a consequence of implementation and other internal and external factors.

emergent strategy
A pattern of action that develops over time in an organization in the absence of vision, mission, and goals, or despite missions and goals, or in addition to what was conceived of in the intended and deliberate strategies.

deliberate strategy
A plan of action, flowing from the intended strategy, that an organization chooses and implements to support its vision, mission, and goals.

1. What is an intended strategy?
2. What is a realized strategy?
3. Why is it important to understand the difference between intended and realized strategies?
4. Why is there not a perfect match-up between realized and intended strategies?
5. What might interfere with the realization of an intended strategy?

3. STRATEGY AS TRADE-OFFS, DISCIPLINE, AND FOCUS

LEARNING OBJECTIVES

1. **Understand the nature of strategic focus.**
2. **Strategy as trade-offs (Porter).**
3. **Strategy as discipline (Treacy and Wiersema).**

A strategy provides a company with focus. Strategy is ultimately about choice—what the organization does and does not do. While vision and mission provide a good sense of direction for the organization, they are not meant to serve as, or take the place of, the actual strategy. Strategy is about choices, and that eventually means making trade-offs such that the strategy and the firm are distinctive in the eyes of stakeholders. In this section, we explain strategic focus—that is, how trade-offs are reconciled—as well as two frameworks for thinking about what such focus might entail.

3.1 What Is Strategic Focus?

strategic focus

When an organization is clear about its mission and vision and has a coherent, well-articulated strategy for achieving those.

While there are different schools of thought about how strategy comes about, researchers generally agree that **strategic focus** is a common characteristic across successful organizations. Strategic focus is seen when an organization is very clear about its mission and vision and has a coherent, well-articulated strategy for achieving those. When a once high-flying firm encounters performance problems, it is not uncommon to hear business analysts say that the firm's managers have lost focus on the customers or markets where they were once highly successful. For instance, Dell Computer's strategy is highly focused around the efficient sale and manufacture of computers and computer peripheral devices. However, during the mid-2000s, Dell started branching out into other products such as digital cameras, DVD players, and flat-screen televisions. As a result, it lost focus on its core sales and manufacturing business, and its performance flagged. As recently as mid-2008, however, Dell has realized a tremendous turnaround: "We are executing on all points of our strategy to drive growth in every product category and in every part of the world," said a press release from Michael Dell, chairman and CEO. "These results are early signs of our progress against our five strategic priorities. Through a continued focus, we expect to continue growing faster than the industry and increase our revenue, profitability and cash flow for greater shareholder value."[10]

Dell provides an excellent example of what is meant by strategic focus. This spirit of focus is echoed in the following two parts of this section where we introduce you to the complementary notions of *strategy as trade-offs* and *strategy as discipline*.

3.2 Strategy as Trade-Offs

Three of the most widely read books on competitive analysis in the 1980s were Michael Porter's *Competitive Strategy*, *Competitive Advantage*, and *Competitive Advantage of Nations*.[11] In his various books, Porter developed three generic strategies that, he argues, can be used singly or in combination to create a defendable position and to outperform competitors, whether they are within an industry or across nations. The strategies are (1) overall cost leadership, (2) differentiation, and (3) focus on a particular market niche.

Cost Leadership, Differentiation, and Scope

These strategies are termed *generic* because they can be applied to any size or form of business. We refer to them as trade-off strategies because Porter argues that a firm must choose to embrace one strategy or risk not having a strategy at all. **Overall lower cost or cost leadership** refers to the strategy where a firm's competitive advantage is based on the bet that it can develop, manufacture, and distribute products more efficiently than competitors. **Differentiation strategy** refers to the strategy where competitive advantage is based on superior products or service. Superiority arises from factors other than low cost, such as customer service, product quality, or unique style. To put these strategies into context, you might think about Walmart as pursuing a cost-leadership strategy and Nordstrom as pursuing a differentiation strategy.

Porter suggests that another factor affecting a company's competitive position is its competitive scope. Competitive scope defines the breadth of a company's target market. A company can have a broad (mass market) competitive scope or a narrow (niche market) competitive scope. A firm following the **focus strategy** concentrates on meeting the specialized needs of its customers. Products and services can be designed to meet the needs of buyers. One approach to focusing is to service either industrial buyers or consumers but not both. Martin-Brower, the third-largest food distributor in the United States, serves only the eight leading fast-food chains. It is the world's largest distributor of products to the world's largest restaurant company—McDonald's. With its limited customer list, Martin-Brower need only stock a limited product line; its ordering procedures are adjusted to match those of its customers; and its warehouses are located so as to be convenient to customers.

Firms using a narrow focus strategy can also tailor advertising and promotional efforts to a particular market niche. Many automobile dealers advertise that they are the largest volume dealer for a specific geographic area. Other car dealers advertise that they have the highest customer satisfaction scores within their defined market or the most awards for their service department.

Another differentiation strategy is to design products specifically for a customer. Such customization may range from individually designing a product for a single customer to offering a menu from which customers can select options for the finished product. Tailor-made clothing and custom-built houses include the customer in all aspects of production, from product design to final acceptance, and involve customer input in all key decisions. However, providing such individualized attention to customers may not be feasible for firms with an industry-wide orientation. At the other end of the customization scale, customers buying a new car, even in the budget price category, can often choose between many features and customizations.

By positioning in either broad scope or narrow scope and a low-cost strategy or differentiation strategy, an organization will fall into one of the following generic competitive strategies: cost leadership, cost focus, differentiation, and focused differentiation.

overall cost-leadership strategy

A strategy in which an organization attempts to gain a competitive advantage by reducing its costs below the costs of competing firms.

differentiation strategy

A strategy in which an organization seeks to distinguish itself from competitors through the perceived quality of its products or services.

focus strategy

A strategy in which an organization concentrates on a specific regional market, product line, or group of buyers in combination with its pursuit of either an overall cost leadership or differentiation strategy.

FIGURE 5.12 Business-Level Strategies

Firms compete on two general dimensions – the source of competitive advantage (cost or uniqueness) and the scope of operations (broad or narrow). Four possible generic business-level strategies emerge from these decisions. An example of each generic business-level strategy from the retail industry is illustrated below.

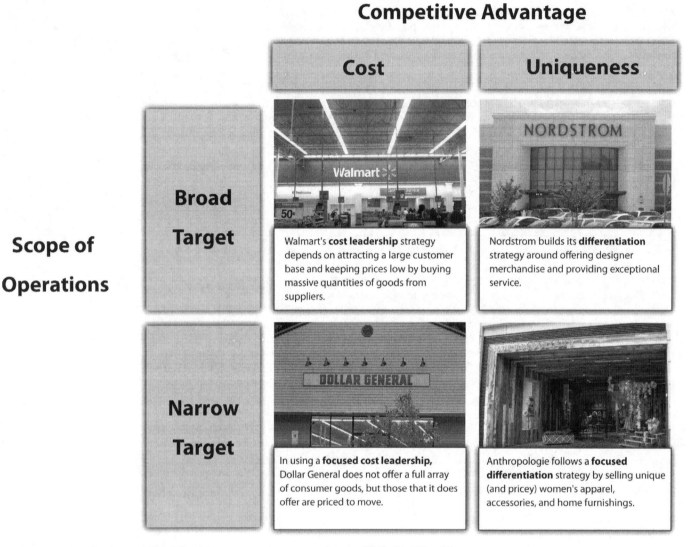

Source: Image courtesy of Ketchen, D., & Short, J. (2011). Mastering strategic management. Irvington, NY: Flat World Knowledge.

Cost Leadership/Low Cost

Cost leadership is a low-cost, broad-based market strategy. Firms pursuing this type of strategy must be particularly efficient in engineering tasks, production operations, and physical distribution. Because these firms focus on a large market, they must also be able to minimize costs in marketing and research and development (R&D). A low-cost leader can gain significant market share enabling it to procure a more powerful position relative to both suppliers and competitors. This strategy is particularly effective for organizations in industries where there is limited possibility of product differentiation and where buyers are very price sensitive.

Overall cost leadership is not without potential problems. Two or more firms competing for cost leadership may engage in price wars that drive profits to very low levels. Ideally, a firm using a cost-leader strategy will develop an advantage that others cannot easily copy. Cost leaders also must maintain their investment in state-of-the-art equipment or face the possible entry of more cost-effective competitors. Major changes in technology may drastically change production processes so that previous investments in production technology are no longer advantageous. Finally, firms may become so concerned with maintaining low costs that they overlook needed changes in production or marketing.

The cost-leadership strategy may be more difficult in a dynamic environment because some of the expenses that firms may seek to minimize are research and development costs or marketing research costs—expenses the firm may need to incur to remain competitive.

Focused Low Cost

A cost-focus strategy is a low-cost, narrowly focused market strategy. Firms employing this strategy may focus on a particular buyer segment or a particular geographic segment and must locate a niche market that wants or needs an efficient product and is willing to forgo extras to pay a lower price for the product. A company's costs can be reduced by providing little or no service, providing a low-cost method of distribution, or producing a no-frills product.

Differentiation

A differentiation strategy involves marketing a unique product to a broad-based market. Because this type of strategy involves a unique product, price is not the most significant factor because consumers may be willing to pay a higher price for a product they perceive as different. The product difference may be based on product design, method of distribution, or any aspect of the product that is valued by a broad group of consumers. A company choosing this strategy must develop and maintain a product perceived as different enough from the competitors' products to warrant the price difference.

Focused Differentiation

A differentiation-focus strategy is the marketing of a differentiated product to a narrow market, often involving a unique product and a unique market. This strategy is viable for a company that can convince consumers that its narrow focus allows it to provide better goods and services than its competitors.

Differentiation does not allow a firm to ignore costs; it makes a firm's products less susceptible to cost pressures from competitors because customers see the product as unique and are willing to pay extra to have the product with the desirable features. Differentiation can be achieved through real product features or through advertising that causes the customer to perceive that the product is unique.

Differentiation may lead to customer brand loyalty, resulting in customers being less sensitive to changes in price. Differentiation may also lead to higher profit margins. Since customers see the product as different from competing products, customers are willing to pay a premium for these features. As long as the firm can increase the selling price by more than the marginal cost of adding the features, the profit margin is increased. Firms must be able to charge more for their differentiated product than it costs them to make it distinct, or else they may be better off making generic, undifferentiated products. Firms must remain sensitive to cost differences. They must carefully monitor the incremental costs of differentiating their product and make certain the difference is reflected in the price.

Firms pursuing a differentiation strategy are vulnerable to different competitive threats than firms pursuing a cost-leader strategy. Customers may sacrifice features, service, or image for cost savings. Price-sensitive customers may be willing to forgo desirable features in favor of a less costly alternative. This can be seen in the growth in popularity of store brands and private labels. Often, the same firms that produce name-brand products produce the private-label products. The two products may be physically identical, but stores are able to sell the private-label products for a lower price because very little money was put into advertising to differentiate the private-label product.

Imitation may also reduce the perceived differences between products when competitors copy product features. Thus, for firms to be able to recover the cost of marketing research or R&D, they may need to add a product feature that is not easily copied by a competitor.

A final risk for firms pursuing a differentiation strategy is changing consumer tastes. The feature that customers like and find attractive about a product this year may not make the product popular next year. Changes in customer tastes are especially obvious in the fashion industry, where consumer tastes change with the seasons and fads can make certain clothes extremely popular for short time periods.

Straddling Positions or Stuck in the Middle?

Can forms of competitive advantage be combined? That is, can a firm straddle strategies so that it is simultaneously the low-cost leader and a differentiator? Porter asserts that a successful strategy requires a firm to stake out a market position aggressively and that different strategies involve distinctly different approaches to competing and operating the business. Some research suggests that straddling strategies is a recipe for below-average profitability compared to the industry. Porter also argues that straddling strategies is an indication that the firm's managers have not made necessary choices about the business and its strategy. A straddling strategy may be especially dangerous for narrow scope firms that have been successful in the past, but then start neglecting their focus.

An organization pursuing a differentiation strategy seeks competitive advantage by offering products or services that are unique from those offered by rivals, either through design, brand image, technology, features, or customer service. Alternatively, an organization pursuing a cost-leadership strategy attempts to gain competitive advantage based on being the overall low-cost provider of a product or service. To be "all things to all people" can mean becoming "stuck in the middle" with no distinct competitive advantage. The difference between being "stuck in the middle" and successfully

FIGURE 5.13

Denny's focuses on low-cost food offerings for customers with late-night cravings.

Source: http://en.wikipedia.org/wiki/ File:Denny%27s_Sign.JPG

FIGURE 5.14

Kellogg's hopes to convince consumers that their frosted flakes are greater than generic alternatives.

Source: http://www.flickr.com/ photos/infrogmation/7324049742.

pursuing combination strategies merits discussion. Although Porter describes the dangers of not being successful in either cost control or differentiation, some firms have been able to succeed using combination strategies.

Research suggests that, in some cases, it is possible to be a cost leader while maintaining a differentiated product. Southwest Airlines has combined cost-cutting measures with differentiation. The company has been able to reduce costs by not assigning seating and by eliminating meals on its planes. It has also been able to promote in its advertising that its fares are so low that checked bags fly free, in contrast to the fees that competitors such as American and United charge for checked luggage. Southwest's consistent low-fare strategy has attracted a significant number of passengers, allowing the airline to succeed.

Some industry environments may actually call for combination strategies. Trends suggest that executives operating in highly complex environments, such as health care, do not have the luxury of choosing exclusively one strategy over another. The hospital industry may represent such an environment, as hospitals must compete on a variety of fronts. Combination strategies are both feasible and necessary to compete successfully. For instance, reimbursement to diagnosis-related groups, and the continual lowering of reimbursement ceilings have forced hospitals to compete on the basis of cost. At the same time, many of them jockey for position with differentiation based on such features as technology and birthing rooms. Thus many hospitals may need to adopt some form of hybrid strategy to compete successfully.[12]

KEY TAKEAWAY

Strategic focus seems to be a common element in the strategies across successful firms. Two prevalent views of strategy where focus is a key component are strategy as trade-offs and strategy as discipline. Michael Porter identifies three flavors of strategy: (1) cost leadership, (2) differentiation, or (3) focus of cost leadership or differentiation on a particular market niche. Firms can straddle these strategies, but such straddling is likely to dilute strategic focus.

EXERCISES

1. What is strategic focus and why is it important?
2. What are Porter's three generic strategies?
3. Can a firm simultaneously pursue a low-cost and a differentiation strategy?

4. DEVELOPING STRATEGY THROUGH INTERNAL ANALYSIS

LEARNING OBJECTIVES

1. Learn about internal analysis.
2. Understand resources, capabilities, and core competencies.
3. See how to evaluate resources, capabilities, and core competencies using VRIO analysis.

In this section, we will focus on three aspects of internal analysis. The primary purpose for internal analysis is to understand the unique resources, capabilities, and core competencies of organizations that may enable them to outperform their competitors over time.

4.1   Internal Analysis

By exploiting internal resources and capabilities and meeting the demanding standards of global competition, firms create value for customers.[13] Value is measured by a product's performance characteristics and by its attributes for which customers are willing to pay.[14] Those particular bundles of resources and capabilities that provide unique advantages to the firm are considered **core competencies**.[15] Core competencies are resources and capabilities that serve as a source of a firm's competitive advantage over rivals. Core competencies distinguish a company competitively and reflect its personality. Core competencies emerge over time through an organizational process of accumulating and learning how to deploy different resources and capabilities. As the capacity to take action, core competencies are "crown jewels of a company," the activities the company performs especially well compared with competitors and through which the firm adds unique value to its goods or services over a long period of time.[16] For example, Black & Decker Corporation has developed an excellence in producing products with small electric motors.

Sometimes consistency and predictability provide value to customers, such as the type of value Walgreens drugstores provides. As a *Fortune* magazine writer noted, "Do you realize that from 1975 to today, Walgreens beat Intel? It beat Intel nearly two to one, GE almost five to one. It beat 3M, Coke, Boeing, Motorola."[17] Walgreens was able to do this by using its core competencies to offer value desired by its target customer group. Instead of responding to the trends of the day, "During the Internet scare of 1998 and 1999, when slogans of 'Change or Die!' were all but graffitied on the subway, Walgreens obstinately stuck to its corporate credo of 'Crawl, walk, run.' Its refusal to act until it thoroughly understood the implications of e-commerce was deeply unfashionable, but…Walgreens is the epitome of the inner-directed company."[18] Thus Walgreens creates value by focusing on the unique capabilities it has built, nurtured, and continues to improve across time.

4.2   Resources and Capabilities

Resources

Broad in scope, *resources* cover a spectrum of individual, social, and organizational assets.[19] Typically, resources alone do not yield a competitive advantage.[20] Instead, core competencies that yield a competitive advantage are often created through the *unique bundling of several resources*.[21] For example, Amazon.com has combined service and distribution resources to develop its competitive advantages. The firm started as an online bookseller, directly shipping orders to customers. It quickly grew large and established a distribution network through which it could ship "millions of different items to millions of different customers." Compared with Amazon's use of combined resources, traditional bricks-and-mortar companies found it hard to establish an effective online presence. These difficulties led many retailers to develop partnerships with Amazon. Retailers such as Eddie Bauer and Foot Locker now sell merchandise on Amazon.com, and Amazon now handles the entire online presence and shipping for retailers including Sears Canada and Britain's Marks & Spencer. Arrangements such as these are useful to the bricks-and-mortar companies because they are not accustomed to shipping so much diverse merchandise directly to individuals.

Some resources are tangible while others are intangible. *Tangible resources* are assets that can be seen and quantified. Production equipment, manufacturing plants, and formal reporting structures are examples of tangible resources. *Intangible resources* typically include assets that are rooted deeply in the firm's history and have accumulated over time. Because they are embedded in unique patterns of routines, intangible resources are relatively difficult for competitors to analyze and imitate. Knowledge, trust between managers and employees, ideas, the capacity for innovation, managerial capabilities, organizational routines (the unique ways people work together), scientific capabilities, and the firm's reputation for its goods or services and how it interacts with people (such as employees, customers, and suppliers) are all examples of intangible resources.[22] The four types of tangible resources are financial, organizational, physical, and technological. The three types of intangible resources are human, innovation, and reputational.

core competency

A particular bundle of resources and capabilities that provides unique competitive advantages to the firm.

FIGURE 5.15 Resources and Capabilities

Resources and capabilities are the basic building blocks that organizations use to create strategies. These two building blocks are tightly linked—capabilities tend to arise from using resources over time.

Resources can be divided into two main types:

Tangible resources are resources than can be readily seen, touched, and quantified. Physical assets such as a firm's property, plant, and equipment are considered to be tangible resources, as is cash.

Intangible resources are quite difficult to see, touch, or quantify. Intangible resources include, for example, the knowledge and skills of employees, a firm's reputation, and a firm's culture. In a nod to Southwest Airlines' outstanding reputation, the firm ranks fourth in *Fortune* magazine's 2011 list of the "World's Most Admired Companies." Only Apple, Google, and Berkshire Hathaway enjoy a stronger reputation.

While resources refer to what an organization *owns*, capabilities refer to what the organization can *do*. More specifically, capabilities refer to the firm's ability to bundle, manage, or otherwise exploit resources in a manner that provides value added and, hopefully, advantage over competitors.

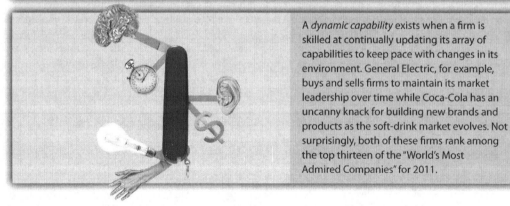

A *dynamic capability* exists when a firm is skilled at continually updating its array of capabilities to keep pace with changes in its environment. General Electric, for example, buys and sells firms to maintain its market leadership over time while Coca-Cola has an uncanny knack for building new brands and products as the soft-drink market evolves. Not surprisingly, both of these firms rank among the top thirteen of the "World's Most Admired Companies" for 2011.

Source: Image courtesy of Ketchen, D., & Short, J. (2011). Mastering strategic management. Irvington, NY: Flat World Knowledge.

Capabilities

Capabilities are the firm's capacity to deploy resources that have been purposely integrated to achieve a desired end state.[23] Capabilities emerge over time through complex interactions among tangible and intangible resources. Capabilities can be tangible, like a business process that is automated, but most of them tend to be tacit and intangible. Critical to forming competitive advantages, capabilities are often based on developing, carrying, and exchanging information and knowledge through the firm's human capital.[24] Because a knowledge base is grounded in organizational actions that may not be explicitly understood by all employees, repetition and practice increase the value of a firm's capabilities.

Knowledge possessed by human capital is among the most significant of an organization's capabilities and may ultimately be at the root of all competitive advantages. But firms must also be able to use the knowledge that they have and transfer it among their operating businesses.[25] "A company's value derives not from things, but from knowledge, know-how, intellectual assets, competencies—all of it embedded in people."[26] Given this reality, the firm's challenge is to create an environment that allows people to fit their individual pieces of knowledge together so that, collectively, employees possess as much organizational knowledge as possible.[27]

To help firms develop an environment in which knowledge is widely spread across all employees, some organizations have created the new upper-level managerial position of chief learning officer (CLO). Establishing a CLO position highlights a firm's belief that "future success will depend on competencies that traditionally have not been actively managed or measured—including creativity and the speed with which new ideas are learned and shared."[28] In general, the firm should manage knowledge in ways that will support its efforts to create value for customers.[29]

FIGURE 5.16 The Value Chain

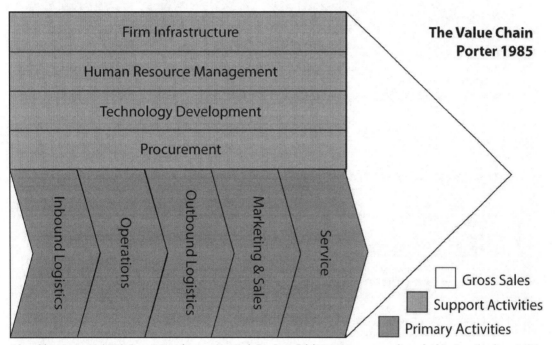

Adapted from Porter, M. (1985). Competitive Advantage. New York: Free Press. Exhibit is creative commons licensed at http://en.wikipedia.org/wiki/ Image:ValueChain.PNG.

Capabilities are often developed in specific functional areas (such as manufacturing, R&D, and marketing) or in a part of a functional area (for example, advertising). The value chain, popularized by Michael Porter's book *Competitive Advantage*, is a useful tool for taking stock of organizational capabilities. A value chain is a chain of activities. In the value chain, some of the activities are deemed to be primary, in the sense that these activities add direct value. In the preceding figure, primary activities are logistics (inbound and outbound), marketing, and service. Support activities include how the firm is organized (infrastructure), human resources, technology, and procurement. Products pass through all activities of the chain in order, and at each activity, the product gains some value. A firm is effective to the extent that the chain of activities gives the products more added value than the sum of added values of all activities.

It is important not to mix the concept of the value chain with the costs occurring throughout the activities. A diamond cutter can be used as an example of the difference. The cutting activity may have a low cost, but the activity adds much of the value to the end product, since a rough diamond is significantly less valuable than a cut, polished diamond. Research suggests a relationship between capabilities developed in particular functional areas and the firm's financial performance at both the corporate and business-unit levels,[30] suggesting the need to develop capabilities at both levels.

value chain

The primary and support activities that an organization uses to create value in the form of products or services.

FIGURE 5.17 Adding Value within a Value Chain

Doughnut shops buy commodity products (such as flour and grease) and transform them into delectable treats. Consumers are willing to pay much more for doughnuts than they would for flour and grease. Below we illustrate how primary and support activities in the value chain can add value for doughnut shops.

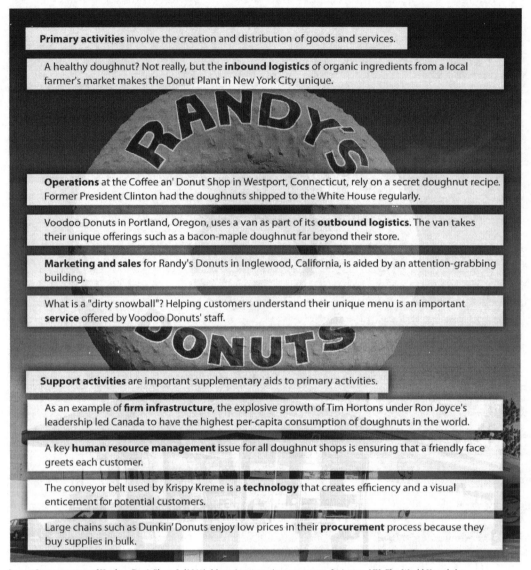

Source: Image courtesy of Ketchen, D., & Short, J. (2011). Mastering strategic management. Irvington, NY: Flat World Knowledge.

4.3 VRIO Analysis

Given that almost anything a firm possesses can be considered a resource or capability, how should you attempt to narrow down the ones that are core competencies, and explain why firm performance differs? To lead to a sustainable competitive advantage, a resource or capability should be valuable, rare, inimitable (including nonsubstitutable), and organized. This VRIO framework is the foundation for internal analysis.[31] VRIO is an acronym for *valuable, rare, inimitable,* and *organization.*

If you ask managers why their firms do well while others do poorly, a common answer is likely to be "our people." What is it about people that is especially valuable? Why do competitors employ dissimilar people? Can competitors hire excellent employees away? Or is there something special about the organization that brings out the best in people? These kinds of questions form the basis of VRIO and get to the heart of why some resources help firms more than others.

FIGURE 5.18 VRIO and Relative Firm Performance

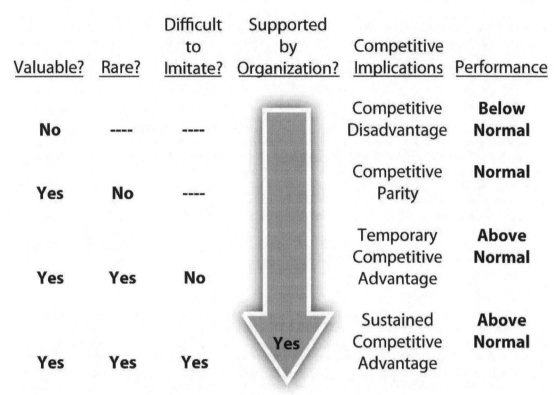

Valuable?	Rare?	Difficult to Imitate?	Supported by Organization?	Competitive Implications	Performance
No	----	----		Competitive Disadvantage	Below Normal
Yes	No	----		Competitive Parity	Normal
Yes	Yes	No		Temporary Competitive Advantage	Above Normal
Yes	Yes	Yes	Yes	Sustained Competitive Advantage	Above Normal

The ability to identify whether an organization has VRIO resources will also likely explain their competitive position. In Figure 5.18 a firm's performance relative to industry peers is likely to vary according to the level to which resources, capabilities, and ultimately core competences satisfy VRIO criteria. The four criteria are explored next.

Valuable

A resource or capability is said to be valuable if it allows the firm to exploit opportunities or negate threats in the environment. Union Pacific's extensive network of rail-line property and equipment in the Gulf Coast of the United States is valuable because it allows the company to provide a cost-effective way to transport chemicals. Because the Gulf Coast is the gateway for the majority of chemical production in the United States, the rail network allows the firm to exploit a market opportunity. If a resource does not allow a firm to minimize threats or exploit opportunities, it does not enhance the competitive position of the firm. In fact, some scholars suggest that owning resources that do not meet the VRIO test of value actually puts the firm at a competitive disadvantage.[32]

Rare

A resource is rare simply if it is not widely possessed by other competitors. Of the criteria this is probably the easiest to judge. For example, Coke's brand name is valuable but most of Coke's competitors (Pepsi, 7Up, RC) also have widely recognized brand names, making it not that rare. Of course, Coke's brand may be the most recognized, but that makes it more valuable, not more rare, in this case.

A firm that possesses valuable resources that are not rare is not in a position of advantage relative to competitors. Rather, valuable resources that are commonly held by many competitors simply allow firms to be at par with competitors. However, when a firm maintains possession of valuable resources that are rare in the industry they are in a position of competitive advantage over firms that do not possess the resource. They may be able to exploit opportunities or negate threats in ways that those lacking the resource will not be able to do. Delta's virtual control of air traffic through Cincinnati gives it a valuable and rare resource in that market.

How rare do the resources need to be for a firm to have a competitive advantage? If only one firm possesses the resource, it has significant advantage over all other competitors. For instance, Monsanto had such an advantage for many years because they owned the patent to aspartame, the chemical compound in NutraSweet; they had a valuable and extremely rare resource. Because during the lifetime of the patent they were the only firm that could sell aspartame, they had an advantage in the artificial sweetener market. However, meeting the condition of rarity does not always require exclusive ownership. When only a few firms possess the resource, they will have an advantage over the remaining competitors. For instance, Toyota and Honda both have the capabilities to build cars of high quality at relatively low cost.[33] Their products regularly beat rival firms' products in both short-term and long-term quality ratings.[34] Thus the criterion of rarity requires that the resource not be widely possessed in the industry. It also suggests that the more exclusive a firm's access to a particularly valuable resource, the greater the benefit.

Inimitable

An inimitable (the opposite of *imitable*) resource is difficult to imitate or to create ready substitutes for. A resource is inimitable and nonsubstitutable if it is difficult for another firm to acquire it or to substitute something else in its place. A valuable and rare resource or capability will grant a competitive advantage as long as other firms do not gain subsequent possession of the resource or a close substitute. If a resource is valuable and rare and responsible for a market leader's competitive advantage, it is likely that competitors lacking the resource or capability will do all that they can to obtain the resource or capability themselves. This leads us to the third criterion—*inimitability*. The concept of imitation includes any form of *acquiring* the lacking resource or *substituting* a similar resource that provides equivalent benefits. The criterion important to be addressed is whether competitors face a *cost disadvantage* in acquiring or substituting the resource that is lacking.

Organized

The fourth and final VRIO criterion that determines whether a resource or capability is the source of competitive advantage recognizes that mere possession or control is necessary but not sufficient to gain an advantage. The firm must likewise have the *organizational* capability to exploit the resources. The question of organization is broad and encompasses many facets of a firm but essentially means that the firm is able to capture any value that the resource or capability might generate. Organization, essentially the same form as that taken in the P-O-L-C framework, spans such firm characteristics as control systems, reporting relationships, compensation policies, and management interface with both customers and value-adding functions in the firm. Although listed as the last criterion in the VRIO tool, the question of organization is a necessary condition to be satisfied if a firm is to reap the benefits of any of the three preceding conditions. Thus a valuable but widely held resource only leads to competitive parity for a firm if they also possess the capabilities to exploit the resource. Likewise, a firm that possesses a valuable and rare resource will not gain a competitive advantage unless it can actually put that resource to effective use.

Many firms have valuable and rare resources that they fail to exploit (the question of imitation is not relevant until the firm exploits valuable and rare resources). For instance, for many years Novell had a significant competitive advantage in computer networking based on its core NetWare product. In high-technology industries, remaining at the top requires continuous innovation. Novell's decline during the mid- to late 1990s led many to speculate that Novell was unable to innovate in the face of changing markets and technology. However, shortly after new CEO Eric Schmidt arrived from Sun Microsystems to attempt to turnaround the firm, he arrived at a different conclusion. Schmidt commented: "I walk down Novell hallways and marvel at the incredible potential of innovation here. But, Novell has had a difficult time in the past turning innovation into products in the marketplace."[35] He later commented to a few key executives that it appeared the company was suffering from "organizational constipation."[36] Novell appeared to still have innovative resources and capabilities, but they lacked the organizational capability (e.g., product development and marketing) to get those new products to market in a timely manner.

Likewise, Xerox proved unable to exploit its innovative resources. Xerox created a successful research team housed in a dedicated facility in Palo Alto, California, known as Xerox PARC. Scientists in this group invented an impressive list of innovative products, including laser printers, Ethernet, graphical interface software, computers, and the computer mouse. History has demonstrated that these technologies were commercially successful. Unfortunately, for Xerox shareholders, these commercially successful innovations were exploited by other firms. Xerox's organization was not structured in a way that information about these innovations flowed to the right people in a timely fashion. Bureaucracy was also suffocating ideas once they were disseminated. Compensation policies did not reward managers for adopting these new innovations but rather rewarded current profits over long-term success. Thus Xerox was never able to exploit the innovative resources and capabilities embodied in their off-site Xerox PARC research center.[37]

KEY TAKEAWAY

Internal analysis begins with the identification of resources and capabilities. Resources can be tangible and intangible; capabilities may have such characteristics as well. VRIO analysis is a way to distinguish resources and capabilities from core competencies. Specifically, VRIO analysis should show you the importance of value, rarity, inimitability, and organization as building blocks of competitive advantage.

EXERCISES

1. What is the objective of internal analysis?
2. What is the difference between a resource and a capability?
3. What is the difference between a tangible and an intangible resource or capability?
4. What is a core competency?
5. What framework helps you identify those resources, capabilities, or core competencies that provide competitive advantage?
6. Why might competitive advantage for a firm be fleeting?

5. DEVELOPING STRATEGY THROUGH EXTERNAL ANALYSIS

LEARNING OBJECTIVES

1. **Understand the basics of general environment analysis.**
2. **See the components of microenvironment analysis that support industry analysis.**
3. **Learn the features of Porter's Five Forces industry analysis.**

In this section, you will learn about some of the basic external inputs for strategy formulation—the determinants of a firm's opportunities and threats. Specifically, we focus on several aspects of external analysis.

5.1 The General Environment

When appraising the external environment of the organization, managers often start with its general environment. The general environment is composed of dimensions in the broader society that influence an industry and the firms within it.[38] We group these dimensions into six segments that compose the acronym PESTEL (political, economic, social, technical or technological, environmental, and legal).

Firms cannot directly control the general environment's segments and elements. Accordingly, successful companies gather the information required to understand each segment and its implications for the selection and implementation of the appropriate strategies. For example, the terrorist attacks in the United States on September 11, 2001, surprised businesses throughout the world. This single set of events had substantial effects on the U.S. economy. Although individual firms were affected differently, none could control the U.S. economy. Instead, companies around the globe were challenged to understand the effects of this economy's decline on their current and future strategies.

Although the degree of impact varies, these environmental segments affect each industry and its firms. The challenge to the firm is to evaluate those elements in each segment that are of the greatest importance. Resulting from these efforts should be a recognition of environmental changes, trends, opportunities, and threats.

5.2   Analyzing the Organization's Microenvironment

Microenvironment refers primarily to an organization's industry and the markets related to it. An **industry** is a group of firms producing products that are close substitutes. In the course of competition, these firms influence one another. Typically, industries include a rich mix of competitive strategies that companies use in pursuing strategic competitiveness and above-average returns. In part, these strategies are chosen because of the influence of an industry's characteristics.[39] *Upstream* markets are the industries that provide the raw material or inputs for the focal industry, while *downstream* markets are the industries (sometimes consumer segments) that consume the industry outputs. For example, the oil production market is upstream of the oil-refining market (and, conversely, the oil refiners are downstream of the oil producers), which in turn is upstream of the gasoline sales market. Instead of upstream and downstream, the terms *wholesale* and *retail* are often used. Accordingly, the **industry microenvironment** consists of stakeholder groups that a firm has regular dealings with. The way these relationships develop can affect the costs, quality, and overall success of a business.

5.3   Porter's Five-Forces Analysis of Market Structure

FIGURE 5.19   Porter's Five Forces

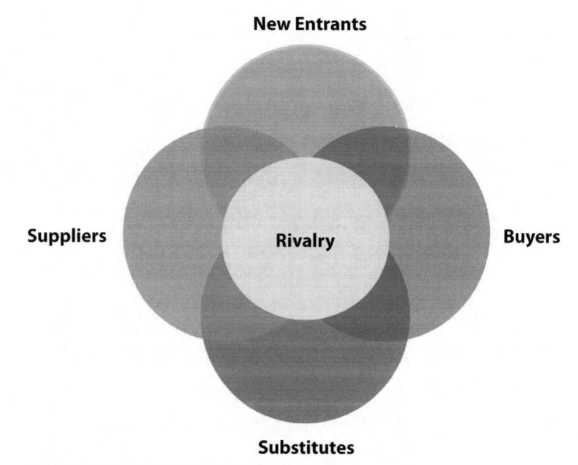

Adapted from Porter, M. (1980). Competitive strategy. New York: Free Press.

One of the most well-known frameworks used to analyze industries is Michael Porter's five forces. Porter's model attempts to analyze the attractiveness of an industry by considering five forces within a market. According to Porter, the likelihood of firms making profits in a given industry depends on five factors: (1) barriers to entry and the threat of potential new entrants, (2) buyer power, (3) supplier power, (4) threat from substitutes, and (5) rivalry among industry competitors.[40]

FIGURE 5.20 Industry Analysis

*Understanding the dynamics that shape how much profit potential exists within an industry is key to knowing how
likely a particular firm is to succeed within the industry. There are five key forces that determine the profitability of a
particular industry.*

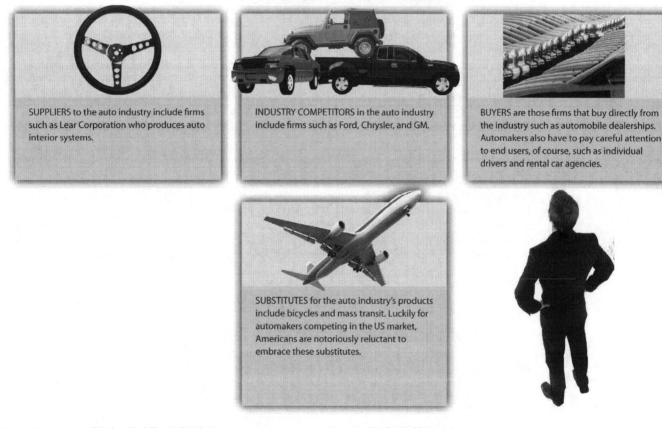

POTENTIAL ENTRANTS are firms that are
not currently considered viable competitors
in the industry but that may become viable
competitors in the future. For example, Tesla
Motors' production of electric vehicles poses
a threat to displace the traditional powers in
the auto industry, and Chinese auto makers
are rumored to be eyeing the US market.

SUPPLIERS to the auto industry include firms
such as Lear Corporation who produces auto
interior systems.

INDUSTRY COMPETITORS in the auto industry
include firms such as Ford, Chrysler, and GM.

BUYERS are those firms that buy directly from
the industry such as automobile dealerships.
Automakers also have to pay careful attention
to end users, of course, such as individual
drivers and rental car agencies.

SUBSTITUTES for the auto industry's products
include bicycles and mass transit. Luckily for
automakers competing in the US market,
Americans are notoriously reluctant to
embrace these substitutes.

Source: Image courtesy of Ketchen, D., & Short, J. (2011). Mastering strategic management. Irvington, NY: Flat World Knowledge.

Compared with the general environment, the industry environment has a more direct effect on the
firm's strategic competitiveness and above-average returns. Porter's five-forces model of competition
expands the arena for competitive analysis. Historically, when studying the competitive environment,
firms concentrated on companies with which they competed directly. However, firms must search
more broadly to identify current and potential competitors by identifying potential customers as well
as the firms serving them. Competing for the same customers and thus being influenced by how customers value location and firm capabilities in their decisions is referred to as the market microstructure.[41] Understanding this area is particularly important because, in recent years, industry boundaries
have become blurred. For example, in the electrical utilities industry, cogenerators (firms that also produce power) are competing with regional utility companies. Moreover, telecommunications companies
now compete with broadcasters, software manufacturers provide personal financial services, airlines
sell mutual funds, and automakers sell insurance and provide financing.[42] In addition to focusing on
customers rather than specific industry boundaries to define markets, geographic boundaries are also

relevant. Research suggests that different geographic markets for the same product can have considerably different competitive conditions.[43]

The five-forces model recognizes that suppliers can become a firm's competitors (by integrating forward), as can buyers (by integrating backward). Several firms have integrated forward in the pharmaceutical industry by acquiring distributors or wholesalers. In addition, firms choosing to enter a new market and those producing products that are adequate substitutes for existing products can become competitors of a company.

Another way to think about industry market structure is that these five sets of stakeholders are competing for profits in the given industry. For instance, if a supplier to an industry is powerful, they can charge higher prices. If the industry member can't pass those higher costs onto their buyers in the form of higher prices, then the industry member makes less profit. For example, if you have a jewelry store, but are dependent on a monopolist like De Beers for diamonds, then De Beers actually is extracting more relative value from your industry (i.e., the retail jewelry business).

New Entrants

The likelihood of new entry is a function of the extent to which barriers to entry exist. Evidence suggests that companies often find it difficult to identify new competitors.[44] Identifying new entrants is important because they can threaten the market share of existing competitors. One reason new entrants pose such a threat is that they bring additional production capacity. Unless the demand for a good or service is increasing, additional capacity holds consumers' costs down, resulting in less revenue and lower returns for competing firms. Often, new entrants have a keen interest in gaining a large market share. As a result, new competitors may force existing firms to be more effective and efficient and to learn how to compete on new dimensions (for example, using an Internet-based distribution channel).

The more difficult it is for other firms to enter a market, the more likely it is that existing firms can make relatively high profits. The likelihood that firms will enter an industry is a function of two factors: barriers to entry and the retaliation expected from current industry participants. Entry barriers make it difficult for new firms to enter an industry and often place them at a competitive disadvantage even when they are able to enter. As such, high-entry barriers increase the returns for existing firms in the industry.[45]

Buyer Power

The stronger the power of buyers in an industry, the more likely it is that they will be able to force down prices and reduce the profits of firms that provide the product. Firms seek to maximize the return on their invested capital. Alternatively, buyers (customers of an industry or firm) want to buy products at the lowest possible price—the point at which the industry earns the lowest acceptable rate of return on its invested capital. To reduce their costs, buyers bargain for higher-quality, greater levels of service, and lower prices. These outcomes are achieved by encouraging competitive battles among the industry's firms.

Supplier Power

The stronger the power of suppliers in an industry, the more difficult it is for firms within that sector to make a profit because suppliers can determine the terms and conditions on which business is conducted. Increasing prices and reducing the quality of its products are potential means used by suppliers to exert power over firms competing within an industry. If a firm is unable to recover cost increases by its suppliers through its pricing structure, its profitability is reduced by its suppliers' actions.

Substitutes

This measures the ease with which buyers can switch to another product that does the same thing, such as using aluminum cans rather than glass or plastic bottles to package a beverage. The ease of switching depends on what costs would be involved (e.g., while it may be easy to sell Coke or Pepsi in bottles or cans, transferring all your data to a new database system and retraining staff could be expensive) and how similar customers perceive the alternatives to be. Substitute products are goods or services from outside a given industry that perform similar or the same functions as a product that the industry produces. For example, as a sugar substitute, NutraSweet places an upper limit on sugar manufacturers' prices—NutraSweet and sugar perform the same function but with different characteristics.

Other product substitutes include fax machines instead of overnight deliveries, plastic containers rather than glass jars, and tea substituted for coffee. Recently, firms have introduced to the market several low-alcohol fruit-flavored drinks that many customers substitute for beer. For example, Smirnoff's Ice was introduced with substantial advertising of the type often used for beer. Other firms have introduced lemonade with 5% alcohol (e.g., Doc Otis Hard Lemon) and tea and lemon combinations with alcohol (e.g., BoDean's Twisted Tea). These products are increasing in popularity and, as product substitutes, have the potential to reduce overall sales of beer.[46]

In general, product substitutes present a strong threat to a firm when customers face few, if any, switching costs and when the substitute product's price is lower or its quality and performance capabilities are equal to or greater than those of the competing product. Differentiating a product along dimensions that customers value (such as price, quality, service after the sale, and location) reduces a substitute's attractiveness.

Rivalry

This measures the degree of competition between existing firms. The higher the degree of rivalry, the more difficult it is for existing firms to generate high profits. The most prominent factors that experience shows to affect the intensity of firms' rivalries are (1) numerous competitors, (2) slow industry growth, (3) high fixed costs, (4) lack of differentiation, (5) high strategic stakes and (6) high exit barriers.

Numerous or Equally Balanced Competitors

Intense rivalries are common in industries with many companies. With multiple competitors, it is common for a few firms to believe that they can act without eliciting a response. However, evidence suggests that other firms generally are aware of competitors' actions, often choosing to respond to them. At the other extreme, industries with only a few firms of equivalent size and power also tend to have strong rivalries. The large and often similar-sized resource bases of these firms permit vigorous actions and responses. The Coca-Cola/Pepsi and Airbus/Boeing competitive battles exemplify intense rivalries between pairs of relatively equivalent competitors.

Slow Industry Growth

When a market is growing, firms try to use resources effectively to serve an expanding customer base. Growing markets reduce the pressure to take customers from competitors. However, rivalry in non-growth or slow-growth markets becomes more intense as firms battle to increase their market shares by attracting their competitors' customers.

Typically, battles to protect market shares are fierce. The instability in the market that results from these competitive engagements reduces profitability for firms throughout the industry, as is demonstrated by the commercial aircraft industry. The market for large aircraft is expected to decline or grow only slightly over the next few years. To expand market share, Boeing and Airbus will compete aggressively in terms of the introduction of new products and product and service differentiation.

High Fixed Costs or High Storage Costs

When fixed costs account for a large part of total costs, companies try to maximize the use of their productive capacity. Doing so allows the firm to spread costs across a larger volume of output. However, when many firms attempt to maximize their productive capacity, excess capacity is created on an industry-wide basis. To then reduce inventories, individual companies typically cut the price of their product and offer rebates and other special discounts to customers. These practices, however, often intensify competition. The pattern of excess capacity at the industry level followed by intense rivalry at the firm level is observed frequently in industries with high storage costs. Perishable products, for example, lose their value rapidly with the passage of time. As their inventories grow, producers of perishable goods often use pricing strategies to sell products quickly.

Lack of Differentiation or Low Switching Costs

When buyers find a differentiated product that satisfies their needs, they frequently purchase the product loyally over time. Industries with many companies that have successfully differentiated their products have less rivalry, resulting in lower competition for individual firms.[47] However, when buyers view products as commodities (as products with few differentiated features or capabilities), rivalry intensifies. In these instances, buyers' purchasing decisions are based primarily on price and, to a lesser degree, service.

The effect of switching costs is identical to that described for differentiated products. The lower the buyers' switching costs, the easier it is for competitors to attract buyers through pricing and service offerings. High switching costs, however, at least partially insulate the firm from rivals' efforts to attract customers. Interestingly, the switching costs—such as pilot and mechanic training—are high in aircraft purchases, yet, the rivalry between Boeing and Airbus remains intense because the stakes for both are extremely high.

High Strategic Stakes

Competitive rivalry is likely to be high when it is important for several of the competitors to perform well in the market. For example, although it is diversified and is a market leader in other businesses,

Samsung has targeted market leadership in the consumer electronics market. This market is quite important to Sony and other major competitors such as Hitachi, Matsushita, NEC, and Mitsubishi. Thus we can expect substantial rivalry in this market over the next few years.

High strategic stakes can also exist in terms of geographic locations. For example, Japanese automobile manufacturers committed to a significant presence in the U.S. marketplace. A key reason for this is that the United States is the world's single largest market for auto manufacturers' products. Because of the stakes involved in this country for Japanese and U.S. manufacturers, rivalry among firms in the U.S. and global automobile industry is highly intense. While close proximity tends to promote greater rivalry, physically proximate competition has potentially positive benefits as well. For example, when competitors are located near one another, it is easier for suppliers to serve them and they can develop economies of scale that lead to lower production costs. Additionally, communications with key industry stakeholders such as suppliers are facilitated and more efficient when they are close to the firm.[48]

High Exit Barriers

Sometimes companies continue competing in an industry even though the returns on their invested capital are low or negative. Firms making this choice likely face high exit barriers, which include economic, strategic, and emotional factors, causing companies to remain in an industry when the profitability of doing so is questionable.

Attractiveness and Profitability

Using Porter's analysis firms are likely to generate higher profits if

- the industry is difficult to enter,
- there is limited rivalry,
- buyers are relatively weak,
- suppliers are relatively weak,
- there are few substitutes.

Profits are likely to be low if

- the industry is easy to enter,
- there is a high degree of rivalry between firms within the industry,
- buyers are strong,
- suppliers are strong,
- it is easy to switch to alternatives.

Effective industry analyses are products of careful study and interpretation of data and information from multiple sources. A wealth of industry-specific data is available to be analyzed. Because of globalization, international markets and rivalries must be included in the firm's analyses. In fact, research shows that in some industries, international variables are more important than domestic ones as determinants of strategic competitiveness. Furthermore, because of the development of global markets, a country's borders no longer restrict industry structures. In fact, movement into international markets enhances the chances of success for new ventures as well as more established firms.[49]

Following a study of the five forces of competition, the firm can develop the insights required to determine an industry's attractiveness in terms of its potential to earn adequate or superior returns on its invested capital. In general, the stronger competitive forces are, the lower the profit potential for an industry's firms. An unattractive industry has low entry barriers, suppliers and buyers with strong bargaining positions, strong competitive threats from product substitutes, and intense rivalry among competitors. These industry characteristics make it very difficult for firms to achieve strategic competitiveness and earn above-average returns. Alternatively, an attractive industry has high entry barriers, suppliers and buyers with little bargaining power, few competitive threats from product substitutes, and relatively moderate rivalry.[50]

KEY TAKEAWAY

External environment analysis is a key input into strategy formulation. PESTEL is an external environment analysis framework that helps guide your prospecting in the political, economic, social, technological, environmental, and legal spheres of an organization's external environment. Working inward to the focal organization, we discussed the broad dimensions of the stakeholders feeding into the firm. Porter's five forces analysis considers (1) barriers to entry and new entry threats, (2) buyer power, (3) supplier power, (4) threat from substitutes, and (5) rivalry as key external environmental forces in developing strategy.

E X E R C I S E S

1. What are the six dimensions of the environment that are of broad concern when you conduct a PESTEL analysis?
2. Which of the PESTEL dimensions do you believe to be most important, and why?
3. What are the key dimensions of a firm's microenvironment?
4. What are the five forces referred to in the Porter framework?
5. Is there a dimension of industry structure that Porter's model appears to omit?

6.   FORMULATING ORGANIZATIONAL AND PERSONAL STRATEGY WITH THE STRATEGY DIAMOND

L E A R N I N G   O B J E C T I V E S

1. **Learn about the strategy diamond.**
2. **See how you can add staging, pacing, and vehicles to the strategy.**
3. **Use the diamond to formulate your personal strategy.**

This section introduces you to the strategy diamond, a tool that will help you understand how clearly and completely you have crafted a strategy. The diamond relates to both business and corporate strategy, and regardless of whether you are a proponent of design or emergent schools of strategizing, it provides you with a good checklist of what your strategy should cover. The section concludes by walking you through the application of the strategy diamond to the task of developing your personal strategy.

6.1   The Strategy Diamond

The **strategy diamond** was developed by strategy researchers Don Hambrick and Jim Fredrickson as a framework for checking and communicating a strategy.[51] In critiquing the field of strategy, these researchers noted that "after more than 30 years of hard thinking about strategy, consultants and scholars have provided executives with an abundance of frameworks for analyzing strategic situations....Missing, however, has been any guidance as to what the product of these tools should be—or what actually constitutes a strategy."[52]

   Because of their critique and analysis, they concluded that if an organization must have a strategy, then the strategy must necessarily have parts. The figure summarizes the parts of their diamond model, its facets, and some examples of the different ways that you can think about each facet. The diamond model consists of an integrated set of choices. In this section we discuss each facet, addressing first the traditional strategy facets of *arenas*, *differentiators*, and *economic logic*; then we will discuss *vehicles* and finally the *staging and pacing* facet.

strategy diamond

A framework comprising five facets for understanding the content of a strategy; the facets are arenas, differentiators, vehicles, staging and pacing, and economic logic.

FIGURE 5.21 The Strategy Diamond

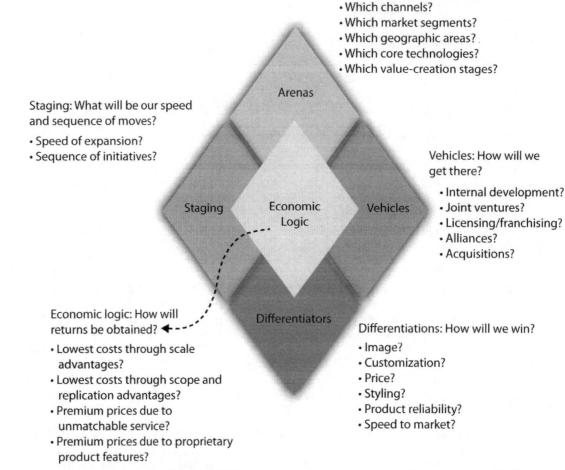

Arenas: Where will we be active
(and with how much emphasis)?

• Which product categories?
• Which channels?
• Which market segments?
• Which geographic areas?
• Which core technologies?
• Which value-creation stages?

Staging: What will be our speed
and sequence of moves?

• Speed of expansion?
• Sequence of initiatives?

Vehicles: How will we
get there?

• Internal development?
• Joint ventures?
• Licensing/franchising?
• Alliances?
• Acquisitions?

Economic logic: How will
returns be obtained?

• Lowest costs through scale
  advantages?
• Lowest costs through scope and
  replication advantages?
• Premium prices due to
  unmatchable service?
• Premium prices due to proprietary
  product features?

Differentiations: How will we win?

• Image?
• Customization?
• Price?
• Styling?
• Product reliability?
• Speed to market?

Adapted from Hambrick, D. C., & Fredrickson, J. W. (2001). Are you sure you have a strategy? Academy of Management Executive, 19 (4), 51–62.

Arenas, Differentiators, and Economic Logic

We refer to the first three facets of the strategy diamond—arenas, differentiators, and economic logic—as traditional in the sense that they address three longstanding hallmarks of strategizing. Specifically, strategy matches up market needs and opportunities (located in arenas) with unique features of the firm (shown by its differentiators) to yield positive performance (economic logic). While performance is typically viewed in financial terms, it can have social or environmental components as well.

Let's start with *arenas*. Answers to strategy questions about arenas tell managers and employees *where* the firm will be active. For instance, Nike is headquartered in Washington County, on the outskirts of Beaverton, Oregon. Today, Nike's geographic market arenas are most major markets around the globe, but in the early 1960s, Nike's arenas were limited to Pacific Northwest track meets accessible by founder Phil Knight's car. In terms of product markets (another part of *where*), the young Nike company (previously Blue Ribbon Sports) sold only track shoes and not even shoes it manufactured.

Beyond geographic-market and product-market arenas, an organization can also make choices about the value-chain arenas in its strategy. To emphasize the *choice* part of this value-chain arena, Nike's competitor New Balance manufactures nearly all the athletic shoes that it sells in the United States. Thus these two sports-shoe companies compete in similar geographic- and product-market arenas but differ greatly in terms of their choice of value-chain arenas.

What about *differentiators*? Differentiators are the things that are supposedly unique to the firm such that they give it a competitive advantage in its current and future arenas. A differentiator could be asset based—that is, it could be something related to an organization's tangible or intangible assets. A **tangible asset** has a value and physically exists. Land, machines, equipment, automobiles, and even currencies, are examples of tangible assets. For instance, the oceanfront land on California's Monterey Peninsula, where the Pebble Beach Golf Course and Resort is located, is a differentiator for it in the premium golf-course market. An **intangible asset** is a nonphysical resource that provides gainful advantages in the marketplace. Brands, copyrights, software, logos, patents, goodwill, and other intangible factors afford name recognition for products and services. The Nike brand has become a valuable intangible asset because of the broad awareness and reputation for quality and high performance that it has built. Differentiators can also be found in capabilities—that is, *how* the organization does something. Walmart, for instance, is very good at keeping its costs low. Nike, in contrast, focuses on developing leading-edge, high-performance athletic performance technologies, as well as up-to-the-minute fashion in active sportswear.

The third facet of the strategy diamond in this traditional view is *economic logic*, which explains how the firm makes money. Economic logic tells us how profits will be generated above the firm's cost of capital. The collapse in the late 1990s of stock market valuations for Internet companies lacking in profits—or any prospect of profits—marked a return to economic reality. Profits above the firm's cost of capital are required to yield sustained or longer-term shareholder returns. While the economic logic can include environmental and social profits (benefits reaped by society), the strategy must earn enough financial profits to keep investors (owners, tax payers, governments, and so on) willing to continue to fund the organization's costs of doing business. A firm performs well (i.e., has a strong, positive economic logic) when its differentiators are well aligned with its chosen arenas.

Vehicles

The first three facets of the strategy diamond—arenas, differentiators, and economic logic—might be considered the traditional facets of strategizing in that they cover the basics: (1) external environment, (2) internal organizational characteristics, and (3) some fit between them that has positive performance consequences. The fourth facet of the strategy diamond is called *vehicles*. If arenas and differentiators show where you want to go, then vehicles communicate how the strategy will get you there.

Specifically, vehicles refer to how you might pursue a new arena through internal means, through help from a new partner or some other outside source, or even through acquisition. In the context of vehicles, this is where you determine whether your organization is going to grow organically, acquisitively, or through a combination of both. *Organic growth* is the growth rate of a company excluding any growth from takeovers, acquisitions, or mergers. *Acquisitive growth*, in contrast, refers precisely to any growth from takeovers, acquisitions, or mergers. Augmenting either organic or acquisitive growth is growth through partnerships with other organizations. Sometimes such partnership-based growth is referred to as *co-opetition*, because an organization cooperates with others, even some competitors, in order to compete and grow.

Vehicles are considered part of the strategy because there are different skills and competencies associated with different vehicles. For instance, acquisitions fuel rapid growth, but they are challenging to negotiate and put into place. Similarly, alliances are a great way to spread the risk and let each partner focus on what it does best. But at the same time, to grow through alliances also means that you must be really good at managing relationships in which you are dependent on another organization over which you do not have direct control. Organic growth, particularly for firms that have grown primarily through partnering or acquisition, has its own distinct challenges, such as the fact that the organization is on its own to put together everything it needs to fuel its growth.

Staging and Pacing

Staging and pacing constitute the fifth and final facet of the strategy diamond. *Staging and pacing* reflect the sequence and speed of strategic moves. This powerful facet of strategizing helps you think about timing and next steps, instead of creating a strategy that is a static, monolithic plan. As an example, the managers of Chuy's, a chain of Austin, Texas-based Tex-Mex restaurants, wanted to grow the business outside of Austin, but at the same time, they knew it would be hard to manage these restaurants that were farther away. How should they identify in which cities to experiment with new outlets? Their creative solution was to choose cities that were connected to Austin by Southwest Airlines. Since Southwest is inexpensive and its point-to-point system means that cities are never much more than an hour apart, the Austin managers could easily and regularly visit their new ventures out of town. Remember, strategizing is about making choices, and sequencing and speed should be key choices along with the other facets of the strategy. The staging and pacing facet also helps to reconcile the designed and emergent portions of your strategy.

---

tangible asset

An asset that has a value and physically exists.

intangible asset

An asset that cannot be physically touched, or is not physical in nature.

6.2 The Strategy Diamond and Your Personal Growth and Development Strategy

The strategy diamond is a useful professional and personal tool for managers. How might it benefit them personally? Figure 5.22 maps out how your strategy fits in the planning aspect of P-O-L-C. Remember that, like in P-O-L-C, personal strategy should be guided by your own mission and vision. Let's look at how you might apply the strategy diamond to your personal growth and development objectives.

FIGURE 5.22 Planning and Your Personal Growth and Development Strategy

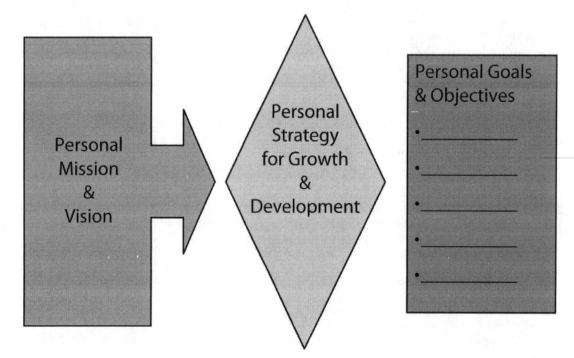

Personal Arenas and Differentiators

Your arenas and differentiators will answer such personal growth and development questions as the following:

- What type of work do I want to do?
- What leisure activities do I like?
- Where do I want to live?
- What capabilities (differentiators) do I need to participate in these arenas?
- What organizations value these capabilities (differentiators)?
- What capabilities (differentiators) do I want to have and excel in?

Your personal arenas can be an activity you want to do, a specific job, or simply a geographic location. For instance, do you want to be a store manager, an accountant, an entrepreneur, or a CEO? Or do you want to live in a certain locale? It can also be a combination of several criteria. For example, perhaps you want to be a software designer for Google and live in San Francisco.

The more specific you are about the arenas in your strategy, the better you will be able to plot out the other facets. Using Google as an example, your personal differentiators would likely have to include the demonstration of excellence in software design and an affinity for the Google corporate culture. More broadly, the differentiators facet of your personal strategy should map on to your arenas facet—that is, they should clearly fit together. Recognize, too, that your differentiators are subject to VRIO, in that where your capabilities are valuable and rare, you may be more likely to economically benefit from them with employers (this foreshadows the link between personal differentiators and personal economic logic).

Personal Vehicles

The personal vehicles facet of your strategy answers questions such as the following:

- What do I need to accomplish on my own?
- What do I want to accomplish on my own?
- What do I need to accomplish with the help of others?
- Who are they?

We often think that our careers and quality of life are up to us—will be based on our choices and actions alone. If that is your belief (i.e., you are a rugged individualist), then your personal growth and development strategy seems to be highly dependent on what you do but not on the contributions of others.

It is true that we have to develop our own knowledge and capabilities to move forward. However, in reality, we also typically get most things done through and with others. You have friends and family outside of work and colleagues, employees, and bosses at work.

The vehicles component of your personal strategy diamond should spell out how your growth and development is a function of what you do (when we talk about organizations, we refer to this as organic growth), and what you depend on others to do. The better you understand your dependence on others, the better you will likely be able to manage those relationships.

Personal Staging and Pacing

You can think of personal staging and pacing as the implications of your strategy for your own Outlook calendar. Personal staging and pacing answers questions such as the following:

- What sequence of events does my strategy require?
- What are the financial requirements and consequences of each event?
- What is my deadline for the first event?
- Is the deadline flexible? Can I manage the pacing of the achievement of each event?
- How will timing affect achievement of my personal growth and development strategy?
- Do some events provide an opportunity to reconsider or adjust my strategy?

For instance, if you want to be a manager of a retail store it is likely you might need a related college degree and experience. Your personal staging and pacing would answer questions about how you would achieve these, the financial implications of each, as well as their timing.

Personal Economic Logic

Finally, your personal growth and development strategy will likely have an economic logic. Personal economic logic answers questions such as the following:

- How does achievement of my strategy help me pay the bills?
- What dimensions of my strategy, like arenas or differentiators, is the economic logic of my strategy most dependent on?
- How sustainable is the economic logic of my strategy?

We can see this most clearly when magazines publish lists of high-demand jobs. When employees have skills that are in high demand by employers, the price of those skills in the form of a paycheck, is usually bid up in the market. For organizations, economic logic is typically viewed in terms of financial performance. However, increasingly, firms target social and environmental performance as well—similarly, the economic logic of your strategy can have implications for what you do to improve social and environmental conditions. This can happen directly through your volunteer hours or indirectly through your financial support of causes you believe in.

KEY TAKEAWAY

In this section, we discussed how to put together a strategy diamond. The first step involves identifying the organization's arenas, differentiators, and economic logic. This step involves a basic understanding of strategy and summarizes many of the traditional views in strategic management. The second step involves contemplating how the organization would compete or grow in existing or new arenas, and this is where the vehicles came into play. Finally, you considered the sequencing and speed of strategic initiatives by learning about the strategy diamond facet of staging and pacing. Together, these five facets (i.e., arenas, differentiators, economic logic, vehicles, staging, and pacing) constitute the strategy diamond. We concluded the chapter with an application of the strategy diamond to your personal situation.

EXERCISES

1. What are the five facets of the Hambrick and Fredrickson strategy diamond?
2. What is the relationship between arenas and differentiators if the strategy yields a positive economic logic?
3. If a firm is performing poorly financially, what might this say about the differentiators, arenas, or both?
4. Why is it important to consider vehicles as part of an organization's strategy?
5. What is the difference between staging and pacing in terms of the strategy diamond?
6. What are some ways that you might apply staging and pacing to an organization's strategy?

7. CASE IN POINT: FLAT WORLD KNOWLEDGE'S TEXTBOOK REVOLUTION

FIGURE 5.23

Source: Used by permission from Flat World Knowledge Inc.

The traditional textbook publishing model no longer serves the interests of students, educators, and authors. Textbooks are too expensive for students and too inflexible for instructors. And authors, the major, initial source of value in the industry, are increasingly confused by faster revision demands and their compensation for those revisions. Flat World addresses all these industry pain points.

- Jeff Shelstad

In 2007, two textbook publishing industry veterans, Jeff Shelstad and Eric Frank, started Flat World Knowledge (FWK), a privately held company, to be a new and disruptive model for the college textbook market. Traditional business textbook publishers carry a portfolio of 5 to 10 titles per subject and charge premium prices for new textbooks, an average of $1,000 in textbooks for a college student's first year, according to a recent General Accounting Office (GAO) report. FWK's strategy was aimed at turning the traditional model on its head by providing online textbook access free to students (http://www.flatworldknowledge.com). FWK earns revenues by selling students the digital textbooks in alternate formats, print and audio initially, and also by selling highly efficient and mobile study aids. Despite the fact that professors have rated the academic quality of FWK textbooks as equal to or higher than that of textbooks from traditional publishers, the cost to students is a fraction of current market prices due to the efficiencies of the FWK business model. Moreover, with FWK's platform, instructors who adopt FWK books for their classes are able to pick and choose the material provided to their students, even if it is from earlier versions of textbooks that have since been revised.

Shelstad and Frank previously served as the editorial director and the marketing director, respectively, at Prentice Hall, a major U.S. publisher of educational materials and a division of Pearson PLC. They resigned from Prentice Hall in January 2007 with plans to start a higher education publishing business together. During the first several months, they met with many students, professors, authors, advisors, and potential angel investors. The result was Flat World Knowledge. Shelstad became the CEO; Frank was the chief marketing officer. They also added David Wiley as the chief openness officer.

Asked why he started FWK, Shelstad said, "I was convinced the college textbook publishing industry model was broken." He added, "When more and more students are running from your core product, you have a problem. For example, many leading business school textbooks sell in the college bookstore or on various Internet sites for $150 or more. Students by and large don't see that value. So they search frantically for substitutes, and the Internet has made the availability and pricing of substitutes very obvious." In its first term (fall of 2009), FWK had 40,000 students using its textbooks. This steadily continued to rise as faculty discovered the low-priced alternative that combined quality and affordability for their students. As of January 2013, FWK has published more than 100 books, with faculty customers at more than 2000 institutions in 44 countries. As a result, more than 600,000 students have benefited from affordable textbook choices that lower costs, increase access, and personalize learning.

Media attention regarding the fledgling FWK was generally very favorable. Social media experts also gave the company accolades. For example, Chris Anderson devoted a page to the FWK business model in his bestselling book "Free: The Future of a Radical Price." Moreover, early user reviews of the product were also very positive. For instance, an instructor who adopted an early FWK text, *Principles of Management*, noted, "I highly recommend this book as a primary textbook for…business majors. The overall context is quite appropriate and the search capability within the context is useful. I have been quite impressed [with] how they have highlighted the key areas." At the same time, opportunities to improve the Web interface still existed, with the same reviewer noting, "The navigation could be a bit more user friendly, however." FWK uses user input like this to better adjust the strategy and delivery of its model. This type of feedback led the FWK design squad to improve its custom Web interface, so that instructors can more easily change the book.

Further changes occurred in late 2012, when the company announced it would no longer offer free online access to its textbooks. Moving from "free to fair" (the entry point for students is now $19.95) was a difficult but necessary decision. On its website, the company explained:

"As the transition to digital has changed student buying trends, the free format has become a barrier to our long-term growth and ability to offer a fair and affordable model that works for all our customers, from individual students and instructors to our institutional partners."

In December 2012, the company announced the appointment of Christopher Etesse as CEO. Etesse is a former senior executive and Chief Technology Officer with Blackboard Inc. Shelstad will remain with the company in a strategic role as Founder.

Only time will tell if the $30 million invested in FWK by 2012 will result in the establishment of a new titan in textbook publishing or will be an entrepreneurial miss.

Case written by Mason Carpenter and adapted by Talya Bauer with permission to accompany Carpenter, M., Bauer, T., Erdogan, B., & Short, J. (2013). Principles of management (2nd ed.). New York: Flat World Knowledge. Based on information from United States Government Accountability Office. (2005, July). College textbooks: Enhanced offering appear to drive recent price increases (GAO-05-806). Retrieved April 22, 2010, from http://www.gao.gov/cgi-bin/getrpt?GAO-05-806; Flat World Knowledge Web site: http://www.flatworldknowledge.com; Community College Open Textbook Collaborative. (2009). Business reviews. Retrieved April 22, 2010, from http://www.collegeopentextbooks.org/reviews/business.html; Personal interviews with Jeff Shelstad and Eric Frank.

CASE DISCUSSION QUESTIONS

1. Planning is a key component to the P-O-L-C framework. What type of planning do you think the founders of Flat World Knowledge engaged in?
2. What competitive advantages does Flat World Knowledge possess?
3. What are Flat World Knowledge's key strengths, weaknesses, opportunities, and threats?
4. How might the extensive textbook industry experience that the Flat World Knowledge founders possess help or hinder their strategy formulation and ultimate success or failure?
5. Based on Porter's strategies, which type of strategy do you see Flat World Knowledge employing? Support your response.

ENDNOTES

1. Carpenter, M. A., & Sanders, W. G. (2009). *Strategic management* (p. 8). Upper Saddle River, NJ: Pearson/Prentice-Hall.

2. Carpenter, M. A., & Sanders, W. G. (2009). *Strategic management* (p. 10). Upper Saddle River, NJ: Pearson/Prentice-Hall.

3. Mintzberg, H. (1978). Patterns in strategy formulation. *Management Science, 24,* 934–949.

4. Carpenter, M. A., & Sanders, W. G. (2008). Fast food chic? The Chipotle burrito. University of Wisconsin Business Case.

5. Retrieved September 12, 2012, from http://www.secinfo.com/dRqWm.89X3.htm#34f.

6. Andrews, K. (1971). *The concept of corporate strategy.* Homewood, IL: R. D. Irwin.

7. Mintzberg, H. (1987, July–August). Crafting strategy. *Harvard Business Review,* 66–75; Mintzberg, H. (1996). The entrepreneurial organization. In H. Mintzberg & J. B. Quinn (Eds.), *The strategy process* (3rd ed.). Englewood Cliffs, NJ: Prentice-Hall; Mintzberg, H., & Waters, J. A. (1985). Of strategies, deliberate and emergent. *Strategic Management Journal, 6,* 257–272.

8. See Mintzberg, H. (1978). Patterns in strategy formulation. *Management Science, 24,* 934–948; Mintzberg, H., & Waters, J. A. (1985). Of strategies, deliberate and emergent. *Strategic Management Journal, 6,* 257–272; and Mintzberg, H. (1988). *Mintzberg on management: Inside our strange world of organizations.* New York: Free Press.

9. The two views of Honda are captured in two Harvard cases: *Honda [A].* (1989). Boston: Harvard Business School, Case 384049, and *Honda [B].* (1989). Boston: Harvard Business School, Case 384050.

10. Dell increases revenue and earnings, lowers operating expenses. (2008, May 28). Dell press release. Retrieved November 3, 2008, from http://www.dell.com/content/topics/global.aspx/corp/pressoffice/en/2008/2008_05_29_rr_000?c=us&l=en's=corp.

11. Porter, M. (1985). *Competitive advantage: Creating and sustaining superior performance.* New York: Free Press; Porter, M. (1989). *Competitive advantage of nations.* New York: Free Press; Porter, M. (1980). *Competitive strategy: Techniques for analyzing industries and companies.* New York: Free Press; Porter, M. (2001, March). Strategy and the Internet. *Harvard Business Review,* 63–78; Retrospective on Michael Porter's (2002). *Competitive strategy* [Special section]. *Academy of Management Executive, 16,* 40–65.

12. Walters, B. A., & Bhuian, S. (2004). Complexity absorption and performance: A structural analysis of acute-care hospitals. *Journal of Management, 30,* 97–121.

13. McEvily, S. K., & Chakravarthy, B. (2002). The persistence of knowledge-based advantage: An empirical test for product performance and technological knowledge. *Strategic Management Journal, 23,* 285–305; Buckley, P. J., & Carter, M. J. (2000). Knowledge management in global technology markets: Applying theory to practice. *Long Range Planning, 33*(1), 55–71.

14. Pocket Strategy. (1998). *Value* (p. 165). London: The Economist Books.

15. Prahalad, C. K., & Hamel, G. (1990). The core competence of the organization. *Harvard Business Review, 90,* 79–93.

16. Hafeez, K., Zhang, Y. B., & Malak, N. (2002). Core competence for sustainable competitive advantage: A structured methodology for identifying core competence. *IEEE Transactions on Engineering Management, 49*(1), 28–35; Prahalad, C. K., & Hamel, G. (1990). The core competence of the corporation. *Harvard Business Review, 68*(3), 79–93.

17. Useem, J. (2001, February 19). Most admired: Conquering vertical limits. *Fortune,* pp. 84–96.

18. Useem, J. (2001, February 19). Most admired: Conquering vertical limits. *Fortune,* pp. 84–96.

19. Eisenhardt, K., & Martin, J. (2000). Dynamic capabilities: What are they? *Strategic Management Journal, 21,* 1105–1121; Michalisin, M. D., Kline, D. M., & Smith. R. D. (2000). Intangible strategic assets and firm performance: A multi-industry study of the resource-based view, *Journal of Business Strategies, 17,* 91–117.

20. West, G. P., & DeCastro, J. (2001). The Achilles heel of firm strategy: Resource weaknesses and distinctive inadequacies. *Journal of Management Studies, 38,* 26–45; Deeds, D. L., DeCarolis, D., & J. Coombs. (2000). Dynamic capabilities and new product development in high technology ventures: An empirical analysis of new biotechnology firms. *Journal of Business Venturing, 15,* 211–229; Chi, T. (1994). Trading in strategic resources: Necessary conditions, transaction cost problems, and choice of exchange structure. *Strategic Management Journal, 15,* 271–290.

21. Berman, S., Down, J., & Hill, C. (2002). Tacit knowledge as a source of competitive advantage in the National Basketball Association. *Academy of Management Journal, 45,* 13–31.

22. Feldman, M. S. (2000). Organizational routines as a source of continuous change, *Organization Science, 11,* 611–629; Knott, A. M., & McKelvey, B. (1999). Nirvana efficiency: A comparative test of residual claims and routines. *Journal of Economic Behavior & Organization, 38,* 365–383.

23. Helfat, C. E., & Raubitschek, R. S. (2000). Product sequencing: Co-evolution of knowledge, capabilities, and products. *Strategic Management Journal, 21,* 961–979.

24. Hitt, M. A., Bierman, L., Shimizu, K., & Kochhar, R. (2001) Direct and moderating effects of human capital on strategy and performance in professional service firms: A resource-based perspective. *Academy of Management Journal, 44,* 13–28; Hitt, M. A., Ireland, R. D., & Lee, H. (2000). Technological learning, knowledge management, firm

growth and performance: An introductory essay. *Journal of Engineering and Technology Management, 17,* 231–246; Hoopes, D. G., & Postrel, S. (1999). Shared knowledge: "Glitches," and product development performance. *Strategic Management Journal, 20,* 837–865; Quinn, J. B. (1994). *The Intelligent Enterprise.* New York: Free Press.

25. Argote, L., & Ingram, P. (2000). Knowledge transfer: A basis for competitive advantage in firms. *Organizational Behavior and Human Decision Processes, 82,* 150–169.

26. Dess, G. G., & Picken, J. C. (1999). *Beyond productivity.* New York: AMACOM.

27. Coy, P. (2002, Spring). High turnover, high risk [Special Issue]. *Business Week,* p. 24.

28. Baldwin, T. T., & Danielson, C. C. (2000). Building a learning strategy at the top: Interviews with ten of America's CLOs. *Business Horizons, 43,* 5–14.

29. Kuratko, D. F., Ireland, R. D., & Hornsby, J. S. (2001). Improving firm performance through entrepreneurial actions: Acordia's corporate entrepreneurship strategy. *Academy of Management Executive, 15,* 60–71; Hansen, M. T., Nhoria, N., & Tierney T. (1999). What's your strategy for managing knowledge? *Harvard Business Review, 77*(2), 106–116.

30. Hitt, M. A., & Ireland, R. D. (1986). Relationships among corporate level distinctive competencies, diversification strategy, corporate structure, and performance. *Journal of Management Studies, 23,* 401–416; Hitt, M. A., & Ireland, R. D. (1985). Corporate distinctive competence, strategy, industry, and performance. *Strategic Management Journal, 6,* 273–293; Hitt, M. A., Ireland, R. D., & Palia, K. A. (1982). Industrial firms' grand strategy and functional importance. *Academy of Management Journal, 25,* 265–298; Hitt, M. A., Ireland, R. D., & Stadter, G. (1982). Functional importance and company performance: Moderating effects of grand strategy and industry type. *Strategic Management Journal, 3,* 315–330; Snow, C. C., & Hrebiniak, E. G. (1980). Strategy, distinctive competence, and organizational performance. *Administrative Science Quarterly, 25,* 317–336.

31. VRIO analysis is at the core of the resource-based view of the firm. Wernerfelt, B. (1984). A resource-based view of the firm. *Strategic Management Journal, 5,* 171–180; Barney, J. B. (1991). Firm resources and sustained competitive advantage. *Journal of Management, 19,* 99–120.

32. Barney, J. B. (1991). Firm resources and sustained competitive advantage. *Journal of Management, 17,* 99–120.

33. Dyer, J. H., Kale, P., & Singh, H. (2004, July–August). When to ally and when to acquire. *Harvard Business Review,* 109–115.

34. Dyer, J. H., & Hatch, N. (2004). Using Supplier Networks to Learn Faster. *Sloan Management Review, 45*(3), 57–63.

35. Personal communication between Mason Carpenter and Margaret Haddox. (2003). Novell Corporate Librarian.

36. Personal communication between Mason Carpenter former executives.

37. Kearns, D. T., & Nadler, D. A. (1992). *Prophets in the dark.* New York: HarperColllins; Barney, J. B. (1995). Looking inside for competitive advantage. *Academy of Management Executive, 9,* 49–61.

38. Fahey, L. (1999). *Competitors.* New York: Wiley; Walters, B. A., & Priem, R. L. (1999). Business strategy and CEO intelligence acquisition. *Competitive Intelligence Review, 10*(2), 15–22.

39. Spanos, Y. E., & Lioukas, S. (2001). An examination into the causal logic of rent generation: Contrasting Porter's competitive strategy framework and the resource-based perspective. *Strategic Management Journal, 22,* 907–934.

40. Porter, M. E. (1980). *Competitive strategy.* New York: Free Press.

41. Zaheer, S., & Zaheer, A. (2001). Market microstructure in a global b2b network. *Strategic Management Journal, 22,* 859–873.

42. Hitt, M. A., Ricart I Costa, J., & Nixon, R. D. (1999). *New managerial mindsets.* New York: Wiley.

43. Pan, Y., & Chi, P. S. K. (1999). Financial performance and survival of multinational corporations in China. *Strategic Management Journal, 20,* 359–374; Brooks, G. R. (1995). Defining market boundaries. *Strategic Management Journal, 16,* 535–549.

44. Geroski, P. A. (1999). Early warning of new rivals. *Sloan Management Review, 40*(3), 107–116.

45. Robinson, K. C., & McDougall, P. P. (2001). Entry barriers and new venture performance: A comparison of universal and contingency approaches. *Strategic Management Journal, 22,* 659–685.

46. Khermouch, G. (2001, March 5). Grown-up drinks for tender taste buds. *Business Week,* 96.

47. Deephouse, D. L. (1999). To be different, or to be the same? It's a question (and theory) of strategic balance. *Strategic Management Journal, 20,* 147–166.

48. Chung, W., & Kalnins, A. (2001). Agglomeration effects and performance: Test of the Texas lodging industry. *Strategic Management Journal, 22,* 969–988.

49. Kuemmerle, W. (2001). Home base and knowledge management in international ventures. *Journal of Business Venturing, 17,* 99–122; Lorenzoni, G., & Lipparini, A. (1999). The leveraging of interfirm relationships as a distinctive organizational capability: A longitudinal study. *Strategic Management Journal, 20,* 317–338.

50. Porter, M. E. (1980). *Competitive strategy.* New York: Free Press.

51. Hambrick, D. C., & Fredrickson, J. W. (2001). Are you sure you have a strategy? *Academy of Management Executive, 19,* 51–62.

52. Hambrick, D. C., & Fredrickson, J. W. (2001). Are you sure you have a strategy? *Academy of Management Executive, 19,* 51–62, esp. 53.

CHAPTER 6
Goals and Objectives

FIGURE 6.1

Amazon has set an aggressive goal of enabling their readers to download "every book ever printed in any language...in less than 60 seconds."

Source: http://www.flickr.com/photos/kodomut/6736940485/; caption retrieved from http://www.itwire.com/your-it-news/entertainment/
17762-amazons-kindle-vision-every-book-in-any-language-in-60-seconds

---

CHAPTER LEARNING OBJECTIVES

Reading this chapter will help you do the following:

1. Demonstrate an understanding of the nature of goals and objectives and their importance to effective management.
2. Learn how our thinking about goals and objectives has evolved.
3. Explain what characterizes good goals and objectives.
4. Show an understanding of the roles of goals and objectives in employee performance reviews.
5. Map out relationships among economic, social, and environmental goals and objectives.
6. Learn how to set and manage your own goals and objectives.

Goals and objectives are a critical component of management, both in terms of planning and in terms of the larger planning-organizing-leading-controlling (P-O-L-C) framework. Their role is summarized in Figure 6.2. Despite their importance, goals are often neglected in managerial practice, and at times, individuals' goals are poorly aligned with the organization's strategy. This practice is problematic because one of a manager's key functions is to evaluate employee performance—such evaluations should be based on how the achievement of individual goals and objectives contributes to those critical to the organization's survival and success. In this chapter, we introduce you to the basics of creating effective goals and objectives and provide you with an understanding of how their usage has evolved. We also show you how to develop a personalized set of goals and objectives to help you achieve your personal and professional aspirations.

FIGURE 6.2 Goals and Objectives in the P-O-L-C Framework

Planning	Organizing	Leading	Controlling
1. Vision & Mission	1. Organization Design	1. Leadership	1. Systems/Processes
2. Strategizing	2. Culture	2. Decision Making	2. Strategic Human Resources
3. Goals & Objectives	3. Social Networks	3. Communications	
		4. Groups/Teams	
		5. Motivation	

1. THE NATURE OF GOALS AND OBJECTIVES

LEARNING OBJECTIVES

1. **Know the difference between goals and objectives.**
2. **Know the relationship between goals and objectives.**
3. **See how goals and objectives fit in the P-O-L-C framework.**

1.1 What Are Goals and Objectives?

goals

Outcome statements that define what an organization is trying to accomplish, both programmatically and organizationally.

Goals are outcome statements that define what an organization is trying to accomplish. Goals are a reflection of major actions of the organization, and provide rallying points for managers. For example, Walmart might state a financial goal of growing its revenues 20% per year or have a goal of growing internationally. Research has found the acquisition of business skills relevant to accomplishing organizational goals to be one of the most critical skills for developing effective leaders.[1]

In contrast to goals, **objectives** are very precise, time-based, measurable actions that support the completion of a goal. Objectives typically must (1) be related directly to the goal; (2) be clear, concise, and understandable; (3) be stated in terms of results; (4) begin with an action verb; (5) specify a date for accomplishment; and (6) be measurable. For example, while Walmart may hold a 20% revenue growth goal, one specific objective to achieve that goal might be to "open 20 new stores in the next six months." Without specific objectives, the general goal cannot be accomplished.

objectives

Very precise, time-based, and measurable actions that support the completion of a goal.

Measures are the actual metrics used to gauge performance on objectives. For instance, the *objective* of improved financial performance can be *measured* using a number of metrics, ranging from improvement in total sales, profitability, efficiencies, or stock price. Colleges and universities might measure performance by using subjective rankings, such as those found in *U.S. News & World Report*, or more objective measures, such as the percentage of faculty with doctoral degrees.[2] An old management adage says, "What gets measured, gets done." Measurement is critical to today's organizations. It is a fundamental requirement and an integral part of strategic planning and of principles of management more generally. Without measures, the accomplishment of goals and objectives is difficult to ascertain.

measures

The actual metrics used to gauge performance on objectives.

1.2 Measurement Challenges

Organizations make three common mistakes related to measurement. First, many organizations emphasize historic financial goals and objectives, which may no longer be relevant. Second, financial outcomes are often short term in nature; consequently, focusing too much on financial measures may lead managers to overlook other key factors that might be important to the longer-term viability of the organization. For instance, *return on sales* (ROS, or net profit divided by total sales) is a commonly used measure of financial performance, and firms often set goals and objectives related to return on sales.

However, an organization can increase return on sales by cutting investments in marketing and research and development (since they are costs that lessen the "return" dimension of ROS). It may be a good thing to cut such costs, but that type of cost-cutting typically hurts the organization's longer-term prospects. Decreases in marketing may reduce brand awareness, and decreases in research and development (R&D) will likely stifle new product or service development. Lastly, goals and objectives, even when they cover more than short-term financial metrics, are not often tied to strategy and ultimately to vision and mission. Instead, managers often create a laundry list of goals and objectives that lack any larger organizing logic.

1.3   Goals and Objectives in P-O-L-C

Goals and objectives are an essential part of planning. They also have implications for all the aspects of organizing, leading, and controlling. Broadly speaking, goals and objectives serve to:

- Gauge and report performance
- Improve performance
- Align effort
- Manage accountabilities

Goals, Objectives, and Planning

Planning typically starts with a vision and a mission. Managers then develop a strategy for realizing the vision and mission; their success and progress in achieving vision and mission will be indicated by how well the underlying goals and objectives are achieved. A vision statement usually describes some broad set of goals—what the organization aspires to look like in the future. Mission statements too have stated goals—what the organization aspires to be for its stakeholders. For instance, Mars, Inc., the global food giant, sets out five mission statement goals in the areas of quality, responsibility, mutuality, efficiency, and freedom. Thus goals are typically set for the organization as a whole and set the stage for a hierarchy of increasingly specific and narrowly set goals and objectives.

Unless the organization consists of only a single person, there are typically many working parts in terms of functional areas and product or service areas. Functional areas like accounting and marketing will need to have goals and objectives that, if measured and tracked, help show if and how those functions are contributing to the organization's goals and objectives. Similarly, product and service areas will likely have goals and objectives. Goals and objectives can also be set for the way that functions and product or service areas interact. For instance, are the accounting and marketing functions interacting in a way that is productive? Is marketing delivering value to product or service initiatives?

Goals, Objectives, and Organizing, Leading, and Controlling

Within the planning facet of P-O-L-C alone, goals and objectives tend to become more specific as you move down the levels of the organization. Similarly, the time horizon for accomplishing goals is often shorter as you move down the organization.

The way that the firm is organized can affect goals and objectives in a number of ways. For instance, a functional organizational structure, where departments are broken out by finance, marketing, operations, and so on, will likely want to track the performance of each department, but exactly what constitutes performance will probably vary from function to function.

In terms of leadership, it is usually top managers who set goals and objectives for the entire organization. Ideally, then, lower-level managers would set or have input into the goals and objectives relevant to their respective parts of the business. For example, a CEO might believe that the company can achieve a sales growth goal of 20% per year. With this organizational goal, the marketing manager can then set specific product sales goals, as well as pricing, volume, and other objectives, throughout the year that show how marketing is on track to deliver its part of organizational sales growth. Goal setting is thus a primary function of leadership, along with holding others accountable for their respective goals and objectives.

FIGURE 6.3 Goals and Objectives in Planning

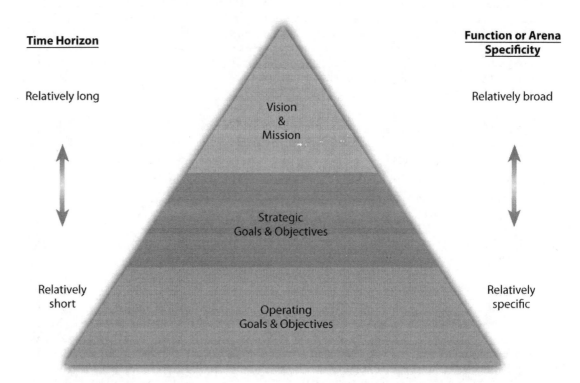

Finally, goals and objectives can provide a form of control since they create a feedback opportunity regarding how well or how poorly the organization executes its strategy. Goals and objectives also are a basis for reward systems and can align interests and accountability within and across business units.

KEY TAKEAWAY

Goals are typically outcome statements, while objectives are very precise, time-based, and measurable actions that support the completion of goals. Goals and objectives are an essential element in planning and are a key referent point in many aspects of organizing, leading, and controlling. Broadly speaking, within the P-O-L-C framework, goals and objectives serve to (1) gauge and report performance, (2) improve performance, (3) align effort and, (4) manage accountabilities.

EXERCISES

1. What is the difference between a goal and an objective?
2. Alone or in a group, think of some specific objectives related to something you care about deeply. Now, what is the relationship between your objectives and the potential specific goals you may have?
3. What characteristics should a good objective have?
4. What four broad ways do goals and objectives fit in the P-O-L-C framework?
5. How are goals and objectives relevant to leadership?
6. In what ways do goals and objectives help managers control an organization?

2. MANAGEMENT BY OBJECTIVES AND THE BALANCED SCORECARD

LEARNING OBJECTIVES

1. Be able to describe management by objectives.
2. Be able to describe the Balanced Scorecard.
3. Understand the evolution of performance measurement systems.

Organizations use a variety of measurement approaches to go about setting and managing goals and objectives. In this section, we focus on two key approaches to setting goals. **Management by objectives (MBO)** is a goal-setting framework primarily used when managers and employees collaborate on setting goals. The **Balanced Scorecard**, in constrast, is used by top managers to make sense of multiple performance measures at the organizational level.

2.1 Management by Objectives

Management by objectives (MBO) is a systematic and organized approach that aims to increase organizational performance by aligning the subordinate objectives throughout the organization with the overall goals set by management. Ideally, employees get strong input to identify their objectives, time lines for completion, and so on. MBO includes ongoing tracking and feedback in the process to reach objectives.

MBO was first outlined by Peter Drucker in 1954 in *The Practice of Management*. One of Drucker's core ideas in MBO was to create a better focus regarding where managers should spend their time and energy. According to Drucker, managers should focus on the result, not the activity. Managers should delegate tasks by "negotiating a contract of objectives" with their subordinates and by refraining from dictating a detailed road map for implementation. MBO is about setting goals and then breaking these down into more specific objectives or key results. MBO involves (1) setting company-wide goals derived from corporate strategy, (2) determining team- and department-level goals, (3) collaboratively setting individual-level goals that are aligned with corporate strategy, (4) developing an action plan, and (5) periodically reviewing performance and revising goals.[3] A review of the literature shows that 68 out of the 70 studies conducted on this topic showed performance gains as a result of MBO implementation.[4] It also seems that top management commitment to the process is the key to successful implementation of MBO programs.[5] Of course, MBO may not work in all contexts. For example, a study of Swedish secondary schools that instituted the program as a national policy found that MBO had little effect on student success.[6]

The broader principle behind MBO is to make sure that everybody within the organization has a clear understanding of the organization's goals, as well as awareness of their own roles and responsibilities in achieving objectives that will help to attain those goals. The complete MBO system aims to get managers and empowered employees acting to implement and achieve their plans, which automatically achieves the organization's goals.

management by objectives (MBO)

A systematic and organized approach that allows management to focus on achievable goals and to attain the best possible results from available resources.

Balanced Scorecard

A framework designed to translate an organization's vision and mission statements and overall business strategy into specific, quantifiable goals and objectives and to monitor the organization's performance in terms of achieving these goals.

FIGURE 6.4 The Importance of Carefully Setting Rewards

In 1975, Steve Kerr published an article now considered a classic within the management field titled "On the Folly of Rewarding A, While Hoping for B." In it, he noted numerous examples where systems rewarded an outcome much different than what the organization hoped to achieve. Here, we illustrate several reward follies.

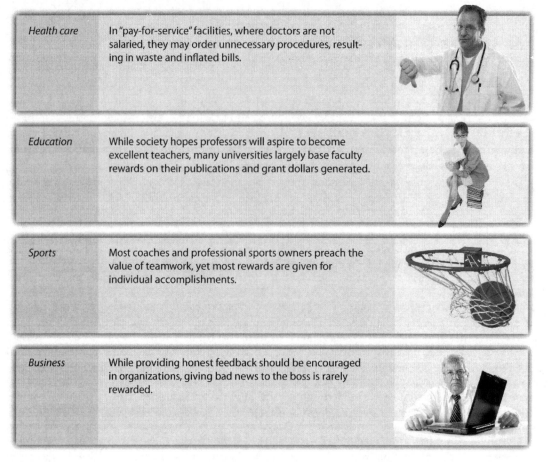

© *Thinkstock*

2.2 The Balanced Scorecard

The Balanced Scorecard is a framework designed to translate an organization's mission and vision statements and overall business strategy into specific, quantifiable goals and objectives and to monitor the organization's performance in terms of achieving these goals. Developed by Robert Kaplan and David Norton in 1992, the Balanced Scorecard approach to management has gained worldwide popularity since the 1996 release of their book *The Balanced Scorecard: Translating Strategy into Action*. In 2001, the Gartner Group estimated that at least 40% of all *Fortune* 1000 companies were using the Balanced Scorecard.

FIGURE 6.5 The Balanced Scorecard

Because the concept of organizational performance is multidimensional, wise managers realize that understanding organizational performance is like flying a plane: pilots must be on track in terms of altitude, air speed, and oil pressure and make sure they have enough gas to finish their flight plan. For tracking organizational performance, assessing how the organization is doing financially is just a starting point. The "balanced scorecard" encourages managers to also monitor how well the organization is serving customers, managing internal activities, and setting the stage for future improvements. This provides a fast but comprehensive view of the organization. As shown below, monitoring these four dimensions also can help individuals assess themselves.

Financial measures – such as *return on assets* and *stock price* – relate to effectiveness and profits.

You could ask yourself: How can I improve my personal wealth? Measures might include cash, savings account, and retirement.

Customer measures – such as *number of new or repeat customers* and *percentage of repeat customers –* relate to customer attraction and satisfaction.

You could ask yourself: How strong is my social network? The number of new contacts you make over time might reflect this dimension.

Internal business process measures – such *as speed at serving a customer* and *time it takes to create a new product and get it to market* – relate to organizational efficiency.

You could ask yourself: Am I getting better at my current job? Tracking improvements in personal efficiency such as the time needed to complete a task can be helpful.

Learning and growth measures – such as the *average number of new skills learned by each employee every year –* relate to the future and emphasize that employee learning is often more important than formal training.

You could ask yourself: What skills should I develop now for the future? Although the acquisition of new skills is hard to measure, the attainment of specialized licenses or earning of a graduate degree are tangible benchmarks.

Source: Image courtesy of Ketchen, D., & Short, J. (2011). Mastering strategic management. Irvington, NY: Flat World Knowledge.

One of the Balanced Scorecard's innovations is explicit attention to vision and strategy in setting goals and objectives. Stemming from the idea that assessing performance through financial returns only provides information about how well the organization did prior to the assessment, the Balanced Scorecard is a comprehensive approach that analyzes an organization's overall performance in four ways, so that future performance can be predicted and proper actions taken to create the desired future.

Balanced Scorecard Dimensions

Performance measures in the Balanced Scorecard can include both leading and lagging indicators; leading indicators include measures that might be examined to predict poor performance of the organization in the future, such as an increase in employee turnover, whereas lagging indicators, such as a decrease in sales, reflect that performance is in decline.[7] The Balanced Scorecard focuses on four types of measures: customers, learning and growth, internal processes, and financial performance. The customer area looks at customer satisfaction and retention. Learning and growth explore the effectiveness of management in terms of measures of employee satisfaction and retention and information system performance. The internal area looks at production and innovation, measuring performance in terms of maximizing profit from current products and following indicators for future productivity. Finally, financial performance, the most traditionally used category of performance indicators, includes assessments of measures such as operating costs and return-on-investment.

As a structure, the Balanced Scorecard breaks broad goals down successively into objectives, measures, and tactical activities. As an example of how the method might work, an organization might include in its mission or vision statement a goal of maintaining employee satisfaction (for instance, the mission statement might say something like "our employees are our most valuable asset"). This would be a key part of the organization's mission but would also provide an "internal" target area for that goal in the Balanced Scorecard. Importantly, this goal, when done correctly, would also be linked to the organization's total strategy where other parts of the scorecard would show how having great employees provides economic, social, and environmental returns. Strategies for achieving that human resources vision might include approaches such as increasing employee-management communication. Tactical activities undertaken to implement the strategy could include, for example, regularly scheduled meetings with employees. Finally, metrics could include quantifications of employee suggestions or employee surveys.

The Balanced Scorecard in Practice

In practice, the Balanced Scorecard is more than simply a framework for thinking about goals and objectives. In its broadest scope, where the scorecard operates much like a map of the firm's vision, mission, and strategy, the Balanced Scorecard relies on four processes to bind short-term activities to long-term objectives:

1. *Translating the vision.* By relying on measurement, the scorecard forces managers to come to an agreement on the metrics they will use to translate lofty visions into everyday realities.

2. *Communicating and linking.* When a scorecard is disseminated to others in the organization, strategy becomes a tool available to everyone. As the high-level scorecard cascades down to individual business units, overarching strategic objectives and measures are translated into objectives and measures appropriate to each particular group. Tying these targets to individual performance and compensation systems yields "personal scorecards." Thus individual employees understand how their own productivity supports the overall strategy.

3. *Business planning.* Most companies have separate procedures (and sometimes units) for strategic planning and budgeting. The discipline of creating a Balanced Scorecard forces companies to integrate the two functions, thereby ensuring that financial budgets indeed support strategic goals. After agreeing on performance measures for the four scorecard perspectives, companies identify the most influential "drivers" of the desired outcomes and then set milestones for gauging the progress they make with these drivers.

4. *Feedback and learning.* By supplying a mechanism for strategic feedback and review, the Balanced Scorecard helps an organization foster a kind of learning often missing in companies: the ability to reflect on inferences and adjust theories about cause-and-effect relationships.

KEY TAKEAWAY

The way that goals and objectives are managed in the P-O-L-C process has evolved over time. While organizations can have very simple performance measurement systems, these systems typically track multiple goals and objectives. The management by objectives (MBO) approach is perhaps one of the earliest systematic approaches to working with goals and objectives. The Balanced Scorecard is aimed at tying goals and objectives to vision, mission, and strategy by branching out beyond purely financial goals and objectives.

EXERCISES

1. Provide an example of a job where management by objectives (MBO) would be challenging to use. Defend your answer.
2. What are the advantages and disadvantages of MBO?
3. Apply the Balanced Scorecard to your college or university.
4. Provide examples of performance measures for each Balanced Scorecard dimension relevant to understanding the performance of a coffee shop.

3. USING GOALS AND OBJECTIVES IN EMPLOYEE PERFORMANCE EVALUATION

LEARNING OBJECTIVES

1. Understand where goals and objectives fit in employee development.
2. See how goals and objectives are part of an effective employee performance evaluation process.

3.1 Goals, Objectives, and Performance Reviews

A **performance evaluation** is a constructive process to acknowledge an employee's performance. Goals and objectives are critical components of effective performance evaluations because evaluation forms need to have a set of measurable goals and objectives spelled out for each area. Some of these, such as *attendance*, are more easy to describe and quantify than others, such as *knowledge*. Research suggests that individual and organizational performance increase 16% when an evaluation system based on specific goals and objectives is implemented.[8]

Role and Limitations of Performance Evaluations

Most organizations conduct employee performance evaluations at least once a year, but they can occur more frequently when there is a clear rationale for doing so—for instance, at the end of a project, at the end of each month, and so on. For example, McKinsey, a leading strategy consulting firm, has managers evaluate employees at the end of every consulting engagement. So, in addition to the annual performance evaluation, consultants can receive up to 20 mini-evaluations in a year. Importantly, the timing should coincide with the needs of the organization and the development needs of the employee. In fact, the concept of performance management, or continuously assessing and developing performance with the goal of aligning individual performance with strategic objectives, is slowly replacing the idea of yearly performance assessments.[9]

Performance evaluations are critical, as they help managers feel more honest in their relationships with their subordinates and better about themselves in their supervisory roles. Subordinates are assured clear understanding of what goals and objectives are expected from them, their own personal strengths and areas for development, and a solid sense of their relationship with their supervisor. Avoiding performance issues ultimately decreases morale, decreases credibility of management, decreases the organization's overall effectiveness, and wastes more of management's time to do what is not being done properly.

It is important to recognize that performance evaluations are a not without their challenges. Studies show that performance-appraisal errors are extremely difficult to eliminate.[10] Training to eliminate certain types of errors often introduces other types of errors and sometimes reduces accuracy. The most common appraisal error is leniency, and managers often realize they are committing this error.

performance evaluation

The constructive process to acknowledge an employee's performance.

FIGURE 6.6 Sample Employee Evaluation Form

EMPLOYEE INFORMATION

Name:	Employee ID:
Department:	Employee Job Title:
Supervisor:	Supervisor Job:

RATINGS

	Poor	Fair	Satisfactory	Good	Excellent
Job Knowledge—Understands duties, responsibilities, has ability to use materials needed, and has the level of proficiency required to accomplish the work.	☐	☐	☐	☐	☐
Comments					
Work Quality—Accuracy, thoroughness, dependability of results.	☐	☐	☐	☐	☐
Comments					
Attendance—Reports to work as scheduled. Follows established procedures for breaks. Notifies supervisor in advance of scheduling changes.	☐	☐	☐	☐	☐
Comments					
Initiative—Ability to be self-directed, efficient, creative, and resourceful. Assumes extra work on own initiative, adapts quickly to new responsibilities.	☐	☐	☐	☐	☐
Comments					
Work Attitude and Cooperation—Extent to which employee demonstrates a positive attitude, and promotes cooperation with supervisors, peers and others.	☐	☐	☐	☐	☐
Comments					
Dependability—Extent to which employee can be counted on to carry out instructions and fulfill job responsibilities accurately and efficiently.	☐	☐	☐	☐	☐
Comments					
Overall Rating					

Source: Image courtesy of Ketchen, D., & Short, J. (2011). Mastering strategic management. Irvington, NY: Flat World Knowledge.

An Example of the Performance Review Process

For example, assume that the organization has determined that annual performance evaluations fit the strategic needs of the organization and the developmental needs of employees. This does not mean however that management and employees discuss goals, objectives, and performance only once a year. In our example, the organization has opted to have a midyear information meeting and then an end-of-year performance evaluation meeting.

At some point in the year, the supervisor should hold a formal discussion with each staff member to review individual activities to date and to modify the goals and objectives that employee is account-able for. This agreed-upon set of goals and objectives is sometimes called an employee performance plan. There should be no surprises at this meeting. The supervisor should have been actively involved in continual assessment of his or her staff through regular contact and coaching. If major concerns arise, the performance plan can be modified or the employees can receive development in areas in which they may be weak. This also is a time for the employee to provide formal feedback to the supervisor on the coaching, on the planning, and on how the process seems to be working.

At the end of the year, a final review of the activities and plans for developing the next year's objectives begin. Again, this is a chance to provide constructive and positive feedback and to address any ongoing concerns about the employee's activities and competencies. Continuing education opportunities can be identified, and for those systems linked to compensation, salary raises will be linked to the employee's performance during the year. Again, there should be no surprises to either employee or supervisor, as continual assessment and coaching should take place throughout the year. Supervisors and managers are involved in the same series of activities with their own supervisors to ensure that the entire organization is developing and focused on the same common objectives.

There are many varieties of performance management systems available, but you must be aware that you will need to tailor any system to suit the needs of the organization and the staff. As the organization and its competitive environment change over time, the system will also need to develop to reflect changes to employee competencies, ranking systems, and rewards linked to the plan.

How do you handle your reviews—that is, when you are the focus of the review process? "Your Performance Review" summarizes some key ideas you might keep in mind for your next review.

Your Performance Review

There are typically three areas to consider when reviewing performance: (1) preparation for the review, (2) what to do if the review is negative, and (3) what should you ultimately take away from the review.

Prepare for an upcoming review. Document achievements and list anything you want to discuss at the review. If you have not kept track of your achievements, you may have to spend some time figuring out what you have accomplished since your last review and, most importantly, how your employer has benefited, such as increased profits, grown the client roster, maintained older clients, and so on. These are easier to document when you have had clear goals and objectives.

What should you do if you get a poor review? If you feel you have received an unfair review, you should consider responding to it. You should first try to discuss the review with the person who prepared it. Heed this warning, however. Wait until you can look at the review objectively. Was the criticism you received really that off the mark or are you just offended that you were criticized in the first place? If you eventually reach the conclusion that the review was truly unjust, then set an appointment to meet with your reviewer. If there are any points that were correct, acknowledge those. Use clear examples that counteract the criticisms made. A paper trail is always helpful. Present anything you have in writing that can back you up. If you didn't leave a paper trail, remember to do this in the future.

What should you take away from a performance review? Ultimately, you should regard your review as a learning opportunity. For instance, did you have clear goals and objectives such that your performance was easy to document? You should be able to take away valuable information, whether it is about yourself or your reviewer.

Best Practices

While there is no single best way to manage performance evaluations, the collective actions across a number of high-performing firms suggests a set of best practices.

1. Decide what you are hoping to achieve from the system. Is it to reward the stars and to correct problems? Or is its primary function to be a tool in focusing all staff activities through better planning?

2. Develop goals and objectives that inspire, challenge, and stretch people's capabilities. Once goals and objectives are clearly communicated and accepted, enlist broad participation, and do not shut down ideas. Support participation and goal attainment through the reward system, such as with gainsharing or other group incentive programs.

3. Ensure you have commitment from the top. Planning must begin at the executive level and be filtered down through the organization to ensure that employees' plans are meaningful in the context of the organization's direction. Top managers should serve as strong role models for the performance evaluation process and attach managerial consequences to the quality of performance reviews (for instance, McKinsey partners are evaluated on how well they develop their consultants, not just the profitability of their particular practice).

4. Ensure that all key staff are involved in the development of the performance management processes from the early phases. Provide group orientations to the program to decrease anxiety over the implementation of a new system. It will ensure a consistent message communicated about the performance management system.

5. If the performance management system is not linked to salary, be sure employees are aware of it. For example, university business school professors are paid salaries based on highly competitive external labor markets, not necessarily the internal goals and objectives of the school such as high teaching evaluations, and so on. Make sure employees know the purpose of the system and what they get out of it.

6. Provide additional training for supervisors on how to conduct the midyear and year-end performance reviews. Ensure that supervisors are proficient at coaching staff. Training, practice, and feedback about how to avoid appraisal errors are necessary, but often insufficient, for eliminating appraisal errors. Eliminating errors may require alternative approaches to evaluation, such as forced distribution (for instance, General Electric must rank the lowest 10% of performers and often ask them to find work with another employer).

7. Plan to modify the performance management system over time, starting with goals and objectives, to meet your organization's changing needs. Wherever possible, study employee behaviors in addition to attitudes; the two do not always converge.

KEY TAKEAWAY

This section outlined the relationship between goals and objectives and employee performance evaluation. Performance evaluation is a tool that helps managers align individual performance with organizational goals and objectives. You saw that the tool is most effective when evaluation includes well-developed goals and objectives that are developed with the needs of both the organization and employee in mind. The section concluded with a range of best practices for the performance evaluation process, including the revision of goals and objectives when the needs of the organization change.

EXERCISES

1. How are goals and objectives related to employee performance evaluation?
2. How often should performance evaluations be performed?
3. What kinds of goals and objectives might be best for performance evaluation to be most effective?
4. What should be included in an employee performance plan?
5. What performance evaluation best practices appear to most directly involve goals and objectives?

4. INTEGRATING GOALS AND OBJECTIVES WITH CORPORATE SOCIAL RESPONSIBILITY

LEARNING OBJECTIVES

1. **Understand the nature of corporate social responsibility.**
2. **See how corporate social responsibility can be incorporated using the Balanced Scorecard.**
3. **Understand that corporate social responsibility, like other goals and objectives, helps the firm only when aligned with its strategy, vision, and mission.**

One of the overarching lessons of this chapter is that goals and objectives are only effective to the extent that they reinforce the organization's strategy and therefore the realization of its vision and mission. This section provides knowledge about the ways that goals and objectives related to social and environmental issues can be tied back into strategy using a Balanced Scorecard approach.

4.1   Corporate Social Responsibility

The movement to embrace **corporate social responsibility (CSR)** has been gathering momentum for well over a decade, with 72% of all companies having formal programs in 2012. A review of 82 published studies finds a positive link between corporate social performance and firm financial performance.[11] However, research examining the relationship between corporate social responsibility and company stock valuation across Asia, Europe, and the United States found significant links to stock price performance only for European firms.[12] More recently, the New York Stock Exchange found that companies able to measure the bottom-line impact of their CR programs enhanced both their profitability and their competitive position.

   CSR is about how companies manage their business processes to produce an overall positive effect on society. This growth has raised questions—how to define the concept and how to integrate it into the larger body of an organization's goals and objectives. The Dow Jones Sustainability Index created a commonly accepted definition of CSR: "a business approach that creates long-term shareholder value by embracing opportunities and managing risks deriving from economic, environmental and social developments."[13] Specifically, the Dow Jones Sustainability Index looks at competence in five areas:

- *Strategy*: Integrating long-term economic, environmental, and social aspects in their business strategies while maintaining global competitiveness and brand reputation.

- *Financial*: Meeting shareholders' demands for sound financial returns, long-term economic growth, open communication, and transparent financial accounting.

- *Customer and Product*: Fostering loyalty by investing in customer relationship management, and product and service innovation that focuses on technologies and systems, which use financial, natural, and social resources in an efficient, effective, and economic manner over the long term.

- *Governance and Stakeholder*: Setting the highest standards of corporate governance and stakeholder engagement, including corporate codes of conduct and public reporting.

- *Human*: Managing human resources to maintain workforce capabilities and employee satisfaction through best-in-class organizational learning and knowledge management practices and remuneration and benefit programs.

A number of academic authors as well as global management consulting firms like McKinsey and KPMG have written about the pressures facing firms with regard to social and environmental issues. For instance, KPMG's "International Survey of Corporate Responsibility Reporting 2011" reflects the growing importance of corporate responsibility as a key indicator of nonfinancial performance, as well as a driver of financial performance.[14] In the 2011 survey, KPMG noted a significant increase in the publication of corporate responsibility reports in the United States, with 95% of the 250 largest companies reporting their corporate social responsibility. KPMG also noted that large companies not reporting corporate social responsibility activities will soon risk not being as transparent as their competitors and that smaller companies may distinguish themselves from their peers by reporting their corporate social responsibility.

Measuring Corporate Social Performance

Corporate social performance (CSP) reflects the measure of an organization's commitment to individuals, communities, and the natural environment. Although measuring a firm's social responsibility is subjective, this challenge has been addressed by Kinder, Lydenberg and Domini & Co. (KLD), a firm based in Boston that rates businesses on a number of stakeholder-related issues. KLD conducts research on publicly traded firms for various metrics of CSP and reports such statistics to potential investors. Their database provides ratings for each firm's numerous "strengths" and "concerns" along a number of dimensions associated with corporate social performance. The results of KLD's assessment are used to develop a social investments fund and have been used extensively in academic research.[15]

corporate social responsibility (CSR)

How companies manage the business processes to produce an overall positive impact on society.

corporate social performance (CSP)

How companies reflect their commitment to individuals, communities, and the natural environment.

FIGURE 6.7　Measuring Corporate Social Performance

Corporate social performance is defined as the degree to which a firm's actions honor ethical values that respect individuals, communities, and the natural environment. Determining whether a firm is socially responsible is somewhat subjective, but one popular approach has been developed by KLD Research & Analytics. Their work tracks "strengths" and "concerns" for hundreds of firms over time. KLD's findings are used by investors to screen socially responsible firms and by scholars who are interested in explaining corporate social performance. We illustrate the six key dimensions tracked by KLD below.

Community strengths include engagement in charitable giving, while involvement in tax controversies exemplifies a community concern.

Product quality/ safety strengths include actions such as the establishment of a well-developed quality program, while concerns arise if a firm receives fines related to product quality and/or safety.

Diversity strengths include progressive programs for the employment of the disabled, whereas fines or civil penalties that result from an affirmative action constitute a concern.

A no-layoff policy is a strength in regard to **employee relations**, while poor union relations are a concern.

Environmental strengths include engaging in recycling, while concerns arise when penalties for air or water violations are documented.

Corporate governance strengths include equitable levels of compensation for top management and board members, while concerns are raised if controversies related to accounting, transparency, or political accountability are discovered.

Source: Image courtesy of Ketchen, D., & Short, J. (2011). Mastering strategic management. Irvington, NY: Flat World Knowledge.

KEY TAKEAWAY

This section explored the challenges and opportunities of incorporating social and environmental goals and objectives into the P-O-L-C process. Many organizations refer to social and environmental activities as corporate social responsibility (CSR), and measures of such activities are considered corporate social performance (CSP).

EXERCISES

1. What does corporate social responsibility mean?
2. Why might it be challenging for organizations to effectively set and achieve social and environmental goals and objectives, in addition to their operating goals and objectives?
3. Why might an organization pay greater attention to adding social and environmental goals and objectives today than, say, 10 years ago?
4. What is meant by "virtuous cycle" with respect to CSR?
5. How does a Balanced Scorecard help managers develop social and environmental goals and objectives?
6. In what ways does achievement of CSR goals and objectives strategically differentiate an organization?

5. YOUR PERSONAL BALANCED SCORECARD

LEARNING OBJECTIVES

1. **Develop a more personalized understanding of the Balanced Scorecard concept.**
2. **See how your vision and mission can be linked to your goals and objectives.**
3. **Be able to develop S-M-A-R-T goals and objectives.**

One of the powerful tools in a manager's tool kit is the Balanced Scorecard, a model that groups goals, objectives, and metrics into the areas of financial, customer, internal business process, and learning and growth. The scorecard is effective because it helps managers link vision, mission, and strategy to the goals and objectives that employees strive to achieve. The scorecard concept can also be applied to personal and professional objectives, and we illustrate how in this section. Someone who does this regularly is Denise Sullivan Morrison, the CEO of Campbell Soup Company since 2011. She has publicly stated, "I believe that when you have goals you declare them, and I believe in setting long-term goals and working to achieve them. I always had a long-term plan for my career and I was willing to do many different positions along the way to develop the skills to not only get the job, but to be great at the job."[16]

5.1   From an Organizational Scorecard to a Personal One

The Balanced Scorecard can be translated into an individual scorecard that helps in the achievement of personal and professional goals and objectives. An organization's scorecard starts with vision and mission, followed by goals (financial, internal business processes, customer, and learning and growth), which have corresponding objectives, metrics, and tactical activities.

Personal Mission, Vision, and Strategy

As with an organization's mission and vision, your personal mission and vision reflect who you are and where you want to go. Mission reflects your values and philosophy of life. Vision captures what you want to achieve. Which values and principles guide your way? What are your most deeply cherished aspirations? What do you want to achieve? How do you distinguish yourself in society and among your peers and family? If you were to read your biography in 20 years, what would you want it to say about you?

Personal Goals and Key Roles

Goals and roles are set out with respect to the areas of financial, others, individual strengths, and learning and growth. Financial, for instance, captures your needs and aspirations about money, as well as the financial obligations that you might have as a result of your role of caring for a parent, sibling, or child. Others reflect goals that you have in relation to other individuals or society at large. How do you want to be seen? Also, in terms of roles, what do relations with your partner, children, friends, employer, colleagues, and others imply for your goals? Individual strengths represent the internal perspective, reflecting goals related to your health and well-being. This category also reflects those strengths that you wish to be distinguishing features. Finally, learning and growth refer to your skills, abilities, and aims with regard to personal and professional learning and growth. How can you learn and remain successful in the future? What type of skills and learning are required now, for future aspired roles?

5.2   Using SMART Criteria

SMART

A goal that is specific, measurable, aggressive, yet attainable, realistic, and timely.

These portions of the scorecard get more specific in terms of which measurable short-term personal results you want to achieve. What are the most important changes you want to tackle in your career? Similarly, you will want to answer how you can measure your personal results. What values do you have to obtain, and what are your specific targets?

For personal objectives and performance measures to be most effective, you might try seeing how they measure up to SMART criteria. These characteristics—specific, measurable, aggressive yet attainable, realistic, and time bound—yield the acronym SMART.[17] Here is how to tell if your objectives, measures, and targets are SMART.

FIGURE 6.8 Creating SMART Goals

While missions and visions provide an overall sense of the organization's direction, goals are narrower aims that should provide clear and tangible guidance to employees. The most effective goals are those that are SMART (specific, measurable, aggressive, realistic, and time-bound). SMART goals help provide clarity, transparency, and accountability. As detailed below, one SMART goal is Coca-Cola's aim to "by 2012, improve our water efficiency by 20%, compared with a 2004 baseline."

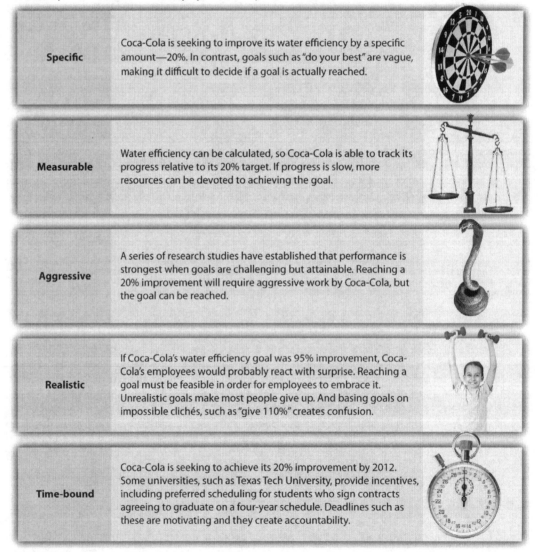

Specific	Coca-Cola is seeking to improve its water efficiency by a specific amount—20%. In contrast, goals such as "do your best" are vague, making it difficult to decide if a goal is actually reached.
Measurable	Water efficiency can be calculated, so Coca-Cola is able to track its progress relative to its 20% target. If progress is slow, more resources can be devoted to achieving the goal.
Aggressive	A series of research studies have established that performance is strongest when goals are challenging but attainable. Reaching a 20% improvement will require aggressive work by Coca-Cola, but the goal can be reached.
Realistic	If Coca-Cola's water efficiency goal was 95% improvement, Coca-Cola's employees would probably react with surprise. Reaching a goal must be feasible in order for employees to embrace it. Unrealistic goals make most people give up. And basing goals on impossible clichés, such as "give 110%" creates confusion.
Time-bound	Coca-Cola is seeking to achieve its 20% improvement by 2012. Some universities, such as Texas Tech University, provide incentives, including preferred scheduling for students who sign contracts agreeing to graduate on a four-year schedule. Deadlines such as these are motivating and they create accountability.

Source: Image courtesy of Ketchen, D., & Short, J. (2011). Mastering strategic management. Irvington, NY: Flat World Knowledge.

Specific

A specific objective has a much greater chance of being accomplished than a general one. To set a specific objective, you must answer the six "W" questions:

- Who: Who is involved?

- What: What do I want to accomplish?
- Where: Identify a location.
- When: Establish a time frame.
- Which: Identify requirements and constraints.
- Why: Specific reasons, purpose or benefits of accomplishing the objective.

For example, a personal goal would be, "Get in shape." But a specific objective would say, "Get into good enough shape that 6 months from now I can hike to the summit of a 14,000-foot mountain and back in one day. To do so, by next Monday I will join a health club within 5 miles of home and work out for at least 45 minutes 3 days a week for 3 months, then reassess my progress."[18]

Measurable

Establish concrete criteria for measuring progress toward the attainment of each objective you set. When you measure your progress, you stay on track, reach your target dates, and experience the exhilaration of achievement that spurs you on to continued effort required to reach your objective.

To determine whether your objective is measurable, ask questions such as: How much? How many? How will I know when it is accomplished? Notice that the specific version of the "get in shape" objective includes metrics of time and distance.

Aggressive Yet Attainable

When you identify objectives that are most important to you, you begin to figure out ways you can make them come true. You develop the attitudes, abilities, skills, and financial capacity to reach them. You begin seeing previously overlooked opportunities to bring yourself closer to the achievement of your goals and objectives.

You can attain most any objective you set when you plan your steps wisely and establish a time frame that allows you to carry out those steps. Goals that may have seemed far away and out of reach eventually move closer and become attainable, not because your goals shrink but because you grow and expand to match them through the achievement of nearer-term objectives. When you list your objectives, you build your self-image. You see yourself as worthy of these goals and objectives and develop the traits and personality that allow you to possess them.

Notice that the "get in shape" example outlines steps toward being able to climb the mountain.

Realistic

To be realistic, an objective must represent an objective toward which you are both willing and able to work. An objective can be both high and realistic; you are the only one who can decide just how high your objective should be. But be sure that every objective represents substantial progress. A high objective is frequently easier to reach than a low one because a low objective exerts low motivational force. Some of the hardest jobs you ever accomplished actually seem easy simply because they were a labor of love.

Your objective is probably realistic if you truly believe that it can be accomplished. Additional ways to know whether your objective is realistic is to determine whether you have accomplished anything similar in the past or ask yourself what conditions would have to exist to accomplish this objective.

You might decide whether an objective to climb a 14,000-foot mountain is realistic by considering whether people of your age and ability have been able to do it.

Time Bound

An objective should be grounded within a time frame. With no time frame tied to it, there's no sense of urgency. If you want to lose 10 pounds, when do you want to lose it by? "Someday" won't work. But if you anchor it within a time frame, "by May 1st," then you've set your unconscious mind into motion to begin working on the objective. SMART goals can also be used to help balance work and life; for example, you might commit to leaving work (a specific action) by 6 p.m. at least three days a week (a specific time period that is realistic and measurable).[19]

T can also stand for *Tangible*. An objective is tangible when you can experience it with one of the senses—that is, taste, touch, smell, sight, or hearing. When your objective is tangible, you have a better chance of making it specific and measurable and thus attainable. The objective of climbing the mountain is both grounded in a time frame—six months from now—and tangible, in that you will either experience climbing the mountain successfully or not.

FIGURE 6.9 Be SMART: Vision, Mission, Goals, and You

Many of the principles for effective organizational vision, missions, and goals apply to individuals too. Here are some ideas that might help you think differently about your own aspirations and how you are working to reach them.

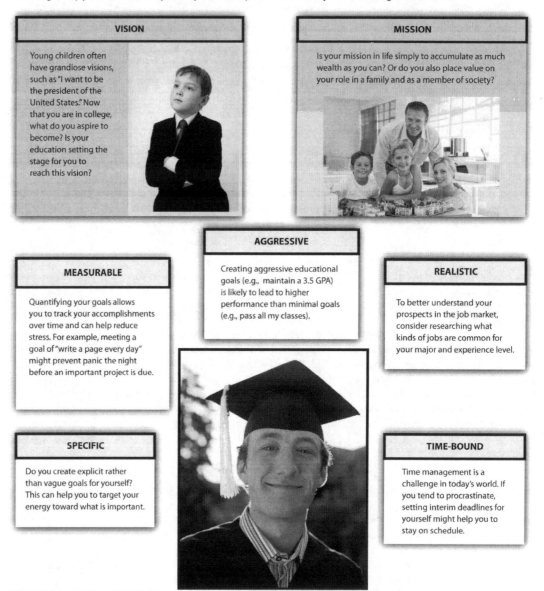

VISION
Young children often have grandiose visions, such as "I want to be the president of the United States." Now that you are in college, what do you aspire to become? Is your education setting the stage for you to reach this vision?

MISSION
Is your mission in life simply to accumulate as much wealth as you can? Or do you also place value on your role in a family and as a member of society?

AGGRESSIVE
Creating aggressive educational goals (e.g., maintain a 3.5 GPA) is likely to lead to higher performance than minimal goals (e.g., pass all my classes).

MEASURABLE
Quantifying your goals allows you to track your accomplishments over time and can help reduce stress. For example, meeting a goal of "write a page every day" might prevent panic the night before an important project is due.

REALISTIC
To better understand your prospects in the job market, consider researching what kinds of jobs are common for your major and experience level.

SPECIFIC
Do you create explicit rather than vague goals for yourself? This can help you to target your energy toward what is important.

TIME-BOUND
Time management is a challenge in today's world. If you tend to procrastinate, setting interim deadlines for yourself might help you to stay on schedule.

Source: Image courtesy of Ketchen, D., & Short, J. (2011). Mastering strategic management. Irvington, NY: Flat World Knowledge.

KEY TAKEAWAY

The purpose of this section was to help you translate the Balanced Scorecard to your own personal and professional situation. You learned how you might construct the scorecard, and take action to achieve personal results. Through this process, you might also learn more about where and how a Balanced Scorecard can be applied in an organizational context in your role as a manager or employee.

6.   CASE IN POINT: NUCOR ALIGNS COMPANY GOALS WITH EMPLOYEE GOALS

FIGURE 6.10

© 2010 Jupiterimages Corporation

The steel manufacturing industry has long been beset by many problems; thus many steel manufacturers have filed for bankruptcy in recent years. Most young employees do not view working at a steel mill as their dream job. Yet one company distinguished itself from all the rest by remaining profitable for over 130 quarters and by providing an over 350% return on investment (ROI) to shareholders. Despite its first year of loss in 2009, the company is clearly doing well by every financial metric available and is the most profitable in its industry.

How do they achieve these amazing results? For one thing, every one of Nucor Corporation's (NYSE: NUE) 20,000 employees behaves like an owner of the company. Employees are treated with dignity and respect, and the company shows its commitment to employees at every turn. For example, when the company was running at 50% capacity in 2009, it still did not lay off any workers or reduce their benefits. Instead, they let go of external contractors, leaving Nucor employees to take care of such tasks as mowing the lawn. In return, employees are expected to act like owners of the company. Specifically, they are encouraged to fix the things they see as wrong and have real power in their jobs. When there is a breakdown in a plant, a supervisor does not have to ask employees to work overtime; employees volunteer for it. In fact, the company is famous for its decentralized structure and for pushing authority and responsibility down to lower levels in the hierarchy. Tasks that previously belonged to management are performed by line workers. Management listens to lower-level employees and routinely implements their new ideas.

The reward system in place at Nucor is also unique, and its employees may be the highest-paid steelworkers in the world. In 2005, the average Nucor employee earned $79,000, followed by a $2,000 bonus decided by the company's annual earnings and $18,000 in the form of profit sharing. At the same time, a large percentage of these earnings are based on performance. People have the opportunity to earn more money if the company is doing well, and there is no upward limit to how much they can make. However, they will do much worse than their counterparts in other mills if the company does poorly. Thus it is to everyone's advantage to help the company perform well. The same incentive system exists at all levels of the company. CEO pay is clearly tied to three-year corporate performance metrics, including return on equity and relative revenue growth. The incentive system penalizes low performers while increasing commitment to the company as well as to high performance.

Nucor's formula for success seems simple: align company goals with employee goals and give employees real power to make things happen. The results seem to work for the company and its employees. Evidence of this successful method is that the company has one of the lowest employee turnover rates in the industry and remains one of the few remaining nonunionized environments in manufacturing. Nucor is the largest U.S. mini-mill with the capacity to produce 26 million tons of new and recycled steel.

Case written by Berrin Erdogan and Talya Bauer to accompany Carpenter, M., Bauer, T., & Erdogan, B., & Short, J. (2013). Principles of management (2nd ed.). New York: Flat World Knowledge. Based on information from Byrnes, N., & Arndt, M. (2006, May 1). The art of motivation. BusinessWeek. Retrieved September 12, 2012, from http://www.businessweek.com/magazine/content/06_18/b3982075.htm; Foust, D. (2008, April 7). The best performers of 2008. BusinessWeek. Retrieved September 12, 2012, from http://www.businessweek.com/magazine/toc/08_14/B4078bw50.htm?chan=magazine+channel_top+stories; Helman, C. (2009, May 11). Test of mettle. Forbes Asia, 5(8); Jennings, J. (2003). Ways to really motivate people: Authenticity is a huge hit with Gen X and Y. The Secured Lender, 59, 62–70; Marks, S. J. (2001). Incentives that really reward and motivate. Workforce, 80, 108–114.

CASE DISCUSSION QUESTIONS

1. How do goals and objectives at Nucor relate to the planning facet of the P-O-L-C framework?
2. What negative consequences might arise at Nucor as a result of tying pay to company performance?
3. What effects does penalizing low performers have on Nucor employees?
4. In addition to monetary incentives, what other ways can a company motivate employees to increase productivity?
5. How might the different reward systems at Nucor, individual empowerment and economic incentives, motivate people differently? Or do they have the same effect?
6. How would unionization at Nucor impact the organization's dynamic?

ENDNOTES

1. Kalargyrou, V., Pescosolido, A., & Kalargiros, E. A. (2012). Leadership skills in management education. *Academy of Educational Leadership Journal, 16*, 39–63.

2. Palmer, T. B., & Short, J. C. (2008). Mission statements in U.S. colleges of business: An empirical examination of their content with linkages to configurations and performance. *Academy of Management Learning and Education, 7*, 454–470.

3. Greenwood, R. G. (1981). Management by objectives: As developed by Peter Drucker, assisted by Harold Smiddy. *Academy of Management Review, 6*, 225–230; Muczyk, J. P., & Reimann, B. C. (1989). MBO as a complement to effective leadership. *Academy of Management Executive, 3*, 131–138; Reif, W. E., & Bassford, G. (1975). What MBO really is: Results require a complete program. *Business Horizons, 16*, 23–30.

4. Rodgers, R., & Hunter, J. E. (1991). Impact of management by objectives on organizational productivity. *Journal of Applied Psychology, 76*, 322–336.

5. Rodgers, R., Hunter, J. E., & Rogers, D. L. (1993). Influence of top management commitment on management program success. *Journal of Applied Psychology, 78*, 151–155.

6. Lindberg, E., & Wilson, T. L. (2011). Management by objectives: The Swedish experience in upper secondary schools. *Journal of Educational Administration, 49*(1), 62–75.

7. Denton, D. K. (2006, March). Measuring relevant things. *Performance Improvement, 45*(3).

8. Rynes, S., Brown, K., & Colbert, A. (2002). Seven common misconceptions about human resource practices: Research findings versus practitioner beliefs. *Academy of Management Executive, 16*(3), 92–102.

9. Aguinis, H., Joo, H., & Gottfredson, R. K. (2011). Why we hate performance management—And why we should love it. *Business Horizons, 54*, 503–507.

10. Rynes, S., Brown, K., & Colbert, A. (2002). Seven common misconceptions about human resource practices: Research findings versus practitioner beliefs. *Academy of Management Executive, 16*(3), 92–102.

11. Allouche, J., & Laroche, P. (2005). A meta-analytic investigation of the relationship between corporate social and financial performance. *Revue de Gestion des Ressources Humaines, 57*, 18–41.

12. Hill, R. P., Ainscough, T., Shank, T., & Manullang, D. (2007). Corporate social responsibility and socially responsible investing: A global perspective. *Journal of Business Ethics, 70*(2), 165–174.

13. Retrieved September 12, 2012, from http://www.sustainability-indexes.com/sustainability-assessment/corporate-sustainability.jsp.

14. Retrieved September 12, 2012, from http://www.kpmg.com/Global/en/IssuesAndInsights/ArticlesPublications/corporate-responsibility/Documents/2011-survey.pdf; Retrieved September 12, 2012, from http://www.csrwire.com/News/13565.html.

15. Cho, S., Lee, C., & Park, C. K. (2012, June). Measuring corporate social responsibility: Certified public accountant. *The CPA Journal, 82*(6), 54–60.

16. Deitsch, R. (2012, September). Soup-er woman: Spelling out Campbell's success strategy. *The Costco Connection.*

17. Drucker, P. (1954). *The Practice of management.* New York: HarperCollins. Drucker coined the usage of the acronym for SMART objectives while discussing objective-based management.

18. We thank Elsa Peterson, our developmental editor, for providing this example based on one of her friend's personal experiences. Another real-life comparable example is shown here: Manochio, M. (2008, September 30). Retrieved September 12, 2012, from http://www.dailyrecord.com/apps/pbcs.dll/article?AID=/20080930/COMMUNITIES12/809300311.

19. Joelle, J. (2011, December). Make your SMART goals WISE goals. *Agency Sales, 41*(11), 36.

CHAPTER 7
Organizational Structure and Change

FIGURE 7.1

The manner in which organizations are structured has important implications for the performance of firms and the individuals within organizations.

© 2010 Jupiterimages Corporation

CHAPTER LEARNING OBJECTIVES

Reading this chapter will help you do the following:

1. Define organizational structure and its basic elements.
2. Describe matrix, boundaryless, and learning organizations.
3. Describe why and how organizations change.
4. Understand reasons why people resist change, and strategies for planning and executing change effectively.
5. Build your own organizational design skills.

FIGURE 7.2 The P-O-L-C Framework

Planning	Organizing	Leading	Controlling
1. Vision & Mission	1. Organization Design	1. Leadership	1. Systems/Processes
2. Strategizing	2. Culture	2. Decision Making	2. Strategic Human Resources
3. Goals & Objectives	3. Social Networks	3. Communications	
		4. Groups/Teams	
		5. Motivation	

Organizational design is one of the three tasks that fall into the organizing function in the planning-organizing-leading-controlling (P-O-L-C) framework. The organization's structure can have a powerful influence on employee actions. This chapter provides details on the types of structures used in organizations and their implications for individual and firm performance.

1. ORGANIZATIONAL STRUCTURE

LEARNING OBJECTIVES

1. Explain the roles of formalization, centralization, levels in the hierarchy, and departmentalization in employee attitudes and behaviors.
2. Describe how the elements of organizational structure can be combined to create mechanistic and organic structures.
3. Understand the advantages and disadvantages of mechanistic and organic structures for organizations.

organizational structure

How individual and team work within an organization are coordinated.

Organizational structure refers to how work is coordinated between individuals and teams within an organization. To achieve organizational goals and objectives, individual work needs to be coordinated and managed. Structure is a valuable tool in achieving coordination, as it specifies reporting relationships (who reports to whom), describes formal communication channels, and explains how separate actions of individuals are linked together. Organizations can function within a number of different structures, each possessing distinct advantages and disadvantages. Although any structure that is not properly managed will have challenges, certain organizational structures are better equipped for particular environments and tasks.

1.1 Building Blocks of Structure

We review four aspects of structure that have been frequently studied in the literature: centralization, formalization, hierarchical levels, and departmentalization. We view these four elements as the building blocks, or elements, making up a company's structure. Then we will examine how these building blocks come together to form two different configurations of structures.

Centralization

centralization

The degree to which decision-making authority is concentrated at higher levels in an organization.

Centralization is the degree to which decision-making authority is concentrated at higher levels in an organization. In centralized companies, many important decisions are made at higher levels of the hierarchy, whereas in decentralized companies, decisions are made and problems are solved at lower levels by employees who are closer to the problem in question.

Decentralized companies give more authority to lower-level employees, resulting in a sense of empowerment. Decisions can be made more quickly, and employees often believe that decentralized companies provide greater levels of procedural fairness to employees. Decentralization is also good for creativity, bringing out the best in employees who have an eagerness to learn new things.[1] Job candidates are more likely to be attracted to decentralized organizations. Because centralized organizations assign decision-making responsibility to higher-level managers, they place greater demands on the judgment capabilities of CEOs and other high-level managers.

Many companies find that the centralization of operations leads to inefficiencies in decision making. For example, in the 1980s, the industrial equipment manufacturer Caterpillar suffered the consequences of centralized decision making. At the time, all pricing decisions were made in the corporate headquarters in Peoria, Illinois. This meant that if a sales representative working in Africa wanted to give a discount on a product, they needed to check with headquarters. Headquarters did not always have accurate or timely information about the subsidiary markets to make an effective decision. As a result, Caterpillar was at a disadvantage against competitors such as the Japanese firm Komatsu. Seeking to overcome this centralization paralysis, Caterpillar underwent several dramatic rounds of reorganization in the 1990s and 2000s.[2] In 2011, Caterpillar had sales and revenues of more than $60 billion. Changing their decision-making approach to a more decentralized style has helped Caterpillar compete at the global level.

Centralization has its advantages. Some employees are more comfortable in an organization where their manager confidently gives instructions and makes decisions. Centralization may also lead to more efficient operations, particularly if the company is operating in a stable environment.[3]

In fact, organizations can suffer from extreme decentralization. For example, some analysts believe that the Federal Bureau of Investigation (FBI) experiences some problems because all its structure and systems are based on the assumption that crime needs to be investigated *after* it happens. Over time, this assumption led to a situation where, instead of following an overarching strategy, each FBI unit is completely decentralized and field agents determine how investigations should be pursued. It has been argued that due to the change in the nature of crimes, the FBI needs to gather accurate intelligence *before* a crime is committed; this requires more centralized decision making and strategy development.[4] Figure 7.3 illustrates the U.S. government's organizational chart. The difficulties faced in coordinating among different branches of government, departments, and thousands of employees highlight the challenges of creating effective organizational structures in which some elements are centralized and others are decentralized.

FIGURE 7.3

The U.S. government's organizational structure is complex yet fairly simple to understand.

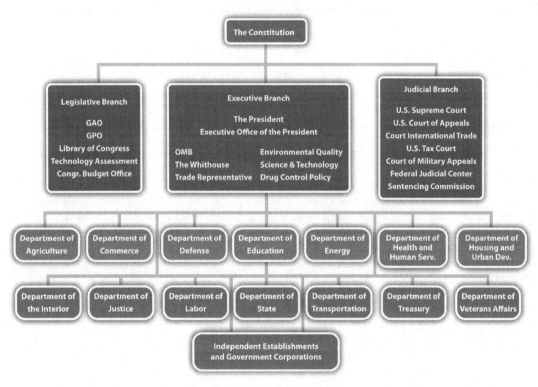

Source: Image courtesy of Ketchen, D., & Short, J. (2011). Mastering strategic management. Irvington, NY: Flat World Knowledge.

Hitting the right balance between decentralization and centralization is a challenge for many organizations as well. At Home Depot, the retail giant with more than 2,200 stores across the United States, Canada, Mexico, and China, one of the major changes instituted by former CEO Bob Nardelli was to centralize most of its operations. Before Nardelli's arrival in 2000, Home Depot store managers made a number of decisions autonomously and each store had an entrepreneurial culture. Nardelli's changes initially saved the company a lot of money. For example, for a company of that size, centralizing purchasing operations led to big cost savings because the company could negotiate important discounts from suppliers. At the same time, many analysts think that the centralization went too far, leading to the loss of the service-oriented culture at the stores. Ultimately, it seemed Home Depot did not feel that Nardelli found the right balance: he was dismissed from the company after seven years.[5]

Formalization

Formalization is the extent to which an organization's policies, procedures, job descriptions, and rules are written and explicitly articulated. Formalized structures are those in which there are many written rules and regulations. These structures control employee behavior using written rules, so that employees have little autonomy to decide on a case-by-case basis. An advantage of formalization is that it makes employee behavior more predictable. Whenever a problem at work arises, employees know to turn to a handbook or a procedure guideline. Therefore, employees respond to problems in a similar way across the organization; this leads to consistency of behavior.

While formalization reduces ambiguity and provides direction to employees, it is not without disadvantages. A high degree of formalization may actually lead to reduced innovativeness because employees are used to behaving in a certain manner. In fact, strategic decision making in such organizations often occurs only when there is a crisis. A formalized structure is associated with reduced motivation and job satisfaction as well as a slower pace of decision making.[6] The service industry is particularly susceptible to problems associated with high levels of formalization. Sometimes employees who are listening to a customer's problems may need to take action, but the answer may not be specified in any procedural guidelines or rulebook. For example, while a handful of airlines such as Southwest do a good job of empowering their employees to handle complaints, in many airlines, lower-level employees have limited power to resolve a customer problem and are constrained by stringent rules that outline a limited number of acceptable responses.

FIGURE 7.4

Peter Gibbons lamented the formalized policy of filling out time-consuming yet unimportant "TPS reports" in the 1999 film *Office Space*.

Source: http://en.wikipedia.org/wiki/ File:RonLivingstonMay10.jpg

Hierarchical Levels

Another important element of a company's structure is the number of levels it has in its hierarchy. In general, **tall structures** have several layers of management between frontline employees and the top level, while **flat structures** consist of only a few layers. In tall structures, the number of employees reporting to each manager tends to be smaller, resulting in greater opportunities for managers to supervise and monitor employee activities. In contrast, flat structures involve a larger number of employees reporting to each manager. In such a structure, managers will be relatively unable to provide close supervision, leading to greater levels of freedom of action for each employee.

Research indicates that flat organizations provide greater satisfaction for employees.[7] At the same time, there may be some challenges associated with flat structures. Research shows that when managers supervise a large number of employees (which is more likely to happen in flat structures), employees experience greater levels of role ambiguity—the confusion that results from being unsure of what is expected of a worker on the job.[8] This is especially a disadvantage for employees who need closer guidance from managers. Moreover, in a flat structure, advancement opportunities will be more limited because there are fewer management layers. Finally, while employees report that flat structures are better at satisfying their higher-order needs such as self-actualization, they also report that tall structures are better at satisfying security needs of employees.[9] Because tall structures are typical in large and well-established companies, it is possible that when working in such organizations employees feel a greater sense of job security.

FIGURE 7.5

Companies such as IKEA, the Swedish furniture manufacturer and retailer, are successfully using flat structures within stores to build an employee attitude of job involvement and ownership.

Source: http://commons.wikimedia.org/wiki/File:IKEA_Regensburg.jpg

Departmentalization

Organizational structures differ in terms of departmentalization, which is broadly categorized as either functional or divisional.

Organizations using **functional structures** group jobs based on similarity in functions. Such structures may have departments such as marketing, manufacturing, finance, accounting, human resources, and information technology. In these structures, each person serves a specialized role and handles large volumes of transactions. For example, in a functional structure, an employee in the marketing department may serve as an event planner, planning promotional events for all the products of the company.

functional structures

Structures in which jobs are grouped based on similarity in functions.

FIGURE 7.6 Functional Structure

Functional structures rely on a division of labor whereby groups of people handle activities related to a specific function of the overall business. We illustrate functional structures in action within two types of organizations that commonly use them.

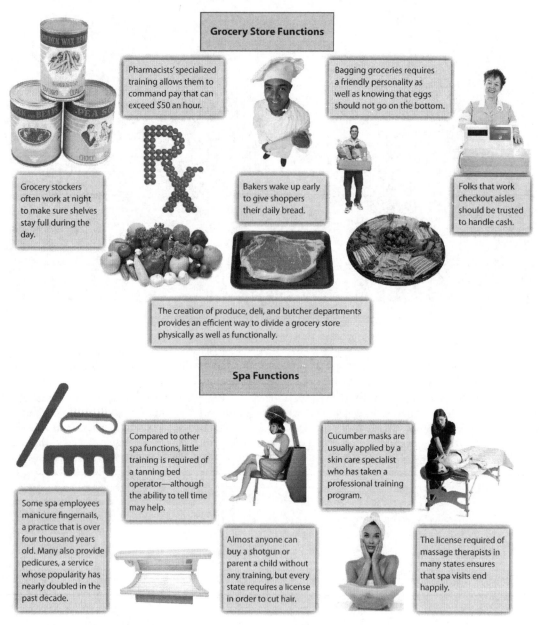

Source: Image courtesy of Ketchen, D., & Short, J. (2011). Mastering strategic management. Irvington, NY: Flat World Knowledge.

divisional structures

When departments represent the unique products, services, customers, or geographic locations the company is serving.

In organizations using **divisional structures**, departments represent the unique products, services, customers, or geographic locations the company is serving. Thus each unique product or service the company is producing will have its own department. Within each department, functions such as marketing, manufacturing, and other roles are replicated. In these structures, employees act like generalists as opposed to specialists. Instead of performing specialized tasks, employees will be in charge of performing many different tasks in the service of the product. For example, a marketing employee in a company with a divisional structure may be in charge of planning promotions, coordinating relations with advertising agencies, and planning and conducting marketing research, all for the particular product line handled by his or her division. General Electric (GE) is an example of a large, multidivisional organization that has enjoyed tremendous success over the past century despite their involvement in numerous different industries.

FIGURE 7.7 Divisional Structure

GE fits a dizzying array of businesses into a relatively simple organizational chart.

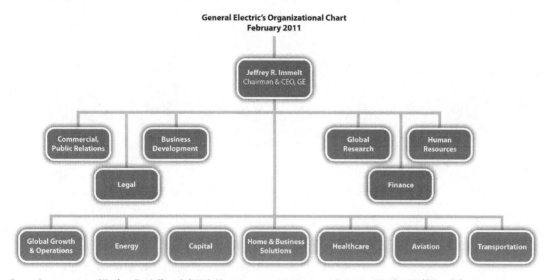

Source: *Image courtesy of Ketchen, D., & Short, J. (2011). Mastering strategic management. Irvington, NY: Flat World Knowledge.*

In reality, many organizations are structured according to a mixture of functional and divisional forms. For example, if the company has multiple product lines, departmentalizing by product may increase innovativeness and reduce response times. Each of these departments may have dedicated marketing, manufacturing, and customer service employees serving the specific product; yet, the company may also find that centralizing some operations and retaining the functional structure makes sense and is more cost effective for roles such as human resources management and information technology. The same organization may also create geographic departments if it is serving different countries.

Each type of departmentalization has its advantages. Functional structures tend to be effective when an organization does not have a large number of products and services requiring special attention. When a company has a diverse product line, each product will have unique demands, deeming divisional (or product-specific) structures more useful for promptly addressing customer demands and anticipating market changes. Functional structures are more effective in stable environments that are slower to change. In contrast, organizations using product divisions are more agile and can perform better in turbulent environments. The type of employee who will succeed under each structure is also different. Research shows that when employees work in product divisions in turbulent environments, because activities are diverse and complex, their performance depends on their general mental abilities.[10]

FIGURE 7.8 An Example of a Pharmaceutical Company with a Functional Departmentalization Structure

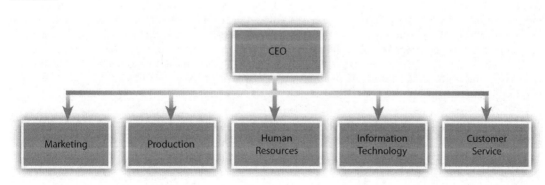

FIGURE 7.9 An Example of a Pharmaceutical Company with a Divisional Departmentalization Structure

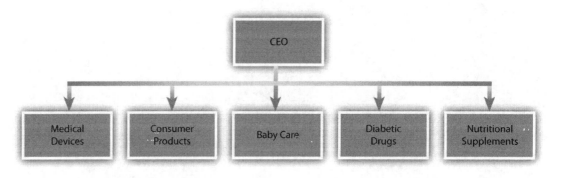

1.2 Two Configurations: Mechanistic and Organic Structures

The different elements making up organizational structures in the form of formalization, centralization, number of levels in the hierarchy, and departmentalization often coexist. As a result, we can talk about two types of organizational structures, depending on how these elements are arranged.

Mechanistic structures are those that resemble a bureaucracy. These structures are highly formalized and centralized. Communication tends to follow formal channels and employees are given specific job descriptions delineating their roles and responsibilities. Mechanistic organizations are often rigid and resist change, making them unsuitable for innovativeness and taking quick action. These forms have the downside of inhibiting entrepreneurial action and discouraging the use of individual initiative on the part of employees. Not only do mechanistic structures have disadvantages for innovativeness, but they also limit individual autonomy and self-determination, which will likely lead to lower levels of intrinsic motivation on the job.[11]

Despite these downsides, however, mechanistic structures have advantages when the environment is more stable. The main advantage of a mechanistic structure is its efficiency. Therefore, in organizations that are trying to maximize efficiency and minimize costs, mechanistic structures provide advantages. For example, McDonald's has a famously bureaucratic structure where employee jobs are highly formalized, with clear lines of communication and specific job descriptions. This structure is an advantage for them because it allows McDonald's to produce a uniform product around the world at minimum cost. Mechanistic structures can also be advantageous when a company is new. New businesses often suffer from a lack of structure, role ambiguity, and uncertainty. The presence of a mechanistic structure has been shown to be related to firm performance in new ventures.[12]

In contrast to mechanistic structures, **organic structures** are flexible and decentralized, with low levels of formalization. In organizations with an organic structure, communication lines are more fluid and flexible. Employee job descriptions are broader and employees are asked to perform duties based on the specific needs of the organization at the time as well as their own expertise levels. Organic structures tend to be related to higher levels of job satisfaction on the part of employees. These structures are conducive to entrepreneurial behavior and innovativeness.[13] An example of a company that has an organic structure is the diversified technology company 3M. The company is strongly committed to decentralization. At 3M, there are close to 100 profit centers, with each division feeling like a small company. Each division manager acts autonomously and is accountable for his or her actions. As operations within each division get too big and a product created by a division becomes profitable, the operation is spun off to create a separate business unit. This is done to protect the agility of the company and the small-company atmosphere.[14]

KEY TAKEAWAY

The degree to which a company is centralized and formalized, the number of levels in the company hierarchy, and the type of departmentalization the company uses are key elements of a company's structure. These elements of structure affect the degree to which the company is effective and innovative as well as employee attitudes and behaviors at work. These elements come together to create mechanistic and organic structures. Mechanistic structures are rigid and bureaucratic and help companies achieve efficiency, while organic structures are decentralized, flexible, and aid companies in achieving innovativeness.

EXERCISES

1. What are the advantages and disadvantages of decentralization?
2. All else being equal, would you prefer to work in a tall or flat organization? Why?
3. What are the advantages and disadvantages of departmentalization by product?

2. CONTEMPORARY FORMS OF ORGANIZATIONAL STRUCTURES

LEARNING OBJECTIVES

1. **Explain what a matrix structure is and the challenges of working in a structure such as this.**
2. **Define boundaryless organizations.**
3. **Define learning organizations, and list the steps organizations can take to become learning organizations.**

For centuries, technological advancements that affected business came in slow waves. Over 100 years passed between the invention of the first reliable steam engine and the first practical internal combustion engine. During these early days of advancement, communication would often go hand in hand with transportation. Instead of delivering mail hundreds of miles by horse, messages could be transported more quickly by train and then later by plane. Beginning in the 1900s, the tides of change began to rise much more quickly. From the telegraph to the telephone to the computer to the Internet, each advancement brought about a need for an organization's structure to adapt and change. While earlier organizations often involved the work of individuals (such as masons or blacksmiths) or small family businesses (such as taverns and inns), the Industrial Revolution created the need to manage thousands of employees on a regular basis.

Business has become global, moving into new economies and cultures. Industries that were not even in existence a century ago (such as those related to high technology) demand flexibility by organizations in ways never before seen. The diverse and complex nature of the current business environment has led to the emergence of several types of organizational structures. Beginning in the 1970s, management experts began to propose organizational designs that they believed were better adapted to the needs of the emerging business environment. Each structure has unique qualities to help businesses handle their particular environment.

2.1 Matrix Organizations

Matrix organizations have a design that combines a traditional functional structure with a product structure. Instead of completely switching from a product-based structure, a company may use a matrix structure to balance the benefits of product-based and traditional functional structures. Specifically, employees reporting to department managers are also pooled together to form project or product teams. As a result, each person reports to a department manager as well as a project or product manager. In a matrix structure, product managers have control and say over product-related matters, while department managers have authority over matters related to company policy. Matrix structures are created in response to uncertainty and dynamism of the environment and the need to give particular attention to specific products or projects. Using the matrix structure as opposed to product departments may increase communication and cooperation among departments because project managers will need to coordinate their actions with those of department managers. In fact, research shows that matrix structure increases the frequency of informal and formal communication within the organization.[15] Matrix structures also have the benefit of providing quick responses to technical problems and customer demands. The existence of a project manager keeps the focus on the product or service provided.

matrix organizations

Organizations that cross a traditional functional structure with a product structure. Specifically, employees reporting to department managers are also pooled together to form project or product teams.

FIGURE 7.10

An example of a matrix structure at a software development company. Business analysts, developers, and testers each report to a functional department manager and to a project manager simultaneously.

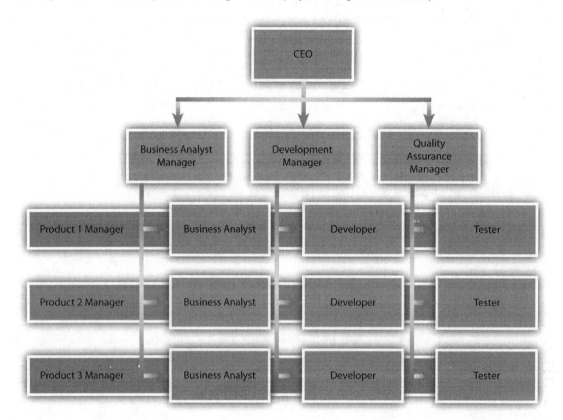

Despite these potential benefits, matrix structures are not without costs. In a matrix, each employee reports to two or more managers. In the movie *Office Space*, the matrix structure is parodied at the fictitious software firm Initech, where Peter Gibbons claims to have eight bosses. Although exaggerated in the film, this situation is ripe for conflict in matrix structures. Because multiple managers are in charge of guiding the behaviors of each employee, there may be power struggles or turf wars among managers. As managers are more interdependent compared to a traditional or product-based structure, they will need to spend more effort coordinating their work. From the employee's perspective, there is potential for interpersonal conflict with team members as well as with leaders. The presence of multiple leaders may create role ambiguity or, worse, role conflict—being given instructions or objectives that cannot all be met because they are mutually exclusive. The necessity to work with a team consisting of employees with different functional backgrounds increases the potential for task conflict at work.[16] Solving these problems requires a great level of patience and proactivity on the part of the employee.

The matrix structure is used in many information technology companies engaged in software development. Sportswear manufacturer Nike is another company that uses the matrix organization successfully. New product introduction is a task shared by regional managers and product managers. While product managers are in charge of deciding how to launch a product, regional managers are allowed to make modifications based on the region.[17]

2.2 Boundaryless Organizations

Boundaryless organization is a term coined by Jack Welch during his tenure as CEO of GE; it refers to an organization that eliminates traditional barriers between departments as well as barriers between the organization and the external environment.[18] Many different types of boundaryless organizations exist. One form is the **modular organization**, in which all nonessential functions are outsourced. The idea behind this format is to retain only the value-generating and strategic functions in-house, while the rest of the operations are outsourced to many suppliers. An example of a company that does this is Toyota. By managing relationships with hundreds of suppliers, Toyota achieves efficiency and quality in its operations. **Strategic alliances** constitute another form of boundaryless design. In this form, similar to a joint venture, two or more companies find an area of collaboration and combine their efforts to create a partnership that is beneficial for both parties. In the process, the traditional boundaries between two competitors may be broken. As an example, Starbucks formed a highly successful partnership with PepsiCo to market its Frappuccino cold drinks. Starbucks has immediate brand-name recognition in this cold coffee drink, but its desire to capture shelf space in supermarkets required marketing savvy and experience that Starbucks did not possess at the time. By partnering with PepsiCo, Starbucks gained an important head start in the marketing and distribution of this product. Finally, boundaryless organizations may involve eliminating the barriers separating employees; these may be intangible barriers, such as traditional management layers, or actual physical barriers, such as walls between different departments. Structures such as self-managing teams create an environment where employees coordinate their efforts and change their own roles to suit the demands of the situation, as opposed to insisting that something is "not my job."[19]

boundaryless organization

An organization that eliminates traditional barriers between departments as well as barriers between the organization and the external environment.

modular organization

An organization where all the nonessential functions are outsourced.

strategic alliances

A form of boundaryless design where two or more companies find an area of collaboration and combine their efforts to create a partnership that is beneficial for all parties.

2.3 Learning Organizations

A learning organization is one whose design actively seeks to acquire knowledge and change behavior as a result of the newly acquired knowledge. In learning organizations, experimenting, learning new things, and reflecting on new knowledge are the norms. At the same time, there are many procedures and systems in place that facilitate learning at all organization levels.

In learning organizations, experimentation and testing potentially better operational methods are encouraged. This is true not only in response to environmental threats but also as a way of identifying future opportunities. 3M is one company that institutionalized experimenting with new ideas in the form of allowing each engineer to spend one day a week working on a personal project. At IBM, learning is encouraged by taking highly successful business managers and putting them in charge of emerging business opportunities (EBOs). IBM is a company that has no difficulty coming up with new ideas, as evidenced by the number of patents it holds. Yet commercializing these ideas has been a problem in the past because of an emphasis on short-term results. To change this situation, the company began experimenting with the idea of EBOs. By setting up a structure where failure is tolerated and risk taking is encouraged, the company took a big step toward becoming a learning organization.[20]

Learning organizations are also good at learning from experience—their own or a competitor's. To learn from past mistakes, companies conduct a thorough analysis of them. Some companies choose to conduct formal retrospective meetings to analyze the challenges encountered and areas for improvement. To learn from others, these companies vigorously study competitors, market leaders in different industries, clients, and customers. By benchmarking against industry best practices, they constantly look for ways of improving their own operations. Learning organizations are also good at studying customer habits to generate ideas. For example, Xerox uses anthropologists to understand and gain insights to how customers are actually using their office products.[21] By using these techniques, learning organizations facilitate innovation and make it easier to achieve organizational change.

KEY TAKEAWAY

The changing environment of organizations creates the need for newer forms of organizing. Matrix structures are a cross between functional and product-based divisional structures. They facilitate information flow and reduce response time to customers but have challenges because each employee reports to multiple managers. Boundaryless organizations blur the boundaries between departments or the boundaries between the focal organization and others in the environment. These organizations may take the form of a modular organization, strategic alliance, or self-managing teams. Learning organizations institutionalize experimentation and benchmarking.

3. ORGANIZATIONAL CHANGE

LEARNING OBJECTIVES

1. **Identify the external forces creating change on the part of organizations.**
2. **Understand how organizations respond to changes in the external environment.**
3. **Understand why people resist change.**

3.1 Why Do Organizations Change?

organizational change

The movement of an organization from one state of affairs to another.

Organizational change is the movement of an organization from one state of affairs to another. A change in the environment (such as a stock market drop or a dramatic change in technology) often requires change within the organization operating within that environment. Change in almost any aspect of a company's operation can be met with resistance, and different cultures can have different reactions to both the change and the means to promote the change. To better facilitate necessary changes, several steps can be taken that have been proved to lower the anxiety of employees and ease the transformation process. Often, the simple act of including employees in the change process can drastically reduce opposition to new methods. In some organizations, this level of inclusion is not possible, and instead organizations can recruit a small number of opinion leaders to promote the benefits of coming changes.

Organizational change can take many forms. It may involve a change in a company's structure, strategy, policies, procedures, technology, or culture. The change may be planned years in advance or may be forced on an organization because of a shift in the environment. Organizational change can be radical and swiftly alter the way an organization operates, or it may be incremental and slow. In any case, regardless of the type, change involves letting go of the old ways in which work is done and adjusting to new ways. Therefore, fundamentally, it is a process that involves effective people management.

Managers carrying out any of the P-O-L-C functions often find themselves faced with the need to manage organizational change effectively. Oftentimes, the planning process reveals the need for a new or improved strategy, which is then reflected in changes to tactical and operational plans. Creating a new organizational design (the organizing function) or altering the existing design entails changes that may affect from a single employee up to the entire organization, depending on the scope of the changes. Effective decision making, a Leadership task, takes into account the change-management implications of decisions, planning for the need to manage the implementation of decisions. Finally, any updates to controlling systems and processes will potentially involve changes to employees' assigned tasks and performance assessments, which will require astute change management skills to implement. In short, change management is an important leadership skill that spans the entire range of P-O-L-C functions.

Workplace Demographics

Organizational change is often a response to changes to the environment. For example, agencies that monitor workplace demographics such as the U.S. Department of Labor and the Organization for Economic Co-operation and Development have reported that the average age of the U.S. workforce will increase as the baby boom generation nears retirement age and the numbers of younger workers are insufficient to fill the gap.[22] What does this mean for companies? Organizations may realize that as the workforce gets older, the types of benefits workers prefer may change. Work arrangements such as flexible work hours and job sharing may become more popular as employees remain in the workforce even after retirement. It is also possible that employees who are unhappy with their current work situation will choose to retire, resulting in a sudden loss of valuable knowledge and expertise in

FIGURE 7.11

British insurance giant Lloyd's of London has seen dramatic change from its humble beginnings as a coffee house in 1688.

© Thinkstock

organizations. Therefore, organizations will have to devise strategies to retain these employees and plan for their retirement. Finally, a critical issue is finding ways of dealing with age-related stereotypes which act as barriers in the retention of these employees.

Technology

Sometimes change is motivated by rapid developments in technology. Moore's law (a prediction by Gordon Moore, cofounder of Intel) dictates that the overall complexity of computers will double every 18 months with no increase in cost.[23] Such change is motivating corporations to change their technology rapidly. Sometimes technology produces such profound developments that companies struggle to adapt. A recent example is from the music industry. When music CDs were first introduced in the 1980s, they were substantially more appealing than the traditional LP vinyl records. Record companies were easily able to double the prices, even though producing CDs cost a fraction of what it cost to produce LPs. For decades, record-producing companies benefited from this status quo. Yet when peer-to-peer file sharing through software such as Napster and Kazaa threatened the core of their business, companies in the music industry found themselves completely unprepared for such disruptive technological changes. Their first response was to sue the users of file-sharing software. They also investigated ways to make it impossible to copy a CD or DVD. Until Apple's iTunes came up with a new way to sell music online, it was doubtful that consumers would ever be willing to pay for music that was otherwise available for free (albeit illegally so).

Globalization

Globalization can be either a threat or an opportunity for organizations, depending on their ability to adapt to relevant changes. Because of differences in national economies and standards of living from one country to another, organizations in developed countries are finding that it is often cheaper to produce goods and deliver services in less-developed countries. This has led many companies to outsource (or "offshore") their manufacturing operations to countries such as China and Mexico. In the 1990s, knowledge work was thought to be safe from outsourcing, but in the 21st century we are also seeing many service operations moved to places with cheaper wages. For example, many companies have outsourced software development to India, with Indian companies such as Wipro and Infosys emerging as global giants. Given these changes, understanding how to manage a global workforce is a necessity. Many companies realize that outsourcing forces them to operate in an institutional environment that is radically different from what they are used to at home. Many companies are now dealing with employee stress resulting from jobs being moved overseas.

Changes in the Market Conditions

Market changes may also create internal changes as companies struggle to adjust. For example, tobacco companies faced dramatic changes and threats to their products as the harmful effects of tobacco became well known. The market forces they face today are dramatically different from the times when they were able to take advantage of the 1920s women's liberation movement and encourage women to smoke under the slogan "torches of freedom." Similar changes are occurring in fast food and snack markets in response to the increasing health consciousness of customers, forcing businesses to consider healthier alternatives to their products and diversify their operations; for example, McDonald's now offers apple slices rather than fries in children's Happy Meals. How does a change in the environment create change within an organization? Environmental change does not automatically change how business is done. Whether the organization changes or not in response to environmental challenges and threats depends on the decision makers' reactions to what is happening in the environment.

FIGURE 7.12

Worker needs and health benefits may change in the United States as the workforce ages.

© *Thinkstock*

FIGURE 7.13

Kurzweil expanded Moore's law (the idea that technology speed nearly doubles every two years) from integrated circuits to earlier technologies, such as transistors, vacuum tubes, relays, and electromechanical computers, to show that his trend applies there as well.

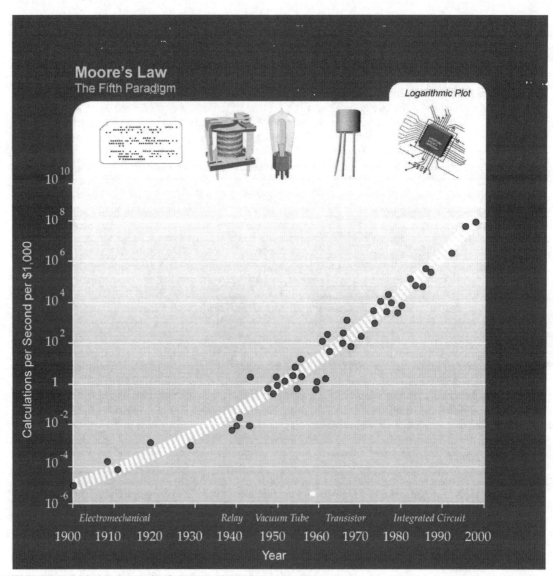

Source: http://upload.wikimedia.org/wikipedia/commons/c/c5/PPTMooresLawai.jpg

Growth

It is natural for small start-up companies to grow as they become successful. An example of this growth is the evolution of the Widmer Brothers Brewing Company, which grew from two brothers brewing beer in their garage to become the ninth largest brewery in the United States by 2012. This growth happened over time as the popularity of their key product—Hefeweizen—grew in popularity and the company had to expand to meet demand. In 2007, Widmer Brothers merged with Redhook Ale Brewery. Anheuser-Busch continues to have a minority stake in both beer companies. So, while 50% of all new small businesses fail in their first year,[24] those that succeed have the potential to evolve into large, complex organizations over time.

Poor Performance

Change can also occur if the company is performing poorly and if there is a perceived threat from the environment. In fact, poorly performing companies often find it easier to change compared with successful companies when high performance leads to overconfidence and failure to change. As a result, successful companies often keep doing what made them successful in the first place. When it comes to the relationship between company performance and organizational change, the saying "nothing fails like success" may be fitting. To combat this potential problem, Finnish cell phone maker Nokia finds that it is important to periodically change the perspective of key decision makers. For this purpose, they rotate heads of businesses to different posts to give them a fresh perspective. In addition to the success of a business, change in a company's upper-level management is a motivator for change at the organization level. Research shows that long-tenured CEOs are unlikely to change their formula for success. Instead, new CEOs and new top management teams create change in a company's culture and structure.[25]

3.2   Resistance to Change

Changing an organization is often essential for a company to remain competitive. Failure to change may influence the ability of a company to survive. Yet employees do not always welcome changes in methods. According to a 2007 survey conducted by the Society for Human Resource Management (SHRM), employee resistance to change is one of the top reasons change efforts fail. In fact, reactions to organizational change may range from resistance to compliance to enthusiastic support of the change, with the latter being the exception rather than the norm.[26]

FIGURE 7.14

In 1984, brothers Kurt (on the left) and Rob Widmer (on the right) quit their jobs and founded Widmer Brothers Brewery. These types of "garage" start-ups tend to increase during economic downturns.

Source: Photo and permission given by Widmer Brothers Brewing Co.

FIGURE 7.15

Reactions to change may take many forms.

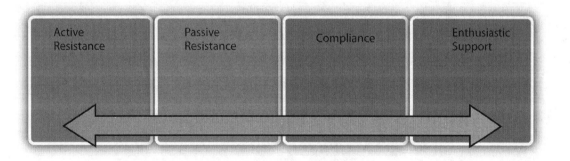

Active resistance is the most negative reaction to a proposed change attempt. Those who engage in active resistance may sabotage the change effort and be outspoken objectors to the new procedures. In contrast, **passive resistance** involves being disturbed by changes without necessarily voicing these opinions. Instead, passive resisters may dislike the change quietly, feel stressed and unhappy, and even look for a new job without necessarily bringing their concerns to the attention of decision makers. **Compliance**, however, involves going along with proposed changes with little enthusiasm. Finally, those who show **enthusiastic support** are defenders of the new way and actually encourage others around them to give support to the change effort as well.

To be successful, any change attempt will need to overcome resistance on the part of employees. Otherwise, the result will be loss of time and energy as well as an inability on the part of the organization to adapt to the changes in the environment and make its operations more efficient. Resistance to change also has negative consequences for the people in question. Research shows that when people react negatively to organizational change, they experience negative emotions, use sick time more often, and are more likely to voluntarily leave the company.[27] These negative effects can be present even when the proposed change clearly offers benefits and advantages over the status quo.

Figure 7.16 is a dramatic example of how resistance to change may prevent improving the status quo. Have you ever wondered why the keyboards we use are shaped the way they are? The QWERTY keyboard, named after the first six letters in the top row, was actually engineered to slow us down. When the typewriter was first invented in the 19th century, the first prototypes of the keyboard would jam if the keys right next to each other were hit at the same time. Therefore, it was important for manufacturers to slow typists down. They achieved this by putting the most commonly used letters to the left-hand side and scattering the most frequently used letters all over the keyboard. Later, the issue of letters being stuck was resolved. In fact, an alternative to the QWERTY developed in the 1930s by educational psychologist August Dvorak provides a much more efficient design and allows individuals to double traditional typing speeds. Yet the Dvorak keyboard never gained wide acceptance. The reasons? Large numbers of people resisted the change. Teachers and typists resisted because they would lose their specialized knowledge. Manufacturers resisted due to costs inherent in making the switch and the initial inefficiencies in the learning curve.[28] In short, the best idea does not necessarily win, and changing people requires understanding why they resist.

FIGURE 7.16

The Dvorak keyboard, shown here, is an efficient alternative to the standard keyboard design in use today. However, due to resistance from typists, teachers, manufacturers, and salespeople, a switch never occurred.

© 2010 Jupiterimages Corporation

3.3 Why Do People Resist Change?

Disrupted Habits

People often resist change for the simple reason that change disrupts our habits. When many individuals hop into their cars for the daily commute to work, little thought is given to their driving because the activity has become routine over time. Individuals may even realize they have reached their destination without noticing the roads used or without conscious thoughts about body movements. Now imagine driving a truck cross-country. The loss of familiar habits and patterns would be jarring given the changes in vehicle, road conditions, purpose, and goals of driving. For this simple reason, people are

Goals   Brandon Tangray

- Graduate with high GPA, earn an MBA

- Possibly earn a CPA

- Get involved in Real Estate

- Own my own business within 7 years

sometimes surprisingly outspoken when confronted with simple changes such as updating to a newer version of a particular software or a change in their voice mail system.

Personality

Some people are more resistant to change than others. Recall that one of the Big Five personality traits is Openness to Experience; people who rank high on this trait will tend to accept change readily. Research also shows that people who have a positive self-concept are better at coping with change, probably because those who have high self-esteem may feel that whatever the changes are, they are likely to adjust to it well and be successful in the new system. People with a more positive self-concept and those who are more optimistic may also view change as an opportunity to shine as opposed to a threat that is overwhelming. Finally, risk tolerance is another predictor of how resistant someone will be to stress. For people who are risk avoidant, the possibility of a change in technology or structure may be more threatening.[29]

Feelings of Uncertainty

Change inevitably brings feelings of uncertainty. Perhaps you just found out that a class you need to graduate was cancelled. What would be your reaction? Such change is often turbulent, and it is often unclear what is going to happen to each individual. The ultimate outcome may be better—or it may be worse. The feeling that the future is unclear is enough to create stress for people because it leads to a sense of lost control and requires greater attention and problem-solving effort.[30]

Fear of Failure

People also resist change when they feel that their performance may be affected under the new system. People who are experts in their jobs may be less than welcoming of the changes because they may be unsure whether their success would last under the new system. Studies show that people who feel that they can perform well under the new system are more likely to be committed to the proposed change, while those who have lower confidence in their ability to perform after changes are less committed.[31]

Personal Impact of Change

It would be too simplistic to argue that people resist all change, regardless of its form. In fact, people tend to be more welcoming of change that is favorable to them on a personal level (such as giving them more power over others or change that improves quality of life such as bigger and nicer offices). Research also shows that commitment to change is highest when proposed changes affect the work unit with a low impact on how individual jobs are performed.[32]

Prevalence of Change

Any change effort should be considered within the context of all the other changes that are introduced in a company. Does the company have a history of making short-lived changes? If the company structure went from functional to product-based to geographic to matrix within the past five years and the top management is in the process of going back to a functional structure again, a certain level of resistance is to be expected because employees are likely to be fatigued as a result of the constant changes. Moreover, the lack of a history of successful changes may cause people to feel skeptical toward the newly planned changes. Therefore, considering the history of changes in the company is important to understanding why people resist. The size of the change is also an important factor. If the company is considering a simple switch to a new computer program, such as introducing Microsoft Access for database management, the change may not be as extensive or stressful compared with a switch to an enterprise resource planning (ERP) system such as SAP or PeopleSoft, which require a significant time commitment and can fundamentally affect how business is conducted.[33]

Perceived Loss of Power

One other reason people may resist change is that change may affect their power and influence in the organization. Imagine that your company moved to a more team-based structure, turning supervisors into team leaders. In the old structure, supervisors were in charge of hiring and firing all those reporting to them. Under the new system, this power is given to the team. Instead of monitoring the progress the team is making toward goals, the job of a team leader is to provide support and mentoring to the team in general and ensure that the team has access to all resources to be effective. Given the loss in prestige and status in the new structure, some supervisors may resist the proposed changes even if it is better for the organization to operate around teams.

FIGURE 7.17

Baseball icon Babe Ruth once said, "Never let the fear of striking out get in your way." Ruth is an excellent example of someone confident in the face of change, as he originally entered baseball as a pitcher, not the star hitter he ultimately became.

Source: http://en.wikipedia.org/wiki/ File:Babe_Ruth2.jpg

3.4 Is All Resistance Bad?

Resistance to change may be a positive force in some instances. In fact, resistance to change is a valuable feedback tool that should not be ignored. Why are people resisting the proposed changes? Do they believe that the new system will not work? If so, why not? By listening to people and incorporating their suggestions into the change effort, it is possible to make a more effective change. Some of a company's most committed employees may be the most vocal opponents of a change effort. They may fear that the organization they feel such a strong attachment to is being threatened by the planned change effort and the change will ultimately hurt the company. In contrast, people who have less loyalty to the organization may comply with the proposed changes simply because they do not care enough about the fate of the company to oppose the changes. As a result, when dealing with those who resist change, it is important to avoid blaming them for a lack of loyalty.[34]

KEY TAKEAWAY

Organizations change in response to changes in the environment and in response to the way decision makers interpret these changes. When it comes to organizational change, one of the biggest obstacles is resistance to change. People resist change because change disrupts habits, conflicts with certain personality types, causes a fear of failure, can have potentially negative effects, can result in a potential for loss of power, and, when done too frequently, can exhaust employees.

EXERCISES

1. Can you think of an organizational or personal change that you had to go through? Have you encountered any resistance to this change? What were the reasons?
2. How would you deal with employees who are resisting change because their habits are threatened? How would you deal with them if they are resisting because of a fear of failure?

---

4. PLANNING AND EXECUTING CHANGE EFFECTIVELY

LEARNING OBJECTIVES

1. **Describe Lewin's three-stage model of planned change.**
2. **Describe how organizations may embrace continuous change.**

How do you plan, organize, and execute change effectively? Some types of change, such as mergers, often come with job losses. In these situations, it is important to remain fair and ethical while laying off otherwise exceptional employees. Once change has occurred, it is vital to take any steps necessary to reinforce the new system. Employees can often require continued support well after an organizational change.

One of the most useful frameworks in this area is the three-stage model of planned change developed in the 1950s by psychologist Kurt Lewin.[35] This model assumes that change will encounter resistance. Therefore, executing change without prior preparation is likely to lead to failure. Instead, organizations should start with **unfreezing**, or making sure that organizational members are ready for and receptive to change. This is followed by **change**, or executing the planned changes. Finally, **refreezing** involves ensuring that change becomes permanent and the new habits, rules, or procedures become the norm.

unfreezing

Making sure that organizational members are ready for and receptive to change.

change

Executing the planned changes.

refreezing

Ensuring that change becomes permanent and the new habits, rules, or procedures become the norm.

FIGURE 7.18 Lewin's Three-Stage Process of Change

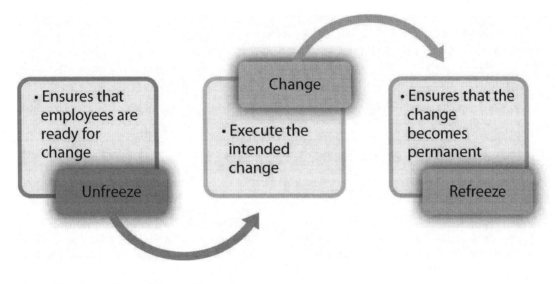

4.1   Unfreezing before Change

Many change efforts fail because people are insufficiently prepared for change. When employees are not prepared, they are more likely to resist the change effort and less likely to function effectively under the new system. What can organizations do before change to prepare employees? There are a number of things that are important at this stage.

Communicate a Plan for Change

Do people know what the change entails, or are they hearing about the planned changes through the grapevine or office gossip? When employees know what is going to happen, when, and why, they may feel more comfortable. Research shows that those who have more complete information about upcoming changes are more committed to a change effort.[36] Moreover, in successful change efforts, the leader not only communicates a plan but also an overall vision for the change.[37] When this vision is exciting and paints a picture of a future that employees would be proud to be a part of, people are likely to be more committed to change.

Ensuring that top management communicates with employees about the upcoming changes also has symbolic value.[38] When top management and the company CEO discuss the importance of the changes in meetings, employees are provided with a reason to trust that this change is a strategic initiative. For example, while changing the employee performance appraisal system, the CEO of Kimberly Clark made sure to mention the new system in all meetings with employees, indicating that the change was supported by the CEO.

Develop a Sense of Urgency

People are more likely to accept change if they feel that there is a need for it. If employees feel their company is doing well, the perceived need for change will be smaller. Those who plan the change will need to make the case that there is an external or internal threat to the organization's competitiveness, reputation, or sometimes even its survival and that failure to act will have undesirable consequences. For example, Lou Gerstner, the former CEO of IBM, executed a successful transformation of the company in the early 1990s. In his biography *Elephants Can Dance*, Gerstner highlights how he achieved cooperation as follows: "Our greatest ally in shaking loose the past was IBM's eminent collapse. Rather than go with the usual impulse to put on a happy face, I decided to keep the crisis front and center. I didn't want to lose the sense of urgency."[39]

Build a Coalition

To convince people that change is needed, the change leader does not necessarily have to convince every person individually. In fact, people's opinions toward change are affected by opinion leaders or those people who have a strong influence over the behaviors and attitudes of others.[40] Instead of trying to get everyone on board at the same time, it may be more useful to convince and prepare the opinion leaders. Understanding one's own social networks as well as the networks of others in the organization can help managers identify opinion leaders. Once these individuals agree that the proposed change is needed and will be useful, they will become helpful allies in ensuring that the rest of the organization is ready for change.[41]

Provide Support

Employees should feel that their needs are not ignored. Therefore, management may prepare employees for change by providing emotional and instrumental support. Emotional support may be in the form of frequently discussing the changes, encouraging employees to voice their concerns, and simply expressing confidence in employees' ability to perform effectively under the new system. Instrumental support may be in the form of providing a training program to employees so that they know how to function under the new system. Effective leadership and motivation skills can assist managers to provide support to employees.

Allow Employees to Participate

Studies show that employees who participate in planning change efforts tend to have more positive opinions about the change. Why? They will have the opportunity to voice their concerns. They can shape the change effort so that their concerns are addressed. They will be more knowledgeable about the reasons for change, alternatives to the proposed changes, and why the chosen alternative was better than the others. Finally, they will feel a sense of ownership of the planned change and are more likely to be on board.[42] Participation may be more useful if it starts at earlier stages, preferably while the problem is still being diagnosed. For example, assume that a company suspects there are problems with manufacturing quality. One way of convincing employees that there is a problem that needs to be solved would be to ask them to take customer calls about the product quality. Once employees experience the problem firsthand, they will be more motivated to solve the problem.

4.2 Executing Change

The second stage of Lewin's three-stage change model is executing change. At this stage, the organization implements the planned changes on technology, structure, culture, or procedures. The specifics of how change should be executed will depend on the type of change. However, there are three tips that may facilitate the success of a change effort.

Continue to Provide Support

As the change is under way, employees may experience high amounts of stress. They may make mistakes more often or experience uncertainty about their new responsibilities or job descriptions. Management has an important role in helping employees cope with this stress by displaying support, patience, and continuing to provide support to employees even after the change is complete.

Create Small Wins

During a change effort, if the organization can create a history of small wins, change acceptance will be more likely.[43] If the change is large in scope and the payoff is a long time away, employees may not realize change is occurring during the transformation period. However, if people see changes, improvements, and successes along the way, they will be inspired and motivated to continue the change effort. For this reason, breaking up the proposed change into phases may be a good idea because it creates smaller targets. Small wins are also important for planners of change to make the point that their idea is on the right track. Early success gives change planners more credibility while early failures may be a setback.[44]

Eliminate Obstacles

When the change effort is in place, many obstacles may crop up along the way. There may be key people who publicly support the change effort while silently undermining the planned changes. There may be obstacles rooted in a company's structure, existing processes, or culture. It is the management's job to identify, understand, and remove these obstacles.[45] Ideally, these obstacles would have been eliminated before implementing the change, but sometimes unexpected roadblocks emerge as change is under way.

4.3 Refreezing

After the change is implemented, the long-term success of a change effort depends on the extent to which the change becomes part of the company's culture. If the change has been successful, the revised ways of thinking, behaving, and performing should become routine. To evaluate and reinforce ("refreeze") the change, there are a number of things management can do.

Publicize Success

To make change permanent, the organization may benefit from sharing the results of the change effort with employees. What was gained from the implemented changes? How much money did the company save? How much did the company's reputation improve? What was the reduction in accidents after new procedures were put in place? Sharing concrete results with employees increases their confidence that the implemented change was a right decision.

Reward Change Adoption

To ensure that change becomes permanent, organizations may benefit from rewarding those who embrace the change effort (an aspect of the controlling function). The rewards do not necessarily have to be financial. The simple act of recognizing those who are giving support to the change effort in front of their peers may encourage others to get on board. When the new behaviors employees are expected to demonstrate (such as using a new computer program, filling out a new form, or simply greeting customers once they enter the store) are made part of an organization's reward system, those behaviors are more likely to be taken seriously and repeated, making the change effort successful.[46]

Embracing Continuous Change

While Lewin's three-stage model offers many useful insights into the process of implementing change, it views each organizational change as an episode with a beginning, middle, and end. In contrast with this episodic change assumption, some management experts in the 1990s began to propose that change is—or ought to be—a continuous process.

The learning organization is an example of a company embracing continuous change. By setting up a dynamic feedback loop, learning can become a regular part of daily operations. If an employee implements a new method or technology that seems to be successful, a learning organization is in a good position to adopt it. By constantly being aware of how employee actions and outcomes affect others as well as overall company productivity, the inevitable small changes throughout organizations can be rapidly absorbed and tailored for daily operations. When an organization understands that change does indeed occur constantly, it will be in a better position to make use of good changes and intervene if a change seems detrimental.

KEY TAKEAWAY

Effective change effort can be conceptualized as a three-step process in which employees are first prepared for change, then change is implemented, and finally the new behavioral patterns become permanent. According to emerging contemporary views, it can also be seen as a continuous process that affirms the organic, ever-evolving nature of an organization.

EXERCISES

1. What are the benefits of employee participation in change management?
2. Imagine that you are introducing a new system to college students where they would have to use a special ID number you create for them for activities such as logging on to campus computers or using library resources. How would you plan and implement the change? Explain using Lewin's three-stage framework.
3. Why are successful companies less likely to change? What should companies do to make organizational change part of their culture?

FIGURE 7.20

In the 1980s , British Airways was known for its on-time departures but poor treatment of passengers, earning it the nickname "Bloody Awful." In 10 years, as a result of significant changes in its reward system and training managers to motivate and empower front-line employees, it built a service culture, now often referred to as "Bloody Awesome."

Source: http://en.wikipedia.org/wiki/File:British_Airways_747-400_G-CIVI.jpg

5. BUILDING YOUR CHANGE MANAGEMENT SKILLS

5.1 Overcoming Resistance to Your Proposals

At some point in your education or career, you may find yourself in a situation where you feel change is needed. You might have a great idea, but people around you do not seem convinced or express resistance. How do you make change happen?

- *Listen to naysayers.* You may think that your idea is great, but listening to those who resist may give you valuable ideas about why it may not work and how to design it more effectively.

- *Is your change revolutionary?* If you are trying to change dramatically the way things are done, you will find that resistance is greater. If your proposal involves incrementally making things better, you may have better luck.

- *Involve those around you in planning the change.* Instead of providing the solutions, make them part of the solution. If they admit that there is a problem and participate in planning a way out, you would have to do less convincing when it is time to implement the change.

- *Assess your credibility.* When trying to persuade people to change their ways, it helps if you have a history of suggesting implementable changes. Otherwise, you may be ignored or met with suspicion. This means you need to establish trust and a history of keeping promises over time before you propose a major change.

- *Present data to your audience.* Be prepared to defend the technical aspects of your ideas and provide evidence that your proposal is likely to work.

- *Appeal to your audience's ideals.* Frame your proposal around the big picture. Are you going to create happier clients? Is this going to lead to a better reputation for the company? Identify the long-term goals you are hoping to accomplish that people would be proud to be a part of.

- *Understand the reasons for resistance.* Is your audience resisting because they fear change? Does the change you propose mean more work for them? Does it affect them in a negative way? Understanding the consequences of your proposal for the parties involved may help you tailor your pitch to your audience.[47]

KEY TAKEAWAY

There are several steps you can take to help you overcome resistance to change. Many of them share the common theme of respecting those who are resistant so you can understand and learn from their concerns.

EXERCISES

1. What do you think are some key reasons why people resist change?
2. Do you think some people are more resistant to change regardless of what it is? Why do you think this is?

6. CASE IN POINT: TOYOTA STRUGGLES WITH ORGANIZATIONAL STRUCTURE

FIGURE 7.21

Source: http://en.wikipedia.org/wiki/File:Toyota_Group_Pavilion.jpg

Toyota Motor Corporation (TYO: 7203) has been enjoying the enviable position of being referred to as the gold standard of the automotive industry. Worldwide they employ nearly 318,000 individuals. In the first quarter of 2007, Toyota (NYSE: TM) overtook General Motors Corporation in sales for the first time as the top automotive manufacturer in the world. Toyota reached success in part because of its exceptional reputation for quality and customer care. Despite the global recession and the tough economic times that American auto companies such as General Motors and Chrysler faced in 2009, Toyota enjoyed profits of $16.7 billion and a sales growth of 6% that year. Toyota's manufacturing system is seen as the chief reason for the company's reputation for quality. Using the Toyota Production system (TPS), built on the principles of "just-in-time" production, Toyota is able to deliver raw materials and supplies to the assembly line at exactly the time they need to be used. In this system, assembly line workers are empowered to pull a cord to stop the manufacturing line when they see a problem. The company also relies on Kaizen, or the philosophy of continuous improvement. These practices have resulted in a reputation for quality that is a key competitive advantage for the company.

The reputation that took Toyota decades to build was severely endangered by the end of 2010. Late 2009 and early 2010 witnessed Toyota's recall of 8 million vehicles due to unintended acceleration. How could this happen to a company known for quality and structured to solve problems as soon as they arise? Later investigations revealed that the manufacturing system was not really at fault and the accidents could be explained by floor mats and sticky pedals. However, by not acknowledging quality problems and failing to act quickly, Toyota alienated its customer base, resulting in the loss of its leadership position in the automotive market and leaving it in third place behind GM and Volkswagen.

While investigations failed to reveal manufacturing problems, they did reveal structural and cultural problems. One key issue was the rapid growth of the company. Expansion strained resources across the organization and slowed response time. Toyota's CEO, Akio Toyoda, the grandson of its founder, has conceded, "Quite frankly, I fear the pace at which we have grown may have been too quick." The company had begun to put growth-related goals in front of quality goals, rewarding those who reached their growth-related metrics. Rapid growth also meant that the company had to hire new employees quickly, with little time spent on training them on the "Toyota way," and hire a large number of contract employees. These changes in the composition of employees meant that communication, coordination, and trust suffered.

Another key problem was the centralized, Japanese-controlled organizational structure. At the time of the crisis, Toyota was a highly centralized organization that did not delegate much authority or decision-making power to its U.S. operations, even though the U.S. market provided 2/3 of its profits. Every time there was a quality issue that necessitated a recall, the problem needed to be communicated to the headquarters using a highly bureaucratic process, and then the headquarters would provide the solution. All U.S. executives were assigned a Japanese boss to mentor them, and no Toyota executive in the United States was authorized to issue a recall. Most information flow was one way, always going back to Japan, where decisions were made. Often, the upper management dismissed quality concerns raised by lower management. In short, Toyota had become too bureaucratic, too centralized, and too big for the challenges it was facing.

Toyota's woes did not end with the safety crisis—a strong yen, and the 2011 tsunami disaster both exacerbated its difficulties. Yet there seems to be cause for hope. Akio Toyoda, who had recently become the CEO toward the beginning of the safety scandal, seems to be taking steps to turn around the structure and culture. Seen as an atypical Japanese executive (for example, he was educated at Babson College in the United States), Toyoda took action by delegating more authority to the North American operations, setting goals to reduce the number of outside engineers to 10%, and expanding the rapid quality response team. Most telling may be the company's reaction to the tsunami. When some of their suppliers were affected by the disaster, affecting Toyota's own operations, teams were sent to the sites of suppliers with the charge to restore production without worrying about reporting back.

Case written by Berrin Erdogan, Carlene Reynolds, and Talya Bauer to accompany Carpenter, M., Bauer, T., Erdogan, B., & Short, J. (2013). Principles of Management (2nd ed.). New York: Flat World Knowledge. Based on information from Cole, R. E. (2011, June 22). What really happened to Toyota? MIT Sloan Review; Liker, J. K., & Ogden, T. N. (2011, November/December). The Toyota recall: Missing the forest for the trees. Ivey Business Journal, 75(6); Saporito, B., Schuman, M., Szczesny, J. R., & Altman, A. (2010, February 22). Toyota tangled. Time, 175(7); Taylor, A., III. (2010, July 26). How Toyota lost its way. Fortune, 162(2).

CASE DISCUSSION QUESTIONS

1. What changes in the organizing facet of the P-O-L-C framework might you make at Toyota to prevent future mishaps like the massive recalls related to brake and accelerator failures?
2. Do you think Toyota's organizational structure and norms are explicitly formalized in rules, or do the norms seem to be more inherent in the culture of the organization?
3. What are the pros and cons of Toyota's structure?
4. What business elements would you suggest remain the same and what elements might need revising?
5. What are the most important elements of Toyota's organizational structure?

ENDNOTES

1. Hirst, G., Van Knippenberg, D., Chen, C. H., & Sacramento, C. A. (2011). How does bureaucracy impact individual creativity? A cross-level investigation of team contextual influences on goal orientation-creativity relationships. *Academy of Management Journal, 54*, 624–641.

2. Nelson, G. L., & Pasternack, B. A. (2005). *Results: Keep what's good, fix what's wrong, and unlock great performance.* New York: Crown Business.

3. Ambrose, M. L., & Cropanzano, R. S. (2000). The effect of organizational structure on perceptions of procedural fairness. *Journal of Applied Psychology, 85*, 294–304; Miller, D., Droge, C., & Toulouse, J. (1988). Strategic process and content as mediators between organizational context and structure. *Academy of Management Journal, 31*, 544–569; Oldham, G. R., & Hackman, R. J. (1981). Relationships between organizational structure and employee reactions: Comparing alternative frameworks. *Administrative Science Quarterly, 26*, 66–83; Pierce, J. L., & Delbecq, A. L. (1977). Organization structure, individual attitudes, and innovation. *Academy of Management Review, 2*, 27–37; Schminke, M., Ambrose, M. L., & Cropanzano, R. S. (2000). The effect of organizational structure on perceptions of procedural fairness. *Journal of Applied Psychology, 85*, 294–304; Turban, D. B., & Keon, T. L. (1993). Organizational attractiveness: An interactionist perspective. *Journal of Applied Psychology, 78*, 184–193; Wally, S., & Baum, J. R. (1994). Personal and structural determinants of the pace of strategic decision making. *Academy of Management Journal, 37*, 932–956.

4. Brazil, J. J. (2007, April). Mission: Impossible? *Fast Company, 114*, 92–109.

5. Charan, R. (2006, April). Home Depot's blueprint for culture change. *Harvard Business Review, 84*(4), 60–70; Marquez, J. (2007, January 15). Big bucks at door for Depot HR leader. *Workforce Management, 86*(1).

6. Fredrickson, J. W. (1986). The strategic decision process and organizational structure. *Academy of Management Review, 11*, 280–297; Oldham, G. R., & Hackman, R. J. (1981). Relationships between organizational structure and employee reactions: Comparing alternative frameworks. *Administrative Science Quarterly, 26*, 66–83; Pierce, J. L., & Delbecq, A. L. (1977). Organization structure, individual attitudes, and innovation. *Academy of Management Review, 2*, 27–37; Wally, S., & Baum, R. J. (1994). Strategic decision speed and firm performance. *Strategic Management Journal, 24*, 1107–1129.

7. Ghiselli, E. E., & Johnson, D. A. (1970). Need satisfaction, managerial success, and organizational structure. *Personnel Psychology, 23*, 569–576; Porter, L. W., & Siegel, J. (2006). Relationships of tall and flat organization structures to the satisfactions of foreign managers. *Personnel Psychology, 18*, 379–392.

8. Chonko, L. B. (1982). The relationship of span of control to sales representatives' experienced role conflict and role ambiguity. *Academy of Management Journal, 25*, 452–456.

9. Porter, L. W., & Lawler, E. E. (1964). The effects of tall versus flat organization structures on managerial job satisfaction. *Personnel Psychology, 17*, 135–148.

10. Hollenbeck, J. R., Moon, H., Ellis, A. P. J., West, B. J., Ilgen, D. R., Sheppard, L.,...Wagner, J. A., III. (2002). Structural contingency theory and individual differences: Examination of external and internal person-team fit. *Journal of Applied Psychology, 87*, 599–606.

11. Burns, T., & Stalker, M. G. (1961). *The Management of innovation.* London: Tavistock; Covin, J. G., & Slevin, D. P. (1988). The influence of organizational structure. *Journal of Management Studies, 25*, 217–234; Schollhammer, H. (1982). *Internal corporate entrepreneurship.* Englewood Cliffs, NJ: Prentice-Hall; Sherman, J. D., & Smith, H. L. (1984). The influence of organizational structure on intrinsic versus extrinsic motivation. *Academy of Management Journal, 27*, 877–885; Slevin, D. P., & Covin, J. G. (1990). Juggling entrepreneurial style and organizational structure—how to get your act together. *Sloan Management Review, 31*(2), 43–53.

12. Sine, W. D., Mitsuhashi, H., & Kirsch, D. A. (2006). Revisiting Burns and Stalker: Formal structure and new venture performance in emerging economic sectors. *Academy of Management Journal, 49*, 121–132.

13. Burns, T., & Stalker, M. G. (1961). *The Management of Innovation.* London: Tavistock; Covin, J. G., & Slevin, D. P. (1988). The influence of organizational structure. *Journal of Management Studies, 25*, 217–234.

14. Adair, J. (2007). *Leadership for innovation: How to organize team creativity and harvest ideas.* London: Kogan Page.

15. Joyce, W. F. (1986). Matrix organization: A social experiment. *Academy of Management Journal, 29*, 536–561.

16. Ford, R. C., & Randolph, W. A. (1992). Cross-functional structures: A review and integration of matrix organization and project management. *Journal of Management, 18*, 267–294.

17. Anand, N., & Daft, R. L. (2007). What is the right organization design? *Organizational Dynamics, 36*(4), 329–344.

18. Ashkenas, R., Ulrich, D., Jick, T., & Kerr, S. (1995). *The Boundaryless organization: Breaking the chains of organizational structure.* San Francisco: Jossey-Bass.

19. Dess, G. G., Rasheed, A. M. A., McLaughlin, K. J., & Priem, R. L. (1995). The new corporate architecture. *Academy of Management Executive, 9*(3), 7–18; Rosenbloom, B. (2003). Multi-channel marketing and the retail value chain. *Thexis, 3*, 23–26.

20. Deutschman, A. (2005, March). Building a better skunk works. *Fast Company, 92*, 68–73.

21. Garvin, D. A. (1993, July/August). Building a learning organization. *Harvard Business Review, 71*(4), 78–91.

22. Lerman, R. I., & Schmidt, S. R. (2006). Trends and challenges for work in the 21st century. Retrieved September 29, 2012, from U.S. Department of Labor Web site, http://www.dol.gov/oasam/programs/history/herman/reports/futurework/conference/trends/trendsl.htm.

23. Anonymous. Moore's Law. *Answers.com.* Retrieved September 5, 2008, from http://www.answers.com/topic/moore-s-law.

24. Get ready. United States Small Business Association. Retrieved September 7, 2012, from http://www.sba.gov/smallbusinessplanner/plan/getready/SERV_SBPLANNER_ISENTFORU.html.

25. Barnett, W. P., & Carroll, G. R. (1995). Modeling internal organizational change. *Annual Review of Sociology, 21*, 217–236; Boeker, W. (1997). Strategic change: The influence of managerial characteristics and organizational growth. *Academy of Management Journal, 40*, 152–170; Deutschman, A. (2005, March). Building a better skunk works. *Fast Company, 92*, 68–73.

26. Anonymous. (2007, December). Change management: The HR strategic imperative as a business partner. *HR Magazine, 52*(12); Huy, Q. N. (1999). Emotional capability, emotional intelligence, and radical change. *Academy of Management Review, 24*, 325–345.

27. Fugate, M., Kinicki, A. J., & Prussia, G. E. (2008). Employee coping with organizational change: An examination of alternative theoretical perspectives and models. *Personnel Psychology, 61*, 1–36.

28. Diamond, J. (2005). *Guns, germs, and steel: The fates of human societies.* New York: W. W. Norton.

29. Judge, T. A., Thoresen, C. J., Pucik, V., & Welbourne, T. M. (1999). Managerial coping with organizational change. *Journal of Applied Psychology, 84*, 107–122; Wanberg, C. R., & Banas, J. T. (2000). Predictors and outcomes of openness to changes in a reorganizing workplace. *Journal of Applied Psychology, 85*, 132–142.

30. Ashford, S. J., Lee, C. L., & Bobko, P. (1989). Content, causes, and consequences of job insecurity: A theory-based measure and substantive test. *Academy of Management Journal, 32*, 803–829; Fugate, M., Kinicki, A. J., & Prussia, G. E. (2008). Employee coping with organizational change: An examination of alternative theoretical perspectives and models. *Personnel Psychology, 61*, 1–36.

31. Herold, D. M., Fedor, D. B., & Caldwell, S. (2007). Beyond change management: A multilevel investigation of contextual and personal influences on employees' commitment to change. *Journal of Applied Psychology, 92*, 942–951.

32. Fedor, D. M., Caldwell, S., & Herold, D. M. (2006). The effects of organizational changes on employee commitment: A multilevel investigation. *Personnel Psychology, 59*, 1–29.

33. Labianca, G., Gray, B., & Brass D. J. (2000). A grounded model of organizational schema change during empowerment. *Organization Science, 11*, 235–257; Rafferty, A. E., & Griffin. M. A. (2006). Perceptions of organizational change: A stress and coping perspective. *Journal of Applied Psychology, 91*, 1154–1162.

34. Ford, J. D., Ford, L. W., & D'Amelio, A. (2008). Resistance to change: The rest of the story. *Academy of Management Review, 33*, 362–377.

35. Lewin K. (1951). *Field theory in social science.* New York: Harper & Row.

36. Wanberg, C. R., & Banas, J. T. (2000). Predictors and outcomes of openness to changes in a reorganizing workplace. *Journal of Applied Psychology, 85*, 132–142.

37. Herold, D. M., Fedor D. B., Caldwell, S., & Liu, Y. (2008). The effects of transformational and change leadership on employees' commitment to a change: A multilevel study. *Journal of Applied Psychology, 93*, 346–357.

38. Armenakis, A. A., Harris, S. G., & Mossholder, K. W. (1993). Creating readiness for organizational change. *Human Relations, 46*, 681–703.

39. Gerstner, L. V. (2002). *Who says elephants can't dance? Inside IBM's historic turnaround.* New York: HarperCollins; Kotter, J. P. (1996). *Leading change.* Boston: Harvard Business School Press.

40. Burkhardt, M. E. (1994). Social interaction effects following a technological change: A longitudinal investigation. *Academy of Management Journal, 37*, 869–898; Kotter, J. P. (1995, March–April). Leading change: Why transformations fail. *Harvard Business Review, 73*(2), 59–67.

41. Armenakis, A. A., Harris, S. G., & Mossholder, K. W. (1993). Creating readiness for organizational change. *Human Relations, 46*, 681–703.

42. Wanberg, C. R., & Banas, J. T. (2000). Predictors and outcomes of openness to changes in a reorganizing workplace. *Journal of Applied Psychology, 85*, 132–142.

43. Kotter, J. P. (1996). *Leading change.* Boston: Harvard Business School Press; Reay, T., Golden-Biddle, K., & Germann, K. (2006). Legitimizing a new role: Small wins and microprocesses of change. *Academy of Management Journal, 49*, 977–998.

44. Hamel, G. (2000, July/August). Waking up IBM. *Harvard Business Review, 78*(4), 137–146.

45. Kotter, J. P. (1995, March–April). Leading change: Why transformations fail. *Harvard Business Review, 73*(2), 59–67.

46. Gale, S. F. (2003). Incentives and the art of changing behavior. *Workforce Management, 82*(11), 48–54.

47. Based on: McGoon, C. (1995, March). Secrets of building influence. *Communication World, 12*(3), 16; Michelman, P. (2007, July). Overcoming resistance to change. *Harvard Management Update, 12*(7), 3–4; Stanley, T. L. (2002, January). Change: A common-sense approach. *Supervision, 63*(1), 7–10.

CHAPTER 8
Organizational Culture

FIGURE 8.1

3M Corporation has been able to continue their innovative culture by allowing employees to use up to 15% of their workweek to develop new innovations such as their famous Post-it Notes.

© *Thinkstock*

CHAPTER LEARNING OBJECTIVES

Reading this chapter will help you do the following:

1. Describe what organizational culture is and why it is important for an organization.
2. Understand the dimensions that make up a company's culture.
3. Understand the creation and maintenance of organizational culture.
4. Understand the factors that create cultural change.
5. Develop personal culture management skills.

Organizations, like individuals, have their own personalities—often referred to as organizational cultures.

Understanding how culture is created, communicated, and changed will help you be a more effective manager.

FIGURE 8.2 The P-O-L-C Framework

Planning	Organizing	Leading	Controlling
1. Vision & Mission	1. Organization Design	1. Leadership	1. Systems/Processes
2. Strategizing	2. Culture	2. Decision Making	2. Strategic Human Resources
3. Goals & Objectives	3. Social Networks	3. Communications	
		4. Groups/Teams	
		5. Motivation	

1. UNDERSTANDING ORGANIZATIONAL CULTURE

LEARNING OBJECTIVES

1. Define organizational culture.
2. Understand why organizational culture is important.
3. Understand the different levels of organizational culture.

1.1 What Is Organizational Culture?

Organizational culture refers to a system of shared assumptions, values, and beliefs that indicate appropriate and inappropriate behavior within a given organization.[1] These values have a strong influence on employee behavior as well as organizational performance. The concept of organizational culture was first made popular in the 1980s when Peters and Waterman's best-selling book *In Search of Excellence* made the argument that company success could be attributed to an organizational culture that was decisive, customer-oriented, empowering, and people-oriented. Since then, organizational culture has become the subject of numerous research studies, books, and articles. Organizational culture is still a relatively new concept in contrast to a topic such as leadership, which has a history spanning several centuries.

Culture is largely invisible to individuals, since many elements of an organization's culture are a function of intangible social cues rather than explicit written policies. Even though culture affects all employee behaviors, thinking, and behavioral patterns, individuals tend to become more aware of their organization's culture when they have the opportunity to compare it to other organizations. Culture is related to the organizational facet of the P-O-L-C framework. The organizing function involves creating and implementing organizational design decisions. The culture of the organization is closely linked to organizational design. For instance, a culture that empowers employees to make decisions could prove extremely resistant to a centralized organizational design, hampering the manager's ability to enact such a design. However, a culture that supports the organizational structure (and vice versa) can be very powerful.

1.2 Why Does Organizational Culture Matter?

An organization's culture may be one of its strongest assets or its biggest liability. In fact, it has been argued that organizations that have a rare and hard-to-imitate culture enjoy a competitive advantage.[2] In a recent survey conducted by the management consulting firm Bain & Company, worldwide business leaders identified corporate culture to be as important as corporate strategy for business success.[3] This comes as no surprise to leaders of successful businesses, who are quick to attribute their company's success to their organization's culture.

Culture, or shared values within the organization, may be related to increased performance. Researchers find a relationship between organizational cultures and company performance with respect to success indicators such as revenues, sales volume, market share, and stock prices.[4] At the same time, it is important to have a culture that fits with the demands of the company's environment. To the extent that shared values are proper for the company in question, company performance may benefit from culture.[5] For example, if a company is in the high-tech industry, having a culture that encourages innovativeness and adaptability will support its performance. However, if a company in the same industry has a culture characterized by stability, a high respect for tradition, and a strong preference for upholding rules and procedures, the company may suffer because of its culture. In other words, just as having the "right" culture may be a competitive advantage for an organization, having the "wrong" culture may lead to performance difficulties, may be responsible for organizational failure, and may act as a barrier preventing the company from changing and taking risks.

In addition to having implications for organizational performance, *organizational culture is an effective control mechanism dictating employee behavior.* Culture is a more powerful way of controlling and managing employee behaviors than organizational rules and regulations. For example, when a company is trying to improve the quality of its customer service, rules may not be helpful, particularly when the problems customers present are unique. Instead, creating a culture of customer service may achieve better results by encouraging employees to think like customers, knowing that the company priorities in this case are clear: Keeping the customer happy is preferable to other concerns, such as saving the cost of a refund. Therefore, the ability to understand and influence organizational culture is an important item for managers to have in their tool kit when they are carrying out their controlling P-O-L-C function as well as their organizing function.

1.3   Levels of Organizational Culture

Organizational culture consists of some aspects that are relatively more visible, as well as aspects that may lie below one's conscious awareness. Organizational culture can be thought of as consisting of three interrelated levels.[6]

At the deepest level, below our awareness, lie basic **assumptions**. These assumptions are taken for granted and reflect beliefs about human nature and reality. At the second level, **values** exist. Values are shared principles, standards, and goals. Finally, at the surface, we have **artifacts**, or visible, tangible aspects of organizational culture. For example, in an organization, a basic assumption employees and managers share might be that happy employees benefit their organizations. This might be translated into values such as egalitarianism, high-quality relationships, and having fun. The artifacts reflecting such values might be an executive "open door" policy, an office layout that includes open spaces and gathering areas equipped with pool tables, and frequent company picnics.

Understanding the organization's culture may start from observing its artifacts: its physical environment, employee interactions, company policies, reward systems, and other observable characteristics. When you are interviewing for a position, observing the physical environment, how people dress, where they relax, and how they talk to others is definitely a good start to understanding the company's culture. However, simply looking at these tangible aspects is unlikely to give a full picture of the organization, since an important chunk of what makes up culture exists below one's degree of awareness. The values and, deeper, the assumptions that shape the organization's culture can be uncovered by observing how employees interact and the choices they make, as well as by inquiring about their beliefs and perceptions regarding what is right and appropriate behavior.

FIGURE 8.3 Organizational Culture Levels

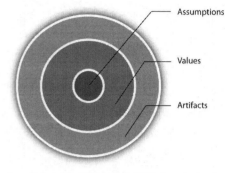

Source: Adapted from Schein, E. H. (1992). Organizational Culture and Leadership. San Francisco: Jossey-Bass.

assumptions

Beliefs about human nature and reality that are taken for granted.

values

Shared principles, standards, and goals.

artifacts

The visible and tangible elements of culture.

KEY TAKEAWAY

Organizational culture is a system of shared assumptions, values, and beliefs that help individuals understand which behaviors are and are not appropriate within an organization. Cultures can be a source of competitive advantage for organizations. Strong organizational cultures can be an organizing as well as a controlling mechanism for organizations. And finally, organizational culture consists of three levels: assumptions that are below the surface, values, and artifacts.

EXERCISES

1. Why do companies need culture?
2. Give an example of a company culture being a strength as well as a weakness.
3. In what ways does culture serve as a controlling mechanism?
4. If assumptions are below the surface, why do they matter?
5. Share examples of artifacts you have noticed at different organizations.

2. MEASURING ORGANIZATIONAL CULTURE

LEARNING OBJECTIVES

1. Understand different dimensions of organizational culture.
2. Understand the role of culture strength.
3. Explore subcultures within organizations.

2.1 Dimensions of Culture

Which values characterize an organization's culture? Even though culture may not be immediately observable, identifying a set of values that might be used to describe an organization's culture helps us identify, measure, and manage culture more effectively. For this purpose, several researchers have proposed various culture typologies. One popular typology is the Organizational Culture Profile (OCP), where culture is represented by seven distinct values.[7]

Innovative Cultures

innovative cultures

Cultures that are flexible, adaptable, and experiment with new ideas.

According to the OCP framework, companies that have **innovative cultures** are flexible, adaptable, and experiment with new ideas. These companies are characterized by a flat hierarchy and titles and other status distinctions tend to be downplayed. For example, Apple has been named by *Fast Company* magazine as the most innovative company in the world. While they do not invent new technology, the innovations they introduced to personal computers, mobile phones, and tablets, with products such as the iPhone and iPad, changed the daily life of consumers and created entire industries working on Apple platforms. This is a culture that values accountability and agility. With a simple organizational chart and clearly defined responsibilities, they are able to achieve clear focus on a small number of products and engage in quick course corrections. In order to maintain agility, the company uses small teams—for example, putting two engineers in charge of writing the code for converting the Safari browser into iPad.[8]

Aggressive Cultures

aggressive cultures

Cultures that value competitiveness and outperforming competitors.

Companies with **aggressive cultures** value competitiveness and outperforming competitors. For example, Microsoft is often identified as a company with an aggressive culture. The company has faced a number of antitrust lawsuits and disputes with competitors over the years. In aggressive companies, people may use language such as "we will kill our competition." In the past, Microsoft executives made statements such as "we are going to cut off Netscape's air supply…Everything they are selling, we are going to give away," and its aggressive culture is cited as a reason for getting into new legal troubles before old ones are resolved.[9]

Outcome-Oriented Cultures

outcome-oriented cultures

Cultures that emphasize achievement, results, and action.

The OCP framework describes **outcome-oriented cultures** as those that emphasize achievement, results, and action as important values. A good example of an outcome-oriented culture may be the electronics retailer Best Buy. Having a culture emphasizing sales performance, Best Buy tallies revenues and other relevant figures daily by department. Employees are trained and mentored to sell company products effectively, and they learn how much money their department made every day.[10] In 2005, the company implemented a Results Oriented Work Environment (ROWE) program that allows employees to work anywhere and anytime; they are evaluated based on results and fulfillment of clearly outlined objectives.[11] Outcome-oriented cultures hold employees as well as managers accountable for success and use systems that reward employee and group output. In these companies, it is more common to see rewards tied to performance indicators as opposed to seniority or loyalty. Research indicates that organizations that have a performance-oriented culture tend to outperform companies that are lacking such a culture.[12] At the same time, when performance pressures lead to a culture where unethical behaviors become the norm, individuals see their peers as rivals, and short-term results are rewarded, the resulting unhealthy work environment serves as a liability.[13]

FIGURE 8.4 Dimensions of the Organizational Culture Profile

Organizational culture is reflected in the different "personalities" exhibited by organizational members. Here, we illustrate how different cultures are reflected in one popular framework for examining such differences—the Organizational Culture Profile (OCP).

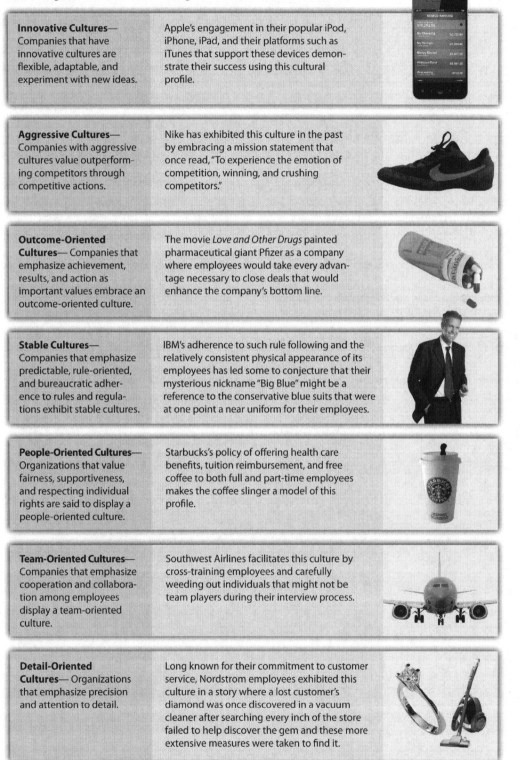

Innovative Cultures— Companies that have innovative cultures are flexible, adaptable, and experiment with new ideas.

Apple's engagement in their popular iPod, iPhone, iPad, and their platforms such as iTunes that support these devices demonstrate their success using this cultural profile.

Aggressive Cultures— Companies with aggressive cultures value outperforming competitors through competitive actions.

Nike has exhibited this culture in the past by embracing a mission statement that once read, "To experience the emotion of competition, winning, and crushing competitors."

Outcome-Oriented Cultures— Companies that emphasize achievement, results, and action as important values embrace an outcome-oriented culture.

The movie *Love and Other Drugs* painted pharmaceutical giant Pfizer as a company where employees would take every advantage necessary to close deals that would enhance the company's bottom line.

Stable Cultures— Companies that emphasize predictable, rule-oriented, and bureaucratic adherence to rules and regulations exhibit stable cultures.

IBM's adherence to such rule following and the relatively consistent physical appearance of its employees has led some to conjecture that their mysterious nickname "Big Blue" might be a reference to the conservative blue suits that were at one point a near uniform for their employees.

People-Oriented Cultures— Organizations that value fairness, supportiveness, and respecting individual rights are said to display a people-oriented culture.

Starbucks's policy of offering health care benefits, tuition reimbursement, and free coffee to both full and part-time employees makes the coffee slinger a model of this profile.

Team-Oriented Cultures— Companies that emphasize cooperation and collaboration among employees display a team-oriented culture.

Southwest Airlines facilitates this culture by cross-training employees and carefully weeding out individuals that might not be team players during their interview process.

Detail-Oriented Cultures— Organizations that emphasize precision and attention to detail.

Long known for their commitment to customer service, Nordstrom employees exhibited this culture in a story where a lost customer's diamond was once discovered in a vacuum cleaner after searching every inch of the store failed to help discover the gem and these more extensive measures were taken to find it.

Source: Retrieved October 8, 2012 from (second from top) Vincent van der Heijden, http://www.flickr.com/photos/flo_and_me/3836753819/; (third from bottom) Cherrysweetdeal, http://www.flickr.com/photos/cherrysweetdeal/4322582205/; all other images © Thinkstock.

Stable Cultures

stable cultures

Cultures that are predictable, rule-oriented, and bureaucratic.

Stable cultures are predictable, rule-oriented, and bureaucratic. When the environment is stable and certain, these cultures may help the organization to be effective by providing stable and constant levels of output.[14] These cultures prevent quick action and, as a result, may be a misfit to a changing and dynamic environment. Public sector institutions may be viewed as stable cultures. In the private sector, GM is cited as having a bureaucractic culture, something the automaker has been struggling to change while recovering from its bankruptcy in 2009. The company is characterized by slow decision making, with several meetings and premeetings for key decisions, resulting in slow adoption of new technology and decision-making failures, such as allowing engineers to continue working on a Hummer sports utility vehicle long after they realized the project would fail.[15]

People-Oriented Cultures

FIGURE 8.5

From their social initiatives to extensive support of their own employees, Starbucks is the epitome of a people-oriented culture.

Source: http://www.flickr.com/ photos/montagecomms/2328936178

People-oriented cultures value fairness, supportiveness, and respecting individual rights. In these organizations, there is a greater emphasis on and expectation of treating people with respect and dignity.[16] One study of new employees in accounting companies found that employees, on average, stayed 14 months longer in companies with people-oriented cultures.[17] Starbucks is an example of a people-oriented culture. The company pays employees above minimum wage, offers health care and tuition reimbursement benefits to its part-time as well as full-time employees, and has creative perks such as weekly free coffee for all associates. As a result of these policies, the company benefits from a turnover rate lower than the industry average.[18]

Team-Oriented Cultures

Companies with a **team-oriented culture** are collaborative and emphasize cooperation among employees. For example, Southwest Airlines facilitates a team-oriented culture by cross-training its employees so that they are capable of helping one another when needed. The company also emphasizes training intact work teams.[19] In Southwest's selection process, applicants who are not viewed as team players are not hired as employees.[20] In team-oriented organizations, members tend to have more positive relationships with their coworkers and particularly with their managers.[21]

FIGURE 8.6

The growth in the number of passengers flying with Southwest Airlines from 1973 to 2012 shows Southwest as one of the most-flown U.S. airlines. While price has played a role in this, their emphasis on service has been a key piece of their culture and competitive advantage and has helped Southwest remain profitable for more than 39 consecutive years.

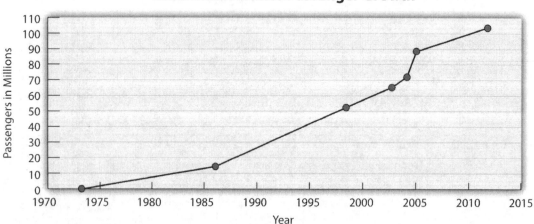

Source: Adapted from http://upload.wikimedia.org/wikipedia/commons/6/69/Southwest-airlines-passengers.jpg

people-oriented cultures

Cultures that value fairness, supportiveness, and respecting individual rights.

team-oriented cultures

Cultures that are collaborative and emphasize cooperation among employees.

Detail-Oriented Cultures

detail-oriented cultures

Cultures that emphasize precision and paying attention to details.

Organizations with a **detail-oriented culture** are characterized in the OCP framework as emphasizing precision and paying attention to details. Such a culture gives a competitive advantage to companies in the hospitality industry by helping them differentiate themselves from others. For example, Four Seasons and Ritz Carlton are among hotels who keep records of all customer requests such as which newspaper the guest prefers or what type of pillow the customer uses. This information is put into a computer system and used to provide better service to returning customers. Any requests hotel employees receive, as well as overhear, might be entered into the database to serve customers better.

2.2 Strength of Culture

A **strong culture** is one that is shared by organizational members[22] —that is, a culture in which most employees in the organization show consensus regarding the values of the company. The stronger a company's culture, the more likely it is to affect the way employees think and behave. For example, cultural values emphasizing customer service will lead to higher-quality customer service if there is widespread agreement among employees on the importance of customer-service-related values.[23]

It is important to realize that a strong culture may act as an asset or a liability for the organization, depending on the types of values that are shared. For example, imagine a company with a culture that is strongly outcome-oriented. If this value system matches the organizational environment, the company may perform well and outperform its competitors. This is an asset as long as members are behaving ethically. However, a strong outcome-oriented culture coupled with unethical behaviors and an obsession with quantitative performance indicators may be detrimental to an organization's effectiveness. Movies such as *Wall Street*, *Glengarry Glen Ross*, and *Boiler Room* illustrate the dangers associated with strong organizational cultures, where the need to "always be closing" a deal overshadows ethical concerns of other stakeholders. Enron is an extreme example of this dysfunctional type of strong culture.

One limitation of a strong culture is the difficulty of changing established organizational behaviors. In an organization where certain values are widely shared, if the organization decides to adopt a different set of values, unlearning the old values and learning the new ones will be a challenge because employees will need to adopt new ways of thinking, behaving, and responding to critical events. For example, Home Depot had a decentralized, autonomous culture where many business decisions were made using "gut feelings" while ignoring the available data. When Robert Nardelli became CEO of the company in 2000, he decided to change its culture starting with centralizing many of the decisions that were previously left to individual stores. This initiative met with substantial resistance, and many high-level employees left during Nardelli's first year. Despite getting financial results such as doubling the sales of the company, many of the changes he made were criticized. He left the company in January 2007.[24]

A strong culture may also be a liability during a merger. During mergers and acquisitions, companies inevitably experience a clash of cultures, as well as a clash of structures and operating systems. Culture clash becomes more problematic if both parties have unique and strong cultures. For example, during the 2010 merger of United Airlines and Continental, one of the key issues was the integration of corporate cultures. United Airlines had consumer satisfaction ratings below industry average, whereas Continental had above-average ratings and a quality focus. United employees had contentious relations with management and unionization rates exceeding 80%, while Continental employees enjoyed more positive relations with management and were 40% unionized. The creation of a unique, unified company culture is key to the success of such a merger.[25]

2.3 Do Organizations Have a Single Culture?

So far, the examples we have mentioned may suggest that a company has a single culture that is shared throughout the organization. In reality there might be multiple cultures within the organization. For example, people working on the sales floor may experience a different culture from that experienced by people working in the warehouse. Cultures that emerge within different departments, branches, or geographic locations are called **subcultures**. Subcultures may arise from the personal characteristics of employees and managers, as well as the different conditions under which work is performed. In addition to understanding the broader organization's values, managers will need to make an effort to understand subculture values to see their effect on workforce behavior and attitudes.

Sometimes, a subculture may take the form of a **counterculture**. Defined as shared values and beliefs that are in direct opposition to the values of the broader organizational culture,[26] countercultures are often shaped around a charismatic leader. For example, within a largely bureaucratic organization, an enclave of innovativeness and risk taking may emerge within a single department. A counterculture may be tolerated by the organization as long as it is bringing in results and contributing positively to the effectiveness of the organization. However, its existence may be perceived as a threat to the broader organizational culture. In some cases, this may lead to actions that would take away the autonomy of the managers and eliminate the counterculture.

strong culture
A culture that is shared by organizational members.

FIGURE 8.7

Walt Disney created a strong culture at his company that has evolved since its founding in 1923.

Source: http://en.wikipedia.org/wiki/ Image:Walt_disney_portrait.jpg

subculture
A set of values unique to a limited cross section of the organization.

counterculture
Shared values and beliefs that are in direct opposition to the values of the broader organizational culture.

EXERCISES

1. Think about an organization you are familiar with. On the basis of the dimensions of OCP, how would you characterize its culture?
2. Out of the culture dimensions described, which dimension do you think would lead to higher levels of employee satisfaction and retention? Which one would be related to company performance?
3. What are pros and cons of an outcome-oriented culture?
4. When bureaucracies were first invented, they were considered quite innovative. Do you think that different cultures are more or less effective at different points in time and in different industries? Why or why not?
5. Can you imagine an effective use of subcultures within an organization?

3. CREATING AND MAINTAINING ORGANIZATIONAL CULTURE

LEARNING OBJECTIVES

1. **Understand how cultures are created.**
2. **Learn how to maintain a culture.**
3. **Recognize organizational culture signs.**

3.1 How Are Cultures Created?

Where do cultures originate? Understanding this question is important in understanding how they can be changed. An organization's culture is shaped as the organization faces and deals with external and internal challenges. When the organization's way of doing business provides a successful adaptation to environmental challenges and ensures success, those values are retained. These values and ways of doing business are taught to new members as *the* way to do business.[27]

The factors that are most important in the creation of an organization's culture include founders' values, preferences, and industry demands.

FIGURE 8.8 Model Describing How Cultures Are Created and Maintained

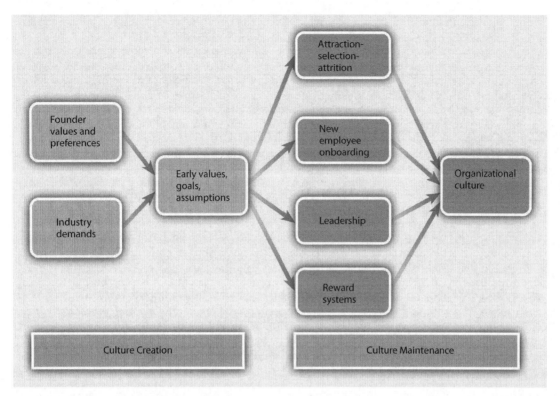

Founder Values

A company's culture, particularly during its early years, is inevitably tied to the personality, background, and values of its founder or founders, as well as their vision for the future of the organization. When entrepreneurs establish their own businesses, the way they want to do business determines the organization's rules, the structure set up in the company, and the people they hire to work with them. For example, some of the existing corporate values of the ice cream company Ben & Jerry's Homemade Holdings Inc. can easily be traced to the personalities of its founders Ben Cohen and Jerry Greenfield. In 1978, the two high school friends opened up their first ice-cream shop in a renovated gas station in Burlington, Vermont. Their strong social convictions led them to buy only from the local farmers and devote a certain percentage of their profits to charities. The core values they instilled in their business can still be observed in the current company's devotion to social activism and sustainability, its continuous contributions to charities, use of environmentally friendly materials, and dedication to creating jobs in low-income areas. Even though Unilever acquired the company in 2000, the social activism component remains unchanged, and Unilever has expressed its commitment to traditional Ben & Jerry's values.[28]

Founder values become part of the corporate culture to the degree to which they help the company be successful. For example, the social activism of Ben and Jerry's was instilled in the company because the founders strongly believed in these issues. However, these values probably would not be surviving three decades later if they had not helped the company in its initial stages. In the case of Ben and Jerry's, these values helped distinguish their brand from larger corporate brands and attracted a loyal customer base. Thus, by providing a competitive advantage, these values were retained as part of the corporate culture and were taught to new members as the right way to do business.

FIGURE 8.9

Ben & Jerry's managed to preserve the most unique aspects of its organizational culture despite being acquired by Unilever. The success of a merger often depends on successful harmonizing of the cultures of two distinct organizations.

Source:

http://commons.wikimedia.org/wiki/ Image:BenJerry-UnitedSquare.jpg

Industry Demands

While founders undoubtedly exert a powerful influence over corporate cultures, the industry characteristics also play a role. Companies within the same industry can sometimes have widely differing cultures. At the same time, the industry characteristics and demands act as a force to create similarities among organizational cultures. For example, despite some differences, many companies in the insurance and banking industries are stable and rule-oriented, many companies in the high-tech industry have innovative cultures, and those in nonprofit industry may be people-oriented. If the industry is one with a large number of regulatory requirements—for example, aviation, banking, health care, and high-reliability (such as nuclear power) industries—then we might expect the presence of a large number of rules and regulations, a bureaucratic company structure, and a stable culture. The industry influence over culture is also important to know because this shows that it may not be possible to imitate the culture of a company in a different industry, even though it may seem admirable to outsiders.

3.2   How Are Cultures Maintained?

As a company matures, its cultural values are refined and strengthened. The early values of a company's culture exert influence over its future values. It is possible to think of organizational culture as an organism that protects itself from external forces. Organizational culture determines what types of people are hired by an organization and what types of people are left out. Moreover, once new employees are hired, the company assimilates new employees and teaches them the way things are done in the organization. We call these processes *attraction-selection-attrition* and *onboarding* processes. We will also examine the role of *leaders* and *reward systems* in shaping and maintaining an organization's culture.

Attraction-Selection-Attrition

Organizational culture is maintained through a process known as attraction-selection-attrition (ASA). First, employees are *attracted* to organizations where they will fit in. Someone who has a competitive nature may feel comfortable in and may prefer to work in a company where interpersonal competition is the norm. Others may prefer to work in a team-oriented workplace. Research shows that employees with different personality traits find different cultures attractive. For example, out of the Big Five personality traits, employees who demonstrate neurotic personalities were less likely to be attracted to innovative cultures, whereas those who had openness to experience were more likely to be attracted to innovative cultures.[29]

Of course, this process is imperfect, and value similarity is only one reason a candidate might be attracted to a company. There may be other, more powerful attractions such as good benefits. At this point in the process, the second component of the ASA framework prevents them from getting in: *selection*. Just as candidates are looking for places where they will fit in, companies are also looking for people who will fit into their current corporate culture. Many companies are hiring people for fit with their culture, as opposed to fit with a certain job. For example, Southwest Airlines prides itself for hiring employees based on personality and attitude rather than specific job-related skills, which they learn after they are hired. Companies use different techniques to weed out candidates who do not fit with corporate values. For example, Google relies on multiple interviews with future peers. By introducing the candidate to several future coworkers and learning what these coworkers think of the candidate, it becomes easier to assess the level of fit.

FIGURE 8.10 The ASA Framework

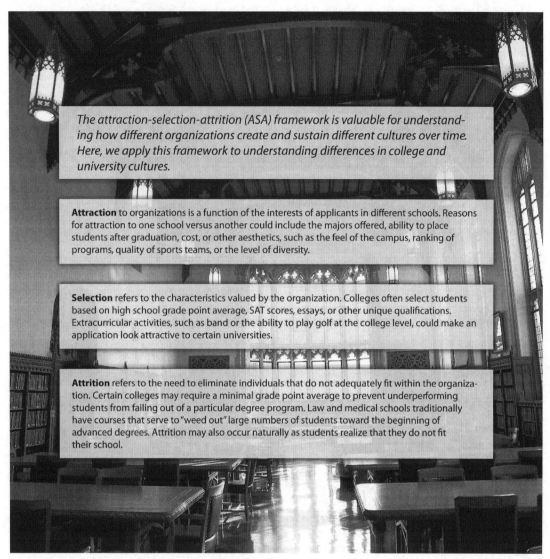

The attraction-selection-attrition (ASA) framework is valuable for understanding how different organizations create and sustain different cultures over time. Here, we apply this framework to understanding differences in college and university cultures.

Attraction to organizations is a function of the interests of applicants in different schools. Reasons for attraction to one school versus another could include the majors offered, ability to place students after graduation, cost, or other aesthetics, such as the feel of the campus, ranking of programs, quality of sports teams, or the level of diversity.

Selection refers to the characteristics valued by the organization. Colleges often select students based on high school grade point average, SAT scores, essays, or other unique qualifications. Extracurricular activities, such as band or the ability to play golf at the college level, could make an application look attractive to certain universities.

Attrition refers to the need to eliminate individuals that do not adequately fit within the organization. Certain colleges may require a minimal grade point average to prevent underperforming students from failing out of a particular degree program. Law and medical schools traditionally have courses that serve to "weed out" large numbers of students toward the beginning of advanced degrees. Attrition may also occur naturally as students realize that they do not fit their school.

Source: http://en.wikipedia.org/wiki/File:OU_Great_Reading_Room.jpg

Even after a company selects people for person-organization fit, there may be new employees who do not fit in. Some candidates may be skillful in impressing recruiters and signal high levels of culture fit even though they do not necessarily share the company's values. In any event, the organization is eventually going to eliminate candidates who do not fit in through *attrition*. Attrition refers to the natural process where the candidates who do not fit in will leave the company. Research indicates that person-organization misfit is one of the important reasons for employee turnover.[30]

Because of the ASA process, the company attracts, selects, and retains people who share its core values, whereas those people who are different in core values will be excluded from the organization either during the hiring process or later on through naturally occurring turnover. Thus, organizational culture will act as a self-defending organism where intrusive elements are kept out. Supporting the existence of such self-protective mechanisms, research shows that organizations demonstrate a certain level of homogeneity regarding personalities and values of organizational members.[31]

New Employee Onboarding

Another way in which an organization's values, norms, and behavioral patterns are transmitted to employees is through **onboarding** (also referred to as the *organizational socialization process*).[32] Onboarding refers to the process through which new employees learn the attitudes, knowledge, skills, and behaviors required to function effectively within an organization. If an organization can successfully socialize new employees into becoming organizational insiders, new employees will feel accepted by their peers and confident regarding their ability to perform; they will also understand and share the assumptions, norms, and values that are part of the organization's culture. This understanding and confidence in turn translate into more effective new employees who perform better and have higher job

onboarding

The process through which new employees learn the attitudes, knowledge, skills, and behaviors required to function effectively within an organization.

satisfaction, stronger organizational commitment, and longer tenure within the company.[33] Organizations engage in different activities to facilitate onboarding, such as implementing orientation programs or matching new employees with mentors.

What Can Employees Do during Onboarding?

New employees who are proactive, seek feedback, and build strong relationships tend to be more successful than those who do not.[34] For example, *feedback seeking* helps new employees. Especially on a first job, a new employee can make mistakes or gaffes and may find it hard to understand and interpret the ambiguous reactions of coworkers. By actively seeking feedback, new employees may find out sooner rather than later any behaviors that need to be changed and gain a better understanding of whether their behavior fits with the company culture and expectations.

Relationship building or *networking* (a facet of the organizing function) is another important behavior new employees may demonstrate. Particularly when a company does not have a systematic approach to onboarding, it becomes more important for new employees to facilitate their own onboarding by actively building relationships. According to one estimate, 35% of managers who start a new job fail in the new job and either voluntarily leave or are fired within one and a half years. Of these, over 60% report not being able to form effective relationships with colleagues as the primary reason for this failure.[35]

What Can Organizations Do during Onboarding?

Many organizations, including Microsoft, UPS, and Bank of America, take a more structured and systematic approach to new employee onboarding, while others follow a "sink or swim" approach where new employees struggle to figure out what is expected of them and what the norms are.

A **formal orientation program** indoctrinates new employees to the company culture, as well as introducing them to their new jobs and colleagues. An orientation program has a role in making new employees feel welcome in addition to imparting information that may help them be successful in their new jobs. Many large organizations have formal orientation programs consisting of lectures, videotapes, and written material, while some may follow more informal approaches. According to one estimate, most orientations last anywhere from one to five days, and some companies are currently switching to a computer-based orientation. Ritz Carlton Hotel Company uses a very systematic approach to employee orientation and views orientation as the key to retention. In the 2-day classroom orientation, employees spend time with management, dine in the hotel's finest restaurant, and witness the attention to customer service detail firsthand. During these two days, they are introduced to the company's intensive service standards, team orientation, and its own language. Later, on their 21st day, they are tested on the company's service standards and are certified.[36] Research shows that formal orientation programs are helpful in teaching employees about the goals and history of the company, as well as communicating the power structure. Moreover, these programs may also help with a new employee's integration to the team. However, these benefits may not be realized to the same extent in computer-based orientations. In fact, compared to those taking part in a regular, face-to-face orientation, those undergoing a computer-based orientation were shown to have lower understanding of their job and the company, indicating that different formats of orientations may not substitute for each other.[37]

What Can Organizational Insiders Do during Onboarding?

One of the most important ways in which organizations can help new employees adjust to a company and a new job is through *organizational insiders*—namely, supervisors, coworkers, and mentors. Leaders have a key influence over onboarding and the information and support they provide determine how quickly employees learn about the company politics and culture, while coworker influence determines the degree to which employees adjust to their teams. Mentors can be crucial to helping new employees adjust by teaching them the ropes of their jobs and how the company really operates. A mentor is a trusted person who provides an employee with advice and support regarding career-related matters. Although a mentor can be any employee or manager who has insights that are valuable to the new employee, mentors tend to be relatively more experienced than their protégés. Mentoring can occur naturally between two interested individuals or organizations can facilitate this process by having formal mentoring programs. These programs may successfully bring together mentors and protégés who would not come together otherwise.

Research indicates that the existence of these programs does not guarantee their success, and there are certain program characteristics that may make these programs more effective. For example, when mentors and protégés feel that they had input in the mentor-protégé matching process, they tend to be more satisfied with the arrangement. Moreover, when mentors receive training beforehand, the outcomes of the program tend to be more positive.[38] Because mentors may help new employees interpret and understand the company's culture, organizations may benefit from selecting mentors who

---

formal orientation program

A program used to indoctrinate new employees to the company culture, as well as introducing them to their new jobs and colleagues.

---

mentor

A trusted person who provides an employee with advice and support regarding career-related matters.

personify the company's values. Thus, organizations may need to design these programs carefully to increase their chance of success.

Leadership

Leaders are instrumental in creating and changing an organization's culture. There is a direct correspondence between the leader's style and an organization's culture. For example, when leaders motivate employees through inspiration, corporate culture tends to be more supportive and people-oriented. When leaders motivate by making rewards contingent on performance, the corporate culture tended to be more performance-oriented and competitive.[39] In these and many other ways, what leaders do directly influences the cultures of their organizations. This is a key point for managers to consider as they carry out their leading P-O-L-C function.

Part of the leader's influence over culture is through role modeling. Many studies have suggested that leader behavior, the consistency between organizational policy and leader actions, and leader role modeling determine the degree to which the organization's culture emphasizes ethics.[40] The leader's own behaviors will signal to individuals what is acceptable behavior and what is unacceptable. In an organization in which high-level managers make the effort to involve others in decision making and seek opinions of others, a team-oriented culture is more likely to evolve. By acting as role models, leaders send signals to the organization about the norms and values that are expected to guide the actions of its members.

Leaders also shape culture by their reactions to the actions of others around them. For example, do they praise a job well done or do they praise a favored employee regardless of what was accomplished? How do they react when someone admits to making an honest mistake? What are their priorities? In meetings, what types of questions do they ask? Do they want to know what caused accidents so that they can be prevented, or do they seem more concerned about how much money was lost because of an accident? Do they seem outraged when an employee is disrespectful to a coworker, or does their reaction depend on whether they like the harasser? Through their day-to-day actions, leaders shape and maintain an organization's culture.

Reward Systems

Finally, the company culture is shaped by the type of reward systems used in the organization and the kinds of behaviors and outcomes it chooses to reward and punish. One relevant element of the reward system is *whether the organization rewards behaviors or results*. Some companies have reward systems that emphasize intangible elements of performance as well as more easily observable metrics. In these companies, supervisors and peers may evaluate an employee's performance by assessing the person's behaviors as well as the results. In such companies, we may expect a culture that is relatively people- or team-oriented, and employees act as part of a family.[41] However, in companies in which goal achievement is the sole criterion for reward, there is a focus on measuring only the results without much regard to the process. In these companies, we might observe outcome-oriented and competitive cultures. *Whether the organization rewards performance or seniority* would also make a difference in culture. When promotions are based on seniority, it would be difficult to establish a culture of outcome orientation. Finally, *the types of behaviors that are rewarded or ignored* set the tone for the culture. Which behaviors are rewarded, which ones are punished, and which are ignored will determine how a company's culture evolves. A reward system is one tool managers can wield when undertaking the controlling function.

FIGURE 8.11

One of the most famous mentor-protégé relationships in history is that of Socrates and his equally famous student, Plato.

Source: http://en.wikipedia.org/wiki/File:Socrates_and_Plato.jpg

3.3   Signs of Organizational Culture

How do you find out about a company's culture? We emphasized earlier that culture influences the way members of the organization think, behave, and interact with one another. Thus, one way of finding out about a company's culture is by observing employees or interviewing them. At the same time, culture manifests itself in some visible aspects of the organization's environment. In this section, we discuss five ways in which culture shows itself to observers and employees.

FIGURE 8.12 Visual Elements of Culture

Although numerous elements that define an organization's culture are tacit and difficult to define, culture does manifest itself in some visible aspects of the organization's environment. Here, we illustrate five ways in which culture shows itself to observers and employees.

Mission statements provide tangible declarations of purpose, describing who the company is and what it does. The lack of incentives for doctors helps physicians at the Mayo Clinic execute their organization's mission statement of "the needs of the patient come first."

Rituals are repetitive activities within an organization that have symbolic meaning. To show camaraderie with his employees, Sam Adams founder Jim Koch volunteers each year to sit in a dunking booth full of stale beer.

Rules and policies determine acceptable and unacceptable behavior within an organization. Starbucks' policy of giving each employee a free pound of coffee a week encourages a culture where customers and employees alike enjoy a caffeinated beverage.

Physical layout—such as a company's building and layout of employee offices and other workspaces—communicates important messages about a company's culture. Lego, for example, utilizes a number of project rooms to inspire employees to continually innovate and create.

Stories and language provide another way to identify an organization's culture. The story of Apple's humble beginnings, with Steve Jobs and Steve Wozniak creating their first personal computer inside Jobs's garage in Los Altos, California, epitomizes the open, creative culture of innovation and experimentation that continues at Apple today.

Source: (From top to bottom) © Thinkstock; http://www.flickr.com/photos/revjim5000/2349161623/; http://www.flickr.com/photos/ell-r-brown/ 4374203580/; http://www.flickr.com/photos/lilivanili/6990868344/; http://www.flickr.com/photos/37796451@N00/4857349094/.

Mission Statement

A mission statement is a statement of purpose, describing who the company is and what it does. It serves an important function for organizations as part of the first facet of the planning P-O-L-C function. But while many companies have mission statements, they do not always reflect the companies' values and purposes. An effective mission statement is well known by employees, is transmitted to all employees starting from their first day at work, and influences employee behavior.

Some mission statements reflect who the company wants to be as opposed to who they actually are. If the mission statement does not affect employee behavior on a day-to-day basis, it has little usefulness as a tool for understanding the company's culture. Enron provided an often-cited example of a disconnect between a company's mission statement and how the company actually operated. Their missions and values statement started with "As a partner in the communities in which we operate, Enron believes it has a responsibility to conduct itself according to certain basic principles." Their values statement included such ironic declarations as "We do not tolerate abusive or disrespectful treatment. Ruthlessness, callousness and arrogance don't belong here."[42]

A mission statement that is taken seriously and widely communicated may provide insights into the corporate culture. For example, the Mayo Clinic's mission statement is "The needs of the patient come first." This mission statement evolved from the founders who are quoted as saying, "The best interest of the patient is the only interest to be considered." Mayo Clinics have a corporate culture that puts patients first. For example, no incentives are given to physicians based on the number of patients they see. Because doctors are salaried, they have no interest in retaining a patient for themselves, and they refer the patient to other doctors when needed.[43] Walmart may be another example of a company that lives its mission statement and therefore its mission statement may give hints about its culture: "Saving people money so they can live better."[44]

Rituals

Rituals refers to repetitive activities within an organization that have symbolic meaning.[45] Usually rituals have their roots in the history of a company's culture. They create camaraderie and a sense of belonging among employees. They also serve to teach employees corporate values and create identification with the organization. For example, at the cosmetics firm Mary Kay Inc., employees attend ceremonies recognizing their top salespeople with an award of a new car—traditionally a pink Cadillac. These ceremonies are conducted in large auditoriums where participants wear elaborate evening gowns and sing company songs that create emotional excitement. During this ritual, employees feel a connection to the company culture and its values such as self-determination, willpower, and enthusiasm.[46] Another example of rituals is the Saturday-morning meetings of Walmart. This ritual was first created by the company founder Sam Walton, who used these meetings to discuss which products and practices were doing well and which required adjustment. He was able to use this information to make changes in Walmart stores before the start of the week, which gave him a competitive advantage over rival stores who would make their adjustments based on weekly sales figures during the middle of the following week. Today, hundreds of Walmart associates attend the Saturday-morning meetings in the Bentonville, Arkansas, headquarters. The meetings, which run from 7:00 a.m. to 9:30 a.m., start and end with the Walmart cheer; the agenda includes a discussion of weekly sales figures and merchandising tactics. As a ritual, the meetings help maintain a small-company atmosphere, ensure employee involvement and accountability, communicate a performance orientation, and demonstrate taking quick action.[47]

Rules and Policies

Another way in which an observer may find out about a company's culture is to examine its rules and policies. Companies create rules to determine acceptable and unacceptable behavior and, thus, the rules that exist in a company will signal the type of values it has. Policies about issues such as decision making, human resources, and employee privacy reveal what the company values and emphasizes. For example, a company that has a policy such as "all pricing decisions of merchandise will be made at corporate headquarters" is likely to have a centralized culture that is hierarchical, as opposed to decentralized and empowering. Swiss Bank UBS has a 43-page dress code that advises employees on how long their skirts should be, how to "enhance personality" using makeup, and what not to eat to have fresh breath, which could be taken as signs of its customer-oriented, detail-oriented, and rule-oriented corporate culture.[48] The presence or absence of policies on sensitive issues such as English-only rules, bullying and unfair treatment of others, workplace surveillance, open-door policies, sexual harassment, workplace romances, and corporate social responsibility all provide pieces of the puzzle that make up a company's culture. This highlights how interrelated the P-O-L-C functions are in practice. Through rules and policies, the controlling function affects the organization's culture, a facet of organizing.

Impact of HR Practices on Organizational Culture

The following are scenarios of critical decisions you may need to make as a manager one day. Read each question and select one response from each pair of statements. Then think about the effect your choice would have on the company's culture (your organizing function) as well as on your controlling function.

1. Your company needs to lay off 10 people. Would you

   a. lay off the newest 10 people?

   b. lay off the 10 people who have the lowest performance evaluations?

2. You're asked to establish a dress code. Would you

   a. ask employees to use their best judgment?

   b. create a detailed dress code highlighting what is proper and improper?

3. You need to monitor employees during work hours. Would you

    a. not monitor them because they are professionals and you trust them?
    b. install a program monitoring their Web usage to ensure that they are spending work hours actually doing work?

4. You're preparing performance appraisals. Would you

    a. evaluate people on the basis of their behaviors?
    b. evaluate people on the basis of the results (numerical sales figures, etc.)?

5. Who will be promoted? Would you promote individuals based on

    a. seniority?
    b. objective performance?

Physical Layout

A company's building, layout of employee offices, common areas, and other workspaces communicate important messages about a company's culture. For example, visitors walking into the Nike campus in Beaverton, Oregon, can witness firsthand some of the distinguishing characteristics of the company's culture. The campus is set on 74 acres and boasts an artificial lake, walking trails, soccer fields, and cutting-edge fitness centers. The campus functions as a symbol of Nike's values such as energy, physical fitness, an emphasis on quality, and a competitive orientation. In addition, at fitness centers on the Nike headquarters, only those using Nike shoes and apparel are allowed in. This sends a strong signal that loyalty is expected. The company's devotion to athletes and their winning spirit are manifested in campus buildings named after famous athletes, photos of athletes hanging on the walls, and their statues dotting the campus.[49]

The layout of the office space also is a strong indicator of a company's culture. A company that has an open layout where high-level managers interact with employees may have a culture of team orientation and egalitarianism, whereas a company where most high-level managers have their own floor may indicate a higher level of hierarchy. Microsoft employees tend to have offices with walls and a door because the culture emphasizes solitude, concentration, and privacy. In contrast, Intel is famous for its standard cubicles, which reflect its egalitarian culture. The same value can also be observed in its avoidance of private and reserved parking spots.[50] The degree to which playfulness, humor, and fun are part of a company's culture may be indicated in the office environment. For example, Jive Software boasts a colorful, modern, and comfortable office design. Their break room is equipped with a keg of beer, free snacks and sodas, an Xbox 360, and Nintendo Wii. A casual observation of their work environment sends the message that employees who work there see their work as fun.[51]

Stories and Language

Perhaps the most colorful and effective way in which organizations communicate their culture to new employees and organizational members is through the skillful use of stories. A story can highlight a critical event an organization faced and the organization's response to it, or a heroic effort of a single employee illustrating the company's values. The stories usually engage employee emotions and generate employee identification with the company or the heroes of the tale. A compelling story may be a key mechanism through which managers motivate employees by giving their behavior direction and by energizing them toward a certain goal.[52] Moreover, stories shared with new employees communicate the company's history, its values and priorities, and create a bond between the new employee and the organization. For example, Arthur Fry, a scientist at 3M, was using slips of paper to mark the pages of hymns in his church choir, but they kept falling off. He remembered a superweak adhesive that had been invented in 3M's labs, and he coated the markers with this adhesive. Thus, Post-it Notes were born. However, marketing surveys showed that interest in such a product was weak and the distributors were not convinced that it had a market. Instead of giving up, Fry distributed samples of the small yellow sticky notes to secretaries throughout his company. Once they tried them, people loved them and asked for more. Word spread and this led to the ultimate success of the product. As you can see, this story does a great job of describing the core values of a 3M employee: Being innovative by finding unexpected uses for objects, persevering, and being proactive in the face of negative feedback.[53]

Language is another way to identify an organization's culture. Companies often have their own acronyms and buzzwords that are clear to them and help set apart organizational insiders from outsiders. In business, this code is known as jargon. Jargon is the language of specialized terms used by a group or profession. Every profession, trade, and organization has its own specialized terms.

FIGURE 8.14

Google promotes a creative and fun atmosphere by enhancing their buildings with a vast array of visual stimuli, such as this dinosaur sculpture of "Stan" and his pink friends who reside at the Googleplex.

Source:

http://commons.wikimedia.org/wiki/ File:Don%27t_be_evil_-_Googleplex _-_IMG_2445.JPG

Organizational cultures are created by a variety of factors, including founders' values and preferences, industry demands, and early values, goals, and assumptions. Culture is maintained through attraction-selection-attrition, new employee onboarding, leadership, and organizational reward systems. Signs of a company's culture include the organization's mission statement, stories, physical layout, rules and policies, and rituals.

EXERCISES

1. Do you think it is a good idea for companies to emphasize person-organization fit when hiring new employees? What advantages and disadvantages do you see when hiring people who fit with company values?
2. What is the influence of company founders on company culture? Give examples based on your personal knowledge.
3. What are the methods companies use to aid with employee onboarding? What is the importance of onboarding for organizations?
4. What type of a company do you feel you would fit in? What type of a culture would be a misfit for you? In your past work experience, were there any moments when you felt that you did not fit in? Why?
5. What is the role of physical layout as an indicator of company culture? What type of a physical layout would you expect from a company that is people-oriented? Team-oriented? Stable?

4. CREATING CULTURE CHANGE

LEARNING OBJECTIVE

1. Understand the process of culture change.

4.1 How Do Cultures Change?

Culture is a product of its founder's values, its history, and collective experiences. Hence culture is part of a company's DNA and is resistant to change efforts. Many organizations realize that their current culture constitutes a barrier against organizational productivity and performance. Particularly when there is a mismatch between an organization's values and the demands of its environment, changing the culture becomes the key to the company turnaround.

Achieving culture change is challenging, and there are many companies that ultimately fail in this mission. Research and case studies of companies that successfully changed their culture indicate that the following six steps increase the chances of success.[54]

FIGURE 8.15 Process of Culture Change

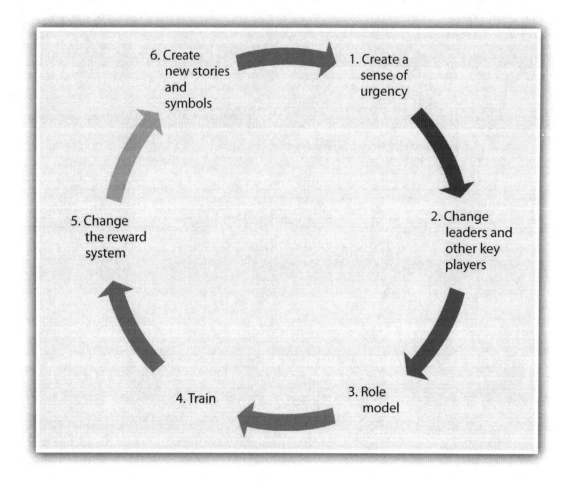

Creating a Sense of Urgency

For the change effort to be successful, it is important to communicate the need for change to employees. One way of doing this is to create a sense of urgency on the part of employees, explaining to them why changing the fundamental way in which business is done is so important. In successful culture change efforts, leaders communicate with employees and present a case for culture change as the essential element that will lead the company to eventual success. As an example, consider the situation at IBM in 1993 when Lou Gerstner was brought in as CEO and chairman. After decades of dominating the market for mainframe computers, IBM was rapidly losing market share to competitors, and its efforts to sell personal computers—the original PC—were seriously undercut by cheaper "clones." In the public's estimation, the name IBM had become associated with obsolescence. Gerstner recalls that the crisis IBM was facing became his ally in changing the organization's culture. Instead of spreading optimism about the company's future, he used the crisis at every opportunity to get buy-in from employees.[55] While IBM sold its personal computer business in 2005, the company continues to be known for exceptional innovation and leadership.

Changing Leaders and Other Key Players

A leader's vision is an important factor that influences how things are done in an organization. Thus, culture change often follows changes at the highest levels of the organization. Moreover, to implement the change effort quickly and efficiently, a company may find it helpful to remove managers and other powerful employees who are acting as a barrier to change. Because of political reasons, self-interest, or habits, managers may create powerful resistance to change efforts. In such cases, replacing these positions with employees and managers giving visible support to the change effort may increase the likelihood that the change effort succeeds. For example, when Robert Iger replaced Michael Eisner as CEO of the Walt Disney Company, one of the first things he did was to abolish the central planning unit, which was staffed by people close to ex-CEO Eisner. This department was viewed as a barrier to creativity at Disney and its removal from the company was helpful in ensuring the innovativeness of the company culture.[56]

Role Modeling

Role modeling is the process by which employees modify their own beliefs and behaviors to reflect those of the leader.[57] CEOs can model the behaviors that are expected of employees to change the culture because these behaviors will trickle down to lower-level employees. For example, when Robert Iger took over Disney, to show his commitment to innovation, he personally became involved in the process of game creation, attended summits of developers, and gave feedback to programmers about the games. Thus, he modeled his engagement in the idea creation process. In contrast, the modeling of inappropriate behavior from the top will lead to the same behavior trickling down to lower levels. A recent example to this type of role modeling is the scandal involving Hewlett-Packard board members. In 2006, when board members were suspected of leaking confidential company information to the press, the company's top-level executives hired a team of security experts to find the source of the leak. The investigators sought the phone records of board members, looking for links to journalists. For this purpose, they posed as board members and called phone companies to obtain itemized home phone records of board members and journalists. When the investigators' methods came to light, HP's chairman and four other top executives faced criminal and civil charges. When such behavior is modeled at top levels, it is likely to have an adverse effect on the company culture.[58]

Training

Well-crafted training programs may be instrumental in bringing about culture change by teaching employees the new norms and behavioral styles. For example, when auto repairer Midas felt the need to change its culture to be more committed to customers, they developed a program to train employees to be more familiar with customer emotions and connect better with them. Customer reports have been overwhelmingly positive in stores that underwent this training.[59]

Changing the Reward System

The criteria with which employees are rewarded and punished have a powerful role in determining the cultural values of an organization. Switching from a commission-based incentive structure to a straight salary system may be instrumental in bringing about customer focus among sales employees. Moreover, by rewarding and promoting employees who embrace the company's new values and promoting these employees, organizations can make sure that changes in culture have a lasting effect. If the company wants to develop a team-oriented culture where employees collaborate with one another, then using individual-based incentives may backfire. Instead, distributing bonuses to intact teams might be more successful in bringing about culture change.

Creating New Symbols and Stories

Finally, the success of the culture change effort may be increased by developing new rituals, symbols, and stories. Prior to its recent merger with United Airlines, Continental Airlines was a company that successfully changed its culture to be less bureaucratic and more team-oriented in the 1990s. One of the first things management did to show employees that they really meant to abolish many of the company's detailed procedures and create a culture of empowerment was to burn the heavy 800-page company policy manual in their parking lot. The new manual was only 80 pages. This action symbolized the upcoming changes in the culture and served as a powerful story that circulated among employees. Another early action was redecorating waiting areas and repainting all their planes, again symbolizing the new order of things.[60] By replacing the old symbols and stories, the new symbols and stories will help enable the culture change and ensure that the new values are communicated.

KEY TAKEAWAY

Organizations need to change their culture to respond to changing conditions in the environment, to remain competitive, and to avoid complacency or stagnation. Culture change often begins by the creation of a sense of urgency. Next, a change of leaders and other key players may enact change and serve as effective role models of new behavior. Training can also be targeted toward fostering these new behaviors. Reward systems are changed within the organization. Finally, the organization creates new stories and symbols. Successful culture change requires managers that are proficient at all of the P-O-L-C functions. Creating and communicating a vision is part of planning; leadership and role modeling are part of leading; designing effective reward systems is part of controlling; all of which combine to influence culture, a facet of organizing.

5. DEVELOPING YOUR PERSONAL SKILLS: LEARNING TO FIT IN

LEARNING OBJECTIVES

1. Understand what you can proactively do to understand a new organizational environment.
2. Some guidelines for proactive onboarding.

5.1 Before You Join

How do you find out about a company's culture before you join? Here are several tips that will allow you to more accurately gauge the culture of a company you are interviewing with.

First, *do your research*. Talking to friends and family members who are familiar with the company, doing an online search for news articles about the company, browsing the company's Web site, and reading its mission statement would be a good start.

Second, *observe the physical environment*. Do people work in cubicles or in offices? What is the dress code? What is the building structure? Do employees look happy, tired, or stressed? The answers to these questions are all pieces of the puzzle.

Third, *read between the lines*. For example, the absence of a lengthy employee handbook or detailed procedures might mean that the company is more flexible and less bureaucratic.

Fourth, *reflect on how you are treated*. The recruitment process is your first connection to the company. Were you treated with respect? Do they maintain contact with you or are you being ignored for long stretches at a time?

Fifth, *ask questions*. What happened to the previous incumbent of this job? What does it take to be successful in this firm? What would their ideal candidate for the job look like? The answers to these questions will reveal a lot about the way they do business.

Finally, *listen to your gut*. Your feelings about the place in general, and your future manager and coworkers in particular, are important signs that you should not ignore.[61]

FIGURE 8.16 Managing Workplace Impressions

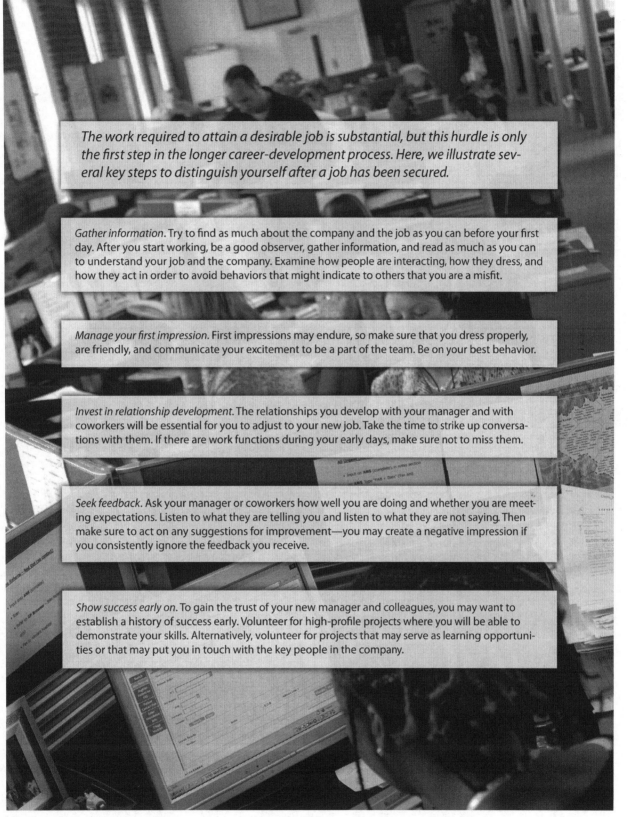

The work required to attain a desirable job is substantial, but this hurdle is only the first step in the longer career-development process. Here, we illustrate several key steps to distinguish yourself after a job has been secured.

Gather information. Try to find as much about the company and the job as you can before your first day. After you start working, be a good observer, gather information, and read as much as you can to understand your job and the company. Examine how people are interacting, how they dress, and how they act in order to avoid behaviors that might indicate to others that you are a misfit.

Manage your first impression. First impressions may endure, so make sure that you dress properly, are friendly, and communicate your excitement to be a part of the team. Be on your best behavior.

Invest in relationship development. The relationships you develop with your manager and with coworkers will be essential for you to adjust to your new job. Take the time to strike up conversations with them. If there are work functions during your early days, make sure not to miss them.

Seek feedback. Ask your manager or coworkers how well you are doing and whether you are meeting expectations. Listen to what they are telling you and listen to what they are not saying. Then make sure to act on any suggestions for improvement—you may create a negative impression if you consistently ignore the feedback you receive.

Show success early on. To gain the trust of your new manager and colleagues, you may want to establish a history of success early. Volunteer for high-profile projects where you will be able to demonstrate your skills. Alternatively, volunteer for projects that may serve as learning opportunities or that may put you in touch with the key people in the company.

EXERCISES

1. What clues does your college or school give about its culture?
2. What are four things you could do today to learn more about an organization you are interested in?
3. Imagine that your good friend is starting a new job next week. What recommendations would you give your friend to help him or her do a great job onboarding into the organization?

6. CASE IN POINT: GOOGLE CREATES UNIQUE CULTURE

FIGURE 8.17

Source: Used with permission from Google, Inc.

Google (NASDAQ: GOOG) is one of the best-known and most admired companies around the world, so much so that "googling" is the term many use to refer to searching for information on the Web. What started out as a student project by two Stanford University graduates—Larry Page and Sergey Brin—in 1996 became the most frequently used Web search engine on the Internet with 4.7 billion searches per day in 2011 alone. Furthermore, Google fosters other innovative applications such as Gmail, Google Earth, Google Maps, and YouTube. Google grew from 10 employees working in a garage in Palo Alto to 33,000 employees operating around the world by 2012. What is the formula behind this success?

Google strives to operate based on solid principles that may be traced back to its founders. Their mission statement summarizes their commitment to end-user needs: "To organize the world's information and to make it universally accessible and useful." While other companies were focused on marketing their sites and increasing advertising revenues, Google stripped the search page of all distractions and presented users with a blank page consisting only of a company logo and a search box. Google resisted pop-up advertising because the company felt that it was annoying to end-users. They insisted that all their advertisements would be clearly marked as "sponsored links." This emphasis on improving the user experience and always putting it before making more money in the short term may have been critical to their success.

Keeping their employees happy is also a value they take to heart. Google created a unique work environment that attracts, motivates, and retains the best players in the field. Google was ranked as the number 1 "Best Place to Work For" by *Fortune* magazine in 2012, up from its number 4 spot in 2011. This is not surprising if one looks closer at how Google treats employees. On their Mountain View, California campus called the "Googleplex," employees are treated to free gourmet food options in the company's 25 cafes, with one employee noting that they are never more than 150 feet away from a stocked pantry. In fact, many employees complain that once they started working for Google, they gained 10 to 15 pounds! Employees have access to gyms, a bowling alley, video games, on-site child care, sleep pods, massages, and doctors. Google provides four months of paternal leave with 75% of full pay and offers $500 for take-out meals for families with a newborn. These perks create a place where employees feel that they are treated well and their needs are met. Moreover, they contribute to the feeling that they are working at a unique and cool place that is different from everywhere else they may have worked.

In addition, Google encourages employee risk taking and innovation. In fact, one of the key reasons Google is an attractive employer is that individuals have the opportunity to work on potentially industry-changing and life-altering projects that are interesting and meaningful. How is the risk-taking orientation maintained? When a vice president in charge of the company's advertising system made a mistake costing the company millions of dollars, she apologized for the mistake, yet was commended by Larry Page, who congratulated her for making the mistake, noting that he would rather run a company where they are moving quickly and doing too much, as opposed to one where they are being too cautious and doing too little. This attitude toward acting fast and accepting the cost of resulting mistakes as a natural consequence of working on the cutting edge may explain why the company is performing so far ahead of competitors such as Microsoft and Yahoo! One of Google's current challenges is to expand to new fields outside of their Web search engine business. To promote new ideas, Google encourages all engineers to spend 20% of their time working on their own ideas.

Google's culture is reflected in their decision making as well. Decisions at Google are made in teams. It is common for several small teams to attack each problem and for employees to try to influence each other using rational persuasion and data. Gut feeling has little impact on how decisions are made. In some meetings, people reportedly are not allowed to say "I think…" but instead must say "the data suggest…." To facilitate teamwork, employees work in open office environments where private offices are assigned only to a select few.

How do they maintain these unique values? In a company emphasizing hiring the smartest people, it is very likely that they will attract big egos that may be difficult to work with. Google realizes that its strength comes from its "small company" values that emphasize risk taking, agility, and cooperation. Therefore, they take their hiring process very seriously. Hiring is extremely competitive, and getting to work at Google is not unlike applying to a college. As they expanded, they relaxed their admission standards a little bit, but this means instead of conducting 12 screening interviews with the same job candidate, they may now conduct four or five. Candidates may be asked to write essays about how they will perform their future jobs. Recently, they targeted potential new employees using billboards featuring brainteasers directing potential candidates to a Web site where they were subjected to more brainteasers. Each candidate may be interviewed by as many as eight people on several occasions. Through this scrutiny, they try to select "Googley" employees who will share the company's values, perform at high levels, and be liked by others within the company.

Will this culture survive in the long run? It may be too early to tell, given that the company was only founded in 1998. The founders emphasized that their initial public offering (IPO) would not change their culture and they would not introduce more rules or change the way things are done at Google to please Wall Street, and so far, they seem to be right. But can a public corporation really act like a start-up? Can a global giant facing scrutiny on issues including privacy, copyright, and censorship maintain its culture rooted in its days spent in a Palo Alto garage? Larry Page is quoted as saying, "We have a mantra: don't be evil, which is to do the best things we know how for our users, for our customers, for everyone. So I think if we were known for that, it would be a wonderful thing."

Case written by Berrin Erdogan and Talya Bauer to accompany Carpenter, M., Bauer, T., Erdogan, B., & Short, J. (2013). Principles of Management (2nd ed.). New York: Flat World Knowledge. Based on information from Elgin, B., Hof, R. D., & Greene, J. (2005, August 8). Revenge of the nerds—again. BusinessWeek. Retrieved September 13, 2012, from http://www.businessweek.com/technology/content/jul2005/tc20050728_5127_tc024.htm; Hardy, Q. (2005, November 14). Google thinks small. Forbes, 176(10); Lashinky, A. (2006, October 2). Chaos by design. Fortune, 154(7); Mangalindan, M. (2004, March 29). The grownup at Google: How Eric Schmidt imposed better management tactics but didn't stifle search giant. Wall Street Journal (p. B1); Lohr, S. (2005, December 5). At Google, cube culture has new rules. New York Times. Retrieved September 13, 2012, from http://www.nytimes.com/2005/12/05/technology/05google.html; Schoeneman, D. (2006, December 31). Can Google come out to play? New York Times. Retrieved September 13, 2012, from http://www.nytimes.com/2006/12/31/fashion/31google.html; Tkaczyk, C., Keating, C., Konrad, A., Vandermey, A., & Kapelke, C. (2012, February 6). The 100 best companies to work for. Fortune, 165(2); Warner, M. (2004, June). What your company can learn from Google. Business 2.0, 5(5).

CASE DISCUSSION QUESTIONS

1. Culture is an essential element of organizing in the P-O-L-C framework. Do you think Google has a strong culture? What would it take to make changes in that culture for better or for worse?
2. Do you think Google's unique culture will help or hurt Google in the long run?
3. What factors are responsible for the specific culture that exists at Google?
4. What type of decision-making approach has Google taken? Do you think this will remain the same over time? Why or why not?
5. Do you see any challenges Google may face in the future because of its emphasis on having a risk-taking culture?

ENDNOTES

1. Chatman, J. A., & Eunyoung Cha, S. (2003). Leading by leveraging culture. *California Management Review, 45*, 19–34; Kerr, J., & Slocum, J. W. (2005). Managing corporate culture through reward systems. *Academy of Management Executive, 19*, 130–138.

2. Barney, J. B. (1986). Organizational culture: Can it be a source of sustained competitive advantage? *Academy of Management Review, 11*, 656–665.

3. Why culture can mean life or death for your organization. (2007, September). *HR Focus, 84*, 9.

4. Kotter, J. P., & Heskett, J. L. (1992). *Corporate culture and performance*. New York: Free Press; Marcoulides, G. A., & Heck, R. H. (1993, May). Organizational culture and performance: Proposing and testing a model. *Organizational Science, 4*, 209–225.

5. Arogyaswamy, B., & Byles, C. H. (1987). Organizational culture: Internal and external fits. *Journal of Management, 13*, 647–658.

6. Schein, E. H. (1992). *Organizational culture and leadership*. San Francisco: Jossey-Bass.

7. Chatman, J. A., & Jehn, K. A. (1991). Assessing the relationship between industry characteristics and organizational culture: How different can you be? *Academy of Management Journal, 37*, 522–553; O'Reilly, C. A., III, Chatman, J. A., & Caldwell, D. F. (1991). People and organizational culture: A profile comparison approach to assessing person-organization fit. *Academy of Management Journal, 34*, 487–516.

8. Lashinsky, A., Burke, D. (2011, May 23). Inside Apple. *Fortune, 163*(7).

9. Greene, J., Reinhardt, A., & Lowry, T. (2004, May 31). Teaching Microsoft to make nice? *Business Week, 3885*, 80–81; Schlender, B. (1998, June 22). Gates's crusade. *Fortune, 137*, 30–32.

10. Copeland, M. V. (2004, July). Best Buy's selling machine. *Business 2.0, 5*, 92–102.

11. Thompson, J. (2005, September). The time we waste. *Management Today*, 44–47.

12. Nohria, N., Joyce, W., & Roberson, B. (2003, July). What really works. *Harvard Business Review, 81*, 42–52.

13. Probst, G., & Raisch, S. (2005). Organizational crisis: The logic of failure. *Academy of Management Executive, 19*, 90–105.

14. Westrum, R. (2004, August). Increasing the number of guards at nuclear power plants. *Risk Analysis: An International Journal, 24*, 959–961.

15. Terlep, S. (2011, June 15). GM's latest change agent tackles designs, red tape. *Wall Street Journal, 257*(138), B1; Welch, D. (2009, June 29). A salvage plan at GM. *BusinessWeek, 4137*.

16. Erdogan, B., Liden, R. C., & Kraimer, M. L. (2006). Justice and leader-member exchange: The moderating role of organizational culture. *Academy of Management Journal, 49*, 395–406.

17. Sheridan, J. (1992). Organizational culture and employee retention. *Academy of Management Journal, 35*, 1036–1056.

18. Weber, G. (2005, February). Preserving the counter culture. *Workforce Management, 84*, 28–34; Motivation secrets of the 100 best employers. (2003, October). *HR Focus, 80*, 1–15.

19. Bolino, M. C., & Turnley, W. H. (2003). Going the extra mile: Cultivating and managing employee citizenship behavior. *Academy of Management Executive, 17*, 60–71.

20. Miles, S. J., & Mangold, G. (2005). Positioning Southwest Airlines through employee branding. *Business Horizons, 48*, 535–545.

21. Erdogan, B., Liden, R. C., & Kraimer, M. L. (2006). Justice and leader-member exchange: The moderating role of organizational culture. *Academy of Management Journal, 49*, 395–406.

22. Arogyaswamy, B., & Byles, C. M. (1987). Organizational culture: Internal and external fits. *Journal of Management, 13*, 647–658; Chatman, J. A., & Eunyoung Cha, S. (2003). Leading by leveraging culture. *California Management Review, 45*, 20–34.

23. Schneider, B., Salvaggio, A., & Subirats, M. (2002). Climate strength: A new direction for climate research. *Journal of Applied Psychology, 87*, 220–229.

24. Charan, R. (2006, April). Home Depot's blueprint for culture change. *Harvard Business Review, 84*, 60–70; Herman, J., & Wernle, B. (2007, August 13). The book on Bob Nardelli: Driven, demanding. *Automotive News, 81*, 42.

25. Flint, P. (2010, June). Merger of equals. *Air Transport World, 47*(6), 47–49.

26. Kerr, J., & Slocum, J. W., Jr. (2005). Managing corporate culture through reward systems. *Academy of Management Executive, 19*, 130–138.

27. Schein, E. H. (1992). *Organizational culture and leadership*. San Francisco: Jossey-Bass.

28. Kiger, P. J. (2005, April). Corporate crunch. *Workforce Management, 84*, 32–38; Rubis, L., Fox, A., Pomeroy, A., Leonard, B., Shea, T. F., Moss, D., …Overman, S. (2005). 50 for history. *HR Magazine, 50*(13), 10–24; Smalley, S. (2007, December 3). Ben & Jerry's bitter crunch. *Newsweek, 150*, 50.

29. Judge, T. A., & Cable, D. M. (1997). Applicant personality, organizational culture, and organization attraction. *Personnel Psychology, 50*, 359–394.

30. Kristof-Brown, A. L., Zimmerman, R. D., & Johnson, E. C. (2005). Consequences of individuals' fit at work: a meta-analysis of person–job, person–organization, person–group, and person–supervisor fit. *Personnel Psychology, 58*, 281–342; O'Reilly, C. A., III, Chatman, J. A., & Caldwell, D. F. (1991). People and organizational culture: A profile comparison approach to assessing person-organization fit. *Academy of Management Journal, 34*, 487–516.

31. Giberson, T. R., Resick, C. J., & Dickson, M. W. (2005). Embedding leader characteristics: An examination of homogeneity of personality and values in organizations. *Journal of Applied Psychology, 90*, 1002–1010.

32. Bauer, T. N., & Erdogan, B. (2010). Organizational socialization: The effective onboarding of new employees. In S. Zedeck, H. Aguinis, W. Cascio, M. Gelfand, K. Leong, S. Parker, & J. Zhou (Eds.), *APA Handbook of industrial and organizational psychology* (Vol. 3, pp. 51–64). Washington, DC: American Psychological Association.

33. Bauer, T. N., Bodner, T., Erdogan, B., Truxillo, D. M., & Tucker, J. S. (2007). Newcomer adjustment during organizational socialization: A meta-analytic review of antecedents, outcomes, and methods. *Journal of Applied Psychology, 92*, 707–721.

34. Bauer, T. N., & Green, S. G. (1998). Testing the combined effects of newcomer information seeking and manager behavior on socialization. *Journal of Applied Psychology, 83*, 72–83; Kammeyer-Mueller, J. D., & Wanberg, C. R. (2003). Unwrapping the organizational entry process: Disentangling multiple antecedents and their pathways to adjustment. *Journal of Applied Psychology, 88*, 779–794; Wanberg, C. R., & Kammeyer-Mueller, J. D. (2000). Predictors and outcomes of proactivity in the socialization process. *Journal of Applied Psychology, 85*, 373–385.

35. Fisher, A. (2005, March 7). Starting a new job? Don't blow it. *Fortune, 151*, 48.

36. Durett, J. (2006, March 1). Technology opens the door to success at Ritz-Carlton. Retrieved September 13, 2012, from http://www.managesmarter.com/msg/search/article_display.jsp?vnu_content_id=100215774; Elswick, J. (2000, February). Puttin' on the Ritz: Hotel chain touts training to benefit its recruiting and retention. *Employee Benefit News, 14*, 9; The Ritz-Carlton Company: How it became a "legend" in service. (2001, January–February). *Corporate University Review, 9*, 16.

37. Klein, H. J., & Weaver, N. A. (2000). The effectiveness of an organizational level orientation training program in the socialization of new employees. *Personnel Psychology, 53*, 47–66; Moscato, D. (2005, April). Using technology to get employees on board. *HR Magazine, 50*, 107–109; Wesson, M. J., & Gogus, C. I. (2005). Shaking hands with a computer: An examination of two methods of organizational newcomer orientation. *Journal of Applied Psychology, 90*, 1018–1026.

38. Allen, T. D., Eby, L. T., & Lentz, E. (2006). Mentorship behaviors and mentorship quality associated with formal mentoring programs: Closing the gap between research and practice. *Journal of Applied Psychology, 91*, 567–578.

39. Sarros, J. C., Gray, J., & Densten, I. L. (2002). Leadership and its impact on organizational culture. *International Journal of Business Studies, 10*, 1–26.

40. Driscoll, K., & McKee, M. (2007). Restorying a culture of ethical and spiritual values: A role for leader storytelling. *Journal of Business Ethics, 73*, 205–217.

41. Kerr, J., & Slocum, J. W., Jr. (2005). Managing corporate culture through reward systems. *Academy of Management Executive, 19*, 130–138.

42. Kunen, J. S. (2002, January 19). Enron's vision (and values) thing. *New York Times*, 19.

43. Jarnagin, C., & Slocum, J. W., Jr. (2007). Creating corporate cultures through mythopoetic leadership. *Organizational Dynamics, 36*, 288–302.

44. Wal-Mart Stores, Inc. (2008). Investor frequently asked questions. Retrieved November 20, 2008, from http://walmartstores.com/Investors/7614.aspx

45. Anand, N. (2005). *Blackwell encyclopedic dictionary of management*. Cambridge: Wiley.

46. Jarnagin, C., & Slocum, J. W., Jr. (2007). Creating corporate cultures through mythopoetic leadership. *Organizational Dynamics, 36*, 288–302.

47. Schlender, B. (2005, April 18). Walmart's $288 billion meeting. *Fortune, 151*, 90–106; Wal around the world. (2001, December 8). *Economist, 361*, 55–57.

48. Dress to impress, says UBS to staff. Retrieved on September 13, 2012, from http://online.wsj.com/article/SB10001424052748704694004576019783931381042.html.

49. Capowski, G. S. (1993, June). Designing a corporate identity. *Management Review, 82*, 37–41; Collins, J., & Porras, J. I. (1996). Building your company's vision. *Harvard Business Review, 74*, 65–77; Labich, K., & Carvell, T. (1995, September 18). Nike vs. Reebok. *Fortune, 132*, 90–114; Mitchell, C. (2002). Selling the brand inside. *Harvard Business Review, 80*, 99–105.

50. Clark, D. (2007, October 15). Why Silicon Valley is rethinking the cubicle office. *Wall Street Journal, 250*, B9.

51. Jive Software. (2008). Careers. Retrieved September 13, 2012, from http://www.jivesoftware.com/company.

52. Beslin, R. (2007). Story building: A new tool for engaging employees in setting direction. *Ivey Business Journal, 71*, 1–8.

53. Higgins, J. M., & McAllester, C. (2002). Want innovation? Then use cultural artifacts that support it. *Organizational Dynamics, 31*, 74–84.

54. Schein, E. H. (1990). Organizational culture. *American Psychologist, 45*, 109–119.

55. Gerstner, L. V. (2002). *Who says elephants can't dance?* New York: HarperCollins.

56. McGregor, J., McConnon, A., Weintraub, A., Holmes, S., & Grover, R. (2007, May 14). The 25 most innovative companies. *Business Week, 4034*, 52–60.

57. Kark, R., & Van Dijk, D. (2007). Motivation to lead, motivation to follow: The role of the self-regulatory focus in leadership processes. *Academy of Management Review, 32*, 500–528.

58. Barron, J. (2007, January). The HP way: Fostering an ethical culture in the wake of scandal. *Business Credit, 109*, 8–10.

59. BST to guide culture change effort at NASA. (2004, June). *Professional Safety, 49*, 16; J. B. (2001, June). The Midas touch. *Training, 38*, 26.

60. Higgins, J., & McAllester, C. (2004). If you want strategic change, don't forget to change your cultural artifacts. *Journal of Change Management, 4*, 63–73.

61. Adapted from ideas in Daniel, L., & Brandon, C. (2006). Finding the right job fit. *HR Magazine, 51*, 62–67; Sacks, D. (2005). Cracking your next company's culture. *Fast Company, 99*, 85–87.

CHAPTER 9
Leading People and Organizations

LEADING PEOPLE AND ORGANIZATIONS

CHAPTER LEARNING OBJECTIVES

Reading this chapter will help you do the following:

1. **Define what leadership is and identify traits of effective leaders.**
2. **Describe behaviors that effective leaders demonstrate.**
3. **Specify the contexts in which various leadership styles are effective.**
4. **Explain the concepts of transformational, transactional, charismatic, servant, and authentic leadership.**
5. **Develop your own leadership skills.**

The P-O-L-C Framework

Planning	Organizing	Leading	Controlling
1. Vision & Mission	1. Organization Design	1. Leadership	1. Systems/Processes
2. Strategizing	2. Culture	2. Decision Making	2. Strategic Human Resources
3. Goals & Objectives	3. Social Networks	3. Communications	
		4. Groups/Teams	
		5. Motivation	

Leadership, by definition, is a key part of the P-O-L-C framework. Leadership may be defined as the act of influencing others to work toward a goal. Leaders exist at all levels of an organization. Some leaders hold a position of authority and may use the power that comes from their position, as well as their personal power, to influence others; they are called **formal leaders**. In contrast, **informal leaders** are without a formal position of authority within the organization but demonstrate leadership by influencing others through personal forms of power. One caveat is important in explaining the nature of leaders: true leaders do not rely on the use of force to influence people. Instead, people willingly adopt the leader's goal as their own goal. If a person is relying on force and punishment, the person is a dictator, not a leader.

formal leaders

Those who hold a position of authority and may utilize the power that comes from their position, as well as their personal power to influence others.

informal leaders

Those without a formal position of authority within the organization but demonstrate leadership by influencing those around them through personal forms of power.

FIGURE 9.2

Abraham Lincoln is frequently ranked in surveys as the greatest U.S. president for his leadership during the American Civil War and famous speeches he gave during his political career.

Source:
http://commons.wikimedia.org/wiki/ File:Abraham_Lincoln_head _on_shoulders_photo_portrait.jpg

What makes leaders effective? What distinguishes people who are perceived as leaders from those who are not perceived as leaders? More importantly, how do we train future leaders and improve their leadership ability? These are important questions that have attracted scholarly attention in the past several decades. In this chapter, we will review the history of leadership studies and summarize the major findings relating to these important questions. Around the world, leaders are at least partly responsible for their team's or company's success and failure. Company chief executive officers (CEOs) are paid millions of dollars in salaries and stock options with the assumption that they hold their company's future in their hands. In politics, education, sports, and profit and nonprofit sectors, influence of leaders over the behaviors of individuals and organizations is rarely questioned. When people and organizations fail, managers and CEOs are often viewed as responsible. Some people criticize the assumption that leadership always matters and call this belief "the romance of leadership." However, research evidence points to the importance of leaders for organizational success.[1]

1. WHO IS A LEADER? TRAIT APPROACHES TO LEADERSHIP

LEARNING OBJECTIVES

1. Learn the position of trait approaches in the history of leadership studies.
2. Explain the traits that are associated with leadership.
3. Discuss the limitations of trait approaches to leadership.

The earliest approach to the study of leadership sought to identify a set of traits that distinguished leaders from nonleaders. What were the personality characteristics and physical and psychological attributes of people who are viewed as leaders? Because of the problems in measurement of personality traits at the time, different studies used different measures. By 1940, researchers concluded that the search for leadership-defining traits was futile. In recent years, though, after advances in personality literature such as the development of the Big Five personality framework, researchers have had more success in identifying traits that predict leadership.[2] Most importantly, charismatic leadership, which is among the contemporary approaches to leadership, may be viewed as an example of a trait approach.

The traits that show relatively strong relations with leadership are as follows:[3]

FIGURE 9.3 Traits Associated with Leadership

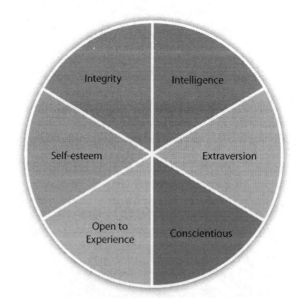

1.1 Intelligence

General mental ability, which psychologists refer to as "g" and which is synonymous with IQ, has been related to a person's emerging as a leader within a group. Specifically, people who have high mental abilities are more likely to be viewed as leaders in their environment.[4] We should caution, though, that intelligence is a positive but modest predictor of leadership. In addition to having high IQ, effective leaders tend to have high emotional intelligence (EQ). People with high EQ demonstrate a high level of self-awareness, motivation, empathy, and social skills. The psychologist who coined the term emotional intelligence, Daniel Goleman, believes that IQ is a threshold quality: it matters for entry- to high-level management jobs, but once you get there, it no longer helps leaders because most leaders already have high IQ. According to Goleman, what differentiates effective leaders from ineffective ones becomes their ability to control their own emotions and understand other people's emotions, their internal motivation, and their social skills.[5] Many observers believe that Carly Fiorina, the ousted CEO of HP, demonstrated high levels of intelligence but low levels of empathy for the people around her, which led to an overreliance on numbers while ignoring the human cost of her decisions.[6]

1.2 Big Five Personality Traits

FIGURE 9.5 Big Five Personality Traits

Trait	Description
Openness	Being curious, original, intellectual, creative, and open to new ideas.
Conscientiousness	Being organized, systematic, punctual, achievement-oriented, and dependable.
Extraversion	Being outgoing, talkative, sociable, and enjoying social situations.
Agreeableness	Being affable, tolerant, sensitive, trusting, kind, and warm.
Neuroticism	Being anxious, irritable, temperamental, and moody.

Source: Goldberg, L. R. (1990). An alternative "description of personality": The big-five factor structure. Journal of Personality & Social Psychology, 59, 1216–1229.

Psychologists have proposed various systems for categorizing the characteristics that make up an individual's unique personality; one of the most widely accepted is the Big Five model, which rates an individual according to openness to experience, conscientiousness, extraversion, agreeableness, and neuroticism. Several of the Big Five personality traits have been related to leadership emergence (whether someone is viewed as a leader by others) and leadership effectiveness.

For example, extraversion is related to leadership. *Extraverts* are sociable, assertive, and energetic. They enjoy interacting with others in their environment and demonstrate self-confidence. Because they are both dominant and sociable in their environment, they emerge as leaders in a wide variety of situations. Out of all personality traits, extraversion has the strongest relationship to both leader emergence and leader effectiveness. This is not to say that all effective leaders are extraverts, but you are more likely to find extraverts in leadership positions. An example of an introverted leader is Jim Buckmaster, CEO of Craigslist. Known as an introvert, he admits to not having meetings because he does not like them.[7] Moreover, recent research has shown that introverted leaders are better than

FIGURE 9.4

An engineering graduate of Stanford, Marissa Mayer was the first female employee at Google. In 2012, she became the CEO of Yahoo! at the age of 37. A "math wiz with a photographic memory," she is the holder of several artificial intelligence patents.

Source:
http://commons.wikimedia.org/wiki/
File:Marissa_Mayer.jpg

extraverted leaders in leading followers who display independent action and initiative, so it is important to recognize that different personality traits may be effective for different followers.[8]

Another personality trait related to leadership is *conscientiousness*. Conscientious people are organized, take initiative, and demonstrate persistence in their endeavors. Conscientious people are more likely to emerge as leaders and be effective as leaders. Finally, people who have *openness to experience*—those who demonstrate originality, creativity, and are open to trying new things—tend to emerge as leaders and tend to be effective as leaders.

1.3 Self-Esteem

Self-esteem is not one of the Big Five personality traits, but it is an important aspect of one's personality. The degree to which people are at peace with themselves and have an overall positive assessment of their self-worth and capabilities seems to be relevant to whether they will be viewed as a leader. Leaders with high self-esteem support their subordinates more, and when punishment needs to be administered, they punish more effectively.[9] It is possible that those with high self-esteem have greater levels of self-confidence and this affects their image in the eyes of their followers. Self-esteem may also explain the relationship between some physical attributes and emerging as a leader. For example, research shows a strong relationship between height and being viewed as a leader (as well as one's career success over life). It is proposed that self-esteem may be the key to the connection of height with leadership, because people who are taller are also found to have higher self-esteem and therefore may project greater levels of charisma as well as confidence to their followers. In fact, research shows that when it comes to height, it is rewarded. One study found that each inch above average was related to $789 more per year in salary for leaders.[10]

1.4 Integrity

Research also shows that people who are effective as leaders tend to have a moral compass and demonstrate honesty and integrity.[11] Leaders whose integrity is questioned lose their trustworthiness, and they hurt their company's business along the way. For example, when it was revealed that Whole Foods CEO John Mackey was using a pseudonym to make negative comments online about the company's rival Wild Oats, his actions were heavily criticized, his leadership was questioned, and the company's reputation was affected.[12]

There are also some traits that are negatively related to emerging as a leader and being successful as a leader. For example, agreeable people who are modest, good natured, and avoid conflict are less likely to be *perceived* as leaders, as they may be perceived as naïve or submissive.[13] The key to benefiting from the findings of trait researchers is to be aware that not all traits are equally effective in predicting leadership potential across all circumstances. Some organizational situations allow leader traits to make a greater difference.[14] For example, in small, entrepreneurial organizations where leaders have a lot of leeway to determine their own behavior, the type of traits leaders have may make a difference in leadership potential. In large, bureaucratic, and rule-bound organizations, such as the government and the military, a leader's traits may have less to do with how the person behaves and whether the person is a successful leader.[15] Moreover, some traits become relevant in specific circumstances. For example, bravery is likely to be a key characteristic in military leaders but not necessarily in business leaders. Scholars now conclude that instead of trying to identify a few traits that distinguish leaders from nonleaders, it is important to identify the conditions under which different traits affect a leader's performance, as well as whether a person emerges as a leader.[16]

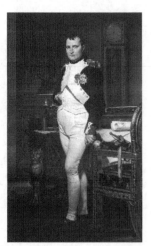

KEY TAKEAWAY

Many studies searched for a limited set of personal attributes, or traits, which would make someone be viewed as a leader and be successful as a leader. Some traits are consistently related to leadership, such as intelligence (both mental ability and emotional intelligence), personality (extraversion, conscientiousness, openness to experience, self-esteem), and integrity. The main limitation of the trait approach was that it ignored the situation in which leadership occurred. Therefore, it is more useful to specify the conditions under which different traits are needed.

EXERCISES

1. What traits are evident in leaders you admire? Are they consistent with the traits discussed in this chapter? If not, why is this person effective despite the presence of different traits?
2. Can the findings of trait approaches be used to train potential leaders? Which traits seem easier to teach? Which are more stable?
3. How can organizations identify future leaders with a given set of traits? Which methods would be useful for this purpose?
4. What other traits can you think of that would be relevant to leadership?

2. WHAT DO LEADERS DO? BEHAVIORAL APPROACHES TO LEADERSHIP

LEARNING OBJECTIVES

1. **Explain the behaviors that are associated with leadership.**
2. **Identify the three alternative decision-making styles leaders use and the conditions under which they are more effective.**
3. **Discuss the limitations of behavioral approaches to leadership.**

When the trait researchers became disillusioned in 1940s, their attention turned to studying leader behaviors. What did effective leaders actually do? Which behaviors helped them to be perceived as leaders? Which behaviors increased their success?

2.1 Leader Behaviors

In order to understand behaviors of effective leaders, researchers at Ohio State University and University of Michigan used many different techniques, such as observing leaders in laboratory settings as well as surveying them directly in workplace settings. This research stream led to the discovery of two broad categories of behaviors: task-oriented behaviors (sometimes called *initiating structure*) and people-oriented behaviors (also called *consideration*). **Task-oriented leader behaviors** involve structuring the roles of subordinates, providing them with instructions, and behaving in ways that will increase the performance of the group. Task-oriented behaviors are directives given to employees to get things done and to ensure that organizational goals are met. **People-oriented leader behaviors** include showing concern for employee feelings and treating employees with respect. People-oriented leaders genuinely care about the well-being of their employees and they demonstrate their concern in their actions and decisions. At the time, researchers thought that these two categories of behaviors were the keys to the puzzle of leadership.[17] However, research did not support the argument that demonstrating both of these behaviors would necessarily make leaders effective.[18]

task-oriented leader behaviors

Behaviors involving structuring the roles of subordinates, providing them with instructions and behaving in ways that will increase the performance of the group. (Also called initiating structure.)

people-oriented leader behaviors

Behaviors that include showing concern for employee feelings and treating employees with respect. (Also called consideration.)

FIGURE 9.8

Laura Chinchilla was elected president of Costa Rica in 2010. She had vastly different responsibilities as a nongovernmental organization (NGO) consultant in Latin America and Africa compared to her roles as minister of justice and then president for Costa Rica. Do you think these differences affected her behavior as a leader?

Source: http://commons.wikimedia.org/wiki/File:Chinchilla_Adelante.jpg

When we look at the overall findings regarding these leader behaviors, it seems that both types of behaviors, in the aggregate, are beneficial to organizations but for different purposes. For example, when leaders demonstrate people-oriented behaviors, employees tend to be more satisfied and react more positively. However, when leaders are task-oriented, productivity tends to be a bit higher.[19] Moreover, the situation in which these behaviors are demonstrated seems to matter. In small companies, task-oriented behaviors were found to be more effective than in large companies.[20] There is also some evidence that working under a leader with very high levels of task-oriented behaviors may cause burnout on the part of employees.[21]

2.2   Leader Decision Making

Another question behavioral researchers focused on was how leaders actually make decisions, and the influence of decision-making styles on leader effectiveness and employee reactions. Three types of decision-making styles were studied. In **autocratic decision making**, leaders make the decision alone without necessarily involving employees in the decision-making process. When leaders use **democratic decision making**, employees participate in the making of the decision. Finally, leaders using **laissez-faire decision making** leave employees alone to make the decision; the leader provides minimum guidance and involvement in the decision.

As with other lines of research on leadership, research did not identify one decision-making style as the best one. It seems that the effectiveness of the style the leader is using depends on the circumstances. A review of the literature shows that when leaders use more democratic decision-making styles, employees tend to be more satisfied, but the effects on decision quality or employee productivity are weaker. Moreover, instead of expecting to be involved in every single decision, employees seem to care more about the overall participativeness of the organizational climate.[22] Different types of employees may also expect different levels of involvement. In a study conducted in a research organization, scientists viewed democratic leadership most favorably and authoritarian leadership least favorably,[23] but employees working in large groups where opportunities for member interaction was limited preferred authoritarian leader decision making.[24]

Finally, the effectiveness of each style seems to depend on who is using it and how they are using it. There are examples of effective leaders using both authoritarian and democratic styles. For example, Larry Page and Sergey Brin at Google are known for their democratic decision-making styles, while Apple's cofounder and former CEO Steve Jobs was renowned for his autocratic leadership style. Through their decision-making styles, all three founders left their mark on these very successful businesses.

FIGURE 9.9 Leaders on Leadership

Here, we illustrate classic quotes from great leaders.

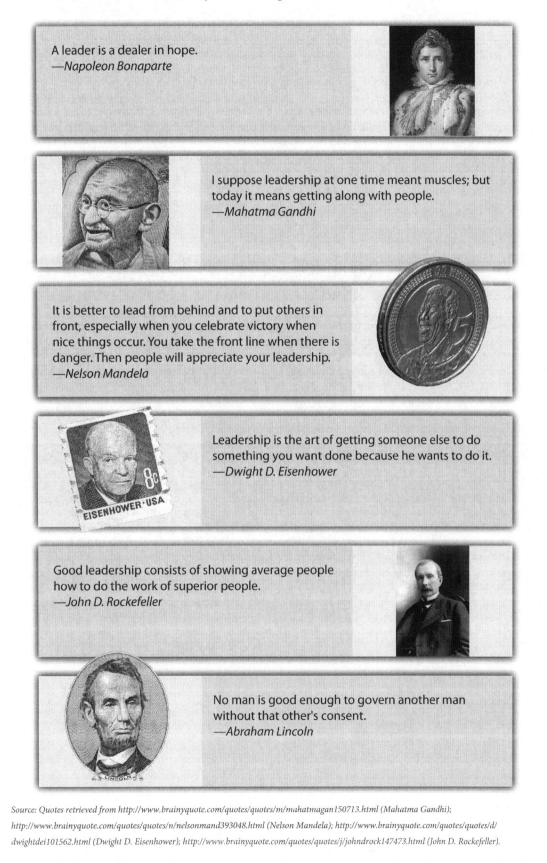

A leader is a dealer in hope.
—*Napoleon Bonaparte*

I suppose leadership at one time meant muscles; but today it means getting along with people.
—*Mahatma Gandhi*

It is better to lead from behind and to put others in front, especially when you celebrate victory when nice things occur. You take the front line when there is danger. Then people will appreciate your leadership.
—*Nelson Mandela*

Leadership is the art of getting someone else to do something you want done because he wants to do it.
—*Dwight D. Eisenhower*

Good leadership consists of showing average people how to do the work of superior people.
—*John D. Rockefeller*

No man is good enough to govern another man without that other's consent.
—*Abraham Lincoln*

Source: Quotes retrieved from http://www.brainyquote.com/quotes/quotes/m/mahatmagan150713.html (Mahatma Gandhi);
http://www.brainyquote.com/quotes/quotes/n/nelsonmand393048.html (Nelson Mandela); http://www.brainyquote.com/quotes/quotes/d/
dwightdei101562.html (Dwight D. Eisenhower); http://www.brainyquote.com/quotes/quotes/j/johndrock147473.html (John D. Rockefeller).

FIGURE 9.10

Google cofounders Larry
Page and Sergey Brin
(shown here with Eric
Schmidt) are known for their
democratic decision-making
styles.

Source:

http://commons.wikimedia.org/wiki/
File:Schmidt-Brin-Page-20080520.jpg

The track record of the laissez-faire decision-making style is more problematic. Research shows that this style is negatively related to employee satisfaction with leaders and leader effectiveness.[25] Laissez-faire leaders create high levels of ambiguity about job expectations on the part of employees, and employees also engage in higher levels of conflict when leaders are using the laissez-faire style.[26]

2.3 Limitations of Behavioral Approaches

Behavioral approaches, similar to trait approaches, fell out of favor because they neglected the environment in which behaviors are demonstrated. The hope of the researchers was that the identified behaviors would predict leadership under all circumstances, but it may be unrealistic to expect that a given set of behaviors would work under all circumstances. What makes a high school principal effective on the job may be very different from what makes a military leader, which would be different from behaviors creating success in small or large business enterprises. It turns out that specifying the conditions under which these behaviors are more effective may be a better approach.

KEY TAKEAWAY

When researchers failed to identify a set of traits that would distinguish effective from ineffective leaders, research attention turned to the study of leader behaviors. Leaders may demonstrate task-oriented and people-oriented behaviors. Both seem to be related to important outcomes, with task-oriented behaviors more strongly relating to leader effectiveness and people-oriented behaviors leading to employee satisfaction. Leaders can also make decisions using authoritarian, democratic, or laissez-faire styles. While laissez-faire has certain downsides, there is no best style and the effectiveness of each style seems to vary across situations. Because of the inconsistency of results, researchers realized the importance of the context in which leadership occurs, which paved the way to contingency theories of leadership.

EXERCISES

1. Give an example of a leader you admire whose behavior is primarily task-oriented, and one whose behavior is primarily people-oriented.
2. What are the limitations of authoritarian decision making? Under which conditions do you think authoritarian style would be more effective?
3. What are the limitations of democratic decision making? Under which conditions do you think democratic style would be more effective?
4. What are the limitations of laissez-faire decision making? Under which conditions do you think laissez-faire style would be more effective?
5. Examine your own leadership style. Which behaviors are you more likely to demonstrate? Which decision-making style are you more likely to use?

3. WHAT IS THE ROLE OF THE CONTEXT? CONTINGENCY APPROACHES TO LEADERSHIP

LEARNING OBJECTIVES

1. Learn about the major situational conditions that determine the effectiveness of different leadership styles.
2. Identify the conditions under which highly task-oriented and highly people-oriented leaders can be successful based on Fiedler's contingency theory.
3. Discuss the main premises of the Path-Goal theory of leadership.
4. Describe a method by which leaders can decide how democratic or authoritarian their decision making should be.

What is the best leadership style? After decades of management research, scholars have learned that more knowledge can be gained by asking, "Under which conditions are different leadership styles more effective?" After the disappointing results of trait and behavioral approaches, several scholars developed leadership theories that specifically incorporated the role of the environment. Researchers started following a contingency approach to leadership—rather than trying to identify traits or behaviors that would be effective under all conditions, the attention moved toward specifying the situations under which different styles would be effective.

3.1 Fiedler's Contingency Theory

The earliest and one of the most influential contingency theories was developed by Frederick Fiedler.[27] According to the theory, a leader's style is measured by a scale called Least Preferred Coworker (LPC) scale. People who are filling out this survey are asked to think of a person who is their least preferred coworker. Then they rate this person in terms of how friendly, nice, and cooperative this person is. Imagine someone you did not enjoy working with. Can you describe this person in positive terms? If you can say that the person you hated working with was still a nice person, you would have a high LPC score. This means that you have a people-oriented personality and you can separate your liking of a person from your ability to work with that person. However, if you think that the person you hated working with was also someone you did not like on a personal level, you would have a low LPC score. To you, being unable to work with someone would mean that you also dislike that person. In other words, you are a task-oriented person.

According to Fiedler's theory, different people can be effective in different situations. The LPC score is akin to a personality trait and is not likely to change. Instead, placing the right people in the right situation or changing the situation is important to increase a leader's effectiveness. The theory predicts that in "favorable" and "unfavorable" situations, a low LPC leader—one who has feelings of dislike for coworkers who are difficult to work with—would be successful. When situational favorableness is medium, a high LPC leader—one who is able to personally like coworkers who are difficult to work with—is more likely to succeed.

How does Fiedler determine whether a situation is favorable, medium, or unfavorable? There are three conditions creating situational favorableness: (1) leader-subordinate relations, (2) position power, and (3) task structure. If the leader has a good relationship with most people, has high position power, and the task is structured, the situation is very favorable. When the leader has low-quality relations with employees, has low position power, and the task is relatively unstructured, the situation is very unfavorable.

Research partially supports the predictions of Fiedler's contingency theory.[28] Specifically, there is more support for the theory's predictions about when low LPC leadership should be used, but there is less support for situations when high LPC leadership should be more effective. Even though the theory was not supported in its entirety, it is a useful framework to think about when task- versus people-oriented leadership may be more effective. Moreover, the theory is important because of its explicit recognition of the importance of the context of leadership.

FIGURE 9.11 Situational Favorableness

Situational favorableness	Leader-subordinate relations	Position Power	Task structure	Best Style
Favorable	Good	High	High	Low LPC Leader
	Good	High	Low	
	Good	Low	High	
Medium	Good	Low	Low	High LPC Leader
	Poor	High	High	
	Poor	High	Low	
	Poor	Low	High	
Unfavorable	Poor	Low	Low	Low LPC leader

Source: Based on information in Fiedler, F. (1967). A Theory of Leadership Effectiveness. New York: McGraw-Hill; Fiedler, F. E. (1964). A contingency model of leader effectiveness. In L. Berkowitz (Ed.), Advances in Experimental Social Psychology (Vol. 1, pp. 149–190). New York: Academic Press.

3.2 Situational Leadership

FIGURE 9.12

Ken Blanchard, a developer of the situational leadership theory, is also known for his best-selling book *The One Minute Manager*, in which he asserts that effective managers provide goals, reprimands, and praises in one-minute increments.

© *Thinkstock*

Another contingency approach to leadership is Kenneth Blanchard and Paul Hersey's Situational Leadership Theory (SLT), which argues that leaders must use different leadership styles depending on their followers' development level.[29] According to this model, employee readiness (defined as a combination of their competence and commitment levels) is the key factor determining the proper leadership style. This approach has been highly popular with 14 million managers across 42 countries undergoing SLT training and 70% of *Fortune* 500 companies employing its use.[30]

The model summarizes the level of directive and supportive behaviors that leaders may exhibit. The model argues that to be effective, leaders must use the right style of behaviors at the right time in each employee's development. It is recognized that followers are key to a leader's success. Employees who are at the earliest stages of developing are seen as being highly committed but with low competence for the tasks. Thus, leaders should be highly directive and less supportive. As the employee becomes more competent, the leader should engage in more coaching behaviors. Supportive behaviors are recommended once the employee is at moderate to high levels of competence. And finally, delegating is the recommended approach for leaders dealing with employees who are both highly committed and highly competent. While the SLT is popular with managers, relatively easy to understand and use, and has endured for decades, research has been mixed in its support of the basic assumptions of the model.[31] Therefore, while it can be a useful way to think about matching behaviors to situations, over-reliance on this model, at the exclusion of other models, is premature.

TABLE 9.1

Situational Leadership Theory helps leaders match their style to follower readiness levels.

Follower Readiness Level	Competence (Low)	Competence (Low)	Competence (Moderate to High)	Competence (High)
	Commitment (High)	Commitment (Low)	Commitment (Variable)	Commitment (High)
Recommended Leader Style	Directing Behavior	Coaching Behavior	Supporting Behavior	Delegating Behavior

3.3 Path-Goal Theory of Leadership

Robert House's path-goal theory of leadership is based on the expectancy theory of motivation.[32] Expectancy theory of motivation suggests that employees are motivated when they believe—or expect—that (1) their effort will lead to high performance, (2) their high performance will be rewarded, and (3) the rewards they will receive are valuable to them. According to the path-goal theory of leadership, the leader's main job is to make sure that all three of these conditions exist. Thus, leaders will create satisfied and high-performing employees by making sure that employee effort leads to performance, and their performance is rewarded. The leader removes roadblocks along the way and creates an environment that subordinates find motivational.

The theory also makes specific predictions about what type of leader behavior will be effective under which circumstances.[33] The theory identifies four leadership styles. Each of these styles can be effective, depending on the characteristics of employees and characteristics of the work environment.

Four Leadership Styles

Path-goal theory of leadership identifies four styles leaders may adopt. **Directive leaders** provide specific directions to their employees. They lead employees by clarifying role expectations, setting schedules, and making sure that employees know what to do on a given workday. The theory predicts that the directive style will work well when employees are experiencing role ambiguity on the job. If people are unclear about how to go about doing their jobs, giving them specific directions will motivate them. However, if employees already have role clarity, and if they are performing boring, routine, and highly structured jobs, giving them direction does not help. In fact, it may hurt them by creating an even more restricting atmosphere. Directive leadership is also thought to be less effective when employees have high levels of ability. When managing professional employees with high levels of expertise and job-specific knowledge, telling them what to do may create a low empowerment environment, which impairs motivation.

Supportive leaders provide emotional support to employees. They treat employees well, care about them on a personal level, and are encouraging. Supportive leadership is predicted to be effective when employees are under a lot of stress or when they are performing boring and repetitive jobs. When employees know exactly how to perform their jobs but their jobs are unpleasant, supportive leadership may also be effective.

Participative leaders make sure that employees are involved in making important decisions. Participative leadership may be more effective when employees have high levels of ability and when the decisions to be made are personally relevant to them. For employees who have a high internal locus of control, or the belief that they can control their own destinies, participative leadership gives employees a way of indirectly controlling organizational decisions, which will be appreciated.

Achievement-oriented leaders set goals for employees and encourage them to reach their goals. Their style challenges employees and focuses their attention on work-related goals. This style is likely to be effective when employees have both high levels of ability and high levels of achievement motivation.

path-goal theory of leadership
Theory stating that a leader's main job is to motivate employees with the beliefs that (1) their effort will lead to high performance, (2) their high performance will be rewarded, and (3) the rewards they will receive are valuable to them.

directive leaders
Those leaders who provide specific directions to their employees.

supportive leaders
Those leaders who provide emotional support to employees.

participative leaders
Those leaders who make sure that employees are involved in making important decisions.

achievement-oriented leaders
Those leaders who set goals for employees and encourage them to reach their goals.

FIGURE 9.13 Predictions of Path-Goal Theory

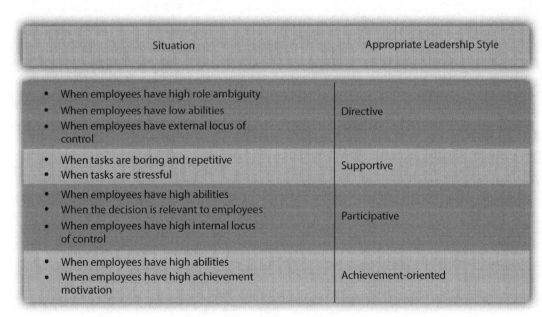

Situation	Appropriate Leadership Style
• When employees have high role ambiguity • When employees have low abilities • When employees have external locus of control	Directive
• When tasks are boring and repetitive • When tasks are stressful	Supportive
• When employees have high abilities • When the decision is relevant to employees • When employees have high internal locus of control	Participative
• When employees have high abilities • When employees have high achievement motivation	Achievement-oriented

Source: On the basis of information presented in House, R. J. (1996). Path-goal theory of leadership: Lessons, legacy, and a reformulated theory. Leadership Quarterly, 7, 323–352; House, R. J., & Mitchell, T. R. (1974). Path-goal theory of leadership. Journal of Contemporary Business, 3, 81–97.

The path-goal theory of leadership has received partial but encouraging levels of support from researchers. Because the theory is highly complicated, it has not been fully and adequately tested.[34] The theory's biggest contribution may be that it highlights the importance of a leader's ability to change styles, depending on the circumstances. Unlike Fiedler's contingency theory, in which the leader's style is assumed to be fixed and only the environment can be changed, House's path-goal theory underlines the importance of varying one's style, depending on the situation.

3.4 Vroom and Yetton's Normative Decision Model

Yale School of Management professor Victor Vroom and his colleagues Philip Yetton and Arthur Jago developed a decision-making tool to help leaders determine how much involvement they should seek when making decisions.[35] The model starts by having leaders answer several key questions and working their way through a funnel based on their responses.

Imagine that you want to help your employees lower their stress so that you can minimize employee absenteeism. There are a number of approaches you could take to reduce employee stress, such as offering gym memberships, providing employee assistance programs, establishing a nap room, and so forth. Refer to the model and start with the first question. As you answer each question as high (H) or low (L), follow the corresponding path down the funnel in Figure 9.14.

FIGURE 9.14

Vroom and Yetton's leadership decision tree shows leaders which styles will be most effective in different situations.

PROBLEM STATEMENT

Decision Significance	Importance of Commitment	Leader Expertise	Likelihood of Commitment	Goal Alignment	Group Expertise	Team Competance	
H	H	H	H	-	-	-	Decide
H	H	H	L	H	H	H	Facilitate
H	H	H	L	H	H	L	Consult (Group)
H	H	H	L	H	L	-	Consult (Group)
H	H	H	L	L	-	-	Consult (Group)
H	H	L	H	H	H	H	Delegate
H	H	L	H	H	H	L	Consult (Individually)
H	H	L	H	H	L	-	Consult (Individually)
H	H	L	H	L	-	-	Consult (Individually)
H	H	L	L	H	H	H	Facilitate
H	H	L	L	H	H	L	Consult (Group)
H	H	L	L	H	L	-	Consult (Group)
H	H	L	L	L	-	-	Consult (Group)
H	L	H	-	-	-	-	Decide
H	L	L	-	H	H	H	Facilitate
H	L	L	-	H	H	L	Consult (Individually)
H	L	L	-	H	L	-	Consult (Individually)
H	L	L	-	L	-	-	Consult (Individually)
L	H	-	H	-	-	-	Decide
L	H	-	L	-	-	H	Delegate
L	H	-	L	-	-	L	Facilitate
L	L	-	-	-	-	-	Decide

Used by permission from Victor H. Vroom.

1. *Decision significance*. The decision has high significance because the approach chosen needs to be effective at reducing employee stress for the insurance premiums to be lowered. In other words, there is a quality requirement to the decision. Follow the path through H.

2. *Importance of commitment.* Does the leader need employee cooperation to implement the decision? In our example, the answer is high, because employees may simply ignore the resources if they do not like them. Follow the path through H.

3. *Leader expertise.* Does the leader have all the information needed to make a high-quality decision? In our example, leader expertise is low. You do not have information regarding what your employees need or what kinds of stress reduction resources they would prefer. Follow the path through L.

4. *Likelihood of commitment.* If the leader makes the decision alone, what is the likelihood that the employees would accept it? Let's assume that the answer is Low. Based on the leader's experience with this group, they would likely ignore the decision if the leader makes it alone. Follow the path from L.

5. *Goal alignment.* Are the employee goals aligned with organizational goals? In this instance, employee and organizational goals may be aligned because you both want to ensure that employees are healthier. So let's say the alignment is high, and follow H.

6. *Group expertise.* Does the group have expertise in this decision-making area? The group in question has little information about which alternatives are costlier or more user friendly. We'll say group expertise is low. Follow the path from L.

7. *Team competence.* What is the ability of this particular team to solve the problem? Let's imagine that this is a new team that just got together and they have little demonstrated expertise to work together effectively. We will answer this as low, or L.

Based on the answers to the questions we gave, the normative approach recommends consulting employees as a group. In other words, the leader may make the decision alone after gathering information from employees and is not advised to delegate the decision to the team or to make the decision alone with no input from the team members.

Vroom and Yetton's model is somewhat complicated, but research results support the validity of the model. On average, leaders using the style recommended by the model tend to make more effective decisions compared with leaders using a style not recommended by the model.[36]

KEY TAKEAWAY

The contingency approaches to leadership describe the role the situation would play in choosing the most effective leadership style. Fiedler's contingency theory argued that task-oriented leaders would be most effective when the situation was the most and the least favorable, whereas relationship-oriented leaders would be effective when situational favorableness was moderate. Situational Leadership Theory takes the maturity level of followers into account. House's path-goal theory states that the leader's job is to ensure that employees view their effort as leading to performance and increase the belief that performance would be rewarded. For this purpose, leaders would use directive, supportive, participative, and achievement-oriented leadership styles, depending on what employees needed to feel motivated. Vroom and Yetton's normative decision model is a guide leaders can use to decide how participative they should be given decision environment characteristics.

EXERCISES

1. Do you believe that the least preferred coworker technique is a valid method of measuring someone's leadership style? Why or why not?

2. Do you believe that leaders can vary their style to demonstrate directive, supportive, achievement-oriented and participative styles with respect to different employees? Or does each leader tend to have a personal style that he or she regularly uses toward all employees?

3. What do you see as the limitations of the Vroom-Yetton leadership decision-making approach?

4. Which of the leadership theories covered in this section do you think are most useful, and least useful, to practicing managers? Why?

4. CONTEMPORARY APPROACHES TO LEADERSHIP

LEARNING OBJECTIVES

1. Learn about the difference between transformational and transactional leaders.
2. Find out about charismatic leadership and how it relates to leader performance.
3. Describe how high-quality leader-subordinate relationships develop.
4. Define servant leadership and evaluate its potential for leadership effectiveness.
5. Define authentic leadership and evaluate its potential for leadership effectiveness.

What leadership theories make the greatest contributions to today's business environment? In this section, we will review the most recent developments in the field of leadership.

FIGURE 9.15 Breaking Through

The glass ceiling refers to the concept of an "invisible barrier" that keeps women and minorities from occupying positions at the top levels of many corporations. While women now comprise more than half of the workforce, in 2012, only 4% of Fortune 500 organizations were headed by female CEOs. Here are a few examples of individuals that have broken through to the other side

A graduate of Princeton University and Harvard Business School, **Meg Whitman** now studies the changing landscape of technology as president and CEO of Hewlett-Packard.

Ranked in *Fortune* magazine's "50 Most Powerful Women in Business" for seven consecutive years, **Virginia Rometty** is also distinguished as the first female CEO of IBM.

The toast of PepsiCo's empire is **Indra Nooyi**, who has doubled net profit since she started as chief financial officer in 2000; she currently serves as chairperson and CEO.

Irene Rosenfeld is in a good position to school her stakeholders on the merits of the Kraft Foods empire she leads as chairperson and CEO; Rosenfeld holds multiple degrees—including a PhD in Marketing and Statistics from Cornell University.

The first African American female head of a Fortune 500 company, the accomplishments of Xerox CEO and chairperson **Ursula Burns** cannot be copied.

Avon Products, Inc., has operated with the goal of serving women for more than 125 years, and this tradition is carried today by the work of current CEO **Sheri McCoy**, whose previous experience was as a research scientist for Johnson & Johnson.

Source: Meg Whitman photo courtesy of http://www8.hp.com/us/en/company-information/executive-team/meg-whitman.html; Virginia Rometty photo courtesy of http://www-03.ibm.com/ press/us/en/biographies.wss; Indra Nooyi image used by permission of PepsiCo Incorporated; Irene Rosenfeld photo courtesy of http://www.kraftfoodscompany.com/MediaCenter/image-gallery/ index.aspx; Ursula Burns photo courtesy of http://www.xerox.com/about-xerox/executive-leadership/ceo/enus.html; Sheri McCoy photo courtesy of http://media.avoncompany.com/ index.php?s=22969&cat=74; background image © Thinkstock.

4.1 Transformational Leadership

Transformational leadership theory is a relatively recent addition to the literature, but more research has been conducted on this theory than all the contingency theories combined. The theory distinguishes between transformational and transactional leaders. **Transformational leaders** lead employees by aligning employee goals with the leader's goals. Thus, employees working for transformational leaders start focusing on the company's well-being rather than on what is best for them as individual employees. However, **transactional leaders** ensure that employees demonstrate the right behaviors because the leader provides resources in exchange.[37]

Transformational leaders have four tools in their possession, which they use to influence employees and create commitment to the company goals.[38] First, transformational leaders are charismatic. **Charisma** refers to behaviors leaders demonstrate that inspire confidence, commitment, and admiration toward the leader.[39] Charismatic individuals have a "magnetic" personality that is appealing to followers. Leaders such as John F. Kennedy, Ronald Reagan, Mahatma Gandhi, Mustafa Kemal Ataturk (founder of the Republic of Turkey), and Winston Churchill are viewed as charismatic. Second, transformational leaders use **inspirational motivation** or come up with a vision that is inspiring to others. Third is the use of **intellectual stimulation**, which means that they challenge organizational norms and status quo, and they encourage employees to think creatively and work harder. Finally, they use **individualized consideration**, which means that they show personal care and concern for the well-being of their followers. Examples of transformational business leaders include the late Steve Jobs of Apple; Lee Iacocca, who transformed Chrysler in the 1980s; and Jack Welch, who was the CEO of General Electric for 20 years. Each of these leaders is charismatic and is held responsible for the turnarounds of their companies.

While transformational leaders rely on their charisma, persuasiveness, and personal appeal to change and inspire their companies, transactional leaders use three other methods. **Contingent rewards** mean rewarding employees for their accomplishments. **Active management by exception** involves leaving employees to do their jobs without interference, but at the same time proactively predicting potential problems and preventing them from occurring. **Passive management by exception** is similar in that it involves leaving employees alone, but in this method, the manager waits until something goes wrong before coming to the rescue.

Research shows that transformational leadership is a powerful influence over leader effectiveness as well as employee satisfaction.[40] In fact, transformational leaders increase the intrinsic motivation of their followers, build more effective relationships with employees, increase performance and creativity of their followers, increase team performance, and create higher levels of commitment to organizational change efforts.[41] However, except for passive management by exception, the transactional leadership styles are also effective, and they also have positive influences over leader performance as well as employee attitudes.[42] To maximize their effectiveness, leaders are encouraged to demonstrate both transformational and transactional styles. They should also monitor themselves to avoid demonstrating passive management by exception or leaving employees to their own devices until problems arise.

Why is transformational leadership more effective? The key factor may be **trust**. Trust is the belief that the leader will show integrity, fairness, and predictability in his or her dealings with others. Research shows that when leaders demonstrate transformational leadership behaviors, followers are more likely to trust the leader. The tendency to trust in transactional leaders is substantially lower. Because transformational leaders express greater levels of concern for people's well-being, and appeal to people's values, followers are more likely to believe that the leader has a trustworthy character.[43]

Some people assume that charisma is something people are born with. However, research does not support this idea. We must acknowledge that there is a connection between some personality traits and charisma. Specifically, people who have a neurotic personality tend to demonstrate lower levels of charisma, and people who are extraverted tend to have higher levels of charisma. However, personality explains only around 10% of the variance in charisma.[44] A large body of research has shown that it is possible to train people to increase their charisma and increase their transformational leadership.[45]

transformational leaders

Those leaders who lead employees by aligning employee goals with the leader's goals.

transactional leaders

Those leaders who ensure that employees demonstrate the right behaviors because the leader provides resources in exchange.

charisma

Behaviors leaders demonstrate that create confidence, commitment, and admiration to the leader.

inspirational motivation

When leaders come up with a vision that is inspiring to others.

intellectual stimulation

When leaders challenge organizational norms and status quo and encourage employees to think creatively and work harder.

individualized consideration

When leaders show personal care and concern for the well-being of their followers.

contingent rewards

Rewarding employees for their accomplishments.

active management by exception

Leaving employees alone but at the same time proactively predicting potential problems and preventing them from occurring.

passive management by exception

Leaving employees alone but then coming to the rescue if anything goes wrong.

trust

The belief that the other party will show integrity, fairness, and predictability in one's actions toward the other.

Even if charisma may be teachable, a more fundamental question remains: is it really needed? Charisma is only one element of transformational leadership and leaders can be effective without charisma. In fact, charisma has a dark side. For every charismatic hero such as Lee Iacocca, Indra Nooyi, and Virgin's Sir Richard Branson, there are charismatic personalities who harmed their organizations or nations, such as Adolph Hitler of Germany and Jeff Skilling of Enron. Leadership experts warn that when organizations are in a crisis, a board of directors or hiring manager may turn to heroes who they hope will save the organization and sometimes hire people who have no other particular qualifications outside of perceived charisma.[46]

An interesting study shows that when companies have performed well, their CEOs are perceived as charismatic, but CEO charisma has no relation to the future performance of a company.[47] So, what we view as someone's charisma may be largely because of their association with a successful company, and the success of a company depends on a large set of factors, including industry effects and historical performance. While it is true that charismatic leaders may sometimes achieve great results, the search for charismatic leaders under all circumstances may be fruitless.

TABLE 9.2

Transformational Leaders		Transactional Leaders	
Charisma	Inspire commitment and confidence	**Contingent rewards**	Reward employees for accomplishments
Inspirational motivation	Develop a vision that inspires others	**Active management by exception**	Leave employees alone but proactively predict problems
Intellectual stimulation	Challenge the status quo	**Passive management by exception**	Leave employees alone and come to their rescue when things go wrong
Individualized consideration	Show support to employees		

4.2 Leader-Member Exchange Theory

Leader-member exchange (LMX) theory proposes that the type of relationship leaders have with their followers (members of the organization) is the key to understanding how leaders influence employees. Leaders form different types of relationships with their employees. In **high-quality LMX relationships**, the leader forms a trust-based relationship with the member. The leader and member like each other, help each other when needed, and respect one another. In these relationships, the leader and the member are both ready to go above and beyond their job descriptions to promote the other's ability to succeed. In contrast, in **low-quality LMX relationships**, the leader and the member have lower levels of trust, liking, and respect toward each other. These relationships do not have to involve actively disliking each other, but the leader and member do not go beyond their formal job descriptions in their exchanges. In other words, the member does his or her job, the leader provides rewards and punishments, and the relationship does not involve high levels of loyalty or obligation toward each other.[48]

FIGURE 9.17 Factors Contributing to the Development of a High-Quality Leader-Member Exchange and Its Consequences

If you have work experience, you may have witnessed the different types of relationships managers form with their employees. In fact, many leaders end up developing differentiated relationships with their followers. Within the same work group, they may have in-group members who are close to them and out-group members who are more distant. If you have ever been in a high-quality LMX relationship with your manager, you may attest to its advantages. Research shows that high-quality LMX members are more satisfied with their jobs, more committed to their companies, have higher levels of clarity about what is expected of them, and perform at a higher level.[49] Their high levels of performance may not be a surprise because they may receive higher levels of resources and help from their managers as well as more information and guidance. If they have questions, these employees feel more comfortable seeking feedback or information.[50] Because of all the help, support, and guidance they receive, those employees who have a good relationship with the manager are in a better position to perform well. Given all they receive, these employees are motivated to reciprocate to the manager, and therefore they demonstrate higher levels of citizenship behaviors such as helping the leader and coworkers.[51] Being in a high-quality LMX relationship is also advantageous because a high-quality relationship is a buffer against many stressors, such as being a misfit in a company, having personality traits that do not match job demands, and having unmet expectations.[52] The list of benefits high-quality LMX employees receive is long, and these employees are less likely to leave their jobs.[53]

Not all employees have a high-quality relationship, and those who are in the leader's out-group may suffer as a result. But how do you end up developing such a high-quality relationship with the leader? That seems to depend on many factors. Managers can help develop such a high-quality and trust-based relationship by treating their employees in a fair and dignified manner.[54] They can also test to see whether the employee is trustworthy by delegating certain tasks when the employee first starts working with the manager.[55] Employees also have an active role in developing the relationship. Employees can seek feedback to improve their performance, be open to learning new things on the job, and engage in political behaviors such as flattery.[56]

Interestingly, high performance on the employee's part does not seem to be enough to develop a high-quality exchange with the leader. Instead, interpersonal factors such as personality similarity and liking are more powerful influences over how the relationship develops.[57] Finally, the relationship development occurs in a slightly different manner in different types of companies; corporate culture matters in how leaders develop these relationships. In performance-oriented cultures, how the leader distributes rewards seem to be the relevant factor, whereas in people-oriented cultures, whether the leader treats people with dignity is more relevant.[58]

Should you worry if you do not have a high-quality relationship with your manager? One problem in a low-quality exchange is that you may not have access to the positive work environment available to the high-quality LMX members. Second, low LMX employees may feel that their situation is unfair. Even when their objective performance does not warrant it, those who have a good relationship with the leader tend to receive positive performance appraisals.[59] Moreover, they are more likely to be given the benefit of the doubt. For example, when they succeed, the manager is more likely to think that they succeeded because they put forth a lot of effort and they had high abilities, whereas for low LMX members who perform objectively well, the manager is less likely to think so.[60] In other words, the leader may interpret the same situation differently, depending on which employee is involved and may reward low LMX employees less even when they are performing well. In short, those with a low-quality relationship with the leader may experience a work environment that may not be very supportive or fair.

Despite its negative consequences, we cannot say that all employees want to have a high-quality relationship with the leader. Some employees may genuinely dislike the leader and may not value the rewards in the leader's possession. If the leader is not well liked in the company and is known as abusive or unethical, being close to such a person may imply guilt by association. For employees who have no interest in advancing their careers in the current company (such as a student employee who is working in retail but has no interest in retail as a career), having a low-quality exchange may afford the opportunity to just do one's job without having to go above and beyond these job requirements. Finally, not all leaders are equally capable of influencing their employees by having a good relationship with their employees: It also depends on the power and influence of the leader in the overall company and how the leader himself or herself is treated within the company. Leaders who are more powerful will have more to share with employees who are close to them. Research shows that when leaders are unable to build high-quality relations with all team members, creating a culture of fairness within the group becomes even more important for performance and employee retention.[61]

What LMX theory implies for leaders is that one way of influencing employees is through the types of relationships leaders form with their employees. These relationships develop naturally because of the work-related and personal interactions between the manager and the employee. Because they occur naturally, some leaders may not be aware of the power that lies in them. These relationships have an important influence over employee attitudes and behaviors. In the worst case, they have the potential to create a negative work environment characterized by favoritism and unfairness. Therefore, managers are advised to be aware of how they build these relationships; put forth effort in cultivating these relationships consciously; be open to forming good relationships with people from all backgrounds regardless of their permanent characteristics such as sex, race, age, or disability status; and prevent these relationships from leading to an unfair work environment.

Self-Assessment: Rate Your LMX

Answer the following questions using 1 = not at all, 2 = somewhat, 3 = fully agree

1. _____ I like my supervisor very much as a person.
2. _____ My supervisor is the kind of person one would like to have as a friend.
3. _____ My supervisor is a lot of fun to work with.
4. _____ My supervisor defends my work actions to a superior, even without complete knowledge of the issue in question.
5. _____ My supervisor would come to my defense if I were "attacked" by others.
6. _____ My supervisor would defend me to others in the organization if I made an honest mistake.
7. _____ I do work for my supervisor that goes beyond what is specified in my job description.
8. _____ I am willing to apply extra efforts, beyond those normally required, to further the interests of my work group.
9. _____ I do not mind working my hardest for my supervisor.
10. _____ I am impressed with my supervisor's knowledge of his/her job.
11. _____ I respect my supervisor's knowledge of and competence on the job.
12. _____ I admire my supervisor's professional skills.

Scoring:

Add your score for 1, 2, 3 = _____ This is your score on the *Liking* factor of LMX.

A score of 3 to 4 indicates a low LMX in terms of liking. A score of 5 to 6 indicates an average LMX in terms of liking. A score of 7+ indicates a high-quality LMX in terms of liking.

Add your score for 4, 5, 6 = _____ This is your score on the *Loyalty* factor of LMX.

A score of 3 to 4 indicates a low LMX in terms of loyalty. A score of 5 to 6 indicates an average LMX in terms of loyalty. A score of 7+ indicates a high-quality LMX in terms of loyalty.

Add your score for 7, 8, 9 = _____ This is your score on the *Contribution* factor of LMX.

A score of 3 to 4 indicates a low LMX in terms of contribution. A score of 5 to 6 indicates an average LMX in terms of contribution. A score of 7+ indicates a high-quality LMX in terms of contribution.

Add your score for 10, 11, 12 = _____ This is your score on the *Professional Respect* factor of LMX.

A score of 3 to 4 indicates a low LMX in terms of professional respect. A score of 5 to 6 indicates an average LMX in terms of professional respect. A score of 7+ indicates a high-quality LMX in terms of professional respect.

Source: Adapted from Liden, R. C., & Maslyn, J. M. (1998). Multidimensionality of leader-member exchange: An empirical assessment through scale development. *Journal of Management, 24*, 43–72. Used by permission of Sage Publications.

4.3   Servant Leadership

The early 21st century has been marked by a series of highly publicized corporate ethics scandals: between 2000 and 2003, Enron, WorldCom, Arthur Andersen, Qwest, and Global Crossing shook investor confidence in corporations and leaders. The importance of ethical leadership and keeping long-term interests of stakeholders in mind is becoming more widely acknowledged.

servant leadership

A leadership approach that defines the leader's role as serving the needs of others.

The **servant leadership** approach defines the leader's role as serving the needs of others. According to this approach, the primary mission of the leader is to develop employees and help them reach their goals. Servant leaders put their employees first, understand their personal needs and desires, empower them, and help them develop in their careers. Unlike mainstream management approaches, the overriding objective in servant leadership is not necessarily getting employees to contribute to organizational goals. Instead, servant leaders feel an obligation to their employees, customers, and the external community. Employee happiness is seen as an end in itself, and servant leaders sometimes sacrifice their own well-being to help employees succeed. In addition to a clear focus on having a moral compass, servant leaders are also interested in serving the community. In other words, their efforts to help others are not restricted to company insiders, and they are genuinely concerned about the broader community surrounding their company.[62] According to historian Doris Kearns Goodwin, Abraham Lincoln was a servant leader because of his balance of social conscience, empathy, and generosity.[63]

Even though servant leadership has some overlap with other leadership approaches, its explicit focus on ethics, community development, and self-sacrifice are distinct characteristics of this leadership style. Research shows that servant leadership has a positive effect on employee commitment, employee citizenship behaviors toward the community (such as participating in community volunteering), and job performance.[64] Leaders who follow the servant leadership approach create a climate of fairness in their departments, which leads to higher levels of interpersonal helping behavior.[65]

Servant leadership is a tough transition for many managers who are socialized to put their own needs first, emphasize success, and tell people what to do. However, leaders who have adopted this approach attest to its effectiveness. David Wolfskehl, of Action Fast Print in New Jersey, founded his printing company when he was 24. He marks the day he started asking employees what he can do for them as the beginning of his company's new culture. In the next two years, his company increased its productivity by 30%.[66]

4.4 Authentic Leadership

Effective leaders have to stay true to themselves. The **authentic leadership approach** embraces this value: its key advice is "be yourself." Individuals all have different backgrounds, different life experiences, and different role models. Events over the course of our lifetime shape our values, preferences, and priorities. Instead of trying to fit into societal expectations about what a leader should be like, act like, or look like, authentic leaders derive their strength from their own past experiences. Thus, one key characteristic of authentic leaders is that they are self-aware. They are introspective, understand where they are coming from, and have a thorough understanding of their own values and priorities. Second, they are not afraid to act the way they are. In other words, they have high levels of personal integrity. They say what they think. They behave in a way consistent with their values—they practice what they preach. Instead of trying to imitate other great leaders, they find their style in their own personality and life experiences.[67]

One example of an authentic leader is Howard Schultz, the founder of Starbucks coffeehouses. As a child, Schultz witnessed the job-related difficulties his father experienced because of medical problems. Even though he had no idea he would have his own business one day, the desire to protect people was shaped in those years and became one of his foremost values. When he founded Starbucks, he became an industry pioneer in providing health insurance and retirement coverage to part-time as well as full-time employees.[68]

Authentic leadership requires understanding oneself. Therefore, in addition to self-reflection, feedback from others is needed to gain a true understanding of one's behavior and effect on others. Authentic leadership is viewed as a potentially influential style because employees are more likely to trust such a leader. Moreover, working for authentic leaders is likely to lead to greater levels of satisfaction, performance, and overall well-being on the part of employees.[69] Best-selling author Jim Collins studied companies that had, in his opinion, gone from good to great, and he found they had one thing in common.[70] All of these companies had what he calls Level 5 leaders who build organizations through their personal humility and professional will. He notes that Level 5 leaders are modest and understated. In many ways, they can be seen as truly authentic leaders.

authentic leadership approach

Effective leaders who stay true to themselves.

FIGURE 9.18

An example of an authentic leader is Howard Schultz, the founder of Starbucks coffeehouses. Witnessing his father losing jobs because of medical problems, he became passionate about a company's need to care for its employees.

Source: http://upload.wikimedia.org/wikipedia/commons/ archive/a/ae/20081006001508!Howard-Schultz- Starbucks.jpg

KEY TAKEAWAY

Contemporary approaches to leadership include transformational leadership, leader-member exchange, servant leadership, and authentic leadership. The transformational leadership approach highlights the importance of leader charisma, inspirational motivation, intellectual stimulation, and individualized consideration as methods of influence. Its counterpart is the transactional leadership approach, in which the leader focuses on getting employees to achieve organizational goals. According to leader-member exchange (LMX) approach, the unique, trust-based relationships leaders develop with employees is the key to leadership effectiveness. Recently, leadership scholars started to emphasize the importance of serving others and adopting a customer-oriented view in leadership; another recent focus is on the importance of being true to oneself as a leader. While each leadership approach focuses on a different element of leadership, effective leaders will need to change their style based on the demands of the situation as well as using their own values and moral compass.

EXERCISES

1. What are the characteristics of transformational leaders? Are transformational leaders more effective than transactional leaders?
2. What is charisma? What are the advantages and disadvantages of charismatic leadership? Should organizations look for charismatic leaders when selecting managers?
3. What are the differences (if any) between a leader having a high-quality exchange with employees and being friends with employees?
4. What does it mean to be a servant leader? Do you know any leaders whose style resembles servant leaders? What are the advantages of adopting such a leadership style?
5. What does it mean to be an authentic leader? How would such a style be developed?
6. Fred Fiedler once quipped, "We need a pretzel-shaped theory for a pretzel-shaped world." Do you agree or disagree with this statement? Why or why not?

5.   DEVELOPING YOUR LEADERSHIP SKILLS

LEARNING OBJECTIVES

1. **Develop your charismatic leadership.**
2. **Learn how to be a servant leader.**
3. **Follow a process to develop your own authentic leadership.**

In this section, we provide tips to help develop charismatic, servant, and authentic leadership skills. Each of these contemporary approaches to leadership is believed to be related to employee attitudes and a healthy work environment.

5.1   Develop Your Charismatic Leadership Skills

Charismatic individuals have a "magnetic" personality that is appealing to followers. While many people assume that charisma is innate, it is possible to improve your charisma by following these suggestions:[71]

Have a vision around which people can gather. When framing requests or addressing to others, instead of emphasizing short-term goals, stress the importance of the long-term vision. When giving a message, think about the overarching purpose. What is the ultimate goal? Why should people care? What are you trying to achieve?

Tie the vision to history. In addition to stressing the ideal future, charismatic leaders bring up the history and how the shared history ties to the future.

Watch your body language. Charismatic leaders are passionate about their ideas. This involves truly believing in your own ideas. When talking to others, you may want to look confident, look them in the eye, and express your belief in your ideas.

Make sure that employees have confidence in themselves. You can achieve this by showing that you believe in them and trust their abilities. If they have real reason to doubt their abilities, make sure that you help them address the underlying issue, such as through training and mentoring.

Challenge the status quo. Charismatic leaders solve current problems by radically rethinking the way things are done and suggesting alternatives that are risky, novel, and unconventional.

5.2   Develop Your Servant Leadership Skills

One of the influential leadership paradigms involves leaders putting others first. This could be a challenging transition for an achievement-oriented and success-driven manager who rises to high levels. Here are some tips to achieve servant leadership.[72]

Don't ask what your employees can do for you. Think of what you can do for them. Your job as a leader is to be of service to them. How can you relieve their stress? Protect them from undue pressure? Pitch in to help them? Think about creative ways of helping ease their lives.

One of your key priorities should be to help employees reach their goals. This involves getting to know them personally. Learn about who they are and what their values and priorities are.

Be humble. You are not supposed to have all the answers and dictate to others. One way of achieving this humbleness may be to do volunteer work.

Be open with your employees. Ask them questions. Give them information so that they understand what is going on in the company.

Find ways of helping the external community. Give employees opportunities to be involved in community volunteer projects or strategize about making a positive impact on the greater community.

5.3   Develop Your Authentic Leadership Skills

Authentic leaders have high levels of self-awareness and their behavior is driven by their core personal values. This leadership approach recognizes the importance of self-reflection and understanding one's life history. Address the following questions to gain a better understanding of your own core values and authentic leadership style.

FIGURE 9.19

Former Microsoft CEO Bill Gates, founder of the Bill and Melinda Gates Foundation, is transforming the face of philantrophy by following a visionary, data-driven approach to identify and solve key issues in health, poverty, and literacy around the world.

Source: http://en.wikipedia.org/wiki/ File:BillGates2012.jpg

Understand Your History

- *Review your life history*. What are the major events in your life? How did these events make you the person you are right now?
- *Think about your role models*. Who were your role models as you were growing up? What did you learn from your role models?

Take Stock of Who You Are Now

- *Describe your personality*. How does your personality affect your life?
- *Know your strengths and weaknesses*. What are they and how can you continue to improve yourself?

Reflect on Your Successes and Challenges

- *Keep a journal*. Research shows that journaling is an effective tool for self-reflection. Write down challenges you face and how you will surmount them; periodically review your entries to check your progress.

Make Integrity a Priority

- *Understand your core values*. What are your core values? Name three of your most important values.
- *Do an ethics check*. Are you being consistent with your core values? If not, how can you get back on track?

Understand the Power of Words

- *Words shape reality*. Keep in mind that the words you use to describe people and situations matter. For example, how might the daily reality be different if you refer to those you manage as associates or team members rather than employees or subordinates?

In view of your answers to the questions above, what kind of a leader would you be if you truly acted out your values? How would people working with you respond to such a leadership style?

KEY TAKEAWAY

The various leadership styles have their pros and cons. It is valuable to be able to assess them in light of your situation and your personal style. Authenticity has become recognized as being important regardless of the other leadership styles one uses. Anyone can be an authentic leader if he or she develops those skills. There is no time like the present to start!

EXERCISES

1. What is the connection between leadership and ethics?
2. Do you believe that ethical leaders are more successful in organizations?
3. Have you ever had an authentic leader? What did this person do that made you consider him or her to be authentic? How effective was his or her leadership?

6. CASE IN POINT: INDRA NOOYI DRAWS ON VISION AND VALUES TO LEAD

FIGURE 9.20

Source: http://www.pepsico.com/images/bio_hires_indra_nooyi.jpg

She was among the top 100 most influential people according to *Time* magazine's 2008 list. In 2012, she was ranked number 4 in *Forbes*'s "Most Influential Women in the World" (2012) and number 2 in *Fortune*'s "50 Most Powerful Women." To those familiar with her work and style, this comes as no surprise. Even before she became the CEO of PepsiCo Inc. (NYSE: PEP) in 2006, she was one of the most powerful executives at PepsiCo and one of two candidates being groomed for the coveted CEO position. Born in Chennai, India, Nooyi graduated from Yale's School of Management and worked in companies such as the Boston Consulting Group Inc., Motorola Inc., and ABB Inc. She also led an all-girl rock band in high school, but that is a different story.

What makes her one of the top leaders in the business world today? To start with, when she took her role at the helm of PepsiCo, she had a clear vision for the company, which seemed to be a timely vision at that point in time. Her vision was framed under the term "performance with purpose," which was based on two key ideas: tackling the obesity epidemic by improving the nutritional status of PepsiCo products and making PepsiCo an environmentally sustainable company. She is an inspirational speaker and rallies people around her vision for the company. She has the track record to show that she means what she says. She was instrumental in PepsiCo's acquisition of the food conglomerate Quaker Oats Company and the juice maker Tropicana Products Inc., both of which have healthy product lines. She is bent on reducing PepsiCo's reliance on high-sugar, high-calorie beverages, and she made sure that PepsiCo removed trans fats from all its products before its competitors did. To facilitate her vision, she also emphasized the role of research and development by hiring the chief of the diabetes and nutritional trials department at the Mayo Clinic and charging him with building a large R&D program. On the environmental side, she is striving for a net-zero impact on the environment. Among her priorities are plans to reduce the plastic used in beverage bottles and find biodegradable packaging solutions for PepsiCo products. While these investments affected short-term profitability and led to criticisms by Wall Street analysts, the overall financial situation of the company has been healthy.

Those who work with her feel challenged by her high performance standards and expectation of excellence. She is not afraid to give people negative feedback—and with humor, too. She pushes people until they come up with a solution to a problem and does not take "I don't know" for an answer. For example, she insisted that her team find an alternative to expensive palm oil and did not stop urging them forward until the alternative arrived: rice bran oil.

Nooyi is well liked and respected because she listens to those around her, even when they disagree with her. Her background cuts across national boundaries, which gives her a true appreciation for diversity, and she expects those around her to bring their values to work. In fact, when she graduated from college, she wore a sari to a job interview at Boston Consulting, where she got the job. She is an unusually collaborative person in the top suite of a *Fortune* 500 company, and she seeks help and information when she needs it. She has friendships with three ex-CEOs of PepsiCo who serve as her informal advisors, and when she was selected to the top position at PepsiCo, she made sure that her rival for the position got a pay raise and was given influence in the company, so she retained him for three years. She says the best advice she received was from her father, who taught her to assume that people have good intentions. Nooyi notes that expecting people to have good intentions helps her prevent misunderstandings and show empathy for them. It seems that she is a role model to other business leaders around the world, and PepsiCo is well positioned to tackle the challenges the future may bring.

Case written by Berrin Erdogan and Talya Bauer to accompany Carpenter, M., Bauer, T., Erdogan, B., & Short, J. (2013). Principles of Management (2nd ed.). New York: Flat World Knowledge. Based on information from Byrnes, N., & Arndt, M. (2006, May 1). The art of motivation. BusinessWeek. Retrieved September 29, 2012, from http://www.businessweek.com/magazine/content/06_18/b3982075.htm; Colvin, G. (2012, June 11). Indra Nooyi's challenge, Fortune, 165(8); Jennings, J. (2003). Ways to really motivate people: Authenticity is a huge hit with Gen X and Y. The Secured Lender, 59, 62–70; Marks, S. J. (2001). Incentives that really reward and motivate. Workforce, 80, 108–114.

CASE DISCUSSION QUESTIONS

1. How might a leader like Nooyi influence PepsiCo's use of P-O-L-C tools beyond her obvious role in the leadership dimension?
2. Do you think Nooyi's vision of "performance with purpose" has been effective? Why or why not?
3. How does charisma relate to leadership? Do you think the CEO of PepsiCo possesses this characteristic?
4. What makes Nooyi so successful at her job? Is it her level of authority, or is it something else?
5. What do the types of advisors that Nooyi relies on tell you about her values?
6. How much passion does Nooyi seem to bring to her role as CEO of PepsiCo?

ENDNOTES

1. Hogan, R., Curphy, G. J., & Hogan, J. (1994). What we know about leadership: Effectiveness and personality. *American Psychologist, 49*, 493–504.
2. House, R. J., & Aditya, R. N. (1997). The social scientific study of leadership: Quo Vadis? *Journal of Management, 23*, 409–473.
3. Judge, T. A., Bono, J. E., Ilies, R., & Gerhardt, M. W. (2002). Personality and leadership: A qualitative and quantitative review. *Journal of Applied Psychology, 87*, 765–780.
4. House, R. J., & Aditya, R. N. (1997). The social scientific study of leadership: Quo Vadis? *Journal of Management, 23*, 409–473; Ilies, R., Gerhardt, M. W., & Huy, L. (2004). Individual differences in leadership emergence: Integrating meta-analytic findings and behavioral genetics estimates. *International Journal of Selection and Assessment, 12*, 207–219; Lord, R. G., De Vader, C. L., & Alliger, G. M. (1986). A meta-analysis of the relation between personality traits and leadership perceptions: An application of validity generalization procedures. *Journal of Applied Psychology, 71*, 402–410; Taggar, S., Hackett, R., & Saha, S. (1999). Leadership emergence in autonomous work teams: Antecedents and outcomes. *Personnel Psychology, 52*, 899–926.
5. Goleman, D. (2004, January). What makes a leader? *Harvard Business Review, 82*(1), 82–91.
6. Karlgaard, R. (2002, February 18). Vote Carly. *Forbes, 169*(4), 37.
7. Buckmaster, J. (2008, May). How does he manage? Classified Web site boss. *Management Today*, 15.
8. Grant, A. M., Gino, F., & Hofmann, D. A. (2011). Reversing the extraverted leadership advantage: The role of employee proactivity. *Academy of Management Journal, 54*, 528–550.
9. Atwater, L. E., Dionne, S. D., Camobreco, J. F., Avolio, B. J., & Lau, A. (1998). Individual attributes and leadership style: Predicting the use of punishment and its effects. *Journal of Organizational Behavior, 19*, 559–576; Niebuhr, R. E., & Davis, K. R. (1984). Self-esteem: Relationship with leader behavior perceptions as moderated by the duration of the superior-subordinate dyad association, *Personality and Social Psychology Bulletin, 10*, 51–59.
10. Judge, T. A., & Cable, D. M. (2004). The effect of physical height on workplace success and income: Preliminary test of a theoretical model. *Journal of Applied Psychology, 89*, 428–441.
11. Reave, L. (2005). Spiritual values and practices related to leadership effectiveness. *Leadership Quarterly, 16*, 655–687.
12. Farrell, G., & Davidson, P. (2007, July 13). Whole Foods' CEO was busy guy online. *USA Today*, Section: Money, 04B.
13. Judge, T. A., Bono, J. E., Ilies, R., & Gerhardt, M. W. (2002). Personality and leadership: A qualitative and quantitative review. *Journal of Applied Psychology, 87*, 765–780; Toegel, G., & Barsoux, J. L. (2012). How to become a better leader. *MIT Sloan Management Review, 53*(3), 51–60.
14. House, R. J., & Aditya, R. N. (1997). The social scientific study of leadership: Quo Vadis? *Journal of Management, 23*, 409–473.
15. Judge, T. A., Bono, J. E., Ilies, R., & Gerhardt, M. W. (2002). Personality and leadership: A qualitative and quantitative review. *Journal of Applied Psychology, 87*, 765–780.
16. Hackman, J. R., & Wageman, R. (2007). Asking the right questions about leadership: Discussion and conclusions. *American Psychologist, 62*, 43–47.
17. See House, R. J., & Aditya, R. N. (1997). The social scientific study of leadership: Quo Vadis? *Journal of Management, 23*, 409–473.
18. Nystrom, P. C. (1978). Managers and the hi-hi leader myth. *Academy of Management Journal, 21*, 325–331.
19. Judge, T. A., Piccolo, R. F., & Ilies, R. (2004). The forgotten ones? The validity of consideration and initiating structure in leadership research. *Journal of Applied Psychology, 89*, 36–51.
20. Miles, R. H., & Petty, M. M. (1977). Leader effectiveness in small bureaucracies. *Academy of Management Journal, 20*, 238–250.
21. Seltzer, J., & Numerof, R. E. (1988). Supervisory leadership and subordinate burnout. *Academy of Management Journal, 31*, 439–446.
22. Miller, K. I., & Monge, P. R. (1986). Participation, satisfaction, and productivity: A meta-analytic review. *Academy of Management Journal, 29*, 727–753.
23. Baumgartel, H. (1957). Leadership style as a variable in research administration. *Administrative Science Quarterly, 2*, 344–360.
24. Vroom, V. H., & Mann, F. C. (1960). Leader authoritarianism and employee attitudes. *Personnel Psychology, 13*, 125–140.
25. Judge, T. A., & Piccolo, R. F. (2004). Transformational and transactional leadership: A meta-analytic test of their relative validity. *Journal of Applied Psychology, 89*, 755–768.
26. Skogstad, A., Einarsen, S., Torsheim, T., Aasland, M. S., & Hetland, H. (2007). The destructiveness of laissez-faire leadership behavior. *Journal of Occupational Health Psychology, 12*, 80–92.
27. Fiedler, F. (1967). *A theory of leadership effectiveness*. New York: McGraw-Hill; Fiedler, F. E. (1964). A contingency model of leader effectiveness. In L. Berkowitz (Ed.), *Advances in experimental social psychology* (Vol. 1, pp. 149–190). New York: Academic Press.
28. Peters, L. H., Hartke, D. D., & Pohlmann, J. T. (1985). Fiedler's contingency theory of leadership: An application of the meta-analysis procedures of Schmidt and Hunter. *Psychological Bulletin, 97*, 274–285; Strube, M. J., & Garcia, J. E. (1981). A meta-analytic investigation of Fiedler's contingency model of leadership effectiveness. *Psychological Bulletin, 90*, 307–321; Vecchio, R. P. (1983). Assessing the validity of Fiedler's contingency model of leadership effectiveness: A closer look at Strube and Garcia. *Psychological Buletin, 93*, 404–408.
29. Hersey, P. H., Blanchard, K. H., & Johnson, D. E. (2007). *Management of Organizational Behavior: Leadership human resources*. Upper Saddle River, NJ: Prentice Hall.
30. Retrieved from http://www.situational.com/Views/SituationalLeadership/RightHereRightNow.aspx.
31. Blank, W., Green, S. G., & Weitzel, J. R. (1990). A test of the situational leadership theory. *Personnel Psychology, 43*, 579–597; Graeff, C. L. (1983). The situational leadership theory: A critical review. *Academy of Management Review, 8*, 285–291; Fernandez, C. F., & Vecchio, R. P. (2002). Situational leadership theory revisited: A test of an across-jobs perspective. *Leadership Quarterly, 8*, 67–84.
32. House, R. J. (1971). A path goal theory of leader effectiveness. *Administrative Science Quarterly, 16*(3), 321–338.
33. House, R. J. (1996). Path-goal theory of leadership: Lessons, legacy, and a reformulated theory. *Leadership Quarterly, 7*, 323–352; House, R. J., & Mitchell, T. R. (1974). Path-goal theory of leadership. *Journal of Contemporary Business, 3*, 81–97.
34. House, R. J., & Aditya, R. N. (1997). The social scientific study of leadership: Quo Vadis? *Journal of Management, 23*, 409–473; Stinson, J. E., & Johnson, T. W. (1975). The path-goal theory of leadership: A partial test and suggested refinement. *Academy of Management Journal, 18*, 242–252; Wofford, J. C., & Liska, L. Z. (1993). Path-goal theories of leadership: A meta-analysis. *Journal of Management, 19*, 857–876.
35. Vroom, V. H. (2000). Leadership and the decision making process. *Organizational Dynamics, 68*, 82–94; Vroom, V. H., & Yetton, P. W. (1973). *Leadership and decision-making*. Pittsburgh: University of Pittsburgh Press; Jago, A., & Vroom, V. H. (1980). An evaluation of two alternatives to the Vroom/Yetton Normative Model. *Academy of Management Journal, 23*, 347–355; Vroom, V. H., & Jago, A. G. (1988). *The new leadership: Managing participation in organizations*. Englewood Cliffs, NJ: Prentice Hall.
36. Vroom, V. H., & Jago, G. (1978). On the validity of the Vroom Yetton model. *Journal of Applied Psychology, 63*, 151–162.
37. Bass, B. M. (1985). *Leadership and performance beyond expectations*. New York: Free Press; Burns, J. M. (1978). *Leadership*. New York: Harper & Row.
38. Bass, B. M. (1985). *Leadership and performance beyond expectations*. New York: Free Press; Burns, J. M. (1978). *Leadership*. New York: Harper & Row; Bycio, P., Hackett, R. D., & Allen, J. S. (1995). Further assessment of Bass's (1985) conceptualization of transactional and transformational leadership. *Journal of Applied Psychology, 80*, 468–478; Judge, T. A., & Piccolo, R. F. (2004). Transformational and transactional leadership: A meta-analytic test of their relative validity. *Journal of Applied Psychology, 89*, 755–768.
39. Shamir, B., House, R. J., & Arthur, M. B. (1993). The motivational effects of charismatic leadership: A self-concept based theory. *Organization Science, 4*, 577–594.
40. Judge, T. A., & Piccolo, R. F. (2004). Transformational and transactional leadership: A meta-analytic test of their relative validity. *Journal of Applied Psychology, 89*, 755–768.
41. Herold, D. M., Fedor, D. B., Caldwell, S., & Liu, Y. (2008). The effects of transformational and change leadership on employees' commitment to a change: A multilevel study. *Journal of Applied Psychology, 93*, 346–357; Piccolo, R. F., & Colquitt, J. A. (2006). Transformational leadership and job behaviors: The mediating role of core job characteristics. *Academy of Management Journal, 49*, 327–340; Schaubroeck, J., Lam, S. K., & Cha, S. E. (2007). Embracing transformational leadership: Team values and the impact of leader behavior on team performance. *Journal of Applied Psychology, 92*, 1020–1030; Shin, S. J., & Zhou, J. (2003). Transformational leadership, conservation, and creativity: Evidence from Korea. *Academy of Management Journal, 46*, 703–714; Wang, H., Law, K. S., Hackett, R. D., Duanxu, W., & Zhen, X. C. (2005). Leader-member exchange as a mediator of the relationship between transformational leadership and followers' performance and organizational citizenship behavior. *Academy of Management Journal, 48*, 420–432.
42. Judge, T. A., & Piccolo, R. F. (2004). Transformational and transactional leadership: A meta-analytic test of their relative validity. *Journal of Applied Psychology, 89*, 755–768.
43. Dirks, K. T., & Ferrin, D. L. (2002). Trust in leadership: Meta-analytic findings and implications for research and practice. *Journal of Applied Psychology, 87*, 611–628.
44. Bono, J. E., & Judge, T. A. (2004). Personality and transformational and transactional leadership: A meta-analysis. *Journal of Applied Psychology, 89*, 901–910.
45. Barling, J., Weber, T., & Kelloway, E. K. (1996). Effects of transformational leadership training on attitudinal and financial outcomes: A field experiment. *Journal of Applied Psychology, 81*, 827–832; Dvir, T., Eden, D., Avolio, B. J., & Shamir, B. (2002). Impact of transformational leadership on follower development and performance: A field experiment. *Academy of Management Journal, 45*, 735–744; Frese, M., Beimel, S., & Schoenborg, S. (2003). Action training for charismatic leadership: Two evaluations of studies of a commercial training module on inspirational communication of a vision. *Personnel Psychology, 56*, 671–697.
46. Khurana, R. (2002, September). The curse of the superstar CEO. *Harvard Business Review, 80*(9), 60–66.
47. Agle, B. R., Nagarajan, N. J., Sonnenfeld, J. A., & Srinivasan, D. (2006). Does CEO charisma matter? An empirical analysis of the relationships among organizational performance, environmental uncertainty, and top management team perceptions of CEO charisma. *Academy of Management Journal, 49*, 161–174.
48. Dansereau, F., Jr., Graen, G., & Haga, W. J. (1975). A vertical dyad linkage approach to leadership within formal organizations: A longitudinal investigation of the role making process. *Organizational Behavior & Human Performance, 13*(1), 46–78; Erdogan, B., & Liden, R. C. (2002). Social exchanges in the workplace: A review of recent developments and future research directions in leader-member exchange theory. In L. L. Neider & C. A. Schriesheim (Eds.), *Leadership* (pp. 65–114). Greenwich, CT: Information Age Press; Gerstner, C. R., & Day, D. V. (1997). Meta-analytic review of leader-member exchange theory: Correlates and construct issues. *Journal of Applied Psychology, 82*, 827–844; Graen, G. B., & Uhl-Bien, M. (1995). Relationship-based approach to leadership: Development of leader-member exchange (LMX) theory over 25 years: Applying a multi-level multi-domain perspective. *Leadership Quarterly, 6*(2), 219–247; Liden, R. C., & Maslyn, J. M. (1998). Multidimensionality of leader-member exchange: An empirical assessment through scale development. *Journal of Management, 24*, 43–72.

49. Gerstner, C. R., & Day, D. V. (1997). Meta-analytic review of leader-member exchange theory: Correlates and construct issues. *Journal of Applied Psychology, 82*, 827–844; Hui, C., Law, K. S., & Chen, Z. X. (1999). A structural equation model of the effects of negative affectivity, leader-member exchange, and perceived job mobility on in-role and extra-role performance: A Chinese case. *Organizational Behavior and Human Decision Processes, 77*, 3–21; Kraimer, M. L., Wayne, S. J., & Jaworski, R. A. (2001). Sources of support and expatriate performance: The mediating role of expatriate adjustment. *Personnel Psychology, 54*, 71–99; Liden, R. C., Wayne, S. J., & Sparrowe, R. T. (2000). An examination of the mediating role of psychological empowerment on the relations between the job, interpersonal relationships, and work outcomes. *Journal of Applied Psychology, 85*, 407–416; Settoon, R. P., Bennett, N., & Liden, R. C. (1996). Social exchange in organizations: Perceived organizational support, leader-member exchange, and employee reciprocity. *Journal of Applied Psychology, 81*, 219–227; Tierney, P., Farmer, S. M., & Graen, G. B. (1999). An examination of leadership and employee creativity: The relevance of traits and relationships. *Personnel Psychology, 52*, 591–620; Wayne, S. J., Shore, L. M., & Liden. R. C. (1997). Perceived organizational support and leader-member exchange: A social exchange perspective. *Academy of Management Journal, 40*, 82–111.

50. Chen, Z., Lam, W., & Zhong, J. A. (2007). Leader-member exchange and member performance: A new look at individual-level negative feedback seeking behavior and team-level empowerment climate. *Journal of Applied Psychology, 92*, 202–212.

51. Ilies, R., Nahrgang, J. D., & Morgeson, F. P. (2007). Leader-member exchange and citizenship behaviors: A meta-analysis. *Journal of Applied Psychology, 92*, 269–277.

52. Bauer, T. N., Erdogan, B., Liden, R. C., & Wayne, S. J. (2006). A longitudinal study of the moderating role of extraversion: Leader-member exchange, performance, and turnover during new executive development. *Journal of Applied Psychology, 91*, 298–310; Erdogan, B., Kraimer, M. L., & Liden, R. C. (2004). Work value congruence and intrinsic career success. *Personnel Psychology, 57*, 305–332; Major, D. A., Kozlowski, S. W., Chao, G. T., & Gardner, P. D. (1995). A longitudinal investigation of newcomer expectations, early socialization outcomes, and the moderating effects of role development factors. *Journal of Applied Psychology, 80*, 418–431.

53. Ferris, G. R. (1985). Role of leadership in the employee withdrawal process: A constructive replication. *Journal of Applied Psychology, 70, 777*, 781; Graen, G. B., Liden, R. C., & Hoel, W. (1982). Role of leadership in the employee withdrawal process. *Journal of Applied Psychology, 67*, 868–872.

54. Masterson, S. S., Lewis, K., Goldman, B. M., & Taylor, M. S. (2000). Integrating justice and social exchange: The differing effects of fair procedures and treatment on work relationships. *Academy of Management Journal, 43*, 738–748.

55. Bauer, T. N., & Green, S. G. (1996). Development of a leader-member exchange: A longitudinal test. *Academy of Management Journal, 39*, 1538–1567.

56. Colella, A., & Varma, A. (2001). The impact of subordinate disability on leader-member exchange relationships. *Academy of Management Journal, 44*, 304–315; Maslyn, J. M., & Uhl-Bien, M. (2001). Leader-member exchange and its dimensions: Effects of self-effort and other's effort on relationship quality. *Journal of Applied Psychology, 86*, 697–708; Janssen, O., & Van Yperen, N. W. (2004). Employees' goal orientations, the quality of leader-member exchange, and the outcomes of job performance and job satisfaction. *Academy of Management Journal, 47*, 368–384; Wing, L., Xu, H., & Snape, E. (2007). Feedback-seeking behavior and leader-member exchange: Do supervisor-attributed motives matter? *Academy of Management Journal, 50*, 348–363.

57. Engle, E. M., & Lord, R. G. (1997). Implicit theories, self-schemas, and leader-member exchange. *Academy of Management Journal, 40*, 988–1010; Liden, R. C., Wayne, S. J., & Stilwell, D. (1993). A longitudinal study on the early development of leader-member exchanges. *Journal of Applied Psychology, 78*, 662–674; Wayne, S. J., Shore, L. M., & Liden. R. C. (1997). Perceived organizational support and leader-member exchange: A social exchange perspective. *Academy of Management Journal, 40*, 82–111.

58. Erdogan, B., Liden, R. C., & Kraimer, M. L. (2006). Justice and leader-member exchange: The moderating role of organizational culture. *Academy of Management Journal, 49*, 395–406.

59. Duarte, N. T., Goodson, J. R., & Klich, N. R. (1994). Effects of dyadic quality and duration on performance appraisal. *Academy of Management Journal, 37*, 499–521.

60. Heneman, R. L., Greenberger, D. B., & Anonyuo, C. (1989). Attributions and exchanges: The effects of interpersonal factors on the diagnosis of employee performance. *Academy of Management Journal, 32*, 466–476.

61. Erdogan, B., & Bauer, T. N. (2010). Differentiated leader-member exchanges (LMX): The buffering role of justice climate. *Journal of Applied Psychology, 95*, 1104–1120; Erdogan, B., & Enders, J. (2007). Support from the top: Supervisors' perceived organizational support as a moderator of leader-member exchange to satisfaction and performance relationships. *Journal of Applied Psychology, 92*, 321–330; Sparrowe, R. T., & Liden, R. C. (2005). Two routes to influence: Integrating leader-member exchange and social network perspectives. *Administrative Science Quarterly, 50*, 505–535.

62. Greenleaf, R. K. (1977). *Servant leadership: A journey into the nature of legitimate power and greatness* (p. 335). Mahwah, NJ: Paulist Press; Liden, R. C., Wayne, S., J., Zhao, H., & Henderson, D. (2008). Servant leadership: Development of a multidimensional measure and multi-level assessment. *Leadership Quarterly, 19*, 161–177.

63. Goodwin, D. K. (2005, June 26). The master of the game. *Time*. Retrieved September 13, 2012, from http://www.time.com/time/printout/0,8816,1077300,00.html.

64. Liden, R. C., Wayne, S., J., Zhao, H., & Henderson, D. (2008). Servant leadership: Development of a multidimensional measure and multi-level assessment. *Leadership Quarterly, 19*, 161–177.

65. Ehrhart, M. G. (2004). Leadership and procedural justice climate as antecedents of unit-level organizational citizenship behavior. *Personnel Psychology, 57*, 61–94.

66. Buchanan, L. (2007, May). In praise of selflessness: Why the best leaders are servants. *Inc, 29*(5), 33–35.

67. Avolio, B. J., & Gardner, W. L. (2005). Authentic leadership development: Getting to the root of positive forms of leadership. *Leadership Quarterly, 16*, 315–338; Gardner, W. L., Avolio, B. J., Luthans, F., May, D. R., & Walumbwa, F. (2005). "Can you see the real me?" A self-based model of authentic leader and follower development. *Leadership Quarterly, 16*, 343–372; George, B. (2007). Authentic leaders: They inspire and empower others. *Leadership Excellence, 24*(9), 16–17; Ilies, R., Morgeson, F. P., & Nahrgang, J. D. (2005). Authentic leadership and eudaemonic well-being: Understanding leader-follower outcomes. *Leadership Quarterly, 16*, 373–394; Sparrowe, R. T. (2005). Authentic leadership and the narrative self. *Leadership Quarterly, 16*, 419–439.

68. Shamir, B., & Eilam, G. (2005). What's your story? A life-stories approach to authentic leadership development. *Leadership Quarterly, 16*, 395–417.

69. Walumbwa, F. O., Avolio, B. J., Gardner, W. L., Wernsing, T. S., & Peterson, S. J. (2008). Authentic leadership: Development and validation of a theory-based measure. *Journal of Management, 34*, 89–126.

70. Collins, J. (2001). *Good to great: Why some companies make the leap…and others don't*. London: Random House Business Books.

71. Frese, M., Beimel, S., & Schoenborg, S. (2003). Action training for charismatic leadership: Two evaluations of studies of a commercial training module on inspirational communication of a vision. *Personnel Psychology, 56*, 671–697; Shamir, B., House, R. J., & Arthur, M. B. (1993). The motivational effects of charismatic leadership: A self-concept based theory. *Organization Science, 4*, 577–594.

72. Buchanan, L. (2007, May). In praise of selflessness: Why the best leaders are servants. *Inc, 29*(5), 33–35; Douglas, M. E. (2005, March). Service to others. *Supervision, 66*(3), 6–9; Ramsey, R. D. (2005, October). The new buzz word. *Supervision, 66*(10), 3–5.

CHAPTER 10
Decision Making

DECISION MAKING

Decca records distributed music by Bing Crosby, Count Basie, and the Rolling Stones—but their decision to pass on signing British band the Beatles tops many experts' lists of worst business decisions of all time. The Beatles sold a historic 15 million records in 1964 alone and had the top 5 singles as well as 12 of the Billboard Hot 100 songs that same year. To date, no other artist or band has topped these accomplishments or reached over 1.6 billion album sales like the Beatles.

Source: http://en.wikipedia.org/wiki/File:The_Beatles_in_America.JPG

CHAPTER LEARNING OBJECTIVES

Reading this chapter will help you do the following:

1. **Understand the meaning of decision making.**
2. **Know key causes of faulty decision making.**
3. **Compare and contrast individual and group decision making.**
4. **Understand how to develop your own personal decision-making skills.**

The P-O-L-C Framework

Planning	Organizing	Leading	Controlling
1. Vision & Mission	1. Organization Design	1. Leadership	1. Systems/Processes
2. Strategizing	2. Culture	2. Decision Making	2. Strategic Human Resources
3. Goals & Objectives	3. Social Networks	3. Communications	
		4. Groups/Teams	
		5. Motivation	

Leadership effectiveness is often a reflection of the decisions that leaders make or fail to make. In this chapter, we explain both ideal and actual decision-making processes within organizations. Understanding how decisions are made, how they can be biased, and how to make the decision-making process run smoothly are key to becoming an effective manager.

0.1   Understanding Decision Making

LEARNING OBJECTIVES

1. Define decision making.
2. Understand different types of decisions.

0.2   Decision Making Defined

decision making

Making choices among alternative courses of action, including inaction.

Decision making refers to selecting choices among alternative courses of action—which may also include inaction. While it can be argued that management *is* decision making, half of the decisions made by managers within organizations lead to negative outcomes.[1] Therefore, increasing effectiveness in decision making is an important part of maximizing effectiveness at work. This chapter provides insights regarding decision making alone or in a group while avoiding common decision-making traps.

Individuals throughout organizations use the information they gather to make a wide range of decisions. These decisions may affect the lives of others and change the course of an organization. For example, the decisions made by executives and consulting firms for Enron ultimately resulted in a $60 billion loss for investors, thousands of employees without jobs, and the loss of all employee retirement funds. But Sherron Watkins, a former Enron employee and now-famous whistleblower, uncovered the accounting problems and tried to enact change. Similarly, the decisions made by firms to trade in mortgage-backed securities is having negative consequences for the entire U.S. economy. Each of these people made a decision, and each person, as well as others, is now living with the consequences of his or her decisions.

Because many decisions involve an ethical component, one of the most important considerations in management is whether the decisions you are making as an employee or manager are ethical. Here are some basic questions you can ask yourself to assess the ethics of a decision.[2]

FIGURE 10.3

Legendary scientist Albert Einstein was known for his tendency to incorporate a programmed decision into his dressing choices by wearing very similar outfits daily and not wearing socks.

Source: http://en.wikipedia.org/wiki/File:Einstein_1921_portrait2.jpg

- Is this decision fair?
- Will I feel better or worse about myself after I make this decision?
- Does this decision break any organizational rules?
- Does this decision break any laws?
- How would I feel if this decision was broadcast on the news?

0.3   Types of Decisions

programmed decisions

Choices that occur frequently enough that we develop an automated response to them.

decision rules

Automated responses used to make programmed decisions.

Despite the far-reaching nature of the decisions, not all decisions have major consequences or even require extensive thought. For example, individuals make simple and habitual decisions such as what to wear, what to eat, and which route to take to and from home and work. These mundane decisions usually do not consume much time. These types of straightforward decisions are termed **programmed decisions**; these are decisions that occur frequently enough that we develop an automated response to them. The automated response we use to make these decisions is called a **decision rule**. For example, many restaurants face customer complaints as a routine part of doing business. Because this is a recurring problem for restaurants, it may be regarded as a programmed decision. To deal with this problem, the restaurant might have a policy stating that every time they receive a valid customer complaint, the customer should receive a free dessert, which represents a decision rule. Making strategic, tactical, and operational decisions is an integral part of the planning function in the P-O-L-C (planning-organizing-leading-controlling) model.

Decisions that are unique and important require conscious thinking, information gathering, and careful consideration of alternatives. These are called **nonprogrammed decisions**. For example, in 2005, McDonald's became aware of a need to respond to growing customer concerns regarding foods high in fat and calories. This is a nonprogrammed decision because for several decades, customers of fast-food restaurants were more concerned with the taste and price of the food, rather than the healthiness. Recognizing the change in public sentiment, McDonald's decided to offer healthier alternatives, such as substituting french fries in Happy Meals for apple slices and discontinuing the use of trans fats.

Decision making can also be classified into three categories based on the level at which they occur. Strategic decisions set the course for organization. Changing strategic direction or introducing a new product that requires years of development would represent a strategic decision. Tactical decisions are decisions about how things will get done. For example, issuing a coupon to increase sales would fall into this category. Operational decisions are decisions that employees make each day to run the organization. Helping serve customer needs through routine interactions or order fulfillment would be an example of this type of decision.

Different decision-making models have been designed to understand and evaluate the effectiveness of nonprogrammed decisions. We explain four decision-making approaches including the rational decision-making model, the bounded rationality decision-making model, the intuitive decision-making model, and the creative decision-making model.

> **nonprogrammed decisions**
> Unique, nonroutine, and important decisions that require conscious thinking, information gathering, and careful consideration of alternatives.

FIGURE 10.4 Decisions Commonly Made within Organizations

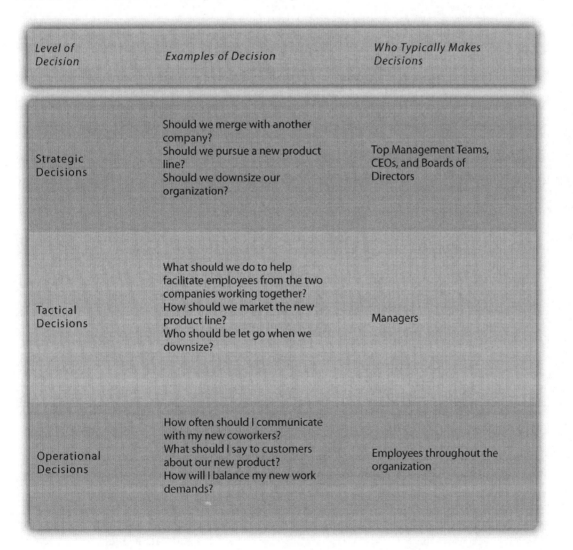

Level of Decision	Examples of Decision	Who Typically Makes Decisions
Strategic Decisions	Should we merge with another company? Should we pursue a new product line? Should we downsize our organization?	Top Management Teams, CEOs, and Boards of Directors
Tactical Decisions	What should we do to help facilitate employees from the two companies working together? How should we market the new product line? Who should be let go when we downsize?	Managers
Operational Decisions	How often should I communicate with my new coworkers? What should I say to customers about our new product? How will I balance my new work demands?	Employees throughout the organization

0.4 Making Rational Decisions

rational decision-making model

A decision making model which describes the series of steps that decision makers should consider if their goal is to maximize their outcome.

FIGURE 10.5

To ensure consistency around the globe, such as at this St. Petersburg, Russia, location, McDonald's trains all restaurant managers (more than 80,000 by 2013) at Hamburger University, where they take the equivalent of two years of college courses and learn how to make decisions. The curriculum is taught in 28 languages.

Source: http://upload.wikimedia.org/ wikipedia/commons/a/a2/ McDonalds_in_St_Petersburg_2004.JPG

The **rational decision-making model** describes a series of steps that decision makers should consider if their goal is to maximize the quality of their outcomes. This model presents formal steps with the goal of achieving an optimal result in terms of the quality of a decision.

The rational decision-making model is best applied to major decisions where the costs are high and the consequences of different decision outcomes are significant. For example, the model can be applied to the decision to purchase a new car. Step 1 involves the recognition that a new vehicle is needed. Step 2 involves selecting factors that are important, such as fuel economy, cost, and number of passengers that the vehicle can accommodate comfortably.

Step 3 involves deciding how important each factor is in the decision outcome. For example, if price and gas mileage are key factors, they might outweigh other factors, with color or other options given medium or low importance. Step 4 requires generation of all alternatives concerning options. In step 5, information is used to evaluate each alternative against established criteria. Step 6 involves selecting the most attractive alternative. Step 7 involves executing the decision by completing the car purchase. Step 8 entails evaluating the decision; if you purchase a car and have a good experience, you are more likely to buy another car of the same model and manufacturer.

FIGURE 10.6 Steps in the Rational Decision-Making Model

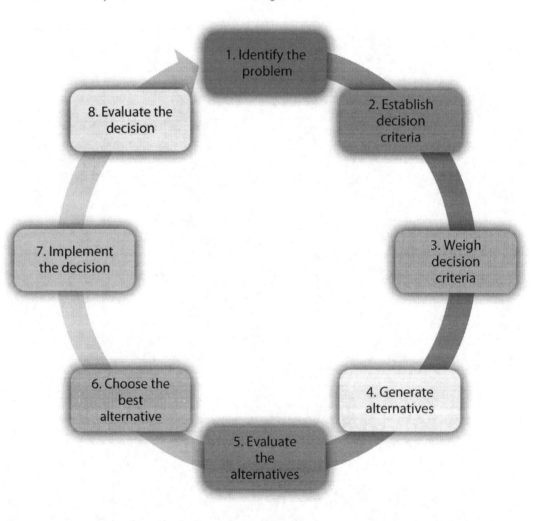

While decision makers can get off track during any of these steps, research shows that limiting the search for alternatives in the fourth step can be the most challenging and lead to failure. In fact, one researcher found that in 85% of the decisions studied, no alternatives were identified.[3] Conversely, successful managers are clear about what they want at the outset of the decision-making process, set objectives for others to respond to, carry out an unrestricted search for solutions, get key people to participate, and avoid using their power to influence the decision outcome.[4]

The rational decision-making model has important lessons for decision makers. First, when making a decision, establish decision criteria before beginning the search for alternatives. This prevents decision makers from favoring one option too much and setting criteria accordingly. For example, let's say someone started browsing for cars before setting decision criteria. They may come across a car that reflects their sense of style and form an emotional bond with the car. This bond might convince them that the fuel economy of the car and the innovative braking system are the most important criteria. After purchasing it, they may realize that the car is too small for their friends, which limits their ability to take long trips. Setting criteria before searching for alternatives can prevent individuals from making such mistakes. Another advantage of the rational model is that it urges decision makers to generate an exhaustive set of alternatives instead of only a few. By generating a large number of alternatives that cover a wide range of possibilities, individuals are likely to make a more effective decision that does not sacrifice one criterion for the sake of another.

Despite all its benefits, the rational decision-making model involves a number of unrealistic assumptions. It assumes that people understand what decision is to be made, that they know all their available choices, that they have no perceptual biases, and that they want to make optimal decisions. Nobel Prize–winning economist Herbert Simon observed that while the rational decision-making model may be a helpful tool for working through problems, it does not represent how decisions are frequently made within organizations. In fact, Simon argued that more can be learned from studying how and when individuals deviate from the model than examining how to follow it more closely.

In most day-to-day decisions, individuals rarely sit down and complete all eight steps in the rational decision-making model. For example, the search for all possible alternatives can be time consuming and individuals are often under time pressure to make decisions. Moreover, even when access to all information is possible, it can be challenging to compare the pros and cons of each alternative and rank them according to preferences. Anyone who has recently purchased a new laptop computer or cell phone can attest to the challenge of sorting through the different strengths and limitations of each brand, model, and plans offered for support and arriving at the solution that best meets their needs.

The availability of too much information and too many choices can lead to **analysis paralysis**, where more and more time is spent on gathering information and thinking about it, but no decisions actually get made. A senior executive at Hewlett-Packard admits his company suffered from this spiral of analyzing things for too long to the point where data gathering led to "not making decisions, instead of us making decisions."[5] Moreover, individuals may not always be interested in reaching an optimal decision. Home buyers may be willing and able to invest a great deal of time and energy in finding and creating their dream home, but students looking for an apartment to rent for the academic year may be willing to take the first one that meets acceptable criteria of being clean, close to campus, and within a certain price range.

> **analysis paralysis**
>
> A decision-making process where more and more time is spent on gathering information and thinking about it but no decisions actually get made.

0.5   Making "Good Enough" Decisions

The **bounded rationality model** of decision making recognizes the limitations of decision-making processes. According to this model, individuals knowingly limit their options to a manageable set and choose the best alternative without conducting an exhaustive search for alternatives. An important part of the bounded rationality approach is the tendency to **satisfice**, which refers to accepting the first alternative that meets your minimum criteria. For example, many college graduates do not conduct a national or international search for potential job openings; instead, they focus their search on a limited geographic area and tend to accept the first offer in their chosen area, even if it may not be the ideal job situation. Satisficing is similar to rational decision making, but it differs in that rather than choosing the best choice and maximizing the potential outcome, the decision maker saves time and effort by accepting the first alternative that meets the minimum threshold.

> **bounded rationality model**
>
> A model that recognizes the limitations of decision-making processes. According to this model, individuals knowingly limit their options to a manageable set and choose the best alternative without conducting an exhaustive search for alternatives.
>
> **satisficing**
>
> Accepting the first alternative that meets minimum criteria.

FIGURE 10.7

Mattel's Magic 8 Ball may be a useful toy when making "good enough" decisions.

Source:

http://commons.wikimedia.org/wiki/
File:Magic8ball.jpg

intuitive decision-making model

Arriving at decisions without conscious reasoning. The model argues that in a given situation, experts making decisions scan the environment for cues to recognize patterns.

0.6 Making Intuitive Decisions

The **intuitive decision-making model** has emerged as an important decision-making model. It refers to arriving at decisions without conscious reasoning. Eighty-nine percent of managers surveyed admitted to using intuition to make decisions at least sometimes, and 59% said they used intuition often.[6] When we recognize that managers often need to make decisions under challenging circumstances with time pressures, constraints, a great deal of uncertainty, highly visible and high-stakes outcomes, and within changing conditions, it makes sense that they would not have the time to formally work through all the steps of the rational decision-making model. Yet when CEOs, financial analysts, and health care workers are asked about the critical decisions they make, seldom do they attribute success to luck. To an outside observer, it may seem like they are making guesses as to the course of action to take, but it turns out that they are systematically making decisions using a different model than was earlier suspected. Research on life-or-death decisions made by fire chiefs, pilots, and nurses finds that these experts do not choose among a list of well-thought-out alternatives. The intuitive decision-making model argues that, in a given situation, experts making decisions scan the environment for cues to recognize patterns.[7] Once a pattern is recognized, they can play a potential course of action through to its outcome based on their prior experience. Due to training, experience, and knowledge, these decision makers have an idea of how well a given solution may work. If they run through the mental model and find that the solution will not work, they alter the solution and retest it before setting it into action. If it still is not deemed a workable solution, it is discarded as an option and a new idea is tested until a workable solution is found. Once a viable course of action is identified, the decision maker puts the solution into motion. The key point is that only one choice is considered at a time. Novices are not able to make effective decisions this way because they do not have enough prior experience to draw upon.[8]

FIGURE 10.8

Firefighters rarely have the luxury of applying the rational decision-making model given their need to respond quickly and decisively.

© Thinkstock

0.7 Making Creative Decisions

In addition to the rational decision making, bounded rationality, and intuitive decision making models, creative decision making is a vital part of being an effective decision maker. Creativity is the generation of new, imaginative ideas. With the flattening of organizations and intense competition among organizations, individuals and organizations are driven to be creative in decisions ranging from cutting costs to creating new ways of doing business. While creativity is the first step in the innovation process, creativity and innovation are not the same thing. Innovation begins with creative ideas, but it also involves realistic planning and follow-through.

The five steps to creative decision making are similar to the previous decision-making models in some keys ways. All of the models include **problem identification**, which is the step in which the need for problem solving becomes apparent. If individuals do not recognize that a problem exists, it is impossible to solve any potential dilemma. **Immersion** is the step in which the decision maker thinks about the problem consciously and gathers information. A key to success in creative decision making is having or acquiring expertise in the area being studied. Then **incubation** occurs. During incubation, the individual sets the problem aside and does not think about it for a while. At this time, the brain is actually working on the problem unconsciously. Then comes **illumination**, or the insight moment, when the solution to the problem becomes apparent to the person, usually when it is least expected. This is the "Eureka!" (meaning, "I have found it!") moment similar to what happened to the ancient Greek inventor Archimedes, who discovered how to measure the density of an object while taking a bath. Finally, the **verification and application** stage happens when the decision maker consciously verifies the feasibility of the solution and implements the decision.

A NASA scientist describes his decision-making process leading to a creative outcome as follows: He had been trying to figure out a better way to de-ice planes to make the process faster and safer. After recognizing the problem, he had immersed himself in the literature to understand all the options, and he worked on the problem for months trying to figure out a solution. It was not until he was sitting outside of a McDonald's restaurant with his grandchildren that it dawned on him. The golden arches of the "M" of the McDonald's logo inspired his solution: he would design the de-icer as a series of M's![9] This represented the illumination stage. After he tested and verified his creative solution, he was done with that problem except to reflect on the outcome and process.

FIGURE 10.9 The Creative Decision-Making Process

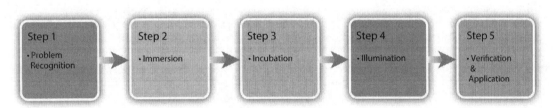

How Do You Know If Your Decision-Making Process Is Creative?

Researchers focus on three factors to evaluate the level of creativity in the decision-making process. **Fluency** refers to the number of ideas a person is able to generate. **Flexibility** refers to how different the ideas are from one another. **Originality** refers to an idea's uniqueness. Reed Hastings, founder and CEO of Netflix, shows at least two elements of creativity: originality and flexibility. After teaching math in Africa with the Peace Corps, Hastings was accepted at Stanford University, where he earned a master's degree in computer science. Soon after starting work at a software company, he invented a successful debugging tool, which led to his founding the computer troubleshooting company Pure Software in 1991. After a merger and the subsequent sale of the resulting company in 1997, Hastings founded Netflix, which revolutionized the DVD rental business through online rentals with no late fees.[10]

FIGURE 10.10 Dimensions of Creativity

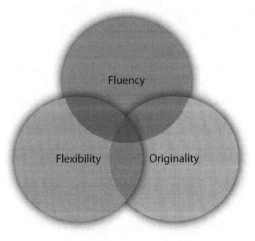

Experts have proposed that creativity occurs as an interaction among three factors: (1) people's personality traits (openness to experience, risk taking), (2) their attributes (expertise, imagination, motivation), and (3) the context (encouragement from others, time pressure, and physical structures).[11] For example, research shows that individuals who are open to experience, are less conscientious, are more self-accepting, seek more feedback, and are more impulsive tend to be more creative.[12]

There are many techniques available that enhance and improve creativity. Linus Pauling, the Nobel prize winner who popularized the idea that vitamin C could help build the immunity system, said, "The best way to have a good idea is to have a lot of ideas." One popular way to generate ideas is to use brainstorming. **Brainstorming** is a group process of generating ideas that follows a set of guidelines that include no criticism of ideas during the brainstorming process, the idea that no suggestion is too crazy, and building on other ideas (piggybacking). Research shows that the quantity of ideas actually leads to better idea quality in the end, so setting high **idea quotas** where the group must reach a set number of ideas before they are done is recommended to avoid process loss and to maximize the effectiveness of brainstorming. Another unique aspect of brainstorming is that the more people are included in brainstorming, the better the decision outcome will be because the variety of backgrounds and approaches give the group more to draw from. Interestingly, research also shows that having group members brainstorm alone without interaction with each other before engaging in team brainstorming results in higher quality and quantities of ideas.[13] A variation of brainstorming is **wildstorming** where the group focuses on ideas that are impossible and then imagines what would need to happen to make them possible.[14] A recent alternative to brainstorming is **crowdsourcing**. For some problems, gathering experts into the same room may not be feasible because the organization may not have the diversity of skills or expertise needed. Therefore, organizations are relying on the power of the masses to creatively solve business problems. Crowdsourcing is outsourcing a problem to a crowd. This process enlists the help of experts, amateurs, and those with a passion for problem solving. For example, Netflix announced in 2006 that they would pay $1 million to someone who would improve the match between their movie recommendations and customers' own ratings. The winning team improved Netflix's own recommendation algorithm by more than 10% and was awarded the cash prize in 2009. Companies are using crowdsourcing for identifying new markets and new trends, solving complex technical problems, and generating ideas for specific problems. Many individuals may work on the same problem alone and in isolation, or they may break up into small groups to collaborate.[15]

0.8 Ideas for Enhancing Organizational Creativity

Organizational creativity is vital to organizations. Here are some guidelines for enhancing organizational creativity within teams.[16]

Team Composition (Organizing/Leading)

- *Diversify your team* to give them more inputs to build on and more opportunities to create functional conflict while avoiding personal conflict.
- *Change group membership* to stimulate new ideas and new interaction patterns.
- *Leaderless teams* can allow teams freedom to create without trying to please anyone up front.

Team Process (Leading)

- *Engage in brainstorming* to generate ideas—but remember to set a high goal for the number of ideas the group should come up with, encourage wild ideas, and allow individuals to brainstorm alone before brainstorming in a group.
- *Use the nominal group technique in person or electronically* to avoid some common group process pitfalls. Consider anonymous feedback as well.
- *Use analogies* to envision problems and solutions.

Leadership (Leading)

- *Challenge teams* so that they are engaged but not overwhelmed.
- *Let people decide how to achieve goals*, rather than telling them what goals to achieve.
- *Support and celebrate creativity* even when it leads to a mistake. But set up processes to learn from mistakes as well.
- *Model* creative behavior.

---

brainstorming

A process of generating ideas that follows a set of guidelines, which includes no criticism of ideas during the process, the idea that no suggestion is too crazy, and building on other ideas (piggybacking).

idea quotas

A set number of ideas a group must reach before they are done with brainstorming.

wildstorming

A variation of brainstorming where the group focuses on ideas that are impossible and then imagines what would need to happen to make them possible.

crowdsourcing

Outsourcing a problem to a crowd.

Culture (Organizing)

- *Create routines* so that individuals do not spend time on routine tasks.
- *Build a physical space conducive to creativity* that is playful and humorous—this is a place where ideas can thrive.
- *Incorporate creative behavior* into the performance appraisal process.

FIGURE 10.11

Which decision-making model should I use?

Decision Making Model	Use This Model When:
Rational	• Information on alternatives can be gathered and quantified. • The decision is important. • You are trying to maximize your outcome.
Bounded Rationality	• The minimum criteria are clear. • You do not have or you are not willing to invest much time to making the decision. • You are not trying to maximize your outcome.
Intuitive	• Goals are unclear. • There is time pressure and analysis paralysis would be costly. • You have experience with the problem.
Creative	• Solutions to the problem are not clear. • New solutions need to be generated. • You have time to immerse yourself in the issues.

The four different decision-making models—rational, bounded rationality, intuitive, and creative—vary in terms of how experienced or motivated a decision maker is to make a choice. Choosing the right approach will make you more effective at work and improve your ability to carry out all the P-O-L-C functions.

KEY TAKEAWAY

Decision making is choosing among alternative courses of action, including inaction. There are different types of decisions, ranging from automatic, programmed decisions to more intensive nonprogrammed decisions. Structured decision-making processes include rational decision making, bounded rationality, intuitive, and creative decision making. Each of these can be useful, depending on the circumstances and the problem that needs to be solved.

EXERCISES

1. What do you see as the main difference between a successful and an unsuccessful decision? How much does luck versus skill have to do with it? How much time needs to pass to answer the first question?
2. Research has shown that over half of the decisions made within organizations fail. Does this surprise you? Why or why not?
3. Have you used the rational decision-making model to make a decision? What was the context? How well did the model work?
4. Share an example of a decision where you used satisficing. Were you happy with the outcome? Why or why not? When would you be most likely to engage in satisficing?
5. Do you think intuition is respected as a decision-making style? Do you think it should be? Why or why not?

1. FAULTY DECISION MAKING

LEARNING OBJECTIVES

1. Understand overconfidence bias and how to avoid it.
2. Understand hindsight bias and how to avoid it.
3. Understand anchoring and how to avoid it.
4. Understand framing bias and how to avoid it.
5. Understand escalation of commitment and how to avoid it.

Daniel Kahneman (another Nobel prize winner) and Amos Tversky spent decades studying how people make decisions. They found that individuals are influenced by a number of biases. Understanding the nature of decision biases helps individuals avoid areas where their decision processes may be flawed. In this section, we explain the biases of anchoring and adjustment, availability bias, escalation of commitment, fundamental attribution error, hindsight bias, judgments about correlation and causality, misunderstandings about sampling, overconfidence bias, framing bias, and satisficing.

1.1 Potential Challenges to Decision Making

Anchoring and Adjustment Bias

anchoring and adjustment bias

The tendency for individuals to rely too heavily on a single piece of information.

Anchoring and adjustment bias refers to the tendency for individuals to rely too heavily on arbitrary numbers, irrelevant traits, or facts when making decisions. Job seekers often fall into this trap by focusing on a desired salary while ignoring other aspects of the job offer, such as additional benefits, fit with the job, and working environment. Similarly, but more dramatically, lives were lost in the Great Bear Wilderness disaster when the coroner declared all five passengers of a small plane dead within five minutes of arriving at the accident scene. This halted the search effort for potential survivors when, in fact, two survivors walked out of the forest the next day. How could a mistake like this have been made? One theory is that decision biases played a large role in this serious error; anchoring on the fact that the plane had been consumed by flames led the coroner to call off the search for any possible survivors.[17]

Availability Bias

availability bias

A situation in which information that is more readily available is viewed as more likely to occur.

Availability bias refers to a situation where information that is more readily available is seen as more likely to occur. For example, an illustrative study asked participants if they thought individuals were more likely to die of auto accidents or stomach cancer and, if so, by how much. Most people reported that auto accidents caused more deaths—likely because auto accidents are reported more in the news compared to stomach cancer fatalities at a rate of more than 100 to 1, while the true difference between them is actually less than 2 to 1.

FIGURE 10.12 Decision Biases

Nobel prize–winner Herbert Simon argued that we can learn much about decision making by examining where we deviate from ideal decisions. We summarize a number of the most common decision biases below.

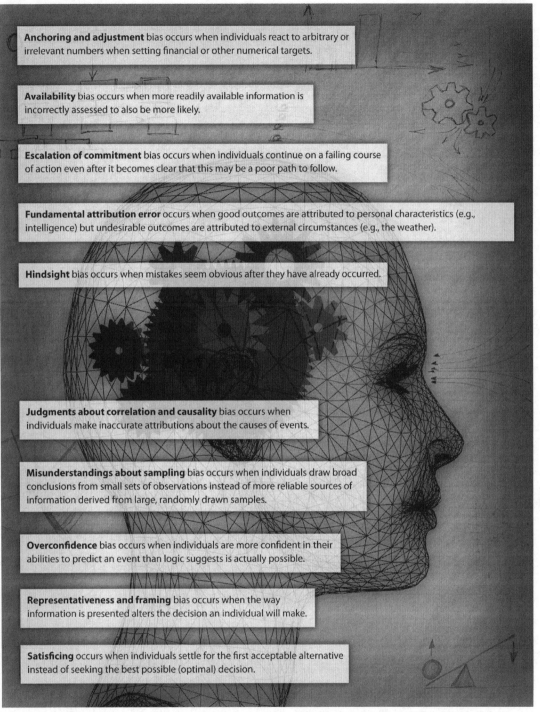

Anchoring and adjustment bias occurs when individuals react to arbitrary or irrelevant numbers when setting financial or other numerical targets.

Availability bias occurs when more readily available information is incorrectly assessed to also be more likely.

Escalation of commitment bias occurs when individuals continue on a failing course of action even after it becomes clear that this may be a poor path to follow.

Fundamental attribution error occurs when good outcomes are attributed to personal characteristics (e.g., intelligence) but undesirable outcomes are attributed to external circumstances (e.g., the weather).

Hindsight bias occurs when mistakes seem obvious after they have already occurred.

Judgments about correlation and causality bias occurs when individuals make inaccurate attributions about the causes of events.

Misunderstandings about sampling bias occurs when individuals draw broad conclusions from small sets of observations instead of more reliable sources of information derived from large, randomly drawn samples.

Overconfidence bias occurs when individuals are more confident in their abilities to predict an event than logic suggests is actually possible.

Representativeness and framing bias occurs when the way information is presented alters the decision an individual will make.

Satisficing occurs when individuals settle for the first acceptable alternative instead of seeking the best possible (optimal) decision.

Source: Image courtesy of Ketchen, D., & Short, J. (2011). Mastering strategic management. Irvington, NY: Flat World Knowledge; © Thinkstock

Escalation of Commitment Bias

Escalation of commitment bias occurs when individuals continue on a failing course of action after information reveals this may be a poor path to follow. It is sometimes called *sunk costs fallacy* because the continuation is often based on the idea that one has already invested in this course of action. For example, imagine a person purchases a used car that turns out to need another repair every few weeks. An effective way of dealing with this situation might be to sell the car without incurring further losses, donate the car, or drive it without repairing it until it falls apart. However, many people spend hours of their time and hundreds, even thousands, of dollars repairing the car in the hopes that they will justify their initial investment in buying the car.

escalation of commitment bias

When individuals continue on a failing course of action after information reveals this may be a poor path to follow.

FIGURE 10.13

Source: Short, J., Bauer, T. N., Simon, L., & Ketchen, D. (2011). Atlas Black: The Complete Adventure. New York: Flat World Knowledge. Reprinted by permission.

FIGURE 10.14

Comedian W. C. Fields once gave wise advice to avoid escalating commitment: "If at first you don't succeed, try, try again. Then quit. There's no point in being a damn fool about it."

Source: http://en.wikipedia.org/wiki/ File:Wcfields36682u.jpg

fundamental attribution error

A situation in which good outcomes are attributed to personal characteristics, such as intelligence, but undesirable outcomes are attributed to external circumstances, such as weather.

A classic example of escalation of commitment from the corporate world may be Motorola's Iridium project. In the 1980s, the phone coverage around the world was weak—it could take hours of dealing with a chain of telephone operators in several different countries to get a call through from, say, Cleveland to Calcutta. Thus there was a real need within the business community to improve phone access around the world. Motorola envisioned solving this problem using 66 low-orbiting satellites, enabling users to place a direct call to any location around the world. At the time of idea development, the project was technologically advanced and sophisticated and made financial sense. Motorola spun off Iridium as a separate company in 1991. It took researchers 15 years to develop the product from idea to market release. However, in the 1990s, the landscape for cell phone technology was dramatically different from the 1980s, and the widespread cell phone coverage around the world eliminated a large contingency of the projected customer base for Iridium. Had they been paying attention to these developments, the decision makers would probably have abandoned the project at some point in the early 1990s. Instead, they released the Iridium phone to the market in 1998. The phone cost $3,000 and was literally the size of a brick. Moreover, it was not possible to use the phone in moving cars or inside buildings! Not surprisingly, the launch was a failure, and Iridium filed for bankruptcy in 1999.[18] The company ultimately was purchased for $25 million by a group of investors (whereas it cost the company $5 billion to develop its product) and scaled down its operations; the product was modified for use by the Department of Defense to connect soldiers in remote areas not served by landlines or cell phones.

A variety of reasons exist for escalation of commitment.[19] Two reasons are particularly important. First, decision makers may not want to admit they were wrong because of personal pride or fear of the consequences of such an admission. Second, decision makers may incorrectly believe that spending more time and energy might somehow help them recover their losses. Effective decision makers avoid escalation of commitment by distinguishing between when persistence may actually pay off versus when persistence might mean escalation of commitment.

FIGURE 10.15

Motorola's original Iridium phone now resides at the Smithsonian National Air and Space Museum in Chantilly, Virginia.

Source: http://upload.wikimedia.org/wikipedia/commons/b/b0/Iridium_phone.jpg

Fundamental Attribution Error

Fundamental attribution error refers to a bias that exists when positive outcomes are seen as a function of personal characteristics while negative outcomes are attributed to external circumstances. In a classroom setting, a student who received a good grade in a class might be tempted to attribute this outcome to his or her own intelligence or exceptional work ethic. On the other hand, a poor-performing student might blame course testing procedures or the quality of education provided by the instructor.

Hindsight Bias

Hindsight bias occurs when looking backward in time where mistakes made seem obvious after they have already occurred. In other words, after a surprising event, many individuals are likely to think that they already knew this was going to happen. Once we know the outcome of a situation, it is hard for us to imagine how we would have acted without such knowledge. Hindsight bias becomes a problem especially when judging someone else's decisions. For example, the term "Monday morning quarterback" has become a common phrase associated with individuals that criticize the decisions of football players in hindsight of games played the previous weekend. Therefore, it is important for decision makers to remember this bias before passing judgments on other people's actions.

Judgments about Correlation and Causality Bias

How does employee satisfaction impact a firm's sales? Three elements are necessary to understand why one thing affects another. These elements, which show **judgments about correlation and causality bias**, include (1) correlation (Do sales increase when employees are satisfied? Do sales decrease when employees are dissatisfied?), (2) temporal order (Does an increase in employee satisfaction occur before sales increase?), and (3) ruling out other potential causes (Is something else causing increases in both satisfaction of employees and firm sales?). The first two items can be easily tracked, while the third can be difficult to isolate.

Misunderstandings about Sampling Bias

Sampling misunderstanding bias occurs when individuals make generalizations from a small sample (or a single source) of information rather than through large, randomly drawn samples that represent a wide audience. Rumors within the workplace provide an example of the type of information that could lead to such misunderstandings.

Overconfidence Bias

Overconfidence bias occurs when individuals overestimate their ability to predict future events. Many people exhibit signs of overconfidence. For example, 82% of surveyed drivers feel they are in the top 30% of safe drivers, 86% of students at the Harvard Business School say they are better looking than their peers, and doctors consistently overestimate their ability to detect problems.[20] Much like individuals who are 100% sure they can pick the winners of this week's football games despite evidence to the contrary, these individuals are suffering from overconfidence bias. People who purchase lottery tickets as a way to make money are probably suffering from overconfidence bias: it is three times more likely for a person driving 10 miles to buy a lottery ticket to be killed in a car accident than to win the jackpot.[21]

Framing Bias

Framing bias refers to the tendency of decision makers to be influenced by the way a situation or problem is presented. For example, when making a purchase, customers find it easier to let go of a discount as opposed to accepting a surcharge, even though they both might cost the person the same amount of money. Similarly, customers tend to prefer a statement such as "85% lean beef" as opposed to "15% fat"![22] It is important to be aware of this tendency because, depending on how a problem is presented, individuals choose an alternative that is disadvantageous simply because of how it is framed.

Satisficing

Satisficing refers to a situation in which individuals select the first acceptable alternative instead of seeking the best possible decision. While this bias might actually be desirable when making simple decisions such as what to wear during an informal event, this bias can be problematic during big decisions such as choosing between competing job offers or making a major purchase with long-term impact.

---

hindsight bias

The opposite of overconfidence bias, as it occurs when a person, looking at the past, judges that a mistake that was made should have been recognized as a mistake at the time.

judgments about correlation and causality bias

A situation in which individuals make inaccurate attributions about the causes of events.

sampling misunderstanding bias

When individuals draw broad conclusions from small sets of observations instead of more reliable sources of information derived from large, randomly drawn samples.

overconfidence bias

When individuals overestimate their ability to predict future events.

framing bias

The tendency of decision makers to be influenced by the way that problems are framed.

FIGURE 10.16

Many retail stores utilize the principles of framing to make shoppers feel like they are getting a bargain and entice them to spend more.

© Thinkstock

KEY TAKEAWAY

Understanding decision-making traps can help you avoid and manage them. Common biases include anchoring and adjustment, availability bias, escalation of commitment, fundamental attribution error, hindsight bias, judgments about correlation and causality, misunderstandings about sampling, overconfidence bias, framing bias, and satisficing.

EXERCISES

1. Describe a time when you fell into one of the decision-making traps. How did you come to realize that you had made a poor decision?
2. How can you avoid escalation of commitment?
3. Share an example of anchoring.
4. Which of the traps seems the most dangerous for decision makers and why?

---

2. DECISION MAKING IN GROUPS

LEARNING OBJECTIVES

1. **Understand the pros and cons of individual and group decision making.**
2. **Learn to recognize the signs of groupthink.**
3. **Recognize different tools and techniques for making better decisions.**

2.1   When It Comes to Decision Making, Are Two Heads Better Than One?

When it comes to decision making, are two heads better than one? Group decision making has the advantages of drawing from the experiences and perspectives of a larger number of individuals. Hence they have the potential to be more creative and lead to a more effective decision. In fact, groups may sometimes achieve results beyond what they could have done as individuals. Groups also make the task more enjoyable for members in question. Finally, when the decision is made by a group rather than a single individual, implementation of the decision will be easier because group members will be invested in the decision. If the group is diverse, better decisions may be made because different group members may have different ideas based on their background and experiences. Research shows that for top management teams, groups that debate issues and that are diverse make decisions that are more comprehensive and better for the bottom line in terms of profitability and sales.[23]

Despite its popularity within organizations, group decision making suffers from a number of disadvantages. For example, groups rarely outperform their best member.[24] While groups have the potential to arrive at an effective decision, they often suffer from process losses. One reason is that groups may suffer from coordination problems. Anyone who has worked with a team of individuals on a project can attest to the difficulty of coordinating members' work or even coordinating everyone's presence in a team meeting. Furthermore, groups can suffer from social loafing, or the tendency of some members to put forth less effort while working within a group. Groups may also suffer from groupthink, the tendency to avoid critical evaluation of ideas the group favors. Finally, group decision making takes a longer time compared with individual decision making, given that all members need to discuss their thoughts regarding different alternatives.

Thus whether an individual or a group decision is preferable will depend on the specifics of the situation. For example, if there is an emergency and a decision needs to be made quickly, individual decision making might be preferred. Individual decision making may also be appropriate if the individual in question has all the information needed to make the decision and if implementation problems are not expected. However, if one person does not have all the information and skills needed to make the decision, if implementing the decision will be difficult without the involvement of those who will be affected by the decision, and if time urgency is more modest, then decision making by a group may be more effective.

social loafing

The tendency of individuals to put in less effort when working in a group context.

groupthink

A group pressure phenomenon that increases the risk of the group making flawed decisions by allowing reductions in mental efficiency, reality testing, and moral judgment.

FIGURE 10.17 Advantages and Disadvantages of Different Levels of Decision Making

Individual Decision Making		Group Decision Making	
Pros	Cons	Pros	Cons
Typically faster than group decision making	Fewer ideas	Diversity of ideas and can piggyback on others' ideas	Takes longer
Best individual in a group usually outperforms the group	Identifying the best individual can be challenging	Greater commitment to ideas	Group dynamics such as groupthink can occur
Accountability is easier to determine	Possible to put off making decisions if left alone to do it	Interaction can be fun and serves as a team building task	Social loafing- harder to identify responsibility for decisions

2.2   Groupthink

Have you ever been in a decision-making group that you felt was heading in the wrong direction, but you restrained yourself from speaking up? If so, you have already been a victim of groupthink. Groupthink is a group pressure phenomenon that increases the risk of the group making flawed decisions by leading to reduced mental efficiency, reality testing, and moral judgment. Groupthink is characterized by eight symptoms:[25]

1. *Illusion of invulnerability* shared by most or all of the group members that creates excessive optimism and encourages them to take extreme risks.

2. *Collective rationalizations* where members downplay negative information or warnings that might cause them to reconsider their assumptions.

3. *An unquestioned belief in the group's inherent morality* that may incline members to ignore ethical or moral consequences of their actions.

4. *Stereotyped views of out-groups* are seen when groups discount rivals' abilities to make effective responses.

5. *Direct pressure* on any member who expresses strong arguments against any of the group's stereotypes, illusions, or commitments.

6. *Self-censorship* when members of the group minimize their own doubts and counterarguments.

7. *Illusions of unanimity* based on self-censorship and direct pressure on the group; the lack of dissent is viewed as unanimity.

8. *The emergence of self-appointed mindguards* where one or more members protect the group from information that runs counter to the group's assumptions and course of action.

While research on groupthink has not confirmed all of the theory, groups do tend to suffer from symptoms of groupthink when they are large and when the group is cohesive because the members like each other.[26] The assumption is that the more frequently a group displays one or more of the eight symptoms, the worse the quality of their decisions will be.

However, if your group is cohesive, it is not necessarily doomed to engage in groupthink.

Recommendations for Avoiding Groupthink

Groups Should

- Discuss the symptoms of groupthink and how to avoid them.
- Assign a rotating **devil's advocate** to every meeting. A devil's advocate is someone who is assigned the role of challenging and questioning the group, and may prevent the group from premature agreement.
- Invite experts or qualified colleagues who are not part of the core decision-making group to attend meetings, and get reactions from outsiders on a regular basis and share these with the group.
- Encourage a culture of difference where different ideas are valued.
- Debate the ethical implications of the decisions and potential solutions being considered.

Individuals Should

- Monitor their own behavior for signs of groupthink and modify behavior if needed.
- Check themselves for self-censorship.
- Carefully avoid mindguard behaviors.
- Avoid putting pressure on other group members to conform.
- Remind members of the ground rules for avoiding groupthink if they get off track.

Group Leaders Should

- Break the group into two subgroups from time to time.
- Have more than one group work on the same problem if time and resources allow it. This makes sense for highly critical decisions.
- Remain impartial and refrain from stating preferences at the outset of decisions.
- Set a tone of encouraging critical evaluations throughout deliberations.
- Create an anonymous feedback channel where all group members can contribute to if desired.

2.3 Tools and Techniques for Making Better Decisions

Nominal Group Technique (NGT) was developed to help with group decision making by ensuring that all members participate fully. NGT is not a technique to be used at all meetings routinely. Rather, it is used to structure group meetings when members are grappling with problem solving or idea generation. It follows four steps.[27] First, each member of the group engages in a period of independently and silently writing down ideas. Second, the group goes in order around the room to gather all the ideas that were generated. This continues until all ideas have been shared. Third, a discussion takes place around each idea and members ask for and give clarification and make evaluative statements. Finally, individuals vote for their favorite ideas by using either ranking or rating techniques. Following the four-step NGT helps to ensure that all members participate fully and avoids group decision-making problems such as groupthink.

Delphi Technique is unique because it is a group process using written responses to a series of questionnaires instead of physically bringing individuals together to make a decision. The first questionnaire asks individuals to respond to a broad question, such as stating the problem, outlining objectives, or proposing solutions. Each subsequent questionnaire is built from the information gathered in the previous one. The process ends when the group reaches a consensus. Facilitators can decide whether to keep responses anonymous. This process is often used to generate best practices from experts. For example, Purdue University professor Michael Campion used this process when he was editor of the

FIGURE 10.18

Avoiding groupthink can be a matter of life or death. In January 1986, the space shuttle *Challenger* exploded 73 seconds after liftoff, killing all seven astronauts aboard. The decision to launch *Challenger* that day, despite problems with mechanical components of the vehicle and unfavorable weather conditions, is cited as a tragic example of groupthink.

Source: http://en.wikipedia.org/wiki/ Image:Challenger_flight_51-l_crew.jpg

devil's advocate

Someone who is assigned the role of challenging and questioning the group. This person may prevent the group from premature agreement.

Nominal Group Technique (NGT)

A technique designed to help with group decision making by ensuring that all members participate fully.

Delphi Technique

A group process that uses written responses to a series of questionnaires instead of physically bringing individuals together to make a decision.

research journal *Personnel Psychology* and wanted to determine the qualities that distinguished a good research article. Using the Delphi Technique, he was able to gather responses from hundreds of top researchers from around the world without ever having to leave his office and distill them into a checklist of criteria that he could use to evaluate articles submitted to the journal.[28]

Majority rule refers to a decision-making rule where each member of the group is given a single vote, and the option that receives the greatest number of votes is selected. This technique has remained popular, perhaps because of its simplicity, speed, ease of use, and representational fairness. Research also supports majority rule as an effective decision-making technique.[29] However, those who did not vote in favor of the decision will be less likely to support it.

Consensus is another decision-making rule that groups may use when the goal is to gain support for an idea or plan of action. While consensus tends to take longer in the first place, it may make sense when support is needed to enact the plan. The process works by discussing the issues, generating a proposal, calling for consensus, and discussing any concerns. If concerns still exist, the proposal is modified to accommodate them. These steps are repeated until consensus is reached. Thus this decision-making rule is inclusive, participatory, cooperative, and democratic. Research shows that consensus can lead to better accuracy,[30] and it helps members feel greater satisfaction with decisions[31] and to have greater acceptance. However, groups take longer with this approach and groups that cannot reach consensus become frustrated.[32]

Group decision support systems (GDSS) are interactive computer-based systems that are able to combine communication and decision technologies to help groups make better decisions. Organizations know that having effective **knowledge management systems** to share information is important. Research shows that a GDSS can actually improve the output of group collaborative work through higher information sharing.[33] Organizations know that having effective knowledge management systems to share information is important, and their spending reflects this reality. As the popularity of these systems grows, they risk becoming counterproductive. Humans can only process so many ideas and information at one time. As virtual meetings grow larger, it is reasonable to assume that information overload can occur and good ideas will fall through the cracks, essentially recreating a problem that the GDSS was intended to solve that is to make sure every idea is heard. Another problem is the system possibly becoming too complicated. If the systems evolve to a point of uncomfortable complexity, it has recreated the problem of the bully pulpit and shyness. Those who understand the interface will control the narrative of the discussion, while those who are less savvy will only be along for the ride.[34] Lastly, many of these programs fail to take into account the factor of human psychology. These systems could make employees more reluctant to share information due to lack of control, lack of immediate feedback, the fear of "flaming" or harsher than normal criticism, and the desire to have original information hence more power.[35]

Decision trees are diagrams in which answers to yes or no questions lead decision makers to address additional questions until they reach the end of the tree. Decision trees are helpful in avoiding errors such as framing bias.[36] Decision trees tend to be helpful in guiding the decision maker to a predetermined alternative and ensuring consistency of decision making—that is, every time certain conditions are present, the decision maker will follow one course of action as opposed to others if the decision is made using a decision tree.

majority rule

A decision-making rule where each member of the group is given a single vote and the option that receives the greatest number of votes is selected.

consensus

A decision-making rule that groups may use when the goal is to gain support for an idea or plan of action. The ideas are discussed and proposals are modified until a unanimous decision is reached.

group decision support systems

Interactive computer-based systems that are able to combine communication and decision technologies to help groups make better decisions.

knowledge management systems

Systems for managing knowledge in organizations, supporting creation, capture, storage, and dissemination of information.

decision trees

Diagrams where answers to yes or no questions lead decision makers to address additional questions until they reach the end of the tree.

KEY TAKEAWAY

There are trade-offs between making decisions alone and within a group. Groups have greater diversity of experiences and ideas than individuals, but they also have potential process losses such as groupthink. Groupthink can be avoided by recognizing the eight symptoms discussed. Finally, there are a variety of tools and techniques available for helping to make more effective decisions in groups, including the Nominal Group Technique, Delphi Technique, majority rule, consensus, GDSS, and decision trees. Understanding the link between managing teams and making decisions is an important aspect of a manager's leading function.

3. DEVELOPING YOUR PERSONAL DECISION-MAKING SKILLS

3.1 Perform a Project "Premortem" to Fix Problems before They Happen

Doctors routinely perform postmortems to understand what went wrong with a patient who has died. The idea is for everyone to learn from the unfortunate outcome so that future patients will not meet a similar fate. In a similar vein, research suggests that the simple exercise of imagining what could go wrong with a given decision can increase the ability to identify reasons for future successes or failures by 30%.[37] A "premortem" is a way to imagine and to avoid what might go wrong before spending a cent or having to change course along the way.[38]

Gary Klein, an expert on decision making in fast-paced, uncertain, complex, and critical environments, recommends that decision makers follow this six-step premortem process to increase their chances of success.

1. A planning team comes up with an outline of a plan, such as the launching of a new product.
2. Either the existing group or a unique group is then told to imagine looking into a crystal ball and seeing that the new product failed miserably. They then write down all the reasons they can imagine that might have led to this failure.
3. Each team member shares items from their list until all the potential problems have been identified.
4. The list is reviewed for additional ideas.
5. The issues are sorted into categories in the search for themes.
6. The plan should then be revised to correct the flaws and avoid these potential problems.

The premortem technique allows groups to truly delve into "what if" scenarios. For example, in a premortem session at a *Fortune* 50 company, an executive imagined that a potential billion-dollar environmental sustainability project might fail because the CEO had retired.

4. CASE IN POINT: HOW ANGRY BIRDS TOOK FLIGHT

FIGURE 10.19

Source: Retrieved October 8, 2012 from http://en.wikipedia.org/wiki/File:Angry_Birds_soft_drink.JPG

What animal does not have wings or feet, looks mean, and attacks harmless-looking pigs, all while costing the inhabitants of our planet 200 million minutes every day? We are, of course, talking about Angry Birds, the mobile game that has been downloaded 1 billion times and earned its maker, Rovio Entertainment, $106 million in revenue as of 2012. How does a company produce such a blockbuster hit? The so-called overnight success of Rovio actually took eight years to achieve and was a unique combination of rational, intuitive, and creative decisions, and not an insignificant amount of luck.

Finnish cousins Mikael and Niklas Hed spent a lot of time talking about video games while growing up. Niklas actually made his first game when he was 12, using the programming language Pascal. When the pair won a 2003 competition organized by Nokia and HP to write a game for an early smartphone, they decided to start their own business. They had little idea how the business would make money, but they knew this was what they wanted to do. In 2004, they founded the company Relude, later renamed Rovio, or "bonfire" in Finnish. A graduate of Tulane University's business school, Mikael brought the business expertise to this partnership, while Niklas was the computer scientist, bringing technical expertise. Mikael's father, Kaj, an entrepreneur who had founded other companies before, later invested €1 million, resulting in an expansion of the company. Mikael left the company in 2005 due to disagreements with his father about the company's future and growth strategy. By 2009, the company was in dire straits, with their once 50-employee office shrunk to 12. Up to this point, they had mainly done work for hire, developing 51 games for big-name companies. None of the games they developed were hits, and they desperately needed a hit.

When Niklas decided to reboot the company, his first act of business was to bring back Mikael, which was a challenge due to the father-son conflict. Once Mikael was convinced to come back on board, the duo outlined how they would come up with the perfect game. In the meantime, a key change in their business environment was working in their favor. While in the past there were a large number of platforms game developers could build on, Apple had revolutionized the business with the iPhone release as well as the iTunes store. Now they could create a game focusing on a single platform and reach a large number of paying customers.

Their criteria for creating a hit game were these: It had to be a physics-based game, which was popular at the time. It had to be easy enough to learn without a tutorial. Users should be able to play it a short while and then put it aside. Loading time had to be brief. It needed an eye-grabbing icon to stand out in the iTunes store. And it needed to appeal to everyone—not just teenagers or science geeks or men, but all demographics. Keeping these criteria in mind, they started reviewing several concepts being pitched to them by their game designers, dismissing them one after the other.

One day in March 2009, their principal game designer brought a sketch of a feetless, wingless, angry-looking bird, and the entire company fell in love with it. Then they started going through iterations to perfect the game. At first the birds were matched to blocks by color, making the game confusing and leading to the decision to give the birds an enemy. The enemy that was a blob turned into a pig after the swine flu epidemic. The question of why the birds were so merciless toward the cute pigs resulted in the back story that the pigs stole the birds' eggs. Niklas knew they had a winner in their hands when he showed the game to his mom over Christmas dinner and did not get his phone back all night.

The game actually flopped when it was first released in the app store. Realizing that breaking into the U.S. and U.K. market would be a challenge, Rovio concentrated on becoming number one in smaller markets such as Finland, Sweden, and Czech Republic, which gave them leverage to talk to Apple executives and convince them to make Angry Birds the featured game of the week in the U.K. They timed this week to coincide with the release of a YouTube video, a free version of the game, and a new version adding 42 levels; this resulted in the application moving from number 600 to number 1. The result is now history, with Rovio building one of the most successful franchises in the world and giving the mean birds themselves celebrity status. The next game in the franchise—Angry Birds Space—was downloaded 10 million times the first three days it was available.

Case written by Berrin Erdogan and Talya Bauer to accompany Carpenter, M., Bauer, T., Erdogan, B., & Short, J. (2013). Principles of Management (2nd ed.). New York: Flat World Knowledge. Based on Ante, S. (2012, August 3). Apps make leap from phones to toys. Wall Street Journal, B6; Cheshire, T. (2011, April). In depth: How Rovio made Angry Birds a winner (and what's next). Wired Magazine; Geron, T. (2012, July 10). Can Rovio repeat angry birds success with new "Amazing Alex" franchise? Forbes; Olson, P. (2012, May 8). A billionaire could quietly hatch from angry birds IPO. Forbes; Rose, V. (2012, January/February). The bird watcher. Discover, 33(1).

CASE DISCUSSION QUESTIONS

1. What do you believe is the role of luck in Rovio Entertainment's success?
2. How did Mikael and Niklas engage in rational decision making? Explain.
3. Which of the Heds' decisions may be characterized as an intuitive decision?
4. Did the founders of Rovio engage in creative decision making? Explain your answer using examples.

ENDNOTES

1. Ireland, R. D., & Miller, C. C. (2004). Decision making and firm success. *Academy of Management Executive, 18*, 8–12; Nutt, P. C. (2002). *Why decisions fail*. San Francisco: Berrett-Koehler; Nutt, P. C. (1999). Surprising but true: Half the decisions in organizations fail. *Academy of Management Executive, 13*, 75–90.

2. Adapted from ideas contained in Blanchard, K., & Peale, N. V. (1988). *The power of ethical management*. New York: William Morrow.

3. Nutt, P. C. (1994). Types of organizational decision processes. *Administrative Science Quarterly, 29*, 414–550.

4. Nutt, P. C. (1998). Surprising but true: Half the decisions in organizations fail. *Academy of Management Executive, 13*, 75–90.

5. Zell, D. M., Glassman, A. M., & Duron, S. A. (2007). Strategic management in turbulent times: The short and glorious history of accelerated decision making at Hewlett-Packard. *Organizational Dynamics, 36*, 93–104.

6. Burke, L. A., & Miller, M. K. (1999). Taking the mystery out of intuitive decision making. *Academy of Management Executive, 13*, 91–98.

7. Breen, B. (2000, August). "What's your intuition?" *Fast Company*, 290; Klein, G. (2003). *Intuition at work*. New York: Doubleday; Salas, E., & Klein, G. (2001). *Linking expertise and naturalistic decision making*. Mahwah, NJ: Lawrence Erlbaum.

8. Dane, E., Rockmann, K. W., & Pratt, M. G. (2012). When should I trust my gut? Linking domain expertise to intuitive decision-making effectiveness. *Organizational Behavior and Human Decision Processes, 119*, 187–194.

9. Interview by author Talya Bauer at Ames Research Center, Mountain View, CA, 1990.

10. Conlin, M. (2007, September 14). Netflix: Recruiting and retaining the best talent. *Business Week Online*. Retrieved September 8, 2012, from http://www.businessweek.com/managing/content/sep2007/ca20070913_564868.htm?campaign_id=rss_null.

11. Amabile, T. M. (1988). A model of creativity and innovation in organizations. In B. M. Staw & L. L. Cummings (Eds.), *Research in Organizational Behavior, 10*, 123–167. Greenwich, CT: JAI Press; Amabile, T. M., Conti, R., Coon, H., Lazenby, J., & Herron, M. (1996). Assessing the work environment for creativity. *Academy of Management Journal, 39*, 1154–1184; Ford, C. M., & Gioia, D. A. (2000). Factors influencing creativity in the domain of managerial decision making. *Journal of Management, 26*, 705–732; Tierney, P., Farmer, S. M., & Graen, G. B. (1999). An examination of leadership and employee creativity: The relevance of traits and relationships. *Personnel Psychology, 52*, 591–620; Woodman, R. W., Sawyer, J. E., & Griffin, R. W. (1993). Toward a theory of organizational creativity. *Academy of Management Review, 18*, 293–321.

12. De Stobbeleir, K. E. M., Ashford, S. J., & Buyens, D. (2011). Self-regulation of creativity at work: The role of feedback-seeking behavior in creative performance. *Academy of Management Journal, 54*, 811–831; Feist, G. J. (1998). A meta-analysis of personality in scientific and artistic creativity. *Personality and Social Psychology Review, 2*, 290–309.

13. Girotra, K., Terwiesch, C., & Ulrich, K. T. (2010). Idea generation and the quality of the best idea. *Management Science, 56*, 591–605.

14. Scott, G., Leritz, L. E., & Mumford, M. D. (2004). The effectiveness of creativity training: A quantitative review. *Creativity Research Journal, 16*, 361–388.

15. Afuah, A., & Tucci, C. L. (2012). Crowdsourcing as a solution to distant search. *Academy of Management Review, 37*, 355–375; Lohr, S. (2009, July 19). The crowd is wise (when focused). *New York Times. Business News*.

16. Adapted from ideas in Amabile, T. M. (1998). How to kill creativity. *Harvard Business Review, 76*, 76–87; Gundry, L. K., Kickul, J. R., & Prather, C. W. (1994). Building the creative organization. *Organizational Dynamics, 22*, 22–37; Hoever, I. J., van Knippenberg, D., van Ginkel, W. P., & Barkema, H. G. (2012). Fostering team creativity: Perspective taking as key to unlocking diversity's potential. *Journal of Applied Psychology, 97*, 982–996; Keith, N., & Frese, M. (2008). Effectiveness of error management training: A meta-analysis. *Journal of Applied Psychology, 93*, 59–69; Pearsall, M. J., Ellis, A. P. J., & Evans, J. M. (2008). Unlocking the effects of gender faultlines on team creativity: Is activation the key? *Journal of Applied Psychology, 93*, 225–234; Thompson, L. (2003). Improving the creativity of organizational work groups. *Academy of Management Executive, 17*, 96–109.

17. Becker, W. S. (2007). Missed opportunities: The Great Bear Wilderness Disaster. *Organizational Dynamics, 36*, 363–376.

18. Finkelstein, S., & Sanford, S. H. (2000, November). Learning from corporate mistakes: The rise and fall of Iridium. *Organizational Dynamics, 29*, 138–148.

19. Sleesman, D. J., Conlon, D. E., McNamara, G., & Miles, J. E. (2012). Cleaning up the big muddy: A meta-analytic review of the determinants of escalation of commitment. *Academy of Management Journal, 55*, 541–562.

20. Tilson, W. (1999, September 20). The perils of investor overconfidence. Retrieved September 8, 2012, from http://www.fool.com/BoringPort/1999/BoringPort990920.htm.

21. Orkin, M. (1991). *Can you win? The real odds for casino gambling, sports betting and lotteries*. New York: W. H. Freeman.

22. Li, S., Sun, Y., & Wang, Y. (2007). 50% off or buy one get one free? Frame preference as a function of consumable nature in dairy products. *Journal of Social Psychology, 147*, 413–421.

23. Simons, T., Pelled, L. H., & Smith, K. A. (1999). Making use of difference: Diversity, debate, decision comprehensiveness in top management teams. *Academy of Management Journal, 42*, 662–673.

24. Miner, F. C. (1984). Group versus individual decision making: An investigation of performance measures, decision strategies, and process losses/gains. *Organizational Behavior and Human Performance, 33*, 112–124.

25. Janis, I. L. (1972). *Victims of groupthink*. New York: Houghton Mifflin.

26. Esser, J. K. (1998). Alive and well after 25 years: A review of groupthink research. *Organizational Behavior and Human Decision Processes, 73*, 116–141; Mullen, B., Anthony, T., Salas, E., & Driskell, J. E. (1994). Group cohesiveness and quality of decision making: An integration of tests of the groupthink hypothesis. *Small Group Research, 25*, 189–204.

27. Delbecq, A. L., Van de Ven, A. H., & Gustafson, D. H. (1975). *Group techniques for program planning: A guide to nominal group and Delphi processes*. Glenview, IL: Scott, Foresman.

28. Campion, M. A. (1993). Article review checklist: A criterion checklist for reviewing research articles in applied psychology. *Personnel Psychology, 46*, 705–718.

29. Hastie, R., & Kameda, T. (2005). The robust beauty of majority rules in group decisions. *Psychological Review, 112*, 494–508.

30. Roch, S. G. (2007). Why convene rater teams: An investigation of the benefits of anticipated discussion, consensus, and rater motivation. *Organizational Behavior and Human Decision Processes, 104*, 14–29.

31. Mohammed, S., & Ringseis, E. (2001). Cognitive diversity and consensus in group decision making: The role of inputs, processes, and outcomes. *Organizational Behavior and Human Decision Processes, 85*, 310–335.

32. Peterson, R. (1999). Can you have too much of a good thing? The limits of voice for improving satisfaction with leaders. *Personality and Social Psychology, 25*, 313–324.

33. Lam, S. S. K., & Schaubroeck, J. (2000). Improving group decisions by better pooling information: A comparative advantage of group decision support systems. *Journal of Applied Psychology, 85*, 565–573.

34. Nunamaker, J. F., Jr., Dennis, A. R., Valacich, J. S., Vogel, D. R., George, J. F. (1991, July). Electronic meetings to support group work. *Communications of the ACM, 34*(7), 40–61.

35. Babock, P. (2004, May). Shedding light on knowledge management. *HR Magazine*, 47–50.

36. Wright, G., & Goodwin, P. (2002). Eliminating a framing bias by using simple instructions to "think harder" and respondents with managerial experience: Comment on "breaking the frame." *Strategic Management Journal, 23*, 1059–1067.

37. Mitchell, D. J., Russo, J., & Pennington, N. (1989). Back to the future: Temporal perspective in the explanation of events. *Journal of Behavioral Decision Making, 2*, 25–38.

38. Breen, B. (2000, August). What's your intuition? *Fast Company*, 290; Klein, G. (2007, September). Performing a project premortem. *Harvard Business Review*, 18–19; Klein, G. (2003). *The power of intuition: How to use your gut feelings to make better decisions at work*. New York: Random House; Pliske, R., McCloskey, M., & Klein, G. (2001). Decision skills training: Facilitating learning from experience. In E. Salas & G. Klein (Eds.), *Linking expertise and naturalistic decision making* (pp. 37–53). Mahwah, NJ: Lawrence Erlbaum.

CHAPTER 11
Communication in Organizations

FIGURE 11.1

A sender's choice of communication channel affects the quality of what is actually understood by the receiver.

© 2010 Jupiterimages Corporation

CHAPTER LEARNING OBJECTIVES

Reading this chapter will help you do the following:

1. Define communication and understand the communication process.
2. Understand and overcome barriers to effective communication.
3. Compare and contrast different types of communication.
4. Compare and contrast different communication channels.
5. Develop your own communication skills.

FIGURE 11.2 The P-O-L-C Framework

Planning	Organizing	Leading	Controlling
1. Vision & Mission	1. Organization Design	1. Leadership	1. Systems/Processes
2. Strategizing	2. Culture	2. Decision Making	2. Strategic Human Resources
3. Goals & Objectives	3. Social Networks	3. Communications	
		4. Groups/Teams	
		5. Motivation	

1. UNDERSTANDING COMMUNICATION

Communication supports each of a manager's P-O-L-C functions. The ability to effectively communicate is a necessary condition for successfully planning, organizing, leading, and controlling. Communication is vital to organizations—it's how we coordinate actions and achieve goals. Communication is defined as "a process by which information is exchanged between individuals through a common system of symbols, signs, or behavior."[1] We know that 50%–90% of a manager's time is spent communicating[2] and that communication ability is related to a manager's performance.[3] In most work environments, miscommunication is an annoyance—it can interrupt workflow by causing delays and interpersonal strife. And in some work arenas, like operating rooms and airplane cockpits, communication can be a matter of life and death.

Unfortunately, miscommunication is common in the workplace, and the relationship between miscommunication and negative outcomes is strong. A NASA study suggests that deficient interpersonal communication was a causal factor in approximately 70%–80% of aviation accidents over a 20-year period.[4]

Poor communication can also lead to lawsuits. For example, while malpractice suits are commonly filed against doctors based on the outcome of their treatments, a study of malpractice suits found that a primary influence on whether a doctor is sued is that doctor's communication style. While the combination of a bad outcome and patient unhappiness can quickly lead to litigation, a warm, personal communication style leads to greater patient satisfaction. And satisfied patients are less likely to sue.[5]

For leaders and organizations, poor communication costs money and wastes time. One study found that 14% of each workweek is wasted on poor communication.[6] In contrast, effective communication is an asset for organizations and individuals alike. Effective communication skills, for example, are an asset for job seekers. A study of recruiters at 85 business schools ranked communication and interpersonal skills as one of most important skills they were looking for, with 89% of the recruiters saying they were important.[7] Good communication can help a company retain star employees. Surveys find that when employees think their organizations do a good job of keeping them informed about matters that affect them and they have ready access to the information they need to do their jobs, they are more satisfied with their employers.[8] Good communication can also increase a company's market value. "When you foster ongoing communications internally, you will have more satisfied employees who will be better equipped to effectively communicate with your customers," says Susan Meisinger, former President/CEO of the Society for Human Resource Management, citing research findings that for organizations that are able to improve their communication integrity, their market value increases by as much as 7.1%.[9]

FIGURE 11.3

Success on complicated missions at NASA depends on strong communication.

Source: http://en.wikipedia.org/wiki/File:Cheering-full-br2.jpg

1.1   The Communication Process

Communication fulfills three main functions within an organization: (1) transmitting information, (2) coordinating effort, and (3) sharing emotions and feelings. All these functions are vital to a successful organization. Transmitting information is vital to an organization's ability to function. Coordinating effort within the organization helps people work toward the same goals. Sharing emotions and feelings bonds teams and unites people in times of celebration and crisis. Effective communication helps people grasp issues, build rapport with coworkers, and achieve consensus.

We all exchange information with others countless times a day, by phone, e-mail, print, and of course in person. Understanding how individuals communicate effectively is the first step in understanding the communication process. We explain one well-known model of communication—the Process Model of Communication—in Figure 11.5.

FIGURE 11.5   The Process Model of Communication

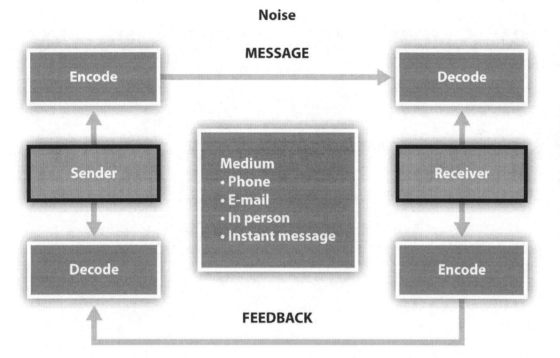

A **Sender**, such as a boss, coworker, or customer, originates the Message with a thought. For example, the boss's thought could be *"Get more printer toner cartridges!"*

The Sender **encodes** the Message, translating the idea into words.

The boss may communicate this thought by saying, *"Hey you guys, we need to order more printer toner cartridges."*

The **medium** of this encoded Message may be spoken words, written words, or signs.

The **receiver** is the person who receives the Message.

The Receiver **decodes** the Message by assigning meaning to the words.

In this example, our Receiver, Bill, has a to-do list a mile long. *"The boss must know how much work I already have,"* the Receiver thinks. Bill's mind translates his boss's Message as, *"Could you order some printer toner cartridges, in addition to everything else I asked you to do this week…if you can find the time?"*

FIGURE 11.4

Famed Irish writer George Bernard Shaw once quipped, "The single biggest problem in communication is the illusion that it has taken place." As the only person to ever win both a Nobel Prize and an Oscar, his advice on communication is noteworthy.

Source: http://en.wikipedia.org/wiki/ File:GBShaw_1909.jpg

encoding

The translation of ideas into words.

medium

The way that a Sender's Message is conveyed.

receiver

The person who a Message is intended to reach.

decoding

The process of assigning meaning to a received Message.

noise

Anything that interferes with or distorts the Message being transformed.

The meaning that the Receiver assigns may not be the meaning that the Sender intended because of such factors as noise. Noise is anything that interferes with or distorts the Message being transformed. Noise can be external in the environment (such as distractions) or it can be within the Receiver. For example, the Receiver may be highly nervous and unable to pay attention to the Message. Noise can even occur within the Sender: the Sender may be unwilling to take the time to convey an accurate Message or the words she chooses can be ambiguous and prone to misinterpretation.

Picture the next scene. The place: a staff meeting. The time: a few days later. The boss believes her Message has been received.

"Are the printer toner cartridges here yet?" she asks.

"You never said it was a rush job!" the Receiver protests.

"But!"

"But!"

Miscommunications like these happen in the workplace every day. But how does a miscommunication happen? It helps to think of the communication process. The series of arrows pointing the way from the Sender to the Receiver and back again can, and often do, fall short of their target.

KEY TAKEAWAY

Communication is vital to organizations. Poor communication is prevalent and can have serious repercussions. Communication fulfills three functions within organizations: transmitting information, coordinating, and sharing emotions and feelings. Noise can disrupt or distort communication.

EXERCISES

1. Where have you seen the communication process break down—at work? At school? At home?
2. Explain how miscommunication might be related to an accident at work.
3. Give an example of noise during the communication process.

2. COMMUNICATION BARRIERS

LEARNING OBJECTIVES

1. Understand different ways that the communication process can be sidetracked.
2. Understand the problem of poor listening and how to promote active listening.

2.1 Barriers to Effective Communication

Several barriers stand in the way of effective communication. These include filtering, selective perception, information overload, emotional disconnects, lack of source familiarity or credibility, workplace gossip, semantics, gender differences, differences in meaning between Sender and Receiver, and biased language. In this section, we explain each of these barriers.

Filtering

Filtering is the distortion or withholding of information to manage a person's reactions. Some examples of filtering include a manager who keeps her division's poor sales figures from her boss, the vice president, fearing that the bad news will make him angry. The old saying, "Don't shoot the messenger!" illustrates the tendency of Receivers (in this case, the vice president) to vent their negative response to unwanted Messages on the Sender. A gatekeeper (the vice president's assistant, perhaps) who doesn't pass along a complete Message is also filtering. The vice president may delete the e-mail announcing the quarter's sales figures before reading it, blocking the Message before it arrives.

Filtering prevents members of an organization from getting a complete picture of reality. To maximize the possibility of sending and receiving effective communications, it's helpful to deliver a Message in multiple ways and to seek information from multiple sources. In this way, the effect of any one person's filtering the Message will be diminished.

Since people tend to filter bad news more often when communicating with a superior, it is also helpful to remember that subordinates in an organization may be wary of sharing bad news. One way to defuse the tendency to filter is to reward employees who clearly convey information, regardless of whether the news is good and bad.

Here are some of the criteria that individuals may use when deciding whether to filter a Message or pass it on:

- **Past experience.** Was the Sender rewarded for passing along news of this kind in the past, or was she criticized?
- **Knowledge, perception of the speaker.** Has the Receiver's direct superior made it clear that "no news is good news?"
- **Emotional state, involvement with the topic, level of attention.** Does the Sender's fear of failure or criticism prevent him from conveying the Message? Is the topic within his realm of expertise, increasing his confidence in his ability to decode it, or is he out of his comfort zone when it comes to evaluating the Message's significance? Are personal concerns impacting his ability to judge the Message's value?

Selective Perception

Selective perception refers to filtering information to suit our own needs. This process is often unconscious. Small things can command our attention when we're visiting a new city or a new company. Over time, however, we begin to make assumptions about the way things are on the basis of our past experience. Often, much of this process is unconscious. "We simply are bombarded with too much stimuli every day to pay equal attention to everything so we pick and choose according to our own needs." Selective perception is a necessary tool that provides efficiency in a complex culture, but it can also lead to mistakes. A classic study on selective perception involved participants watching a particularly violent football game between Princeton and Dartmouth. Participants rooting for a specific team counted more infractions committed by the other team.

filtering
The distortion or withholding of information to manage a person's reactions.

selective perception
The personal filtering of what we see and hear to suit our own needs.

information overload

This occurs when the information processing demands on an individual's time to perform interactions and internal calculations exceed the supply or capacity of time available for such processing.

grapevine

The informal gossip network within a given organization.

semantics

The meanings of words and the study of meaning in communication.

Information Overload

Information overload can be defined as "occurring when the information processing demands on an individual's time to perform interactions and internal calculations exceed the supply or capacity of time available for such processing."[10] Messages reach us in countless ways every day. Some are societal—advertisements that we may hear or see in the course of our day. Others are professional—e-mails, and memos, voice mails, and conversations from our colleagues. Others are personal—messages and conversations from our loved ones and friends.

Experts note that information overload is "A symptom of the high-tech age, which is too much information for one human being to absorb in an expanding world of people and technology. The sources of information overload include TV, newspapers, and magazines as well as wanted and unwanted regular mail, e-mail, and faxes. It has been exacerbated enormously because of the formidable number of results obtained from Web search engines."[11] Other research shows that working in such fragmented fashion has a significant negative effect on efficiency, creativity, and mental acuity.[12]

Emotional Disconnects

Emotional disconnects happen when the Sender or the Receiver is upset, whether about the subject at hand or about some unrelated incident that may have happened earlier. An effective communication requires a Sender and a Receiver who are open to speaking and listening to one another, despite possible differences in opinion or personality. One or both parties may have to put their emotions aside to achieve the goal of communicating clearly. A Receiver who is emotionally upset tends to ignore or distort what the Sender is saying. A Sender who is emotionally upset may be unable to present ideas or feelings effectively.

Lack of Source Credibility

Lack of source familiarity or credibility can derail communications, especially when humor is involved. Sarcasm and irony are subtle and have a high potential to be misunderstood. Lack of familiarity with the source of a joke can lead to misinterpreting humor, especially in less-rich information channels like e-mail.

Similarly, if the Sender lacks credibility or is untrustworthy, the Message will not get through. Receivers may be suspicious of the Sender's motivations ("Why am I being told this?"). Likewise, if the Sender has communicated erroneous information in the past, or has created false emergencies, his current Message may be filtered.

Workplace gossip, also known as the **grapevine**, is a lifeline for many employees seeking information about their company.[13] Researchers agree that the grapevine is an inevitable part of organizational life with 70% of all organizational communication occurring at the grapevine level.[14]

Employees trust their peers as a source of Messages, but the grapevine's informal structure can be a barrier to effective communication from the managerial point of view. Its grassroots structure gives it greater credibility in the minds of employees than information delivered through official channels, even when that information is false.

A study of the positive side of gossip found that the likelihood that information would be shared made individuals less likely to act in a selfish manner.[15] Some downsides of the office grapevine are that gossip offers politically minded insiders a powerful tool for disseminating communication (and self-promoting miscommunications) within an organization. In addition, the grapevine lacks a specific Sender, which can create a sense of distrust among employees—who is at the root of the gossip network? When the news is volatile, suspicions may arise as to the person or persons behind the Message. Managers who understand the grapevine's power can use it to send and receive Messages of their own. They also decrease the grapevine's power by sending official Messages quickly and accurately, should big news arise.

Semantics

Semantics is the study of meaning in communication. Words can mean different things to different people, or they might not mean anything to other people. For example, companies often have their own acronyms and buzzwords (called business jargon) that are clear to them but impenetrable to outsiders. For example, at IBM, GBS is focusing on BPTS, using expertise acquired from the PwC purchase (which had to be sold to avoid conflicts of interest in light of SOX) to fend other BPO providers and inroads by the Bangalore tiger. Translation: IBM's Global Business Services (GBS) division is focusing on offering companies Business Process Transformation Services (BPTS), using the expertise it acquired from purchasing the management consulting and technology services arm of PricewaterhouseCoopers (PwC), which had to sell the division because of the Sarbanes-Oxley Act (SOX, enacted in response to the major accounting scandals like the Enron). The added management expertise puts it above business process outsourcing (BPO) vendors who focus more on automating processes rather than transforming and improving them. Chief among these BPO competitors is Wipro, often called the "Bangalore tiger" because of its geographic origin and aggressive growth.

Given the amount of Messages we send and receive every day, it makes sense that humans try to find shortcuts—a way to communicate things in code. In business, this code is known as **jargon**. Jargon is the language of specialized terms used by a group or profession. It is common shorthand among experts and if used sensibly can be a quick and efficient way of communicating. Most jargon consists of unfamiliar terms, abstract words, nonexistent words, acronyms, and abbreviations, with an occasional euphemism thrown in for good measure. Every profession, trade, and organization has its own specialized terms.[16] At first glance, jargon seems like a good thing—a quicker way to send an effective communication, the way text message abbreviations can send common messages in a shorter, yet understandable way. But that's not always how things happen. Jargon can be an obstacle to effective communication, causing listeners to tune out or fostering ill-feeling between partners in a conversation. When jargon rules the day, the Message can get obscured.

A key question to ask before using jargon is, "Who is the Receiver of my Message?" If you are a specialist speaking to another specialist in your area, jargon may be the best way to send a message while forging a professional bond—similar to the way best friends can communicate in code. For example, an information technology (IT) systems analyst communicating with another IT employee may use jargon as a way of sharing information in a way that reinforces the pair's shared knowledge. But that same conversation should be held in Standard English, free of jargon, when communicating with staff members outside the IT group.

Online Follow-Up

Here is a Web site of 25 buzz words in business:

http://www.businessnewsdaily.com/1846-business-buzzwords-2012.html.

And here is a discussion of why slang is a problem:

http://sbinfocanada.about.com/od/speakforsuccesscourse/a/speechlesson5.htm.

Gender Differences

Men and women work together every day. But their different styles of communication can sometimes work against them. Generally speaking, women like to ask questions before starting a project, while men tend to "jump right in." A male manager who's unaware of how many women communicate their readiness to work may misperceive a ready employee as not ready.

Another difference that has been noticed is that men often speak in sports metaphors, while many women use their home as a starting place for analogies. Women who believe men are "only talking about the game" may be missing out on a chance to participate in a division's strategy and opportunities for teamwork and "rallying the troops" for success.[17]

"It is important to promote the best possible communication between men and women in the workplace," notes gender policy adviser Dee Norton. "As we move between the male and female cultures, we sometimes have to change how we behave (speak the language of the other gender) to gain the best results from the situation. Clearly, successful organizations of the future are going to have leaders and team members who understand, respect, and apply the rules of gender culture appropriately."[18]

Being aware of these gender differences can be the first step in learning to work with them, as opposed to around them. For example, keep in mind that men tend to focus more on competition, data, and orders in their communications, while women tend to focus more on cooperation, intuition, and requests. Both styles can be effective in the right situations, but understanding the differences is a first step in avoiding misunderstandings based on them.

Differences in meaning often exist between the Sender and Receiver. "*Mean what you say, and say what you mean.*" While this advice may seem straightforward, different words mean different things to different people. Age, education, and cultural background are all factors that influence how a person interprets words. The less we consider our audience, the greater our chances of miscommunication will be. When communication occurs in the cross-cultural context, extra caution is needed given that different words will be interpreted differently across cultures and different cultures have different norms regarding nonverbal communication. Eliminating jargon is one way of ensuring that our words will convey real-world concepts to others. Speaking to our audience, as opposed to ourselves, is another. Nonverbal Messages can also have different meanings.

FIGURE 11.7

Excessive jargon in business led to the creation of buzzword bingo, where business words or phrases substitute for traditional bingo squares.

Source: http://www.flickr.com/ photos/keasone/2001471860

jargon

A specific set of acronyms or words unique to a specific group or profession.

FIGURE 11.8

Gender differences in communication have been documented by a number of experts, including linguistics professor Deborah Tannen in her best-selling book *You Just Don't Understand: Women and Men in Conversation.*

© Thinkstock

FIGURE 11.9 Watch Your Language

Cultural differences rooted in language—even across English-speaking countries—can affect how firms do business internationally. Below we provide a few examples.

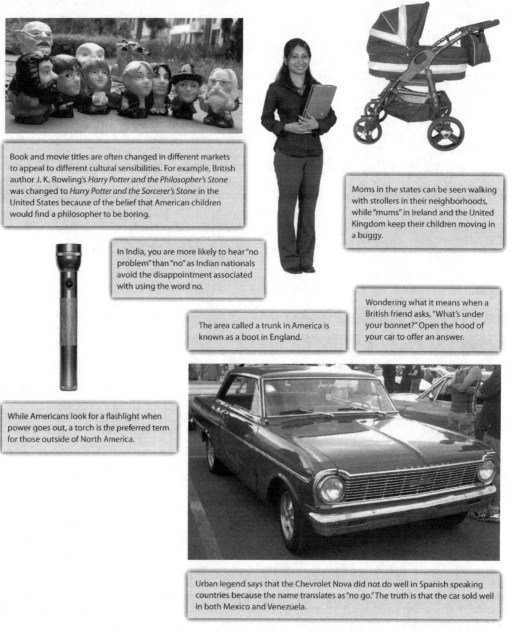

Book and movie titles are often changed in different markets to appeal to different cultural sensibilities. For example, British author J. K. Rowling's *Harry Potter and the Philosopher's Stone* was changed to *Harry Potter and the Sorcerer's Stone* in the United States because of the belief that American children would find a philosopher to be boring.

In India, you are more likely to hear "no problem" than "no" as Indian nationals avoid the disappointment associated with using the word no.

Moms in the states can be seen walking with strollers in their neighborhoods, while "mums" in Ireland and the United Kingdom keep their children moving in a buggy.

The area called a trunk in America is known as a boot in England.

Wondering what it means when a British friend asks, "What's under your bonnet?" Open the hood of your car to offer an answer.

While Americans look for a flashlight when power goes out, a torch is the preferred term for those outside of North America.

Urban legend says that the Chevrolet Nova did not do well in Spanish speaking countries because the name translates as "no go." The truth is that the car sold well in both Mexico and Venezuela.

Source: Image courtesy of Ketchen, D., & Short, J. (2011). Mastering strategic management. Irvington, NY: Flat World Knowledge.

Managers who speak about "long-term goals and profits" to a staff that has received scant raises may find their core Message ("You're doing a great job—and that benefits the folks in charge!") has infuriated the group they hoped to inspire. Instead, managers who recognize the "contributions" of their staff and confirm that this work is contributing to company goals in ways "that will benefit the source of our success—our employees as well as executives," will find their core Message ("You're doing a great job—we really value your work") is received as opposed to being misinterpreted.

Biased language can offend or stereotype others on the basis of their personal or group affiliation. The figure below provides a list of words that have the potential to be offensive in the left-hand column. The right-hand column provides more neutral words that you can use instead.[19]

FIGURE 11.10 Avoiding Biased Language

Avoid	Consider Using
black attorney	attorney
businessman	business person
chairman	chair or chairperson
cleaning lady	cleaner or maintenance worker
male nurse	nurse
manpower	staff or personnel
secretary	assistant or associate

Effective communication is clear, factual, and goal-oriented. It is also respectful. Referring to a person by one adjective (a *brain*, a *diabetic*, an *invalid*) reduces that person to that one characteristic. Language that belittles or stereotypes a person poisons the communication process. Language that insults an individual or group based on age, ethnicity, sexual preference, or political beliefs violates public and private standards of decency, ranging from civil rights to corporate regulations.

The effort to create a neutral set of terms to refer to heritage and preferences has resulted in a debate over the nature of "political correctness." Proponents of political correctness see it as a way to defuse the volatile nature of words that stereotyped groups and individuals in the past. Critics of political correctness see its vocabulary as stilted and needlessly cautious.

Many companies offer new employees written guides on standards of speech and conduct. These guides, augmented by common sense and courtesy, are solid starting points for effective and respectful workplace communication. Tips for appropriate workplace speech include but are not limited to

- alternating the use of "he" and "she" when referring to people in general,
- relying on guidelines generated by human resources,
- remembering that terms that feel respectful or comfortable to us may not be comfortable or respectful to others.

2.2   Poor Listening and Active Listening

Former Chrysler CEO Lee Iacocca lamented, "I only wish I could find an institute that teaches people how to listen. After all, a good manager needs to listen at least as much as he needs to talk."[20] Research shows that listening skills are related to promotions.[21] A Sender may strive to deliver a Message clearly. But the Receiver's ability to listen effectively is equally vital to effective communication. The average worker spends 55% of his or her workdays listening. Managers listen up to 70% each day. But listening does not lead to understanding in every case. Listening takes practice, skill, and concentration.

According to University of San Diego professor Phillip Hunsaker, "The consequences of poor listening are lower employee productivity, missed sales, unhappy customers, and billions of dollars of increased cost and lost profits. Poor listening is a factor in low employee morale and increased turnover because employees do not feel their managers listen to their needs, suggestions, or complaints."[22] Clearly, if you hope to have a successful career in management, it behooves you to learn to be a good listener.

Alan Gulick, a Starbucks spokesperson, puts better listening to work in pursuit of better profits. If every Starbucks employee misheard one $10 order each day, he calculates, their errors would cost the company a billion dollars annually. To teach its employees to listen, Starbucks created a code that helps employees taking orders hear the size, flavor, and use of milk or decaf coffee. The person making the drink echoes the order aloud.

How can you improve your listening skills? The Roman philosopher Cicero said, "Silence is one of the great arts of conversation." How often have we been in conversation with someone else where we are not really listening but itching to convey our portion? This behavior is known as "rehearsing." It suggests the Receiver has no intention of considering the Sender's Message and intends to respond to an earlier point instead. Clearly, rehearsing is an impediment to the communication process. Effective communication relies on another kind of listening: active listening.

Active listening can be defined as giving full attention to what other people are saying, taking time to understand the points being made, asking questions as appropriate, and not interrupting at inappropriate times.[23] Active listening creates a real-time relationship between the Sender and the Receiver by acknowledging the content and receipt of a Message. For example, repeating and confirming a Message's content offers a way to confirm that the correct content is flowing between colleagues. The process creates a bond between coworkers while increasing the flow and accuracy of messaging.

Carl Rogers, founder of the "person-centered" approach to psychology, formulated five rules for active listening:

1. Listen for message content
2. Listen for feelings
3. Respond to feelings
4. Note all cues
5. Paraphrase and restate

Fortunately, listening is a skill that can be learned.[24] The first step is to decide that we want to listen. Casting aside distractions, such as by reducing background or internal noise, is critical. The Receiver takes in the Sender's Message silently, without speaking. Second, throughout the conversation, show the speaker that you're listening. This can be accomplished nonverbally by nodding your head and keeping your attention focused on the speaker. You can also do it verbally, by saying things like, "Yes," "That's interesting," or other such verbal cues. As you're listening, pay attention to the Sender's body language for additional cues about how they're feeling. Interestingly, silence plays a major role in active listening. During active listening, we are trying to understand what has been said, and in silence, we can consider the implications. Finally, if anything is not clear, ask questions. Confirm that you've heard the message accurately, by repeating back a crucial piece like, "Great, I'll see you at 2 p.m. in my office." At the end of the conversation, a "thank you" from both parties communicates mutual respect.

In summary, active listening creates a more dynamic relationship between a Receiver and a Sender. It strengthens personal investment in the information being shared. It also forges healthy working relationships among colleagues by making Speakers and Listeners equally valued members of the communication process.

KEY TAKEAWAY

Many barriers to effective communication exist. Examples include filtering, selective perception, information overload, emotional disconnects, lack of source familiarity or credibility, workplace gossip, semantics, gender differences, differences in meaning between Sender and Receiver, and biased language. The Receiver can enhance the probability of effective communication by engaging in active listening, which involves (1) giving one's full attention to the Sender and (2) checking for understanding by repeating the essence of the Message back to the Sender.

EXERCISES

1. Most individuals are poor listeners. Do you agree or disagree with this statement? Please support your position.
2. Please share an example of how differences in shared meaning have affected you.
3. Give an example of selective perception.
4. Do you use jargon at or in your classes? If so, do you think it helps or hampers communication? Why or why not?
5. In your experience, how is silence used in communication? How does your experience compare with the recommended use of silence in active listening?

3.   DIFFERENT TYPES OF COMMUNICATION

LEARNING OBJECTIVES

1. Understand the features and advantages of verbal communication.
2. Understand the features and advantages of written communication.
3. Understand the features of nonverbal communication and how it interacts with verbal and written communications.

Communication can be categorized into three basic types: (1) verbal communication, in which you listen to a person to understand their meaning; (2) written communication, in which you read their meaning; and (3) nonverbal communication, in which you observe a person and infer meaning. Each has its own advantages and disadvantages.

3.1   Verbal Communication

Verbal communications in business may take place over the phone, in person, or via video conferencing. With verbal communication, the medium of the Message is *oral*. Research shows that individuals tend to enjoy verbal communication, and it is effective in helping to build relationships at work.[25] In addition, oral communication has a special place at work, including the role of storytelling and crucial conversations.

Storytelling

Storytelling has been shown to be an effective form of verbal communication; it serves an important organizational function by helping to construct common meanings for individuals within the organization. Stories can help clarify key values and help demonstrate how things are done within an organization, and story frequency, strength, and tone are related to higher organizational commitment.[26] The quality of the stories entrepreneurs tell is related to their ability to secure capital for their firms.[27] Stories can serve to reinforce and perpetuate an organization's culture, part of the organizing P-O-L-C function.

Crucial Conversations

While the process may be the same, high-stakes communications require more planning, reflection, and skill than normal day-to-day interactions at work. Examples of high-stakes communication events include asking for a raise or presenting a business plan to a venture capitalist. In addition to these events, there are also many times in our professional lives when we have **crucial conversations**—discussions in which not only are the stakes high but opinions vary and emotions run strong.[28] One of the most consistent recommendations from communications experts is to work toward using "and" instead of "but" as you communicate under these circumstances. In addition, be aware of your communication style and practice flexibility; it is under stressful situations that communication styles can become the most rigid.

crucial conversations

Discussions where the stakes are high, opinions vary, and emotions run strong.

3.2   Written Communication

In contrast to verbal communications, written business communications are *printed messages*. Examples of written communications include memos, proposals, e-mails, letters, training manuals, and operating policies. They may be printed on paper, handwritten, or appear on the screen. Normally, a verbal communication takes place in real time. Written communication, by contrast, can be constructed over a longer period of time. Written communication is often asynchronous (occurring at different times). That is, the Sender can write a Message that the Receiver can read at any time, unlike a conversation that is carried on in real time. A written communication can also be read by many people (such as all employees in a department or all customers). It's a "one-to-many" communication, as opposed to a one-to-one verbal conversation. There are exceptions, of course: a voicemail is an oral Message that is asynchronous. Conference calls and speeches are oral one-to-many communications, and e-mails may have only one recipient or many.

FIGURE 11.11

Communication mediums have come a long way since Alexander Graham Bell's original telephone.

Source:

http://wikimediafoundation.org/wiki/ File:CNAM-IMG_0564.jpg

Most jobs involve some degree of writing. According to the National Commission on Writing, 67% of salaried employees in large American companies and professional state employees have some writing responsibility. Half of responding companies reported that they take writing into consideration when hiring professional employees, and 91% take writing into account when hiring for any position.[29]

Luckily, it is possible to learn to write clearly. Here are some tips on writing well. Thomas Jefferson summed up the rules of writing well with this idea "Don't use two words when one will do." One of the oldest myths in business is that writing more will make us sound more important; in fact, the opposite is true. Leaders who can communicate simply and clearly project a stronger image than those who write a lot but say nothing.

3.3 Nonverbal Communication

What you say is a vital part of any communication. But what you *don't say* can be even more important. Research also shows that 55% of in-person communication comes from nonverbal cues like facial expressions, body stance, and tone of voice. According to one study, only 7% of a Receiver's comprehension of a Message is based on the Sender's actual words; 38% is based on paralanguage (the tone, pace, and volume of speech), and 55% is based on *nonverbal cues* (body language).[30]

Research shows that nonverbal cues can also affect whether you get a job offer. Judges examining videotapes of actual applicants were able to assess the social skills of job candidates with the sound turned off. They watched the rate of gesturing, time spent talking, and formality of dress to determine which candidates would be the most successful socially on the job.[31] For this reason, it is important to consider how we appear in business as well as what we say. The muscles of our faces convey our emotions. We can send a silent message without saying a word. A change in facial expression can change our emotional state. Before an interview, for example, if we focus on feeling confident, our face will convey that confidence to an interviewer. Adopting a smile, even when feeling stressed, can reduce the body's stress levels.

To be effective communicators, one's body language, appearance, and tone need to be aligned with the words one is trying to communicate. Research shows that when individuals are lying, they are more likely to blink more frequently, shift their weight, and shrug.[32]

Another element of nonverbal communication is tone. A different tone can change the perceived meaning of a message. Figure 11.12 demonstrates how clearly this can be true, whether in verbal or written communication. If we simply read these words without the added emphasis, we would be left to wonder, but the emphasis shows us how the tone conveys a great deal of information. Now you can see how changing one's tone of voice or writing can incite or defuse a misunderstanding.

FIGURE 11.12 Don't Use That Tone with Me!

Changing your tone can dramatically change your meaning.

Placement of the emphasis	What it means
I did not tell John you were late.	Someone else told John you were late.
I did **not** tell John you were late.	This did not happen.
I did not **tell** John you were late.	I may have implied it.
I did not tell **John** you were late.	But maybe I told Sharon and José.
I did not tell John **you** were late.	I was talking about someone else.
I did not tell John you **were** late.	I told him you still are late.
I did not tell John you were **late**.	I told him you were attending another meeting.

Source: Based on ideas in Kiely, M. (1993, October). When "no" means "yes." Marketing, 7–9.

Here, we present several examples of nonverbal cues that can support or detract from effective communication.

Body Language

A simple rule of thumb is that simplicity, directness, and warmth convey sincerity. And sincerity is key to effective communication. A firm handshake, given with a warm, dry hand, is a great way to establish trust. A weak, clammy handshake conveys a lack of trustworthiness. Gnawing one's lip conveys uncertainty. A direct smile conveys confidence.

Eye Contact

In business, the style and duration of eye contact considered appropriate vary greatly across cultures. In the United States, looking someone in the eye (for about a second) is considered a sign of trustworthiness.

Facial Expressions

The human face can produce thousands of different expressions. These expressions have been decoded by experts as corresponding to hundreds of different emotional states.[33] Our faces convey basic information to the outside world. Happiness is associated with an upturned mouth and slightly closed eyes; fear with an open mouth and wide-eyed stare. Flitting ("shifty") eyes and pursed lips convey a lack of trustworthiness. The effect of facial expressions in conversation is instantaneous. Our brains may register them as "a feeling" about someone's character.

Posture

The position of our body relative to a chair or another person is another powerful silent messenger that conveys interest, aloofness, professionalism—or lack thereof. Head up, back straight (but not rigid) implies an upright character. In interview situations, experts advise mirroring an interviewer's tendency to lean in and settle back in her seat. The subtle repetition of the other person's posture conveys that we are listening and responding.

Touch

The meaning of a simple touch differs between individuals, genders, and cultures. In Mexico, when doing business, men may find themselves being grasped on the arm by another man. To pull away is seen as rude. In Indonesia, to touch anyone on the head or touch anything with one's foot is considered highly offensive. In the Far East, according to business etiquette writer Nazir Daud, "it is considered impolite for a woman to shake a man's hand."[34] Americans, as we have noted, place great value in a firm handshake. But handshaking as a competitive sport ("the bone-crusher") can come off as needlessly aggressive, at home and abroad.

Space

Anthropologist Edward T. Hall coined the term *proxemics* to denote the different kinds of distance that occur between people. These distances vary between cultures. Figure 11.13 outlines the basic proxemics of everyday life and their meaning.[35]

Standing too far away from a colleague (such as a public speaking distance of more than seven feet) or too close to a colleague (intimate distance for embracing) can thwart effective verbal communication in business.

FIGURE 11.13 Interpersonal Distances

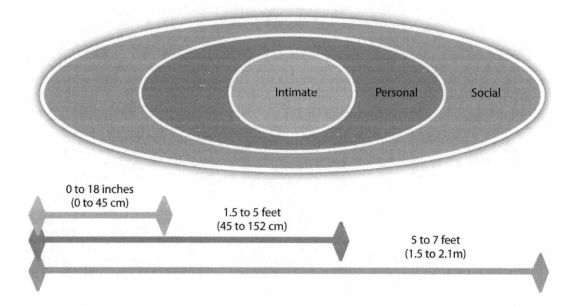

FIGURE 11.14 Cultural Risk: When in Rome

The phrase "When in Rome, do as the Romans do" is used to encourage travelers to embrace local customs. An important part of fitting in is avoiding behaviors that locals consider offensive. Below we illustrate a number of activities that would go largely unnoticed in the United States but could raise concerns in other countries.

If you want to signal "Check please!" to catch the attention of your garçon in France and Belgium, remember that snapping your fingers is vulgar there.

In many Asian and Arabian countries, showing the sole of your shoe is considered rude.

Provocative dress is embraced by many Americans, but many people in Muslim countries consider a woman's clothing to be inappropriate if it reveals anything besides the face and hands.

If everything is OK when you're in Brazil, avoid making this hand signal. It's the equivalent to giving someone the middle finger.

Do you pride yourself on your punctuality? You may be wasting your time in Latin American countries, where the locals tend to be about 20 minutes behind schedule.

Do not clean your plate in China. Leaving food on the plate indicates the host was so generous that the meal could not be finished.

Do not eat with your left hand in India or Malaysia. That hand is associated with unclean activities reserved for the bathroom.

In Japan, direct eye contact is viewed as impolite.

KEY TAKEAWAY

Types of communication include verbal, written, and nonverbal. Verbal communications have the advantage of immediate feedback, are best for conveying emotions, and can involve storytelling and crucial conversations. Written communications have the advantage of asynchronicity, of reaching many readers, and are best for conveying information. Both verbal and written communications convey nonverbal messages through tone; verbal communications are also colored by body language, eye contact, facial expression, posture, touch, and space.

EXERCISES

1. When you see a memo or e-mail full of typos, poor grammar, or incomplete sentences, how do you react? Does it affect your perception of the Sender? Why or why not?

2. How aware of your own body language are you? Has your body language ever gotten you into trouble when you were communicating with someone?

3. If the meaning behind verbal communication is only 7% words, what does this imply for written communication?

4. COMMUNICATION CHANNELS

LEARNING OBJECTIVES

1. **Understand how communication channels affect communication.**
2. **Recognize different communication directions within organizations.**

The channel, or medium, used to communicate a message affects how accurately the message will be received. Verbal, written, and nonverbal communications have different strengths and weaknesses. In business, the decision to communicate verbally or in written form can be a powerful one. In addition, a smart manager is aware of the nonverbal messages conveyed by either type of communication—as noted earlier, only 7% of verbal communication comes from the words themselves.

4.1 Information Richness

Channels vary in their *information richness*. Information-rich channels convey more nonverbal information. Research shows that effective managers tend to use more information-rich communication channels than less effective managers.[36] Figure 11.15 illustrates the information richness of different information channels.

FIGURE 11.15 Information Richness

This figure illustrates the information richness of different information channels.

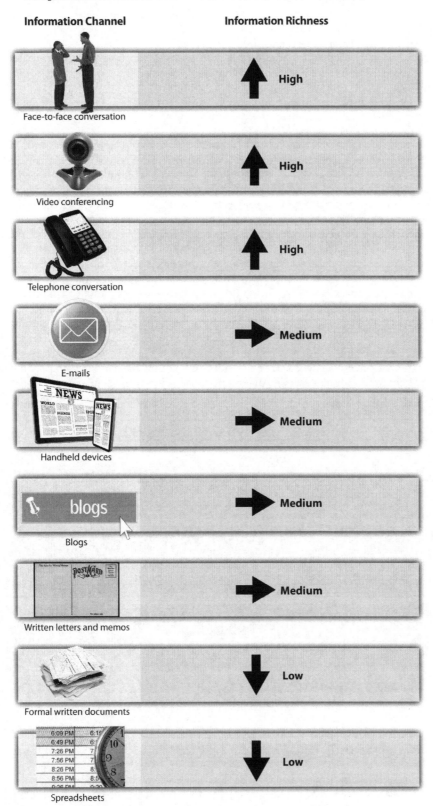

Source: Adapted from information in Daft, R. L., & Lenge, R. H. (1984). Information richness: A new approach to managerial behavior and organizational design. In B. Staw & L. Cummings (Eds.), Research in organizational behavior (Vol. 6, pp. 191–233). Greenwich, CT: JAI Press; and Lengel, R. H., & Daft, D. L. (1988). The selection of communication media as an executive skill. Academy of Management Executive, 11, 225–232. All images © Thinkstock.

Like face-to-face and telephone conversation, videoconferencing has high information richness because Receivers and Senders can see or hear beyond just the words—they can see the Sender's body language or hear the tone of their voice. Handheld devices, blogs, and written letters and memos offer medium-rich channels because they convey words and pictures/photos. Formal written documents, such as legal documents, and spreadsheets, such as the division's budget, convey the least richness because the format is often rigid and standardized. As a result, nuance is lost.

The decision to communicate verbally or in written form can be powerful. In addition, a smart manager is aware of the nonverbal messages conveyed by either type of communication—as noted earlier, only 7% of verbal communication comes from the words themselves.

When determining whether to communicate verbally or in writing, ask yourself, *Do I want to convey facts or feelings?* Verbal communications are a better way to convey feelings. Written communications do a better job of conveying facts.

Picture a manager making a speech to a team of 20 employees. The manager is speaking at a normal pace. The employees appear interested. But how much information is being transmitted? Humans listen much faster than they speak. The average public speaker communicates at a speed of about 125 words a minute. And that pace sounds fine to the audience. (In fact, anything faster than that probably would sound strange. To put that figure in perspective, someone having an excited conversation speaks at about 150 words a minute.) On the basis of these numbers, we could assume that the employees have more than enough time to take in each word the manager delivers. The average person in the audience can hear 400–500 words a minute.[37] Consequently, the audience has *more than enough time* to hear. As a result, they will each be processing many thoughts of their own, on totally different subjects, while the manager is speaking. As this example demonstrates, oral communication is an inherently flawed medium for conveying specific facts. Knowing this information allows individuals to make more intelligent communication choices based on the kind of information those individuals desire to convey.

The key to effective communication is to match the communication channel with the goal of the communication.[38] For example, written media may be a better choice when the Sender wants a record of the content, has less urgency for a response, is physically separated from the Receiver, does not require a lot of feedback from the Receiver, or the Message is complicated and may take some time to understand. Oral communication, however, makes more sense when the Sender is conveying a sensitive or emotional Message, needs feedback immediately, and does not need a permanent record of the conversation.

FIGURE 11.16 Guide for When to Use Written versus Verbal Communication

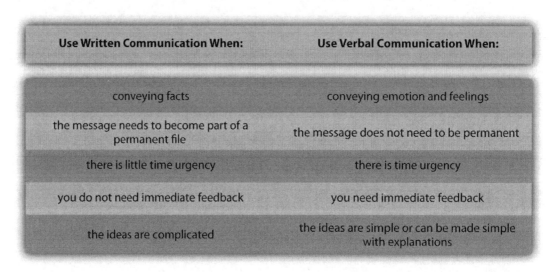

Use Written Communication When:	Use Verbal Communication When:
conveying facts	conveying emotion and feelings
the message needs to become part of a permanent file	the message does not need to be permanent
there is little time urgency	there is time urgency
you do not need immediate feedback	you need immediate feedback
the ideas are complicated	the ideas are simple or can be made simple with explanations

4.2 Business Use of E-Mail

The growth of e-mail has been spectacular, but it has also created challenges in managing information and an ever-increasing speed of doing business. By 2013, over 34% of the world's population used the Internet, for a total of 2,405 million users.[39] Internet users around the world send an estimated 294 billion e-mails every day, and many of those are spam or scam attempts. That makes e-mail the second most popular medium of communication worldwide, second only to voice. A 2005 study estimated that less than 1% of all written human communications even reached paper—and we can imagine that this percentage has gone down even further since then.[40] To combat the overuse of e-mail, companies such as Intel have even instituted "no e-mail Fridays," where all communication is done via other communication channels. Learning to be more effective in your e-mail communications is an important skill.

Business E-Mail Do's and Don'ts

1. DON'T send or forward chain e-mails.

2. DON'T put anything in an e-mail that you don't want the world to see.

3. DON'T write a Message in capital letters—this is the equivalent of SHOUTING.

4. DON'T routinely "cc" everyone all the time. Reducing inbox clutter is a great way to increase communication.

5. DON'T hit Send until you spell-check your e-mail.

6. DO use a subject line that summarizes your Message, adjusting it as the Message changes over time.

7. DO make your request in the first line of your e-mail. (And if that's all you need to say, stop there!)

8. DO end your e-mail with a brief sign-off such as, "Thank you," followed by your name and contact information.

9. DO think of a work e-mail as a binding communication.

10. DO let others know if you've received an e-mail in error.

Source: Adapted from information in Leland, K., & Bailey, K. (2000). Customer service for dummies. New York: Wiley; Information Technology Services (1997). Top 10 email dos and top ten email don'ts. Retrieved July 1, 2008, from the University of Illinois at Chicago Medical Center Web site: http://www.uic.edu/hsc/uicmc/its/customers/email-tips.htm; Kawasaki, G. (2006, February 3). The effective emailer. Retrieved September 13, 2012, from How to Change the World Web site: http://blog.guykawasaki.com/2006/02/the_effective_e.html.

An important, although often ignored, rule when communicating emotional information is that e-mail's lack of richness can be your loss. E-mail is a medium-rich channel. It can convey facts quickly. But when it comes to emotion, e-mail's flaws make it far less desirable a choice than oral communication—the 55% of nonverbal cues that make a conversation comprehensible to a listener are missing. E-mail readers do not pick up on sarcasm and other tonal aspects of writing as much as the writer believes they will.[41]

The Sender may believe she has included these emotional signifiers in her Message. But, with words alone, those signifiers are not there. This gap between the form and content of e-mail inspired the rise of emoticons—symbols that offer clues to the emotional side of the words in each Message. Generally speaking, however, emoticons are not considered professional in business communication.

Individuals often feel uncomfortable conveying an emotionally laden message verbally, especially when the message contains unwanted news. Sending an e-mail to your staff that there will be no bonuses this year may seem easier than breaking the bad news face-to-face, but that does not mean that e-mail is an effective or appropriate way to deliver this kind of news. When the Message is emotional, the Sender should use verbal communication. Indeed, a good rule of thumb is that the more emotionally laden messages require more thought in the choice of channel and how they are communicated.

4.3 Direction of Communication Within Organizations

Information can move horizontally, from a Sender to a Receiver, or vertically, down from top management or up from the front line. Information can also move diagonally between and among levels of an organization, such as a Message from a customer service representative up to a manager in the manufacturing department, or a Message from the chief financial officer sent down to all department heads.

FIGURE 11.17

Communication flows in many different directions within an organization.

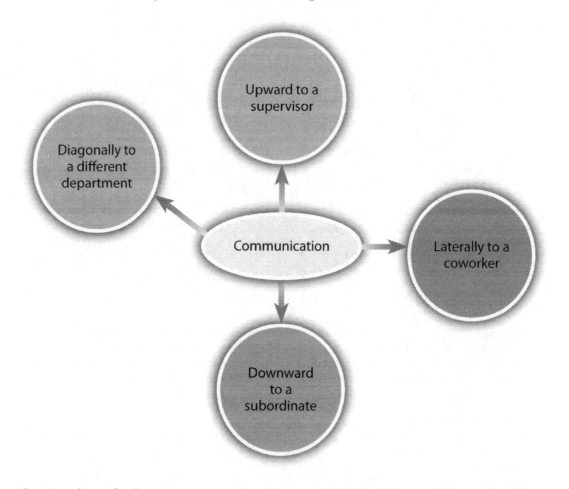

There is a chance for these arrows to go awry, of course. As Mihaly Csikszentmihalyi, author of best-selling books such as *Flow*, has noted, "In large organizations the dilution of information as it passes up and down the hierarchy, and horizontally across departments, can undermine the effort to focus on common goals." Managers need to keep this in mind when they make organization design decisions as part of the organizing function.

The organizational status of the Sender can affect the Receiver's attentiveness to the Message. For example, consider the following: A senior manager sends a memo to a production supervisor. The supervisor, who has a lower status within the organization, is likely to pay close attention to the Message. The same information, conveyed in the opposite direction, however, might not get the attention it deserves. The Message would be filtered by the senior manager's perception of priorities and urgencies.

Requests are just one kind of communication in business. Other communications, both verbal and written, may seek, give, or exchange information. Research shows that frequent communications with one's supervisor is related to better job performance ratings and overall organizational performance.[42] Research also shows that lateral communication done between peers can influence important organizational outcomes such as turnover.[43]

FIGURE 11.18 Who Managers Spend Time Communicating with at Work

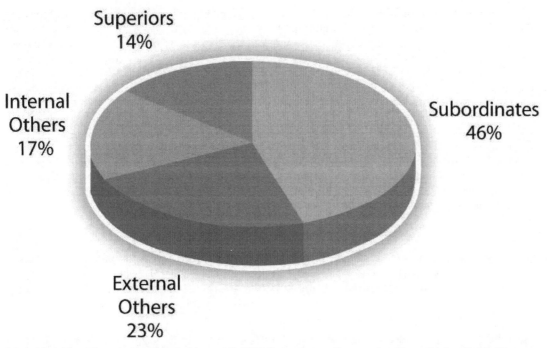

Source: *Adapted from information in Luthans, F., & Larsen, J. K. (1986). How managers really communicate. Human Relations, 39, 161–178.*

4.4   External Communications

External communications deliver specific business messages to individuals outside an organization. They may announce changes in staff or strategy, earnings, and more. The goal of an external communication is to create a specific Message that the Receiver will understand and share with others. Examples of external communications include the following.

Press Releases

Public relations professionals create external communications about a client's product, services, or practices for specific Receivers. These Receivers, it is hoped, will share the Message with others. In time, as the Message is passed along, it should *appear* to be independent of the Sender, creating the illusion of an independently generated consumer trend, public opinion, and so on.

The Message of a public relations effort may be *b2b* (business to business), *b2c* (business to consumer), or media related. The Message can take different forms. Press releases try to convey a newsworthy message, real or manufactured. It may be constructed like a news item, inviting editors or reporters to reprint the Message in part, or as a whole, with or without acknowledgment of the Sender's identity. Public relations campaigns create Messages over time, through contests, special events, trade shows, and media interviews in addition to press releases.

Ads

Advertising places external business Messages before target Receivers through media buys. A media buy is a fee that is paid to a television network, Web site, or magazine by an advertiser for an on-air, site, or publication ad. The fee is based on the perceived value of the audience who watches, reads, or frequents the space where the ad will appear.

In recent years, Receivers have begun to filter advertiser's Messages, a phenomenon that is perceived to be the result of the large amount of ads the average person sees each day and a growing level of consumer wariness of paid Messaging. Advertisers, in turn, are trying to create alternative forms of advertising that Receivers won't filter. The *advertorial* is one example of an external communication that combines the look of an article with the focused Message of an ad. Product placements in videos, movies, and games are other ways that advertisers strive to reach Receivers with commercial Messages.

Web Pages

A Web page's external communication can combine elements of public relations, advertising, and editorial content, reaching Receivers on multiple levels and in multiple ways. Banner ads, blogs, and advertiser-driven "click-through" areas are just a few of the elements that allow a business to deliver a Message to a Receiver online. The perceived flexibility of online communications can impart a less formal (and, therefore, more believable) quality to an external communication. A Message relayed in a daily blog post will reach a Receiver differently than if it is delivered in an annual report, for example. The popularity and power of blogs is growing, with 23% of *Fortune* 500 companies having official blogs (up from 4% in 2005). In fact, blogs have become so important to some companies as Coca-Cola, Kodak, and Marriott that they have created official positions within their organizations titled "Chief Blogging Officer."[44]

The "real-time" quality of Web communications may appeal to Receivers who might filter out a traditional ad and public relations message because of its "prefab" quality. Despite their "spontaneous" feel, many online pages can be revisited in perpetuity. For this reason, clear and accurate external communications are as vital for online use as they are in traditional media.

Customer Communications

Customer communications can include letters, catalogs, direct mail, e-mails, text messages, and telemarketing messages. Some Receivers automatically filter bulk messages like these. Others will be receptive. The key to a successful external communication to customers is to convey a business message in a personally compelling way—dramatic news, a money-saving coupon, and so forth.

KEY TAKEAWAY

Different communication channels are more or less effective at transmitting different kinds of information. Some types of communication are information rich while others are medium rich. In addition, communications flow in different directions within organizations. A major internal communication channel is e-mail, which is convenient but needs to be handled carefully. External communication channels include PR/press releases, ads, Web pages, and customer communications such as letters and catalogs.

EXERCISES

1. How could you use your knowledge of communication richness to be more effective in your own communications?
2. What are the three biggest advantages and disadvantages you see regarding technology and communications?
3. Explain the difference between internal and external communications in an organization, giving examples of each.

5. DEVELOPING YOUR PERSONAL COMMUNICATION SKILLS

LEARNING OBJECTIVES

1. Learn how to improve your own listening habits.
2. Learn how to handle personal communications in a career-friendly manner.
3. Learn what communication freezers are and how to avoid them.

By being sensitive to the errors outlined in this chapter and adopting active listening skills, you may increase your communication effectiveness, increasing your ability to carry out the managerial functions of planning, organizing, leading, and controlling. The following are additional tools for helping you increase your communication effectiveness.

Ten Ways to Improve Your Listening Habits

1. **Start by stopping.** Take a moment to inhale and exhale quietly before you begin to listen. Your job as a listener is to receive information openly and accurately.

2. **Don't worry about what you'll say when the time comes.** Silence can be a beautiful thing.

3. **Join the Sender's team.** When she pauses, summarize what you believe she has said. "What I'm hearing is that we need to focus on marketing as well as sales. Is that correct?" Be attentive to physical as well as verbal communications. "I hear you saying that we should focus on marketing. But the way you're shaking your head tells me the idea may not really appeal to you—is that right?"

4. **Don't multitask while listening.** Listening is a full-time job. It's tempting to multitask when you and the Sender are in different places, but doing that is counterproductive. The human mind can only focus on one thing at a time. Listening with only half your brain increases the chances that you'll have questions later, requiring more of the Speaker's time. (And when the speaker is in the same room, multitasking signals a disinterest that is considered rude.)

5. **Try to empathize with the Sender's point of view.** You don't have to agree; but can you find common ground?

6. **Confused? Ask questions.** There's nothing wrong with admitting you haven't understood the Sender's point. You may even help the Sender clarify the Message.

7. **Establish eye contact.** Making eye contact with the speaker (if appropriate for the culture) is important.

8. **What is the goal of this communication?** Ask yourself this question at different points during the communication to keep the information flow on track. Be polite. Differences in opinion can be the starting point of consensus.

9. **It's great to be surprised.** Listen with an open mind, not just for what you **want** to hear.

10. **Pay attention to what is not said.** Does the Sender's body language seem to contradict the Message? If so, clarification may be in order.

Source: Adapted from information in Barrett, D. J. (2006). Leadership communication. New York: McGraw-Hill/Irwin; Improving verbal skills. Retrieved September 13, 2012, from http://www.itstime.com/aug97.htm; Ten tips: Active Listening from Communication at work. (2007, June 4). Retrieved September 13, 2012, from http://communication.atwork-network.com/2007/06/04/ten-tips-active-listening.

5.1   Professional Communications

Communication can occur without your even realizing it. Consider the following: Is your e-mail name professional? The typical convention for business e-mail contains some form of your name. While an e-mail name like "LazyGirl" or "DeathMonkey" may be fine for chatting online with your friends, they may send the wrong signal to individuals you e-mail such as professors and prospective employers.

- *Is your outgoing voice mail greeting professional?* If not, change it. Faculty and prospective recruiters will draw certain conclusions if, upon calling you, they hear a message that screams, "Party, party, party!"

- *Do you have a "private" social networking Web site on Pinterest, Google+, or Facebook?* If so, consider what it says about you to employers or clients. If it is information you would not share at work, it probably shouldn't be there.

- *Googled yourself lately?* If not, you probably should. Potential employers have begun searching the Web as part of background checking and you should be aware of what's out there about you. It is possible to set up automated reports so that every time your name is mentioned on the Web, you are alerted.

5.2   Communication Freezers

Communication freezers put an end to effective communication by making the Receiver feel judged or defensive. Typical communication stoppers include criticizing, blaming, ordering, judging, or shaming the other person. The following are some examples of things to avoid saying:[45]

1. Telling people what to do:

   - "You must…"
   - "You cannot…"

2. Threatening with "or else" implied:

- "You had better…"
- "If you don't…"

3. Making suggestions or telling other people what they ought to do:

- "You should…"
- "It's your responsibility to…"

4. Attempting to educate the other person:

- "Let me give you the facts."
- "Experience tells us that…"

5. Judging the other person negatively:

- "You're not thinking straight."
- "You're wrong."

6. Giving insincere praise:

- "You have so much potential."
- "I know you can do better than this."

7. Psychoanalyzing the other person:

- "You're jealous."
- "You have problems with authority."

8. Making light of the other person's problems by generalizing:

- "Things will get better."
- "Behind every cloud is a silver lining."

9. Asking excessive or inappropriate questions:

- "Why did you do that?"
- "Who has influenced you?"

10. Making light of the problem by kidding:

- "Think about the positive side."
- "You think *you've* got problems!"

KEY TAKEAWAY

By practicing the skills associated with active listening, you can become more effective in your personal and professional relationships. Managing your online communications appropriately can also help you avoid career pitfalls. Finally, be aware of the types of remarks that freeze communication and try not to use them.

EXERCISES

1. How can you assess if you are engaging in active listening?
2. How does it feel when someone does not seem to be listening to you?
3. Some companies have internal social networking pages where employees can mingle and share ideas and information. Do you think this practice is a good idea? Why or why not?
4. What advice would you give to someone who is going to become a first-time manager in terms of communication?

6.   CASE IN POINT: EDWARD JONES COMMUNICATES CARING

FIGURE 11.20

© *Thinkstock*

Because of the economic turmoil that most financial institutions find themselves in today, it might come as a surprise that an individual investment company came in at number 5 on *Fortune* magazine's "100 Best Companies to Work For" list in 2012. Edward Jones was originally founded in St. Louis, Missouri, where its headquarters remain today. With more than 12,000 offices across the United States and Canada, they are able to serve nearly 7 million investors. This is the 13th year Edward Jones has made the Best Companies list. In addition, Edward Jones ranked highest in client satisfaction among full-service investment firms, according to an annual survey released by J. D. Power and Associates in 2012. How has Edward Jones maintained this favorable reputation in the eyes of both its employees and its customers?

It begins with the perks offered, including profit sharing and telecommuting. But if you ask the company's leadership, they will likely tell you that it goes beyond the financial incentives, and at the heart of it is the culture of honest communication that they adamantly promote. Top management work with senior managers and team members in what makes up an open floor plan that always tries to maintain approachability. Examples of this philosophy include direct communication, letters to staff, video, and Internet-posted talks. In addition, regular meetings are held to celebrate achievements and reinforce the firm's ethos. Staff surveys are frequently administered and feedback is widely taken into consideration so that the 31,000 employees feel heard and respected.

According to *Fortune*'s managing editor, Hank Gilman, "The most important considerations for this year's list were hiring and the ways in which companies are helping their employees weather the recession." Edward Jones was able to persevere through the trauma of the recent financial crisis with no layoffs and an 8% one-year job growth. While a salary freeze was enacted, profit sharing continued. They feel the best approach to the recent economic downturn is to remain honest with employees even when the news being delivered is not what employees want to hear.

Edward Jones was established in 1922 by Edward D. Jones Sr., and long ago, the company recognized the importance of a satisfied workforce and how that has the ability to translate into customer satisfaction and long-term growth. The company's internal policy of open communication seems to carry over to how advisors value their relationship with individual customers. Investors are most likely to contact their advisor by directly visiting them at a local branch or by picking up the phone and calling them directly. Edward Jones's managing partner, Jim Weddle, explains it best himself: "We are able to stay focused on the long-term because we are a partnership and we know who we are and what we do. When you respect the people who work here, you take care of them—not just in the good times, but in the difficult times as well."

Case written by Carlene Reynolds, Talya Bauer, and Berrin Erdogan to accompany Carpenter, M., Bauer, T., Erdogan, B., & Short, J. (2013). Principles of Management (2nd ed.). New York: Flat World Knowledge. Based on information from 100 best companies to work for. (2010, February 8). Fortune. Retrieved September 21, 2012, from http://money.cnn.com/magazines/fortune/best-companies/2012/full_list; St. Louis firms make Fortune's best workplaces (2009, January 22). St. Louis Business Journal. Retrieved September 21, 2012, from http://www.bizjournals.com/stlouis/stories/2009/01/19/daily40.html; Rodrigues, N., & Clayton, C. (2009). A positive difference in the office and the world. Sunday Times, pp. 10, 11. Retrieved from LexisNexis Academic database; Lawlor, A. (2008, March 13). Edward Jones is one to work for. Sunday Times, Financial Adviser. Retrieved February 2, 2010, from LexisNexis Academic database; Keeping clients happy (2009, August 1). Registered Rep. Retrieved September 21, 2012, from http://registeredrep.com/planner-ria-practice/finance-keeping-clients-happy-0801.

CASE DISCUSSION QUESTIONS

1. Communication is a key part of the leading facet of the P-O-L-C framework. What other things could Edward Jones do to increase its effectiveness in the area of communications?

2. As an organization, what qualities do you think Edward Jones looks for when hiring new financial advisors? How do you think that affects its culture over time?

3. With its success in North America, why do you think Edward Jones has not expanded across the Pacific or Atlantic Oceans?

4. How has technology enabled Edward Jones to become more effective at communicating with its employees and customers?

5. What types of customer service policies do you think Edward Jones has in place? How do these relate to its culture over time?

ENDNOTES

1. *Merriam-Webster online dictionary*. (2008). Retrieved September 21, 2012, from http://www.merriam-webster.com/dictionary/communication.

2. Schnake, M. E., Dumler, M. P., Cochran, D. S., & Barnett, T. R. (1990). Effects of differences in subordinate perceptions of superiors' communication practices. *The Journal of Business Communication, 27*, 37–50.

3. Penley, L. E., Alexander, E. R., Jernigan, I. E., & Henwood, C. I. (1991). Communication abilities of managers: The relationship of performance. *Journal of Management, 17*, 57–76.

4. Baron, R. (2004). Barriers to effective communication: Implications for the cockpit. Retrieved September 21, 2012, from AirlineSafety.com: http://www.airlinesafety.com/editorials/BarriersToCommunication.htm.

5. Communications skills cut malpractice risk—study reveals most important reason that patients decide to file malpractice suits is because of poor communication by physicians and not medical errors. (1997, October). *USA Today*.

6. Armour, S. (1998, September 30). Failure to communicate costly for companies. *USA Today*, 1A.

7. Alsop, R. (2006, September 20). The top business schools: Recruiters' M.B.A. picks. *Wall Street Journal Online*. Retrieved September 22, 2012 from http://online.wsj.com/article/SB115860376846766495.html?mod=2_1245_1.

8. Mercer. (2003, June). What are the bottom line results of communicating? *Pay for Performance Report*, p. 1. Retrieved September 21, 2012, from http://www.mercerHR.com.

9. Meisinger, S. (2003, February). Enhancing communications—ours and yours. *HR Magazine*. Retrieved September 21, 2012, from http://www.shrm.org/hrmagazine/archive/0203toc.asp.

10. Schick, A. G., Gordon, L. A., & Haka, S. (1990). Information overload: A temporal approach. *Accounting, Organizations, and Society, 15*, 199–220.

11. Retrieved September 21, 2012, from PC Magazine encyclopedia Web site: http://www.pcmag.com/encyclopedia_term/0,2542,t=information+overload&i=44950,00.asp, and reinforced by information in Dawley, D. D., & Anthony, W. P. (2003). User perceptions of e-mail at work. *Journal of Business and Technical Communication, 17*, 170–200.

12. Based on Overholt, A. (2001, February). Intel's got (too much) mail. *Fast Company*. Retrieved September 21, 2012, from http://www.fastcompany.com/online/44/intel.html and http://blogs.intel.com/it/2006/10/information_overload.php.

13. Kurland, N. B., & Pelled, L. H. (2000). Passing the word: Toward a model of gossip and power in the workplace. *Academy of Management Review, 25*, 428–438.

14. Crampton, S. M. (1998). The informal communication network: factors influencing grapevine activity. *Public Personnel Management*, Retrieved September 21, 2012, from http://www.allbusiness.com/management/735210-1.html.

15. Beersma, B., & Van Kleef, G. (2011). How the grapevine keeps you in line: Gossip increases contributions to the group. *Social Psychological and Personality Science, 2*, 642–649.

16. Wright, N. *Keep it jargon-free*. Retrieved September 21, 2012, from http://www.plainlanguage.gov/howto/wordsuggestions/jargonfree.cfm.

17. Krotz, J. L. (n.d.). 6 tips for bridging the communication gap. Retrieved September 21, 2012, from Microsoft Small Business Center Web site, http://www.microsoft.com/smallbusiness/resources/management/leadership-training/women-vs-men-6-tips-for-bridging-the-communication-gap.aspx.

18. Norton, D. (1998, Spring). Gender and communication—finding common ground. Retrieved September 21, 2012, from http://www.au.af.mil/au/awc/awcgate/uscg/gender_communication.htm.

19. Adapted from information in Ashcraft, K., & Mumby, D. K. (2003). *Reworking gender*. Thousand Oaks, CA: Sage; Miller, C., & Swift, K. (1980). *The handbook of nonsexist writing*. New York: Lippincott & Crowell; Procter, M. (2007, September 11). *Unbiased language*. Retrieved September 21, 2012, from http://www.utoronto.ca/writing/unbias.html.

20. Iacocca, L., & Novak, W. (1984). *Iacocca: An autobiography*. New York: Bantam Press.

21. Sypher, B. D., Bostrom, R. N., & Seibert, J. H. (1989). Listening, communication abilities, and success at work. *Journal of Business Communication, 26*, 293–303.

22. Alessandra, T., Garner, H., & Hunsaker, P. L. (1993). *Communicating at work*. New York: Simon & Schuster.

23. O*NET Resource Center, the nation's primary source of occupational information. Retrieved September 21, 2012, from http://online.onetcenter.org/skills.

24. Brownell, J. (1990). Perceptions of effective listeners: A management study. *Journal of Business Communications, 27*, 401–415.

25. Kacmar, K. M., Witt, L. A., Zivnuska, S., & Gully, S. M. (2003). The interactive effect of leader-member exchange and communication frequency on performance ratings. *Journal of Applied Psychology, 88*, 764–772.

26. McCarthy, J. F. (2008). Short stories at work: Storytelling as an indicator of organizational commitment. *Group & Organization Management, 33*, 163–193.

27. Martens, M. L., Jennings, J. E., & Devereaux, J. P. (2007). Do the stories they tell get them the money they need? The role of entrepreneurial narratives in resource acquisition. *Academy of Management Journal, 50*, 1107–1132.

28. Patterson, K., Grenny, J., McMillan, R., & Switzler, A. (2002). *Crucial conversations: Tools for talking when stakes are high*. New York: McGraw-Hill.

29. Flink, H. (2007, March). Tell it like it is: Essential communication skills for engineers. *Industrial Engineer, 39*, 44–49.

30. Mehrabian, A. (1981). *Silent messages*. New York: Wadsworth.

31. Gifford, R., Ng, C. F., & Wilkinson, M. (1985). Nonverbal cues in the employment interview: Links between applicant qualities and interviewer judgments. *Journal of Applied Psychology, 70*, 729–736.

32. Siegman, A. W. (1985). *Multichannel integrations of nonverbal behavior*. Hillsdale, NJ: Lawrence Erlbaum.

33. Ekman, P., Friesen, W. V., & Hager, J. C. The facial action coding system (FACS). Retrieved September 21, 2012, from http://face-and-emotion.com/dataface/facs/manual.

34. Daud, N. (n.d.). Business etiquette. Retrieved September 21, 2012, from http://ezinearticles.com/?Business-Etiquette---Shaking-Hands-around-the-World&id=746227.

35. Hall, E. T. (1966). *The hidden dimension*. New York: Doubleday.

36. Allen, D. G., & Griffeth, R. W. (1997). Vertical and lateral information processing; Fulk, J., & Boyd, B. (1991). Emerging theories of communication in organizations. *Journal of Management, 17*, 407–446; Yates, J., & Orlikowski, W. J. (1992). Genres of organizational communication: A structurational approach to studying communication and media. *Academy of Management Review, 17*, 299–326.

37. Lee, D., & Hatesohl, D. (1993, October). Listening: Our most used communication skill. *University of Missouri*. Retrieved September 21, 2012, from http://extension.missouri.edu/explore/comm/cm0150.htm.

38. Barry, B., & Fulmer, I. S. (2004). The medium and the Message: The adaptive use of communication media in dyadic influence. *Academy of Management Review, 29*, 272–292.

39. Retrieved January 10, 2013, from http://www.internetworldstats.com/emarketing.htm.

40. http://www.sims.berkeley.edu/research/projects/how-much-info/index.htm, as cited in Isom, D. K. (2005, October 19). Electronic discovery: New power, new risks. Retrieved September 21, 2012, from http://utahbar.org/barjournal2000/html/november_2003_2.html.

41. Kruger, J. (2005). Egocentrism over email: Can we communicate as well as we think? *Journal of Personality and Social Psychology, 89*, 925–936.

42. Snyder, R. A., & Morris, J. H. (1984). Organizational communication and performance. *Journal of Applied Psychology, 69*, 461–465; Kacmar, K. M., Witt, L. A., Zivnuska, S., & Gully, S. M. (2003). The interactive effect of leader-member exchange and communication frequency on performance ratings. *Journal of Applied Psychology, 88*, 764–772.

43. Krackhardt, D., & Porter, L. W. (1986). The snowball effect: Turnover embedded in communication networks. *Journal of Applied Psychology, 71*, 50–55.

44. Chief blogging officer title catching on with corporations. (2008, May 1). *Workforce Management News in Brief*. Retrieved September 21, 2012, from http://www.workforce.com/section/00/article/25/50/77.html.

45. *Source*: Adapted from information in Tramel, M., & Reynolds, H. (1981). *Executive leadership*. Englewood Cliffs, NJ: Prentice Hall; Saltman, D., & O'Dea, N. (n.d.). Conflict management workshop PowerPoint presentation. Retrieved September 21, 2012, from http://www.nswrdn.com.au/client_images/6806.PDF; Communication stoppers. Retrieved September 21, 2012, from *Mental Health Today* Web site: http://www.mental-health-today.com/Healing/communicationstop.htm.

CHAPTER 12
Managing Groups and Teams

FIGURE 12.1

Careful coordination and teamwork is needed to manage the hundred-plus members that make up a modern symphony orchestra such as the Mexico-based Jalisco Philharmonic Orchestra shown here.

Source: http://en.wikipedia.org/wiki/File:Orquesta_Filarmonica_de_Jalisco.jpg

---

CHAPTER LEARNING OBJECTIVES

Reading this chapter will help you do the following:

1. Recognize and understand group dynamics and development.
2. Understand the difference between groups and teams.
3. Understand how to organize effective teams.
4. Recognize and address common barriers to team effectiveness.
5. Build and maintain cohesive teams.

FIGURE 12.2 The P-O-L-C Framework

Planning	Organizing	Leading	Controlling
1. Vision & Mission	1. Organization Design	1. Leadership	1. Systems/Processes
2. Strategizing	2. Culture	2. Decision Making	2. Strategic Human Resources
3. Goals & Objectives	3. Social Networks	3. Communications	
		4. Groups/Teams	
		5. Motivation	

Groups and teams are found everywhere on today's landscape, and team management skills are required within each of the planning-organizing-leading-controlling (P-O-L-C) functions. This is exemplified by the statistic that 91% of high-level managers surveyed agreed with the statement "teams are central to organizational success."[1] For instance, planning may often occur in teams, particularly in less centralized organizations or toward the higher levels of the firm. When making decisions about the structure of the firm and individual jobs, managers conducting their organizing function must determine how teams will be used within the organization. Teams and groups have implications for the controlling function because teams require different performance assessments and rewards. Finally, teams and groups are a facet of the leading function. Today's managers must be both good team members and good team leaders. Managing groups and teams is a key component of leadership.

1.   GROUP DYNAMICS

LEARNING OBJECTIVES

1. Understand the difference between informal and formal groups.
2. Learn the stages of group development.
3. Identify examples of the punctuated equilibrium model.
4. Learn how group cohesion, social loafing, and collective efficacy can affect groups.

Because many tasks in today's world have become so complex, groups and teams have become an essential component of an organization's success. The success of the group depends on the successful management of its members and making sure all aspects of work are fair for each member. Being able to work in a group is a key skill for managers and employees alike.

1.1   Types of Groups: Formal and Informal

group

A collection of individuals who interact with each other such that one person's actions have an impact on the others.

A **group** is a collection of individuals who interact with each other such that one person's actions have an impact on the others. In organizations, most work is done within groups, and managing groups is key to each of the P-O-L-C functions. How groups function has important implications for organizational productivity. Groups where people get along, feel the desire to contribute, and are capable of coordinating their efforts may have high performance levels, whereas those characterized by extreme levels of conflict or hostility may demoralize members of the workforce.

FIGURE 12.3

Employees at Google are encouraged to find micro-communities by joining interest groups with fellow Googlers. There are "Gleeglers" who sing together, "Snowglers" who ski together, and "Greyglers," older Google employees who share interests and support each other.

Source: Used by permission of Google, Inc.

In organizations, groups can be classified into two basic types: informal and formal. **Informal work groups** are made up of two or more individuals who are associated with one another in ways not prescribed by the formal organization. For example, a few people in the company who get together to play tennis on the weekend would be considered an informal group. A **formal work group** is made up of managers, subordinates, or both with close associations among group members that influence the behavior of individuals in the group. We will discuss many different types of formal work groups later on in this chapter.

1.2   Stages of Group Development

American organizational psychologist Bruce Tuckman presented a now well-known model of group development in 1965 that is still widely used today. On the basis of his observations of group behavior in a variety of settings, he proposed a four-stage map of group evolution, known as the **Forming-Storming-Norming-Performing Model**.[2] Later he enhanced the model by adding a fifth and final stage, **adjourning**. The phases are illustrated in Figure 12.4. Just as an individual moves through developmental stages such as childhood, adolescence, and adulthood, so does a group, although in a much shorter period of time.

According to this theory, to facilitate a group successfully, the leader needs to move through various leadership styles over time. Generally, this is accomplished by first being more direct, eventually serving as a coach, and later, once the group is able to assume more power and responsibility for itself, shifting to delegator.

While research has not confirmed that this is descriptive of how groups progress, knowing and following these steps can help groups be more effective. For example, groups that do not go through the storming phase early on will often return to this stage toward the end of the group process to address unresolved issues. Another example of the validity of the group development model involves groups that take the time to get to know each other socially in the forming stage. When this socialization occurs, groups tend to handle future challenges better because the individuals have an understanding of each other's needs.

informal work groups

Groups made up of two or more individuals who are associated with one another in ways not prescribed by the formal organization.

formal work group

A group made up of managers, subordinates, or both with close associations among group members that influence the behavior of individuals in the group.

Forming-Storming-Norming-Performing Model

A model proposed by Bruce Tuckman in 1965 involving a four-stage map of group evolution.

adjourning

The fifth and final stage of the Tuckman model.

FIGURE 12.4 Stages of the Group Development Model

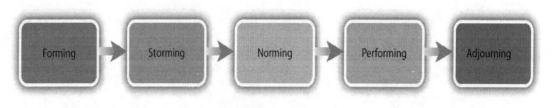

Forming

In the **Forming** stage, the group comes together for the first time. The members may already know each other or they may be total strangers. In either case, there is a level of formality, some anxiety, and a degree of guardedness as group members are not sure how they will fit into the group or how work will be conducted. "Will I be accepted? What will my role be? Who has the power in the group?" These are some of the questions participants think about during this stage of group formation. Because of the large amount of uncertainty, members tend to be polite, conflict avoidant, and observant. They are trying to figure out the "rules of the game" without being too vulnerable. At this point, they may also be quite excited and optimistic about the task, perhaps experiencing a level of pride at being chosen to join a particular group.

Group members are trying to achieve several goals at this stage, although this may not necessarily be done consciously. First, they are trying to get to know one another. Often this can be accomplished by finding some common ground. Members also begin to explore group boundaries to determine what will be considered acceptable behavior. "Can I interrupt? Can I leave when I feel like it?" This trial phase may also involve testing the appointed leader or seeing whether a leader emerges from the group. At this point, group members are also discovering how the group will work in terms of what needs to be done and who will be responsible for each task. This stage is often characterized by abstract discussions about issues to be addressed by the group; those who like to get moving can become impatient with this part of the process. This phase is usually short in duration, perhaps a meeting or two.

Storming

Once group members feel sufficiently safe and included, they tend to enter the **Storming** phase. Participants focus less on keeping their guard up as they shed social facades, becoming more authentic and more argumentative. Group members begin to explore their power and influence, and they often stake out their territory by differentiating themselves from the other group members rather than seeking common ground. Discussions can become heated as participants raise conflicting points of view and values, or disagree over how tasks should be done and who is assigned to them. It is not unusual for group members to become defensive, competitive, or jealous. Group members may take sides or begin to form cliques within the group. Questioning and resisting direction from the leader is also quite common. "Why should I have to do this? Who designed this project in the first place? What gives you the authority to tell me what to do?"

Although little seems to get accomplished at this stage, it actually serves an important purpose: group members are becoming more authentic as they express their deeper thoughts and feelings. What they are really exploring is "Can I truly be me, have power, and be accepted?" During this chaotic stage, a great deal of creative energy that was previously buried is released and available for use, but it takes skill to move the group from Storming to Norming. In many cases, the group gets stuck in the Storming phase.

Once group members discover that they can be authentic and that the group is capable of handling differences without dissolving, they are ready to enter the next stage, **Norming**.

Norming

Group members often feel relief at this point, and they are much more committed to each other and the group's goal. Feeling energized, group members are now ready to get to work. Finding themselves more cohesive and cooperative, participants find it easy to establish their own ground rules (or *norms*) and define their operating procedures and goals. The group tends to make big decisions, while subgroups or individuals handle the smaller decisions. It is hoped at this point the group members are more open and respectful toward each other and willing to ask one another for both help and feedback. They may even begin to form friendships and share more personal information.

At this point, the leader should become more of a facilitator by stepping back and letting the group assume more responsibility for its goal. Since the group's energy is running high, this is an ideal time to host a social or team-building event.

Performing

Galvanized by a sense of shared vision and a feeling of unity, the group is ready to go into high gear. Members are more interdependent, individuality and differences are respected, and group members feel themselves to be part of a greater entity. At the **Performing** stage, participants are not only getting the work done, but they also pay greater attention to *how* they are doing it. They ask such questions as, "Do our operating procedures best support productivity and quality assurance? Do we have suitable means for addressing differences that arise so we can preempt destructive conflicts? Are we relating to and communicating with each other in ways that enhance group dynamics and help us achieve our goals? How can I further develop as a person to become more effective?" By now, the group has matured, becoming more competent, autonomous, and insightful.

Group leaders can finally move into coaching roles and help members grow in skill and leadership. These leadership shifts are essential for managers enacting the Leadership function to keep in mind. In fact, a manager who leads multiple teams may find it necessary to shift leadership styles not only over time but between teams at different stages.

Adjourning

Many groups or teams formed in a business context are project-oriented and therefore are temporary. Alternatively, a working group may dissolve because of an organizational restructuring. As with graduating from school or leaving home for the first time, these endings can be bittersweet, with group members feeling a combination of victory, grief, and insecurity about what is coming next. For those who like routine and bond closely with fellow group members, this transition can be particularly challenging. Group leaders and members alike should be sensitive to handling these endings respectfully and compassionately. An ideal way to close a group is to set aside time to debrief ("How did it all go? What did we learn?"), acknowledge one another, and celebrate a job well done.

performing
The stage in which participants are not only getting the work done, but they also pay greater attention to *how* they are doing it.

FIGURE 12.5 Developing the Avengers

The five phases in the Stages of the Group Development Model can be seen in a number of well-known groups—both real and imagined. Here, we apply the model to the development seen in the 2012 blockbuster The Avengers.

Forming
The Avengers were formed when S.H.I.E.L.D. (Strategic Homeland Intervention, Enforcement, and Logistics Division) agent Phil Coulson brought together superheroes Iron Man, Thor, Captain America, Hulk, Black Widow, and Hawkeye.

Storming
Storming occurs as Avengers members begin to argue over how best to fight their enemy, the dreaded Loki. Storming also arises as several members express concern with Dr. Bruce Banner, who can turn into the uncontrollable Hulk at a moment's notice.

Norming
When S.H.I.E.L.D.'s flying aircraft carrier, the Helicarrier, is attacked, the Avengers begin to search for norms as they fight a common enemy.

Performing
As the Avengers rally to protect New York and defeat Loki, they realize the team must work together to perform at the level necessary to defeat such a powerful foe. The Hulk plays a critical role in the defense of the city.

Adjourning
As the film ends, S.H.I.E.L.D. agent Nick Fury notes that the Avengers will return when they are again needed. The Avengers may not be ready to adjourn, as shown in one of the film's postcredit scenes, where the Avengers dine in silence at a local shawarma restaurant.

Source: (*From top to bottom*) *marvelousRoland, http://www.flickr.com/photos/tales2astonish/6976086464/in/photostream/; Tony Felgueiras, http://www.flickr.com/photos/tonyfelgueiras/ 7134291249/; marvelousRoland, http://www.flickr.com/photos/tales2astonish/7122167899/in/photostream/; marvelousRoland, http://www.flickr.com/photos/tales2astonish/6976087980/in/ photostream/; marvelousRoland, http://www.flickr.com/photos/tales2astonish/6976088794/.*

1.3 The Punctuated-Equilibrium Model

The five-stage model we have just reviewed is a linear process. According to the model, a group progresses to the Performing stage, at which point it finds itself in an ongoing, smooth-sailing situation until the group dissolves. In reality, subsequent researchers, most notably Joy H. Karriker, have found that the life of a group is much more dynamic and cyclical in nature.[3] For example, a group may operate in the Performing stage for several months. Then, because of a disruption, such as a competing emerging technology that changes the rules of the game or the introduction of a new CEO, the group may move back into the Storming phase before returning to Performing. Ideally, any regression in the linear group progression will ultimately result in a higher level of functioning. Proponents of this cyclical model draw from behavioral scientist Connie Gersick's study of **punctuated equilibrium**.[4]

The concept of punctuated equilibrium was first proposed in 1972 by paleontologists Niles Eldredge and Stephen Jay Gould, who both believed that evolution occurred in rapid, radical spurts rather than gradually over time. Identifying numerous examples of this pattern in social behavior, Gersick found that the concept applied to organizational change. She proposed that groups remain fairly static, maintaining a certain equilibrium for long periods. Change during these periods is incremental, largely due to the resistance to change that arises when systems take root and processes become institutionalized. In this model, revolutionary change occurs in brief, punctuated bursts, generally catalyzed by a crisis or a problem that breaks through the systemic inertia and shakes up the deep organizational structures in place. At this point, the organization or group has the opportunity to learn and create new structures that are better aligned with current realities. Whether the group does this is not guaranteed. In sum, in Gersick's model, groups can repeatedly cycle through the Storming and Performing stages, with revolutionary change taking place during short transitional windows. For organizations and groups who understand that disruption, conflict, and chaos are inevitable in the life of a social system, these disruptions represent opportunities for innovation and creativity.[5]

punctuated equilibrium

The theory that change within groups occurs in rapid, radical spurts rather than gradually over time.

FIGURE 12.6 The Punctuated Equilibrium Model

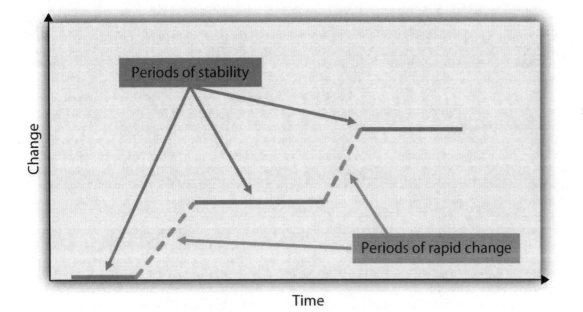

1.4 Cohesion, Social Loafing, and Collective Efficacy

Cohesion can be thought of as a kind of social glue. It refers to the degree of camaraderie within the group. Cohesive groups are those in which members are attached to each other and act as one unit. The more cohesive a group, the more productive it will be and the more rewarding the experience will be for the group's members.[6] Cohesive groups tend to have the following characteristics: they have a collective identity; they experience a moral bond and a desire to remain part of the group; they share a sense of purpose, working together on a meaningful task or cause; and they establish a structured pattern of communication.

The fundamental factors affecting group cohesion include the following:

- **Similarity.** The more similar group members are in terms of age, sex, education, skills, attitudes, values, and beliefs, the more likely the group will bond.

cohesion

The degree of camaraderie within the group.

- **Stability.** The longer a group stays together, the more cohesive it becomes.
- **Size.** Smaller groups tend to have higher levels of cohesion.
- **Support.** When group members receive coaching and are encouraged to support their fellow team members, group identity strengthens.
- **Satisfaction.** Cohesion is correlated with how pleased group members are with one another's performance, behavior, and conformity to group norms.

As you might imagine, there are many benefits in creating a cohesive group. Members are generally more personally satisfied and feel greater self-confidence and self-esteem in a group where they feel they belong. For many, membership in such a group can be a buffer against stress, which can improve mental and physical well-being. Because members are invested in the group and its work, they are more likely to regularly attend and actively participate in the group, taking more responsibility for the group's functioning. In addition, members can draw on the strength of the group to persevere through challenging situations that might otherwise be too hard to tackle alone.

Can a Group Have Too Much Cohesion?

Despite the advantages of cohesion, too much cohesion can be detrimental to a group. Because members can come to value belonging over all else, an internal pressure to conform may arise where some members modify their behavior to adhere to group norms. Members may become conflict avoidant, focusing on trying to please one another so as not to be ostracized. In some cases, members might censor themselves to maintain the party line. As such, the group is dominated by a superficial sense of harmony and discourages diversity of thought. Having less tolerance for deviants, who threaten the group's static identity, cohesive groups will often disapprove of members who dare to disagree. Members attempting to make a change may be criticized, undermined, or even ostracized by other members, who perceive their attempts as a threat to the status quo. The painful possibility of being marginalized can keep many members in line with the majority.

The more strongly members identify with the group, the easier it is to see outsiders as inferior or, in extreme cases, as enemies. It is easy to see how this can lead to increased insularity. This form of prejudice can have a downward spiral effect. The group is not getting corrective feedback from within its own confines, and it is closing itself off from input and a cross-fertilization of ideas from the outside. In such an environment, groups can easily adopt extreme ideas that will not be challenged. Denial increases as problems are ignored and failures are blamed on external factors. With limited, often biased, information and no internal or external opposition, groups like these can make disastrous decisions.

Groupthink is a group pressure phenomenon that increases the risk of the group making flawed decisions by allowing reductions in mental efficiency, reality testing, and moral judgment. A famous example of groupthink is the decision to invade Cuba made by President John F. Kennedy and his cabinet in 1961. In a matter of days, Cuban forces repelled the invaders, whose objective was to overthrow the entire Cuban government, resulting in many casualties and captured troops. In retrospect, there were many reasons why the Bay of Pigs invasion was doomed from the start, but the planning and approval were characterized by a belief that the insiders knew best and did not need to consider "devil's advocate" points of view. As this example illustrates, groupthink is a serious risk in highly cohesive groups.[7]

Cohesive groups can go awry in much milder ways. For example, group members can value their social interactions so much that they have fun together but spend little time on accomplishing their assigned task. Or a group's goal may begin to diverge from the larger organization's goal and those trying to uphold the organization's goal may be criticized (for example, students may tease the class "brain" for doing well in school).

In addition, research shows that cohesion leads to acceptance of group norms.[8] Groups with high task commitment tend to do well, whereas little is accomplished in a group in which the norm is to work as little as possible.

groupthink

A group pressure phenomenon that increases the risk of the group making flawed decisions by allowing reductions in mental efficiency, reality testing, and moral judgment.

FIGURE 12.7

Groups with high cohesion and high task commitment tend to be the most effective.

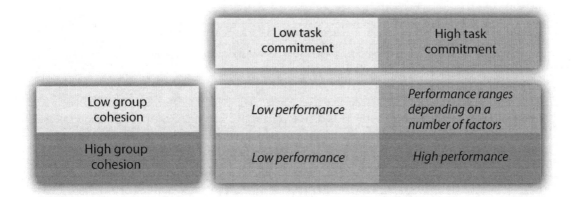

Social Loafing

Social loafing refers to the tendency of individuals to put in less effort when working in a group context. This phenomenon, also known as the Ringelmann effect, was first noted by French agricultural engineer Max Ringelmann in 1913. In one study, he had people pull on a rope individually and in groups. He found that as the number of people pulling increased, the group's total pulling force was less than the sum of individual efforts had been when measured alone.[9]

Why do people work less hard when they are working with other people? Observations show that as the size of the group grows, this effect becomes larger as well.[10] The social loafing tendency is not so much a matter of laziness as a matter of perceiving that one will receive neither one's fair share of rewards if the group is successful nor blame if the group fails. Rationales for this behavior include, "My own effort will have little effect on the outcome." "Others aren't pulling their weight, so why should I?" Or "I don't have much to contribute, and no one will notice anyway." This is a consistent effect across a great number of group tasks and countries.[11] Research also shows that perceptions of fairness are related to less social loafing.[12] Therefore, teams that are deemed as more fair should also see less social loafing.

Collective Efficacy

Collective efficacy refers to a group's perception of its ability to successfully perform well.[13] A group with high collective efficacy is one whose members share a belief in the group's capability to pursue its agreed-upon course of action and attain its goals. Collective efficacy is influenced by a number of factors, including watching others ("that group did it and we're better than them"), verbal persuasion ("we can do this"), and how a person feels ("this is a good group"). Research shows that a group's collective efficacy is positively related to its performance.[14] In addition, this relationship is stronger when task interdependence (the degree an individual's task is linked to someone else's work) is high rather than low.

social loafing

The tendency of individuals to put in less effort when working in a group context.

FIGURE 12.8

The Ringelmann effect found that as the number of group members increases, the effort of each member decreases.

© Thinkstock

collective efficacy

A group's perception of its ability to successfully perform well.

KEY TAKEAWAY

Groups may be either formal or informal. Groups go through developmental stages much like individuals do. The Forming-Storming-Norming-Performing-Adjourning Model is useful in prescribing stages that groups should pay attention to as they develop. The punctuated-equilibrium model of group development argues that groups often move forward during bursts of change after long periods without change. Groups that are similar, stable, small, supportive, and satisfied tend to be more cohesive than groups that are not. Cohesion can help support group performance if the group values task completion, but too much cohesion can also be a concern for groups. Social loafing increases as groups become larger. When collective efficacy is high, groups tend to perform better.

2. UNDERSTANDING TEAM DESIGN CHARACTERISTICS

LEARNING OBJECTIVES

1. **Understand the difference between groups and teams.**
2. **Understand the factors leading to the rise in the use of teams.**
3. **Understand how tasks and roles affect teams.**
4. **Identify different types of teams.**
5. **Identify team design considerations.**

Effective teams give companies a significant competitive advantage. In a high-functioning team, the sum is truly greater than the parts. Team members not only benefit from one another's diverse experiences and perspectives but also stimulate each other's creativity. Plus, for many people, working in a team can be more fun than working alone. In this section, we define a team and its difference from a group and explain different team characteristics, types of teams companies use, and how to design effective teams.

2.1 Differences Between Groups and Teams

process loss

Any aspect of group interaction that inhibits group functioning.

team

A cohesive coalition of people working together to achieve mutual goals.

Organizations consist of groups of people. What exactly is the difference between a group and a team? A group is a collection of individuals. Within an organization, groups might consist of project-related groups such as a product group or division or they can encompass an entire store or branch of a company. The performance of a group consists of the inputs of the group minus any process losses such as the quality of a product, ramp-up time to production, or the sales for a given month. **Process loss** is any aspect of group interaction that inhibits group functioning.

What is the difference between a *group* and a *team*? A collection of people is not a team, though they may learn to function in that way. A **team** is a particular type of group: a cohesive coalition of people working together to achieve mutual goals. Being on a team does not equate to a total suppression of personal agendas, but it does require a commitment to the vision and involves each individual working toward accomplishing the team's objective. Teams differ from other types of groups in that members are focused on a joint goal or product, such as a presentation, discussing a topic, writing a report, creating a new design or prototype, or winning a team Olympic medal. Moreover, teams also tend to be defined by their relatively smaller size. For instance, according to one definition, "A team is a *small* number of people with complementary skills who are committed to a common purpose, performance goals, and approach for which they are mutually accountable."[15]

The purpose of assembling a team is to accomplish larger, more complex goals than what would be possible for an individual working alone or even the simple sum of several individuals working independently. Teamwork is also needed in cases where multiple skills are tapped or where buy-in is required from several individuals. Teams can, but do not always, provide improved performance. Working together to further a team agenda seems to increase mutual cooperation between what are often competing factions. The aim and purpose of a team is to perform, get results, and achieve victory in the workplace. The best managers are those who can gather together a group of individuals and mold them into an effective team.

The key properties of a true team include **collaborative action** where, along with a common goal, teams have collaborative tasks. Conversely, in a group, individuals are responsible only for their own area. They also share the rewards of strong team performance with their **compensation based on shared outcomes**. Compensation of individuals must be based primarily on a shared outcome, not individual performance. Members are also willing to **sacrifice for the common good** in which individuals give up scarce resources for the common good instead of competing for those resources. For example, teams occur in sports such as soccer and basketball, in which the individuals actively help each other, forgo their own chance to score by passing the ball, and win or lose collectively as a team.

2.2 Teams in Organizations

The early 1990s saw a dramatic rise in the use of teams within organizations, along with dramatic results such as the Miller Brewing Company increasing productivity 30% in the plants that used self-directed teams compared with those that used the traditional organization. This same method allowed Texas Instruments in Malaysia to reduce defects from 100 parts per million to 20 parts per million. In addition, Westinghouse reduced its cycle time from 12 weeks to 2 weeks, and Harris Electronics was able to achieve an 18% reduction in costs.[16] The team method has served countless companies over the years through both quantifiable improvements and more subtle individual worker-related benefits.

Companies such as Square D, a maker of circuit breakers, switched to self-directed teams and found that overtime on machines like the punch press dropped 70% under teams. Productivity increased because the setup operators were able to manipulate the work in much more effective ways than a supervisor could dictate.[17] In 2001, clothing retailer Chico's FAS was looking to grow its business. The company hired Scott Edmonds as president, and two years later revenues had almost doubled from $378 million to $760 million. By 2006, revenues were $1.6 billion, and Chico's had nine years of double-digit same-store sales growth. The company has continued to do well even after his departure; in 2012 sales were over $2 billion. What did Edmonds do to get these results? He created a horizontal organization "ruled by high-performance teams with real decision-making clout and accountability for results, rather than by committees that pass decisions up to the next level or toss them over the wall into the nearest silo."

The use of teams also began to increase because advances in technology have resulted in more complex systems that require contributions from multiple people across the organization. Overall, team-based organizations have more motivation and involvement, and teams can often accomplish more than individuals.[18] It is no wonder organizations are relying on teams more and more.

Do We Need a Team?

Teams are not a cure-all for organizations. To determine whether a team is needed, organizations should consider whether a variety of knowledge, skills, and abilities are needed, whether ideas and feedback are needed from different groups within the organization, how interdependent the tasks are, if wide cooperation is needed to get things done, and whether the organization would benefit from shared goals.[19] If the answer to these questions is "yes," then a team or teams might make sense. For example, research shows that the more team members perceive that outcomes are interdependent, the better they share information and the better they perform.[20]

2.3 Team Tasks and Roles

Teams differ in terms of the tasks they are trying to accomplish and the roles team members play.

FIGURE 12.9

Teams are only as strong as their weakest link. While Michael Phelps has been dubbed "the world's greatest swimmer" and received a great deal of personal attention, he could not have achieved his record eight gold medals in a single Olympics and 18 gold medals total without the combined efforts of his teammates in relay events during the 2004, 2008, and 2012 Olympic Games.

Source: http://en.wikipedia.org/wiki/ File:Michael_Phelps_Ryan_Lochte _Laszlo_Cseh_medals_2008 _Olympics.jpg

FIGURE 12.10

The production tasks assigned to construction workers creating a new building often involve tight deadlines and incentives to complete work on schedule.

© Thinkstock

As early as the 1970s, J. R. Hackman identified three major classes of tasks: (1) production tasks, (2) idea generation tasks, and (3) problem-solving tasks.[21] **Production tasks** include actually making something, such as a building, a product, or a marketing plan. **Idea generation tasks** deal with creative tasks, such as brainstorming a new direction or creating a new process. **Problem-solving tasks** refer to coming up with plans for actions and making decisions, both facets of managerial P-O-L-C functions (planning and leading). For example, a team may be charged with coming up with a new marketing slogan, which is an idea generation task, while another team might be asked to manage an entire line of products, including making decisions about products to produce, managing the production of the product lines, marketing them, and staffing their division. The second team has all three types of tasks to accomplish at different points in time.

Task Interdependence

Another key to understanding how tasks are related to teams is to understand their level of task interdependence. **Task interdependence** refers to the degree that team members depend on one another to get information, support, or materials from other team members to be effective. Research shows that self-managing teams are most effective when their tasks are highly interdependent.[22]

There are three types of task interdependence. **Pooled interdependence** exists when team members may work independently and simply combine their efforts to create the team's output. For example, when students meet to divide the sections of a research paper and one person simply puts all the sections together to create one paper, the team is using the pooled interdependence model. However, they might decide that it makes more sense to start with one person writing the introduction of their research paper, then the second person reads what was written by the first person and, drawing from this section, writes about the findings within the paper. Using the findings section, the third person writes the conclusions. If one person's output becomes another person's input, the team would be experiencing **sequential interdependence**. And finally, if the student team decided that in order to create a top notch research paper they should work together on each phase of the research paper so that their best ideas would be captured at each stage, they would be undertaking **reciprocal interdependence**. Another important type of interdependence that is not specific to the task itself is **outcome interdependence**, where the rewards that an individual receives depend on the performance of others.

FIGURE 12.11 Task Interdependence

Task interdependence refers to the degree that team members depend on one another to reach the goals of the team. Interdependence varies significantly based on the type of team. Here, we illustrate the three different types of task interdependence using different types of sports teams.

Pooled interdependence exists when team members work independently and simply combine their efforts to create the team's output. This type of interdependence is seen in football where each player often has a unique "assignment" he is responsible for during a specific play.

Reciprocal interdependence exists when individuals work together and ideas and project assignments are passed back and forth until the project is complete. This type of interdependence is seen in basketball where players must be constantly alert to receive a pass, rebound, or transition between offence and defense.

Sequential interdependence exists when one person's output becomes another person's input. This interdependence is common in baseball where the ball is fielded and then relayed from player to player until it reaches its ultimate destination (hopefully).

© Thinkstock

Team Roles

While relatively little research has been conducted on team roles, some recent studies show that individuals who are more aware of team roles and the behavior required for each role perform better than individuals that do not. This fact remains true for both student project teams as well as work teams, even after accounting for intelligence and personality.[23] Early research found that teams tend to have two categories of roles: those related to the tasks at hand and those related to the team's functioning. For example, teams that only focus on production at all costs may be successful in the short run, but if they pay no attention to how team members feel about working 70 hours a week, they are likely to experience high turnover. Teams also do well when their members have different cognitive styles.[24]

On the basis of decades of research on teams, 10 key roles have been identified.[25] Team leadership is effective when leaders are able to adapt the roles they are contributing to or asking others to contribute to fit what the team needs, given its stage and the tasks at hand.[26] Ineffective leaders might always engage in the same task role behaviors when what they really need to do is focus on social roles, put disagreements aside, and get back to work. While these behaviors can be effective from time to time, if the team doesn't modify its role behaviors as things change, they most likely will not be effective.

FIGURE 12.12

Teams are based on many roles being carried out as summarized by the Team Role Typology. These 10 roles include task roles (contractor, creator, contributor, completer, and critic), social roles (calibrator, communicator, and cooperator), and boundary-spanning roles (consul and coordinator).

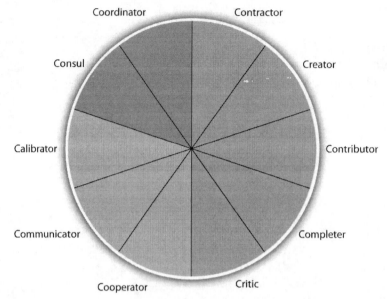

Source: Mumford, T. V., Van Iddekinge, C. H., Morgeson, F. P., & Campion, M. A. (2008). The team role test: Development and validation of a team role knowledge situational judgment test. Journal of Applied Psychology, 93, 250–267; Mumford, T. V., Campion, M. A., & Morgeson, F. P. (2006). Situational judgments in work teams: A team role typology. In J. A. Weekley & R. E. Ployhart (Eds.), Situational judgment tests: Theory, measurement (pp. 319–343). Mahwah, NJ: Lawrence Erlbaum.

Task Roles

Five roles make up the task portion of the role typology. The **contractor role** includes behaviors that serve to organize the team's work, including creating team time lines, production schedules, and task sequencing. The **creator role** deals more with changes in the team's task process structure. For example, reframing the team goals and looking at the context of goals would fall under this role. The **contributor role** is important because it brings information and expertise to the team. This role is characterized by sharing knowledge and training those who have less expertise to strengthen the team. Research shows that teams with highly intelligent members and evenly distributed workloads are more effective than those with uneven workloads.[27] The **completer role** is also important, as it is often where ideas are transformed into action. Behaviors associated with this role include following up on tasks such as gathering needed background information or summarizing the team's ideas into reports. Finally, the **critic role** includes "devil's advocate" behaviors, which go against the assumptions being made by the team.

Social Roles

Social roles serve to keep the team operating effectively. When the social roles are filled, team members feel more cohesive and the group is less prone to suffer process losses or biases, such as social loafing, groupthink, or a lack of participation from all members. Three roles fall under the umbrella of social roles. The **cooperator role** includes supporting those with expertise toward the team's goals. This is a proactive role. The **communicator role** includes behaviors that are targeted at collaboration such as practicing good listening skills and appropriately using humor to diffuse tense situations. Having a good communicator helps the team to feel more open to sharing ideas. And the **calibrator role** is an important one and serves to keep the team on track in terms of suggesting any needed changes to the team's process. This role includes initiating discussions about potential team problems such as power struggles or other tensions. Similarly, this role may involve settling disagreements or pointing out what is working and what is not in terms of team process.

Boundary-Spanning Roles

The final two roles are related to activities outside of the team that help to connect the team to the larger organization.[28] Teams that engage in a greater level of boundary-spanning behaviors increase their team effectiveness.[29] The **consul role** includes gathering information from the larger organization and informing those within the organization about team activities, goals, and successes. Often the consul role is filled by team managers or leaders. The **coordinator role** includes interfacing with others within the organization so that the team's efforts are in line with other individuals and teams within the organization.

2.4   Types of Teams

There are many different types of teams, and a given team may be described according to multiple types. For example, a team of scientists writing a research article for publication may be temporary, virtual, and cross-functional.

Teams may be permanent or long term, but more typically, a team exists for a limited time. In fact, one-third of all teams in the United States are temporary.[30] An example of a temporary team is a **task force** that addresses a specific issue or problem until it is resolved. Other teams may be temporary or ongoing such as **product development teams**. In addition, matrix organizations have **cross-functional teams** where individuals from different parts of the organization staff the team, which may be temporary or long-standing.

Virtual Teams

Virtual teams are teams in which members are not located in the same physical place. They may be in different cities, states, or even different countries. Some virtual teams are formed by necessity, such as to take advantage of lower labor costs in different countries; one study found that upward of 8.4 million individuals worldwide work virtually in at least one team.[31] Often, virtual teams are formed to take advantage of distributed expertise or time—the needed experts may be living in different cities. A company that sells products around the world, for example, may need technologists who can solve customer problems at any hour of the day or night. It may be difficult to find the caliber of people needed who would be willing to work at 2 a.m. on a Saturday, for example. So companies organize virtual technical support teams. BakBone Software, for instance, has a 13-member technical support team. Each member has a degree in computer science and is divided among offices in California, Maryland, England, and Tokyo. BakBone believes it has been able to hire stronger candidates by drawing from a diverse talent pool and hiring in different geographic regions rather than limiting hiring to one region or time zone.[32]

Despite potential benefits, virtual teams present special management challenges, particularly to the controlling function. Managers often think that they have to see team members working to believe that work is being done. Because this kind of oversight is impossible in virtual team situations, it is important to devise evaluation schemes that focus on deliverables. Are team members delivering what they said they would? In self-managed teams, are team members producing the results the team decided to measure itself on?

FIGURE 12.13

College teams are, by their nature, temporary, making Coach Bud Wilkinson's record 47-game winning streak with the University of Oklahoma football program even more impressive.

Source: http://en.wikipedia.org/wiki/ File:JFK-Bud_Wilkinson.jpg

task force

A temporary team that is asked to address a specific issue or problem until it is resolved.

product development teams

A type of team that may be either temporary or ongoing.

cross-functional teams

Teams that involve individuals from different parts of the organization staff.

virtual teams

Teams in which members are not located in the same physical place.

Another special challenge of virtual teams is building trust. Will team members deliver results just as they would in face-to-face teams? Can members trust one another to do what they said they would do? Companies often invest in bringing a virtual team together at least once so members can get to know one another and build trust.[33] In manager-led virtual teams, managers should be held accountable for their team's results and evaluated on their ability as a team leader.

Finally, communication is especially important in virtual teams, through e-mail, phone calls, conference calls, or project management tools that help organize work. If individuals in a virtual team are not fully engaged and tend to avoid conflict, team performance can suffer.[34] A wiki is an Internet-based method for many people to collaborate and contribute to a document or discussion. Essentially, the document remains available for team members to access and amend at any time. The most famous example is Wikipedia, which is gaining traction as a way to structure project work globally and get information into the hands of those that need it. Empowered organizations put information into everyone's hands.[35] Research shows that empowered teams are more effective than those that are not empowered.[36]

Top Management Teams

Top management teams are appointed by the chief executive officer (CEO) and, ideally, reflect the skills and areas that the CEO considers vital for the company. There are no formal rules about top management team design or structure. The top management team often includes representatives from functional areas, such as finance, human resources, and marketing or key geographic areas, such as Europe, Asia, and North America. Depending on the company, other areas may be represented such as legal counsel or the company's chief technologist. Typical top management team member titles include chief operating officer (COO), chief financial officer (CFO), chief marketing officer (CMO), or chief technology officer (CTO). Because CEOs spend an increasing amount of time outside their companies (i.e., with suppliers, customers, regulators, and so on), the role of the COO has taken on a much higher level of internal operating responsibilities. In most American companies, the CEO also serves as chairman of the board and can have the additional title of president. Companies have top management teams to help set the company's vision and strategic direction, key tasks within the planning P-O-L-C function. Top teams make decisions on new markets, expansions, acquisitions, or divestitures. The top team is also important for its symbolic role: how the top team behaves dictates the organization's culture and priorities by allocating resources and by modeling behaviors that will likely be emulated lower down in the organization. Importantly, the top team is most effective when team composition is functionally and demographically diverse and when it can truly operate as a *team*, not just as a *group* of individual executives.[37] The board of directors is an example of one important team within corporations as well as nonprofit organizations that utilize boards as a key decision-making body.

That "the people make the place" holds especially true for members of the top management team. In a study of 15 firms that demonstrated excellence, defined as sustained performance over a 15-year period, leadership researcher Jim Collins noted that those firms attended to people first and strategy second. "They got the right people on the bus, moved the wrong people off the bus, ushered the right people to the right seats—then they figured out where to drive it."[38] The best teams plan for turnover. **Succession planning** is the process of identifying future members of the top management team. Effective succession planning allows the best top teams to achieve high performance today and create a legacy of high performance for the future.

FIGURE 12.14 Board Roles

William Shakespeare once wrote, "All the world's a stage, and the men and women merely players." This analogy applies well to boards of directors. When the performance of board members is impressive, the company is able to put on a dynamic show. But if a board member phones in their role, failure may soon follow. We discuss the different roles board members may play below.

Accountant – Board members may, at times, approve financial objectives.

Lawyer – Ensuring the firm complies with applicable laws is a key role.

Advisor – Providing advice on strategic issues is a critical role that is overlooked by less effective boards.

Activist – Boards must ensure that the rights and interests of stakeholders (especially stockholders) are represented.

Human Resource Manager – Boards must monitor the CEO and engage in hiring, firing, and the administration of CEO compensation.

Agent – Because board members may serve in powerful positions at other companies, a well-networked board member may be able to bring new connections to the firm.

Source: Image courtesy of Ketchen, D., & Short, J. (2011). Mastering strategic management. Irvington, NY: Flat World Knowledge.

2.5 Team Leadership and Autonomy

Teams also vary in terms of how they are led. **Traditional or manager-led teams** are teams in which the manager serves as the team leader. The manager assigns work to other team members. These types of teams are the most natural to form, wherein managers have the power to hire and fire team members and are held accountable for the team's results.

traditional or manager-led teams

Teams where the manager serves as the team leader.

FIGURE 12.15 Building a Better Team Leader at Google

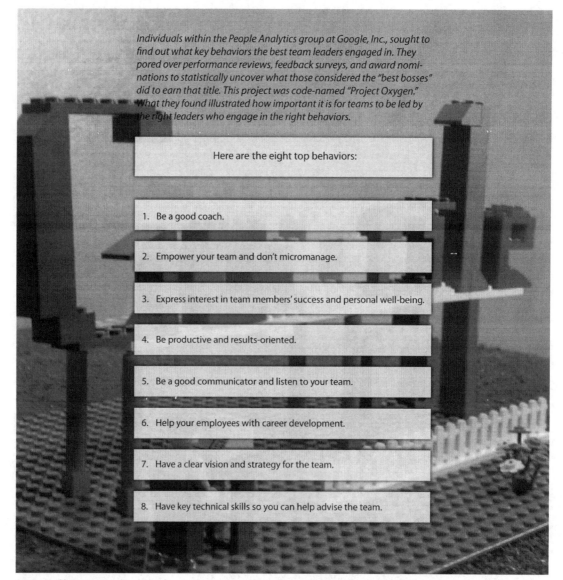

Source: Used by permission of Google, Inc.

self-managed teams

Teams that manage themselves and do not report directly to a supervisor. Instead, team members select their own leader, and they may even take turns in the leadership role.

Self-managed teams are a new form of team that rose in popularity with the Total Quality Movement in the 1980s. Unlike manager-led teams, these teams manage themselves and do not report directly to a supervisor. Instead, team members select their own leader, and they may even take turns in the leadership role. Self-managed teams also have the power to select new team members. As a whole, the team shares responsibility for a significant task, such as assembly of an entire car. The task is ongoing rather than temporary such as a charity fund drive for a given year.

Organizations began to use self-managed teams as a way to reduce hierarchy by allowing team members to complete tasks and solve problems on their own. The benefits of self-managed teams extend much further. Research has shown that employees in self-managed teams have higher job satisfaction, increased self-esteem, and grow more on the job. The benefits to the organization include increased productivity, increased flexibility, and lower turnover. Self-managed teams can be found at all levels of the organization, and they bring particular benefits to lower-level employees by giving them a sense of ownership of their jobs that they may not otherwise have. The increased satisfaction can also reduce absenteeism because employees do not want to let their team members down.

Typical team goals are improving quality, reducing costs, and meeting deadlines. Teams also have a "stretch" goal, which is difficult to reach but important to the business unit. Many teams also have special project goals. Texas Instruments (TI), a company that makes semiconductors, used self-directed teams to make improvements in work processes.[39] Teams were allowed to set their own goals in conjunction with managers and other teams. TI also added an individual component to the typical team compensation system. This individual component rewarded team members for learning new skills that added to their knowledge. These "knowledge blocks" include topics such as leadership, administration, and problem solving. The team decides what additional skills people might need to help the team meet its objectives. Team members would then take classes or otherwise demonstrate their proficiency in that new skill on the job to be certified for mastering the skill. Individuals could then be evaluated based on their contribution to the team and how they are building skills to support the team.

Self-managed teams are **empowered**, which means that they have the *responsibility* as well as the *authority* to achieve their goals. Team members have the power to control tasks and processes and to make decisions. Research shows that self-managed teams may be at a higher risk of suffering from negative outcomes due to conflict, so it is important that they are supported with training to help them deal with conflict effectively.[40] Self-managed teams may still have a leader who helps them coordinate with the larger organization.[41] For a product team composed of engineering, production, and marketing employees, empowerment means that the team can decide everything about a product's appearance, production, and cost without having to get permission or sign-off from higher management. As a result, empowered teams can more effectively meet tighter deadlines. At AT&T, for example, the model 4200 phone team cut development time in half while lowering costs and improving quality by using the empowered team approach.[42] A special form of self-managed teams are **self-directed teams** in which they also determine who will lead them with no external oversight.

empowered teams

Teams that have the responsibility as well as the authority to achieve their goals.

self-directed teams

A special form of self-managed teams in which members determine who will lead them with no external oversight.

FIGURE 12.16

Team leadership is a major determinant of how autonomous a team will be.

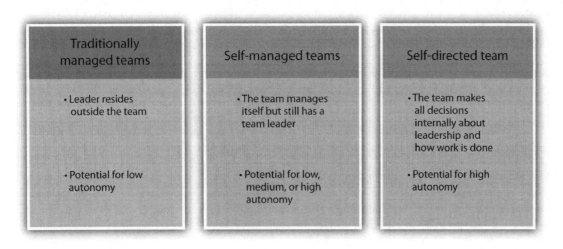

2.6 Designing Effective Teams

Designing an effective team means making decisions about team composition (who should be on the team), team size (the optimal number of people on the team), and team diversity (should team members be of similar background, such as all engineers, or of different backgrounds). Answering these questions will depend, to a large extent, on the type of task that the team will be performing. Teams can be charged with a variety of tasks, from problem solving to generating creative and innovative ideas to managing the daily operations of a manufacturing plant.

Who Are the Best Individuals for the Team?

A key consideration when forming a team is to ensure that all the team members are **qualified** for the roles they will fill for the team. This process often entails understanding the knowledge, skills, and abilities (KSAs) of team members as well as the personality traits needed before starting the selection process.[43] For example, when GE decided to manufacture jet engines after 20 years of not doing so, they staffed the new factory not just with engineers but with engineers holding FAA (Federal Aviation Administration) licenses. The superior qualifications of the engineers allowed the team to effectively make key decisions with minimal oversight. When talking to potential team members, be sure to communicate the job requirements and norms of the team. To the degree that this is not possible, such as when already existing groups are used, think of ways to train the team members as much as possible to help ensure success. In addition to task knowledge, research has shown that individuals who understand the concepts covered in this chapter and in this book such as conflict resolution, motivation, planning, and leadership actually perform better on their jobs. This finding holds for a variety of jobs, including officer in the United States Air Force, an employee at a pulp mill, or a team member at a box manufacturing plant.[44]

How Large Should My Team Be?

Interestingly, research has shown that regardless of **team size**, the most active team member speaks 43% of the time. The difference is that the team member who participates the least in a 3-person team is still active 23% of the time versus only 3% in a 10-person team.[45] When deciding team size, a good rule of thumb is a size of 2 to 20 members. The majority of teams have 10 members or less because the larger the team, the harder it is to coordinate and interact as a team. With fewer individuals, team members are more able to work through differences and agree on a common plan of action. They have a clearer understanding of others' roles and greater accountability to fulfill their roles (remember social loafing?). Some tasks, however, require larger team sizes because of the need for diverse skills or because of the complexity of the task. In those cases, the best solution is to create subteams where one member from each subteam is a member of a larger coordinating team. The relationship between team size and performance seems to greatly depend on the level of task interdependence, with some studies finding larger teams outproducing smaller teams and other studies finding just the opposite.[46] The bottom line is that team size should be matched to the goals of the team.

FIGURE 12.17

The ideal size for a team depends on the task. Groups larger than 10 members tend to be harder to coordinate and often break into subteams to accomplish the work.

© Thinkstock

How Diverse Should My Team Be?

Team composition and **team diversity** often go hand in hand. Teams whose members have complementary skills are often more successful because members can see each other's blind spots. One team member's strengths can compensate for another's weaknesses.[47] For example, consider the challenge that companies face when trying to forecast future sales of a given product. Workers who are educated as forecasters have the analytic skills needed for forecasting, but these workers often lack critical information about customers. Salespeople, in contrast, regularly communicate with customers, which means they're in the know about upcoming customer decisions. But salespeople often lack the analytic skills, discipline, or desire to enter this knowledge into spreadsheets and software that will help a company forecast future sales. Putting forecasters and salespeople together on a team tasked with determining the most accurate product forecast each quarter makes the best use of each member's skills and expertise.

Diversity in team composition can help teams come up with more creative and effective solutions. Research shows that teams that believe in the value of diversity performed better than teams that do not.[48] The more diverse a team is in terms of expertise, gender, age, and background, the more ability the group has to avoid the problems of groupthink.[49] For example, different educational levels for team members were related to more creativity in research and development teams and faster time to market for new products.[50] Members will be more inclined to make different kinds of mistakes, which means that they'll be able to catch and correct those mistakes.

KEY TAKEAWAY

Teams, though similar to groups, are different in both scope and composition. A team is a particular type of group: a cohesive coalition of people working together to achieve mutual goals. In the 21st century, many companies have moved toward the extensive use of teams. The task a team is charged with accomplishing affects how they perform. In general, task interdependence works well for self-managing teams. Team roles consist of task, social, and boundary-spanning roles. Different types of teams include task forces, product development teams, cross-functional teams, and top management teams. Team leadership and autonomy varies depending on whether the team is traditionally managed, self-managed, or self-directed. Teams are most effective when teams consist of members with the right KSAs for the tasks, are not too large, contain diversity across team members. Decisions about where and how to use teams, the leadership of teams, and the structure of teams illustrate the overlap in the design and leading P-O-L-C functions.

EXERCISES

1. Think of the last team you were in. Did the task you were asked to do affect the team? Why or why not?
2. Which of the 10 work roles do you normally take in a team? How difficult or easy do you think it would be for you to take on a different role?
3. Have you ever worked in a virtual team? If so, what were the challenges and advantages of working virtually?
4. How large do you think teams should be and why?

3. ORGANIZING EFFECTIVE TEAMS

LEARNING OBJECTIVES

1. **Understand how to create team norms, roles, and expectations.**
2. **Identify keys to running effective team meetings.**

When a team is well organized, it tends to perform well. Well-designed teams are able to capitalize on positive events while maintaining composure when facing a negative event. There are several strategies that can boost team effectiveness through effective organization.

3.1 Establishing Team Norms and Contracts

A key to successful team design is to have clear norms, roles, and expectations among team members. Problems such as social loafing or groupthink can be avoided by paying careful attention to team member differences and providing clear definitions for roles, expectancy, measurement, and rewards.

Team Norms

Norms are shared expectations about how things operate within a group or team. Just as new employees learn to understand and share the assumptions, norms, and values that are part of an organization's culture, they also must learn the norms of their immediate team. This understanding helps teams be more cohesive and perform better. Norms are a powerful way of ensuring coordination within a team. For example, is it acceptable to be late to meetings? How prepared are you supposed to be at the meetings? Is it acceptable to criticize someone else's work? These norms are shaped early during the life of a team and affect whether the team is productive, cohesive, and successful.

Team Contracts

Scientific research, as well as experience working with thousands of teams, shows that teams that are able to articulate and agree on established ground rules, goals, and roles and develop a **team contract** around these standards are better equipped to face challenges that may arise within the team.[51] Having a team contract does not necessarily mean that the team will be successful, but it can serve as a road map when the team veers off course. Questions that can help to create a meaningful team contract include the following:

- **Team values and goals.** What are our shared team values? What is our team goal?
- **Team roles and leadership.** Who does what within this team? (Who takes notes at the meeting? Who sets the agenda? Who assigns tasks? Who runs the meetings?) Does the team have a formal leader? If so, what are his or her roles?
- **Team decision making.** How are minor decisions made? How are major decisions made?
- **Team communication.** Who do you contact if you cannot make a meeting? Who communicates with whom? How often will the team meet?
- **Team performance.** What constitutes good team performance? What if a team member tries hard but does not seem to be producing quality work? How will poor attendance/work quality be dealt with?

3.2 Team Meetings

Anyone who has been involved in a team knows it involves team meetings. While few individuals relish meetings, they serve an important function in terms of information sharing and decision making. They also serve an important social function and can help to build team cohesion and a task function in terms of coordination. Unfortunately, we've all attended lengthy meetings that were a waste of time and where little happened that couldn't have been accomplished by reading an e-mail in five minutes. To run effective meetings, it helps to think of meetings in terms of three sequential steps.[52]

norms

Shared expectations about how things operate within a group or team.

team contract

A contract that includes agreements on established ground rules, goals, and roles.

Before the Meeting

Much of the effectiveness of a meeting is determined before the team gathers. There are three key things you can do to ensure that the team members get the most out of their meeting.

First, ask yourself, Is a meeting needed? Leaders should do a number of things before the meeting to help make it effective. The first thing is to be sure a meeting is even needed. If the meeting is primarily informational, ask yourself whether it is imperative that the group fully understands the information and whether future decisions will be built on this information. If so, a meeting may be needed. If not, perhaps simply communicating with everyone in a written format will save valuable time. Similarly, decision-making meetings make the most sense when the problem is complex and important, there are questions of fairness to be resolved, and commitment is needed moving forward.

Second, create and distribute an agenda. An agenda is important in helping to inform those invited about the purpose of the meeting. It also helps organize the flow of the meeting and keep the team on track.

Third, send a reminder before the meeting. Reminding everyone of the purpose, time, and location of the meeting helps everyone prepare themselves. Anyone who has attended a team meeting only to find there is no reason to meet because members haven't completed their agreed-upon tasks knows that, as a result, team performance or morale can be negatively affected. Follow up to make sure everyone is prepared. As a team member, inform others immediately if you will not be ready with your tasks so they can determine whether the meeting should be postponed.

During the Meeting

During the meeting, there are several things you can do to make sure the team starts and keeps on track.

Start the meeting on time. Waiting for members who are running late only punishes those who are on time and reinforces the idea that it's OK to be late. Starting the meeting promptly sends an important signal that you are respectful of everyone's time.

Follow the meeting agenda. Veering off agenda communicates to members that it is not important. It also makes it difficult for others to keep track of where you are in the meeting and can facilitate important points not being addressed.

Manage group dynamics for full participation. There are a number of group dynamics that can limit a team's functioning. Be on the lookout for full participation and engagement from all team members as well as any potential problems such as social loafing, group conflict, or groupthink.

Summarize the meeting with action items. Be sure to clarify team member roles moving forward. If individual's tasks are not clear, chances are role confusion will arise later. There should be clear notes from the meeting regarding who is responsible for each action item and the timeframes associated with next steps.

End the meeting on time. This is vitally important as it shows that you respect everyone's time and are organized. If another meeting is needed to follow up, schedule it later, but don't let the meeting run over.

After the Meeting

Follow up on action items. After the meeting you probably have several action items. In addition, it is likely that you'll need to follow up on the action items of others.

FIGURE 12.18

Conducting meetings standing up has been shown to save time and keep information flowing across the team.[53]

© Thinkstock

EXERCISES

1. Have the norms for most of the teams you have belonged to been formal or informal? How do you think that has affected these teams?
2. Have you ever been involved in creating a team contract? Explain how you think that may have influenced how the team functioned.
3. Should the person requesting a meeting always prepare a meeting agenda? Why or why not?
4. Do you think conducting team meetings standing up is a good idea? Why or why not?

4. BARRIERS TO EFFECTIVE TEAMS

LEARNING OBJECTIVE

1. **Recognize common barriers to effective teams and how to address them**

Problems can arise in any team that will hurt the team's effectiveness. Here are some common problems faced by teams and how to deal with them.

4.1 Common Barriers to Effective Teams

Challenges of Knowing Where to Begin

At the start of a project, team members may be at a loss as to how to begin. Also, they may have reached the end of a task but are unable to move on to the next step or put the task to rest.

Floundering often results from a lack of clear goals, so the remedy is to go back to the team's mission or plan and make sure that it is clear to everyone. Team leaders can help move the team past floundering by asking, "What is holding us up? Do we need more data? Do we need assurances or support? Does anyone feel that we've missed something important?"

Dominating Team Members

Some team members may have a dominating personality that encroaches on the participation or airtime of others. This overbearing behavior may hurt the team morale or the momentum of the team.

A good way to overcome this barrier is to design a team evaluation to include a "balance of participation" in meetings. Knowing that fair and equitable participation by all will affect the team's performance evaluation will help team members limit domination by one member and encourage participation from all members, even shy or reluctant ones. Team members can say, "We've heard from Mary on this issue, so let's hear from others about their ideas."

Poor Performance of Some Team Members

Research shows that teams deal with poor performers in different ways, depending on members' perceptions of the reasons for poor performance.[54] In situations in which the poor performer is perceived as lacking in ability, teams are more likely to train the member. In situations in which members perceive the individual as simply being low on motivation, they are more likely to try to motivate or reject the poor performer.

Keep in mind that justice is an important part of keeping individuals working hard for the team.[55] Be sure that poor performers are dealt with in a way that is deemed fair by all the team members.

Poorly Managed Team Conflict

Disagreements among team members are normal and should be expected. Healthy teams raise issues and discuss differing points of view because that will ultimately help the team reach stronger, more well-reasoned decisions. Unfortunately, sometimes disagreements arise because of personality issues or feuds that predated the teams' formation.

Ideally, teams should be designed to avoid bringing adversaries together on the same team. If that is not possible, the next best solution is to have adversaries discuss their issues privately, so the team's progress is not disrupted. The team leader or other team member can offer to facilitate the discussion. One way to make a discussion between conflicting parties meaningful is to form a behavioral contract between the two parties. That is, if one party agrees to do X, the other will agree to do Y.[56]

KEY TAKEAWAY

Barriers to effective teams include the challenges of knowing where to begin, dominating team members, the poor performance of team members, and poorly managed team conflict.

EXERCISES

1. Have you ever been involved in a team where one or more dominating team members hurt the team's performance? Share what happened and how the team dealt with this.

2. Have you ever been involved in a team where conflict erupted between team members? How was the situation handled?

---

5. DEVELOPING YOUR TEAM SKILLS

LEARNING OBJECTIVE

1. **Identify guidelines for developing cohesion in your team.**

5.1 Steps to Creating and Maintaining a Cohesive Team

There are several steps you can take as a manager to help build a cohesive team. For example, you can work to do the following:

- Align the group with the greater organization. Establish common objectives in which members can get involved.

- Let members have choices in setting their own goals. Include them in decision making at the organizational level.

- Define clear roles. Demonstrate how each person's contribution furthers the group goal—everyone is responsible for a special piece of the puzzle.

- Situate group members in proximity to one another. This builds familiarity.

- Give frequent praise, both to individuals and to the group, and encourage them to praise each other. This builds individual self-confidence, reaffirms positive behavior, and creates an overall positive atmosphere.

- Treat all members with dignity and respect. This demonstrates that there are no favorites and everyone is valued.

- Celebrate differences. This highlights each individual's contribution while also making diversity a norm.
- Establish common rituals. Thursday morning coffee, monthly potlucks—these reaffirm group identity and create shared experiences.

KEY TAKEAWAY

There are many things you can do to help build a cohesive team. One key thing to remember is that too much cohesion without strong performance norms can be a problem. Many of the ways to build cohesive groups are also fun, such as celebrating successes and creating rituals.

EXERCISES

1. Think of the most cohesive group you have ever been in. What factors made the group so close?
2. What are some challenges you see to creating a cohesive group?
3. How does team size affect cohesion?

6. CASE IN POINT: PRET A MANGER PUTS PEER PRESSURE TO WORK

FIGURE 12.19

Source: http://commons.wikimedia.org/wiki/File:Pret_A_Manger_HK.JPG

Pret A Manger (meaning "ready to eat" in French) is a UK-based café known for convenient, inexpensive, and healthy food with menu items such as soups, salads, sandwiches, muffins, cakes, and coffee. The first Pret opened in 1986 in London and was founded by two college friends, Sinclair Beecham and Julian Metcalfe, who wanted to avoid additives, preservatives, and chemicals frequently found in fast food. But they are also known for their unique team-based structure, selection, and training techniques.

Pret is structured around the concept of a "Pret Estate," based on small groups of 10 shops. These are led by what Pret calls "imaginative and passionate leaders." In addition, all their shops have trainers within their core staff. It is not unusual to have staff remain for decades. For example, Collins Obamwanyi is a general manager of a Pret shop but began at his very first shop decades earlier. Just like Obamwanyi, a total of 75% of Pret managers began their careers as team members.

Getting a job at Pret is a team process. A newly hired employee goes through a traditional hiring process. However, those who make it that far are asked to work at a shop for a six-hour shift. After that, employees who worked with the hire are asked to vote whether or not they want to work with this person. Most make it through this process, but 10% do not. Those who do not are paid for that day's work and not invited back. Their team-based approach to hiring seems to be working, because while the turnover rate in the fast-food industry can be over 400%, Pret A Manger enjoys a relatively low 60% turnover rate without paying more than other similar businesses who rely on hourly workers. In addition, Pret rewards employees who are promoted or pass training hurdles with a monetary reward. The catch? They must give the reward away to coworkers who helped them succeed. When stores are rated well by the mystery shoppers who anonymously visit and grade the stores each week, the top 10% of stores receive money for a shop party. Twice a year, they also throw a "massive" party to which everyone at Pret is invited.

Pret has "hopped the pond" to the United States with stores in New York, Chicago, and Washington, DC, as well as shops in Hong Kong and Paris. Pret plans to continue expansion around the world. Pret has a shop within a Target store and is in talks to open up further, with Pret retaining full control of its own kitchen, menu, and pricing.

Case written by Talya Bauer and Berrin Erdogan to accompany Carpenter, M., Bauer, T., Erdogan, B., & Short, J. (2013). Principles of Management (2nd ed.). New York: Flat World Knowledge. Based on information from Pret A Manger. Retrieved September 14, 2012, from www.pret.com/about; Clifford, S. (2011). Would you like a smile with that? New York Times. Retrieved September 14, 2012, from http://www.nytimes.com/2011/08/07/business/pret-a-manger-with-new-fast-food-ideas-gains-a-foothold-in-united-states.html; Horovitz, B. (2012). Target to open natural foods restaurant in Chicago store. USA Today. Retrieved September 14, 2012, from http://www.usatoday.com/money/industries/food/story/2012-07-24/target-pret-a-manger-healthier-food/56466400/1.

CASE DISCUSSION QUESTIONS

1. Teams are an essential part of the leading facet of the P-O-L-C framework. Looking at the team role typology, how might you categorize the roles played by the members of Pret in this case?

2. What are the benefits of creating a team whose members hold hiring power over potential new employees? What are the potential negatives?

3. What do you think inspires individuals at Pret to work as a cohesive team?

4. In the case of Pret, do you view the team members or the management leaders as the most important part of the story?

5. How do you think Pret holds team members accountable for their actions?

6. Do you think that Pret offers enough of a support system for its employees in order to create this type of team cohesion?

ENDNOTES

1. Martin, A., & Bal, V. (2006). *The state of teams: CCL research report*. Greensboro, NC: Center for Creative Leadership.

2. Tuckman, B. (1965). Developmental sequence in small groups. *Psychological Bulletin, 63*, 384–399.

3. Karriker, J. H. (2005). Cyclical group development and interaction-based leadership emergence in autonomous teams: an integrated model. *Journal of Leadership & Organizational Studies, 11*, 54–64.

4. Gersick, C. J. G. (1991). Revolutionary change theories: A multilevel exploration of the punctuated equilibrium paradigm. *Academy of Management Review, 16*(1), 10–36.

5. Farh, J., Lee, C., & Farh, C. I. C. (2010). Task conflict and team creativity: A question of how much and when. *Journal of Applied Psychology, 95*, 1173–1180; Hülsheger, U. R., & Anderson, N. (2009). Team-level predictors of innovation at work: A comprehensive meta-analysis spanning three decades of research. *Journal of Applied Psychology, 94*, 1128–1145.

6. Beal, D. J., Cohen, R. R., Burke, M. J., & McLendon, C. L. (2003). Cohesion and performance in groups: A meta-analytic clarification of construct relations. *Journal of Applied Psychology, 88*, 989–1004; Evans, C. R., & Dion, K. L. (1991). Group cohesion and performance: A meta-analysis. *Small Group Research, 22*, 175–186.

7. Janis, I. L. (1972). *Victims of groupthink*. New York: Houghton Mifflin.

8. Goodman, P. S., Ravlin, E., & Schminke, M. (1987). Understanding groups in organizations. *Research in Organizational Behavior, 9*, 121–173.

9. Karau, S. J., & Williams, K. D. (1993). Social loafing: A meta-analytic review and theoretical integration. *Journal of Personality and Social Psychology, 65*, 681–706.

10. Karau, S. J., & Williams, K. D. (1993). Social loafing: A meta-analytic review and theoretical integration. *Journal of Personality and Social Psychology, 65*, 681–706.

11. Gabrenya, W. L., Latane, B., & Wang, Y. (1983). Social loafing in cross-cultural perspective. *Journal of Cross-Cultural Perspective, 14*, 368–384; Harkins, S., & Petty, R. E. (1982). Effects of task difficulty and task uniqueness on social loafing. *Journal of Personality and Social Psychology, 43*, 1214–1229; Taylor, D. W., & Faust, W. L. (1952). Twenty questions: Efficiency of problem-solving as a function of the size of the group. *Journal of Experimental Psychology, 44*, 360–363; Ziller, R. C. (1957). Four techniques of group decision-making under uncertainty. *Journal of Applied Psychology, 41*, 384–388.

12. Price, K. H., Harrison, D. A., & Gavin, J. H. (2006). Withholding inputs in team contexts: Member composition, interaction processes, evaluation structure, and social loafing. *Journal of Applied Psychology, 91*, 1375–1384.

13. Bandura, A. (1997). *Self-efficacy: The exercise of control*. San Francisco: Jossey-Bass.

14. Gully, S. M., Incalcaterra, K. A., Joshi, A., & Beaubien, J. M. (2002). A meta-analysis of team-efficacy, potency, and performance: Interdependence and level of analysis as moderators of observed relationships. *Journal of Applied Psychology, 87*, 819–832; Porter, C. O. L. H (2005). Goal orientation: Effects on backing up behavior, performance, efficacy, and commitment in teams. *Journal of Applied Psychology, 90*, 811–818; Tasa, K., Taggar, S., & Seijts, G. H. (2007). The development of collective efficacy in teams: A multilevel and longitudinal perspective. *Journal of Applied Psychology, 92*, 17–27.

15. Katzenbach, J. R., & Smith, D. K. (1993). *The wisdom of teams: Creating the high-performance organization*. Boston: Harvard Business School Press.

16. Welins, R., Byham, W., & Dixon, G. (1994). *Inside Teams*. San Francisco: Jossey-Bass.

17. Moskal, B. (1988, June 20). Supervisors, begone! *Industry Week*, p. 32.

18. Cannon-Bowers, J. A., & Salas, E. (2001, February). Team effectiveness and competencies. In W. Karwowski (Ed.), *International encyclopedia of ergonomics and human factors* (1383). London: CRC Press.

19. Rees, F. (1997). *Teamwork from start to finish*. San Francisco: Jossey-Bass.

20. De Dreu, C. K. W. (2007). Cooperative outcome interdependence, task reflexivity, and team effectiveness: A motivated information processing perspective. *Journal of Applied Psychology, 92*, 628–638.

21. Hackman, J. R. (1976). Group influences on individuals. In M. D. Dunnette (Ed.), *Handbook of industrial and organizational psychology*. Chicago: Rand-McNally.

22. Langfred, C. W. (2005). Autonomy and performance in teams: The multilevel moderating effect of task interdependence. *Journal of Management, 31*, 513–529; Liden, R. C., Wayne, S. J., & Bradway, L. K. (1997). Task interdependence as a moderator of the relation between group control and performance. *Human Relations, 50*, 169–181.

23. Mumford, T. V., Van Iddekinge, C. H., Morgeson, F. P., & Campion, M. A. (2008). The team role test: Development and validation of a team role knowledge situational judgment test. *Journal of Applied Psychology, 93*, 250–267.

24. Miron-Spektor, E., Erez, M., & Naveh, E. (2011). The effect of conformist and attentive-to-detail members on team innovation: Reconciling the innovation paradox. *Academy of Management Journal, 54*, 740–760.

25. Bales, R. F. (1950). *Interaction process analysis: A method for the study of small groups*. Cambridge, MA: Addison-Wesley; Benne, K. D., & Sheats, P. (1948). Functional roles of group members. *Journal of Social Issues, 4*, 41–49; Belbin, R. M. (1993). *Management teams: Why they succeed or fail*. Oxford: Butterworth-Heinemann.

26. Kozlowski, S. W. J., Gully, S. M., McHugh, P. P., Salas, E., & Cannon-Bowers, J. A. (1996). A dynamic theory of leadership and team effectiveness: Developmental and task contingent roles. In G. Ferris (Ed.), *Research in personnel and human resource management* (Vol. 14, pp. 253–305). Greenwich, CT: JAI Press; Kozlowski, S. W. J., Gully, S. M., Salas, E., & Cannon-Bowers, J. A. (1996). Team leadership and development: Theory, principles, and guidelines for training leaders and teams. In M. M. Beyerlein, D. A. Johnson, & S. T. Beyerlein (Eds.), *Advances in interdisciplinary studies of work teams* (Vol. 3, pp. 253–291). Greenwich, CT: JAI Press.

27. Ellis, A. P. J., Hollenbeck, J. R., Ilgen, D. R., Porter, C. O. L. H., West, B. J., & Moon, H. (2003). Team learning: Collectively connecting the dots. *Journal of Applied Psychology, 88*, 821–835.

28. Anacona, D. G. (1990). Outward bound: Strategies for team survival in an organization. *Academy of Management Journal, 33*, 334–365; Anacona, D. G. (1992). Bridging the boundary: External activity and performance in organizational teams. *Administrative Science Quarterly, 37*, 634–665; Druskat, V. U., & Wheeler, J. V. (2003). Managing from the boundary: The effective leadership of self-managing work teams. *Academy of Management Journal, 46*, 435–457.

29. Marrone, J. A., Tesluk, P. E., & Carson, J. B. (2007). A multi-level investigation of antecedents and consequences of team member boundary-spanning behavior. *Academy of Management Journal, 50*, 1423–1439.

30. Gordon, J. (1992). Work teams: How far have they come? *Training, 29*, 59–62.

31. Ahuja, M., & Galvin, J. (2003). Socialization in virtual group. *Journal of Management, 29*, 161–185.

32. Alexander, S. (2000, November 10). Virtual teams going global. *InfoWorld*. Retrieved September 14, 2012, from http://www.infoworld.com/articles/ca/xml/00/11/13/001113cavirtual.html.

33. Kirkman, B. L., Rosen, B., Gibson, C. B., Tesluk, P. E., & McPherson, S. O. (2002). Five challenges to virtual team success: Lessons from Sabre, Inc. *Academy of Management Executive, 16*, 67–79.

34. Montoya-Weiss, M. M., Massey, A. P., & Song, M. (2001). Getting it together: Temporal coordination and conflict management in global virtual teams. *Academy of Management Journal, 44*, 1251–1262.

35. Kirkman, B. L., & Rosen, B. (2000). Powering up teams. *Organizational Dynamics, 28*(3), 48–66.

36. Mathieu, J. E., Gilson, L. L., & Ruddy, T. M. (2006). Empowerment and team effectiveness: An empirical test of an integrated model. *Journal of Applied Psychology, 91*, 97–108.

37. Carpenter, M. A., Geletkanycz, M. A., & Sanders, W. G. (2004). The upper echelons revisited: The antecedents, elements, and consequences of TMT composition. *Journal of Management, 30*, 749–778.

38. Collins, J. (2001, July–August). Level leadership. *Harvard Business Review*, 66–76.

39. Welins, R., Byham, W., & Dixon, G. (1994). *Inside teams*. San Francisco: Jossey-Bass.

40. Alper, S., Tjosvold, D., & Law, K. S. (2000). Conflict management, efficacy, and performance in organizational teams. *Personnel Psychology, 53*, 625–642; Langfred, C. W. (2007). The downside of self-management: A longitudinal study of the effects of conflict on trust, autonomy, and task interdependence in self-managing teams. *Academy of Management Journal, 50*, 885–900.

41. Morgeson, F. P. (2005). The external leadership of self-managing teams: Intervening in the context of novel and disruptive events. *Journal of Applied Psychology, 90*, 497–508.

42. Parker, G. (1994). *Cross-functional teams*. San Francisco: Jossey-Bass.

43. Humphrey, S. E., Hollenbeck, J. R., Meyer, C. J., & Ilgen, D. R. (2007). Trait configurations in self-managed teams: A conceptual examination of the use of seeding for maximizing and minimizing trait variance in teams. *Journal of Applied Psychology, 92*, 885–892.

44. Hirschfeld, R. R., Jordan, M. H., Field, H. S., Giles, W. F., & Armenakis, A. A. (2006). Becoming team players: Team members' mastery of teamwork knowledge as a predictor of team task proficiency and observed teamwork effectiveness. *Journal of Applied Psychology, 91*, 467–474; Stevens, M. J., & Campion, M. A. (1999). Staffing work teams: Development and validation of a selection test for teamwork settings. *Journal of Management, 25*, 207–228.

45. McGrath, J. E. (1984). *Groups: Interaction and performance*. Englewood Cliffs, NJ: Prentice Hall; Solomon, H. (1960). *Mathematical thinking in the measurement of behavior*. Glencoe, IL: Free Press.

46. Campion, M. A., Medsker, G. J., & Higgs, A. C. (1993). Relations between work group characteristics and effectiveness: Implications for designing effective work groups. *Personnel Psychology, 46*, 823–850; Magjuka, R. J., & Baldwin, T. T. (1991). Team-based employee involvement programs: Effects of design and administration. *Personnel Psychology, 44*, 793–812; Vinokur-Kaplan, D. (1995). Treatment teams that work (and those that don't): An application of Hackman's group effectiveness model to interdisciplinary teams in psychiatric hospitals. *Journal of Applied Behavioral Science, 31*, 303–327.

47. Jackson, S. E., Joshi, A., & Erhardt, N. L. (2003). Recent research on team and organizational diversity: SWOT analysis and implications. *Journal of Management, 29*, 801–830; van Knippenberg, D., De Dreu, C. K. W., & Homan, A. C. (2004). Work group diversity and group performance: An integrative model and research agenda. *Journal of Applied Psychology, 89*, 1008–1022.

48. Homan, A. C., van Knippenberg, D., Van Kleef, G. A., & De Dreu, C. K. W. (2007). Bridging faultlines by valuing diversity: Diversity beliefs, information elaboration, and performance in diverse work groups. *Journal of Applied Psychology, 92*, 1189–1199.

49. Surowiecki. J. (2005). *The wisdom of crowds*. New York: Anchor Books.

50. Eisenhardt, K. M., & Tabrizi, B. N. (1995). Accelerating adaptive processes: Product innovation in the global computer industry. *Administrative Science Quarterly, 4*, 84–110; Shin, S. J., & Zhou, J. (2007). When is educational specialization heterogeneity related to creativity in research and development teams? Transformational leadership as a moderator. *Journal of Applied Psychology, 92*, 1709–1721.

51. Katzenbach, J. R., & Smith, D. K. (1993). *The wisdom of teams: Creating the high-performance organization*. Boston: Harvard Business School Press; Porter, T. W., & Lilly, B. S. (1996). The effects of conflict, trust, and task commitment on project team performance. *International Journal of Conflict Management, 7*, 361–376.

52. Haynes, M. E. (1997). *Effective meeting skills*. Menlo Park, C Crisp.

53. See Bluedorn, A. C., Turban, D. B., & Love, M. S. (1999). The effects of stand-up and sit-down meeting formats on meeting outcomes. *Journal of Applied Psychology, 84,* 277–285. This technique is used by Johnson & Johnson, Ritz-Carlton, ThoughtWorks, Agile Software, and Corning.

54. Jackson, C. L., & LePine, J. A. (2003). Peer responses to a team's weakest link: A test and extension of LePine and Van Dyne's model. *Journal of Applied Psychology, 88,* 459–475.

55. Colquitt, J. A. (2004). Does the justice of the one interact with the justice of the many? Reactions to procedural justice in teams. *Journal of Applied Psychology, 89,* 633–646.

56. Scholtes, P. (1988). *The team handbook*. Madison, WI: Joiner Associates.

CHAPTER 13
Motivating Employees

FIGURE 13.1

Should managers use the carrot or the stick? Research has found that rewards are more effective than punishments in altering individual behavior.

© 2010 Jupiterimages Corporation

CHAPTER LEARNING OBJECTIVES

Reading this chapter will help you do the following:

1. Understand need-based theories of motivation.
2. Understand process-based theories of motivation.
3. Describe how fairness perceptions are determined and their consequences.
4. Learn to use performance appraisals in a motivational way.
5. Learn to apply organizational rewards in a motivational way.
6. Develop your personal motivation skills.

Motivation is defined as "the intention of achieving a goal, leading to goal-directed behavior."[1] When we refer to someone as being motivated, we mean that the person is trying hard to accomplish a certain task. Motivation is clearly important for someone to perform well. However, motivation alone is not sufficient. **Ability**—having the skills and knowledge required to perform the job—is also important and is sometimes the key determinant of effectiveness. Finally, environmental factors—having the resources, information, and support one needs to perform well—are also critical to determine performance.

motivation

The intention of achieving a goal, leading to goal-directed behavior.

ability

The characteristic of having the skills and knowledge required to perform the job.

FIGURE 13.2 The P-O-L-C Framework

Planning	Organizing	Leading	Controlling
1. Vision & Mission	1. Organization Design	1. Leadership	1. Systems/Processes
2. Strategizing	2. Culture	2. Decision Making	2. Strategic Human Resources
3. Goals & Objectives	3. Social Networks	3. Communications	
		4. Groups/Teams	
		5. Motivation	

What makes employees willing to "go the extra mile" to provide excellent service, market a company's products effectively, or achieve the goals set for them? Answering questions like these is of utmost importance to understand and manage the work behavior of our peers, subordinates, and even supervisors. As with many questions involving individuals, the answers are complex and there are several theories explaining the concept of motivation, as we will discuss in this chapter.

FIGURE 13.3

Motivation, ability, and environment are the major influences over employee performance

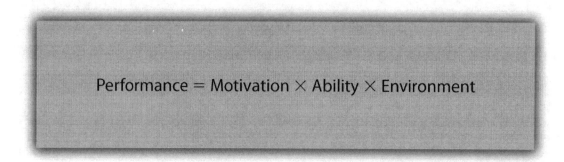

Performance = Motivation × Ability × Environment

Source: Mitchell, T. R. (1982). Motivation: New directions for theory, research, and practice. Academy of Management Review, 7, 80–88; Porter, L. W., & Lawler, E. E. (1968). Managerial attitudes and performance. Homewood, IL: Irwin.

1. NEED-BASED THEORIES OF MOTIVATION

LEARNING OBJECTIVES

1. Explain how employees are motivated according to Maslow's hierarchy of needs.
2. Explain how ERG theory addresses the limitations of Maslow's hierarchy.
3. Describe the difference between factors contributing to employee motivation and how these differ from factors contributing to dissatisfaction.
4. Describe the needs for achievement, power, and affiliation, and how these needs affect work behavior.

The earliest answer to motivation involved understanding individual needs. Specifically, early researchers thought that employees are motivated to satisfy their needs. For example, an employee who is always walking around the office talking to people may have a need for companionship and this behavior may be a way of satisfying that need. There are four major theories in the need-based category: Maslow's hierarchy of needs, ERG theory, Herzberg's dual factor theory, and McClelland's acquired needs theory.

1.1 Maslow's Hierarchy of Needs

Abraham Maslow is among the most prominent psychologists of the 20th century and the hierarchy of needs, accompanied by the pyramid representing how human needs are ranked, is an image familiar to many business students and managers. Maslow's theory is based on a simple premise: Human beings have needs that are hierarchically ranked.[2] There are some needs that are basic to all human beings, and in their absence, other needs are not considered. As we satisfy these basic needs, we start looking to satisfy higher-order needs. Once a lower-level need is satisfied, it no longer serves as a motivator.

The most basic of Maslow's needs are **physiological needs**. Physiological needs refer to the need for air, food, and water. Individuals that are hungry direct their behavior toward finding food. Once fed, the search for sustenance ceases and food no longer serves as a motivator. Once physiological needs are satisfied, people tend to become concerned about safety. Are they safe from danger, pain, or an uncertain future? One level up, social needs refer to the need to bond with other human beings, to be loved, and to form lasting attachments. In fact, having no attachments can negatively affect health and well-being.[3] The satisfaction of social needs makes **esteem needs** more salient. Esteem needs refer to the desire to be respected by one's peers, feeling important, and being appreciated. Finally, at the highest level of the hierarchy, the need for **self-actualization** refers to "becoming all you are capable of becoming." This need manifests itself by acquiring new skills, taking on new challenges, and behaving in a way that will lead to the satisfaction of one's life goals.

So, how can organizations satisfy their employees' various needs? By leveraging the various facets of the planning-organizing-leading-controlling (P-O-L-C) functions. In the long run, physiological needs may be satisfied by a paycheck, but it is important to remember that pay may satisfy other needs such as safety and esteem as well. Providing generous benefits, including health insurance and company-sponsored retirement plans, as well as offering a measure of job security, will help satisfy safety needs. Social needs may be satisfied by having a friendly environment, providing a workplace conducive to collaboration and communication with others. Company picnics and other social get-togethers may also be helpful if the majority of employees are motivated primarily by social needs (but may cause resentment if they are not and if they have to sacrifice a Sunday afternoon for a company picnic). Providing promotion opportunities at work, recognizing a person's accomplishments verbally or through more formal reward systems, and job titles that communicate to the employee that one has achieved high status within the organization are among the ways of satisfying esteem needs. Finally, self-actualization needs may be satisfied by providing development and growth opportunities on or off the job, as well as by assigning interesting and challenging work. By making the effort to satisfy the different needs each employee may have at a given time, organizations may ensure a more highly motivated workforce.

Maslow's hierarchy is a systematic way of thinking about the different needs employees may have at any given point and explains different reactions they may have to similar treatment. An employee who is trying to satisfy her esteem needs may feel gratified when her supervisor praises her. However, another employee who is trying to satisfy his social needs may resent being praised by upper management in front of peers if the praise sets him apart from the rest of the group.

physiological needs

The need for air, food, and water.

safety needs

The need to be safe from danger, pain, or an uncertain future.

social needs

The need to bond with other human beings, to be loved, and to form lasting attachments with them.

esteem needs

The desire to be respected by one's peers, feeling important, and being appreciated.

self-actualization

The quality of "becoming all you are capable of becoming."

FIGURE 13.4 Maslow's Hierarchy of Needs

Maslow's well-known theory argues that needs are arranged in a hierarchy where higher order needs cannot be satisfied until lower order needs have been met. Here, we illustrate this hierarchy.

Self-actualization refers to acquiring new skills that lead to satisfying one's life goals.

Esteem needs refer to the desire to be respected by one's peers, feel important, and be appreciated.

Social needs refer to the need for love, bonding, and lasting attachments.

Safety needs refer to safety from pain or danger.

Physiological needs refer to the need for air, food, and water.

© Thinkstock

1.2 ERG Theory

ERG theory of Clayton Alderfer is a modification of Maslow's hierarchy of needs.[4] Instead of the five needs that are hierarchically organized, Alderfer proposed that basic human needs may be grouped under three categories, namely, **Existence**, **Relatedness**, and **Growth**. Existence need corresponds to Maslow's physiological and safety needs, relatedness corresponds to social needs, and growth need refers to Maslow's esteem and self-actualization.

existence

This need corresponds to Maslow's physiological and safety needs.

relatedness

This need corresponds to social needs.

growth

This need refers to Maslow's esteem and self-actualization.

FIGURE 13.5 ERG Theory

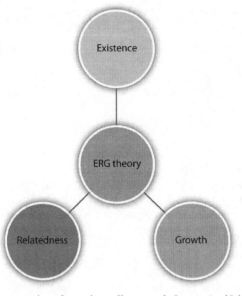

Source: Based on Alderfer, C. P. (1969). An empirical test of a new theory of human needs. Organizational Behavior and Human Performance, 4, 142–175.

ERG theory's main contribution to the literature is its relaxation of Maslow's assumptions. For example, ERG theory does not rank needs in any particular order and explicitly recognizes that more than one need may operate at a given time. Moreover, the theory has a "frustration-regression" hypothesis, suggesting that individuals who are frustrated in their attempts to satisfy one need may regress to another one. For example, someone who is frustrated by the lack of growth opportunities in his job and slow progress toward career goals may regress to relatedness needs and start spending more time socializing with one's coworkers. The implication of this theory is that we need to recognize the multiple needs that may be driving an individual at a given point to understand his behavior and to motivate him.

1.3 Two-Factor Theory

Frederick Herzberg approached the question of motivation by asking individuals what satisfies them on the job and what dissatisfies them. Herzberg came to the conclusion that aspects of the work environment that satisfy employees are very different from aspects that dissatisfy them.[5] Herzberg labeled factors causing dissatisfaction of workers as "hygiene" factors because these factors were part of the context in which the job was performed, as opposed to the job itself. **Hygiene factors** included company policies, supervision, working conditions, salary, safety, and security on the job. For example, if you are working in an unpleasant work environment where your office is too hot in the summer and too cold in the winter, or if you are being harassed and mistreated, you would likely be miserable. However, if these problems were solved (your office temperature is just right and you are not harassed at all), would you be motivated? Most likely, you would take the situation for granted. In fact, many factors in our work environment are things that we miss when they are absent, but take for granted if they are present.

hygiene factors

The factors that include company policies, supervision, working conditions, salary, safety, and security on the job.

motivators

The factors that are intrinsic to the job, such as achievement, recognition, interesting work, increased responsibilities, advancement, and growth opportunities.

In contrast, **motivators** are factors that are intrinsic to the job, such as achievement, recognition, interesting work, increased responsibilities, advancement, and growth opportunities. According to Herzberg's research, motivators, and not hygiene factors, are the conditions that truly motivate employees.

FIGURE 13.6 Two-Factor Theory of Motivation

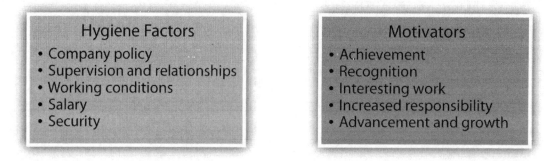

Source: Based on Herzberg, F., Mausner, B., & Snyderman, B. (1959). The motivation to work. New York: Wiley; Herzberg, F. (1965). The motivation to work among Finnish supervisors. Personnel Psychology, 18, 393–402.

FIGURE 13.7

At Hewlett-Packard, one of the most prestigious awards an employee can receive is the Golden Banana Award for technological innovation. This award began when an engineer came to his manager to report that he'd solved a challenging problem. The manager wanted to show his appreciation, looked around his desk, and found the banana he planned to eat for lunch. He handed the banana to the engineer while saying, "Well done! Congratulations!"

© *Thinkstock*

need for achievement

Having a strong need to be successful.

high need for affiliation

The need to be liked and accepted by others.

Herzberg's research, despite its intuitive appeal, has received its share of criticism.[6] One criticism relates to the classification of the factors as hygiene or motivator. For example, pay is viewed as a hygiene factor. However, pay is not necessarily a contextual factor and may have symbolic value by showing employees that they are being recognized for their contributions as well as communicating to them that they are advancing within the company. Similarly, quality of supervision or relationships employees form with their supervisors may determine whether they are assigned interesting work, whether they are recognized for their potential, and whether they take on more responsibilities. Despite its limitations, the two-factor theory can be a valuable aid to managers because it points out that improving the environment in which the job is performed goes only so far in motivating employees.

1.4 Acquired Needs Theory

Among the need-based approaches to motivation, Douglas McClelland's acquired needs theory is the one that has received the greatest amount of support. According to this theory, individuals acquire three types of needs as a result of their life experiences. These needs are need for achievement, need for affiliation, and need for power. All individuals possess a combination of these needs.

Those who have a high **need for achievement** have a strong need to be successful. A worker who derives great satisfaction from meeting deadlines, coming up with brilliant ideas, and planning his or her next career move may be high in need for achievement. Individuals high on need for achievement are well suited to positions such as sales where there are explicit goals, feedback is immediately available, and their effort often leads to success.[7] Because of their success in lower-level jobs, those with a high need for achievement are often promoted to higher-level positions.[8] However, a high need for achievement has important disadvantages in management. Management involves getting work done by motivating others. When a salesperson is promoted to be a sales manager, the job description changes from actively selling to recruiting, motivating, and training salespeople. Those who are high in need for achievement may view managerial activities such as coaching, communicating, and meeting with subordinates as a waste of time. Moreover, they enjoy doing things themselves and may find it difficult to delegate authority. They may become overbearing or micromanaging bosses, expecting everyone to be as dedicated to work as they are, and expecting subordinates to do things exactly the way they are used to doing.[9]

Individuals who have a **high need for affiliation** want to be liked and accepted by others. When given a choice, they prefer to interact with others and be with friends.[10] Their emphasis on harmonious interpersonal relationships may be an advantage in jobs and occupations requiring frequent interpersonal interaction, such as social worker or teacher. In managerial positions, a high need for affiliation may again serve as a disadvantage because these individuals tend to be overly concerned about how they are perceived by others. Thus, they may find it difficult to perform some aspects of a manager's job such as giving employees critical feedback or disciplining poor performers.

Finally, those with a high **need for power** want to influence others and control their environment. Need for power may be destructive of one's relationships if it takes the form of seeking and using power for one's own good and prestige. However, when it manifests itself in more altruistic forms, such as changing the way things are done so that the work environment is more positive or negotiating more resources for one's department, it tends to lead to positive outcomes. In fact, need for power is viewed as important for effectiveness in managerial and leadership positions.[11]

McClelland's theory of acquired needs has important implications for motivating employees. While someone who has a high need for achievement may respond to goals, those with a high need for affiliation may be motivated to gain the approval of their peers and supervisors, whereas those who have a high need for power may value gaining influence over the supervisor or acquiring a position that has decision-making authority. And, when it comes to succeeding in managerial positions, individuals who are aware of the drawbacks of their need orientation can take steps to overcome these drawbacks.

need for power

The desire to influence others and control their environment.

KEY TAKEAWAY

Need-based theories describe motivated behavior as individual efforts to meet needs. According to this perspective, the manager's job is to identify what people need and then to make sure that the work environment becomes a means of satisfying these needs. Maslow's hierarchy categorizes human needs into physiological, safety, social, esteem, and self-actualization needs. ERG theory is a modification of Maslow's hierarchy, where the five needs are collapsed into three categories (existence, relatedness, and growth). The two-factor theory differentiates between factors that make people dissatisfied on the job (hygiene factors) and factors that truly motivate employees. Finally, acquired-needs theory argues that individuals possess stable and dominant motives to achieve, acquire power, or affiliate with others. Each of these theories explains characteristics of a work environment that motivate employees.

EXERCISES

1. Many managers assume that if an employee is not performing well, the reason must be lack of motivation. What is the problem with this assumption?
2. Review Maslow's hierarchy of needs. Do you agree with the particular ranking of employee needs?
3. Review the hygiene factors and motivators in the two-factor theory. Are there any hygiene factors that you would consider to be motivators and vice versa?
4. A friend of yours is competitive, requires frequent and immediate feedback, and enjoys accomplishing things. She has recently been promoted to a managerial position and seeks your advice. What would you tell her?
5. Which motivation theory have you found to be most useful in explaining why people behave in a certain way? Why?

2.   PROCESS-BASED THEORIES

LEARNING OBJECTIVES

1. **Explain how employees evaluate the fairness of reward distributions.**
2. **List the three questions individuals consider when deciding whether to put forth effort at work.**
3. **Describe how managers can use learning and reinforcement principles to motivate employees.**
4. **Learn the role that job design plays in motivating employees.**
5. **Describe why goal setting motivates employees.**

In contrast to the need-based theories we have covered so far, process-based theories view motivation as a rational process. Individuals analyze their environment, develop reactions and feelings, and react in certain ways. Under this category, we will review equity theory, expectancy theory, and reinforcement theory. We will also discuss the concepts of job design and goal setting as motivational strategies.

2.1 Equity Theory

Imagine you are paid $10 an hour working as an office assistant and you have held this job for six months. You are very good at what you do, coming up with creative ways to make things easier in the workplace, and you are a good colleague, willing to help others. You stay late when necessary and are flexible if asked to rearrange priorities or work hours. Now imagine that you find out your manager is hiring another employee who is going to work with you, hold the same job title, and perform the same types of tasks. This employee has more advanced computer skills, but it is unclear whether these will be used on the job. The starting pay for the new hire will be $14 an hour. How would you feel? Would you be as motivated as before, going above and beyond your duties?

If your reaction to this scenario was along the lines of "I would think it's unfair," your feelings may be explained using equity theory.[12] According to this theory, individuals are motivated by a sense of fairness in their interactions. Moreover, our sense of fairness is a result of the social comparisons we make. Specifically, we compare our inputs and outputs with someone else's inputs and outputs. We perceive fairness if we believe that the input-to-output ratio we are bringing into the situation is similar to the input/output ratio of a comparison person, or a **referent**. Perceptions of inequity create tension within us and drive us to action that will reduce perceived inequity. This process is illustrated in Figure 13.8.

What Are Inputs and Outputs?

Inputs are the contributions the person feels he or she is making to the environment. In the previous example, hard work, loyalty to the organization, number of months worked, level of education, training, and skills may have been relevant inputs. Outputs are the rewards the person feels he or she is receiving from the situation. The $10 an hour was a salient output. There may be other outputs, such as the benefits received or the treatment one gets from the boss.

FIGURE 13.8 The Equity Formula

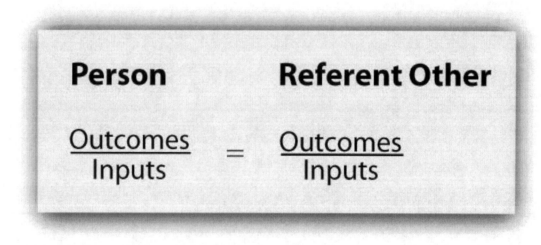

Source: Based on Adams, J. S. (1965). Inequity in social exchange. In L. Berkowitz (Ed.), Advances in experimental social psychology (Vol. 2, pp. 267–299). New York: Academic Press.

We should emphasize that equity perceptions develop as a result of a subjective process. Different people may look at exactly the same situation and perceive different levels of equity. For example, another person may look at the same scenario and decide that the situation is fair because the new hire has computer skills and the company is paying extra for these skills.

Who Is the Referent?

The referent other may be a specific person or an entire category of people. For example, some might look at want ads for entry-level clerical workers and see whether the pay offered is in the $10 per hour range; in this case, the referent other is the category of entry-level clerical workers, including office assistants, in the local area. Referents should be comparable to us—otherwise the comparison is not meaningful. It would be illogical for entry-level employees to compare themselves to the CEO of the company given the differences in the nature of inputs and outcomes. Instead, individuals logically compare themselves to those performing similar tasks within the same organization or a different organization.

Reactions to Unfairness

The theory outlines several potential reactions to perceived inequity, which are summarized in Figure 13.10. Oftentimes, the situation may be dealt with perceptually, by *distorting our perceptions of our own or referent's inputs and outputs*. For example, individuals may justify the situation by downplaying their own inputs ("I don't really work very hard on this job"), valuing the outputs more highly ("I am gaining valuable work experience, so the situation is not that bad"), distorting the other person's inputs ("He really is more competent than I am and deserves to be paid more"), or distorting the other person's outputs ("He gets $14 but will have to work with a lousy manager, so the situation is not unfair").

Another way of addressing perceived inequity is to *reduce one's own inputs or increase one's own outputs*. If individuals reduce their efforts, perceived inequity can be reduced. Indeed, research shows that people who perceive inequity tend to reduce their work performance or reduce the quality of their inputs.[13] Increasing one's outputs can be achieved through legitimate means such as negotiating a pay raise. At the same time, research shows that those feeling inequity sometimes resort to stealing to balance the scales.[14] Other options include *changing the comparison person* (for example, you may learn that others doing similar work in different organizations are paid only minimum wage) and *leaving the situation* by quitting one's job.[15] We might even consider taking legal action as a potential outcome of perceived inequity. For example, if you find out that the main reason behind a pay gap is gender, you may react to the situation by taking legal action because sex discrimination in pay is illegal in the United States.

FIGURE 13.9

The concept of equity helps explain aggressive negotiations in professional sports, such as Alex Rodriquez' 10-year contract that pays more than $27 million annually.

Source: http://en.wikipedia.org/wiki/File:Alex_Rodriguez_2008-04-19.jpg

FIGURE 13.10 Potential Responses to Inequity

Reactions to inequity	Example
Distort perceptions	Changing one's thinking to believe that the referent actually is more skilled than previously thought
Increase referent's inputs	Encouraging the referent to work harder
Reduce own input	Deliberately putting forth less effort at work. Reducing the quality of one's work
Increase own outcomes	Negotiating a raise for oneself or using unethical ways of increasing rewards such as stealing from the company
Change referent	Comparing oneself to someone who is worse off
Leave the situation	Quitting one's job
Seek legal action	Suing the company or filing a complaint if the unfairness in question is under legal protection

Source: Based on research findings reported in Carrell, M. R., & Dittrich, J. E. (1978). Equity theory: The recent literature, methodological considerations, and new directions. Academy of Management Review, 3, 202–210; Goodman, P. S., & Friedman, A. (1971). An examination of Adams's theory of inequity. Administrative Science Quarterly, 16, 271–288; Greenberg, J. (1993). Stealing in the name of justice: Informational and interpersonal moderators of theft reactions to underpayment inequity. Organizational Behavior and Human Decision Processes, 54, 81–103; Schmidt, D. R., & Marwell, G. (1972). Withdrawal and reward reallocation as responses to inequity. Journal of Experimental Social Psychology, 8, 207–211.

Overpayment Inequity

What would you do if you felt you were overrewarded? Originally, equity theory proposed that overrewarded individuals would experience guilt and would increase their effort to restore perceptions of equity. However, research does not provide support for this argument. Instead, it seems that individuals experience less distress as a result of being overrewarded.[16] It is not hard to imagine that individuals find perceptual ways to deal with a situation like this, such as believing that they have more skills and bring more to the situation compared with the referent person. Therefore, research does not support equity theory's predictions with respect to people who are overpaid.[17]

Individual Differences in Reactions to Inequity

Equity theory assumes that once people feel that a situation is inequitable they are motivated to react. However, does inequity disturb everyone equally? Researchers identified a personality trait that explains different reactions to inequity and named this trait **equity sensitivity**.[18] Equity sensitive individuals experience distress when they feel they are overrewarded or underrewarded and expect to maintain equitable relationships. At the same time, there are some individuals who are **benevolents** who give without waiting to receive much in return and **entitleds** who expect to receive a lot without giving much in return. Thus, the theory is more useful in explaining the behavior of equity sensitive individuals, and organizations will need to pay particular attention to how these individuals view their relationships.

Fairness beyond Equity: Procedural and Interactional Justice

Equity theory looks at perceived fairness as a motivator. However, the way equity theory defines fairness is limited to fairness regarding rewards. Starting in the 1970s, researchers of workplace fairness began taking a broader view of justice. Equity theory deals with outcome fairness, and therefore, it is considered to be a distributive justice theory. **Distributive justice** refers to the degree to which the outputs received from the organization are fair. Two other types of fairness have been identified: procedural justice and interactional justice.

Let's assume that you found out you are getting a promotion that will include a pay raise, increased responsibilities, and prestige. If you feel you deserve to be promoted, you would perceive high distributive justice ("getting the promotion is fair"). However, if you later found out that the department manager picked your name randomly out of a hat, how would you feel? You might still like the outcome but feel that the decision-making process was unfair since it was not performance based. This response would involve feelings of procedural injustice. **Procedural justice** refers to the degree to which fair decision-making procedures are used. Research shows that employees care about procedural justice for many organizational decisions, including layoffs, employee selection, surveillance of employees, performance appraisals, and pay decisions.[19] They tend to care about procedural justice particularly when they do not get the outcome they feel they deserve.[20] If you do not get the promotion and find out that management chose the candidate by picking a name out of a hat, you may view this as adding insult to injury. When people do not get the rewards they want, they tend to hold management responsible if procedures are not fair.[21]

Research has identified many ways of achieving procedural justice. For example, giving employees *advance notice* before laying them off, firing them, or disciplining them is perceived as fairer.[22] *Allowing employees' voices into decision making* is also important.[23] When designing a performance appraisal system or implementing reorganization, asking employees for their input may be a good idea because it increases perceptions of fairness. Even when it is not possible to have employees participate, providing *explanations* is helpful in fostering procedural justice.[24] Finally, people expect *consistency* in treatment.[25] If one person is given extra time when taking a test while another is not, individuals would perceive decision making as unfair.

---

equity sensitivity

A personality trait that explains different reactions to inequity.

benevolents

Individuals who give without waiting to receive much in return.

entitleds

Individuals who expect to receive a lot without giving much in return.

distributive justice

The degree to which the outcomes received from the organization are fair.

procedural justice

The degree to which fair decision-making procedures are used to arrive at a decision.

FIGURE 13.11

The idea that "justice is blind" refers to the notion that procedural justice is applied to all who enter the U.S. legal system.

Now let's imagine your boss telling you that you are getting a promotion. The manager uses these exact words: "Yes, we are giving you the promotion. The job is so simple that we thought even you can handle it." Now what is your reaction? The unpleasant feelings you may now experience are explained by interactional justice. **Interactional justice** refers to the degree to which people are treated with respect, kindness, and dignity in interpersonal interactions. We expect to be treated with dignity by our peers, supervisors, and customers. When the opposite happens, we feel angry. Even when faced with negative outcomes such as a pay cut, being treated with dignity and respect serves as a buffer and alleviates our stress.[26]

Employers would benefit from paying attention to all three types of justice perceptions. In addition to being the right thing to do, justice perceptions lead to outcomes companies care about. Injustice is directly harmful to employee psychological health and well-being and contributes to stress.[27] High levels of justice create higher levels of employee commitment to organizations, are related to higher job performance, higher levels of organizational citizenship (behaviors that are not part of one's job description but help the organization in other ways such as speaking positively about the company and helping others), and higher levels of customer satisfaction, whereas low levels of justice lead to retaliation and supporting union certification movements.[28]

2.2 Expectancy Theory

Expectancy theory argues that individual motivation to put forth more or less effort is determined by a rational calculation.[29] According to this theory, individuals ask themselves three questions.

FIGURE 13.12 Summary of Expectancy Theory

Source: Based on Porter, L. W., & Lawler, E. E. (1968). Managerial attitudes and performance. Homewood, IL: Irwin; Vroom, V. H. (1964). Work and motivation. New York: Wiley.

The first question is whether the person believes that high levels of effort will lead to desired outcomes. This perception is labeled as **expectancy**. For example, do you believe that the effort you put forth in a class is related to learning worthwhile material and receiving a good grade? If you do, you are more likely to put forth effort.

The second question is the degree to which the person believes that performance is related to secondary outcomes such as rewards. This perception is labeled as **instrumentality**. For example, do you believe that passing the class is related to rewards such as getting a better job, or gaining approval from your instructor, from your friends, or parents? If you do, you are more likely to put forth effort.

Finally, individuals are also concerned about the value of the rewards awaiting them as a result of performance. The anticipated satisfaction that will result from an outcome is labeled as **valence**. For example, do you value getting a better job or gaining approval from your instructor, friends, or parents? If these outcomes are desirable to you, you are more likely to put forth effort.

As a manager, how can you influence these perceptions to motivate employees? In fact, managers can influence all three perceptions.[30] To influence their expectancy perceptions, managers may train their employees, or hire people who are qualified for the jobs in question. Low expectancy may also be due to employees feeling that something other than effort predicts performance, such as political behaviors on the part of employees. In this case, clearing the way to performance and creating an environment in which employees do not feel blocked will be helpful. The first step in influencing instrumentality is to connect pay and other rewards to performance using bonuses, award systems, and merit pay. Publicizing any contests or award programs is helpful in bringing rewards to the awareness of employees. It is also important to highlight that performance and not something else is being rewarded. For example, if a company has an employee-of-the-month award that is rotated among employees, employees are unlikely to believe that performance is being rewarded. In the name of being egalitarian, such a reward system may actually hamper the motivation of highest performing employees by eroding instrumentality. Finally, to influence valence, managers will need to find out what their employees

interactional justice

The degree to which people are treated with respect, kindness, and dignity in interpersonal interactions.

expectancy

The extent to which a person believes that high levels of effort will lead to outcomes of interest such as performance or success.

instrumentality

The degree to which the person believes that performance is related to secondary outcomes such as rewards.

valence

The value of the rewards awaiting the person as a result of performance.

value. This can be done by talking to employees, or surveying them about what rewards they find valuable.

2.3 Reinforcement Theory

Reinforcement theory is based on the work of Ivan Pavlov in behavioral conditioning and the later work B. F. Skinner did on operant conditioning.[31] According to reinforcement theory, behavior is a function of its consequences. Imagine that even though no one asked you to, you stayed late and drafted a report. When the manager found out, she was ecstatic and took you out to lunch and thanked you genuinely. The consequences following your good deed were favorable, and therefore you are more likely to do similar good deeds in the future. In contrast, if your manager had said nothing about it and ignored the sacrifice you made, you would be less likely to demonstrate similar behaviors in the future, or your behavior would likely become extinct.

Despite the simplicity of reinforcement theory, how many times have you seen positive behavior ignored or, worse, negative behavior rewarded? In many organizations, this is a familiar scenario. People go above and beyond the call of duty, and yet their behaviors are ignored or criticized. People with disruptive habits may receive no punishments because the manager is afraid of the reaction the person will give when confronted. They may even receive rewards such as promotions so that the person is transferred to a different location and becomes someone else's problem. Moreover, it is common for people to be rewarded for the wrong kind of behavior. Steven Kerr labeled this phenomenon as "the folly of rewarding A while hoping for B."[32] For example, a company may make public statements about the importance of quality. Yet, they choose to reward shipments on time regardless of the number of known defects contained in the shipments. As a result, employees are more likely to ignore quality and focus on hurrying the delivery process.

FIGURE 13.13 Reinforcement Methods

While motivating employees is a far cry from training a puppy, much can be learned from understanding the principles of reinforcement theory that apply to both. Here, we discuss applications to people and puppies.

Positive reinforcement refers to adding a reward following good behavior. Puppies enjoy treats while employees favor praise or cold, hard cash.

Negative reinforcement refers to removing a deterrent after good behavior is established. Removing the leash from a puppy who has learned to not run away is valued, much like well-trained employees may value not being watched over their shoulder once they prove their competence.

Extinction refers to actively ignoring or otherwise not rewarding bad behavior. Ignore a puppy when they bark needlessly and they just might stop. The same trick works with ignoring employees who stop by your office to chat for no reason.

Punishment refers to adding a negative consequence following bad behavior. Tap a puppy on the nose if he tries to bite, or issue a written warning for poor employee behavior.

Source: From FWK Atlas Black: The Complete Adventure graphic novel.

Reinforcement Interventions

Reinforcement theory describes four interventions to modify employee behavior. Two of these are methods of increasing the frequency of desired behaviors while the remaining two are methods of reducing the frequency of undesired behaviors.

Positive reinforcement is a method of increasing the desired behavior.[33] Positive reinforcement involves making sure that behavior is met with positive consequences. Praising an employee for treating a customer respectfully is an example of positive reinforcement. If the praise immediately follows the positive behavior, the employee will see a link between behavior and positive consequences and will be motivated to repeat similar behaviors.

Negative reinforcement is also used to increase the desired behavior. Negative reinforcement involves removal of unpleasant outcomes once desired behavior is demonstrated. Nagging an employee to complete a report is an example of negative reinforcement. The negative stimulus in the environment will remain present until positive behavior is demonstrated. The problem with negative reinforcement may be that the negative stimulus may lead to unexpected behaviors and may fail to stimulate the desired behavior. For example, the person may start avoiding the manager to avoid being nagged.

Extinction occurs when a behavior ceases as a result of receiving no reinforcement. For example, suppose an employee has an annoying habit of forwarding e-mail jokes to everyone in the department, cluttering up people's in-boxes and distracting them from their work. Commenting about the jokes, whether in favorable or unfavorable terms, may be encouraging the person to keep forwarding them. Completely ignoring the jokes may reduce their frequency.

Punishment is another method of reducing the frequency of undesirable behaviors. Punishment involves presenting negative consequences following unwanted behaviors. Giving an employee a warning for consistently being late to work is an example of punishment.

FIGURE 13.15

Properly designed sales commissions are widely used to motivate sales employees. The blend of straight salary and commissions should be carefully balanced to achieve optimum sales volume, profitability, and customer satisfaction.

© Thinkstock

positive reinforcement

Reinforcement that involves making sure that behavior is met with positive consequences.

negative reinforcement

Reinforcement that involves removal of unpleasant outcomes once desired behavior is demonstrated.

extinction

The removal of rewards following negative behavior.

punishment

The presentation of negative consequences following unwanted behaviors.

FIGURE 13.14
Principles of Punishment

McGregor's "hot stove rule" argues that punishment should be akin to touching a hot stove, where the result it severe, immediate, enforced with warning, and applied consistently and impartially.

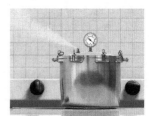

© Thinkstock

Reinforcement Schedules

In addition to types of reinforcements, the timing or schedule on which reinforcement is delivered has a bearing on behavior.[34] Reinforcement is presented on a **continuous schedule** if reinforcers follow all instances of positive behavior. An example of a continuous schedule would be giving an employee a sales commission every time he or she makes a sale. **Fixed ratio schedules** involve providing rewards every nth time the right behavior is demonstrated, for example, giving the employee a bonus for every 10th sale he or she makes. **Fixed interval schedules** involve providing a reward after a specified period of time, such as giving a sales bonus once a month regardless of how many sales have been made. **Variable ratio** involves a random pattern, such as giving a sales bonus every time the manager is in a good mood.

A systematic way in which reinforcement theory principles are applied is called Organizational Behavior Modification (or **OB Mod**).[35] This is a systematic application of reinforcement theory to modify employee behaviors. The model consists of five stages. The process starts with identifying the behavior that will be modified. Let's assume that we are interested in reducing absenteeism among employees. In step 2, we need to measure the baseline level of absenteeism. In step 3, the behavior's antecedents and consequences are determined. Why are employees absent? More importantly, what is happening when an employee is absent? If the behavior is being unintentionally rewarded, we may expect these to reinforce absenteeism behavior. For example, suppose that absences peak each month on the days when a departmental monthly report is due, meaning that coworkers and supervisors must do extra work to prepare the report. To reduce the frequency of absenteeism, it will be necessary to think of financial or social incentives to follow positive behavior and negative consequences to follow negative behavior. In step 4, an intervention is implemented. Removing the positive consequences of negative behavior may be an effective way of dealing with the situation, for example, starting the monthly report preparation a few days earlier, or letting employees know that if they are absent when the monthly report is being prepared, their contribution to the report will be submitted as incomplete until they finish it. Punishments may be used in persistent cases. Finally, in step 5 the behavior is measured periodically and maintained. Studies examining the effectiveness of OB Mod have been supportive of the model in general. A review of the literature found that OB Mod interventions resulted in an average of 17% improvement in performance.[36]

FIGURE 13.16 Timing Is Everything: Utilizing Reinforcement Schedules

The timing (often referred to as a schedule) with which reinforcement is delivered has a bearing on the ensuing behavior. Here, we illustrate different reinforcement schedules.

A **continuous schedule** *reinforces all instances of positive behavior.*

Wise parents stock up on stickers and other rewards to utilize this schedule when potty training their children.

Some companies ring a bell to provide positive feedback or give employees a sales commission every time a sale is made.

Fixed ratio schedules *involve providing rewards every nth time the right behavior is demonstrated.*

Some hair salons hoping to keep regular customers often give away a free haircut after every 10th haircut.

Some companies give an employee a bonus for every 10 sales made.

Fixed interval schedules *involve providing a reward after a specified period of time.*

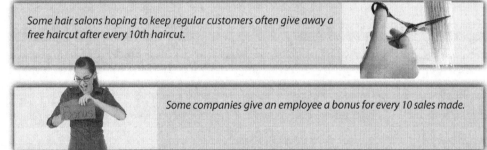

Estée Lauder was the first company to provide a "gift with purchase" certain times of the year to increase cosmetics sales.

Many employers provide an end-of-the-year bonus to align with the holiday season.

Variable ratio *involves a random pattern.*

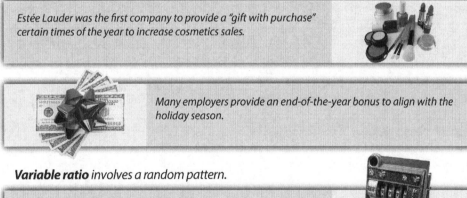

Casino slot machines pay out on a variable ratio schedule to provide an element of chance to their patrons.

Firms that provide a sales bonus every time the manager is in a good mood use this schedule at their own risk.

© *Thinkstock*

2.4   Job Design

Many of us assume that the most important motivator at work would be pay. Yet, studies point to a different factor as the primary influence over worker motivation: job design. How a job is designed has a major impact on employee motivation, job satisfaction, commitment to organization, as well as absenteeism and turnover. Job design is just one of the many organizational design decisions managers must make when engaged in the organizing function.

The question of how to properly design jobs so that employees are more productive and more satisfied has received managerial and research attention since the beginning of the 20th century.

Scientific Management and Job Specialization

job specialization

Breaking down tasks to their simplest components and assigning them to employees so that each person would perform few tasks in a repetitive manner.

Perhaps the earliest attempt to design jobs was presented by Frederick Taylor in his 1911 book *Principles of Scientific Management*. Scientific management proposed a number of ideas that have been influential in job design. One idea was to minimize waste by identifying the best method to perform the job to ensure maximum efficiency. Another one of the major advances of scientific management was **job specialization**, which entails breaking down tasks to their simplest components and assigning them to employees so that each person would perform few tasks in a repetitive manner. While this technique may be very efficient in terms of automation and standardization, from a motivational perspective, these jobs will be boring and repetitive and therefore associated with negative outcomes such as absenteeism.[37] Job specialization is also an ineffective way of organizing jobs in rapidly changing environments where employees close to the problem should modify their approach based on the demands of the situation.[38]

FIGURE 13.17

This Ford panel assembly line in Berlin, Germany, is an example of specialization. Each person on the line has a different job.

© 2010 Jupiterimages Corporation

job rotation

Moving employees from job to job at regular intervals.

Rotation, Job Enlargement, and Enrichment

One of the early alternatives to job specialization was **job rotation**, which involves moving employees from job to job at regular intervals, thereby relieving the monotony and boredom typical in repetitive jobs. For example, Maids International, a company that provides cleaning services to households and businesses, uses job rotation such that maids cleaning the kitchen in one house would clean the bedroom in another house.[39] Using this technique, among others, the company was able to reduce its turnover level. In a study conducted in a supermarket, cashiers were rotated to work in different departments. As a result of the rotation, employee stress level was reduced as measured by their blood pressure. Moreover, they reported fewer pain symptoms in their neck and shoulders.[40]

Job rotation has a number of advantages for organizations. It is an effective way for employees to acquire new skills, as the rotation involves cross-training to new tasks; this means that organizations increase the overall skill level of their employees.[41] In addition, job rotation is a means of knowledge transfer between departments. An interesting side effect of job rotation in some jobs is increased accountability and more ethical behavior. For example, loan officers tend to prepare more accurate and honest reports about their own performance when they anticipate rotation, presumably because they do not want their bad decisions to be exposed by their successor.[42] For employees, rotation is a benefit because they acquire new skills, which keeps them marketable in the long run.

Anecdotal evidence suggests that companies successfully rotate high-level employees to train their managers and increase innovativeness in the company. For example, Marriott International uses strategic movement of management trainees within a property (e.g., from banquet to sales), as well as among its 3,000 lodging properties in 70 countries, to prepare them for future assignments.[43] India's information technology giant Wipro, which employs about 119,000 employees, uses a three-year plan to groom future leaders of the company by rotating them through different jobs.[44]

job enlargement

Expanding the tasks performed by employees to add more variety.

Job enlargement refers to expanding the tasks performed by employees to add more variety. Like job rotation, job enlargement can reduce boredom and monotony as well as use human resources more effectively. When jobs are enlarged, employees view themselves as being capable of performing a broader set of tasks.[45] Job enlargement is positively related to employee satisfaction and higher-quality customer services, and it increases the chances of catching mistakes.[46] At the same time, the effects of job enlargement may depend on the *type* of enlargement. For example, exclusively giving employees simpler tasks had negative consequences on employee satisfaction with the job of catching errors, whereas giving employees more tasks that require them to be knowledgeable in different areas seemed to have more positive effects.[47]

job enrichment

A job redesign technique that allows workers more control over how they perform their own tasks.

Job enrichment is a job redesign technique that allows workers more control over how they perform their own tasks, giving them more responsibility over their jobs. As an alternative to job specialization, companies using job enrichment may experience positive outcomes such as reduced turnover, increased productivity, and reduced absences.[48] This may be because employees who have the authority and responsibility over their own work can be more efficient, eliminate unnecessary tasks, take shortcuts, and overall increase their own performance. At the same time, there is some evidence that job enrichment may sometimes cause employees to be dissatisfied.[49] The reason may be that employees who are given additional autonomy and responsibility may expect greater levels of pay or other types of compensation, and if this expectation is not met, they may feel frustrated. One more thing to remember is that job enrichment may not be suitable for all employees.[50] Not all employees desire to have control over how they work, and if they do not have this desire, they may feel dissatisfied in an enriched job.

A recent approach to job enrichment is job crafting. **Job crafting** refers to the changes employees make to their own job description—expanding certain elements that are a better fit to their own personality or reducing the scope of the job to achieve better work-life balance—all in the service of better meeting the employees' career and life goals. The idea behind job crafting is that oftentimes employees are not passive recipients of their roles and instead take an active role in shaping their own job roles and responsibilities to fit the realities of their interests, passions, and goals. Not all jobs allow job crafting, but some organizations are increasingly encouraging employees to take on an active role in the shaping of job descriptions. As an example, Deloitte employees may renegotiate their roles with management to increase or decrease the scope and visibility of the projects they take on or increase the flexibility of their work hours.[51]

job crafting

Proactive changes employees make in their own job descriptions.

Job Characteristics Model

The **job characteristics model** is one of the most influential attempts to design jobs to increase their motivational properties.[52] Proposed in the 1970s by Hackman and Oldham, the model describes five core job dimensions, leading to three critical psychological states, which lead to work-related outcomes. In this model, shown in Figure 13.18, there are five core job dimensions.

job characteristics model

A model that describes five core job dimensions leading to three critical psychological states, which lead to work-related outcomes.

FIGURE 13.18 Job Characteristics Model

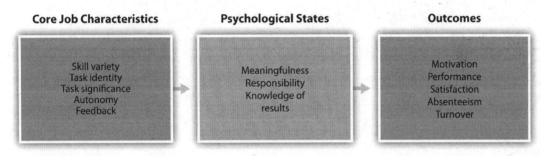

Source: Adapted from Hackman, J. R., & Oldham, G. R. (1975). Development of the job diagnostic survey. Journal of Applied Psychology, 60, 159–170.

Skill variety refers to the extent to which the job requires the person to use multiple high-level skills. A car wash employee whose job consists of directing cars into the automated car wash demonstrates low levels of skill variety, whereas a car wash employee who acts as a cashier, maintains car wash equipment, and manages the inventory of chemicals demonstrates higher skill variety.

skill variety

The extent to which the job requires the person to use multiple high-level skills.

Task identity refers to the degree to which the person completes a piece of work from start to finish. A Web designer who designs parts of a Web site will have low task identity because the work blends in with other Web designers' work, and in the end, it will be hard for the person to claim responsibility for the final output. The Webmaster who designs the entire Web site will have higher task identity.

task identity

The degree to which the person is in charge of completing an identifiable piece of work from start to finish.

Task significance refers to whether the person's job substantially affects other people's work, health, or well-being. A janitor who cleans the floor at an office building may find the job low in significance, thinking it is not an important job. However, janitors cleaning the floors at a hospital may see their role as essential in helping patients recover in a healthy environment. When they see their tasks as significant, employees tend to feel that they are making an impact on their environment and their feelings of self-worth are boosted.[53]

task significance

The degree to which the person's job substantially affects other people's work, health, or well-being.

Autonomy is the degree to which the person has the freedom to decide how to perform tasks. As an example, a restaurant chef working in a small restaurant who has control over the menu, concept, and pricing will have greater autonomy compared to a chef who is working in a chain restaurant who oversees the cooking process without having control over the taste of food, how it is cooked, or where ingredients are acquired from. Autonomy increases motivation at work, but it also has other benefits. Autonomous workers are less likely to adopt a "this is not my job" attitude and instead be proactive and creative.[54] Giving employees autonomy is also a great way to train them on the job. For example, Gucci's former CEO Robert Polet describes the autonomy he received while working at Unilever as the key to his development of leadership talents.[55]

autonomy

The degree to which the person has the freedom to decide how to perform one's tasks.

Feedback refers to the degree to which the person learns how effective he or she is at work. Feedback may come from other people such as supervisors, peers, subordinates, customers, or from the job. A salesperson who makes informational presentations to potential clients but is not informed whether they sign up has low feedback. If this salesperson receives a notification whenever someone who has heard his presentation becomes a client, feedback will be high.

feedback

The degree to which the person learns how effective he or she is being at work.

The mere presence of feedback is not sufficient for employees to feel motivated to perform better, however. In fact, in about one-third of the cases, feedback was detrimental to performance.[56] In addition to whether feedback is present, the character of the feedback (positive or negative), whether the person is ready to receive the feedback, and the manner in which feedback was given will all determine whether employees feel motivated or demotivated as a result of feedback.

2.5 Goal Setting Theory

Goal setting theory[57] is one of the most influential theories of motivation. It has been supported in over 1,000 studies with employees, ranging from blue-collar workers to research and development employees, and there is strong evidence that setting goals is related to performance improvements.[58] In fact, according to one estimate, goal setting improves performance between 10% and 25% or more.[59] On the basis of evidence such as this, thousands of companies around the world are using goal setting in some form, including companies such as Coca-Cola, PricewaterhouseCoopers, Nike, Intel, and Microsoft to name a few.

Setting SMART Goals

The mere presence of a goal does not motivate individuals. Think about New Year's resolutions that many individuals fail to keep. Some decided they should lose some weight but then never put a concrete plan in action. Others decided that they would read more but didn't. Why did 97% of those who set New Year's resolutions fail to meet their goals?

SMART

A goal that is specific, measurable, aggressive/achievable, realistic, and timely.

Accumulating research evidence indicates that effective goals are SMART. SMART goals are specific, measurable, aggressive/achievable, realistic, and timely. Here is a sample SMART goal: Walmart recently set a goal to eliminate 20 million metric tons of greenhouse gas emissions from its supply chain by the year 2015. This goal meets all the conditions of being SMART if we assume that it is an aggressive and achievable goal.[60] Even though it seems like a simple concept, in reality many goals that are set within organizations may not be SMART. For example, Microsoft recently conducted an audit of its goal-setting and performance review system and found that only about 40% of the goals were specific and measurable.[61]

Why Do SMART Goals Motivate?

FIGURE 13.19

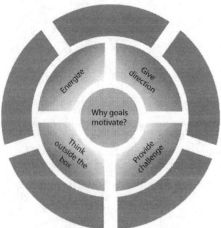

Source: Based on information contained in Latham, G. P. (2004). The motivational benefits of goal setting. Academy of Management Executive, 18, 126–129; Seijts, G. H., & Latham, G. P. (2005). Learning versus performance goals: When should each be used? Academy of Management Executive, 19, 124–131; Shaw, K. N. (2004). Changing the goal-setting process at Microsoft. Academy of Management Executive, 18, 139–142.

There are at least four reasons why goals motivate.[62] First, goals give us direction; therefore, goals should be set carefully. Giving employees goals that are not aligned with company goals will be a problem because goals will direct employee's energy to a certain end. Second, goals energize people and tell them not to stop until they reach that point. Third, having a goal provides a challenge. When people have goals and when they reach them, they feel a sense of accomplishment. Finally, SMART goals urge people to think outside the box and rethink how they are working. If a goal is substantially difficult, merely working harder will not get you the results. Instead, you will need to rethink the way you usually work and devise a creative way of working. It has been argued that this is how designers and engineers in Japan came up with the bullet train. Having a goal that went way beyond the current speed of trains prevented engineers from making minor improvements and urged them to come up with a radically different concept.[63]

Are There Downsides to Goal Setting?

As with any management technique, there may be some downsides to goal setting.[64] First, setting goals for specific outcomes may hamper employee performance if employees lack skills and abilities to reach the goals. In these situations, setting goals for behaviors and for learning may be more effective than setting goals for outcomes. Second, goal setting may motivate employees to focus on a goal and ignore the need to respond to new challenges. For example, one study found that when teams had difficult goals and when employees within the team had high levels of performance orientation, teams had difficulty adapting to unforeseen circumstances.[65] Third, goals focus employee attention on the activities that are measured, which may lead to sacrificing other important elements of performance. When goals are set for production numbers, quality may suffer. As a result, it is important to set goals touching on all critical aspects of performance. Finally, aggressive pursuit of goals may lead to unethical behaviors. Particularly when employees are rewarded for goal accomplishment but there are no rewards whatsoever for coming very close to reaching the goal, employees may be tempted to cheat.

None of these theories are complete by themselves, but each theory provides us with a framework we can use to analyze, interpret, and manage employee behaviors in the workplace, which are important skills managers use when conducting their leading function. In fact, motivation is important throughout the entire P-O-L-C framework because most managerial functions involve accomplishing tasks and goals through others.

KEY TAKEAWAY

Process-based theories use the mental processes of employees as the key to understanding employee motivation. According to equity theory, employees are demotivated when they view reward distribution as unfair. In addition to distributive justice, research identified two other types of fairness (procedural and interactional), which also affect worker reactions and motivation. According to expectancy theory, employees are motivated when they believe that their effort will lead to high performance (expectancy), that their performance will lead to outcomes (instrumentality), and that the outcomes following performance are desirable (valence). Reinforcement theory argues that behavior is a function of its consequences. By properly tying rewards to positive behaviors, eliminating rewards following negative behaviors, and punishing negative behaviors, leaders can increase the frequency of desired behaviors. In job design, there are five components that increase the motivating potential of a job: skill variety, task identity, task significance, autonomy, and feedback. These theories are particularly useful in designing reward systems within a company. Goal-setting theory is one of the most influential theories of motivation. To motivate employees, goals should be SMART (specific, measurable, aggressive/achievable, realistic, and timely). Setting goals and objectives is a task managers undertake when involved in the planning portion of the P-O-L-C function.

EXERCISES

1. Your manager tells you that the best way of ensuring fairness in reward distribution is to keep the pay a secret. How would you respond to this assertion?
2. What are the distinctions among procedural, interactional, and distributive justice? List ways in which you could increase each of these justice perceptions.
3. Using an example from your own experience in school or at work, explain the concepts of expectancy, instrumentality, and valence.
4. Some practitioners and researchers consider OB Mod as unethical because it may be viewed as employee manipulation. What would be your reaction to this criticism?
5. Consider a job you held in the past. Analyze the job using the framework of job characteristics model.
6. If a manager tells you to "sell as much as you can," is this goal likely to be effective? Why or why not?

3. DEVELOPING YOUR PERSONAL MOTIVATION SKILLS

LEARNING OBJECTIVES

1. **Understand what you can do to give feedback through an effective performance appraisal.**
2. **Learn guidelines for proactively seeking feedback.**

3.1 Guidelines for Giving Feedback in a Performance Appraisal Meeting

Before the meeting, ask the person to complete a self-appraisal. This is a great way of making sure that employees become active participants in the process and are heard. Complete the performance appraisal form and document your rating using several examples. Be sure that your review covers the entire time since the last review, not just recent events. Be sure that you devote sufficient time to each meeting. If you schedule too many meetings back to back, you may lose your energy in later meetings. Be sure that the physical location is conducive to a private conversation.

During the meeting, be sure to recognize effective performance through specific praise. Do not start the meeting with a criticism. Starting with positive instances of performance helps establish a better mood and shows that you recognize what the employee is doing right. Give employees opportunities to talk. Ask them about their greatest accomplishments, as well as opportunities for improvement. Show empathy and support. Remember, your job as a manager is to help the person solve performance problems. Identify areas where you can help. Conclude by setting goals and creating an action plan for the future.

After the meeting, continue to give the employee periodic and frequent feedback. Follow through on the goals that were set.[66]

3.2 Five Guidelines for Seeking Feedback

Research shows that receiving feedback is a key to performing well. If you are not receiving enough feedback on the job, it is better to seek it instead of trying to guess how well you are doing.

1. Consider seeking regular feedback from your boss. This also has the added benefit of signaling to the manager that you care about your performance and want to be successful.

2. Be genuine in your desire to learn. When seeking feedback, your aim should be improving yourself as opposed to creating the impression that you are a motivated employee. If your manager thinks that you are managing impressions rather than genuinely trying to improve your performance, feedback seeking may hurt you.

3. Develop a good relationship with your manager as well as the employees you manage. This would have the benefit of giving you more feedback in the first place. It also has the upside of making it easier to ask direct questions about your own performance.

4. Consider finding trustworthy peers who can share information with you regarding your performance. Your manager is not the only helpful source of feedback.

5. Be gracious when you receive unfavorable feedback. If you go on the defensive, there may not be a next time. Remember, even if it may not feel like it sometimes, feedback is a gift. You can improve your performance by using feedback constructively. Consider that the negative feedback giver probably risked your goodwill by being honest. Unless there are factual mistakes in the feedback, do not try to convince the person that the feedback is inaccurate.[67]

KEY TAKEAWAY

Giving effective feedback is a key part of a manager's job. To do so, plan the delivery of feedback before, during, and after the meeting. In addition, there are a number of ways to learn about your own performance. Take the time to seek feedback and act on it. With this information, you can do key things to maximize your success and the success of those you manage.

EXERCISES

1. Why can discussing performance feedback with employees be so hard?
2. What barriers do you perceive in asking for feedback?
3. How would you react if one of your employees came to you for feedback?
4. Imagine that your good friend is starting a new job next week. What recommendations would you give to help your friend do a great job seeking feedback?

4.   CASE IN POINT: ZAPPOS CREATES A MOTIVATING PLACE TO WORK

FIGURE 13.20

Source: http://en.wikipedia.org/wiki/File:Tony_hsieh.jpg

It is unique to hear about a CEO who studies happiness and motivation and builds those principles into the company's core values or to hear about a company with a five-week training course and an offer of $2,000 to quit anytime during that five weeks if you feel the company is not a good fit. Top that off with an on-site life coach who also happens to be a chiropractor and you are really talking about something you don't hear about every day. Zappos is known as much for its 365-day return policy and free shipping as it is for its innovative corporate culture. Although acquired in 2009 by Amazon (NASDAQ: AMZN), Zappos managed to move from number 23 on *Fortune* magazine's "100 Best Companies to Work For" list of 2009 up to number 11 in 2012.

Performance is a function of motivation, ability, and the environment in which you work. Zappos seems to be creating an environment that encourages motivation and builds inclusiveness. The company delivers above and beyond basic workplace needs and addresses the self-actualization needs that most individuals desire from their work experience. CEO Tony Hsieh believes that the secret to customer loyalty is to make a corporate culture of caring a priority. This is reflected in the company's 10 core values and its emphasis on building a team and a family. During the interview process, applicants are asked questions relating to the company's values, such as gauging their own weirdness, open-mindedness, and sense of family. Only 2% to 3% of trainees take the offer to be paid to quit during the training process. Work is structured differently at Zappos as well. For example, there is no limit to the time customer service representatives spend on a phone call, and they are encouraged to make personal connections with the individuals on the other end rather than to try to quickly end the call.

Although Zappos has more than 1,500 employees, the company has been able to maintain a relatively flat organizational structure and prides itself on its extreme transparency. Two of the top executives have no titles, and no one except two in-house lawyers have an office. In an exceptionally detailed and lengthy letter to employees, Hsieh spelled out what the new partnership with Amazon would mean for the company, what would change, and more important, what would remain the same. As a result of this type of company structure, individuals have more freedom, which can lead to greater satisfaction.

In 2010, Zappos had 55,000 job applicants for 200 openings. Although Zappos pays its employees well and offers attractive benefits such as full health-care coverage and a compressed workweek, the desire to work at Zappos seems to go beyond simply their excellent benefits package. As Hsieh would say, happiness is the driving force behind almost any action an individual takes. Whether your goals are for achievement, affiliation, or simply an enjoyable environment in which to work, Zappos strives to address these needs.

Case written by Carlene Reynolds, Talya Bauer, and Berrin Erdogan to accompany Carpenter, M., Bauer, T., Erdogan, B., & Short, J. (2013). Principles of Management (2nd ed.). New York: Flat World Knowledge; Based on information from El Nasser, H. (2012, June 6). What office? Laptops are workspace. USA Today; Gillespie, L. V. (2012, April). Targeting soft skills yields hard returns for employers. Employee Benefits News, 26(5), 18–20; Robischon, N. (2009, July 22). Amazon buys Zappos for $847 million. Fast Company. Retrieved September 14, 2012, from http://www.fastcompany.com/blog/ noah-robischon/editors-desk/amazon-buys-zappos-807-million; Walker, A. (2009, March 14). Zappos' Tony Hsieh on Twitter, phone calls and the pursuit of happiness. Fast Company. Retrieved September 14, 2012, from http://www.fastcompany.com/blog/alissa-walker/member-blog/ tony-hsiehs-zapposcom; Happy feet—Inside the online shoe utopia. (2009, September 14). New Yorker. Retrieved September 14, 2012, from http://about.zappos.com/press-center/media-coverage/happy-feet-inside-online-shoe-utopia; 100 best companies to work for. (2010, February 8). Fortune. Retrieved September 14, 2012, from http://money.cnn.com/magazines/fortune/bestcompanies/2010/snapshots/15.html.

CASE DISCUSSION QUESTIONS

1. Motivation is an essential element of the leading facet of the P-O-L-C framework. Besides those used by Zappos, what are other means that organizations use to motivate employees?

2. What potential organizational changes might result from the acquisition by Amazon?

3. Why do you think Zappos's approach is not utilized more often? In other words, what are the challenges of using these techniques?

4. Why do you think Zappos offers a $2,000 incentive to quit?

5. Would you be motivated to work at Zappos? Why or why not?

ENDNOTES

1. *Columbia encyclopedia.* (2004). New York: Columbia University Press.

2. Maslow, A. H. (1943). A theory of human motivation. *Psychological Review, 50,* 370–396; Maslow, A. H. (1954). *Motivation and personality.* New York: Harper.

3. Baumeister, R. F., & Leary, M. R. (1995). The need to belong: Desire for interpersonal attachments as a fundamental human motivation. *Psychological Bulletin, 117,* 497–529.

4. Alderfer, C. P. (1969). An empirical test of a new theory of human needs. *Organizational Behavior and Human Performance, 4,* 142–175.

5. Herzberg, F., Mausner, B., & Snyderman, B. (1959). *The motivation to work.* New York: Wiley; Herzberg, F. (1965). The motivation to work among Finnish supervisors. *Personnel Psychology, 18,* 393–402.

6. Cummings, L. L., & Elsalmi, A. M. (1968). Empirical research on the bases and correlates of managerial motivation. *Psychological Bulletin, 70,* 127–144; House, R. J., & Wigdor, L. A. (1967). Herzberg's dual-factor theory of job satisfaction and motivation: A review of the evidence and a criticism. *Personnel Psychology, 20,* 369–389.

7. Harrell, A. M., & Stahl, M. J. (1981). A behavioral decision theory approach for measuring McClelland's trichotomy of needs. *Journal of Applied Psychology, 66,* 242–247; Trevis, C. S., & Certo, S. C. (2005). Spotlight on entrepreneurship. *Business Horizons, 48,* 271–274; Turban, D. B., & Keon, T. L. (1993). Organizational attractiveness: An interactionist perspective. *Journal of Applied Psychology, 78,* 184–193.

8. McClelland, D. C., & Boyatzis, R. E. (1982). Leadership motive pattern and long-term success in management. *Journal of Applied Psychology, 67,* 737–743.

9. McClelland, D. C., & Burnham, D. H. (1976). Power is the great motivator. *Harvard Business Review, 25,* 159–166.

10. Wong, M. M., & Csikszentmihalyi, M. (1991). Affiliation motivation and daily experience: Some issues on gender differences. *Journal of Personality and Social Psychology, 60,* 154–164.

11. McClelland, D. C., & Burnham, D. H. (1976). Power is the great motivator. *Harvard Business Review, 25,* 159–166; Spangler, W. D., & House, R. J. (1991). Presidential effectiveness and the leadership motive profile. *Journal of Personality and Social Psychology, 60,* 439–455; Spreier, S. W. (2006). Leadership run amok. *Harvard Business Review, 84,* 72–82.

12. Adams, J. S. (1965). Inequity in social exchange. In L. Berkowitz (Ed.), *Advances in experimental social psychology* (Vol. 2, pp. 267–299). New York: Academic Press.

13. Carrell, M. R., & Dittrich, J. E. (1978). Equity theory: The recent literature, methodological considerations, and new directions. *Academy of Management Review, 3,* 202–210; Goodman, P. S., & Friedman, A. (1971). An examination of Adams' theory of inequity. *Administrative Science Quarterly, 16,* 271–288.

14. Greenberg, J. (1993). Stealing in the name of justice: Informational and interpersonal moderators of theft reactions to underpayment inequity. *Organizational Behavior and Human Decision Processes, 54,* 81–103.

15. Schmidt, D. R., & Marwell, G. (1972). Withdrawal and reward reallocation as responses to inequity. *Journal of Experimental Social Psychology, 8,* 207–211.

16. Austin, W., & Walster, E. (1974). Reactions to confirmations and disconfirmations of expectancies of equity and inequity. *Journal of Personality and Social Psychology, 30,* 208–216.

17. Evan, W. M., & Simmons, R. G. (1969). Organizational effects of inequitable rewards: Two experiments in status inconsistency. *IEEE Engineering Management Review, 1,* 95–108.

18. Huseman, R. C., Hatfield, J. D., & Miles, E. W. (1987). A new perspective on equity theory: The equity sensitivity construct. *Academy of Management Review, 12,* 222–234.

19. Alge, B. J. (2001). Effects of computer surveillance on perceptions of privacy and procedural justice. *Journal of Applied Psychology, 86,* 797–804; Bauer, T. N., Maertz, C. P., Jr., Dolen, M. R., & Campion, M. A. (1998). Longitudinal assessment of applicant reactions to employment testing and test outcome feedback. *Journal of Applied Psychology, 83,* 892–903; Kidwell, R. E. (1995). Pink slips without tears. *Academy of Management Executive, 9,* 69–70.

20. Brockner, J., & Wiesenfeld, B. M. (1996). An integrative framework for explaining reactions to decisions: Interactive effects of outcomes and procedures. *Psychological Bulletin, 120,* 189–208.

21. Brockner, J., Fishman, A. Y., Reb, J., Goldman, B., Spiegel, S., & Garden, C. (2007). Procedural fairness, outcome favorability, and judgments of an authority's responsibility. *Journal of Applied Psychology, 92,* 1657–1671.

22. Kidwell, R. E. (1995). Pink slips without tears. *Academy of Management Executive, 9,* 69–70.

23. Alge, B. J. (2001). Effects of computer surveillance on perceptions of privacy and procedural justice. *Journal of Applied Psychology, 86,* 797–804; Kernan, M. C., & Hanges, P. J. (2002). Survivor reactions to reorganization: Antecedents and consequences of procedural, interpersonal, and informational justice. *Journal of Applied Psychology, 87,* 916–928; Lind, E. A., Kanfer, R., & Earley, C. P. (1990). Voice, control, and procedural justice: Instrumental and noninstrumental concerns in fairness judgments. *Journal of Personality and Social Psychology, 59,* 952–959.

24. Schaubroeck, J., May, D. R., & William, B. F. (1994). Procedural justice explanations and employee reactions to economic hardship: A field experiment. *Journal of Applied Psychology, 79,* 455–460.

25. Bauer, T. N., Maertz, C. P., Jr., Dolen, M. R., & Campion, M. A. (1998). Longitudinal assessment of applicant reactions to employment testing and test outcome feedback. *Journal of Applied Psychology, 83,* 892–903.

26. Greenberg, J. (2006). Losing sleep over organizational injustice: Attenuating insomniac reactions to underpayment inequity with supervisory training in interactional justice. *Journal of Applied Psychology, 91,* 58–69.

27. Greenberg, J. (2004). Managing workplace stress by promoting organizational justice. *Organizational Dynamics, 33,* 352–365; Tepper, B. J. (2001). Health consequences of organizational injustice: tests of main and interactive effects. *Organizational Behavior and Human Decision Processes, 86,* 197–215.

28. Blader, S. L. (2007). What leads organizational members to collectivize? Injustice and identification as precursors of union certification. *Organization Science, 18,* 108–126; Colquitt, J. A., Conlon, D. E., Wesson, M. J., Porter, C. O. L. H., & Ng, K. Y. (2001). Justice at the millennium: A meta-analytic review of 25 years of organizational justice research. *Journal of Applied Psychology, 86,* 425–445; Colquitt, J. A., Rodell, J. B. (2011). Justice, trust, and trustworthiness: A longitudinal analysis integrating three theoretical perspectives. *Academy of Management Journal, 54,* 1183–1206; Masterson, S. S. (2001). A trickle-down model of organizational justice: Relating employees' and customers' perceptions of and reactions to fairness. *Journal of Applied Psychology, 86,* 594–604; Masterson, S. S., Lewis, K., Goldman, B. M., & Taylor, S. M. (2000). Integrating justice and social exchange: The differing effects of fair procedures and treatment on work relationships. *Academy of Management Journal, 43,* 738–748; Skarlicki, D. P., & Folger, R. (1997). Retaliation in the workplace: The roles of distributive, procedural, and interactional justice. *Journal of Applied Psychology, 82,* 434–443.

29. Porter, L. W., & Lawler, E. E. (1968). *Managerial attitudes and performance.* Homewood, IL: Irwin; Vroom, V. H. (1964). *Work and motivation.* New York: Wiley.

30. Cook, C. W. (1980). Guidelines for managing motivation. *Business Horizons, 23,* 61–69.

31. Skinner, B. F. (1953). *Science and human behavior.* New York: Free Press.

32. Kerr, S. (1995). On the folly of rewarding A while hoping for B. *Academy of Management Executive, 9,* 7–14.

33. Beatty, R. W., & Schneier, C. E. (1975). A case for positive reinforcement. *Business Horizons, 18,* 57–66.

34. Beatty, R. W., & Schneier, C. E. (1975). A case for positive reinforcement. *Business Horizons, 18,* 57–66.

35. Luthans, F., & Stajkovic, A. D. (1999). Reinforce for performance: The need to go beyond pay and even rewards. *Academy of Management Executive, 13,* 49–57.

36. Stajkovic, A. D., & Luthans, F. (1997). A meta-analysis of the effects of organizational behavior modification on task performance, 1975–1995. *Academy of Management Journal, 40,* 1122–1149.

37. Campion, M. A., & Thayer, P. W. (1987). Job design: Approaches, outcomes, and trade-offs. *Organizational Dynamics, 15,* 66–78.

38. Wilson, F. M. (1999). Rationalization and rationality: From the founding fathers to eugenics. In *Organizational behaviour: A critical introduction.* Oxford: Oxford University Press.

39. Denton, D. K. (1994). …I hate this job. *Business Horizons, 37,* 46–52.

40. Rissen, D., Melin, B., Sandsjo, L., Dohns, I., & Lundberg, U. (2002). Psychophysiological stress reactions, trapezius muscle activity, and neck and shoulder pain among female cashiers before and after introduction of job rotation. *Work & Stress, 16,* 127–137.

41. Campion, M. A., Cheraskin, L., & Stevens, M. J. (1994). Career-related antecedents and outcomes of job rotation. *Academy of Management Journal, 37,* 1518–1542.

42. Hertzberg, A., Liberti, J. M., & Paravisini, D. (2010). Information and incentives inside the firm: Evidence from loan officer rotation. *Journal of Finance, 65,* 795–828; Kane, A. A., Argote, L., & Levine, J. M. (2005). Knowledge transfer between groups via personnel rotation: Effects of social identity and knowledge quality. *Organizational Behavior and Human Decision Processes, 96,* 56–71.

43. Nalbantian, H. R. (2009, March). Making mobility matter. *Harvard Business Review, 87*(3)

44. Ramamurti, R. (2001). Wipro's chairman Azim Premji on building a world-class Indian company. *Academy of Management Executive, 15,* 13–19.

45. Parker, S. K. (1998). Enhancing role breadth self-efficacy: The roles of job enrichment and other organizational interventions. *Journal of Applied Psychology, 83,* 835–852.

46. Campion, M. A., & McClelland, C. L. (1991). Interdisciplinary examination of the costs and benefits of enlarged jobs: A job design quasi-experiment. *Journal of Applied Psychology, 76,* 186–198.

47. Campion, M. A., & McClelland, C. L. (1993). Follow-up and extension of the interdisciplinary costs and benefits of enlarged jobs. *Journal of Applied Psychology, 78,* 339–351.

48. McEvoy, G. M., & Cascio, W. F. (1985). Strategies for reducing employee turnover. *Journal of Applied Psychology, 70,* 342–353; Locke, E. A., Sirota, D., & Wolfson, A. D. (1976). An experimental case study of the successes and failures of job enrichment in a government agency. *Journal of Applied Psychology, 61,* 701–711.

49. Locke, E. A., Sirota, D., & Wolfson, A. D. (1976). An experimental case study of the successes and failures of job enrichment in a government agency. *Journal of Applied Psychology, 61,* 701–711.

50. Cherrington, D. J., & Lynn, E. J. (1980). The desire for an enriched job as a moderator of the enrichment-satisfaction relationship. *Organizational Behavior and Human Performance, 25,* 139–159; Hulin, C. L., & Blood, M. R. (1968). Job enlargement, individual differences, and worker responses. *Psychological Bulletin, 69,* 41–55.

51. Fitzpatrick, L. (2009, May 25). We're getting off the ladder. *Time, 173*(20); Wrzesniewski, A. Berg, J. M., & Dutton, J. E. (2010). Turn the job you have into the job you want. *Harvard Business Review. 88*(6), 114–117.

52. Hackman, J. R., & Oldham, G. R. (1975). Development of the job diagnostic survey. *Journal of Applied Psychology, 60,* 159–170.

53. Grant, A. M. (2008). The significance of task significance: Job performance effects, relational mechanisms, and boundary conditions. *Journal of Applied Psychology, 93,* 108–124.

54. Morgeson, F. P., Delaney-Klinger, K., & Hemingway, M. A. (2005). The importance of job autonomy, cognitive ability, and job-related skill for predicting role breadth and job performance. *Journal of Applied Psychology, 90,* 399–406; Parker, S. K., Wall, T. D., & Jackson, P. R. (1997). "That's not my job": Developing flexible employee work orientations. *Academy of Management Journal, 40,* 899–929; Parker, S. K., Williams, H. M., & Turner, N. (2006). Modeling the antecedents of proactive behavior at work. *Journal of Applied Psychology, 91,* 636–652; Zhou, J. (1998). Feedback valence, feedback style, task autonomy, and achievement orientation: Interactive effects on creative performance. *Journal of Applied Psychology, 83,* 261–276.

55. Gumbel, P. (2008, January 21). Galvanizing Gucci. *Fortune, 157*(1), 80–88.

56. Kluger, A. N., & DeNisi, A. (1996). The effects of feedback interventions on performance: A historical review, a meta-analysis, and a preliminary feedback intervention theory. *Psychological Bulletin, 119,* 254–284.

57. Locke, E. A., & Latham, G. P. (1990). *A theory of goal setting and task performance.* Englewood Cliffs, NJ: Prentice-Hall.

58. Ivancevich, J. M., & McMahon, J. T. (1982). The effects of goal setting, external feedback, and self-generated feedback on outcome variables: A field experiment. *Academy of Management Journal, 25,* 359–372; Latham, G. P., & Locke, E. A. (2006). Enhancing the benefits and overcoming the pitfalls of goal setting. *Organizational Dynamics, 35,* 332–340; Umstot, D. D., Bell, C. H., & Mitchell, T. R. (1976). Effects of job enrichment and task goals on satisfaction and productivity: Implications for job design. *Journal of Applied Psychology, 61,* 379–394.

59. Pritchard, R. D., Roth, P. L., Jones, S. D., Galgay, P. J., & Watson, M. D. (1988). Designing a goal-setting system to enhance performance: A practical guide. *Organizational Dynamics, 17,* 69–78.

60. Heath, D., & Heath, C. (2008, February). Make goals not resolutions. *Fast Company, 122,* 58–59.

61. Shaw, K. N. (2004). Changing the goal-setting process at Microsoft. *Academy of Management Executive, 18,* 139–142.

62. Latham, G. P. (2004). The motivational benefits of goal-setting. *Academy of Management Executive, 18,* 126–129; Seijts, G. H., & Latham, G. P. (2005). Learning versus performance goals: When should each be used? *Academy of Management Executive, 19,* 124–131; Shaw, K. N. (2004). Changing the goal-setting process at Microsoft. *Academy of Management Executive, 18,* 139–142.

63. Kerr, S., & Landauer, S. (2004). Using stretch goals to promote organizational effectiveness and personal growth: General Electric and Goldman Sachs. *Academy of Management Executive, 18,* 134–138.

64. Locke, E. A. (2004). Linking goals to monetary incentives. *Academy of Management Executive, 18,* 130–133; Pritchard, R. D., Roth, P. L., Jones, S. D., Galgay, P. J., & Watson, M. D. (1988). Designing a goal-setting system to enhance performance: A practical guide. *Organizational Dynamics, 17,* 69–78; Seijts, G. H., & Latham, G. P. (2005). Learning versus performance goals: When should each be used? *Academy of Management Executive, 19,* 124–131.

65. Lepine, J. A. (2005). Adaptation of teams in response to unforeseen change: Effects of goal difficulty and team composition in terms of cognitive ability and goal orientation. *Journal of Applied Psychology, 90,* 1153–1167.

66. Make employee appraisals more productive. (2007, September). *HR Focus, 84*(9), 1, 11–15; Ryan, L. (2007, January 1). Coping with performance-review anxiety. *Business Week Online,* p. 6; Stone, D. L. (1984). The effects of feedback sequence and expertise of the rater on perceived feedback accuracy. *Personnel Psychology, 37,* 487–506; Sulkowicz, K. (2007, September 10). Straight talk at review time. *Business Week,* 16.

67. Adapted from ideas in Jackman, J. M., & Strober, M. H. (2003, April). Fear of feedback. *Harvard Business Review, 81*(4), 101–107; Wing, L., Xu, H., & Snape, E. (2007). Feedback-seeking behavior and leader-member exchange: Do supervisor-attributed motives matter? *Academy of Management Journal, 50,* 348–363; Lee, H. E., Park, H. S., Lee, T. S., & Lee, D. W. (2007). Relationships between LMX and subordinates' feedback-seeking behaviors. *Social Behavior & Personality: An International Journal, 35,* 659–674.

CHAPTER 14
The Essentials of Control

FIGURE 14.1
Control lets managers monitor and regulate actions to align performance with expectations, much like music producers align musicians to create a desired sound.

© 2010 Jupiterimages Corporation

CHAPTER LEARNING OBJECTIVES

Reading this chapter will help you do the following:

1. Understand what is meant by organizational control.
2. Differentiate among different levels, types, and forms of control.
3. Know the essentials of financial controls.
4. Know the essentials of nonfinancial controls.
5. Know the basics of lean control systems.
6. Craft a Balanced Scorecard for an organization or yourself.

With the planning-organizing-leading-controlling (P-O-L-C) framework, organizational controls should serve two basic functions. First, they should help managers determine whether and why their strategy is achieving the desired results. Second, they should be an early warning system in cases where the organization is getting a little (or a lot) off track.

FIGURE 14.2 The P-O-L-C Framework

Planning	Organizing	Leading	Controlling
1. Vision & Mission	1. Organization Design	1. Leadership	1. Systems/Processes
2. Strategizing	2. Culture	2. Decision Making	2. Strategic Human Resources
3. Goals & Objectives	3. Social Networks	3. Communications	
		4. Groups/Teams	
		5. Motivation	

1. ORGANIZATIONAL CONTROL

LEARNING OBJECTIVES

1. Know what is meant by organizational control.
2. Recognize that controls have costs.
3. Understand the benefits of controls.

1.1 What Is Organizational Control?

organizational control

The process by which an organization influences its subunits and members to behave in ways that lead to the attainment of organizational goals and objectives.

The fourth facet of the P-O-L-C framework, **organizational control**, refers to the process by which an organization influences its subunits and members to behave in ways that lead to the attainment of organizational goals and objectives. When properly designed, such controls should lead to better performance because an organization is able to execute its strategy better.[1] As shown in the P-O-L-C framework figure, we typically think of or talk about control in a sequential sense, where controls (systems and processes) are put in place to make sure everything is on track and stays on track. Controls can be as simple as a checklist, such as the ones commonly used by pilots, flight crews, and some doctors.[2]

Organizational control typically involves four steps: (1) establish standards, (2) measure performance, (3) compare performance to standards, and then (4) take corrective action as needed. Corrective action can include changes made to the performance standards—setting them higher or lower or identifying new or additional standards. Organizational controls are often most noticeable when they seem to be absent, as in the 2008 meltdown of U.S. financial markets, the crisis in the U.S. auto industry, or the much earlier demise of Enron and MCI/WorldCom due to fraud and inadequate controls. As shown in these examples, effective controls are relevant to a large spectrum of organizations.

1.2 The Costs and Benefits of Organizational Controls

Organizational controls provide significant benefits, particularly when they help the firm stay on track with respect to its strategy. External stakeholders, too, such as government, investors, and public interest groups have an interest in seeing certain types or levels of control are in place. However, controls also come at a cost. It is useful to know that there are trade-offs between having and not having organizational controls, and even among the different forms of control.

FIGURE 14.3 Organizational Controls: Costs and Benefits

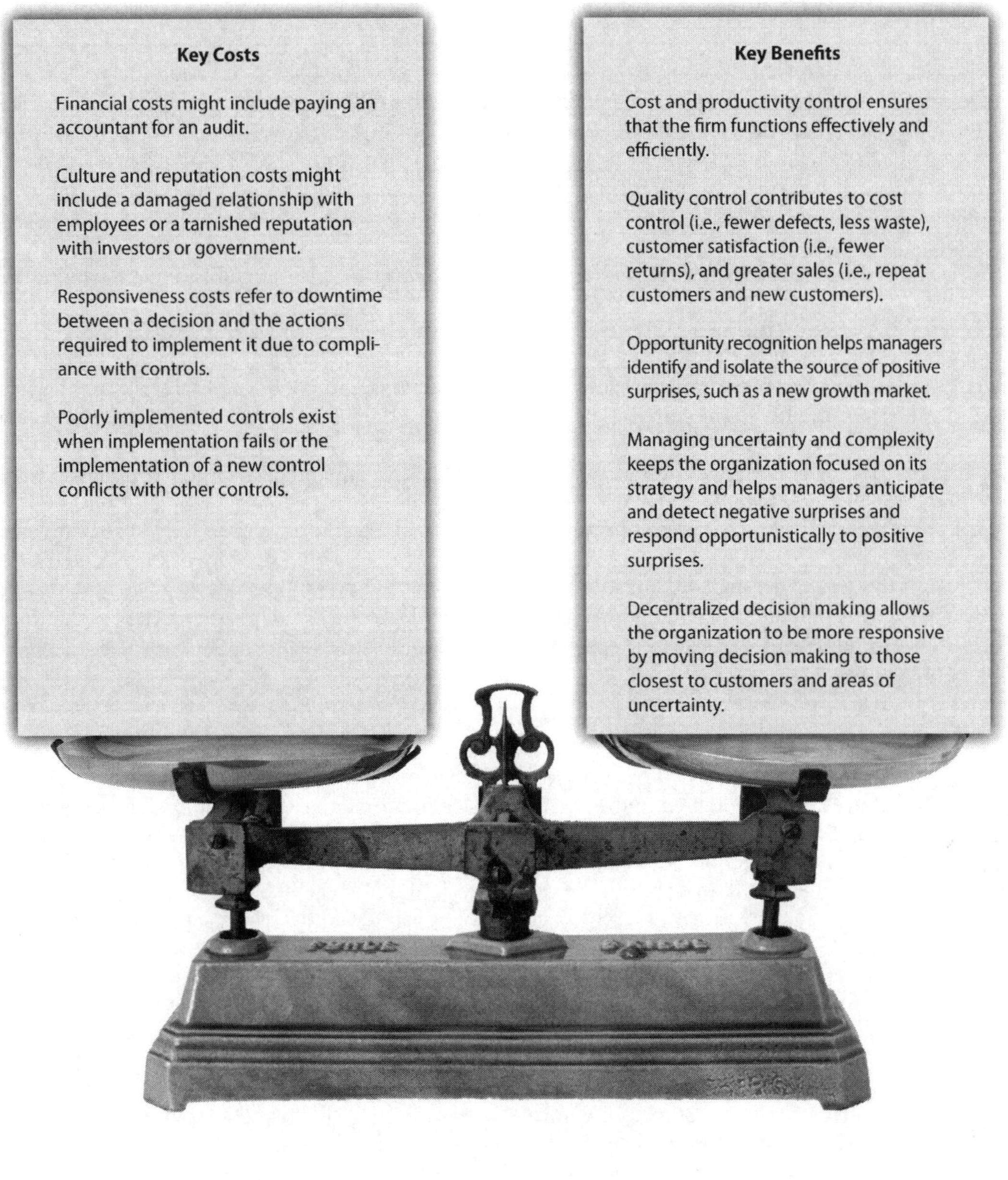

Key Costs

Financial costs might include paying an accountant for an audit.

Culture and reputation costs might include a damaged relationship with employees or a tarnished reputation with investors or government.

Responsiveness costs refer to downtime between a decision and the actions required to implement it due to compliance with controls.

Poorly implemented controls exist when implementation fails or the implementation of a new control conflicts with other controls.

Key Benefits

Cost and productivity control ensures that the firm functions effectively and efficiently.

Quality control contributes to cost control (i.e., fewer defects, less waste), customer satisfaction (i.e., fewer returns), and greater sales (i.e., repeat customers and new customers).

Opportunity recognition helps managers identify and isolate the source of positive surprises, such as a new growth market.

Managing uncertainty and complexity keeps the organization focused on its strategy and helps managers anticipate and detect negative surprises and respond opportunistically to positive surprises.

Decentralized decision making allows the organization to be more responsive by moving decision making to those closest to customers and areas of uncertainty.

© Thinkstock

Costs

Controls can cost the organization in several areas, including (1) financial, (2) damage to culture and reputation, (3) decreased responsiveness, and (4) failed implementation. An example of financial cost is the fact that organizations are often required to perform and report the results of a financial audit. These audits are typically undertaken by external accounting firms, which charge a substantial fee for their services; the auditor may be a large firm like Deloitte or KPMG, or a smaller local accounting office. Such audits are a way for banks, investors, and other key stakeholders to understand the firm's financial health. Thus, if an organization needs to borrow money from banks or has investors, it can only obtain these benefits if it incurs the monetary and staffing costs of the financial audit.

Controls also can have costs in terms of organization culture and reputation. While you can imagine that organizations might want to keep track of employee behavior, or otherwise put forms of strict monitoring in place, these efforts can have undesirable cultural consequences in the form of reduced employee loyalty, greater turnover, or damage to the organization's external reputation. Management researchers such as the late London Business School professor Sumantra Ghoshal have criticized theory that focuses on the economic aspects of man (i.e., assumes that individuals are always opportunistic).

According to Ghoshal, "A theory that assumes that managers cannot be relied upon by shareholders can make managers less reliable."[3] Such theory, he warned, would become a self-fulfilling prophecy.

Evidence of the need for controls is found in Hewlett-Packard's (HP) indictment on charges of spying on its own board of directors. In a letter to HP's board, director Tom Perkins said his accounts were "hacked" and attached a letter from AT&T explaining how the breach occurred. Records of calls made from Perkins's home phone were obtained simply with his home phone number and the last four digits of his Social Security number. His long-distance account records were obtained when someone called AT&T and pretended to be Perkins, according to the letter from AT&T.[4] HP Chairman Patricia Dunn defended this rather extreme form of control as legal, but the amount of damage to the firm's reputation from these charges led the firm to discontinue the practice. It also prompted the resignation of several directors and corporate officers.[5]

The third potential cost of having controls is that they can afford less organizational flexibility and responsiveness. Typically, controls are put in place to prevent problems, but controls can also create problems. For instance, the Federal Emergency Management Agency (FEMA) is responsible for helping people and business cope with the consequences of natural disasters, such as hurricanes. After Hurricane Katrina devastated communities along the U.S. Gulf Coast in 2005, FEMA found that it could not provide prompt relief to the hurricane victims because of the many levels of financial controls that it had in place.[6]

The fourth area of cost, failed implementation, is needed when controls are poorly understood, so that their launch creates significant unintended, negative consequences. For example, when Hershey Foods put a new computer-based control system in place in 1999, there were so many problems with its installation that it was not able to fulfill a large percentage of its Halloween season chocolate sales that year. It did finally get the controls in working order, but the downtime created huge costs for the company in terms of inefficiencies and lost sales.[7] Some added controls may also interfere with others. For instance, a new quality control system may improve product performance but also delay product deliveries to customers.

Benefits

Although organizational controls come at some cost, most controls are valid and valuable management tools. When they are well designed and implemented, they provide at least five possible areas of benefits, including (1) improved cost and productivity control, (2) improved quality control, (3) opportunity recognition, (4) better ability to manage uncertainty and complexity, and (5) better ability to decentralize decision making. In this section, we explain each of these benefits.

First, good controls help the organization act efficiently and effectively by helping managers control costs and productivity levels. Cost can be controlled using budgets, where managers compare actual expenses to forecasted ones. Similarly, productivity can be controlled by comparing how much each person can produce, in terms of service or products. For instance, the productivity of a fast-food restaurant like McDonald's depends on the speed of its order takers and meal preparers. McDonald's can look across all its restaurants to identify the target speed for taking an order or wrapping a burger, then measure each store's performance on these dimensions.

Quality control is a second benefit of controls. Increasingly, quality can be quantified in terms of response time (i.e., How long did it take to prepare a burger?) or accuracy (i.e., Did the burger actually weigh one-quarter pound?). Similarly, Toyota tracks the quality of its cars according to hundreds of quantified dimensions, including the number of defects per car. Some measures of quality are qualitative, however. For instance, Toyota also tries to gauge how "delighted" each customer is with its vehicles and dealer service. One mark of quality control is the reception of the Malcolm Baldrige Performance Excellence Program Award. The Baldrige award is given by the president of the United States to businesses—manufacturing and service, small and large—and to education, health care, and nonprofit organizations that apply and are judged to be outstanding in seven areas: leadership; strategic planning; customer and market focus; measurement, analysis, and knowledge management; human resource focus; process management; and results.[8] Controlling—how well the organization measures and analyzes its processes—is a key criterion for winning the award. The Baldrige award is given to organizations in a wide range of categories and industries, from education to ethics to manufacturing.

The third area in which organizations can benefit from controls is opportunity recognition. Opportunities can come from outside of the organization and typically are the result of a surprise. For instance, when Nestlé purchased the Carnation Company for its ice cream business, it had also planned to sell off Carnation's pet food line of products. However, through its financial controls, Nestlé found that the pet food business was even more profitable than ice cream, which led to the decision to keep both. Opportunities can come from inside the organization too, as would be the case if McDonald's finds that one of its restaurants is exceptionally good at managing costs or productivity. It can then take this learned ability and transfer it to other restaurants through training and other means.

Controls also help organizations manage uncertainty and complexity. This is a fourth area of benefit from well-designed and implemented controls. Perhaps the most easily understood example of this type of benefit is how financial controls help an organization navigate economic downturns. Without budgets and productivity controls in place, the organization might not know it has lost sales or expenses are out of control until it is too late.

FIGURE 14.4 Control Criteria for the Baldrige Performance Excellence Program Award

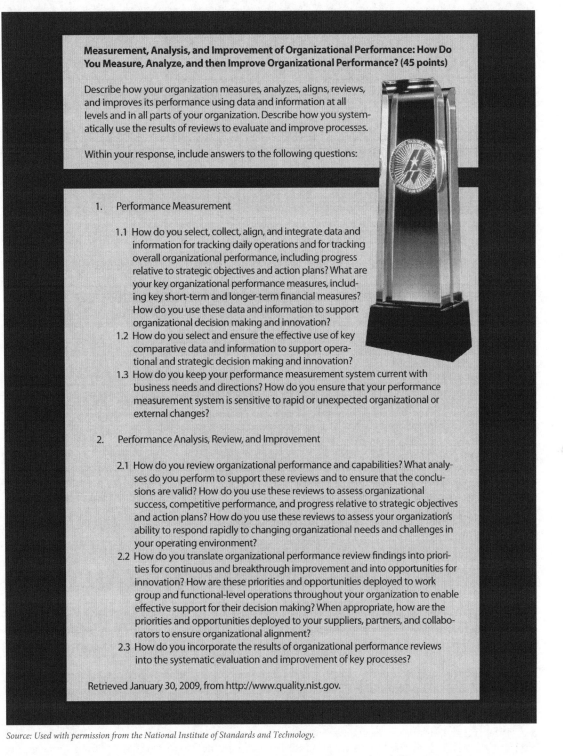

Measurement, Analysis, and Improvement of Organizational Performance: How Do You Measure, Analyze, and then Improve Organizational Performance? (45 points)

Describe how your organization measures, analyzes, aligns, reviews, and improves its performance using data and information at all levels and in all parts of your organization. Describe how you systematically use the results of reviews to evaluate and improve processes.

Within your response, include answers to the following questions:

1.   Performance Measurement

   1.1 How do you select, collect, align, and integrate data and information for tracking daily operations and for tracking overall organizational performance, including progress relative to strategic objectives and action plans? What are your key organizational performance measures, including key short-term and longer-term financial measures? How do you use these data and information to support organizational decision making and innovation?

   1.2 How do you select and ensure the effective use of key comparative data and information to support operational and strategic decision making and innovation?

   1.3 How do you keep your performance measurement system current with business needs and directions? How do you ensure that your performance measurement system is sensitive to rapid or unexpected organizational or external changes?

2.   Performance Analysis, Review, and Improvement

   2.1 How do you review organizational performance and capabilities? What analyses do you perform to support these reviews and to ensure that the conclusions are valid? How do you use these reviews to assess organizational success, competitive performance, and progress relative to strategic objectives and action plans? How do you use these reviews to assess your organization's ability to respond rapidly to changing organizational needs and challenges in your operating environment?

   2.2 How do you translate organizational performance review findings into priorities for continuous and breakthrough improvement and into opportunities for innovation? How are these priorities and opportunities deployed to work group and functional-level operations throughout your organization to enable effective support for their decision making? When appropriate, how are the priorities and opportunities deployed to your suppliers, partners, and collaborators to ensure organizational alignment?

   2.3 How do you incorporate the results of organizational performance reviews into the systematic evaluation and improvement of key processes?

Retrieved January 30, 2009, from http://www.quality.nist.gov.

Source: Used with permission from the National Institute of Standards and Technology.

The fifth area of benefit in organizational control is related to decentralized decision making. Organization researchers have long argued that performance is best when those individuals and areas of the organization that are closest to customers and pockets of uncertainty also have the ability (i.e., the information and authority) to respond to them.[9] It would be difficult to give a McDonald's store manager information about a store's performance and possible choices if information about performance were only compiled at the city, regional, or corporate level. With store-level performance tracking (or, even better, tracking of performance by the hour within a store), McDonald's gives store managers the information they need to respond to changes in local demand. Similarly, it equips McDonald's to give those managers the authority to make local decisions, track that decision-making performance, and feed it back into the control and reward systems.

KEY TAKEAWAY

This chapter introduced the basics of controls, the process by which an organization influences its subunits and members to behave in ways that lead to attaining organizational goals and objectives. When properly designed, controls lead to better performance by enabling the organization to execute its strategy better. Managers must weigh the costs and benefits of control, but some minimum level of control is essential for organizational survival and success.

EXERCISES

1. What do properly conceived and implemented controls allow an organization to do?
2. What are three common steps in organizational control?
3. What are some of the costs of organizational controls?
4. What are some of the benefits of organizational controls?
5. How do managers determine when benefits outweigh costs?

---

2. TYPES AND LEVELS OF CONTROL

LEARNING OBJECTIVES

1. Know the difference between strategic and operational controls.
2. Understand the different types of controls.
3. Be able to differentiate between financial and nonfinancial controls.

Recognizing that organizational controls can be categorized in many ways, it is helpful at this point to distinguish between two sets of controls: (1) strategic controls and (2) management controls—sometimes called operating controls.[10]

2.1 Two Levels of Control: Strategic and Operational

strategic control

The process by which an organization tracks the strategy as it is being implemented, detecting any problem areas or potential problem areas that might suggest that the strategy is incorrect, and making any necessary adjustments.

Two types of controls are utilized when a captain pilots a ship. Strategic controls make sure that the ship is going in the right direction, while management and operating controls make sure the ship is in good condition before, during, and after the voyage. In the context of piloting organizations, **strategic control** is concerned with tracking the strategy as it is being implemented, detecting any problem areas or potential problem areas suggesting that the strategy is incorrect, and making any necessary adjustments.[11] Strategic controls allow managers to step back and look at the big picture and make sure all the pieces of the picture are correctly aligned.

Ordinarily, a significant time span occurs between initial implementation of a strategy and achievement of its intended results. For instance, a ship going from San Diego to Seattle would need a crew, supplies, fuel, and so on. The voyage might be delayed until the weather permits the captain to make the trip safely. Similarly, in larger organizations, numerous projects are undertaken, investments are made, and actions are undertaken to implement the new strategy at the same time. Meanwhile, the environmental situation and the firm's internal situation are developing and evolving. The economy could be booming or perhaps falling into recession. Strategic controls are necessary to steer the firm through these events. They must provide some means of correcting direction on the basis of intermediate performance and new information.

operational control

A process concerned with executing the strategy.

Operational control, in contrast to strategic control, is concerned with executing the strategy. Where operational controls are imposed, they function within the framework established by the strategy. Normally these goals, objectives, and standards are established for major subsystems within the organization, such as business units, projects, products, functions, and responsibility centers.[12]

Typical operational control measures include return on investment, net profit, cost, and product quality. These control measures are essentially summations of finer-grained control measures. Corrective action based on operating controls may have implications for strategic controls when they involve changes in the strategy.

2.2 Types of Control

Within the strategic and operational levels of control, there are several types of control. The first two types can be mapped across two dimensions: level of proactivity and outcome versus behavioral. Figure 14.5 summarizes these along with examples of what such controls might look like.

Proactivity

Proactivity can be defined as the monitoring of problems in a way that provides their timely prevention, rather than after the fact reaction. In management, this is known as **feedforward control**; it addresses what can be done ahead of time to help a plan succeed. The essence of feedforward control is to see the problems coming in time to do something about them. For instance, feedforward controls include preventive maintenance on machinery and equipment and due diligence on investments.

feedforward controls

The active monitoring of problems in a way that provides their timely prevention, rather than after-the-fact reaction.

FIGURE 14.5 Types and Examples of Control

Control Proactivity	Behavioral Control	Outcome Control
Feedforward control	Organizational culture	Market demand or economic forecasts
Concurrent control	Hands-on management supervision during a project	The real-time speed of a production line
Feedback control	Qualitative measures of customer satisfaction	Financial measures such as profitability, sales growth

Concurrent Controls

The process of monitoring and adjusting ongoing activities and processes is known as **concurrent control**. Such controls are not necessarily proactive, but they can prevent problems from becoming worse. For this reason, concurrent controls are thought of as real-time controls because they deal with the present.

concurrent controls

Processes that entail monitoring and adjusting ongoing activities.

Feedback Controls

Feedback controls involve gathering information about a completed activity, evaluating that information, and taking steps to improve the similar activities in the future. This is the least proactive of controls and is generally a basis for reactions. Feedback controls permit managers to use information on past performance to bring future performance in line with planned objectives.

feedback controls

Processes that involve the gathering of information about a completed activity, evaluating that information, and taking steps to improve the similar activities in the future.

Control as a Feedback Loop

In this latter sense, all these types of control function as a feedback mechanism to help leaders and managers make adjustments in the strategy, as perhaps is reflected by changes in the planning, organizing, and leading components. This feedback loop is characterized in Figure 14.6.

FIGURE 14.6 Controls as Part of a Feedback Loop

Why might it be helpful for you to think of controls as part of a feedback loop in the P-O-L-C process? An entrepreneur writing the business plan for a completely new business would likely start with the planning component and work his or her way to the controlling component by spelling out how he or she is going to assess whether the new venture is on track. Most individuals work within an organization that is already operating, and this means that a plan is already in place. With the plan in place, managers continually face the challenge of understanding the organizing, leading, or controlling challenges facing the organization.

Outcome and Behavioral Controls

Outcome controls are generally preferable when performance can be measured through tangible performance metrics. Outcome controls are effective when there's little external interference between managerial decision making on the one hand and business performance on the other.

---

outcome controls

Processes that are generally preferable when just one or two performance measures (say, return on investment or return on assets) are good gauges of a business's health.

FIGURE 14.7 Output Controls

Outcome controls assess measurable production and other tangible results. Often output controls emphasize "bottom-line" performance. We illustrate some outcome controls found in organizations below.

Because real estate agents are paid a percentage of the selling price when a house sells, the number of dollars generated in houses sold is an important metric. Many realty offices have designations like "five million dollar club" to recognize very productive realtors.

Grade point averages provide a tangible means to compare students for employers and graduate schools.

In the movie *Elf*, the main character Buddy leaves Santa's workshop when the number of Etch-A-Sketch toys he produces is nearly nine hundred units lower than the standard pace.

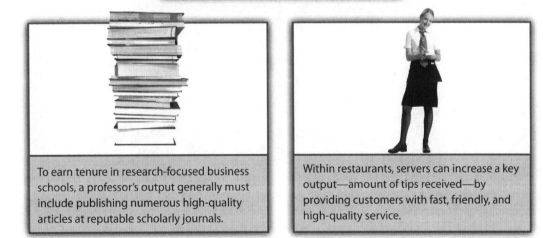

To earn tenure in research-focused business schools, a professor's output generally must include publishing numerous high-quality articles at reputable scholarly journals.

Within restaurants, servers can increase a key output—amount of tips received—by providing customers with fast, friendly, and high-quality service.

Source: Image courtesy of Ketchen, D., & Short, J. (2011). Mastering strategic management. Irvington, NY: Flat World Knowledge.

Behavioral controls involve the direct evaluation of managerial and employee decision making, not of the results of managerial decisions. Behavioral controls are typically more appropriate when the actions of individuals can be clearly tied to the organization's performance.

FIGURE 14.8 Behavioral Controls

Behavioral controls dictate the actions of individuals. Such controls often emphasize rules and procedures. We illustrate some behavioral controls found in organizations below.

No shoes, no shirt, no paycheck. Many food service companies have strict attire requirements to make sure employees are in compliance with the rules of the Food and Drug Administration and those of local health departments.

Casual Fridays provide a welcome break in offices that enforce strict dress codes.

Many businesses require that checks are signed by two people. This prevents a dishonest employee from embezzling money.

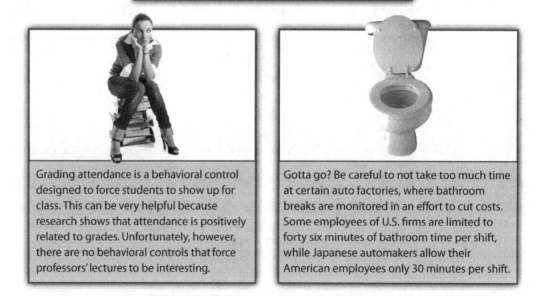

Grading attendance is a behavioral control designed to force students to show up for class. This can be very helpful because research shows that attendance is positively related to grades. Unfortunately, however, there are no behavioral controls that force professors' lectures to be interesting.

Gotta go? Be careful to not take too much time at certain auto factories, where bathroom breaks are monitored in an effort to cut costs. Some employees of U.S. firms are limited to forty six minutes of bathroom time per shift, while Japanese automakers allow their American employees only 30 minutes per shift.

Source: Image courtesy of Ketchen, D., & Short, J. (2011). Mastering strategic management. Irvington, NY: Flat World Knowledge.

Financial and Nonfinancial Controls

Financial control involves the management of a firm's costs and expenses to control them in relation to budgeted amounts. Thus, management determines which aspects of its financial condition, such as assets, sales, or profitability, are most important, tries to forecast them through budgets, and then compares actual performance to budgeted performance. At a strategic level, total sales and indicators of profitability would be relevant strategic controls.

One key mechanism managers rely on to control performance is the use of performance referents that serve as comparison points when understanding if performance is on target. The use of multiple referents is advised, as different measures will provide different insights into the organization's functioning. In a similar manner, multiple performance measures should be utilized when individuals access their own personal finances.

> **financial control**
> The management of a firm's costs and expenses to control them in relation to budgeted amounts.

FIGURE 14.9 How Organizations and Individuals Can Use Financial Performance Measures and Referents

Types of Measures	Applications for Organizations		Application for Individuals	
	Key Measure	Key Referent	Key Measure	Key Referent
Liquidity measures: Helpful for understanding if obligations can be paid when due.	Current ratio (Current assets/ Current liabilities)	A ratio of less than 1.0 suggests the firm does not have enough cash to pay its bills.	Cash in your checking account.	Do you have enough cash to cover your monthly debts?
Leverage measures: Helpful for understanding if debt level is too high. The term *leverage* refers to the extent to which borrowed money is used.	Debt-to-equity ratio	Competitors' debt-to-equity ratios. The use of debt varies across industries. Auto companies, for example, tend to have high debt-to-equity because they must build massive factories.	Debt-to-income ratio (Monthly debt payments / Monthly income)	If you have a debt-to-income ratio higher than 40%, you may be on the verge of becoming a credit risk.
Profitability measures: Helpful for understanding how much profit, if any, is really being made.	Net income (income after taxes)	Last year's net income. An increase shows the firm's profits are moving in the right direction.	Net income (income after taxes)	Are you making enough money to cover your yearly expenses and save for retirement?

Source: Image courtesy of Ketchen, D., & Short, J. (2011). Mastering strategic management. Irvington, NY: Flat World Knowledge.

Increasing numbers of organizations have been measuring customer loyalty, referrals, employee satisfaction, and other such performance areas that are not financial. In contrast to financial controls, **nonfinancial controls** track aspects of the organization that are not immediately financial in nature but are expected to lead to positive performance outcomes. The idea behind such nonfinancial controls is that they should provide managers with a glimpse of the organization's progress well before financial outcomes can be measured.[13] For example, GE has found that highly satisfied customers are the best predictor of future sales in many of its businesses, so it regularly tracks customer satisfaction.

KEY TAKEAWAY

Organizational controls can take many forms. Strategic controls help managers know whether a chosen strategy is working, while operating controls contribute to successful execution of the current strategy. Within these types of strategy, controls can vary in terms of proactivity, where feedback controls were the least proactive. Outcome controls are judged by the result of the organization's activities, while behavioral controls involve monitoring how the organization's members behave on a daily basis. Financial controls are executed by monitoring costs and expenditure in relation to the organization's budget, and nonfinancial controls complement financial controls by monitoring intangibles like customer satisfaction and employee morale.

EXERCISES

1. What is the difference between strategic and operating controls? What level of management would be most concerned with operating controls?
2. If feedforward controls are the most proactive, then why do organizations need or use feedback controls?
3. What is the difference between behavioral and outcome controls?
4. What is the difference between nonfinancial and financial controls? Is a financial control a behavioral or an outcome control?

---

3. FINANCIAL CONTROLS

LEARNING OBJECTIVES

1. **Understand the nature of financial controls.**
2. **Know how a balance sheet works.**
3. **Know how an income profit and loss statement works.**
4. **See the sources of cash flow.**

Financial controls are a key element of organizational success and survival. There are three basic financial reports that all managers need to understand and interpret to manage their businesses successfully: (1) the balance sheet, (2) the income/profit and loss (P&L) statement, and (3) the cash flow statement. These three reports are often referred to collectively as "the financials." Banks often require a projection of these statements to obtain financing.

Financial controls provide the basis for sound management and allow managers to establish guidelines and policies that enable the business to succeed and grow. **Budgeting**, for instance, generally refers to a simple listing of all planned expenses and revenues. An overall budget often includes a monthly or quarterly projection of what the balance sheet and income statement will look like based on your list of planned expenses and revenues.

3.1 The Nature of Financial Controls

Financial statements provide one of the most valuable tools to help manage financial controls. Each year, after the organization has outlined strategies to reach its goals and objectives, funds are budgeted for the necessary resources and labor. As money is spent, statements are updated to reflect how much was spent, how it was spent, and what it obtained. Managers, who report to the board, use these financial statements, such as an income statement or balance sheet, to monitor the progress of programs and plans. Financial statements provide management with information to monitor financial resources and activities. The income statement shows the results of the organization's operations, such as revenues, expenses, and profit or loss. The balance sheet shows what the organization is worth (assets) at a single point in time, and the extent to which those assets were financed through debt (liabilities) or owner's investment (equity).

Organizations often conduct financial audits, or formal investigations, to ensure that financial management practices follow generally accepted procedures, policies, laws, and ethical guidelines. Audits are conducted both internally by members of the company's accounting department and by outside accounting firms hired to conduct an external audit.

Financial ratio analysis examines the relationship between specific figures on the financial statements and helps explain the significance of those figures: By analyzing financial reports, the managers are able to determine how well the business is doing and what may need to be done to improve its financial viability.

While actual financial performance is always historical, proactive managers plan ahead for the problems the business is likely to encounter and the opportunities that may arise. To do this, they use pro forma financials, which are projections; usually these are projected for three fiscal years. Being proactive requires reading and analyzing the financial statements on a regular basis. Monthly, and sometimes daily or weekly, financial analysis is preferred. (In the business world as a whole, quarterly is more common, and some organizations do this only once a year, which is not often enough.) The proactive manager has financial data available based on actual results and compares them to the budget. This process points out weaknesses in the business before they reach crisis proportion and allows the manager to make the necessary changes and adjustments before major problems develop.

A reactive manager waits to react to problems and then solves them by crisis management. This type of manager goes from crisis to crisis with little time in between to notice opportunities that may become available. The reactive manager's business is seldom prepared to take advantage of new opportunities quickly. Businesses that are managed proactively are more likely to be successful, and this result can be aided by the use of company-wide initiatives to promote proactive controls.

Most organizations use computer software programs to do record keeping and develop financials. These programs provide a chart of accounts that can be individualized to the business and the templates for each account ledger, the general ledgers, and the financial reports. These programs strive to be user-friendly, but knowing how to input the data correctly is not enough. A manager must also know where to input each piece of data and how to analyze the reports compiled from the data. Widely accepted accounting guidelines dictate that if you have not learned a manual record-keeping system, you need to do this before attempting to use a computerized system.

3.2 The Balance Sheet

The balance sheet is a snapshot of the business's financial position at a certain point in time. This can be any day of the year, but balance sheets are usually done at the end of each month. With a budget in hand, you project forward and develop pro forma statements to monitor actual progress against expectations.

As shown in Figure 14.11, this financial statement is a listing of total assets (what the business owns—items of value) and total liabilities (what the business owes). The total assets are broken down into subcategories of current assets, fixed assets, and other assets. The total liabilities are broken down into subcategories of current liabilities, long-term liabilities/debt, and owner's equity.

FIGURE 14.10

Financial controls tell you when good organizational performance is reflected in positive financial outcomes.

© 2010 Jupiterimages Corporation

budgeting

A listing of all planned expenses and revenues.

Assets

Current assets are those assets that are cash or can be readily converted to cash in the short term, such as accounts receivable or inventory. In the balance sheet shown in Figure 14.11, the current assets are cash, petty cash, accounts receivable, inventory, and supplies.

FIGURE 14.11 Sample Balance Sheet

December 31, 2013				
Assets			**Liabilities**	
Current Assets			Current Liabilities	
Cash	12,300		Notes Payable	5,000
Petty Cash	100		Accounts Payable	35,900
			Wages Payable	14,600
Accounts Receivable	40,500		Interest Payable	2,900
Inventory	31,000		Warranty Liability	1,100
Supplies	5,300			
Total Current Assets	89,200		Total Current Liabilities	59,500
Investments	36,000		Long-Term Liabilities	
			Notes Payable	20,000
Property, Plant and Equipment			Bonds Payable	400,000
Land	5,500		Total Long-Term Liabilities	420,000
Land Improvements	6,500			
Buildings	180,000			
Equipment	201,000		Total Liabilities	479,500
Less Accum. Depreciation	(56,000)			
Prop., Plant, and Equipment Net	337,000			
Intangible Assets			Stockholders' Equity	
Goodwill	105,000		Common Stocks	110,000
Trade Names	200,000		Retained Earnings	229,000
Total Intangible Assets	305,000		Less Treasury Stock	(50,000)
Other Assets	3,000			
Total Assets	770,200		Total Liability and Stockholder Equity	768,500

Some individuals define current assets as those the business expects to use or consume within the coming fiscal year. Thus, a business's noncurrent assets would be those that have a useful life of more than one year. These include fixed assets and intangible assets.

    Fixed assets are those assets that are not easily converted to cash in the short term; that is, they are assets that only change over the long term. Land, buildings, equipment, vehicles, furniture, and fixtures are some examples of fixed assets. In the Figure 14.11 illustrative balance sheet, the fixed assets shown are furniture and fixtures and equipment. These fixed assets are shown less accumulated depreciation.

Intangible assets (net) may also be shown on a balance sheet. These may be goodwill, trademarks, patents, licenses, copyrights, formulas, and franchises. In this instance, net means the value of intangible assets minus amortization.

Liabilities

Current liabilities are those coming due in the short term, usually the coming year. These are accounts payable; employment, income and sales taxes; salaries payable; federal and state unemployment insurance; and the current year's portion of multiyear debt. A comparison of the company's current assets and its current liabilities reveals its working capital. Many managers use an accounts receivable aging report and a current inventory listing as tools to help them in management of the current asset structure.

Long-term debt, or liabilities, may be bank notes or loans made to purchase the business's fixed asset structure. Long-term debt/liabilities come due in a period of more than 1 year. The portion of a bank note that is not payable in the coming year is long-term debt/liability.

For example, a business owner may take out a bank note to buy land and a building. If the land is valued at $50,000 and the building is valued at $50,000, the business's total fixed assets are $100,000. If $20,000 is made as a down payment and $80,000 is financed with a bank note for 15 years, the $80,000 is the long-term debt.

Owner's Equity

Owner's equity refers to the amount of money the owner has invested in the firm. This amount is determined by subtracting current liabilities and long-term debt from total assets. The remaining capital/owner's equity is what the owner would have left in the event of liquidation, or the dollar amount of the total assets that the owner can claim after all creditors are paid.

3.3 The Income Profit and Loss Statement (P&L)

The profit and loss statement (P&L) shows the relation of income and expenses for a specific time interval. The income/P&L statement is expressed in a 1-month format, January 1 through January 31, or a quarterly year-to-date format, January 1 through March 31. This financial statement is cumulative for a 12-month fiscal period, at which time it is closed out. A new cumulative record is started at the beginning of the new 12-month fiscal period.

The P&L statement is divided into five major categories: (1) sales or revenue, (2) cost of goods sold/cost of sales, (3) gross profit, (4) operating expenses, and (5) net income. Let's look at each category in turn.

Sales or Revenue

The sales or revenue portion of the income statement is where the retail price of the product is expressed in terms of dollars times the number of units sold. This can be product units or service units. Sales can be expressed in one category as total sales or can be broken out into more than one type of sales category: car sales, part sales, and service sales, for instance. In our example, if the company sold 20,000 books at a retail price of $25 each, the total revenues would equal $500,000. If a firm sells all of its books on credit (i.e., you can charge them on your credit card), the company does not collect cash for these sales until the end of the month, or whenever the credit card company settles up with the firm.

Cost of Goods Sold/Cost of Sales

The cost of goods sold/sales portion of the income statement shows the cost of products purchased for resale, or the direct labor cost (service person wages) for service businesses. Cost of goods sold/sales also may include additional categories, such as freight charges cost or subcontract labor costs. These costs also may be expressed in one category as total cost of goods sold/sales or can be broken out to match the sales categories: car purchases, parts, purchases, and service salaries, for example.

intangible asset

An asset that cannot be physically touched, or is not physical in nature.

current liabilities

Liabilities coming due in the short term, usually the coming year.

long-term debt

Liabilities may be bank notes or loans made to purchase the business's fixed asset structure. Long-term debt/liabilities come due in a time period of more than 1 year.

FIGURE 14.12 Sample Income Statement

For the year ended December 31, 2013	
Sales/Revenues (All on Credit):	$500,000
Cost of Goods Sold	$380,000
Gross Profit	120,000
Operating Expenses	
Selling Expenses	35,000
Administrative Expenses	45,000
Total Operating Expenses	(80,000)
Operating Income	40,000
Interest Expense	(12,000)
Income before Taxes	28,000
Income Tax Expense	(5,000)
Net Income	**$23,000**

Breaking out sales and cost of goods sold/sales into separate categories can have an advantage over combining all sales and costs into one category. When you break out sales, you can see how much each product you have sold costs and the gross profit for each product. This type of analysis enables you to make inventory and sales decisions about each product individually.

Gross Profit

The gross profit portion of the income/P&L statement tells the difference between what you sold the product or service for and what the product or service cost you. The goal of any business is to sell enough units of product or service to be able to subtract the cost and have a high enough gross profit to cover operating expenses, plus yield a net income that is a reasonable return on investment. The key to operating a profitable business is to maximize gross profit.

If you increase the retail price of your product too much above the competition, you might lose units of sales to the competition and not yield a high enough gross profit to cover your expenses. However, if you decrease the retail price of your product too much below the competition, you might gain additional units of sales but not make enough gross profit per unit sold to cover your expenses.

While this may sound obvious, a carefully thought out pricing strategy maximizes gross profit to cover expenses and yield a positive net income. At a very basic level, this means that prices are set at a level where marginal and operating costs are covered. Beyond this, pricing should carefully be set to reflect the image you want portrayed and, if desired, promote repeat business.

Operating Expenses

The operating expense section of the income/P&L statement is a measurement of all the operating expenses of the business. There are two types of expenses, fixed and variable. Fixed expenses are those expenses that do not vary with the level of sales; thus, you will have to cover these expenses even if your sales are less than the expenses. The entrepreneur has little control over these expenses once they are set. Some examples of fixed expenses are rent (contractual agreement), interest expense (note agreement), an accounting or law firm retainer for legal services of X amount per month for 12 months, and monthly charges for electricity, phone, and Internet connections.

Variable expenses are those expenses that vary with the level of sales. Examples of variable expenses include bonuses, employee wages (hours per week worked), travel and entertainment expenses, and purchases of supplies. (Note: Categorization of these may differ from business to business.) Expense control is an area where the entrepreneur can maximize net income by holding expenses to a minimum.

Net Income

The net income portion of the income/P&L statement is the bottom line. This is the measure of a firm's ability to operate at a profit. Many factors affect the outcome of the bottom line. Level of sales, pricing strategy, inventory control, accounts receivable control, ordering procedures, marketing of the business and product, expense control, customer service, and productivity of employees are just a few of these factors. The net income should be enough to allow growth in the business through reinvestment of profits and to give the owner a reasonable return on investment.

3.4   The Cash Flow Statement

The cash flow statement is the detail of cash received and cash expended for each month of the year. A projected cash flow statement helps managers determine whether the company has positive cash flow. Cash flow is probably the most immediate indicator of an impending problem, since negative cash flow will bankrupt the company if it continues for a long enough period. If company's projections show a negative cash flow, managers might need to revisit the business plan and solve this problem.

An old joke claims, "How can I be broke if I still have checks in my checkbook (or if I still have a debit/credit card, etc.)?" While perhaps poor humor, many new managers similarly think that the only financial statement they need to manage their business effectively is an income/P&L statement; that a cash flow statement is excess detail. They mistakenly believe that the bottom-line profit is all they need to know and that if the company is showing a profit, it is going to be successful. In the long run, profitability and cash flow have a direct relationship, but profit and cash flow do not mean the same thing in the short run. A business can be operating at a loss and have a strong cash flow position. Conversely, a business can be showing an excellent profit but not have enough cash flow to sustain its sales growth.

The process of reconciling cash flow is similar to the process you follow in reconciling your bank checking account. The cash flow statement is composed of (1) beginning cash on hand, (2) cash receipts/deposits for the month, (3) cash paid out for the month, and (4) ending cash position.

KEY TAKEAWAY

The financial controls provide a blueprint to compare against the actual results once the business is in operation. A comparison and analysis of the business plan against the actual results can tell you whether the business is on target. Corrections, or revisions, to policies and strategies may be necessary to achieve the business's goals. The three most important financial controls are (1) the balance sheet, (2) the income statement (sometimes called a profit and loss statement), and (3) the cash flow statement. Each gives the manager a different perspective on and insight into how well the business is operating toward its goals. Analyzing monthly financial statements is a must since most organizations need to be able to pay their bills to stay in business.

4. NONFINANCIAL CONTROLS

Nonfinancial controls are defined as controls where nonfinancial performance outcomes are measured. Why is it important to measure such outcomes? Because they are likely to affect profitability in the long term.

How do we go about identifying nonfinancial controls? In some areas it is easy to do, and in others more difficult. Some possible nonfinancial controls are described next.

4.1 Common Mistakes with Nonfinancial Controls

FIGURE 14.13

Customer satisfaction is an increasingly important metric in strong nonfinancial controls.

© 2010 Jupiterimages Corporation

In a review of current nonfinancial control practices, Harvard professors Chris Ittner and David Larcker commented, "Tracking things like customer satisfaction and employee turnover can powerfully supplement traditional bookkeeping. Unfortunately, most companies botch the job."[14]

Ittner and Larcker somewhat cynically conclude their study by stating, "The original purpose of nonfinancial performance measures was to fill out the picture provided by traditional accounting. Instead, such measures have become a shabby substitute for financial performance."[15] However, research also shows that those firms that put these nonfinancial controls in place, and can validate them, earn much higher profits than those that fail to utilize such controls.[16] In this section, we will discuss common mistakes that organizations make in their control procedures.

Failure to Use Nonfinancial Controls

While poorly conceived and implemented nonfinancial controls are certainly a cost for organizations, such ineptness is no defense for not including them in every modern organization's system of controls. The world is simply changing too fast and competitors' capabilities are evolving too quickly to rely solely on financial controls. For example, considering the relationship between customer satisfaction and a retail store's sales, a dissatisfied customer is hard to get back (and may have been dissatisfied enough to leave the store before even making that first purchase).

Not Linking Control to Strategy

This mistake appears to be a common one, but its root cause—failure to adapt the control system to the specific strategy of the organization—is not obvious. Growth in interest in nonfinancial controls has led to widespread adoption of such systems as the Balanced Scorecard. However, because such a system can be complex, managers tend to put them in place without tailoring them to the specific needs and characteristics of their organization.

Several things can go wrong when nonfinancial controls are not linked to the strategy. First, control systems tend to be tied to reward systems, and if managers and employees are being paid based on the achievement of certain nonstrategic, nonfinancial outcomes, then the firm's strategy and, hence, performance, could suffer. Second, if the controls are not linked to the strategy, or the linkages are unclear, then managers do not really understand which nonfinancial controls are the most important.

Failing to Validate the Links

There are two big challenges that organizations face when trying to use nonfinancial controls. First, nonfinancial controls are indirectly related to financial performance; the relationship is like a sequence of nonfinancial outcomes that cascade down to financial performance. For instance, (1) good employee recruiting leads to (2) satisfied employees, which leads to (3) an employee base that creates value, which leads to (4) satisfied customers, which leads to (5) profitable customer buying patterns, which lead to (6) good profitability. While these six nonfinancial outcomes might lead to good financial performance, it might be challenging to identify and manage the inputs to each step.

Once managers take the step of identifying these linkages, the second challenge is to show that the linkages actually exist. While more companies are putting such models into place, few are collecting the information to test and validate the actual relationships in their organization. In fact, Ittner and Larcker found that less than a quarter of the firms that they surveyed actually did any formal validation of the nonfinancial model they had developed. Consequently, a nonfinancial control that lacks validity could actually lead to poorer organizational performance than failing to use nonfinancial controls altogether.

Failing to Set Appropriate Performance Targets

The third common area of weakness in the use of nonfinancial controls is the failure to set appropriate performance targets. A firm might want to set high goals, and therefore control, for such things as customer satisfaction or employee turnover, but the cost of achieving 100% customer satisfaction or zero employee turnover may exceed their benefit financially.

Failing to set appropriate performance targets can take on another form. In such cases, instead of setting inappropriate nonfinancial controls and related targets, the organization simply has set too many.[17] This can happen when a new control system is put in place, but the old one is not removed. Just as often, it can occur because management has not made the hard choices about which nonfinancial controls are most important and invested in validating their usage.

Measurement Failure

In many cases, an inappropriate measure is used to assess whether a targeted nonfinancial control is being achieved. This can happen for a number of reasons. First, different parts of the business may assess customer satisfaction differently. This makes it very hard to evaluate consistently the relationship between customer satisfaction (a nonfinancial control) and financial performance. Second, even when a common basis for evaluation is used, the meaning may not be clear in the context of how it is measured. For example, if a firm created a simple survey of customer satisfaction, where individuals were scored on a range from 1 (satisfied) to 7 (unsatisfied), what does each individual score between 1 and 7 mean? Finally, sometimes the nonfinancial control or objective is complex. Customer or employee satisfaction, for instance, are not necessarily easily captured on a scale of 1 to 7. Imagine trying to introduce controls for leadership ability (i.e., we know if we have strong leaders, they make good choices, which eventually lead to good financial performance) or innovativeness (i.e., cool products lead to more customer enthusiasm, which eventually leads to financial performance). Such intangibles are extremely difficult to measure and to track.

KEY TAKEAWAY

Nonfinancial controls, such as those related to employee satisfaction, customer service, and so on, are an important and increasingly applied form of organizational control. While firms that use nonfinancial controls well also perform much better than firms that fail to use them, numerous managerial mistakes are made with regard to their conceptualization, implementation, or both. Beyond simply using nonfinancial controls, best practices around such controls include aligning them with the strategy, validating the links between nonfinancial controls and financial controls, setting appropriate control performance targets, and confirming the right measure of the desired control.

EXERCISES

1. What are nonfinancial controls? Name some examples.
2. What should be the relationship between nonfinancial and financial controls?
3. What are some common mistakes made by managers with regard to nonfinancial controls?
4. What are some solutions to the common mistakes you identified?

5. LEAN CONTROL

lean

A system of nonfinancial controls used to improve product and service quality and decrease waste.

Lean control, or simply lean, has become an immensely popular business control and improvement methodology in recent years. Lean control is a highly refined example of nonfinancial controls in action. **Lean** is a system of nonfinancial controls used to improve product and service quality and decrease waste. Research suggests that up to 70% of manufacturing firms are using some form of lean in their business operations.[18] Lean was initially focused on improving manufacturing operations but is now used to improve product development, order processing, and a variety of other nonmanufacturing processes (sometimes called "lean in the office").

5.1 What Is Meant by Lean Control?

FIGURE 14.14

Developed by Motorola in 1986, the term Six Sigma refers to a process where, statistically, 99.99966% of products manufactured (or 3.4 defects per million operations) are statistically free from defects.

© Thinkstock

Lean's popularity has both resulted from and been driven by an explosion in the volume of lean-related educational resources. Amazon offers almost 1,800 books and other materials about lean, and Yahoo! hosts over 90 online discussion groups relating to lean. Colleges and universities, industry trade associations, and private consulting firms routinely offer courses, seminars, and conferences to explain what lean is and how to implement lean control.

Lean control, according to one definition, "is a process for measuring and reducing inventory and streamlining production. It is a means for changing the way a company measures plant performance. It is a knowledge-based system. It takes years of hard work, preparation and support from upper management. Lean is so named because it purports to use much less of certain resources (space, inventory, workers, etc.) than is used by normal mass-production systems to produce comparable output." The term came into widespread use with the 1990 publication of the book *The Machine That Changed the World*, by James P. Womack, Daniel T. Jones, and Daniel Roos.[19]

This abundance of education resources on the topic of lean is actually a mixed blessing for managers who are just now becoming interested in lean. On the one hand, today's managers do not have to search far to find lean materials or programs. But the wealth of lean resources can also be a source of confusion for two main reasons. First, there is no universal definition of lean and little agreement about what the truly core principles of lean are. For instance, quality programs such as Six-Sigma, or even lean Six Sigma, are other titles competing for the "lean" intellectual space. Therefore, lean experts often approach the subject from differing perspectives and describe lean in different ways. Many experts strongly argue that their particular "brand" of lean is the one right way to implement and use lean.

5.2 Lean Applications

FIGURE 14.15

Lean organizations strive to improve flow by reducing the size of production batches, and in the process, they increase flexibility and lower costs.

© 2010 Jupiterimages Corporation

Lean is often associated with Toyota Motor Corporation because most lean tools and techniques were developed by Toyota in Japan beginning in the 1950s. After World War II, Toyota's leaders were determined to make the company a full-range car and truck manufacturing enterprise, but they faced several serious challenges. The Japanese motor vehicle market was small and yet demanded a fairly wide range of vehicle types. This meant that Toyota needed to find a way to earn a profit while manufacturing a variety of vehicles in low volumes. In addition, capital was extremely scarce, which made it impossible for Toyota to make large purchases of the latest production equipment. To succeed, or even survive, Toyota needed a way to build vehicles that would require fewer resources. To achieve this goal, Toyota's leaders, principally Eiji Toyoda and Taiichi Ohno, began to create and implement the production techniques and tools that came to be known as lean.[20]

To gain the most benefits from lean, managers must be able to determine what specific lean tools and techniques will be effective in their particular business. And to make that determination, they must clearly understand what lean is designed to accomplish (its primary objectives) and what core principles lean is based on. With this understanding, managers can decide which lean tools will work well in their business, which lean tools will need to be modified or adapted to work well, and which tools are simply not appropriate.

FIGURE 14.16 Savings Using Lean Control

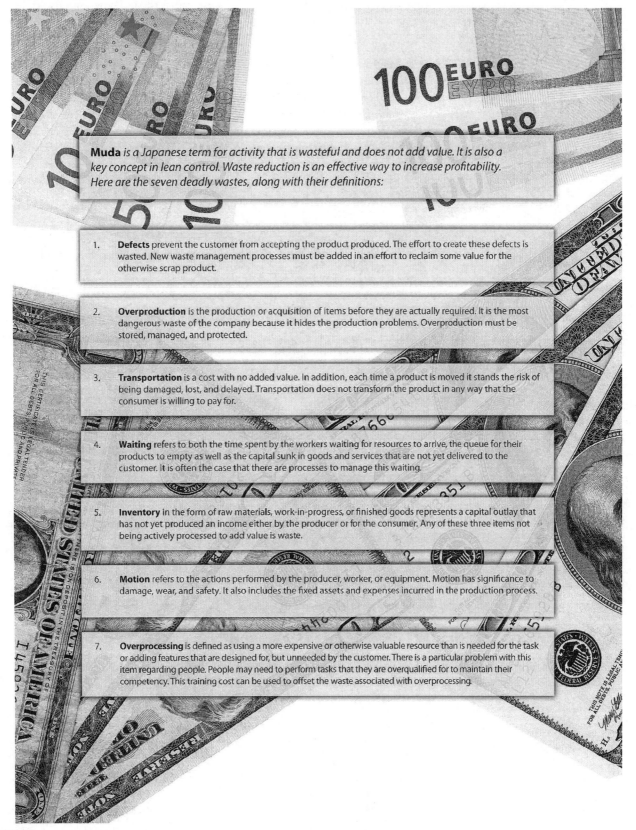

Muda *is a Japanese term for activity that is wasteful and does not add value. It is also a key concept in lean control. Waste reduction is an effective way to increase profitability. Here are the seven deadly wastes, along with their definitions:*

1. **Defects** prevent the customer from accepting the product produced. The effort to create these defects is wasted. New waste management processes must be added in an effort to reclaim some value for the otherwise scrap product.

2. **Overproduction** is the production or acquisition of items before they are actually required. It is the most dangerous waste of the company because it hides the production problems. Overproduction must be stored, managed, and protected.

3. **Transportation** is a cost with no added value. In addition, each time a product is moved it stands the risk of being damaged, lost, and delayed. Transportation does not transform the product in any way that the consumer is willing to pay for.

4. **Waiting** refers to both the time spent by the workers waiting for resources to arrive, the queue for their products to empty as well as the capital sunk in goods and services that are not yet delivered to the customer. It is often the case that there are processes to manage this waiting.

5. **Inventory** in the form of raw materials, work-in-progress, or finished goods represents a capital outlay that has not yet produced an income either by the producer or for the consumer. Any of these three items not being actively processed to add value is waste.

6. **Motion** refers to the actions performed by the producer, worker, or equipment. Motion has significance to damage, wear, and safety. It also includes the fixed assets and expenses incurred in the production process.

7. **Overprocessing** is defined as using a more expensive or otherwise valuable resource than is needed for the task or adding features that are designed for, but unneeded by the customer. There is a particular problem with this item regarding people. People may need to perform tasks that they are overqualified for to maintain their competency. This training cost can be used to offset the waste associated with overprocessing.

muda

A Japanese term for activity that is wasteful and doesn't add value.

What are the major objectives and core principles of lean? Despite the arguments and debates that often surround attempts to define and describe lean, it is clear that the ultimate objective of lean is the avoidance of wasteful activity (dubbed **muda** in Japanese) in all business operations. As shown in Figure 14.16, muda comprises *seven deadly wastes*. In the lean world, waste means any activity or condition that consumes resources but creates no value for customers. Therefore, waste includes the production of defective products that must be remade or fixed, the production of more products than the market will buy, excessive work-in-process inventories, overprocessing (processing steps that are not really needed or that add no value), unnecessary movement of people or products, and unnecessary waiting by employees.

5.3 The Five Core Principles of Lean

Lean methodologies are lean because they enable a business to do more with less. A lean organization uses less human effort, less equipment, less facilities space, less time, and less capital—while always coming closer to meeting customers' exact needs. Therefore, lean is not just another cost-cutting program of the kind we often see in business organizations. Lean is much more about the conservation of valuable resources than it is about cost cutting.

In their best-selling book, *Lean Thinking*, James Womack and Daniel Jones identified five core principles of lean.[21] In this section, we explain each.

Define Value from the Customer's Perspective

The first core principle in the Womack/Jones lean framework is that value must be defined and specified from the customer's perspective. This requires more than high-minded, generic statements. To be meaningful, value must be defined in terms of specific products. This means that managers must understand how each specific product meets the needs of specific customers at a specific price and at a specific time.

Describe the Value Stream for Each Product or Service

The second core principle of lean is to describe the value stream for each product or service (or, in some cases, for groups or families of similar products). The value stream is the set of activities that the business is performing to bring a finished product to a customer. It includes both direct manufacturing activities and indirect activities such as order processing, purchasing, and materials management. Developing a detailed description or map of each value stream usually reveals huge amounts of waste. It enables managers to identify which value stream activities add value to the product, which activities add no value but cannot be immediately eliminated for various reasons, and which activities create no value and can be immediately eliminated (or at least reduced substantially).

Create Flow in Each Value Stream

The third essential principle of lean is embodied in the word flow. When a value stream has been completely described as unnecessary, non-value-adding activities have been eliminated, the basic idea of flow is to arrange the remaining activities sequentially, so that products will move smoothly and continuously from one activity to the next. However, flow means more than ease of movement. Flow is the lean principle that directly challenges the traditional "batch-and-queue" model of manufacturing, where people and equipment are organized and located by function, and products (and component parts) are manufactured in large batches. Lean organizations strive to improve flow by reducing the size of production batches, and in the process, they increase flexibility and lower costs.

Produce at the Pace (Pull) of Actual Customer Demand

Producing at the pace or pull of actual customer demand is the fourth key principle of lean. One of the greatest benefits of moving from traditional batch-and-queue manufacturing to continuous flow production is that lead times fall dramatically. Reduced lead times and increased flexibility mean that lean organizations can respond to actual customer demand rather than attempt to predict in advance what that level of demand will be. This allows lean organizations to substantially lower both finished goods and work-in-process inventories.

Strive to Continuously Improve All Business Operations

The fifth core principle of lean is continuous improvement, expressed in Japanese by the word **kaizen**. Companies that implement lean adopt the mind-set that it is always possible to improve any business activity, and they regularly conduct kaizen events throughout their organizations to improve specific processes or operations. Today, Toyota is recognized as one of the most "lean" business enterprises in the world.

kaizen

The Japanese term for continuous improvement.

KEY TAKEAWAY

Lean control, or simply lean, is the system of nonfinancial controls used to improve product and service quality and decrease waste. While popularized through the dramatic successes of Toyota in auto manufacturing, lean processes are used to improve quality and decrease waste in most service and manufacturing industries around the world. In this section, you saw examples of the seven deadly wastes (*muda*) and the five core principles of lean, which culminate in continuous improvement, or *kaizen*.

EXERCISES

1. What is lean control?
2. What types of industries might find lean controls valuable?
3. What does *muda* mean and what are some examples of it?
4. What are the five lean principles?
5. Pick a company you are familiar with—what would it need to do differently to comply with the five lean principles?

---

6. CRAFTING YOUR BALANCED SCORECARD

LEARNING OBJECTIVES

1. **Understand the Balanced Scorecard concept.**
2. **See how the Balanced Scorecard integrates nonfinancial and financial controls.**
3. **Be able to outline a personal Balanced Scorecard.**

6.1 An Introduction to the Balanced Scorecard

The Balanced Scorecard was originally introduced to integrate financial and nonfinancial controls in a way that provided a balanced understanding of the determinants of firm performance. It is also a strategic performance management tool because it helps managers identify and understand the way that operating controls are tied to strategic controls, and ultimately, firm performance. In this broader sense, a **Balanced Scorecard** is a control system that translates an organization's vision, mission, and strategy into specific, quantifiable goals and to monitor the organization's performance in terms of achieving these goals.

According to Robert S. Kaplan and David P. Norton, the Balanced Scorecard approach "examines performance in four areas. Financial analysis, the most traditionally used performance indicator, includes assessments of measures such as operating costs and return-on-investment. Customer analysis looks at customer satisfaction and retention. Internal analysis looks at production and innovation, measuring performance in terms of maximizing profit from current products and following indicators for future productivity. Finally, learning and growth analysis explores the effectiveness of management in terms of measures of employee satisfaction and retention and information system performance."[22]

Balanced Scorecard

A framework designed to translate an organization's vision and mission statements and overall business strategy into specific, quantifiable goals and objectives and to monitor the organization's performance in terms of achieving these goals.

Whereas the scorecard identifies financial and nonfinancial areas of performance, the second step in the scorecard process is the development of a strategy map. The idea is to identify key performance areas in learning and growth and show how these metrics relate to internal, customer, and financial performance areas. Typically, this is an iterative process where managers test relationships among the different areas of performance. Managers should be able to show how and why the choice made in each area ultimately led to high profitability and stock prices in for-profit businesses and other meaningful outcomes in nonprofit organizations.

FIGURE 14.18 The Balanced Scorecard Hierarchy

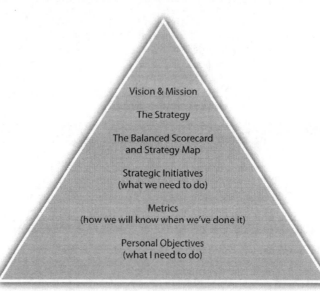

With the scorecard and strategy map in hand, managers then break broad goals down successively into vision, strategies, strategic initiatives, and metrics. As an example, imagine that an organization has a goal of maintaining employee satisfaction in its vision and mission statements. This would be the organization's vision in the domain of learning and growth, since employee satisfaction is indirectly related to financial performance. Strategies for achieving that learning and growth vision might include approaches such as increasing employee-management communication. Initiatives undertaken to implement the strategy could include, for example, regularly scheduled meetings with employees. Metrics could include quantifications of employee suggestions or employee surveys. Finally, managers would want to test their assumptions about the relationship between employee satisfaction and the downstream areas such as internal, customer, and financial performance. For example, satisfied employees may be more productive and less likely to quit (internal), which leads to better products or services and customer relations (customer), which leads to lower employee recruiting and training costs and greater sales and repeat sales (financial). This sequence of causal relationships is summarized in Figure 14.19.

FIGURE 14.19 The Strategy Map: A Causal Relationship between Nonfinancial and Financial Controls

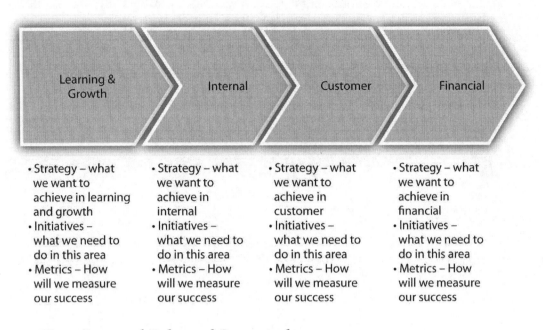

6.2 Your Personal Balanced Scorecard

Now that you have an understanding of nonfinancial and financial controls, and specific cases such as lean control systems and the Balanced Scorecard, it's time to apply the notion of the Balanced Scorecard to individuals. Recall that the figure shows your position in the context of the Balanced Scorecard—it asks you to state your personal objectives, in the context of the organization's objectives. However, in developing your own Balanced Scorecard, you will be laying out a road map to achieve your personal and professional objectives (or mission and vision more broadly), which may overlap a lot or very little with the organization's objectives. While you can choose to focus the scorecard more narrowly on something like your career, you will be much better served by the personal Balanced Scorecard if you pursue a holistic (personal + professional) approach. For example, you may have particular personal goals about financial independence, and this would relate to other choices you might want to make about your personal and professional priorities.

Social psychologist Hubert Rampersad has sought to translate the business Balanced Scorecard into a personal balanced score by providing you with the following four suggestions.[23]

1. **Learning and growth:** your skills and learning ability. How do you learn, and how can you be successful in the future? For example, the course that you are taking in conjunction with this book may lead to a degree, be a prerequisite for other courses, and so on.

2. **Internal:** your physical health and mental state. How can you control these to create value for yourself and others? How can you remain feeling good at work as well as in your spare time? For instance, your objectives and activities related to physical and emotional fitness.

3. **Customer (external):** relations with your spouse, children, friends, employer, colleagues, and others. How do they see you?

4. **Financial:** financial stability. To what degree are you able to fulfill your financial needs? Again, do you seek financial independence, resources to fund other endeavors?

The best way to put these suggestions into action is to work on the scorecard in several sessions, as there is a wide range of factors to consider. Your objective for the first session should be to develop your personal vision statement and list several areas of development in *learning, internal, customer,* and *financial* facets of the scorecard. You should be able to fit the scorecard on a single page, for easy and frequent reference. You can use your next session with the scorecard to refine your developmental objectives and set relevant measures and near-term objectives. Post the scorecard where you can refer to it often. And, just as with organizations, if your circumstances change, then that is the critical time to revalidate or revise your personal Balanced Scorecard.

EXERCISES

1. What is a Balanced Scorecard? What is the difference between a Balanced Scorecard and a simple list of nonfinancial and financial controls?
2. What roles do vision, mission, and strategy play in the development of a Balanced Scorecard?
3. What might be some of the differences between an organization's Balanced Scorecard and your personal Balanced Scorecard? What might be some of the similarities?
4. Under what circumstances should an organization's or an individual's Balanced Scorecard be revised?

7. CASE IN POINT: NEWELL RUBBERMAID LEVERAGES COST CONTROLS TO GROW

FIGURE 14.20

© Thinkstock

Newell Company grew to be a diversified manufacturer and marketer of simple household items, cookware, and hardware. In the early 1950s, Newell Company's business consisted solely of manufactured curtain rods sold through hardware stores and retailers like Sears. Since the 1960s, however, the company has diversified extensively through acquisitions of businesses for paintbrushes, writing pens, pots and pans, hairbrushes, and the like. Over 90% of its growth can be attributed to these many small acquisitions, whose performance Newell improved tremendously through aggressive restructuring and corporate emphasis on cost cutting and cost controls. Usually within a year of the acquisition, Newell would bring in new leadership and install its own financial controller in the acquired unit. Then three standard sets of controls were introduced: an integrated financial accounting system, a sales-and-order processing and tracking system, and a flexible manufacturing system. Once these systems were in place, managers were able to control costs by limiting expenses to those previously budgeted. Administration, accounting, and customer-related financial accounting aspects of the acquired business were also consolidated into Newell's corporate headquarters to further reduce and control costs.

While Newell Company's 16 different lines of business may appear quite different, they all share the common characteristics of being staple manufactured items sold primarily through volume retail channels like Walmart, Target, and Kmart. Because Newell operates each line of business autonomously (separate manufacturing, research and development [R&D], and selling responsibilities for each), it is perhaps best described as pursuing a related, linked diversification strategy. The common linkages are both internal (accounting systems, product merchandising skills, and acquisition competency) and external (distribution channel of volume retailers). Beyond its internal systems and processes, Newell was also able to control costs through outcome controls—that is, business managers were paid a bonus based on the profitability of their particular unit—in fact, the firm's strategy is to achieve profits, not simply growth at the expense of profits. Newell managers could expect a base salary equal to the industry average but could earn bonuses ranging from 35% to 100% based on their rank and unit profitability.

In 1999, Newell acquired Rubbermaid, a U.S.-based manufacturer of flexible plastic products like trash cans, reheatable and freezable food containers, and a broad range of other plastic storage containers designed for home and office use. While Rubbermaid was highly innovative (over 80% of its growth has come from internal new product development), it had difficulty controlling costs and was losing ground against powerful customers like Walmart. Newell believed that the market power it wielded with retailers like Walmart would help it turn Rubbermaid's prospects around. The acquisition deal between these two companies resulted in a single company that was twice as big and became known as Newell Rubbermaid Inc. (NYSE: NWL). In 2012, *Fortune* named Newell Rubbermaid the number 10 "Most Admired Company" in the home equipment and furnishings category.

Case written by Mason Carpenter and Talya Bauer to accompany Carpenter, M., Bauer, T., Erdogan, B., & Short, J. (2013). Principles of Management (2nd ed.). New York: Flat World Knowledge; Based on information retrieved September 14, 2012, from http://www.bain.com/masteringthemerger/ case_example_new_rbbmd_trans.asp and from the Newell Rubbermaid Web site: http://www.newellrubbermaid.com/public/Our-Company/ Our-History.aspx.

CASE DISCUSSION QUESTIONS

1. The controlling facet of the P-O-L-C framework introduces you to a variety of controls. What do other organizations you are familiar with do with regard to control that is similar to or different from what we see in the case of Newell?

2. What types of controls does Newell use?

3. Does Newell use behavioral controls? What are some examples?

4. Does Newell use outcome controls? What are some examples?

5. How do the controls Newell uses fit its strategy?

6. At the end of the case, how has Newell adjusted its strategy? What changes in controls has it made as a result?

ENDNOTES

1. Kuratko, D. F., Ireland, R. D., & Hornsby. J. S. (2001). Improving firm performance through entrepreneurial actions: Acordia's corporate entrepreneurship strategy. *Academy of Management Executive, 15*(4), 60–71.

2. Retrieved September 14, 2012, from http://www.thehealthcareblog.com/the_health_care_blog/2007/12/pilots-use-chec.html.

3. Ghoshal S., & Moran, P. (1996). Bad for practice: A critique of the transaction cost theory. *Academy of Management Review. 21*(1), 13–47.

4. Retrieved September 14, 2012, from http://i.n.com/pdf/ne/2006/perkins_letter.pdf.

5. Retrieved September 14, 2012, from http://news.zdnet.com/2100-9595_22-149452.html.

6. U.S. Government Printing Office. (2006, February 15). Executive summary. Select Bipartisan Committee to Investigate the Preparation for and Response to Hurricane Katrina.

7. Retrieved September 14, 2012, from Hershey profits for 4Q 1999 down 11% due to SAP implementation problem: http://www.greenspun.com/bboard/q-and-a-fetch-msg.tcl?msg_id=002SUM.

8. Retrieved September 14, 2012, from http://www.nist.gov/public_affairs/factsheet/baldfaqs.htm.

9. Galbraith, J. R. (1974). Organization design: An information processing view. *Interfaces, 4,* 28–36. Galbraith believes that "the greater the uncertainty of the task, the greater the amount of information that must be processed between decision makers during the execution of the task to get a given level of performance." Firms can reduce uncertainty through better planning and coordination, often by rules, hierarchy, or goals. Galbraith states that "the critical limiting factor of an organizational form is the ability to handle the non-routine events that cannot be anticipated or planned for."

10. Harrison, J. S., & St. John, C. H. (2002). *Foundations in Strategic Management* (2nd ed., pp. 118–129). Cincinnati, OH: South-Western College.

11. Venkataraman, S., & Sarasvathy, S. D. (2001). Strategy and entrepreneurship: Outlines of an untold story. In M. A. Hitt, R. E. Freeman, & J. S. Harrison (Eds.), *Handbook of strategic management* (pp. 650–668). Oxford: Blackwell.

12. Matthews, J. (1999). Strategic moves. *Supply Management, 4*(4), 36–37.

13. Ittner, C., & Larcker, D. F. (2003, November). Coming up short on nonfinancial performance measurement. *Harvard Business Review,* 2–8.

14. Ittner, C., & Larcker, D. F. (2003, November). Coming up short on nonfinancial performance measurement. *Harvard Business Review,* 2–8.

15. Ittner, C., & Larcker, D. F. (2003, November). Coming up short on nonfinancial performance measurement. *Harvard Business Review,* 2–8.

16. Ittner, C., & Larcker, D. F. (2003, November). Coming up short on nonfinancial performance measurement. *Harvard Business Review,* 2–8.

17. Brown, M. G. (1996). *Keeping score.* New York: Productivity Press.

18. PrintPlanet launches lean manufacturing forum. (2008, August 11). Retrieved September 14, 2012, from http://members.whattheythink.com/home/wttnews080811.cfm.

19. Womack, J. P., Jones, D. T., & Roos, D. (1990). *The machine that changed the world.* New York: Rawson Associates.

20. Retrieved September 14, 2012, from http://www.toyota.co.jp/en/history/index.html.

21. Womack, J. P., & Jones, D. T. (2003). *Lean thinking.* New York: Simon & Schuster.

22. Kaplan, R., & Norton, D. (2001). *The strategy-focused organization.* Boston: Harvard Business School Press.

23. Rampersad, H. K. (2006). *The personal Balanced Scorecard: The way to individual happiness, personal integrity, and organizational effectiveness.* Greenwich, CT: Information Age.

CHAPTER 15
Strategic Human Resource Management

FIGURE 15.1

Just like chess masters who carefully place their pieces to ensure victory, strategic human resource management involves positioning the organization's human resources to secure competitive advantage.

© 2010 Jupiterimages Corporation

CHAPTER LEARNING OBJECTIVES

Reading this chapter will help you do the following:

1. Understand the scope and changing role of strategic human resource management (SHRM) in principles of management.
2. Understand key elements in the war for talent.
3. Engage in effective selection and placement strategies.
4. Understand the roles of pay structure and pay for performance.
5. Understand the components of a high-performance work system.
6. Use the human resources Balanced Scorecard to gauge and proactively manage human capital, including your own.

Management scholars and practicing managers have both argued that *the people make the place*. In today's fast-changing environment, organizations need employees who understand the organization's strategy and are empowered to execute it effectively. To achieve this goal, organizations need to follow a strategic human resource management (SHRM) approach. SHRM ensures that people are a key factor in a firm's competitive advantage. As summarized in Figure 15.2, SHRM is an integral part of the control portion of the planning-organizing-leading-controlling (P-O-L-C) framework.

FIGURE 15.2 The P-O-L-C Framework

Planning	Organizing	Leading	Controlling
1. Vision & Mission	1. Organization Design	1. Leadership	1. Systems/Processes
2. Strategizing	2. Culture	2. Decision Making	2. Strategic Human Resources
3. Goals & Objectives	3. Social Networks	3. Communications	
		4. Groups/Teams	
		5. Motivation	

Organizations need human resources (HR) to be a partner in identifying, attracting, and hiring the type of employees who will be most qualified to help the company achieve its goals. SHRM requires attracting the right employees to the company, identifying metrics to help employees stay on target to meet the company's goals, and rewarding them appropriately for their efforts so that they stay engaged and motivated. Having all these components in place—designing a high-performance work system—improves organizational performance and unleashes employee talent.

1. THE CHANGING ROLE OF STRATEGIC HUMAN RESOURCE MANAGEMENT IN PRINCIPLES OF MANAGEMENT

LEARNING OBJECTIVES

1. **Understand how HR is becoming a strategic partner.**
2. **Understand the importance of an organization's human capital.**
3. **List the key elements of SHRM.**
4. **Explain the importance of focusing on outcomes.**

The role of HR is changing. Previously considered a support function, HR is now becoming a strategic partner in helping a company achieve its goals. A strategic approach to HR means going beyond the administrative tasks like payroll processing. Instead, managers need to think more broadly and deeply about how employees will contribute to the company's success.

1.1 HR as a Strategic Partner

strategic human resource management (SHRM)

An organizational level approach to human resources management with a concern for the effects of HRM practices on firm performance.

Strategic human resource management (SHRM) is an organizational-level approach to human resources management with a concern for the effects of such practices on firm performance. Consequently, SHRM is not just a function of the HR department—all managers and executives need to be involved because the role of human capital (people) is so vital to a company's competitive advantage.[1]

In addition, organizations that value their employees are more profitable than those that do not.[2] Research shows that successful organizations have several things in common, such as providing employment security, engaging in selective hiring, using self-managed teams, being decentralized, paying well, training employees, reducing status differences, and sharing information.[3] When organizations enable, develop, and motivate human capital, they improve accounting profits as well as shareholder value in the process.[4] The most successful organizations manage HR as a strategic asset and measure HR performance in terms of its strategic impact.

SHRM practices should provide answers to the following key questions:[5]

- *Competence.* To what extent does our company have the required knowledge, skills, and abilities to implement its strategy?

- *Consequence.* To what extent does our company have the right measures, rewards, and incentives in place to align people's efforts with the company strategy?

- *Governance.* To what extent does our company have the right structures, communications systems, and policies to create a high-performing organization?

- *Learning and leadership.* To what extent can our company respond to uncertainty and learn and adapt to change quickly?

1.2 The Importance of Human Capital

Employees provide an organization's **human capital**. Human capital refers to a set of skills that individuals have acquired on the job, through training and experience, which increase a person's value in the marketplace. The Society of Human Resource Management defines an organization's human capital as follows: "A company's human capital asset is the collective sum of the attributes, life experience, knowledge, inventiveness, energy and enthusiasm that its people choose to invest in their work."[6]

1.3 Focus on Outcomes

Historically, many HR managers are more effective in the technical or operational aspects of HR than they are in the strategic. In recent years, this trend has begun to change as managers have realized that the strategic aspects have a much larger effect on the company's success.[7] In the past, HR professionals focused on compliance to rules, such as those set by the federal government, and they tracked simple metrics like the number of employees hired or the number of hours of training delivered. The new principles of management, however, require a focus on outcomes and results, not just numbers and compliance. Just as lawyers view their key performance measure as the number of cases they have won—not just the time and effort spent working on cases—so too must HR professionals track how employees are using the skills they have learned to attain goals versus a potentially less impactful measure such as the number of hours employees have engaged in training.[8]

John Murabito, executive vice president and head of HR and Services at Cigna, says that HR executives need to understand the company's goals and strategy and then provide employees with the skills needed. HR executives often get wrapped up in their own initiatives without understanding how their role contributes to the business. That is a concern because when it comes to the HR department, "anything that is administrative or transactional is going to get outsourced," Murabito says.[9] Indeed, the number of HR outsourcing contracts over $25 million has been increasing.[10] For example, Bank of America outsourced its HR administration to Arinso. While Arinso will provide timekeeping, payroll processing, and payroll services for 10,000 Bank of America employees outside the United States, Scotiabank signed a five-year payroll deal with Arinso for over 40,000 employees in more than 50 countries.[11] To avoid outsourcing, HR needs to stay relevant and accept accountability for its business results. In short, the people strategy needs to be fully aligned with the company's business strategy and keep the focus on outcomes.

1.4 Key Elements of HR

In high-performing companies, each element of the HR system is designed to reflect best practice and to maximize employee performance. The different parts of the HR system are strongly aligned with company goals.

FIGURE 15.3

Demonstrating the value of human resources at the top level, former GE CEO Jack Welch personally reviewed the top 500 employees at his company every year.

Source: http://en.wikipedia.org/wiki/ File:GeneralElectricSign.jpg

human capital

The collective sum of the attributes, life experience, knowledge, inventiveness, energy, and enthusiasm that people choose to invest in their work.

FIGURE 15.4 Key Elements of HR

Beyond the basic need for compliance with HR rules and regulations, the four key elements of human resources are illustrated below.

Selection and Placement
Selecting the right individuals for an organization is a critical human resources task thoughtfully considered using the selection process. To tap into individuals with critical thinking skills, IBM's consulting division often asks unique interview questions such as "How many traffic lights are there in New York City?" to assess the potential employee's ability to walk through a logical process and create a reasonable estimate.

Job Design
Job design refers to the process of putting together various elements to form a job, bearing in mind organizational and individual worker requirements, as well as considerations of health, safety, and ergonomics. Workers can thank designer Robert Probst for his well-known (and often bemoaned) invention that has greatly changed how many employees engage in their day-to-day work activities—the cubicle.

Compensation and Rewards
How organizations pay employees represents one of the most tangible elements of human resource management. Such rewards can be found in real estate companies that highlight the commissions earned by their employees through membership in million dollar clubs found around the globe.

Diversity Management
Diversity goes far beyond the idea of avoiding discrimination and involves actively appreciating and using the differing perspectives and ideas that individuals bring to the workplace. When teams include members with complementary skills, the diversity helps companies and teams come up with more creative and effective solutions. More than half of *Fortune* 500 companies now employ a chief diversity officer, or similar executive, with the charge of leveraging the power of diversity. Several international companies such as Ericsson—named after their famed inventor founder—are also well known for their global diversity management initiatives.

Source: http://en.wikipedia.org/wiki/File:Swedish_inventor_Lars_Magnus_Ericsson.jpg (bottom); all other images © Thinkstock.

Selection and Placement

When hiring, acquaint prospective new hires with the nature of the jobs they will be expected to fulfill. This includes explaining the technical competencies needed (for example, collecting statistical data) and defining behavioral competencies. Behavioral competencies may have a customer focus, such as the ability to show empathy and support of customers' feelings and points of view, or a work management focus, such as the ability to complete tasks efficiently or to know when to seek guidance.

In addition, make the organization's culture clear by discussing the values that underpin the organization—describe the organization's "heroes." For example, are the heroes of the company people who go the extra mile to get customers to smile? Are they the people who toil through the night to develop new code? Are they the ones who can network and reach a company president to make the sale? By sharing such stories of company heroes with potential hires, managers help reinforce what makes a company unique. This, in turn, will help the job candidates determine whether they will fit into the organization's culture.

Job Design

Design jobs that involve doing a whole piece of work and are challenging but doable. **Job design** refers to the process of putting together various elements to form a job, bearing in mind organizational and individual worker requirements, as well as considerations of health, safety, and ergonomics. Train employees to have the knowledge and skills to perform all parts of their job and give them the authority and accountability to do so.[12] Job enrichment is important for retaining your employees.

Companies that allow employees growth opportunities and interesting jobs are often desirable places to work, becoming hubs for worldwide talent. For example, Boston-based global consulting firm Bain & Company is rated as the top employer of 2012 according to Glassdoor.com and is number 4 in *Fortune* magazine's top 15 MBA employer list. Bain & Company provides employees with the opportunity to solve some of the most challenging business problems around the world, allows all employees to have a voice in internal conversations, and provides the opportunity to learn from the company's more senior talent. Programs such as Take Two allow consultants to take 2 months off after working for 10 months to fulfill personal or career goals.[13]

> **job design**
>
> The process of putting together various elements to form a job, bearing in mind organizational and individual worker requirements.

Compensation and Rewards

Organizations should carefully evaluate and pay employees based on their performance, not simply for showing up on the job. Offer rewards for skill development and organizational performance, emphasizing teamwork, collaboration, and responsibility for performance. Help employees identify new skills to develop so that they can advance and achieve higher pay and rewards. Compensation systems that include incentives, gainsharing, profit sharing, and skill-based pay reward employees who learn new skills and put those skills to work for the organization. Employees who are trained in a broad range of skills and problem solving are more likely to grow on the job and feel more satisfaction. Such training enables them to make more valuable contributions to the company, which, in turn, gains them higher rewards and greater commitment to the company.[14] The company likewise benefits from employees' increased flexibility, productivity, and commitment.

When employees have access to information and the authority to act on that information, they are more involved in their jobs and more likely to make the right decision and take the necessary actions to further the organization's goals. Similarly, rewards need to be linked to performance, so that employees are naturally inclined to pursue outcomes that will gain them rewards and further the organization's success at the same time.

Diversity Management

Another key to successful SHRM in today's business environment is embracing diversity. In past decades, "diversity" simply meant avoiding discrimination against women, minorities, and those with disabilities in hiring. Today, diversity goes far beyond this limited definition; diversity management involves actively appreciating and using the differing perspectives and ideas that individuals bring to the workplace. Diversity is an invaluable contributor to innovation and problem-solving success. Research shows that the more diverse the group in terms of expertise, gender, age, and background, the more ability the group has to avoid the problems of groupthink.[15] Diversity helps company teams to come up with more creative and effective solutions. Teams whose members have complementary skills are often more successful because members can see one another's blind spots. Members will be more inclined to make different kinds of mistakes, which means that they'll be able to catch and correct those mistakes.

Decision-Making Diversity Pays Off at TIAA-CREF

FIGURE 15.5

Source: http://en.wikipedia.org/wiki/File:RogerWFergusonJr.jpg

Do diverse groups make better decisions? TIAA-CREF believes so. TIAA-CREF is headquartered in New York and offers financial advice, investment information, retirement plans and accounts, college savings plans, annuities, life insurance, brokerage, and trust services for 3.5 million investors. In 2012, it was listed as number 88 on the *Fortune* 500 list. Researchers studying the impact on board of directors' diversity noted that diversity is a key investment criterion for TIAA-CREF because they believe a diverse board will be less beholden to management. Roger W. Ferguson Jr., CEO of TIAA-CREF, believes it too. He recently proclaimed, "You get better answers if you have a diverse work force." This is a powerful statement and he cites a powerful example to make his case. Ferguson explains that executives at his Charlotte, North Carolina-based branch of the company had a "knock-down, drag-out" fight before the 2008 economic crash regarding how much of their then $430 billion portfolio should be invested in the sub-prime mortgage market. He explains that because the company is aggressive about fostering diversity, the discussion included diverse points of view that led to the decision to avoid the risk of investing heavily in the sub-prime market. He argues that such diverse points of view might have been suppressed at other organizations less focused on diversity in terms of ideas as well as more visible types of diversity such as gender or race. Researchers have reached similar conclusions, stating that "after controlling for size, industry, and other corporate governance measures, we find significant positive relationships between the fraction of women and minorities on the board and firm value."

TIAA-CREF has a long history of being recognized as a leader in valuing diversity including being consistently recognized by *Fortune*, *Working Mother*, *Hispanic*, and *Black Enterprise* magazine as a good place to work. Their diversity program states, "Building on our success, our goal is to ensure that we continue to respect the creativity, talents, and experiences that each employee contributes regardless of age, gender, race, ethnicity, religious belief, sexual orientation, mental or physical disability, veteran status, medical condition, or family circumstance. We actively recruit and hire members of underrepresented groups for opportunities in all areas, at all levels in the organization, to achieve our objective of a highly diversified talent pool." Diversity extends to their suppliers as well. The company prefers to do business with suppliers who are in line with their diversity values in practice or because they are owned by diverse individuals.

CEO Ferguson earned a law degree and PhD in economics at Harvard University. He is a former vice chair of the U.S. Federal Reserve's board of governors and is a member of President Barack Obama's Economic Recovery Advisory Board. Ferguson is the second African American CEO at TIAA-CREF after Clifton R. Wharton Jr., who became CEO of the company—and the first African American CEO of a major U.S. corporation—in 1987.

Case written by Talya Bauer and Berrin Erdogan to accompany Carpenter, M., Bauer, T., Erdogan, B., & Short, J. (2013). Principles of Management (2nd ed.). New York: Flat World Knowledge; Based on Diel, S. (2010, November 4). TIAA-CREF chief Roger W. Ferguson Jr. tells Birmingham audience that diverse companies outperform others. Birmingham News; Reuters (2008, April 4). Chief is selected at TIAA-CREF. New York Times; Carter, D. A., Simkins, B. J., & Simpson, W. G. (2003). Corporate governance, board diversity, and firm value. Financial Review. Retrieved September 8, 2012, from https://www.tiaa-cref.org/public/about-us/employee-diversity-inclusion.

KEY TAKEAWAY

Human resources management is becoming increasingly important in organizations because today's knowledge economy requires employees to contribute ideas and be engaged in executing the company's strategy. HR is thus becoming a strategic partner by identifying the skills that employees need and then providing employees with the training and structures needed to develop and deploy those competencies. All the elements of HR—selection, placement, job design, and compensation—need to be aligned with the company's strategy so that the right employees are hired for the right jobs and rewarded properly for their contributions to furthering the company's goals.

EXERCISES

1. What are the advantages of the new SHRM approach?
2. Name three elements of HR.
3. What benefits does a diverse workforce provide the company?
4. Whose responsibility is it to manage human resources in an organization?

---

2. THE WAR FOR TALENT

LEARNING OBJECTIVES

1. **Define talent management.**
2. **Attract the right workers to your organization.**
3. **Understand how to keep your stars.**
4. **Understand the benefits of good talent management.**

The **war for talent** refers to competition among organizations to attract and retain the most able employees. Agencies that track demographic trends have been warning for years that the U.S. workforce will shrink in the second and third decades of the 21st century as the baby boom generation (born 1945–1961) reaches retirement age. Even though many boomers say they want to (or have to) continue working past the traditional age of retirement, those who do retire or who leave decades-long careers to pursue "something I've always wanted to do" will leave employers scrambling to replace well-trained, experienced workers. As workers compete for the most desirable jobs, employers will have to compete even more fiercely to find the right talent.

2.1 What Talent Management Means

Peter Cappelli of the Wharton School defines **talent management** as anticipating the need for human capital and setting a plan to meet it.[16] It goes hand in hand with **succession planning**, the process whereby an organization ensures that employees are recruited and developed to fill each key role within the company. Most companies, unfortunately, do not plan ahead for the talent they need, which means that they face shortages of critical skills at some times and surpluses at other times. Other companies use outdated methods of succession planning that do not accurately forecast the skills they will need in the future.

---

war for talent

Competition between organizations to attract and retain the most able employees.

talent management

Anticipating the need for human capital and setting a plan to meet it.

succession planning

A process whereby an organization ensures that employees are recruited and developed to fill each key role within the company.

FIGURE 15.6

In the business world, executives need not fear headhunters—firms that are in the trenches in the war for talent, such as Ana Dutra, CEO for Korn/Ferry Leadership and Talent Consulting.

Source: Photo © Eric Miller

Several techniques developed to achieve productivity breakthroughs in manufacturing can be applied to talent management. For example, it is expensive to develop all talent internally; training people takes a long time and requires accurate predictions about which skill will be needed. Such predictions are increasingly difficult to make in our uncertain world. Therefore, rather than developing everyone internally, companies can hire talent from the outside when they need to tap specific skills. In manufacturing, this principle is known as "make or buy." In HR, the solution is to make *and* buy; that is, to train some people and to hire others from the external marketplace. In this case, "making" an employee means hiring a person who doesn't yet have all the needed skills to fulfill the role, but who can be trained ("made") to develop them. The key to a successful "make" decision is to distinguish between the high-potential employees who don't yet have the skills but who can learn them from the mediocre employees who merely lack the skills. The "buy" decision means hiring an employee who has all the necessary skills and experience to fulfill the role from day one. The "buy" decision is useful when it is too difficult to predict exactly which skills will be needed in the future.[17]

Another principle from manufacturing that works well in talent management is to run smaller batch sizes. That is, rather than sending employees to three-year-long training programs, companies send their employees to shorter programs more frequently. With this approach, managers do not have to make the training decision so far in advance. They can wait to decide exactly which skills employees will learn closer to the time the skill is needed, thus ensuring that employees are trained on the skills they will actually use.

2.2 Attracting the Right Workers to the Organization

Winning the war for talent means more than simply attracting workers to the company. It means attracting the *right* workers—the ones who will be enthusiastic about their work. Enthusiasm for the job requires more than having a good attitude about receiving good pay and benefits—it means that an employee's goals and aspirations also match those of the company. Therefore, it is important to identify employees' preferences and mutually assess how well they align with the company's strategy. To do this, the organization must first be clear about the type of employee it wants. Companies already do this with customers: marketing executives identify specific segments of the universe of buyers to target for selling products. Red Bull, for example, targets college-age consumers, whereas SlimFast markets to adults of all ages who feel they are overweight. Both companies are selling beverages but to completely different consumer segments. Similarly, companies need to develop a profile of the type of workers they want to attract. Does a company want entrepreneurial types who seek autonomy and continual learning or team players who enjoy collaboration, stability, and structure? Neither employee type is inherently "better" than another, but an employee who craves autonomy may feel constrained within the very same structure in which a team player would thrive.

It is important to "mutually assess" how well employees' preferences align with the company's strategy. One-half of "mutual" refers to the company, but the other half refers to the job candidates. They also need to know whether they will fit well into the company. One way to help prospective hires make this determination is to describe to them the "signature experience" that sets your company apart. As Tamara Erickson and Lynda Gratton define it, your company's signature experience is the distinctive practice that shows what it is really like to work at your company.[18]

Consider the signature experiences of two companies: Whole Foods and Goldman Sachs. At Whole Foods, team-based hiring is a signature experience—employees in each department vote on whether a new employee will be retained after a four-week trial period. This demonstrates to potential hires that Whole Foods is all about collaboration. In contrast, Goldman Sachs's signature experience is multiple one-on-one interviews. The story often told to prospective hires is of the MBA student who went through 60 interviews before being hired. This story signals to new hires that they need to be comfortable meeting endless new people and building networks across the company. Those who enjoy meeting and being interviewed by so many diverse people are exactly the ones who will fit into Goldman's culture. The added benefit of hiring workers who match your organizational culture and are engaged in their work is that they will be less likely to leave a company just to get a higher salary.

2.3 Keeping Star Employees

The war for talent stems from the approaching shortage of workers. Millions of baby boomers reaching retirement age are leaving a gaping hole in the U.S. workforce. In addition, workers are job-hopping more frequently than in the past. According to the U.S. Bureau of Labor Statistics, the average job tenure has dropped from 15 years in 1980 to 4.6 years in 2012.[19] Managers need to give employees reasons to stay with their company. One way to do that is to spend time talking with employees about their career goals. Listening to their likes and dislikes in order to help them use the skills they like using or develop new ones they wish to acquire will go a long way in motivating employees.[20]

Managers are also advised not to be afraid to "grow" employees. Some managers want to keep their employees in their department. They fear that helping employees grow on the job will mean that employees will outgrow their job and leave it.[21] But keeping employees down is a sure way to lose them. If companies help employees advance, it will be easier for the manager to move up in the organization because employees will be better able to take on the role left behind.

In some cases, employees may not be sure what career path they want. Managers can help them identify their goals by asking questions such as the following:[22]

- What assignments have you found most engaging?
- Which of your accomplishments in the last six months made you proudest?
- What makes for a great day at work?

What Employees Want

Employees want to grow and develop, stretching their capabilities. They want projects that engage their heads as well as their hearts, and they want to connect with the people and things that will help them achieve their professional goals.[23] Here are two ways to help employees reach these goals: First, connect people with mentors and help them build their networks. Research suggests that successful managers dedicate 70% more time to networking activities and 10% more time to communication than their less successful counterparts.[24] What makes networks special? Through networks, people energize one another, learn, create, and find new opportunities for growth. Second, help connect people with a sense of purpose. Focusing on the need for purpose is especially important for younger workers, who rank meaningful work and challenging experiences at the top of their job search lists.[25]

Social Networking as a Career-Building Strategy

FIGURE 15.7

© Thinkstock

Penelope Trunk, author of "The Brazen Careerist" column and blog (blog.penelopetrunk.com), views job hunting not as an event but as a lifestyle. She advises that in today's business environment, people change jobs so often that they need to keep their eye on the market even if they just started a new job. In her view, "the people who control their destiny most effectively leave their job when they find a better one, not when they are tossed out because of layoffs or reorganizations." This also means that social networking should be a central element in any job-search strategy. And because many jobs are filled by knowing someone who knows about an open position, Trunk argues that it's more important to network than it is to read the want ads. Trunk evokes the principle of reciprocity when she says, "building a network is adding value to lots of people's lives so that they, in turn, will want to add value to yours." Another useful strategy is to network proactively rather than reacting to concerns about your present job or news of a possible opening. By being proactive, you will increase your chances of being in the right place at the right time.

Career networking opportunities are plentiful; regardless of where you live, you can use the Internet to read blogs, subscribe to e-mail newsletters, and make friends on social networking sites. When you consider the principle of exchange, you realize that your networking possibilities are not limited to people in your chosen field—you can actually gain more by networking with those in related fields or even in jobs far removed from yours. With the exchange principle in mind, even residents of sparsely populated rural areas can network with their neighbors a few miles down the road.

Adapted from Trunk, P. (2008, March 1). Take control of your career destiny. Wisconsin State Journal, B1.

2.4 Benefits of Good Talent Management

Global consulting firm McKinsey & Company conducted a study to identify links between a company's financial performance and its success in managing talent. The survey results show that there was indeed a relationship between a firm's financial performance and its global talent management practices. Three talent management practices in particular correlated highly with exceptional financial performance:

1. Creating globally consistent talent evaluation processes.
2. Achieving cultural diversity in a global setting.
3. Developing and managing global leaders.[26]

The McKinsey survey found that companies achieving scores in the top third in any of these three areas had a 70% chance of achieving financial performance in the top third of all companies.[27]

Having consistent talent evaluation means that employees around the world are evaluated on the same standards. This means that if an employee from one country transfers to another, his or her manager can be assured that the employee has been held to the same level of skills and standards. Second, having cultural diversity means having employees with knowledge about the culture of different countries, not just those with foreign language skills. This helps bring about open-mindedness across cultures. Finally, developing global leaders means rotating employees across different cultures and giving them international experience. Companies who do this best also have policies of giving managers incentives to share their employees with other units.

KEY TAKEAWAY

The coming shortage of workers makes it imperative for managers to find, hire, retain, and develop their employees. Managers first need to define the skills that the company will need for the future. Then, they can "make or buy"—that is, train or hire—employees with the needed skills. Retaining these employees requires engaging them on the job. Good talent management practices translate to improved financial performance for the company as a whole.

EXERCISES

1. How might a manager go about identifying the skills that the company will need in the future?
2. Describe the "make or buy" option and how it can be applied to HR.
3. How would you go about attracting and recruiting talented workers to your organization? Suggest ideas you would use to retain stars and keep them happy working for you.
4. What skills might an organization like a bank need from its employees?

3. EFFECTIVE SELECTION AND PLACEMENT STRATEGIES

LEARNING OBJECTIVES

1. Explain why a good job description benefits the employer and the applicant.
2. Describe how company culture can be used in selecting new employees.
3. Discuss the advantages and disadvantages of personnel testing.
4. Describe some considerations in international staffing and placement

Selecting the right employees and placing them in the right positions within the company is a key HR function and is vital to a company's success. Companies should devote as much care and attention to this "soft" issue as they do to financial planning because errors will have financial impact and adverse effects on a company's strategy.

FIGURE 15.8 Effective Selection and Placement Strategies

Selecting employees that fit with the organization's culture and values is a key HR function with the potential to impact the firm's performance. Equally important is the ability to carefully place employees within specific positions in the company. Here, we illustrate issues related to both selection and placement.

Job Description Best Practices
An accurate and complete job description is a powerful SHRM tool that costs little to produce and can help considerably in reducing turnover. Descriptions should be concise, relevant, and avoid jargon. For example, a job description for a barista (creator of coffee drinks) might say, "Prepare coffee and other hot beverages, maintain equipment, and create a hospitable atmosphere. Various part-time tasks in other areas will often be required."

Tailoring Recruitment and Selection to Match Company Culture
Managers who hire well do not just hire for skills or academic background; they ask about the potential employee's philosophy on life or how the candidate likes to spend free time to assess whether the cultural fit is right. At Google, for example, job candidates are asked questions like "If you could change the world using Google's resources, what would you build?" In fact, you can even see it in their job postings. Marissa Mayer (known as Google employee #20 and now CEO at Yahoo!) wrote a job ad that read, "You're brilliant? We're hiring. Come work at Google." Her ad got eight times more responses than their other ads.

Tools and Methods: Interviewing and Testing
Testing and interviewing are two established methods to gather information about potential employees. Interviews often include "the human being" test where candidates are simply assessed on their personability and ability to interact with others. Situational interviews focus on past experience or future situations to assess what a job candidate might do in a given situation. The rationale behind testing is to give the employer more information—information vital to assessing how well a candidate is suited to a particular job—before making the selection and placement decision. For example, behavioral traits assessments measure energy level, assertiveness, sociability, manageability, and attitude.

International Staffing and Placement
In our increasingly global economy, managers need to decide between using expatriates and hiring locals when staffing international locations. At an estimated cost of $200,000 per failed expatriate, international assignment decisions should be made with careful forethought and consideration. The challenge is to overcome the natural tendency to hire a well-known, corporate insider over an unknown local at the international site. Expatriates are useful when company-specific knowledge is important, while local hires are beneficial when large cultural issues may come into play in the day-to-day business operations. The movie (and short lived TV show) *Outsourced* chronicles the pros and cons of each type of employee when an American manager travels to India to train his replacement, only to experience various forms of cultural shock that require him to heavily rely on the expertise of a call center worker he is hired to manage.

Source: http://www.flickr.com/photos/findyoursearch/7546440028/ (second from top); all other images © Thinkstock.

3.1 Job-Description Best Practices

An accurate and complete job description is a powerful SHRM tool that costs little to produce and can help considerably in reducing turnover. While the realistic description may discourage some applicants (often those who would not do well in the job), those who follow through with the application process are much more likely to be satisfied with the job once hired. In addition to summarizing what the worker will actually be doing all day, here are some additional suggestions for writing an effective job description:

- List the job requirements in bullet form so that job seekers can scan the posting quickly.

- Use common industry terms, which speak to knowledgeable job seekers.

- Avoid organization-specific terms and acronyms, which would confuse job seekers.

- Use meaningful job titles (not the internal job codes of the organization).

- Use key words taken from the list of common search terms (to maximize the chance that a job posting appears on a job seeker's search).

- Include information about the organization, such as a short summary and links to more detailed information.

- Highlight special intangibles and unusual benefits of the job and workplace (e.g., flextime, travel, etc.).

- Specify the job's location (and nearest large city) and provide links to local community pages (to entice job seekers with quality-of-life information).

3.2 Tailoring Selection to Match Company Culture

Managers who hire well do not just hire for skills or academic background; they ask about the potential employee's philosophy on life or how the candidate likes to spend free time. These questions help the manager assess whether the cultural fit is right. A company in which all work is done in teams needs team players, not just students that did well academically. Ask questions like, "Do you have a personal mission statement? If not, what would it be if you wrote one today?"[28] to identify potential hires' preferences.

At Google, for example, job candidates are asked questions like, "If you could change the world using Google's resources, what would you build?"[29] Google wants employees who will think and act on a grand scale, employees who will take on the challenges of their jobs, whatever their job may be. Take Josef DeSimone, Google's executive chef, for example. DeSimone, who's worked everywhere from family-style restaurants to Michelin-caliber ones, was amazed to learn that Google had dozens of cafes for its employees. "Nobody changes the menu daily on this scale," he says. "It's unheard of." When he was hired, DeSimone realized, "Wow, you hire a guy who's an expert in food and let him run with it! You don't get in his way or micromanage."[30] Google applies this approach to all positions and lets employees run with the challenge.

Traditionally, companies have built a competitive advantage by focusing on what they have—structural advantages such as economies of scale, a well-established brand, or dominance in certain market segments. Companies such as Southwest Airlines, by contrast, see its people as their advantage: "Our fares can be matched; our airplanes and routes can be copied. But we pride ourselves on our customer service," said Sherry Phelps, director of corporate employment. That's why Southwest looks for candidates who generate enthusiasm and leans toward extraverted personalities.[31] Southwest hires for attitude. Flight attendants have been known to sing and rap the safety instructions, and pilots tell jokes over the public address system.

Southwest Airlines makes clear right from the start the kind of people it wants to hire. For example, recruitment ads showed Southwest founder Herb Kelleher dressed as Elvis and read, "Work in a Place Where Elvis Has Been Spotted…The qualifications? It helps to be outgoing. Maybe even a bit off-center. And be prepared to stay awhile. After all, we have the lowest employee turnover rate in the industry." People may scoff or question why Southwest indulges in such showy activities. Phelps answers, "We do take our work seriously. It's ourselves that we don't." People who don't have a humane, can-do attitude are fired. Southwest has a probationary period during which it determines the compatibility of new hires with the culture. People may be excellent performers, but if they don't match the culture, they are let go. As Southwest's founder Kelleher once said, "People will write me and complain, 'Hey, I got terminated or put on probation for purely subjective reasons.' And I'll say, 'Right! Those are the important reasons.'"

In many states, employees are covered under what is known as the **at-will employment doctrine**. At-will employment is "a doctrine of American law that defines an employment relationship in which either party can break the relationship with no liability, provided there was no express contract for a definite term governing the employment relationship and that the employee does not belong to a collective bargaining unit (i.e., a union)."[32] However, there are legal restrictions on how subjective the reasons for firing can be. For instance, if the organization has written hiring and firing procedures and does not follow them in selective cases, then those cases might give rise to claims of wrongful termination. Similarly, in situations where termination is clearly illegal—for example, based on age, race, religion, and so on—wrongful termination can be claimed.

3.3   Tools and Methods: Interviewing and Testing

Testing and interviewing are two time-tested methods to get information about a job candidate.

A detailed interview begins by asking the candidate to describe his or her work history and then inquire about the person's most recent position (or the position most similar to the open position). Ask about the candidate's responsibilities and major accomplishments. Then ask in-depth questions about specific job situations. Called **situational interviews**, these types of interviews can focus on past experience or future situations. For example, experience-based questions are "Tell me about a major initiative you developed and the steps you used to get it adopted." Or "Describe a problem you had with someone and how you handled it." In contrast, future-oriented situation interview questions ask candidates to describe how they would handle a future hypothetical situation, such as "Suppose you came up with a faster way to do a task, but your team was reluctant to make the change. What would you do in that situation?"

In addition to what is asked, it is also important that interviewers understand what they should not ask, largely because certain questions lead to answers that may be used to discriminate. There are five particularly sensitive areas. The only times interviewers can ask about age are when it is a requirement of a job duty or if the company needs to determine whether a work permit is required. Second, it is rarely appropriate or legal to ask questions regarding race, color, national origin, or gender. Third, although candidates may volunteer religious or sexually orientated information in an interview, interviewers still need to be careful not to discriminate. Asking questions relevant to work experience or qualifications is always appropriate. Fourth, firms cannot discriminate for health or disabilities; potential employers may not ask about smoking, health, or disabilities in an interview. Finally, interviewers may not ask questions about marital status, children, personal life, pregnancy, or arrest records (although employers may inquire about convictions). Certain kinds of questions could be tempting to ask if you are interviewing for a position requiring travel; however, companies can only explain the travel requirements and confirm that the requirements are acceptable.

In addition to interviews, many employers use testing to select and place job applicants. Any tests given to candidates must be job related and follow guidelines set forth by the Equal Opportunity Employment Commission to be legal. For the tests to be effective, they should be developed by reputable psychologists and administered by professionally qualified personnel who have had training in occupations testing in an industrial setting. The rationale behind testing is to give the employer more information before making the selection and placement decision—information vital to assessing how well a candidate is suited to a particular job. Most pre-employment assessment tests measure thinking styles, behavioral traits, and occupational interests. The results are available almost immediately after a candidate completes the roughly hour-long questionnaire. Thinking styles tests can tell the potential employer how fast someone can learn new things or how well he or she can verbally communicate. Behavioral traits assessments measure energy level, assertiveness, sociability, manageability, and attitude. For example, a high sociability score would be a desirable trait for salespeople.[33]

3.4   International Staffing and Placement

In our increasingly global economy, managers need to decide between using expatriates or hiring locals when staffing international locations. **Expatriates** are employees assigned to a foreign location on a temporary basis. On the surface, this seems a simple choice between the firm-specific expertise of the expatriate and the cultural knowledge of the local hire. In reality, companies often fail to consider the high probability and high cost of expatriates failing to adapt and perform in their international assignments.

FIGURE 15.9

Although upward of 85% of college grads move back home, Washington, DC, ranks #1 as the most desirable place for U.S. graduates to relocate if possible.

© *Thinkstock*

Cultural issues can create misunderstandings between expatriate managers and employees, suppliers, customers, and local government officials. At an estimated cost of $200,000 per failed expatriate, international assignment decisions should be made with careful forethought and consideration. The challenge is to overcome the natural tendency to hire a well-known, corporate insider over an unknown local at the international site. Here are some indications to use to determine whether an expatriate or a local hire would be best.

Managers may want to choose an expatriate when

- company-specific technology or knowledge is important,
- confidentiality in the staff position is an issue,
- there is a need for speed (assigning an expatriate is usually faster than hiring a local),
- work rules regarding local workers are restrictive,
- the corporate strategy is focused on global integration.

Managers may want to staff the position with a local hire when

- the need to interact with local customers, suppliers, employees, or officials is paramount,
- the corporate strategy is focused on multidomestic/market-oriented operations,
- cost is an issue (expatriates often bring high relocation/travel costs),
- immigration rules regarding foreign workers are restrictive,
- there are large cultural distances between the host country and candidate expatriates.[34]

KEY TAKEAWAY

Effective selection and placement means finding and hiring the right employees for your organization and then putting them into the jobs for which they are best suited. Providing an accurate and complete job description is a key step in the selection process. An important determination is whether the candidate's personality is a good fit for the company's culture. Interviewing is a common selection method. Situational interviews ask candidates to describe how they handled specific situations in the past (experience-based situational interviews) and how they would handle hypothetical questions in the future (future-oriented situational interviews). Other selection tools include cognitive tests, personality inventories, and behavioral traits assessments. Specific personalities may be best suited for positions that require sales, teamwork, or entrepreneurship, respectively. In our increasingly global economy, managers need to decide between using expatriates and hiring locals when staffing international locations.

EXERCISES

1. What kind of information would you include in a job description?
2. Do you think it is important to hire employees who fit into the company culture? Why or why not?
3. List questions that you would ask in a future-oriented situational interview.
4. What requirements must personnel tests meet?
5. If you were hiring to fill a position overseas, how would you go about selecting the best candidate?

4.   THE ROLES OF PAY STRUCTURE AND PAY FOR PERFORMANCE

LEARNING OBJECTIVES

1. Explain the factors to be considered when setting pay levels.
2. Understand the value of pay for performance plans.
3. Discuss the challenges of individual versus team-based pay.

Pay can be thought of in terms of the "total compensation package" that includes an individual's base salary, variable pay, share ownership, and other benefits. A **bonus**, for example, is a form of variable play. A bonus is a one-time cash payment, often awarded for exceptional performance. Providing employees with an annual statement of all these benefits they receive can help them understand the full value of what they are getting.[35]

Indirect compensation is far more varied, including everything from legally required public protection programs such as social security to health insurance, retirement programs, paid leave, child care, or housing. Some indirect compensation elements are required by law: social security, unemployment, and disability payments. Other indirect elements are up to the employer and can offer excellent ways to provide benefits to the employees and the employer as well. For example, a working parent may take a lower-paying job with flexible hours that will allow him or her to be home when the children get home from school. A recent graduate may be looking for stable work and a desirable place to live. Both of these individuals have different needs and, therefore, would appreciate different compensation elements.

bonus

A form of variable pay where the employee earns a one-time cash payment based on achieved objectives.

FIGURE 15.10 Pay Systems Elements

Pay can take the form of direct or indirect compensation. Nonmonetary pay can include any benefit an employee receives from an employer or job that does not involve tangible value. This includes career and social rewards, such as job security, flexible hours and opportunity for growth, praise and recognition, task enjoyment, and friendships. Direct pay is an employee's base wage. It can be an annual salary, hourly wage, or any performance-based pay that an employee receives, such as profit-sharing bonuses. Here, we illustrate elements common to many pay systems.

Pay Type	Description	Example
Nonmonetary pay	Includes benefits that do not involve tangible value, such as a desirable location.	
Direct pay	Employee's base wage.	
Indirect pay	Everything from legally required programs to health insurance, retirement, housing, etc.	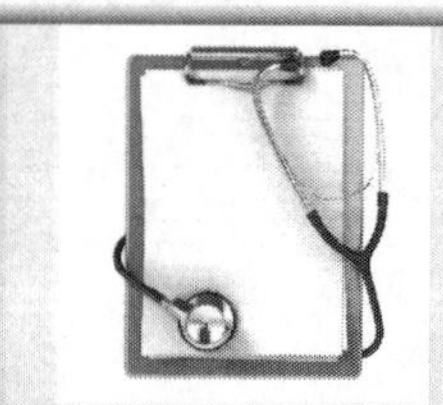
Incentive pay	A bonus paid when specified performance objectives are met, such as the pink Cadillac given to successful Mary Kay employees.	
Stock options	A right to buy a piece of the business that may be given to an employee to reward excellent service. An employee who owns a share of the business is far more likely to go the extra mile for the operation.	
Bonuses	A gift given occasionally to reward exceptional performance or for special occasions. Bonuses can show an employer appreciates his or her employees and ensures that good performance or special events are rewarded.	

Source: (third from bottom) Tim Wang, http://www.flickr.com/photos/jiazi/4824887400/; all other images © Thinkstock.

4.1 Setting Pay Levels

When setting pay levels for positions, managers should make sure that the pay level is fair relative to what other employees in the position are being paid. Part of the pay level is determined by the pay level at other companies. If one company pays substantially less than others, it's going to be a less desirable choice of employment unless it offers something overwhelmingly positive to offset the low pay, such as flexible hours or a fun, congenial work atmosphere. Besides these external factors, companies conduct a **job evaluation** to determine the internal value of the job—"A" positions are those on which the company's value depends, "B" positions are somewhat less important in that they do not deliver as much upside to the company, and "C" positions are those of least importance—in some cases, these are outsourced.

The most vital jobs to one company's success may not be the same as in other companies. For example, information technology companies may put top priority on their software developers and programmers, whereas for retailers such as Nordstrom, the "A" positions are those frontline employees who provide personalized service. For an airline, pilots would be a "B" job because, although they need to be well trained, investing further in their training is unlikely to increase the airline's profits. "C" positions for a retailer might include back office bill processing, while an information technology company might classify customer service as a "C" job.

When setting reward systems, it's important to pay for what the company actually hopes to achieve. Companies often say they want innovative thinking or risk taking, but they reward people who "make the numbers."[36] If companies truly want to achieve what they hope for, they need payment systems aligned with their goals. For example, if retention of star employees is important to your company, reward managers who retain top talent. At PepsiCo, for instance, one-third of a manager's bonus is tied directly to how well the manager did at developing and retaining employees. Tying compensation to retention makes managers accountable for creating a culture that decreases employee turnover.[37]

Pay for Performance

Pay for performance ties pay directly to an individual's performance in meeting specific business goals or objectives. Managers (often together with the employees themselves) design performance targets to which the employee will be held accountable. The targets have accompanying metrics that enable employees and managers to track performance. The metrics can be financial indicators, or they can be indirect indicators such as customer satisfaction or speed of development. Pay-for-performance schemes often combine a fixed base salary with a variable pay component (such as bonuses or stock options) that vary with the individual's performance.

Innovative Employee Recognition Programs

In addition to regular pay structures and systems, companies often create special programs that reward exceptional employee performance. For example, the financial software company Intuit, Inc., instituted a program called Spotlight. The purpose of Spotlight is to "spotlight performance, innovation and service dedication."[38] Unlike regular salaries or year-end bonuses, spotlight awards can be given on the spot for specific behavior that meets the reward criteria, such as filing a patent, inventing a new product, or meeting a milestone for years of service. Rewards can be cash awards of $500 to $3,000 and can be made by managers without high-level approval. In addition to cash and noncash awards, two Intuit awards feature a trip with $500 in spending money.[39]

4.2 Pay Structures for Groups and Teams

Many employers use compensation systems that reward all of the organization's employees as a group or various groups and teams within the organization. In this section, we examine these pay structures.

job evaluation

An evaluation of the positions in an organization to understand job design requirements and identify positions critical to strategy and firm performance.

pay for performance

When pay is tied directly to an individual's performance in meeting specific business goals or objectives.

FIGURE 15.11

Often learned at a young age, the concept of pay for performance remains one of the most effective pay structures.

© Thinkstock

Gainsharing and Profit Sharing

Gainsharing is a form of pay for performance. In gainsharing, the organization shares the financial gains with employees. Employees receive a portion of the profit achieved from their specific efforts and ideas. How much they receive is determined by their performance against the plan. Here's how gainsharing works: First, the organization must measure the historical (baseline) performance. Then, if employees help improve the organization's performance on those measures, they share in the financial rewards achieved. This sharing is typically determined by a formula.

The effectiveness of a gainsharing plan depends on employees seeing a relationship between what they do and how well the organization performs. The larger the size of the organization, the harder it is for employees to see the effect of their work. Therefore, gainsharing plans are more effective in companies with fewer than 1,000 people.[40] Gainsharing success also requires the company to have good performance metrics in place so that employees can track their process. The gainsharing plan can only be successful if employees believe and see that if they perform better, they will be paid more. The pay should be given as soon as possible after the performance so that the tie between the two is established.

While gainsharing divides a portion of cost savings or profit increases that can be directly traced back to cost saving ideas of employees, **profit-sharing** programs are those plans that provide an incentive to employees based on company profits. The assumption behind these programs is that organizations are profitable thanks to the efforts of all employees; hence employees are entitled to a portion of the profits. These programs have the intention to encourage workers to think like owners of a business.

When designing systems to measure performance, realize that performance appraisals need to focus on quantifiable measures. Designing these measures with input from the employees helps make the measures clear and understandable to employees and increases their buy-in that the measures are reasonable.

Team-Based Pay

Many managers seek to build teams but struggle with the challenge of motivating all the members to achieve the team's goals. In response to this challenge, team-based pay is becoming increasingly accepted. In 1992, only 3% of companies had team-based pay; however, the concept quickly took off. By 1999, 80% of companies had implemented it, and this number has continued to climb over time. With increasing acceptance and adoption come different choices and options of how to structure team-based pay. One way to structure the pay is to first identify the type of team and then choose the pay option that is most appropriate to that team type.

4.3 Pay Systems That Reward Both Team and Individual Performance

There are two main theories of how to reward employees. Nancy Katz characterized the theories as two opposing camps.[41] The first camp advocates rewarding individual performance, through plans such as commissions-sales schemes and merit-based-pay. The claim is that this will increase employees' energy, drive, risk taking, and task identification. The disadvantages of rewarding individual performance are that employees will cooperate less, that high performers may be resented by others in the organization, and that low performers may try to undermine top performers.

The second camp believes that organizations should reward team performance, without regard for individual accomplishment. This reward system is thought to bring the advantages of increased helping and cooperation, sharing of information and resources, and mutual-respect among employees. The disadvantages of team-based reward schemes are that they create a lack of drive, that low performers are "free riders," and that high performers may withdraw or act aggressively toward poorer-performing team members.

Katz sought to identify reward schemes that achieve the best of both worlds. These hybrid pay systems would reward individual and team performance, promoting excellence at both levels. Katz suggested two possible hybrid reward systems. The first system features a base rate of pay for individual performance that increases when the group reaches a target level of performance. In this reward system, individuals have a clear pay-for-performance incentive, and their rate of pay increases when the group as a whole does well. In the second hybrid, the pay-for-performance rate also increases when a target is reached. Under this reward system, however, every team member must reach a target level of performance before the higher pay rate takes effect. In contrast with the first hybrid, this reward system clearly incentivizes the better performers to aid poorer performers. Only when the poorest performer reaches the target can all team members benefit from the higher pay rate.

Compensation plans reward employees for contributing to company goals. Pay levels should reflect the value of each type of job to the company's overall success. For some companies, technical jobs are the most vital, whereas for others frontline customer service positions determine the success of the company against its competitors. Pay-for-performance plans tie an individual's pay directly to his or her ability to meet performance targets. These plans can reward individual performance or team performance or a combination of the two.

EXERCISES

1. What factors would you consider when setting a pay level for a particular job?
2. What might be the "A" level positions in a bank?
3. If you were running a business, would you implement a pay-for-performance scheme? Why or why not?
4. Describe the difference between a base salary, a bonus, and a gainsharing plan.
5. Discuss the advantages and disadvantages of rewarding individual versus team performance.

5. DESIGNING A HIGH-PERFORMANCE WORK SYSTEM

LEARNING OBJECTIVES

1. **Define a high-performance work system.**
2. **Describe the role of technology in HR.**
3. **Describe the use of HR systems to improve organizational performance.**
4. **Describe succession planning and its value.**

Now it is your turn to design a high-performance work system (HPWS). HPWS is a set of management practices that attempt to create an environment within an organization where the employee has greater involvement and responsibility. Designing a HPWS involves putting all the HR pieces together. A HPWS is all about determining what jobs a company needs done, designing the jobs, identifying and attracting the type of employee needed to fill the job, and then evaluating employee performance and compensating them appropriately so that they stay with the company.

5.1 e-HRM

FIGURE 15.12

Once the domain of gas stations and food buffets, online HR websites now allow for self-service of HR functions and practices.

© Thinkstock

Technology is changing the way HR is done. The electronic human resource management (e-HRM) business solution is based on the idea that information technologies, including the Web, can be designed for human resources professionals and executive managers who need support to manage the workforce, monitor changes, and gather the information needed in decision making. At the same time, e-HRM can enable all employees to participate in the process and keep track of relevant information. For instance, companies provide employees with a Web site where they can log in; get past and current pay information, including tax forms (i.e., 1099, W-2, and so on); manage investments related to a 401(k); or opt for certain medical record-keeping services.

More generally, for example, many administrative tasks are being done online, including

- providing and describing insurance and other benefit options,
- enrolling employees for those benefits,
- enrolling employees in training programs,
- administering employee surveys to gauge their satisfaction.

Many of these tasks are being done by employees themselves, which is referred to as *employee self-service*. With all the information available online, employees can access it themselves when they need it.

Part of an effective HR strategy is using technology to reduce the manual work performance by HR employees. Simple or repetitive tasks can be performed self-service through e-HRM systems that provide employees with information and let them perform their own updates. Typical HR services that can be formed in an e-HRM system include the following:

- Answer basic compensation questions.
- Look up employee benefits information.
- Process candidate recruitment expenses.
- Receive and scan resumes into recruiting software.
- Enroll employees in training programs.
- Maintain training catalog.
- Administer tuition reimbursement.
- Update personnel files.

Organizations that have invested in e-HRM systems have found that they free up HR professionals to spend more time on the strategic aspects of their job. These strategic roles include employee development, training, and succession planning.

5.2 The Value of High-Performance Work Systems

Employees who are highly involved in conceiving, designing, and implementing workplace processes are more engaged and perform better. For example, a study analyzing 132 U.S. manufacturing firms found that companies using HPWS had significantly higher labor productivity than their competitors. The key finding was that when employees have the power to make decisions related to their performance, can access information about company costs and revenues, and have the necessary knowledge, training, and development to do their jobs—and are rewarded for their efforts—they are more productive.[42]

HPWS can be used globally to good result. For example, Fey and colleagues studied 101 foreign-based firms operating in Russia and found significant linkages between HRM practices, such as incentive-based compensation, job security, employee training, and decentralized decision making, and subjective measures of firm performance.[43]

5.3 Improving Organizational Performance

Organizations that want to improve their performance can use a combination of HR systems to get these improvements. For example, performance measurement systems help underperforming companies improve performance. The utility company Arizona Public Service used a performance measurement system to rebound from dismal financial results. The company developed 17 "critical success indicators," which it measures regularly and benchmarks against the best companies in each category. Of the 17, nine were identified as "major critical success indicators":

- Cost to produce kilowatt hour

- Customer satisfaction
- Fossil plants' availability
- Operations and maintenance expenditures
- Construction expenditures
- Ranking as corporate citizen in Arizona
- Safety all-injury incident rate
- Nuclear performance
- Shareholder value return on assets

Each department sets measurable goals in line with these indicators, and a gainsharing plan rewards employees for meeting the indicators.

In addition, companies can use reward schemes to improve performance. Better-performing firms tend to invest in more sophisticated HRM practices, which further enhance organizational performance.[44] Currently, about 20% of firms link employee compensation to the firm's earnings. They use reward schemes such as employee stock ownership plans, gainsharing, and profit sharing. This trend is increasing.

Is the performance of an organization with a profit-sharing plan better than that of other firms? And, does adoption of a profit-sharing plan lead to improvement in an organization's performance? The reasons profit-sharing plans would improve organizational performance go back to employee motivation theory. A profit-sharing plan will likely encourage employees to monitor one another's behavior because "loafers" would erode the rewards for everyone. Moreover, profit sharing should lead to greater information sharing, which increases the productivity and flexibility of the firm.

Researcher Michel Magnan studied 294 Canadian credit unions in the same region (controlling for regional and sector-specific economic effects). Of the firms studied, 83 had profit sharing plans that paid the bonus in full at the end of the year. This meant that employees felt the effect of the organizational performance reward immediately, so it had a stronger motivational effect than a plan that put profits into a retirement account, where the benefit would be delayed (and essentially hidden) until retirement.

Magnan's results showed that firms with profit-sharing plans had better performance on most facets of organizational performance. They had better performance on asset growth, market capitalization, operating costs, losses on loans, and return on assets than firms without profit-sharing plans. The improved performance was especially driven by activities where employee involvement had a quick, predictable effect on firm performance, such as giving loans or controlling costs.

Another interesting finding was that when firms adopted a profit-sharing plan, their organizational performance went up. Profit-sharing plans appear to be a good turnaround tool because the firms that showed the greatest improvement were those that had not been performing well before the profit-sharing plan. Even firms that had good performance before adopting a profit-sharing plan had better performance after the profit-sharing plan.[45]

Succession Planning

Succession planning is a process whereby an organization ensures that employees are recruited and developed to fill each key role within the company. In a recent survey, HR executives and non-HR executives were asked to name their top human capital challenge. Nearly one-third of both executive groups cited succession planning,[46] but less than 20% of companies with a succession plan addressed non-management positions. Slightly more than 40% of firms did not have a plan in place.

Looking across organizations, succession planning takes a number of forms (including no form at all). An absence of succession planning should be a red flag, since the competitive advantage of a growing percentage of firms is predicated on their stock of human capital and ability to manage such capital in the future. One of the overarching themes of becoming better at succession is that effective organizations become much better at developing and promoting talent from within. The figure "Levels of Succession Planning" summarizes the different levels that firms can work toward.

Levels of Succession Planning

- Level 1: No planning at all.
- Level 2: Simple replacement plan. Typically the organization has only considered what it will do if key individuals leave or become debilitated.
- Level 3: The company extends the replacement plan approach to consider lower-level positions, even including middle managers.

- Level 4: The company goes beyond the replacement plan approach to identify the competencies it will need in the future. Most often, this approach is managed along with a promote-from-within initiative.
- Level 5: In addition to promoting from within, the organization develops the capability to identify and recruit top talent externally. However, the primary source of successors should be from within, unless there are key gaps where the organization does not have key capabilities.

Dow Chemical exemplifies some best practices for succession planning:

- Dow has a comprehensive plan that addresses all levels within the organization, not just executive levels.
- CEO reviews the plan, signaling its importance.
- Managers regularly identify critical roles in the company and the competencies needed for success in those roles.
- Dow uses a grid for succession planning, plotting employees along the two dimensions of potential and performance.
- High potential employees are recommended for training and development, such as Dow Academy or an MBA.

The principles of strategic human resource management and high-performance work systems apply to nonprofit enterprises as well as for-profit companies, and the benefits of good HR practices are just as rewarding. When it comes to succession planning, nonprofits face a particularly difficult challenge of attracting workers to a field known for low pay and long hours. Often, the people attracted to the enterprise are drawn by the cause rather than by their own aspirations for promotion. Thus, identifying and training employees for leadership positions is even more important.

KEY TAKEAWAY

A high-performance work system unites the social and technical systems (people and technology) and aligns them with company strategy. It ensures that all the interrelated parts of HR are aligned with one another and with company goals. Technology and structure supports employees in their ability to apply their knowledge and skills to executing company strategy. HR decisions, such as the type of compensation method chosen, improve performance for organizations and enterprises of all types.

EXERCISES

1. What are some ways in which HR can improve organizational performance?
2. What is the most important aspect of high performance work systems? Name three benefits of high performance work systems.
3. How does e-HRM help a company?
4. If you were designing your company's succession planning program, what guidelines would you suggest?

6. TYING IT ALL TOGETHER: USING THE HR BALANCED SCORECARD TO GAUGE AND MANAGE YOUR HUMAN CAPITAL

LEARNING OBJECTIVES

1. Describe the Balanced Scorecard method and how it can be applied to HR.
2. Discuss what is meant by "human capital."
3. Understand why metrics are important to improving company performance.
4. Consider how your human capital might be mapped on an HR Balanced Scorecard.

The **Balanced Scorecard** helps managers define the performance categories that relate to the company's strategy. The managers then translate those categories into metrics and track performance on those metrics. Besides traditional financial measures and quality measures, companies use employee performance measures to track their people's knowledge, skills, and contribution to the company.[47]

The employee performance aspects of Balanced Scorecards analyze employee capabilities, satisfaction, retention, and productivity. Companies also track whether employees are motivated (for example, the number of suggestions made and implemented by employees) and whether employee performance goals are aligned with company goals.

6.1 Applying the Balanced Scorecard Method to HR

Because the Balanced Scorecard focuses on the strategy and metrics of the business, Mark Huselid and his colleagues developed the HR and Workforce Scorecard to provide framework specific to HR. According to Huselid, the **Workforce Scorecard** identifies and measures the behaviors, skills, mindsets, and results required for the workforce to contribute to the company's success. Specifically, as summarized in Figure 15.13, the Workforce Scorecard has four key sequential elements:[48]

1. **Workforce mind-set and culture.** First, does the workforce understand the strategy, embrace it, and does it have the culture needed to support strategy execution?
2. **Workforce competencies.** Second, does the workforce, especially in the strategically important or "A" positions, have the skills it needs to execute strategy? ("A" positions are those job categories most vital to the company's success.)
3. **Leadership and workforce behaviors.** Third, are the leadership team and workforce consistently behaving in a way that will lead to attaining the company's key strategic objectives?
4. **Workforce success.** Fourth, has the workforce achieved the key strategic objectives for the business? If the organization can answer "yes" to the first three elements, then the answer should be yes here as well.[49]

Balanced Scorecard

A framework designed to translate an organization's vision and mission statements and overall business strategy into specific, quantifiable goals and objectives and to monitor the organization's performance in terms of achieving these goals.

Workforce Scorecard

An application of the Balanced Scorecard concept to an organization's human capital to identify and measure the behaviors, skills, mind-sets, and results required for the workforce to contribute to the company's success.

FIGURE 15.13

The HR Balanced Scorecard bridges HR best practices and the firm's comprehensive Balanced Scorecard.

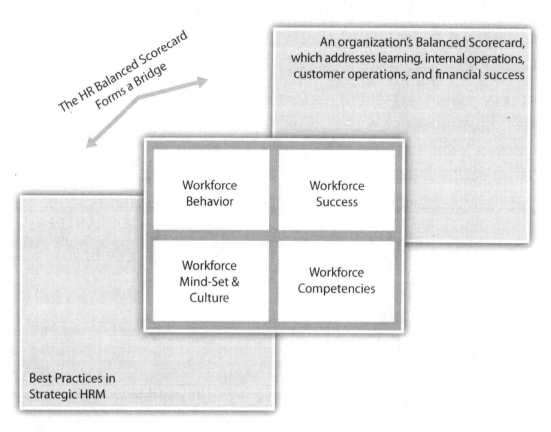

Human Capital

Implementing the HR scorecard requires a change in perspective, from seeing people as a cost to seeing people as the company's most important asset to be managed—**human capital**. According to the Society of Human Resource Management's *Research Quarterly*, "A company's human capital asset is the collective sum of the attributes, life experience, knowledge, inventiveness, energy and enthusiasm that its people choose to invest in their work."[50] Such an asset is difficult to measure because it is intangible, and factors like "inventiveness" are subjective and open to interpretation. The challenge for managers, then, is to develop measurement systems that are more rigorous and provide a frame of reference. The metrics can range from activity-based (transactional) metrics to strategic ones. Transactional metrics are the easiest to measure and include counting the number of new people hired, fired, transferred, and promoted. The measures associated with these include the cost of each new hire, the length of time and cost associated with transferring an employee, and so forth. Typical ratios associated with transactional metrics include the training cost factor (total training cost divided by the employees trained) and training cost percentage (total training cost divided by operating expense).[51] But these transactional measures do not get at the strategic issues such as whether the right employees are being trained and whether they are remembering and using what they learned. Measuring training effectiveness requires not only devising metrics but actually changing the nature of the training.

The Bank of Montreal has taken this step. "What we're trying to do at the Bank of Montreal is to build learning into what it is that people are doing," said Jim Rush of the Bank of Montreal's Institute for Learning. "The difficulty with training as we once conceived it is that you're taken off your job, you're taken out of context, you're taken away from those things that you're currently working on, and you go through some kind of training. And then you've got to come back and begin to apply that. Well, you walk back to that environment and it hasn't changed. It's not supportive or conducive to you behaving in a different kind of way, so you revert back to the way you were, very naturally." To overcome this, the bank conducts training such that teams bring in specific tasks on which they are working, so that they learn by doing. This removes the gap between learning in one context and applying it in another. The bank then looks at performance indices directly related to the bottom line. "If we take an entire business unit through a program designed to help them learn how to increase the market share of a particular product, we can look at market share and see if it improved after the training," Rush said.[52]

Motorola has adopted a similar approach, using action learning in its Senior Executives Program. Action learning teams are assigned a specific project by Motorola's CEO and are responsible for implementing the solutions they design. This approach not only educates the team members but also lets them implement the ideas, so they are in a position to influence the organization. In this way, the training seamlessly supports Motorola's goals.

Organizations need employees to apply the knowledge they have to activities that add value to the company. In planning and applying human capital measures, managers should use both retrospective (lagging) and prospective (leading) indicators. Lagging indicators are those that tell the company what it has accomplished (such as the Bank of Montreal's documenting the effect that training had on a business unit's performance). Leading indicators are forecasts that help an organization see where it is headed. Leading indicators include employee learning and growth indices.[53]

The Payoff

Given the complexity of what we've just discussed, some managers may be inclined to ask, "Why bother doing all this?" Research by John Lingle and William Schiemann provides a clear answer: Companies that make a concerted effort to measure intangibles such as employee performance, innovation, and change in addition to measuring financial measures perform better. Lingle and Schiemann examined how executives measured six strategic performance areas: financial performance, operating efficiency, customer satisfaction, employee performance, innovation and change, and community/environment issues. To evaluate how carefully the measures were tracked, the researchers asked the executives, "How highly do you value the information in each strategic performance area?" and "Would you bet your job on the quality of the information on each of these areas?" The researchers found that the companies that paid the closest attention to the metrics and had the most credible information were the ones identified as industry leaders over the previous three years (74% of measurement-managed companies compared with 44% of others) and reported financial performance in the top one-third of their industry (83% compared with 52%).

The scorecard is vital because most organizations have much better control and accountability over their raw materials than they do over their workforce. For example, a retailer can quickly identify the source of a bad product, but the same retailer can't identify a poor-quality manager whose negative attitude is poisoning morale and strategic execution.[54]

Applying the Balanced Scorecard Method to Your Human Capital

Let's translate the HR scorecard to your own Balanced Scorecard of human capital. As a reminder, the idea behind the HR scorecard is that if developmental attention is given to each area, then the organization will be more likely to be successful. In this case, however, you use the scorecard to better understand why you may or may not be effective in your current work setting. Your scorecard will comprise four sets of answers and activities.

1. **What is your mind-set and values?** Do you understand the organization's strategy and embrace it, and do you know what to do in order to implement the strategy? If you answered "no" to either of these questions, then you should consider investing some time in learning about your firm's strategy. You may need additional coursework or mentoring to understand what it takes to move the firm's strategy forward.

2. **What are your work-related competencies?** Do you have the skills and abilities to get your job done? If you have aspirations to key positions in the organization, do you have the skills and abilities for those higher roles?

3. **What are the leadership and workforce behaviors?** If you are not currently in a leadership position, do you know how consistently your leaders are behaving with regard to the achievement of strategic objectives? If you are one of the leaders, are you behaving strategically?

4. **Your success?** Can you tie your mind-set, values, competencies, and behaviors to the organization's performance and success?

This simple scorecard assessment will help you understand why your human capital is helping the organization or needs additional development itself. With such an assessment in hand, you can act to help the firm succeed and identify priority areas for personal growth, learning, and development.

The Balanced Scorecard, when applied to HR, helps managers align all HR activities with the company's strategic goals. Assigning metrics to the activities lets managers track progress on goals and ensure that they are working toward strategic objectives. It adds rigor and lets managers quickly identify gaps. Companies that measure intangibles such as employee performance, innovation, and change perform better financially than companies that don't use such metrics. Rather than investing equally in training for all jobs, a company should invest disproportionately more in developing the people in the key "strategic" ("A") jobs of the company on which the company's success is most dependent.

EXERCISES

1. Define the Balanced Scorecard method.
2. List the elements of a Workforce Scorecard.
3. Discuss how human capital can be managed like a strategic asset.
4. Why is it important to align HR metrics with company strategy?
5. What kind of metrics would be most useful for HR to track?

7. CASE IN POINT: KRONOS USES SCIENCE TO FIND THE IDEAL EMPLOYEE

FIGURE 15.14

Source: http://commons.wikimedia.org/wiki/File:Kronos-incorporated.jpg by KenSavage.

You are interviewing a candidate for a cashier position in a supermarket. You need someone polite, courteous, patient, and dependable. The candidate you are talking to seems nice. But how do you know who is the right person for the job? Will the job candidate like the job or get bored? Will they have a lot of accidents on the job or be fired for misconduct? Don't you wish you knew before hiring? One company approaches this problem scientifically, saving companies time and money on hiring hourly wage employees.

Retail employers do a lot of hiring, given their growth and high turnover rate. According to one estimate, replacing an employee who leaves in retail costs companies around $4,000. High turnover also threatens the quality of customer service. Therefore retail employers have an incentive to screen people carefully so that they hire people with the best chance of being successful and happy on the job. Unicru, an employee selection company, developed software that quickly became a market leader in screening hourly workers. The company was acquired by Massachusetts-based Kronos Inc. (NASDAQ: KRON) in 2006 and is currently owned by a private equity firm.

The idea behind the software is simple: If you have a lot of employees and keep track of your data over time, you have access to an enormous resource. By analyzing these data, you can identify the profile of the "ideal" employee for a particular company. The software captures the profile of high performers, and applicants are screened to assess their fit with this particular profile. More important, the profile is continually updated as studies that compare employee profiles to job performance are conducted. As the number of employees in the database gets larger, the software does a better job of identifying the right people for the job.

If you ever applied for a job in retail, you may already be a part of this database: The users of the Kronos system include giants such as Universal Studios, Costco Wholesale Corporation, Burger King, and other retailers and chain restaurants. In companies such as Albertsons or Blockbuster, applicants can either use a kiosk in the store to answer a list of questions and to enter their background, salary history, and other information or apply on-line from their home computers. The software screens people on basic criteria such as availability in schedul-ing as well as personality traits.

Candidates are asked to agree or disagree with statements such as "I often make last-minute plans" or "I work best when I am on a team." Additionally, questions about how an applicant would react in specific job-related situations and about person-job fit are included. After the candidates complete the questions, hiring man-agers are sent a report complete with a color-coded suggested course of action. Red means the candidate does not fit the job, yellow indicates the hiring manager should proceed with caution, and green means the candidate is likely a good fit. Because of the use of different question formats and complex scoring methods, the company contends that faking answers to the questions of the software is not easy because it is difficult for candidates to predict the desired profile.

Matching candidates to jobs has long been viewed as a key way of ensuring high performance and low turnover in the workplace. Advances in computer technology are making it easier and more efficient to assess candidate–job fit. Companies using such technology are cutting down the time it takes to hire people, and it is estimated that using such technologies lowers their turnover by 10%–30%.

Case written by Berrin Erdogan and Talya Bauer to accompany Carpenter, M., Bauer, T., Erdogan, B., & Short, J. (2013). Principles of Management (2nd ed.). New York: Flat World Knowledge; Based on information from Berta, D. (2002, February 25). Industry increases applicant screening amid labor surplus, security concerns. Nation's Restaurant News, 36(8), 4; Frauenheim, E. (2006, March 13). Unicru beefs up data in latest screening tool. Workforce Management, 85(5), 9–10; Frazier, M. (2005, April). Help wanted. Chain Store Age, 81(4), 37–39; Haaland, D. E. (2006, April 17). Safety first: Hire conscientious employees to cut down on costly workplace accidents. Nation's Restaurant News, 40(16), 22–24; Overholt, A. (2002, February). True or false? You're hiring the right people. Fast Company, 55, 108–109; Rafter, M. V. (2005, May). Unicru breaks through in the science of "smart hiring." Workforce Management, 84(5), 76–78.

CASE DISCUSSION QUESTIONS

1. Strategic human resource management (SHRM) is included in your P-O-L-C framework as an essential element of control. Based on what you have learned about Kronos, how might SHRM relate to the planning, organizing, and leading facets of the P-O-L-C framework?

2. What can a company do in addition to using techniques like these to determine whether a person is a good candidate for a job?

3. What are potential complicating factors in using personality testing for employee selection?

4. Why do you think that retail companies are particularly prone to high turnover rates?

5. What steps do you take as a job seeker to ensure that an organization is a good fit for you?

ENDNOTES

1. Becker, B. E., & Huselid, M. A. (2006). Strategic human resources management: Where do we go from here? *Journal of Management, 32*, 898–925.

2. Huselid, M. A. (1995). The impact of human resource management practices on turnover, productivity, and corporate financial performance. *Academy of Management Journal, 38*, 635–672; Pfeffer, J. (1998). *The human equation: Building profits by putting people first.* Boston: Harvard Business School Press; Pfeffer, J., & Veiga, J. F. (1999). Putting people first for organizational success. *Academy of Management Executive, 13*, 37–48; Welbourne, T., & Andrews, A. (1996). Predicting performance of initial public offering firms: Should HRM be in the equation? *Academy of Management Journal, 39*, 910–911.

3. Pfeffer, J., & Veiga, J. F. (1999). Putting people first for organizational success. *Academy of Management Executive, 13*, 37–48.

4. Brian, E., Becker, B. E., Huselid, M. A., & Ulrich, D. (2002). *Six key principles for measuring human capital performance in your organization.* University of Maryland Working Paper.

5. Ulrich, D. (1998). *Delivering results.* Boston: Harvard Business School Press.

6. Weatherly, L. (2003, March). Human capital—the elusive asset; measuring and managing human capital: A strategic imperative for HR. *Research Quarterly*, Society for Human Resource Management Web site. Retrieved September 14, 2012, from http://www.shrm.org/research/quarterly/0301capital.pdf.

7. Huselid, M. A., Jackson, S. E., & Schuler, R. S. (1997). Technical and strategic human resource management effectiveness as determinants of firm performance. *Academy of Management Journal, 40*, 171–188.

8. Ulrich, D. (1998). *Delivering results.* Boston: Harvard Business School Press.

9. Marquez, J. (2007, September 10). On the front line: A quintet of 2006's highest-paid HR leaders discuss how they are confronting myriad talent management challenges as well as obstacles to being viewed by their organizations as strategic business partners. *Workforce Management, 86*, 22.

10. TPI Counts 2700+ Outsourcing Contracts. (2007, December). Retrieved September 14, 2012, from http://www.sharedxpertise.org/file/230/trends--research.html.

11. HRO Europe (2006, August 23). Retrieved September 14, 2012, from http://www.hroeurope.com.

12. Lawler, E. (1992). *The ultimate advantage.* San Francisco: Jossey-Bass.

13. Retrieved October 19, 2012, from http://money.cnn.com/galleries/2012/pf/jobs/1205/gallery.top-MBA-employers/4.html.

14. Barnes, W. F. (2001). *The challenge of implementing and sustaining high performance work systems in the United States: An evolutionary analysis of I/N Tek and Kote.* (Doctoral dissertation, University of Notre Dame).

15. Surowiecki. J. (2005). *The wisdom of crowds.* New York: Anchor Books.

16. Cappelli, P. (2008, March). Talent management for the 21st century, Boston. *Harvard Business Review*, 17–36.

17. Buhler, P. M. (2008, March). Managing in the new millennium; succession planning: Not just for the c suite. *Supervision, 69*(3), 19–23.

18. Erickson, T., & Gratton, L. (2007, March). What it means to work here. *Harvard Business Review*, 23–29.

19. Retrieved October 19, 2012, from http://www.bls.gov/news.release/tenure.nr0.htm.

20. Kaye, B. (2008). *Love 'em or lose 'em.* San Francisco: Barrett-Koehler.

21. Field, A. (2008, June). Do your stars see a reason to stay? *Harvard Management Update*.

22. Butler, T. (2007). *Getting unstuck.* Boston: Harvard Business School Press.

23. Deloitte Research. (2007). *Do you know where your talent is? Why acquisition and retention strategies don't work.* Geneva, Switzerland: Deloitte-Touch Research Report.

24. Luthans, F., Yodgetts, R., & Rosenkrantz, S. (1988). *Real managers.* Cambridge: Ballinger.

25. Sheahan, P. (2006). *Generation Y: Thriving (and surviving) with generation Y at work.* Victoria, Australia: Hardie Grant Books.

26. McKinsey global-talent-management survey of over 450 executives. (2007, December). Retrieved September 14, 2012, from http://www.mckinseyquarterly.com/article_print.aspx?L2=18&L3=31&ar=2140.

27. Guthridge, M., & Komm, A. B. (1988, May). Why multinationals struggle to manage talent. *McKinsey Quarterly*, 19–25.

28. Pfeffer, J. (1998). *The human equation: Building profits by putting people first.* Boston: Harvard Business School Press.

29. Slater, C. (2008, March). The faces and voices of Google. *Fast Company*, 37–45.

30. Slater, C. (2008, March). Josef DeSimone—executive chef. *Fast Company*, 46–48.

31. Bruce, A. (1997, March). Southwest: Back to the FUNdamentals. *HR Focus, 74*(3), 11; Freiberg, K., & Freiberg, J. (2003). *Nuts! Southwest Airlines's crazy recipe for business and personal success.* Austin, TX: Bard; Hallowell, R. (1996, Winter). Southwest Airlines: A case study linking employee needs satisfaction and organizational capabilities to competitive advantage. *Human Resource Management, 35*(4), 513–529; Heskett J. L., & Hallowell, R. (1993). Southwest Airlines—1993 (A). *Harvard Business School Case*; Southwest Airlines' Herb Kelleher: Unorthodoxy at work. (1995, January). *Management Review*, 2–9; LaBarre, P. (1996, February 5). Lighten up! Blurring the line between fun and work not only humanizes organizations but strengthens the bottom line. *Industry Week, 245*(3), 53–67; Labich, K. (1994, May 2). Is Herb Kelleher America's best CEO? *Fortune*, 44–45; McNerney, D. J. (1996, August). Employee motivation: Creating a motivated workforce. *HR Focus, 73*(8), 1; Tomkins, R. (1996, November 11). HR: The seriously funny airline. *Financial Times* (33137), 14, A1–A5.

32. Rothstein, M. A., Knapp, Andria S., & Liebman, Lance. (1987). *Cases and materials on employment law* (p. 738). New York: Foundation Press.

33. Mrosko, T. (2006, August). The personnel puzzle: Preemployment testing can help your bottom line. *Inside Business, 8*(8), 60–73.

34. Weems, Rebecca E. (1998). *Ethnocentric staffing and international assignments: A transaction cost theory approach.* Presentation at the Academy of Management Conference, August 9–12.

35. Anderson, I. (2007, August 1). Human resources: War or revolution? *Mondaq Business Briefing*, n.p.

36. Kerr, S. (1995). On the folly of rewarding A, while hoping for B. *Academy of Management Executive, 9*, 25–37.

37. Field, A. (2008, June). Do your starts see a reason to stay? *Harvard Management Update*, 5–6.

38. Hoyt, D. (2008, March). Employee recognition at Intuit; and Spotlight. Global Strategic Recognition Program. Stanford Graduate School of Business Case Study. Retrieved January 30, 2009, from http://www.globoforce.com/corporate/eng/our-customers/case-studies/intuit.html?KeepThis=true&TB_iframe=true&height=400&width=600.

39. Intuit spotlights strategic importance of global employee recognition. (2008, August 15). Retrieved January 30, 2009, from http://howtomanagehumanresources.blogspot.com/2008/08/intuit-spotlights-strategic-importance.html.

40. Lawler, E. (1992). *The ultimate advantage.* San Francisco: Jossey-Bass.

41. Katz, N. R. (1998). Promoting a healthy balance between individual achievement and team success: The impact of hybrid reward systems. Presented at the "Do Rewards Make a Difference?" Session at the Academy of Management Conference, August 9–12.

42. Konrad, A. M. (2006, March/April). Engaging employees through high-involvement work practices. *Ivey Business Journal Online*, 1–6. Retrieved January 30, 2009, from http://www.iveybusinessjournal.com.

43. Fey, C., Bjorkman, I., & Pavlovskaya, A. (2000). The effect of human resource management practices on firm performance in Russia. *International Journal of Human Resource Management, 11*, 1–18.

44. Shih, H.-A., Chiang, Y.-H., & Hsu, C.-C. (2006, August). Can high performance work systems really lead to better performance? *International Journal of Manpower, 27*(8), 741–763.

45. Magnan, M., & St-Onge, S. (1998). Profit sharing and firm performance: A comparative and longitudinal analysis. Presented at the Academy of Management Conference, August 9–12.

46. Buhler, P. M. (2008, March). Managing in the new millennium; succession planning: Not just for the c suite. *Supervision, 69*(3), 19.

47. Kaplan, R., & Norton, D. (1996). *The Balanced Scorecard.* Boston: Harvard Business School Press.

48. Huselid, M., Becker, B., & Beatty, D. (2005). *The workforce scorecard: Managing human capital to execute strategy.* Boston: Harvard Business School Press.

49. Huselid, M.A., Beatty, R.W., & Becker, B.E (2005, December). "A players" or "A positions"? The strategic logic of workforce management. *Harvard Business Review*.

50. Weatherly, L. (2003, March). Human capital—the elusive asset; measuring and managing human capital: A strategic imperative for HR. *Research Quarterly*, Society for Human Resource Management. Retrieved June 1, 2003, from http://www.shrm.org/research/quarterly/0301capital.pdf.

51. Saratoga Institute—2003 SHRM National Conference, as quoted in Weatherly, L. (2003). The value of people: The challenges and opportunities of human capital measurement and reporting. *SHRM Research Quarterly, 3*, 14–25.

52. Rush, J. (1995, July). Interview backgrounder for *Fast Company*.

53. Weatherly, L. A. (2003). The value of people: The challenges and opportunities of human capital measurement and reporting. *SHRM Research Quarterly, 3*, 26–31.

54. Becker, B. E., & Huselid, M. A., (2006). Strategic human resources management: Where do we go from here? *Journal of Management, 32*, 898–925.

Index

Index

stakeholder analysis

109-111

stakeholders

22-24, 55, 93-102, 108-114, 128, 142-144, 155, 207, 246, 358-359

stereotypes

74-76, 83, 89, 187, 269, 285

storming

307-313

strategic alliances

185

strategic control

362

strategic focus

128, 132

strategic human resource management (SHRM)

385-386, 411

strategic human resources management (SHRM)

100

strategic management

2-5, 17, 54, 95-96, 110, 116-152, 159-162, 166-170, 177-181, 199, 265, 275, 284, 291, 321, 365-367, 384

strategic management process

118

strategic planning

20, 118, 126-127, 154, 160, 360

strategy

2, 6-18, 28-33, 51, 87, 91-103, 109-112, 116-132, 139-140, 144-167, 173, 177, 186, 202, 273, 283, 297, 320, 357-358, 362-363, 368, 372-375, 379-387, 391-394, 398-412

strategy diamond

117, 145-150

strategy formulation

110, 117-118, 125, 139, 144, 151-152

strategy implementation

109, 117-118, 125

strong culture

207, 223

subculture

204-208

succession planning

320, 391, 403-406, 412

supportive leaders

237

sustainable competitive advantage

122, 136

SWOT analysis

121, 125, 331

synergy

119

tactical planning

20

talent management

391-394, 412

tall structures

178

tangible asset

147

task force

319

task identity

349-351

task interdependence

313-317, 324, 331

task significance

349-351, 355

task-oriented leader behaviors

231

team

4-6, 12-15, 21, 25-28, 39, 43, 50-52, 58, 72, 87-89, 100-103, 109, 127, 138, 157, 176, 184, 191, 198-199, 206, 210-219, 228, 240-245, 250-254, 262, 269-275, 281-283, 294, 299-301, 305-308, 312-332, 350-356, 392, 396-403, 407-412

team contract

325-327

team-oriented cultures

206, 213, 219

teamwork

21, 27, 115, 223, 283, 305, 314, 331, 389, 398

top management teams

2, 189, 275, 320, 324

traditional or manager-led teams

321

transactional leaders

241-244, 248

transformational leaders

243-244, 248

trust

55, 78, 82-83, 89, 100, 133, 193-197, 216, 243-249, 253, 275, 282, 289, 320, 331, 355, 390

turnover

20, 64, 68, 76, 80-90, 108, 152, 159, 172, 206, 211, 254, 285, 296, 303, 317-322, 329, 348, 355, 359, 374-375, 395-396, 401, 410-412

uncertainty avoidance

50-52

unfreezing

192-193

valence

343, 351, 356

value chain

123, 135-136, 199

values

21, 31-36, 40-41, 50-65, 69-72, 76-78, 87-115, 135, 167-168, 202-219, 223-224, 243, 247-253, 287, 308-313, 325-327, 353, 388-390, 409

values statement

93, 214

variable ratio

346

verification and application

261

virtual organizations

43-45

virtual teams

319-320, 331

vision statement

42, 93, 97-98, 104-114, 155, 159, 381

VRIO

123, 132, 136-139, 148, 152

war for talent

385, 391-392

Warren Bennis

15, 41

wiki

11, 15-19, 23-31, 39-47, 59-61, 65-68, 78, 82, 86, 95-105, 131, 135, 178-179, 191, 195-197, 207-216, 228-234, 244, 249, 255-256, 260, 266, 270-273, 278-279, 288, 305, 315, 319-320, 329, 341, 353, 387-390, 410

wildstorming

262

Workforce Scorecard

407-412